THE GLOBAL ENVIRONMENT

Fourth Edition

*For Lenny, Gregg,
Renee, Sam, and Ari,*

and

*little Sienna,
Laryssa, and Sarah*

THE GLOBAL ENVIRONMENT

INSTITUTIONS, LAW, AND POLICY

Fourth Edition

Edited by

Regina S. Axelrod
Adelphi University

Stacy D. VanDeveer
University of New Hampshire

Los Angeles | London | New Delhi
Singapore | Washington DC

Los Angeles | London | New Delhi
Singapore | Washington DC

FOR INFORMATION:

CQ Press
An Imprint of SAGE Publications, Inc.
2455 Teller Road
Thousand Oaks, California 91320
E-mail: order@sagepub.com

SAGE Publications Ltd.
1 Oliver's Yard
55 City Road
London, EC1Y 1SP
United Kingdom

SAGE Publications India Pvt. Ltd.
B 1/I 1 Mohan Cooperative Industrial Area
Mathura Road, New Delhi 110 044
India

SAGE Publications Asia-Pacific Pte. Ltd.
3 Church Street
#10-04 Samsung Hub
Singapore 049483

Library of Congress Cataloging-in-Publication Data

The global environment : institutions, law, and policy / Edited by Regina S. Axelrod, Adelphi University, Stacy D. VanDeveer, University of New Hampshire. — Fourth edition.

pages cm

Includes bibliographical references and index.

ISBN 978-1-4522-4145-6 (pbk) —
ISBN 978-1-4833-1200-2 (web pdf)

1. Environmental law, International. 2. Environmental policy. I. Axelrod, Regina S., editor of compilation. II. VanDeveer, Stacy D., editor of compilation.

K3585.4.G58 2014

363.7—dc23

2013038357

Acquisitions Editor: Sarah Calabi
Editorial Assistant: Davia Grant
Production Editor: Stephanie Palermini
Copy Editor: Judy Selhorst
Typesetter: Hurix Systems Pvt. Ltd.
Proofreader: Christine Dahlin
Indexer: Judy Hunt
Cover Designer: Candice Harman
Marketing Manager: Amy Whitaker

14 15 16 17 18 10 9 8 7 6 5 4 3 2 1

Contents

Preface   vii
Selected Acronyms in Global Environmental Policy   xi
Global Environmental Policy: A Brief Chronology   xvii
Contributors   xxi

1. Introduction: Governing the Global Environment   1
    Regina S. Axelrod and Stacy D. VanDeveer

Part I. International Environmental Actors and Institutions

2. Architects, Agitators, and Entrepreneurs: International and
    Nongovernmental Organizations in Global Environmental
    Politics   26
    Kate O'Neill

3. International Law and the Protection of
    the Global Environment   53
    Jacqueline Peel

4. International Environmental Regimes and the Success of
    Global Ozone Policy   83
    David Leonard Downie

5. Compliance with Global Environmental Policy: Climate
    Change and Ozone Layer Cases   110
    Michael G. Faure and Jürgen Lefevere

Part II. Big Players in Global Environmental Policy Making

6. Domestic Sources of U.S. Unilateralism   133
    Elizabeth R. DeSombre

7. Environmental Policy Making and Global Leadership in the
    European Union   157
    Regina S. Axelrod and Miranda A. Schreurs

8. Energy and Environment in China: National and Global
    Challenges   187
    Joanna I. Lewis and Kelly Sims Gallagher

9. The View from the South: Developing Countries in Global Environmental Politics   213
Adil Najam

Part III. Cases, Controversies, and Challenges

10. International Climate Change Policy: Complex Multilevel Governance   234
Michele M. Betsill

11. Global Politics and Policy on Hazardous Chemicals   259
Henrik Selin

12. Global Biodiversity Governance: Genetic Resources, Species, and Ecosystems   283
G. Kristin Rosendal

13. Democracy and the Global Nuclear Renaissance: From the Czech Republic to Fukushima   305
Regina S. Axelrod

14. Free Trade and Environmental Protection   330
Daniel C. Esty

15. Consumption, Commodity Chains, and Global and Local Environments   350
Stacy D. VanDeveer

Index   373

Preface

This volume is designed to meet the need for an authoritative collection of readings on international environmental institutions, laws, and policies at the beginning of the twenty-first century. In contrast to the numerous texts available in individual disciplinary fields, this book brings together essays by a distinguished group of international scholars spanning the traditional boundaries of political science, international relations, international law, policy studies, and comparative politics. Only by integrating perspectives from diverse fields can we begin to address the enormous complexities of global environmental problems and their governance.

The introductory chapter explains some of the most important concepts derived from these fields for the study of international environmental law and policy. These include basic perspectives on international cooperation drawn from international relations theory, the nature of international institutions and policy regimes, and the concept of sustainable development. The first two sections of the book focus on the development of global environmental institutions, laws, regimes, and policies and the roles played by major players in global environmental politics, such as the United States, the European Union, China, and the many countries of the global South. The third section presents case studies of national and regional implementation of international environmental and sustainable development policies. Linkages among national and international actors as well as among public institutions, firms, and nongovernmental organizations are discussed throughout the book.

In one sense, all serious environmental threats are now international in scope, given that nearly all forms of pollution, use of resources, and destabilization of natural ecosystems have implications for the sustainability of life as we know it. Global biogeochemical cycles circulate materials and energy throughout the planetary biosphere, and losses of Earth's inherited biodiversity and mineral resources are irreversible. The consumption of resources by one country or group of people ultimately affects the life chances of other—and much larger—segments of the human population, including those in future generations.

The nations of the world began to deal with many of the most obvious environmental threats during the past century, particularly since the twin imperatives of ecological sustainability and development of the world's poorest economies were put on the global agenda at the United Nations Conference on the Human Environment, held in Stockholm in 1972. The concept of sustainable development, articulated in the 1987 report of the World Commission on Environment and Development and at the United Nations Conference on Environment and Development, held in Rio de Janeiro in

1992, established a broad intellectual framework and agenda for action by the international community. Commitments to the implementation of this agenda were discussed by representatives of 191 nations at the World Summit on Sustainable Development, held in Johannesburg in 2002, and again at Rio+20 in 2012.

Despite this progress, the prospects for attaining the levels of international cooperation necessary to manage the impact of humans on the natural life-support systems of the planet remain grim. The contributors to this volume were asked to evaluate initial steps toward strengthening international policies and institutions to achieve the goals of sustainable development. Although some advances are documented, the record to date is not encouraging. The political will to make substantial economic and political changes appears to be lacking in most parts of the world. The declining leadership of the United States in international environmental policy making is even more striking than it was when the first edition of this book was published in 1999, and given the polarization of U.S. politics, increased global leadership seems unlikely in the near term.

Disagreements over the meaning of sustainable development as well as problems in implementing environmental policies are evident throughout this book. Several contributors note the persistence of deep cleavages among developed, developing, and transitional states in various regions of the world. Political differences among the United States, Europe, and the developing world have remained acrimonious, often widening rather than narrowing in recent years (Chapters 6–9) on a host of issues, including climate change (Chapter 10), hazardous chemicals (Chapter 11), biodiversity protection (Chapter 12), and trade (Chapter 14). Projects such as the expansion of nuclear power in the Czech Republic and around the world in the wake of the Fukushima nuclear power plant disaster (Chapter 13) and the ever-growing demands of consumer societies on the Earth's finite resources and fragile ecosystems (Chapter 15) raise profound questions about the trade-offs that may be required to achieve sustainable development—and about the role of international financial interests in promoting incompatible forms of development. Every member of a human population of seven to nine billion will not be able to consume the Earth's resources like the average North American; neither should billions be expected to settle for lives of poverty.

We hope this fourth edition will be even more useful than the previous ones as a text in college and university courses and that this edition will also be of interest to a broad range of scholars, professionals, and citizens concerned about the state of the global environment. We wish to acknowledge the support of our colleagues and staff at Adelphi University and the University of New Hampshire, without whom we would not have been able to complete the project, and the inspiring work of Norm Vig, who coedited the first two editions. Regina S. Axelrod owes thanks to the National Science Foundation for a grant (SBR-9708180) that allowed her to study nuclear power development in the Czech Republic; to colleagues at Charles University, the University of Economics, and the Czech Institute of

International Relations, Prague; and to the many public officials there and in the Environment Directorate of the European Commission, who facilitated her research, as well as Dawn Kelleher, administrative assistant, political science department, Adelphi University, for her technical assistance. Stacy D. VanDeveer is grateful for support from the Transatlantic Academy in Washington, D.C., and to the University of New Hampshire's senior vice provost for academic affairs and senior vice provost for research for supporting aspects of his research. He also wishes to thank his graduate assistant, Michael Cole, and his many undergraduate and graduate students at UNH, Brown, Harvard, and Regent's College (London) for inspiring his continuing interests in environmental, energy, and resource politics. Finally, we express our appreciation to Elise Frasier, Davia Grant, Charisse Kiino, and Stephanie Palermini of CQ Press for their encouragement and assistance throughout this project. We also extend our gratitude to Judy Selhorst for copyediting the manuscript. Any remaining errors are, of course, our own responsibility.

Regina S. Axelrod
Stacy D. VanDeveer

Selected Acronyms in Global Environmental Policy

ABS	access and benefit sharing
AMAP	Arctic Monitoring and Assessment Programme
AOSIS	Alliance of Small Island States
APEC	Asia-Pacific Economic Cooperation Forum
ASEAN	Association of Southeast Asian Nations
BATs	best available techniques
BCM	bromochloromethane
BINGO	business and industry nongovernmental organization
BRICS	Brazil, Russia, India, China, South Africa
CACAM	Central Asia, Caucasus, Albania, Moldova
CAFE	corporate average fuel economy
CAFTA-DR	Dominican Republic–Central America–United States Free Trade Agreement
CAN	Climate Action Network
CBD	Convention on Biological Diversity
CCX	Chicago Climate Exchange
CDM	Clean Development Mechanism
CEC	Commission for Environmental Cooperation
CEE	Central and Eastern Europe
CEZ	Ceske energeticke zavody
CFCs	chlorofluorocarbons
CITES	Convention on International Trade in Endangered Species of Wild Fauna and Flora
CJA	Climate Justice Action
CJN!	Climate Justice Now!
CLRTAP	Convention on Long-Range Transboundary Air Pollution
CMR	carcinogenetic, mutagenic, and toxic for reproduction
CMS	Convention on the Conservation of Migratory Species of Wild Animals (Bonn Convention)
COP	Conference of the Parties
CTK	Czech News Agency
DDT	dichlorodiphenyl trichloroethane
DoE	U.S. Department of Energy
ECJ	European Court of Justice
Eco-AP	Eco-Innovation Action Plan
ECSC	European Coal and Steel Community
EEA	European Environment Agency
EEC	European Economic Community
EIA	environmental impact assessment

EIONET   European Environment Information and Observation Network
EMEP   European Monitoring and Evaluation Programme
ENB   Earth Negotiations Bulletin
ENGO   environmental nongovernmental organization
ENVI   Committee on the Environment, Public Health and Food
           Safety (European Parliament)
EPA   Environmental Protection Agency
EPB   Beijing Environmental Protection Bureau
ERUs   emission reduction units
EU ETS   European Union Emissions Trading System (also known as
           European Union Emissions Trading Scheme)
Euratom   European Atomic Energy Authority
FAO   United Nations Food and Agriculture Organization
FCCC   United Nations Framework Convention on Climate Change
           (also known as UNFCCC)
FSC   Forest Stewardship Council
GATT   General Agreement on Tariffs and Trade
GCC   Global Climate Coalition
GDP   gross domestic product
GEF   Global Environment Facility
GHGs   greenhouse gases
GMOs   genetically modified organisms
GONGO   government-organized nongovernmental organizations
GRASP   Great Apes Survival Project
G-77   Group of 77 (developing countries)
HBFCs   hydrobromofluorocarbons
HCFCs   hydrochlorofluorocarbons
IAEA   International Atomic Energy Agency
ICJ   International Court of Justice
ICLEI   International Council of Local Environmental Initiatives (also
           known as ICLEI–Local Governments for Sustainability)
IEAs   international environmental agreements
IET   International Emissions Trading
IFCS   Intergovernmental Forum on Chemical Safety
IGCC   integrated gasification combined cycle
IGO   intergovernmental organization (or international governmental
           organization)
IGY   International Geophysical Year
ILO   International Labour Organization
IMF   International Monetary Fund
IMO   International Maritime Organization
IMPEL   European Union Network for the Implementation and
           Enforcement of Environmental Law
IPBES   Intergovernmental Panel on Biodiversity and Ecosystem
           Services
IPCC   Intergovernmental Panel on Climate Change

IPOs	indigenous peoples' organizations
IRPTC	International Register of Potentially Toxic Chemicals
ISO	International Organization for Standardization
ISPA	Instrument for Structural Policies for Pre-Accession
ITLOS	International Tribunal for the Law of the Sea
ITPGRFA	International Treaty on Plant Genetic Resources for Food and Agriculture
ITTO	International Tropical Timber Organization
IUCN	International Union for Conservation of Nature
IWC	International Whaling Commission
JI	Joint Implementation
LGMAs	local governments and municipal authorities
LMOs	living modified organisms
MANGO	market advocacy nongovernmental organization
MARPOL	International Convention for the Prevention of Pollution from Ships
MDGs	Millennium Development Goals
MEA	multilateral environmental agreement
MEP	Ministry of Environmental Protection (China)
MOP	Meeting of the Parties
MSY	maximum sustainable yield
NAFTA	North American Free Trade Agreement
NAM	Non-Aligned Movement
NAMAs	nationally appropriate mitigation actions
NCPs	noncompliance procedures
NCSC	National Center for Climate Strategy and International Cooperation of China
NDRC	National Development and Reform Commission (China)
NGO	nongovernmental organization
NIEnvO	new international environmental order
NIEO	new international economic order
NRC	Nuclear Regulatory Commission
ODSs	ozone-depleting substances
OECD	Organisation for Economic Cooperation and Development
OEWG	Open-Ended Working Group
OPEC	Organization of Petroleum Exporting Countries
OSPAR	Convention for the Protection of the Marine Environment of the North-East Atlantic
PBT	persistent, bioaccumulative, and toxic
PCBs	polychlorinated biphenyls
PHARE	Poland-Hungary: Assistance for Restructuring Their Economies
PIC	prior informed consent
PIT	pesticides in international trade
PM	particulate matter
POPs	persistent organic pollutants

PPM	production process or method
REACH	Registration, Evaluation, Authorisation and Restriction of Chemicals
REDD	reducing emissions from deforestation and forest degradation
RGGI	Regional Greenhouse Gas Initiative
RINGO	research and independent nongovernmental organization
RoHS	restriction of the use of certain hazardous substances in electrical and electronic equipment
SAICM	Strategic Approach to International Chemicals Management
SBSTA	Subsidiary Body for Scientific and Technological Advice (of the UN Framework Convention on Climate Change)
SBSTTA	Subsidiary Body on Scientific, Technical, and Technological Advice (of the Convention on Biological Diversity)
SEPA	State Environmental Protection Agency (China)
TANs	transnational activist networks
TCX	Tianjin Climate Exchange
TEDs	turtle excluder devices
TEPCO	Tokyo Electric Power Company
TRIPS	Agreement on Trade-Related Aspects of Intellectual Property Rights
TUNGO	trade union nongovernmental organization
UNCCD	United Nations Convention to Combat Desertification
UNCED	United Nations Conference on Environment and Development
UNCHE	United Nations Conference on the Human Environment
UNCLOS	United Nations Convention on the Law of the Sea
UNCSD	United Nations Commission on Sustainable Development
UNCTAD	United Nations Conference on Trade and Development
UNDP	United Nations Development Programme
UNECE	United Nations Economic Commission for Europe
UNEP	United Nations Environment Programme
UNESCO	United Nations Educational, Scientific and Cultural Organization
UNFCCC	United Nations Framework Convention on Climate Change
UNICEF	United Nations Children's Fund (formerly United Nations International Children's Emergency Fund)
UNIDO	United Nations Industrial Development Organization
UNITAR	United Nations Institute for Training and Research
USTR	United States Trade Representative
vPvB	very persistent and very bioaccumulative
WCED	World Commission on Environment and Development
WEEE	waste electrical and electronic equipment
WHC	World Heritage Convention
WHO	World Health Organization
WIPO	World Intellectual Property Organization
WMO	World Meteorological Organization

WRI	World Resources Institute
WSSD	World Summit on Sustainable Development
WTO	World Trade Organization
WWF	World Wide Fund for Nature (formerly World Wildlife Fund)
YOUNGO	youth nongovernmental organization

Global Environmental Policy: A Brief Chronology

1900	First multinational treaty to protect endangered species signed
1909	Treaty between the United States and Great Britain Respecting Boundary Waters; International Joint Commission formed
1911	Treaty for the Preservation and Protection of Fur Seals
1933	London Convention on the Preservation of Fauna and Flora in Their Natural State
1940	Convention on Nature Protection and Wildlife Preservation in the Western Hemisphere
1941	Final decision of Trail Smelter arbitration
1944	United States and Mexico adopt Treaty on Colorado and Tijuana Rivers
1945	United Nations created
1946	International Bank for Reconstruction and Development (World Bank) created; International Convention on the Regulation of Whaling
1948	International Maritime Organization (IMO) created; International Union for Conservation of Nature (IUCN) founded
1949	International Convention for the Northwest Atlantic Fisheries; United Nations Conference on Conservation and Utilization of Resources
1950	World Meteorological Organization (WMO) created; International Convention for the Protection of Birds
1952	Four thousand people die in the worst of the London "killer fogs"
1954	International Convention for the Prevention of Pollution of the Sea by Oil
1957	International Atomic Energy Agency (IAEA) created; Treaty of Rome establishing European Economic Community
1961	World Wildlife Fund (WWF) established
1963	Agreement for the Protection of the Rhine against Pollution; Nuclear Test Ban Treaty

1965   United Nations Development Programme (UNDP) created

1971   UNESCO's Man and the Biosphere program launched;
        Ramsar Convention on Wetlands of International Importance;
        Greenpeace established

1972   United Nations Conference on the Human Environment
            (UNCHE; often referred to as the Stockholm Conference), the
            first global environmental conference;
        United Nations Environment Programme (UNEP) created;
        UNESCO Convention Concerning the Protection of the World
            Cultural and Natural Heritage (World Heritage Convention)

1973   Convention on International Trade in Endangered Species of
            Wild Fauna and Flora (CITES);
        International Convention for the Prevention of Pollution from
            Ships (MARPOL)

1974   World Population Conference, Bucharest;
        M. J. Molina and F. S. Rowland publish their theory that
            chlorofluorocarbons (CFCs) threaten the ozone layer

1976   Convention for the Protection of the Mediterranean Sea against
            Pollution;
        United Nations Conference on Human Settlements, Vancouver

1977   UNEP International Register of Potentially Toxic Chemicals
            (IRPTC);
        UN Conference on Desertification

1978   CFCs in spray cans banned in the United States

1979   Bonn Convention on the Conservation of Migratory Species of
            Wild Animals (CMS);
        Convention on Long-Range Transboundary Air Pollution (CLRTAP)

1980   Convention on the Conservation of Antarctic Marine Living
            Resources

1982   United Nations Convention on the Law of the Sea (UNCLOS)

1983   International Tropical Timber Agreement

1985   Vienna Convention for the Protection of the Ozone Layer;
        discovery of the Antarctic ozone hole

1987   Montreal Protocol on Substances That Deplete the Ozone Layer;
        World Commission on Environment and Development publishes
            Our Common Future (Brundtland Commission Report)

1989   Basel Convention on the Control of Transboundary Movements
            of Hazardous Wastes and Their Disposal;
        oil spilled in the Gulf of Alaska by the *Exxon Valdez*

1991   Global Environment Facility (GEF) created;
        Convention on the Ban of the Import into Africa and the Control
            of Transboundary Movement and Management of Hazardous
            Wastes within Africa (Bamako Convention)

1992   United Nations Conference on Environment and Development
            (UNCED), also known as the Earth Summit, Rio de Janeiro;
        United Nations Framework Convention on Climate Change
            (UNFCCC);
        Convention on Biological Diversity (CBD);
        Rio Declaration on Environment and Development and Agenda 21;
        Maastricht Treaty establishing the European Union;
        United Nations Commission on Sustainable Development
            (UNCSD) created

1993   North American Free Trade Agreement (NAFTA) signed

1994   United Nations Convention to Combat Desertification
            (UNCCD);
        United Nations Conference on Population and Development,
            Cairo;
        World Trade Organization (WTO) established

1997   Kyoto Protocol to the FCCC

1998   Rotterdam Convention on the Prior Informed Consent (PIC)
            Procedure for Certain Hazardous Chemicals and Pesticides in
            International Trade;
        CLRTAP Persistent Organic Pollutants (POPs) Protocol;
        CLRTAP Heavy Metals Protocol

2000   Millennium Development Goals adopted in UN Millennium
            Declaration
        Cartagena Protocol on Biosafety

2001   Stockholm Convention on Persistent Organic Pollutants

2002   UN World Summit on Sustainable Development (WSSD,
            or Johannesburg Summit)

2005   Millennium Ecosystem Assessment published;
        European Union Emissions Trading System (EU ETS) launched

2006   UNEP-coordinated Strategic Approach to International
            Chemicals Management (SAICM) launched

2009   United Nations Climate Change Conference (Copenhagen Summit)

2010   Nagoya Protocol to the CBD

2012   United Nations Conference on Sustainable Development (Rio+20)

2013   Minamata Convention on Mercury

Contributors

Regina S. Axelrod is professor of political science and chair of the political science department at Adelphi University. She has published numerous articles and books on environmental and energy policy in the United States, the European Union, and Central Europe, including *Conflict between Energy and Urban Environment: Consolidated Edison versus the City of New York* (1982) and *Environment, Energy, Public Policy: Toward a Rational Future* (1981). She has lectured at Charles University, Prague; University of Economics, Prague; and University of Budapest on nuclear power and the transition to democracy. She is an academic associate of the Atlantic Council and past president of the New York Political Science Association. In 2007, she lectured at the University of Economics, Prague, on theories of public policy and on international environmental policy on a Fulbright Senior Specialist grant. She is a research associate at the Czech Institute of International Relations.

Michele M. Betsill is professor of political science at Colorado State University, where she teaches courses on international relations and global environmental politics. Her research focuses on the multiple ways in which climate change is governed, from the global to the local level across the public and private spheres, with a particular focus on questions of politics and authority in global environmental governance. She is coauthor (with Harriet Bulkeley) of *Cities and Climate Change: Urban Sustainability and Global Environmental Governance* (2003) and coeditor (with Elisabeth Corell) of *NGO Diplomacy: The Influence of Nongovernmental Organizations in International Environmental Negotiations* (2008). She is the founder and coleader of the Environmental Governance Working Group at Colorado State University and serves on the Scientific Steering Committee for the Earth System Governance network.

Elizabeth R. DeSombre is Frost Professor of Environmental Studies at Wellesley College, where she directs the Environmental Studies Program. Her research concerns global environmental politics, particularly relating to issues of the global commons, especially protection of the oceans and atmosphere. Her recent books include *Saving Global Fisheries: Reducing Fishing Capacity to Promote Sustainability* (2013) and *Fish* (2011), both coauthored with J. Samuel Barkin. Her first book, *Domestic Sources of International Environmental Policy: Industry, Environmentalists, and U.S. Power* (2000), won several prizes.

David Leonard Downie is director of environmental studies and associate professor of politics at Fairfield University and an adjunct research scholar at Columbia University's Earth Institute. His research focuses on the creation, content, and implementation of national and international environmental policy. He has attended dozens of global environmental negotiations on climate change, stratospheric ozone protection, toxic chemicals, mercury pollution, and sustainable development. During many negotiations on ozone protection, mercury, and toxic chemicals, he has worked with the treaty secretariat drafting in-session and summary documents. He received his B.A. degree from Duke University and his Ph.D. in political science from the University of North Carolina. His recent publications include *Global Environmental Politics* (sixth edition, 2014), coauthored with Pamela S. Chasek and Janet Welsh Brown, and several articles and book chapters. Prior to joining Fairfield University, he taught courses in environmental politics from 1994 to 2008 at Columbia University, where he also served as director of the Global Roundtable on Climate Change, associate director of the Graduate Program in Climate and Society, director of the Earth Institute Fellows Program, and director of environmental policy studies (MIA program) at the School of International and Public Affairs.

Daniel C. Esty is Hillhouse Professor of Environmental Law and Policy at Yale University, currently on leave to serve as commissioner of Connecticut's Department of Energy and Environmental Protection. He holds faculty appointments in both Yale's Environment and Law Schools and serves as director of the Yale Center for Environmental Law and Policy and the Center for Business and the Environment at Yale. He is author or editor of ten books and numerous articles on sustainability and environmental issues and the relationships between environmental protection and corporate strategy, competitiveness, trade, globalization, metrics, governance, and development. His prizewinning book (with Andrew Winston) *Green to Gold: How Smart Companies Use Environmental Strategy to Innovate, Create Value, and Build Competitive Advantage* argues that pollution control and natural resource management have become critical elements of marketplace success and explains how leading-edge companies have folded environmental thinking into their core business strategies. His most recent book (with P. J. Simmons), *The Green to Gold Business Playbook: How to Implement Sustainability Practices for Bottom-Line Results in Every Business Function*, offers practical advice on how to execute a sustainability strategy across a wide range of businesses and activities. Professor Esty has served as an adviser on corporate environmental or sustainability strategy for companies of all sizes and in a wide range of industries, including Ikea, Coca-Cola, Unilever, Boeing, and IBM. Prior to taking up his position at Yale, he was a senior fellow at the Institute for International Economics and held a variety of senior positions in the U.S. Environmental Protection Agency.

Michael G. Faure studied law at the University of Antwerp (licentiate in law 1982) and criminology at the University of Ghent (licentiate in criminology

1983). He obtained a master of laws from the University of Chicago Law School (1984) and a doctor iuris from the University of Freiburg. He was a lecturer and senior lecturer in the department of criminal law of the law faculty of Leyden University from 1988 to 1999 and became academic director of the Maastricht European Institute for Transnational Legal Research and professor of comparative and international environmental law at the law faculty of Maastricht University in September 1991. He still holds both positions today. In addition, he is academic director of the Ius Commune Research School and a member of the board of directors of the European Center of Tort and Insurance Law. Since February 2008 he has been half-time professor of comparative private law and economics at the Rotterdam Institute of Law and Economics of Erasmus University Rotterdam and academic director of the European Doctorate in Law and Economics Program. Since 1982 he has also been an attorney and a member of the Antwerp bar. In 2011, he became a member of the Humanities and Social Sciences Division of the Royal Netherlands Academy of Arts and Sciences.

Kelly Sims Gallagher is associate professor of energy and environmental policy at the Fletcher School of Law and Diplomacy. She directs the Center for International Environment and Resource Policy at Fletcher, as well as its energy, climate, and innovation research program. She is also senior research associate and a member of the board of directors of Belfer Center for Science and International Affairs at Harvard University, where she previously directed the Energy Technology Innovation Policy research group. She focuses on energy and climate policy in both the United States and China and is particularly interested in the role of policy in spurring the development and deployment of cleaner and more efficient energy technologies, domestically and internationally. She is the author of *China Shifts Gears: Automakers, Oil, Pollution, and Development* (2006), editor of *Acting in Time on Energy Policy* (2009) and *The Globalization of Clean Energy Technology: Lessons from China* (2014), and author of numerous academic articles and policy reports.

Jürgen Lefevere has worked on European and international environmental law and policy issues since 1993, initially at the University of Maastricht (the Netherlands) and from 1998 to 2003 at the London-based Foundation for International Environmental Law and Development. He joined the European Commission in 2003 and is currently adviser on international climate negotiations and climate strategy at the Directorate General for Climate Action of the European Commission in Brussels. He has been involved in international climate negotiations since 1998, serving as legal adviser to the Alliance of Small Island States and now heading the delegation of the European Union to the United Nations climate negotiations. He cofacilitated part of the negotiations during the second commitment period of the Kyoto Protocol in the run-up to and during the negotiations in Doha in 2012. He has also played a key role in the development and implementation of the European Union's greenhouse gas emissions trading system.

Joanna I. Lewis is assistant professor of science, technology, and international affairs at Georgetown University's Edmund A. Walsh School of Foreign Service. Her research focuses on energy and environmental issues in China, including renewable energy industry development, climate change policy, and technology acquisition and innovation strategies for energy leapfrogging. Her book *Green Innovation in China: China's Wind Power Industry and the Global Transition to a Low-Carbon Economy* was published in late 2012. She is currently a visiting faculty affiliate in the China Energy Group at Lawrence Berkeley National Laboratory and a lead author of the Intergovernmental Panel on Climate Change's Fifth Assessment Report. She has been a visiting scholar at the Woodrow Wilson International Center for Scholars, the East-West Center, and Tsinghua University's Institute of Energy, Environment and Economy. She holds a Ph.D. in energy and resources from the University of California, Berkeley, and a B.A. in environmental science and policy from Duke University.

Adil Najam is professor of international relations, Earth, and environment at Boston University and until recently held the position of vice chancellor of the Lahore University of Management Sciences (LUMS) in Pakistan. He was a lead author for the Third and Fourth Assessment Reports of the Intergovernmental Panel on Climate Change and currently serves on the Council of the International Institute of Applied Systems Analysis (IIASA) and as a trustee on the boards of WWF-International and The Asia Foundation. His teaching and research have focused on international diplomacy and negotiation, global governance, environmental policy and international development, and long-range global policy challenges. He has published more than one hundred scholarly articles, book chapters, and books, most recently the coedited books *South Asia 2060: Envisioning Regional Futures* (with Moeed Yusuf; 2013), *The Future of South-South Economic Relations* (with Rachel Thrasher; 2012), and *How Immigrants Impact Their Homelands* (with Susan Eckstein; 2013).

Kate O'Neill is associate professor in the department of environmental science, policy, and management at the University of California, Berkeley. Her Ph.D. in political science is from Columbia University. She writes and teaches on matters of global environmental politics and governance. Her first book, *Waste Trading among Rich Nations: Building a New Theory of Environmental Regulation*, was published in 2000. Her second book, *The Environment and International Relations* (2009), is a state-of-the-art examination of the theory and practice of global environmental governance. She has also published a number of peer-reviewed articles and chapters, including work on environmental social movements, and she is coeditor of the journal *Global Environmental Politics*. She is particularly interested in the ways new actors, initiatives, and institutions are emerging onto the global environmental scene. She is currently working on various projects, including the second edition of *The Environment and International Relations* and research concerning the global political economy of wastes.

Jacqueline Peel is a professor at the Melbourne Law School in Australia. She holds the degrees of bachelor of science and bachelor of laws (Hon I) from the University of Queensland; a master of laws from New York University, where she was a Fulbright Scholar; and a Ph.D. in law from the University of Melbourne. Her teaching and research interests lie in the areas of environmental law (domestic and international), risk regulation and the role of science, and climate change law. She has published numerous articles and several books on these topics, including the third edition of *Principles of International Environmental Law* (with Philippe Sands; 2012), *Australian Climate Law in Global Context* (with Alexander Zahar and Lee Godden; 2013), *Environmental Law: Scientific, Policy and Regulatory Dimensions* (with Lee Godden; 2009), *Science and Risk Regulation in International Law* (2010), and *The Precautionary Principle in Practice: Environmental Decision-Making and Scientific Uncertainty* (2005). She is an expert member of the International Law Association's Committee on the Legal Principles Relating to Climate Change and served as rapporteur of that committee during the latter half of 2012. She has also been the recipient of several awards and fellowships, including a Hauser Research Scholarship and Emile Noel Fellowship at New York University, a research associateship from the United States Studies Centre, and two Australian Research Council grants on climate change law-related topics. She is pursuing work on the most recent of these grants—on the topic of climate change litigation—jointly with Professor Hari Osofsky of the Minnesota Law School to undertake a comparative analysis of U.S. and Australian climate change litigation that will be published as a book. In 2013, she was a visiting scholar at Stanford University's Water in the West.

G. Kristin Rosendal is a research professor with the Fridtjof Nansen Institute, Norway, and holds a Ph.D. in political science. She has published extensively on the formation, implementation, and interaction of international regimes for environmental and resource management and trade, in particular issues relating to biodiversity, forestry management, biotechnology, and genetic resources. Most recently, she has coedited the volume *Global Governance of Genetic Resources: Access and Benefit Sharing after the Nagoya Protocol* (with Sebastian Oberthür; 2013).

Miranda A. Schreurs is director of the Environmental Policy Research Center and professor of comparative politics at the Free University of Berlin. She is a member of the Advisory Council on the Environment, a consultative committee of the German federal government, and chair of the European Environment and Sustainable Development Advisory Councils, a network of advisory councils across Europe. She also served on the Ethics Commission on a Safe Energy Supply, which was charged by Chancellor Angela Merkel with advising the German government on how Germany should respond to the Fukushima nuclear accident. She was the 2009–2010 Fulbright New Century Scholar Program's Distinguished Leader, and in that capacity coordinated the program's activities on "the role of the university as knowledge center and innovation driver."

Henrik Selin is associate professor in the department of international relations at Boston University, where he conducts research and teaches classes on global and regional politics and policy making on environment and sustainable development. He is the author of *Global Governance of Hazardous Chemicals: Challenges of Multilevel Management* (2010) and coeditor of *Changing Climates in North American Politics: Institutions, Policymaking, and Multilevel Governance* (with Stacy D. VanDeveer; 2009) and *Transatlantic Environment and Energy Politics: Comparative and International Perspectives* (with Miranda A. Schreurs and Stacy D. VanDeveer; 2009). In addition, he is author or coauthor of more than four dozen reviewed journal articles and book chapters, as well as numerous reports, reviews, and commentaries.

Stacy D. VanDeveer is professor and department chair in political science at the University of New Hampshire. His research interests include international environmental policy making and its domestic impacts, comparative environmental politics, connections between environmental and security issues, the roles of expertise in policy making and the global politics of consumption, and environmental and humanitarian degradation. In addition to authoring or coauthoring more than seventy articles, book chapters, working papers, and reports, he is coeditor of *Comparative Environmental Politics: Theory, Practice, and Prospects* (with Paul F. Steinberg; 2012), *Changing Climates in North American Politics: Institutions, Policymaking, and Multilevel Governance* (with Henrik Selin; 2009), *Transatlantic Environment and Energy Politics: Comparative and International Perspectives* (with Miranda A. Schreurs and Henrik Selin; 2009), *EU Enlargement and the Environment: Institutional Change and Environmental Policy in Central and Eastern Europe* (with JoAnn Carmin; 2005), and *Saving the Seas: Values, Scientists, and International Governance* (with L. Anathea Brooks; 1997). He is also coeditor of the journal *Global Environmental Politics*.

1

Introduction

Governing the Global Environment

Regina S. Axelrod and Stacy D. VanDeveer

Humans change their environments. Environmental change is driven by the things we eat, build, make, buy, and throw away—and by the decisions we make as citizens and voters. Over the past few decades we have acquired the power to change the planet's climate. The early twenty-first century finds the Earth's physical and biological systems under unprecedented strain. The growing human population exceeds seven billion, and the global economy has grown to more than $70 trillion annually. The United Nations estimates that one-third of the world's people live in countries with moderate to high shortages of fresh water. Many of the world's largest cities are choked by pollution. As carbon dioxide and other greenhouse gases build in the atmosphere, the average surface temperature of the Earth has reached the highest level ever recorded, measured on an annual basis, as glaciers and polar ice recede. The biological diversity of the planet is also under heavy stress. Scientists believe that a mass extinction of plants and animals is under way and predict that a quarter of all species could be pushed to extinction by 2050 as a consequence of global warming alone. Without question, human impacts on the biosphere will remain one of the most critical issues of the century.

Scientists and conservationists have recognized the threats to the Earth's flora and fauna, water systems, and atmosphere for more than a century, but only in the past four decades have nations begun to address these issues on a global scale. The 1972 United Nations Conference on the Human Environment (UNCHE) in Stockholm, Sweden, attended by 113 states, marked the beginning of organized international efforts to devise a comprehensive agenda to safeguard the environment while also promoting economic development. Although no binding treaties were adopted at Stockholm, the conference established the United Nations Environment Programme (UNEP), creating a permanent forum for monitoring global environmental trends, convening international meetings and conferences, and negotiating international agreements. Among UNEP's most important achievements are the 1985 Vienna Convention for the Protection of the Ozone Layer and the binding 1987 Montreal Protocol on Substances That Deplete the Ozone Layer.[1] In 1987 the World Commission on Environment and Development (WCED, also known as the Brundtland Commission for its chair, former

Norwegian prime minister Gro Harlem Brundtland) issued its historic report *Our Common Future*, which called for a new era of "sustainable development."[2] To begin implementing this strategy, the United Nations Conference on Environment and Development (UNCED), known as the Earth Summit, was convened in Rio de Janeiro, Brazil, in June 1992. The conference produced major international treaties on climate change and biodiversity, two declarations of principle, and a lengthy action program (Agenda 21) for implementing sustainable development around the world. Ten years later, in August 2002, 191 nations attended the World Summit on Sustainable Development (WSSD) in Johannesburg, South Africa, to reassess and renew commitments to sustainable development.[3] Another ten years found public, private, and civil society actors returning to Rio for the United Nations Conference on Sustainable Development, or Rio+20.

As a result of such diplomatic achievements and the politics, policy making, and activism that surround them, a system for global environmental governance now exists. This system consists of states and hundreds of intergovernmental organizations such as the United Nations and UNEP (and dozens of issue-specific organizations set up by treaty) and thousands of nongovernmental organizations (NGOs) (see Chapter 2), a framework of international environmental law based on several hundred multilateral treaties and agreements (see Chapter 3), and a diverse host of complex international cooperation regimes and other governance arrangements (see Chapter 4).

Hundreds of bilateral and regional treaties and organizations, such as those involving the United Nations Regional Seas Programme and the European Union (see Chapter 7), deal with dozens of transboundary and shared resource issues. By one count, 1,190 multilateral international agreements (MEAs) and more than 1,500 bilateral environmental agreements are currently in effect.[4] Some date back to the nineteenth century, while some were created as recently as 2013, when the Minamata Convention on Mercury was signed in Japan.

Particularly since the 1990s, a host of nongovernmental organizations, including international environmental interest groups, scientific bodies, business and trade associations, women's groups, and indigenous peoples' organizations, have also come to play an important role in international environmental governance (see Chapter 2). Environmental activists and NGOs (small and large) can now be found all around the globe, engaged in politics and social action and organizing from neighborhoods and local communities to national and global politics.[5] These organizations participate in international negotiations, help to monitor treaty compliance, and often play leading roles in implementing policies. At the 2002 Johannesburg summit, more than twenty thousand individuals registered as participants, and countless others attended the parallel Global People's Forum and summit of indigenous peoples.[6] The increased access to and transparency of international environmental governance is one of the most remarkable achievements of the emerging global environmental governance system.

Despite these strides, there is a growing perception that the current international governance system remains weak and ineffective.[7] Many international environmental institutions lack adequate funding and effective enforcement mechanisms. Because no world government or global sovereign political authority exists, international agencies often work at cross-purposes and rely on individual states to carry out their policies. States are reluctant to relinquish their sovereignty and their right to pursue their own national interests. Consequently, many trends and patterns of global environmental degradation have not been reversed, leaving us on a path toward devastating ecological crises unless global institutions are strengthened and public, private-sector, and civil society actors—and individual citizens and consumers—take on far more responsibility for environmental governance.

The role of the United States in international environmental diplomacy has been especially disappointing in recent years. Although the Clinton administration signed the 1997 Kyoto Protocol, which set targets and timetables for reducing greenhouse gas emissions that cause global warming, neither this treaty nor others, such as the Convention on Biological Diversity, the Basel Convention on the trade in hazardous wastes, and agreements covering biosafety and a host of transboundary air pollutants, have been ratified by the U.S. Senate. President George W. Bush repudiated the Kyoto Protocol in 2001 and showed little interest in other multilateral environmental agreements and institutions. U.S. support for many international environmental programs has declined over time. This indifference often results in deep divisions between the United States and both the European Union and the developing nations of the global South (see Chapters 6, 7, 9, 10, and 12).[8] Yet even here the picture is more complex than it might seem at first glance. Although the U.S. federal government largely abandoned environmental policy development in the early years of this century, many U.S. states and cities continued to make policy in response to international environmental challenges. Many states, for example, enacted policies to combat climate change and expand renewable energy generation even when the federal government was opposed to doing so.[9] In 2009, the Obama administration arrived in Washington, D.C., pledging to return to domestic environmental policy making and to steer the United States toward reengagement in global environmental cooperation (and in other areas of multilateral politics). Such changes take time and require the support of Congress and the American people. Congress has repeatedly opposed environmental initiatives—ignoring calls to act to reduce greenhouse gas emissions, to set clear regulations for hydraulic fracturing (fracking) and natural gas extraction, and to enact serious energy efficiency regulation—and has struggled to sustain even modest support for renewable energy generation. While a reelected President Obama pledged to lead on climate change and other environmental issues in both domestic and global politics, his administration's ability to do so remains constrained by congressional inaction and opposition. In 2013, attempting to circumvent congressional hostility toward climate policy, President Obama initiated a series of executive actions and EPA-driven regulatory processes, engendering ongoing opposition.

This book presents an overview of the development of international environmental institutions, laws, and policies and attempts to assess their adequacy. The authors analyze developments since World War II, with an emphasis on trends since the 1992 Earth Summit in Rio. They share both an optimism that people and nations can work together to address global problems and growing concern and pessimism about trends in both global environmental degradation and governance in the past two decades. They also take a longer view in evaluating emerging environmental regimes, because global cooperation is difficult to establish and sustain. Most of the contributors to this volume argue that there are important lessons to learn and reasons for hope. They caution, however, that more serious attention to global environmental governance is required of citizens and governments alike if disturbing and dangerous trends are to be reversed.

The past forty-plus years have seen dramatic and often surprising political and economic changes from which this volume seeks to learn. In addition to the large global summits on the environment and sustainable human development, the past twenty-five years witnessed developments such as the end of apartheid in South Africa, the collapse of Soviet-style communism in Eastern Europe and across the Soviet Union, a host of other transitions to democratic rule in Latin America and elsewhere, and the recent dramatic social and political changes across parts of North Africa and the Middle East. These changes brought unprecedented growth in the number of democracies in the world. The same era witnessed deepening European integration and expansion of the European Union from twelve countries to twenty-eight member states (with more applicants negotiating entry). China, India, Brazil, and a few other developing countries have roared into the global economy, reshaping aspects of their domestic politics, international relations, and global resource and environmental trends. These developments can both affect and inspire global environmental governance. For example, many of these political and economic changes help drive ever-increasing use of the Earth's resources (along with the seemingly never-ending growth in North American–style consumption). Yet if Europeans can overcome generations of war to build a unified Europe and citizens living under nondemocratic governments can demand their democratic and basic human rights and replace dictators with elected officials, then it may be possible for humankind to reverse global environmental degradation and build effective global environmental governance institutions to engender sustainable development around the globe.

The next two sections of this chapter provide a brief overview of the theoretical context for studying international environmental governance. The first of these summarizes the most important perspectives from international relations theory relevant to the emergence of international environmental institutions and law. The second discusses the concept of sustainable development, which became the dominant ideological framework for global environmental policies in the 1990s. The third section below outlines the organization and contents of the book, briefly discussing each of the three parts: (I) international environmental actors and institutions; (II) big players in global environmental policy making; and (III) cases, controversies, and challenges in global environmental governance. A short conclusion summarizes some of the themes of the book.

International Relations, Regimes, and Governance

International politics and governance institutions associated with environmental and sustainable development issues have produced a large and growing body of social science research and analysis.[10] Similarly, a large body of international relations theory is applicable to the development of international environmental institutions and agreements (see Chapter 4).[11] The study of international relations has traditionally been dominated by two broad theoretical schools: realism and liberalism. "Realists" view the world as an anarchic collection of sovereign nation-states, each of which is a unitary actor in pursuing its unique national interests. These interests are largely defined in terms of relative power and security compared with other states. In this perspective, nation-states do not cooperate with one another unless it is clearly in their self-interest to do so, and cooperative behavior will continue only as long as the parties perceive this condition to be met. International laws and institutions are thus essentially instruments for promoting or defending national interests and have little or no independent effect on the behavior of nations. Indeed, such laws and institutions can usually function only if strong or hegemonic states maintain them and enforce their decisions against weaker members or other states. The potential for international cooperation is therefore quite limited, and international laws and institutions are likely to be fragile and impermanent.[12]

This anarchic, state-centered perspective has been increasingly challenged in recent decades by a variety of "liberals," "neoliberals," and "liberal institutionalists." While most of these theorists concede that states are the primary actors on the international level, they hold that the traditional view of state sovereignty and unitary interest cannot explain the steady growth of international cooperation or the persistence of many specialized international institutions in the contemporary world. Although there are many strands of thinking, most liberal theorists hold that states are interdependent and, in fact, have many common interests that lead them to cooperate; moreover, they believe that international institutions not only serve these common interests but also create further incentives for cooperation.[13] In other words, institutions matter, and they influence the preferences and behavior of states by allowing states to improve collective welfare outcomes by cooperating. Whereas realists focus on *relative* status gains (especially regarding military security), liberals tend to emphasize *absolute* benefits (especially mutual economic gains) made possible by international agreements and institutions that solve collective action problems.

Over the past generation, a third, broad theoretical perspective has joined realism and liberalism in the pantheon of common theoretical approaches to understanding global environmental politics: constructivism.[14] Constructivism focuses attention on the influence of ideas, collective values, identities, and norms in international politics. The name given to this perspective refers to the argument that social reality is "constructed" through social interaction—that humans, collectively, construct the world in which they live through their identities and debates about values and norms (about what is justified or appropriate). Because of constructivism's attention to the influence of ideas and values, some international relations theorists view it as the contemporary variant of idealism.[15] For constructivists, international cooperation is more than mere ad hoc coalitions or a reflection of shared interests. It reflects who the participants are (or believe they are), and it can shape how they see themselves over time and what they view as appropriate. In other words, cooperation has the potential to be transformative in constructivism. For example, political scientist Peter Haas argues that a constructivist understanding of the effectiveness or impacts of conferences like the global environmental and sustainable development summits in 1972, 1992, 2002, and 2012 focuses more on how such meetings shape actor understandings, raise awareness, and bring political actors to agreement on norms, values, and ideas (on which they may act later).[16]

In other words, global environmental politics both reveals and shapes emerging, collectively held consensus positions and norms—about policies, problems, and how we understand the global environment and our place in it (and the place of international politics). For example, constructivists might examine scientific and policy debates around climate change to understand how some actors reach consensus or agreement while others continue to question widely held views or understandings. They might also explore the role and use of language and discourse in such debates.

Building on these three approaches to international relations theory during the past two decades, many environmental policy scholars have turned to the concept of regimes. International environmental regimes are composed of the international treaties and agreements, intergovernmental organizations, binding and nonbinding norms and principles, relevant national and local government institutions, and associated nongovernmental and private institutions that define and implement policies in different issue areas, such as climate change, maritime oil pollution, and endangered species protection. In Chapter 4 of this volume, David Leonard Downie explains regime theory in more detail and discusses many prominent examples of international environmental regimes. Drawing on other strands of international relations theory and systems theory, he also analyzes the obstacles to effective international cooperation. His chapter thus reveals the real difficulties of achieving effective international environmental policies.

Some theorists are more optimistic about the potential for a global governance system comprising an increasingly dense and interactive network of international regimes.[17] "Governance" in this sense does not presuppose a central government; rather, that coordination of action can occur through many different institutions, including private social and economic systems and nongovernmental organizations, as well as a variety of governmental institutions at different levels. This concept often presupposes some kind of global "civil society" or decentralized network of autonomous social institutions that represent citizens and organized interests and engage in cooperative actions to achieve broad goals such as sustainable development. Increased communication and exchange of information among individuals and groups around the world through the Internet and other means can magnify the impact of such civic action to the point where common ideas and values begin to influence the actions of governments from the bottom up.[18] Recent work within the "governance turn" in global environmental politics scholarship has begun to catalog and analyze large numbers of transnational or regional governance initiatives—or experiments—around the world involving complex sets of public, private, and civil society actors and a diverse set of institutionalized relationships and environmental goals.[19]

This brief discussion highlights the fact that whatever one's basic theoretical perspective, the development of international environmental cooperation has become one of the most fruitful and dynamic fields of international relations. Although there is no consensus among scholars on the nature of the world system or the autonomy and durability of current international environmental institutions, laws, and policies, it is undeniable that the global environment has become a principal concern of political actors as well as scholars around the world. From this broader vantage point, the halting and confused human response to gathering evidence of potential ecological catastrophe may be less discouraging than short-term observations suggest.

Sustainable Development

Cutting across theoretical disputes are the realities of world economic and social development. Environmental threats are the products not only of individual actions; they are also deeply embedded in our cultural, economic, political, and social systems. Perhaps the most obvious realities are that these systems are highly fragmented and differentiated and that global economic development is grossly uneven. The gap between the world's richer and poorer states is enormous and growing. So, for example, while gross domestic product per capita in the United States is more than $46,000, about a billion people, concentrated mostly in the world's fifty poorest countries, live on less than one dollar per day. These differences among nations at various stages and levels of development have profound implications for the global environment. Recognized since the Stockholm Conference is the fact that the needs and agendas of developed nations ("the North") are often fundamentally different from those of developing countries ("the South"); thus it is difficult to reach consensus on international policies that benefit all parties (see Chapter 9). Essentially, while the North gives substantial political attention to environmental issues that threaten ecological stability, the South has placed greater emphasis on immediate needs for economic growth to raise standards of living. Indeed, developing countries at the Stockholm Conference feared that environmental protection was a plot by the North to limit their development—a concern that still echoes through all international negotiations.[20]

The North-South division raises fundamental issues of international equity.[21] Developing countries (rightly) argue that the developed countries have benefited from environmental exploitation in the past and are responsible for most of the world's pollution and resource depletion, including that leading to ozone depletion and climate change. Thus, the argument goes, it should be primarily their responsibility to deal with these problems. Furthermore, developing countries are not willing to foreclose opportunities for economic growth that would permanently lock them into poverty and dependence while the peoples of the North engage in profligate consumption. Representatives of developing countries (organized as the Group of 77 in the United Nations since 1964 but now actually including more than 130 states) thus usually condition their willingness to participate in international environmental treaties and agreements on concessions from the North, such as guarantees of special funding and transfer of technologies to enable them to reduce their impact on the environment while increasing economic growth.

Another fundamental dimension of global environmental protection concerns intertemporal, or intergenerational, equity. That is, policies must consider the needs of both the present generation and the future. Edith Brown Weiss defines three essential principles: (1) each generation should be required to conserve the diversity of the resource base so that it does not unduly restrict the options available to future generations; (2) each generation should maintain the planet's overall quality so that it is bequeathed in no worse condition than it was received; and (3) members of every generation should have comparable rights of access to the legacy of past generations and should conserve this access for future generations.[22] The third principle implies a degree of intragenerational equity as a condition for intergenerational equity; that is, no group should either be denied a right to present environmental resources or be asked to bear a disproportionate share of environmental burdens (a principle often referred to as *environmental justice*).

The concept of sustainable development was born of these concerns. First set out by Dennis Pirages in 1977 in *The Sustainable Society* and in *World Conservation Strategy*, published by the International Union for Conservation of Nature (IUCN) with the World Wildlife Fund (WWF, now the World Wide Fund for Nature) and UNEP in 1980, the concept was popularized in the Brundtland Commission report of 1987. The famous definition of sustainable development comes from this report: "Sustainable development is development that meets the needs of the present without compromising the ability of future generations to meet their own needs." This is followed immediately by the explication of two key concepts embedded within the definition: "the concept of 'needs,' in particular the essential needs of the world's poor, to which overriding priority should be given"; and "the idea of limitations imposed by the state of technology and social organization on the environment's ability to meet present and future needs."[23]

Several elements in this definition are critical for an understanding of sustainable development. First, the concept clearly represents an attempt to bridge the concerns and interests of developed and developing nations, but it applies to both. That is, both the wealthiest and the less developed countries will need to change their production and consumption patterns. Second, it attempts to reconcile economic growth and environmental protection, not view them as trade-offs. Third, the concept is strongly anthropocentric. It starts from the premise that human needs must be met before a state can address environmental problems. Thus improvement in the living conditions in poor countries, and especially those of women and marginal social and economic groups, is an essential precondition for ecological preservation. Fourth, the limits to growth are not ultimately physical or biological but social and technological; it is assumed that environmental problems can be solved. Finally, the concept is extremely general, lacking specific content on how sustainable development is to be attained or who is responsible for achieving it. This vagueness is deliberate: it allows the idea to be adopted by virtually everyone as a way of bringing people together to seek common ground. In this formulation it is clearly a political and social construct, not a scientific concept or blueprint.[24]

Sustainability is now a ubiquitous term used by governments, the business sector, NGOs, and international organizations. It has become difficult to assess sustainability paradigms or initiatives and to separate serious and potentially transformative ones from "greenwashing" in which the term is used as meaningless jargon for corporate branding.[25] Whatever the conceptual and ideological differences below the surface, there have been numerous attempts to translate sustainable development into policy initiatives. The most important political effort to do so occurred at the UN Conference on Environment and Development in 1992 in Rio de Janeiro. UNCED produced both a general declaration of principles (the Rio Declaration on Environment and Development) and Agenda 21, a massive effort to define strategies and policies for implementing sustainable development. Governments pledged to formulate sustainable development plans and programs, and the Commission on Sustainable Development was established by the UN General Assembly to monitor these commitments. Many regional, national, and local organizations have adopted the principles and goals of sustainable development since 1992. Organizations such as UNEP, the IUCN–World Conservation Union, the World Bank, the Organization for Economic Cooperation and Development, and the U.S. National Academy of Sciences have also been actively working to identify specific empirical "indicators" for measuring progress toward sustainable development.[26]

Despite such efforts, there is a general sense of disappointment, if not despair, regarding implementation of Agenda 21 in the twenty years since the Rio summit. For example, international aid flows for sustainable development have failed to come close to the levels considered necessary; indeed, official development assistance has *declined* in absolute terms.[27] A sense of pessimism pervaded both the 2002 World Summit on Sustainable Development in Johannesburg and Rio+20 in 2012. The WSSD attempted to focus on implementing existing obligations rather than on launching new programs, although some new policy goals, financial commitments, and public-private partnerships were agreed upon. Like most global summits, Rio+20 produced debate about its value, accomplishments, and underlying values and assumptions.[28] At best, one can characterize its accomplishments as modest and its results as mixed. Little sign of the political will and urgency suggested by environmental trends and environmental science was on evidence in the actual commitments made by states. Nothing illustrates this more than the disappointing outcomes of ongoing global climate change cooperation efforts such as the Kyoto Protocol, which expired in 2012 with no serious global agreements to replace it as global greenhouse emissions of all kinds continue to rise.

Overview of the Book

This book's individual contributions are organized into three sections, the themes, concepts, and topics of which are summarized below.

International Environmental Actors and Institutions

International environmental organizations take many forms. Some of the oldest, such as treaties to protect intercontinental migratory bird species, European river basin commissions, and the International Joint Commission formed by the United States and Canada in 1909 to preserve the Great Lakes, are bilateral or multilateral institutions created to encourage cooperation in managing shared resources. Some, like the International Whaling Commission (IWC) and the International Tropical Timber Organization (ITTO), concern the worldwide harvesting and trade of specific categories of living resources, while others protect "common-pool resources," such as Antarctica and the high seas, that are beyond national jurisdictions. The environmental impacts and effectiveness of such cooperation arrangements also vary widely—as in most areas of public policy. So, for example, the fractious and controversial IWC has clearly helped to curtail whaling around the world even if some few states have opted out, while the ITTO has had little discernible impact on deforestation trends. The International Maritime Organization regulates shipping to reduce pollution as a result of both normal operations and accidents, slowly changing shipping standards and practices over decades. Still others, like the World Meteorological Organization and the Intergovernmental Panel on Climate Change (IPCC), conduct scientific research, monitor environmental change, and/or assess ongoing scientific and technical research on a global scale. Finally, many are essentially ad hoc organizations, such as the secretariats and conferences of the parties (COPs) that are created to monitor and develop detailed protocols to treaties and conventions.

Most of these international bodies are *intergovernmental organizations* (IGOs), meaning that they are created by member states and are accountable to them. In most cases member states are formally equal in governing (though not in financing) these institutions, but some (notably the World Bank and the International Monetary Fund) use weighted voting procedures that reflect donor contributions. This has become a contentious issue in negotiations over multilateral funding mechanisms to channel special economic assistance to the South. The Global Environment Facility (GEF), which provides funding primarily for implementation of the climate change and biodiversity conventions in developing countries, was restructured after 1992 to give recipient countries more influence in financial decisions.

In Chapter 2, Kate O'Neill examines both the evolution of global institutions since the 1972 Stockholm era and the increasingly important role that *nongovernmental organizations* play in global environmental politics on local, national, and international levels. The United Nations General Assembly has been key in establishing the scope of environmental problems, principles of international law, and the United Nations Environment Programme, a major international environmental institution. O'Neill traces the development of "Earth summits" and their accomplishments and limits. These state-led international regimes, with UN support, have had significant successes, but as performance demonstrates, although UNEP can respond quickly and engage in long-term monitoring, results can be limited because of inadequate resources and lack of political will. O'Neill explains the roles of crosscutting intergovernmental organizations such as the World Trade Organization (WTO), the IPCC, the GEF, and the World Bank, which establish networks to promote solutions to environmental problems. NGOs have increased in number and significance in recent years, and they are quite diverse in their aims, forms, and structures. Ranging from local activists to professional organizations, they set international agendas, transcend state boundaries, work in partnership with the corporate sector and states, and participate directly in international environmental regimes. It is now a matter of debate whether IGOs and NGOs can successfully supplant states as major actors in global environmental policy, given issues of legitimacy and representativeness. O'Neill explores the breadth and scope of the many international environmental actors operating on multiple levels of governance and the increase in the numbers of international environmental agreements in which states, IGOs, and NGOs interact.

Jacqueline Peel provides a history of the development of international environmental law and its most important principles in Chapter 3. Before the establishment of the United Nations in 1945, there was no international forum in which to raise international environmental issues. Although the UN Charter does not explicitly mention the environment or conservation of resources, the United Nations convened its first environmental conference in 1949 and hosted many negotiations prior to the Stockholm Conference in 1972. Most existing environmental treaties were signed between 1972 and 1992, and recent decisions of the International Court of Justice confirm that the environment is now considered within the mainstream of international law. Peel explains the sources of international law, the roles of different actors in formulating and implementing it, and the most important emerging principles of environmental law. She outlines the development of international legal standards in six broad fields: protection of biodiversity, the marine environment, freshwater resources, air quality and climate change, waste management, and hazardous substances. Finally, she concludes that implementation and enforcement of this body of international law will be the most critical issue in the next phase of its development, suggesting that both international courts and nonjudicial bodies such as tribunals of the World Trade Organization are playing stronger roles than they have in the past.

In Chapter 4, David Leonard Downie analyzes the nature of international environmental policy regimes. Building on previous scholarship, he defines such a regime as "a system of principles, norms, rules, operating procedures, and institutions that actors create or accept to regulate and coordinate action in a particular issue area of international relations." He explains these terms in detail, often using as a generally successful and effective example the global regime to protect the ozone layer. He briefly outlines the structure of several other environmental regimes before discussing a wide range of political, economic, procedural, scientific, and cultural factors that can undermine the effectiveness of regimes and make international cooperation difficult. While not denying the success of some existing regimes, Downie's chapter casts a cold eye of realism on the strategic difficulties in achieving effective international policy, helping to explain the wide variance in effectiveness on display in global environmental governance.

The final chapter in Part I, by Michael G. Faure and Jürgen Lefevere, focuses on the broad problem of improving compliance with international environmental agreements.[29] The authors distinguish among treaty compliance, implementation, enforcement, and effectiveness. *Compliance* refers to the extent to which the behavior of states conforms to the rules set out in a treaty, whereas *implementation* involves specific actions taken by states within their own legal systems to make a treaty operative; *enforcement* denotes measures to force state compliance and implementation, and *effectiveness* focuses on whether the objectives of the treaty are actually achieved. Compliance does not guarantee effectiveness but is usually a necessary condition unless the treaty itself is so weak that compliance requires no changes in behavior. Throughout Chapter 5, Faure and Lefevere present examples from the global climate change and ozone layer regimes to illustrate the concepts and the challenges associated with compliance.

Traditionally, international agreements have included some dispute settlement procedures or other provisions for invoking legal, economic, or political sanctions against noncompliant parties, but in practice such sanctions have rarely been enforced and are seldom effective in achieving treaty objectives. Faure and Lefevere discuss the many factors that can affect rates of compliance, including the number of parties involved, the capacities of national governments, the strength of NGOs, and the nature of the substantive provisions (primary rules) written into the treaties themselves. They show how there has been a shift from the traditional enforcement approach to a "managerial" or "facilitative" approach in some recent environmental agreements such as the Montreal Protocol on ozone-depleting substances and the Kyoto

Protocol on climate change. These new "comprehensive noncompliance response systems" attempt to induce compliance through information and advice, technical assistance, and other incentives rather than by invoking negative sanctions. Nonadversarial approaches—successful in some cases—seem to be gaining in popularity, but the general effectiveness of these methods will be tested as international environmental law and governance shift toward a greater focus on compliance and implementation.

Big Players in Global Environmental Policy Making

Because the concept of sustainable development is broad and has quite different meanings when translated into different cultures and languages, it is difficult to evaluate national policies in terms of specific criteria or indicators of sustainability.[30] Some nations, such as New Zealand and the Netherlands, have adopted far-reaching sustainable development plans and programs, whereas others have dealt with sustainability issues in a piecemeal and ad hoc fashion, if at all.[31] But apart from rhetorical justification of selected measures under the sustainable development label, many policies and projects at the national and local levels do, in fact, have major implications for sustainability. Decisions about energy supply or land use within a given country can have impacts on other nations or the entire global system; this is especially true of very large nations such as China, Brazil, and the United States, and of the European Union. Major projects within countries (even small states) also attract capital and technical support from international banks and corporations, thus involving the international community in what may appear to be local developments. Such linkages between national politics and international action are essential components of global environmental policies and governance.[32]

Among developed nations, the United States has been among the most resistant to the idea of sustainable development and to ratification of multilateral environmental agreements in the past two decades.[33] Although the leader in establishing many of the environmental treaties through the 1980s (including the Montreal Protocol), the United States has generally been an international laggard since the first Bush administration, often becoming openly hostile to multilateral institutions and policies during the George W. Bush administration. American policy sometimes reflected a shift to conservative majorities in the U.S. Congress between 1995 and 2007, making it virtually impossible to ratify any environmental treaties. Although Democratic majorities in Congress briefly ushered in greater attention to environmental issues and regulation, by late 2013 deeply divided Congresses remained unable to change the poor record of U.S. environmental treaty ratification. Thus the United States has not ratified (and is not a party to) the Convention on Biological Diversity and its Biosafety Protocol, the Kyoto Protocol, the Law of the Sea, or the Basel Convention—to name just a few. American avoidance of certain kinds of international environmental agreements predates (and may outlast) the era of conservative ascendancy, requiring a deeper analysis of U.S. behavior.

In Chapter 6, Elizabeth R. DeSombre explores a wide range of hypotheses as to why the United States has initiated or supported some multilateral environmental agreements and opposed others over the past several decades. In particular, why has the United States taken a unilateral course on such major issues as climate change, biodiversity, trade in hazardous wastes, and the law of the sea? In search of a consistent causal explanation, DeSombre examines these cases as well as others in which the United States has preferred a cooperative approach, such as on combating ozone layer depletion and protecting endangered species. After determining that most conventional explanations concerning American culture and ideology, scientific uncertainty, relative vulnerability to harm, and the projected costs of regulation fail to explain all cases, she suggests a more nuanced explanation that focuses on certain aspects of U.S. domestic politics. In general, the United States supports international agreements when it already has enacted domestic regulations in the same areas and opposes international controls that go beyond domestic regulation or would be difficult to implement in the U.S. system. This pattern can in turn be explained by institutional peculiarities of the American system, especially the unique role that Congress plays in shaping foreign policy. DeSombre and others have noted that the Senate, especially, tends to be responsive to domestic business and industry pressures seeking to block international regulation. This pattern may change over time, however, as some major firms and industrial sectors come to favor action on climate change and other issues and because international institutions may, over time, shape the preferences of U.S. domestic actors.

In contrast with the United States, the European Union has increasingly taken the lead—or attempted to lead—domestically and internationally in numerous areas of environmental policy. In Chapter 7, Regina S. Axelrod and Miranda A. Schreurs explain how the European integration process and its evolving institutional structure contribute to this leadership role. Although the Treaty of Rome, which established the European Economic Community (EEC) in 1957, made no mention of environmental policy, beginning in 1972 the EEC adopted a series of environmental action programs and enacted numerous specific environmental laws as a way of harmonizing economic policies. Since 1986 several major treaty revisions have strengthened the legal capacity of the EEC to legislate in the field of environmental protection. The Maastricht Treaty of 1992 transformed the European Economic Community into the broader European Union, which has since grown from twelve to twenty-eight states. The EU has also explicitly incorporated the goal of sustainable development into the treaty and has taken an increasingly active role in international environmental diplomacy on matters such as climate change. In a number of environmental policy areas, EU and U.S. federal policy making has often diverged on global environmental issues during the past fifteen-plus years.[34] The EU has enacted a large set of innovative and ambitious environmental policies over the past twenty years on a wide range of issues—several opposed by U.S. government and corporate actors. This growth, however, has also increased the implementation challenges in both the newer EU member states and longtime member states, presenting the EU with compliance and implementation challenges at home and occasionally threatening its global environmental leadership position.[35]

Axelrod and Schreurs describe the structure and evolution of the EU in detail and analyze policy developments since 1992. Although the European Union is still an intergovernmental organization in the sense that decisions must ultimately be approved by member states, in practice it functions as a supranational governance system in which most policies are adopted by majority voting in the council and the parliament. Moreover, the composition of EU officials and member state representatives can change according to the subject at issue, including environment ministers and technocrats, for example, when the EU considers environmental legislation. As a result, EU environmental policies have been less subject to opposition group pressure than have such policies in the United States. At the same time, EU treaties require integration of environmental policy into other policy sectors in order to promote sustainable development. Several new, innovative policies that go beyond measures in the United States are discussed in the chapter. Yet, as Axelrod and Schreurs make clear, the EU faces major hurdles in implementing sustainable development policies and in adapting governance structures and policy standards to both old and new member states.[36]

In Chapter 8, Joanna I. Lewis and Kelly Sims Gallagher address energy, environmental, and sustainability issues in a large and rapidly developing country: China. They present a wealth of data on China's energy resources, trends, and use, as well as on its transportation and electricity generation infrastructure. They also analyze the political institutions that shape energy issues in China. As Lewis and Gallagher show, providing energy for 1.3 billion people and a growing and modernizing economy in an environmentally sensitive and sustainable manner is an enormous, unprecedented challenge. The environmental and social costs of China's energy and transportation infrastructure are huge. Yet the Chinese central government has demonstrated growing concern about environmental issues and growing interest in serious environmental policy reform and investments in renewable energy generation and air and water quality improvements. The costs of moving China away from coal are enormous, as is the challenge of implementing new environmental standards at the local level. Yet China's automobile efficiency standards are as high as or higher than those in the United States, and its investments in wind and solar power have made it a world leader in only a few years in terms of installed capacity and industrial production. Lewis and Gallagher make it clear that China faces enormous obstacles in transitioning to a more sustainable society, but they also demonstrate that China's environmental politics and regulation are changing rapidly as concern has grown among publics and state leaders.

Chapter 9 shifts the focus to the developing world, or the Global South, more broadly. Adil Najam argues that the South has a well-developed collective identity and sense of purpose dating back to the Stockholm Conference on the Human Environment and the quest for a "new international economic order" in the 1970s. This unity is manifest primarily in the Group of 77 (G-77) bloc in the United Nations, now consisting of some 134 developing countries. Najam explains how preparations for the 1992 UNCED in Rio offered the South an opportunity to revive the North-South dialogue around the theme of sustainable development, and how subsequent UN global summits have offered opportunities to advance the overarching economic and political agendas of the South as well as created disappointment and frustration regarding many results in such global forums. From the South's perspective, the Rio conference provided a high point in its ability to shape the international agenda. Although most of the South's demands were not met, UNCED did link the economic development goals of the South to the environmental agenda of the North, and it established several important new principles of international environmental law, such as the principle of common but differentiated responsibility. Nevertheless, in looking back at the two decades between Rio and Rio+20, Najam concludes that these principles and the "Rio bargain" on sustainable development have been largely abandoned at the global level, leading to widespread disillusionment among developing countries.

Cases, Controversies, and Challenges

The range of international environmental policies currently in force is vast, covering, among other things, protection of endangered plants and animals and biodiversity, broadly; protection against transboundary pollution of air, water, and soil; protection of the atmosphere against acidification, ozone depletion, and climate change; protection of the oceans against oil spills and the dumping of radioactive and other hazardous materials; conservation of fisheries; regulation of trade in dangerous chemicals, pesticides, and hazardous wastes; measures to combat desertification; and protection of Antarctica. In addition, new policies are emerging for consideration of environmental protection under the rules of international trade and for promoting sustainable development initiatives pursuant to Agenda 21.

Policies may take the form of binding treaties or secondary legislation, or they may take the form of policy declarations or voluntary programs to achieve certain results. They usually require implementation by actors at many levels, including businesses, local governments, and grassroots organizations as well as national governments. Evaluation of the *effectiveness* of policies is complex, in part because effectiveness can be measured in many ways: for example, by whether states are in legal compliance with treaties, by whether monetary and other resources are being spent on programs, and by the actual results of the policies in terms of environmental improvements. Policies are also *learning processes* in that the actors involved continually gain new knowledge about problems and engage other parties in parallel efforts to achieve goals.

Climate change resulting from a gradual buildup of greenhouse gases (GHGs) in the Earth's atmosphere is perhaps the most serious, complex, and

contentious of all international environmental policy issues. It is now generally accepted that climate change is resulting from increased GHGs in the
atmosphere and that this is a global problem to be reckoned with from local
to global levels of authority. Scientific and technical expertise plays an important role in global environmental politics around issues such as climate
change, but scientific findings have come under strong and well-funded
attacks, with pockets of explicit denial in some countries. Few things illustrate
these dynamics better than the acrimonious debates about the methods and
language of each IPCC report and the sustained attacks on the credibility and
legitimacy of IPCC participants. In Chapter 10, Michele M. Betsill traces the
origins of concern over the problem of climate change and analyzes policy
responses since the First World Climate Conference in 1979. In the
thirty-plus years of globalizing concern, the impacts of climate change—
temperature changes, weather volatility and extremes, agricultural changes,
ice cap and glacial melt, species migration and biodiversity changes, and rising
sea level (to name only a few)—have become increasingly apparent and
severe. Growing numbers of local and national communities are threatened
by these ongoing and accelerating changes. Betsill discusses the development
of scientific research as a basis for negotiations leading to the United Nations
Framework Convention on Climate Change (FCCC) in 1992. She explains
the principles underlying this historic agreement before analyzing the first
binding agreement restricting GHG emissions made pursuant to the FCCC,
the Kyoto Protocol of 1997. Although the United States neither ratified nor
implemented the Kyoto treaty, the protocol came into legal force because of
other states' ratifications. Betsill argues that the Kyoto agreement and subsequent negotiations have many important indirect effects on policy actors at
many levels of government and in the private sector—in the United States
and in ratifying states. For example, many states and cities and private corporations (in the United States and around the globe) have adopted GHG
reduction strategies despite the lack of international consensus. As negotiations for a climate agreement to follow the Kyoto Protocol progressed, the
role and actions of the United States, and of the largest developing country
emitters, loomed large in global negotiations. Yet, as Betsill makes clear,
global climate change governance is a complex, multilevel process not confined only to multilateral treaty making. Such multilevel governance, she
argues, presents new opportunities to develop effective policy responses
around the world.

A consequence of modern societies' reliance on chemicals and heavy metals
is the release of hazardous substances that produce long-term environmental
damage and pose significant health risks. Many international and regional
treaties address these issues, and the United Nations plays a prominent role.
In Chapter 11, Henrik Selin focuses on four such treaties: the 1989 Basel
Convention on the Control of Transboundary Movements of Hazardous
Wastes and Their Disposal, the 1998 Rotterdam Convention on the Prior
Informed Consent Procedure for Certain Hazardous Chemicals and Pesti-
cides in International Trade, the 1998 Protocol on Persistent Organic

Pollutants to the Convention on Long-Range Transboundary Air Pollution (CLRTAP), and the 2001 Stockholm Convention on Persistent Organic Pollutants. The Basel Convention seeks to regulate trade in hazardous waste through a notification scheme. The Rotterdam Convention focuses on transparency in the trade of chemicals by requiring notification to importers by exporters of such materials. The aim of the CLRTAP Protocol is to reduce the release and long-term transport of persistent organic pollutants. The Stockholm Convention regulates the production of persistent organic chemicals. Selin discusses the accomplishments of these regulatory regimes and the problems they have incurred, suggesting means to strengthen them. Hazardous materials are still produced in large quantities, and many states remain suspicious of relinquishing national authority to international treaty regimes or organizations. Selin's treatment of these issues also demonstrates the tremendous growth in international cooperation over time, from isolated and rather modest agreements to a large and complex set of governance regimes. The European Union has taken a leadership role in adopting regulations targeting hazardous chemicals and electronic waste, but countries all over the world are struggling to manage hazardous substances and wastes. Selin argues for more proactive and precautionary actions, including giving industry greater responsibilities for reducing hazardous waste and the development of greener chemistry.

Biodiversity is often defined as the total variety of all ecosystems and species in the world, including the genetic variation within species. It is declining globally, with serious ecological, moral, and economic ramifications. In the bulk of Chapter 12, G. Kristin Rosendal focuses on the contents, negotiations, and ongoing politics around the 1992 Convention on Biological Diversity, a framework convention, and its associated Cartagena Protocol on Biosafety and Nagoya Protocol on Access and Benefit Sharing. Also part of the global biodiversity regime complex are the older cooperation arrangements focused on wetlands preservation and the protection of migratory and/or endangered species. Global biodiversity politics connects many themes in the volume as a whole, including the challenges associated with North-South politics, differing conceptions of expertise, and the tensions among sustainability, sovereignty, and economic opportunity in international relations.

The formerly socialist countries of Central and Eastern Europe have experienced rapid political and economic transformations over the past generation, moving from Soviet-style communism to capitalist democracy and EU membership.[37] In Chapter 13, Regina S. Axelrod discusses the political controversy surrounding the Temelin nuclear power plant in the Czech Republic. She frames this case in the context of what many call the global renaissance of nuclear power, comparing aspects of Czech nuclear power controversies with ongoing debates in the United States and Japan. Western governments, banks, and corporations and various IGOs were involved in upgrading Soviet-designed nuclear power reactors such as Temelin in Central and Eastern European countries to ensure the reactors' safety and continued operation and to provide alternatives to dirty coal-fired power plants. As Axelrod explains, however, serious technical and environmental problems have raised questions about the wisdom of this strategy and have led to protests both inside and outside the Czech Republic. She finds a troubling rejection of sustainable development policies by Czech governments since 1992, accompanied by an exclusion of environmental NGOs and the reassertion of state bureaucratic and technocratic methods of decision making. Axelrod argues that nuclear power debates demonstrate that the concept of sustainability remains new and rather marginalized in both the Czech Republic and the United States. Pressure to revive nuclear energy in the United States has been stymied by cost and the absence of a solution to the disposal of nuclear waste. The ongoing Fukushima disaster refocused global attention on the safety and environmental impact of nuclear energy, with hundreds of tons of leaking radioactive water and calls for international assistance from Japan, raising questions about the viability of any global nuclear renaissance. All three countries—the Czech Republic, Japan, and the United States—are grappling with the problem of developing their energy futures and questioning the role nuclear energy will play in light of its long-term environmental and safety issues.

International trade in dangerous substances is only one example of how economic globalization has led to a host of new concerns over environmental impacts. Many environmentalists fear that international trade agreements such as the North American Free Trade Agreement (NAFTA) and establishment of the World Trade Organization will accelerate global environmental degradation in several ways: by increasing the consumption of resources and production of wastes as the result of accelerated economic growth, by shifting capital and production to "pollution havens" with weak environmental laws, and by establishing rules of international trade that may conflict with and override existing multilateral environmental agreements and environmental legislation in individual countries. For example, laws restricting trade in endangered species or banning products harvested using environmentally damaging methods might be found to violate international free trade principles.[38]

In Chapter 14, Daniel C. Esty takes a somewhat more optimistic view of the potential for balancing international trade and environmental protection. He analyzes environmentalists' concerns that liberalized trade and increasing competitive pressures will undermine existing environmental protections, and he summarizes the counterarguments of free trade advocates. NAFTA was the first such agreement to integrate aspects of environmental and trade policy. Esty evaluates the Environmental Side Agreement to NAFTA, generally finding it a more successful effort to balance economic and environmental goals than many critics suggest.[39] Moreover, in the trade agreement negotiating authority granted to President George W. Bush in 2002 by the U.S. Congress and in resolutions at the World Summit on Sustainable Development in Johannesburg, linkages between trade and environmental protection were explicitly recognized. Recent U.S. trade agreements also include some environmental commitments. Esty explores the changing role of the WTO in these issues, as it becomes more sensitive to environmental concerns and the location of a growing number of environment-related trade disputes. He concludes that the WTO needs reform—especially to increase transparency and access by NGOs—and that the underlying General Agreement on Tariffs and Trade may have to be revised to ensure the trade regime's compatibility with environmental treaties.[40]

Finally, in Chapter 15, Stacy D. VanDeveer addresses the related issues of consumption, transnational commodity chains, and sustainability. Human consumption of the Earth's resources continues to grow as we use up ever-increasing amounts of material throughput. VanDeveer's analysis rests on some basic facts and arguments: that everything comes from somewhere, that all consumption uses things up, and that every transaction along the webs of social relations for any basic commodity or manufactured good consumes (or uses) resources. This ever-increasing material throughput of consumer societies—societies that are being rapidly replicated around the world—means that the ecological and humanitarian damage done by consumption is globalizing and increasing. The things we eat, drink, buy, use, and throw away in our everyday lives leave long trails of destruction, even if they also accrue benefits for their consumers and producers. VanDeveer explores this destruction through discussion of the long and complex product chains for consumer products such as blue jeans, agricultural commodities, and the industries associated with mining and oil and gas extraction. He offers a list of policies that might combat or reduce such harms as well as some examples of ongoing efforts to meet the challenges posed by global consumerism and its costs.

The Uncertain Future

The contributions to this book convey rather mixed and sobering messages. Although substantial progress was made between the 1971 Stockholm and 1992 Rio conferences in establishing international environmental institutions, laws, and policies to address problems such as marine pollution and depletion of the ozone layer, global environmental governance has often faltered since the mid-1990s. The concept of sustainable development turned out to be enormously complex and difficult to implement in the two decades following the Rio Earth Summit, although efforts to do so continue at the global, national, and local levels around the world, producing thousands of interesting policy and social experiments. Again, while some progress has been made, the most basic requirement of sustainable development—raising the living standards of the world's poorest people—has not yet been achieved, nor have environmental concerns been effectively integrated into most sectors of economic and social development in either the richest or the poorest countries. Even as the truly catastrophic outcomes of climate change loom in the not-too-distant future, states and societies around the world struggle to muster the political will to act to reduce the emissions causing climate change, to adapt to the impacts of global climate change, or both.

Most international agencies, including the United Nations Environment Programme, the Global Environment Facility, and the UN Commission on

Sustainable Development, are inadequately financed and torn by economic and political divisions and other ideological conflicts. With the possible exception of the European Union and a few specific policy regimes, international environmental governance remains weak, even by the standards of international governance. National governments also vary greatly in their interpretation of and commitment to the idea of sustainable development, but few have given high priority to environmental sustainability. While the EU often attempts to lead on global environmental issues, the United States continues to struggle to define its role as a leader or a laggard in global environmental governance, and China and other large and influential developing countries remain similarly conflicted.

Despite this, local governments, private organizations, and a host of NGOs have become increasingly important actors in defining the environmental norms of civil society. Also, without engagement and commitments from large and economically dynamic developing states such as China, global environmental governance is unlikely to succeed. The 2009 Copenhagen Climate Change Summit (and subsequent climate change cooperation efforts) and 2012's Rio+20 summit demonstrated the continuing inability of states to come to agreement on binding commitments designed to stave off the most disastrous impacts of environmental change.

The election of a U.S. administration that placed greater emphasis on building renewable energy infrastructure and industries and showed a greater willingness to support more stringent environmental policies, both domestically and internationally, promised to give sustainability issues a new life in the United States. And many European, North American, and Asian leaders and citizens continue to talk about the need for greater multilateral environmental cooperation and the benefits of states competing to become leaders in renewable energy and cleaner technology development. Yet hoped-for cooperation among big players on the global stage remains elusive. Nevertheless, impressive policy efforts can be found at local and national levels around the globe, including the rapid expansion of renewable energy generation in China and some European countries and accelerating efforts to address air and water pollution in a number of the fastest-growing developing countries. And environmental NGOs and social movements have not stopped pushing for stronger, more dramatic action by public and private actors.

Global environmental issues are becoming more critical as more serious, complex, and long-ranging problems surface, but attempts to address them remain a low priority for governments in a world feeling the impact of economic challenges. Although the numbers of international environmental agreements and regimes, and of international and national NGOs, have grown, improvements in the state of the environment are difficult to achieve. Even though the world's nations have acquired more knowledge and expertise about the state of the environment and how to mitigate environmental problems, they have demonstrated less political will to make serious changes and less effective policy implementation. In recent years, however, large developing countries such as China, India, and Brazil have shown greater willingness than before to engage in global environmental negotiations and governance as well as domestic policy development. Growing awareness of environmental degradation and its public health, economic, and security implications may yet bring countries (North and South) into greater agreement about sustainability. Still, economic issues and interests continue to outcompete environmental ones for political attention and for funding, despite years of sustainable development–inspired assertions and research suggesting that environmental and economic issues need not be at odds.

Whether economic globalization and rising global consumption can be made compatible with the integrity of the Earth's ecological systems and the needs and demands of human social systems remains an open question. Overall, the early years of the twenty-first century have been a period of uncertainty and rather incremental development for international environmental governance. The European Union, some U.S. states, and a few other world leaders demonstrate that environmental policy leadership remains possible and potentially effective and beneficial. Successful cooperation around issues such as the protection of the ozone layer also demonstrates that global environmental governance can be efficient and effective for the public and private sectors. If worrisome environmental trends are to be reversed, such successes and the leadership they require must become the rule rather than the exception. Global environmental problems are becoming more urgent and dangerous. Citizens and public officials need to demonstrate that they can meet these serious challenges if the worst outcomes are to be avoided.

Notes

1. See especially Richard Elliot Benedick, *Ozone Diplomacy: New Directions in Safeguarding the Planet,* enlarged ed. (Cambridge, MA: Harvard University Press, 1998); Edward A. Parson, *Protecting the Ozone Layer: Science and Strategy* (Oxford: Oxford University Press, 2003). See also Chapters 4 and 5 in this volume.
2. World Commission on Environment and Development, *Our Common Future* (New York: Oxford University Press, 1987).
3. On UNCED and WSSD, see Philip Shabecoff, *A New Name for Peace: International Environmentalism, Sustainable Development, and Democracy* (Hanover, NH: University Press of New England, 1996); James Gustave Speth, "Perspectives on the Johannesburg Summit," *Environment* 45, no. 1 (January–February 2003): 24–29.
4. Ronald B. Mitchell, International Environmental Agreements (IEA) Database Project, Version 2013.2, accessed July 2013, http://iea.uoregon.edu/page.php?file=home.htm.
5. Paul F. Steinberg and Stacy D. VanDeveer, *Comparative Environmental Politics: Theory, Practice, and Prospects* (Cambridge: MIT Press, 2012).
6. United Nations Development Programme, *World Resources 2002–2004: Decisions for the Earth—Balance, Voice, and Power* (Washington, DC: World Resources Institute, 2003), 140–141.
7. Ibid., 138–139; James Gustave Speth, *Red Sky at Morning: America and the Crisis of the Global Environment* (New Haven, CT: Yale University Press, 2004), esp. chap. 5, "Anatomy of Failure"; Hilary French, *Vanishing Borders: Protecting the Planet in the Age of Globalization* (New York: W. W. Norton, 2000); Ronnie D. Lipschutz, *Global Environmental Politics: Power, Perspectives, and Practice* (Washington, DC: CQ Press, 2004).

8. See also Miranda A. Schreurs, Henrik Selin, and Stacy D. VanDeveer, eds., *Transatlantic Environment and Energy Politics: Comparative and International Perspectives* (Farnham, UK: Ashgate, 2009); Norman J. Vig and Michael G. Faure, eds., *Green Giants? Environmental Policies of the United States and the European Union* (Cambridge: MIT Press, 2004).

9. See Henrik Selin and Stacy D. VanDeveer, eds., *Changing Climates in North American Politics: Institutions, Policymaking, and Multilevel Governance* (Cambridge: MIT Press, 2009).

10. The quarterly journal *Global Environmental Politics* is the premier example among many such periodicals as well as many university press and commercial books published each year.

11. Kate O'Neill, *The Environment and International Relations* (New York: Cambridge University Press, 2009); Steinberg and VanDeveer, *Comparative Environmental Politics.*

12. See John J. Mearsheimer, "The False Promise of International Institutions," *International Security* 19 (1995): 5–49. Classic realist texts include Hans J. Morgenthau, *Politics among Nations: The Struggle for Power and Peace,* 5th ed. (New York: Knopf, 1978); Kenneth N. Waltz, *Theory of International Politics* (New York: Random House, 1979).

13. For a standard text, see Robert O. Keohane and Joseph S. Nye Jr., *Power and Interdependence: World Politics in Transition* (Boston: Little, Brown, 1977).

14. O'Neill, *The Environment and International Relations;* Kate O'Neill, Joerg Balsiger, and Stacy VanDeveer, "Actors, Norms and Impact," *Annual Review of Political Science* 7 (2004): 149–175.

15. Jack Snyder, "One World, Rival Theories," *Foreign Policy,* November/December 2004, 52–62.

16. Peter Haas, "UN Conferences and the Constructivist Governance of the Environment," *Global Governance* 8 (2002): 73–91.

17. Oran R. Young, ed., *Global Governance: Drawing Insights from the Environmental Experience* (Cambridge: MIT Press, 1997); Paul F. Diehl, ed., *The Politics of Global Governance* (Boulder, CO: Lynne Rienner, 1997); Deborah D. Avant, Martha Finnemore, and Susan K. Sell, eds., *Who Governs the Globe?* (Cambridge: Cambridge University Press, 2010).

18. See, for example, Ronnie D. Lipschutz with Judith Mayer, *Global Civil Society and Global Environmental Governance* (Albany: State University of New York Press, 1996); Margaret E. Keck and Kathryn Sikkink, *Activists beyond Borders: Advocacy Networks in International Politics* (Ithaca, NY: Cornell University Press, 1998); Lipschutz, *Global Environmental Politics.*

19. Mathew J. Hoffmann, *Climate Governance at the Crossroads: Experimenting with a Global Response after Kyoto* (New York: Oxford University Press, 2011); Harriet Bulkeley, Liliana Andonova, Michele Betsill, Daniel Compagnon, Thomas Hale, Mathew Hoffmann, Peter Newell, Matthew Paterson, Charles Roger, and Stacy D. VanDeveer, *Transnational Climate Change Governance* (Cambridge: Cambridge University Press, 2014); Philip Andrews-Speed, Raimund Bleischwitz, Tim Boersma, Corey Johnson, Geoffrey Kemp, and Stacy D. VanDeveer, *The Global Resource Nexus: The Struggles for Land, Energy, Food, Water, and Minerals* (Washington, DC: Transatlantic Academy, 2012).

20. On the conflict preceding the Stockholm Conference, see Lynton K. Caldwell, *International Environmental Policy,* 3rd ed. (Durham, NC: Duke University Press, 1996), 57–62.

21. See, for example, John Lemons and Donald A. Brown, eds., *Sustainable Development: Science, Ethics, and Public Policy* (Dordrecht, Netherlands: Kluwer Academic Publishers, 1995); Ian H. Rowlands, "International Fairness and Justice in Addressing Global Climate Change," *Environmental Politics* 6 (Autumn 1997): 1–30; Keekok Lee, Alan Holland, and Desmond McNeill, eds., *Global Sustainable Development in the 21st Century* (Edinburgh: Edinburgh University Press, 2000).

22. Edith Brown Weiss, "The Emerging Structure of International Environmental Law," in *The Global Environment: Institutions, Law, and Policy*, ed. Norman J. Vig and Regina S. Axelrod (Washington, DC: CQ Press, 1999), 106–107. For a full discussion, see Edith Brown Weiss, *In Fairness to Future Generations: International Law, Common Patrimony, and Intergenerational Equity* (Dobbs Ferry, NY: Transnational Publishers, 1989).
23. WCED, *Our Common Future*, 43.
24. For an excellent collection of essays on this topic, see Susan Baker, Maria Kousis, Dick Richardson, and Stephen Young, eds., *The Politics of Sustainable Development* (London: Routledge, 1997). See also Thomas M. Parris, "Toward a Sustainability Transition: The International Consensus," *Environment* 45, no. 1 (January–February 2003): 12–22; John C. Dernbach, ed., *Stumbling toward Sustainability* (Washington, DC: Environmental Law Institute, 2002).
25. Peter Dauvergne and Jane Lister, *Eco-Business: A Big-Brand Takeover of Sustainability* (Cambridge: MIT Press, 2013).
26. Some of these are discussed in Leslie Paul Thiele, *Sustainability* (London: Polity, 2013); Thaddeus C. Trzyna, *A Sustainable World: Defining and Measuring Sustainable Development* (Sacramento: California Institute of Public Affairs, 1995); and Simon Bell and Stephen Morse, *Measuring Sustainability: Learning from Doing* (London: Earthscan, 2003). See also Joy E. Hecht, "Sustainability Indicators on the Web," *Environment* 45, no. 1 (January–February 2003): 3–4.
27. Paul G. Harris, *International Equity and Global Environmental Politics: Power and Principles of U.S. Foreign Policy* (Aldershot, UK: Ashgate, 2001); Paul G. Harris, "International Development Assistance and Burden Sharing," in Vig and Faure, *Green Giants?*, 252–275; Adil Najam, Janice M. Poling, Naoyuki Yamagishi, Daniel G. Straub, Jillian Sarno, Sara M. DeRitter, and Eonjeong M. Kim, "From Rio to Johannesburg: Progress and Prospects," *Environment* 44, no. 7 (September 2002): 26–38.
28. For nice summaries of such debates, see Maria Ivanova, "The Contested Legacy of Rio+20," *Global Environmental Politics* 13, no. 4 (2013): 1–11; Steven Bernstein, "Rio+20: Sustainable Development in a Time of Multilateral Decline," *Global Environmental Politics* 13, no. 4 (2013): 12–21.
29. See David G. Victor, Kal Raustiala, and Eugene B. Skolnikoff, eds., *The Implementation and Effectiveness of International Environmental Commitments: Theory and Practice* (Cambridge: MIT Press, 1998); Edith Brown Weiss and Harold K. Jacobson, eds., *Engaging Countries: Strengthening Compliance with International Environmental Accords* (Cambridge: MIT Press, 1998).
30. For a comparison of European-language translations of the term *sustainable development*, see Nigel Haigh, "'Sustainable Development' in the European Union Treaties," *International Environmental Affairs* 8 (Winter 1996): 87–91.
31. Huey D. Johnson, *Green Plans: Greenprint for Sustainability* (Lincoln: University of Nebraska Press, 1995). See also Tim O'Riordan and Heather Voisey, eds., "Sustainable Development in Western Europe: Coming to Terms with Agenda 21," special issue, *Environmental Politics* 6 (Spring 1997); William M. Lafferty and James Meadowcroft, eds., *Implementing Sustainable Development: Strategies and Initiatives in High Consumption Societies* (Oxford: Oxford University Press, 2000).
32. For some good examples, see Miranda A. Schreurs and Elizabeth C. Economy, eds., *The Internationalization of Environmental Protection* (Cambridge: Cambridge University Press, 1997); Steinberg and VanDeveer, *Comparative Environmental Politics*.
33. See Gary C. Bryner, "The United States: 'Sorry—Not Our Problem,'" in Lafferty and Meadowcroft, *Implementing Sustainable Development*. There have been many sustainable development projects at the state and local levels, however; see Daniel A. Mazmanian and Michael E. Kraft, eds., *Toward Sustainable Communities: Transitions and Transformations in Environmental Policy* (Cambridge: MIT Press, 1999); Kent E. Portney, *Taking Sustainable Cities Seriously: Economic Development, the Environment,*

and the Quality of Life in American Cities (Cambridge: MIT Press, 2002); Barry G. Rabe, *Statehouse and Greenhouse: The Emerging Politics of American Climate Change Policy* (Washington, DC: Brookings Institution Press, 2004).

34. See Vig and Faure, *Green Giants?*; Schreurs et al., *Transatlantic Environment and Energy Politics.*

35. JoAnn Carmin and Stacy D. VanDeveer, eds., *EU Enlargement and the Environment: Institutional Change and Environmental Policy in Central and Eastern Europe* (London: Routledge, 2005).

36. See Susan Baker and John McCormick, "Sustainable Development: Comparative Understandings and Responses," in Vig and Faure, *Green Giants?*, 277–302.

37. For discussion of developments in this region, see Liliana B. Andonova, *Transnational Politics of the Environment: The European Union and Environmental Policy in Central and Eastern Europe* (Cambridge: MIT Press, 2003); Carmin and VanDeveer, *EU Enlargement and the Environment.*

38. For a collection of essays on the environmental consequences of free trade, see James Gustave Speth, ed., *Worlds Apart: Globalization and the Environment* (Washington, DC: Island Press, 2003).

39. See John J. Audley, *Green Politics and Global Trade: NAFTA and the Future of Environmental Politics* (Washington, DC: Georgetown University Press, 1997); Jerry Mander and Edward Goldsmith, eds., *The Case against the Global Economy* (San Francisco: Sierra Club, 1996). For a more recent assessment of NAFTA, see John J. Audley, Demetrios G. Papademetriou, Sandra Polaski, and Scott Vaughan, *NAFTA's Promise and Reality: Lessons from Mexico for the Hemisphere* (Washington, DC: Carnegie Endowment for International Peace, 2004).

40. See also Daniel Esty, "Toward a Global Environmental Mechanism," in Speth, *Worlds Apart*, 67–82.

2

Architects, Agitators, and Entrepreneurs

International and Nongovernmental Organizations in Global Environmental Politics

Kate O'Neill

This chapter introduces two types of representative organizations active in global environmental politics—international governmental organizations, also known as intergovernmental organizations (IGOs), and nongovernmental organizations (NGOs)—and discusses their roles in instigating, coordinating, and implementing global environmental governance over the past decades. IGOs and NGOs represent very different constituencies: nation-states, and civil society, respectively. As *agitators* for environmental action, *architects* of governance solutions, and *entrepreneurs* for new sorts of initiatives,[1] they have been critical in shaping and directing the international community's response to global environmental challenges. Both IGOs and NGOs have, in the face of intransigence, low capacity, and/or low commitment of national governments, taken on larger and more autonomous roles in global environmental governance than these organizations were initially designed or intended to do. They have played a critical role in building larger visions, or goals, for achieving a sustainable future that have helped frame intergovernmental action on a larger scale, for example, through the eight Millennium Development Goals, established at the United Nations Millennium Summit in 2000.

State-led global environmental governance has been the dominant mode of global environmental governance for the past forty-plus years,[2] whereby national governments cooperate to establish multilateral environmental agreements (MEAs) and the networks of institutions and organizations that manage them. Its history can be traced through four major "Earth Summits" that have been held since 1972 and through the multitude of MEAs that have been negotiated over time, many since the first global environmental conference, held in Stockholm, Sweden, in 1972. Over this time, IGOs and NGOs have multiplied and spread across the arena of global environmental governance. The remainder of this chapter examines and evaluates the emergence and evolution of these two sorts of representative organizations and, through them, global environmental governance. Other chapters in this volume focus in more detail on the roles of treaties and other types of international law (Chapter 3) and international regimes (Chapter 4).

International Governmental Organizations and the Global Environment

Nation-states establish IGOs to ease international cooperation by taking on the tasks of coordinating interstate negotiations and implementing and enforcing resulting agreements. IGOs may be defined as "organizations that include at least three states among their membership, that have activities in several states, and that are created through a formal intergovernmental agreement such as a treaty, charter or statute."[3] Examples range from the United Nations and its associated agencies down to single-issue IGOs such as the International Whaling Commission and regional IGOs such as the Association of Southeast Asian Nations. This section reviews the many forms and functions of IGOs that have a role in global environmental governance.

IGOs can be *agitators*, taking advantage of opportunities to raise governmental concern about the state of the global environment and generating knowledge that informs understanding of the causes of these problems and what to do about them. They are also, of course, *architects* of global environmental governance, given their instigating and coordinating roles delegated to them by member states. They are *managers* of governance regimes and processes established under their auspices, and they are *entrepreneurs* as well, shaping the norms that underlie the overall architecture of global environmental governance and pushing for new directions, often when states are unable or unwilling to push for stronger measures.

The United Nations System

The United Nations and key actors within it have played a central role as instigators and architects of global environmental governance, starting with the first global summit on the environment, held in Stockholm in 1972. The United Nations was established in 1945 as a global security organization to maintain collective security and peace in the wake of World War II. By 2013, it had 193 member states. Its two most important governing bodies are the General Assembly, in which each member country is represented and has a single vote, and the Security Council, which consists of representatives from fifteen countries, including five permanent representatives (from the United States, the United Kingdom, Russia, France, and China) who have veto power over council decisions.[4] The UN's powers include establishing peacekeeping operations, meting out international punitive sanctions, and authorizing military action. The United Nations is administered by the office of the secretary-general. Its specialized agencies and programs are responsible for promoting different aspects of the UN's global mandate, from economic and social development to agriculture to world health.[5]

The UN's early years were marked by Cold War divisions and intransigent interstate disputes. However, as countries in Asia and Africa emerged from colonial rule in the 1950s and 1960s, membership increased dramatically. By 1962, the organization had doubled in size from its initial fifty-one members, including many more developing and nonaligned nations, which were not as invested in the Cold War face-off between the United States and the Soviet Union.[6] These new members pushed for social and economic issues to lead the UN's agenda, partly through the collective influence of the Group of 77 (G-77), which formed in 1964 during the first UN Conference on Trade and Development (UNCTAD).[7] In turn, these developments invigorated the UN's social and economic development programs and helped open the door for the inclusion of global environmental issues in the UN's suite of activities.

Within this same time frame, scientists and environmentalists were converging in their concerns and beginning to see environmental problems as global and transboundary threats. In some cases—such as transboundary air pollution and species loss—the threats were familiar but had come to be understood to exist on a far larger scale than previously thought. Others were newly recognized problems or problems that had been theorized but the impacts and causes of which were now being demonstrated by scientific research—such as climate change and stratospheric ozone layer depletion as a result of human economic activity. These two latter problems, furthermore, could be understood as existential risks: like global nuclear war, each posed a significant—perhaps highly potent—threat to human civilization (as highlighted by the National Oceanic and Atmospheric Administration in 2009). In addition, prior to 1972, existing environmental treaties were not housed under any particular institution, nor had there been much attempt to bring them together as a coherent system with unifying principles, despite the existence of an already extensive body of international environmental law.[8]

During this time, the United Nations was instrumental in helping to raise international concern and to frame ways the international community could move forward and address global environmental concerns in a systematic fashion. First, it sponsored some of the leading international scientific collaborations that generated research on the biosphere and atmosphere in the 1950s, 1960s, and early 1970s.[9] Examples include the World Meteorological Organization's involvement in the 1956–1957 International Geophysical Year and its leadership, with the International Council of Scientific Unions, of the Global Atmospheric Research Program—a fifteen-year multicountry endeavor—and UNESCO's leadership of the Man and the Biosphere program, which began in 1971. The UN was able to take advantage of this and other new scientific research and use it to push for global action on pressing environmental issues at the same time that the environmental movement (see below) was also gathering strength and advocating for global solutions.

The late 1960s and early 1970s were a propitious time for creating a new arena of global politics. Cold War tensions were starting to ease, at least for a time, and the superpowers—the United States and the Soviet Union—were beginning to talk about arms control agreements. The global environment could not only be a new issue for a somewhat embattled UN to claim as its own, but it could also help erode long-standing political rivalries, uniting enemies in a common cause. The United Nations was, therefore, able to provide an effective platform from which efforts to protect the global environment could be launched.

Particular individuals and countries within the UN system took the lead in initiating the process that led to the first global environmental summit in 1972.[10]

Designing Global Environmental Governance: The Role of Global Summits

In 1972 the UN convened the first global "Earth Summit," the UN Conference on the Human Environment (UNCHE), in Stockholm (see Table 2-1), initiating what would prove to be a watershed moment in global environmental governance. UNCHE brought together representatives from 113 countries to discuss how to address the newly recognized global scope of environmental problems. The resulting agreements accomplished several goals. Delegates agreed that the most effective way forward would be through multilateral diplomacy: the negotiation of binding legal agreements among nation-states on an issue-by-issue basis. This decision ratified existing practices, as by then a large number of multilateral environmental agreements were already in existence, from the 1946 International Whaling Convention to other cooperative arrangements dating back to the nineteenth century. Second, the Stockholm Declaration codified twenty-six principles of international environmental law, including the rights of states to use their own resources but also their obligations not to harm the environments of other states.[11] Third, UNCHE established the UN Environment Programme (UNEP), whose job it would be to coordinate global environmental governance through identifying important problems, convening and enabling international negotiations, and monitoring the resulting agreements. UNEP, discussed in more depth below, has remained the most important international institution in the area of global environmental governance, anchoring this highly complex system.[12]

Primarily, but not wholly, under the auspices of UNEP, the ensuing decades saw the negotiation of a large number of MEAs. One database identifies more than four hundred full MEAs, with additional protocols and amendments, many of which have come into being since 1972.[13] These agreements include the "flagship" agreements on issues of global concern—the Vienna Convention for the Protection of the Ozone Layer (1985) and its subsequent Montreal Protocol (1987), the 1992 UN Framework Convention on Climate Change (UNFCCC) and the 1997 Kyoto Protocol, and the 1992 Convention on Biological Diversity (CBD) and its associated Cartagena and Nagoya Protocols (2000 and 2010, respectively). They also include agreements on transboundary issues, such as the 1979 Convention on Long-Range Transboundary Air Pollution (CLRTAP) and the 1989 Basel Convention on the Control of Transboundary Movements of Hazardous Wastes and Their Disposal. Some MEAs drawn up during this period are forty years old or older, such as the 1973 Convention on International Trade in Endangered Species of Wild Fauna and Flora (CITES). Others are more recent, such as the 2001 Stockholm Convention on Persistent Organic Pollutants (POPs) and, most recently, the 2013 Minamata Convention on Mercury, which addresses the production of, trade in, and storage of mercury (see Chapter 11).

Each of these multilateral processes is governed by a secretariat and often involves additional bodies, such as scientific advisory committees. The parties to a given agreement meet every one or two years at a Conference of the Parties (COP), where decisions are made (or are supposed to be made) to strengthen the agreement or to deal with new problems. Each MEA has its own goals, decision-making processes, and underlying norms and engages its own range of actors, including nonstate actors such as NGOs. The combination of these different elements, along with the ongoing processes of negotiation that characterize each MEA, leads analysts to describe each MEA as a regime: a set of rules, norms, principles, decision-making procedures, and organizations that steer actor behavior around a given issue area.[14]

Since 1972, three subsequent "Earth Summits" have been held, each organized by the UN and its agencies. The UN Conference on Environment and Development (UNCED) convened in Rio de Janeiro, Brazil, in 1992; the World Summit on Sustainable Development (WSSD) was held in Johannesburg, South Africa, in 2002; and the UN Conference on Sustainable Development (Rio+20), marking twenty years since UNCED, was held in Rio de Janeiro in June 2012. Table 2-1 provides a brief comparison of the components and outcomes of these four conferences.

The 1992 Rio Summit marked the high point of international environmental diplomacy, with the opening for signature of two major conventions, the CBD and the UNFCCC.[15] The WSSD, held under the looming shadow of the second Iraq War, was a far more subdued event, also reflecting many parties' disillusionment with multilateral diplomacy as the primary global environmental governance tool.[16] Both UNCED and WSSD were marked by the convergence, both at and around the conferences, of civil society actors, some as accredited observers but many more attending parallel summits and other events designed to draw attention to broader social, environmental, and human rights issues not necessarily being addressed by the main delegates.

The 2012 Rio+20 conference was convened by the UN Commission on Sustainable Development (UNCSD).[17] Its theme, "The Green Economy," indicated how much closer together the agendas of global environmental and global economic governance had moved in the preceding decades. Many observers—and indeed many participants—found the agenda and the results of this summit to be rather empty of substantive content and goals. John Vidal, environment correspondent for the British newspaper the *Guardian*, offers an alternative view: that Rio+20 succeeded to the extent that it did not fall apart. He notes that it was "an extraordinary trade fair" of NGOs, business, and other representatives and resulted in the strengthening of UNEP (see below) and reform of the UN Commission on Sustainable Development.[18] Nonetheless, the deep disappointment that was the majority opinion after Rio+20 will probably dampen plans for future megasummits on the global environment.

Table 2-1 The "Earth Summits," 1972–2012

1972: UN Conference on the Human Environment (UNCHE)
- Held in Stockholm, Sweden
- 113 nations represented
- 225 accredited NGOs represented
- Established UNEP
- Produced the Stockholm Declaration: twenty-six principles of international environmental law

---

1992: UN Conference on Environment and Development (UNCED)
- Held in Rio de Janeiro, Brazil
- 172 nations represented; attendees include 108 heads of state
- 1,420 accredited NGOs represented; another 17,000 representatives attend a parallel NGO summit
- Produced the Framework Convention on Climate Change and the Convention on Biological Diversity, but states failed to agree on a Forests Convention; established the UN Commission on Sustainable Development (UNCSD) and the Global Environment Facility (GEF)
- Produced two documents: the 300-page Agenda 21 and the Rio Declaration on Sustainable Development

---

2002: World Summit on Sustainable Development (WSSD)
- Held in Johannesburg, South Africa
- 191 governments represented
- 8,000 accredited NGOs represented; accompanied by two parallel civil society summits
- Produced no major treaties, but reached agreement on a series of smaller-scale initiatives, including "Type II partnerships" among NGOs, governments, and other actors on the ground to meet goals around fresh water, biodiversity, and hazardous chemicals
- Produced the Johannesburg Declaration on Sustainable Development

---

2012: UN Conference on Sustainable Development (Rio+20)
- Held in Rio de Janeiro, Brazil
- 191 governments represented, with 79 heads of state in attendance
- 44,000 badges issued for official events, with strong side events and parallel participation by NGOs, business, and local government representatives
- Institutional reforms included upgrading UNEP and restructuring UNCSD
- Produced the 49-page document "The Future We Want"

These summits are significant for two particular reasons. First, they demonstrate the role of the United Nations and its agencies in setting a longer-term agenda of global environmental governance. This can be seen in the activities at the summits themselves as well as in the documents and declarations they produced. Agenda 21 (1992) has remained a foundational document in state and nonstate circles for developing political goals. "The Future We Want," produced at Rio+20, outlines plans to develop a series of Sustainable Development Goals by 2015, to complement and succeed the Millennium Development Goals.

Second, these summits have articulated the trends that shape the actions of the leading actors in the system, which themselves shape global environmental governance institutions. These trends—the convergence of international environmental, development, and economic norms and agendas; the rising role of nonstate actors; and a shift away from large, flagship agreements—are all important in the stories told in this chapter and others in this volume. The trends sketched here demonstrate that the architecture of state-led global environmental governance is not static. IGOs such as the UN, UNEP, and treaty secretariats, as well as nonstate actors such as NGOs, have played fundamental roles in shaping the direction and strength of global environmental governance regimes.

The United Nations Environment Program

UNEP was established as a UN program under the auspices of the UN General Assembly and UNESCO.[19] As a program, UNEP lacks the authority and autonomy to make binding decisions on its members, as a specialized UN agency such as the World Health Organization can.[20] Nor can it enforce treaty provisions when they are violated or settle disputes, compared with the UN Security Council and the World Trade Organization (WTO). It is, however, designed to be able to respond quickly to global environmental demands.[21]

UNEP is the first UN agency to be based in a developing country, with headquarters in Nairobi, Kenya, although its associated secretariats and offices are distributed worldwide. It serves as a focal point for and coordinator of international environmental initiatives and engages in monitoring, assessment, and early warning, fostering compliance with MEAs and long-term capacity-building efforts.[22] It is funded through voluntary, not mandatory, assessments by member states: in 2010, the funding requirements across UNEP's work programs added up to about $218 million.[23]

Assessments of UNEP's performance are mixed, although many analysts do point out the financial and political constraints the program must operate under.[24] While it has not been able to push much beyond its original mandate, it has been more successful in monitoring and assessing the state of the global environment and in establishing and managing many different international environmental regimes and negotiating processes.[25] It has helped advance existing regimes and has pushed for new ones. However, UNEP's persistent problems of underfunding and inefficiencies, along with that fact that the program is a small player in the universe of UN agencies, have led to calls for reform and/or expansion.

In 2012, following the Rio+20 meeting, the UN General Assembly "upgraded and strengthened" UNEP.[26] Previously its membership was restricted to a governing council of 58 UN member states. Now it is open to all 193 member states and has the promise of enhanced funding and structural capacity to fulfill its mandate. How these changes will play out, and how they will change the status of UNEP compared with other IGOs, remains to be seen, but the changes do demonstrate a significant commitment on the part of nation-states to UNEP's ongoing work.

Treaty Secretariats and Other Regime Bodies

Each international environmental regime is governed by its own secretariat, a permanent body. The secretariat reports to the regime's COP and has its own full-time staff. Many secretariats are nested within UNEP and are housed in its offices in Nairobi, Geneva, Bonn, and other cities. The UN manages some secretariats, such as the secretariat of the UNFCCC, while others, such as the Ramsar Convention secretariat, exist entirely outside the UN system.[27]

Although the secretariats are often dismissed as merely functional bureaucracies, coordinating treaty-related paperwork and COPs, it has become clear that in many cases they have been able to exercise considerable (but usually not explicit) influence, steering their member states toward particular outcomes.[28] For example, the secretariats of the various biodiversity/conservation regimes have worked to manage overlap among them, taking advantage of synergies and reducing conflict.[29] These activities are often undertaken by informal interregime liaison groups. In recent years, the secretariats of UNEP and the WTO have started working together to minimize conflicts and manage overlap between their respective jurisdictions.[30] Secretariat influence varies. While, for example, the ozone regime secretariat, despite its small size, has been an important force behind the success of the regime,[31] others have found themselves limited by the political conflicts between member states that have restricted their mandates. The UNFCCC secretariat has taken on far more of a technocratic role than its more activist equivalents in other regimes for these reasons.[32]

Many treaty-based environmental regimes also contain subsidiary bodies, often for scientific and technical advice.[33] Many of these bodies are permanent; some are ad hoc, established to fulfill particular tasks and then disbanded. The UN Framework Convention on Climate Change and the Kyoto Protocol have a particularly complex combined administrative structure, with permanent and ad hoc committees serving under the overall authority of the UNFCCC secretariat to deal with matters such as scientific advice, implementation, and funding mechanisms. The most prominent international scientific body associated with the climate regime, the Intergovernmental Panel on Climate Change (IPCC), operates outside the UNFCCC. Coestablished by UNEP and the World Meteorological Organization in 1988, the IPCC collects, assesses, and summarizes global scientific research on climate change.[34] The scientific advisory group for the Convention on Biological Diversity is the Subsidiary Body on Scientific, Technical and Technological

Advice (SBSTTA). The CBD also has a working group, established under Article 8j of the convention, whose mandate is to integrate local knowledge and knowledge holders into the regime. Even in regimes that are not anchored by multilateral agreements, more informal international bodies—such as the UN Forum on Forests—provide venues and assistance for multilateral dialogue and advice.

Crosscutting Environmental IGOs

Some IGOs work across environmental regimes. The Global Environment Facility (GEF), founded in 1991 and restructured in 1993, coordinates funding and capacity-building projects across several regimes and issue areas: climate change, ozone depletion, biodiversity, oceans, persistent organic pollutants, and desertification or land degradation. It is the main funding mechanism of the CBD, the POPs treaties, the UNFCCC, and the UN Convention to Combat Desertification, and it supplements the activities of the Multilateral Fund of the ozone regime. The GEF is administered by UNEP and the United Nations Development Programme (UNDP), with funding coordinated by the World Bank, and has its own council and decision-making body. Over the twenty-plus years since its founding, the GEF has provided $11.5 billion in grants and leveraged $57 billion in cofinancing for more than 3,215 projects in over 165 developing countries and economies in transition. Through its Small Grants Programme, the GEF has also made more than 16,030 small grants directly to civil society and community–based organizations totaling $653.2 million.[35] It is funded by its member states, with replenishments every four years.

Critiques of the GEF often revolve around the nature of its funding and its size relative to other sorts of international aid and spending.[36] The GEF funds projects according to the principle of additionality—the extent to which a local project is expected to generate global benefits in one of the GEF's focal areas. Additionality is hard to measure, and it is hard to tell what projects might have gone ahead even without GEF funding. It is also true that the GEF's budget fund adds up to only a small fraction of global aid spending, although it is the only aid agency directly responsible for funding a range of global environmental commitments. The GEF has, however, been lauded as an example of cooperation among three international agencies and as an entity that has been able to learn and adapt, to give recipient countries significant voice in its decision-making processes, and to incorporate NGOs.

As it moves forward, the GEF will need to find its place in the ever more complex landscape of global climate (and environmental) funding. This arena has boomed in recent years, as governments, aid agencies, NGOs, and private actors have sought to develop funding mechanisms that can protect the environment, mitigate greenhouse gas emissions (for example, through carbon sequestration), and encourage green investment. Such initiatives include the Clean Development Mechanism and the Green Climate Fund, established in 2011, both part of the UNFCCC process. The UN-administered Reducing

Emissions from Deforestation and forest Degradation (REDD) seeks to preserve and enhance forest stocks, and thus also reduce the amount of carbon dioxide entering the atmosphere, by paying forest owners/authorities.[37] Altogether, dozens of bilateral and multilateral initiatives have emerged in recent years and will need to compete for scarce funding.

On a smaller scale, other environmental IGOs do important work. The Green Customs Initiative trains customs officials in developing countries to be able to identify and prevent the smuggling of various goods and substances prohibited across different environmental regimes, from ozone-depleting substances to hazardous wastes to wildlife and genetically modified organisms. Although by no means exclusively environmental, the UN Institute for Training and Research (UNITAR) plays an important role in building capacity at local and national levels to address a variety of environmental problems—from climate change to chemicals management.

Nonenvironmental IGOs with Environmental Functions

Finally, issues of global environmental change and sustainable development have spilled over into the activities of IGOs that traditionally have had little association—in practice or by mandate—with these issues. The World Meteorological Organization, for example, worked with UNEP to set up the early meetings that led to the 1985 Vienna Convention for the Protection of the Ozone Layer and with the UN to set up the Intergovernmental Panel on Climate Change in 1988. UNESCO oversees the 1972 World Heritage Convention, an early conservation agreement that protects sites of natural and cultural importance worldwide. The International Maritime Organization (IMO), among other important functions to do with maritime security and safety, oversees the International Convention for the Prevention of Pollution from Ships (MARPOL, 1973/1978).

The major international trade, development, and finance organizations have, somewhat unwillingly but very significantly, taken on environmental responsibilities in recent years. Set up after World War II, the World Bank, the International Monetary Fund (IMF), and the General Agreement on Tariffs and Trade (GATT)—known as the Bretton Woods institutions, after the town in New Hampshire where Allied leaders met to establish them—were designed to foster postwar reconstruction and economic development.

The World Bank provides aid and loans at different terms to developing nations. Among its most high-profile activities, it funds large-scale development projects, such as dams, power plants, and roads. The IMF was designed to intervene in fiscal and monetary crises and has taken on a powerful role in lending to countries in trouble, imposing structural adjustment conditions as part of its terms. The GATT, signed in 1948, fostered trade liberalization among signatory states by lowering tariffs on traded goods and forbidding discrimination between trading partners and between domestically produced and foreign-produced goods. In 1995, signatories to the GATT created the

WTO in order to rationalize and strengthen the capacity of the GATT and related trade and services agreements.

None of these organizations had an environmental mandate when they were first established. In the late 1940s there was little real awareness of resource constraints, and in the 1950s, theories of development optimistically assumed that all countries could follow an upward trajectory under the right conditions. These assumptions turned out to be wrong, and by the late 1970s and early 1980s, the environmental impacts of rapid and unequal global economic growth and development began to become apparent, with subsequent impacts on the policies and actions of the World Bank and the GATT/WTO.

Starting in the late 1980s, a concerted campaign by NGOs, targeting both the World Bank and the national legislatures that authorize its funding, forced the World Bank to address the environmental degradation and social dislocation that had followed many of the large-scale infrastructure projects it had funded in developing countries.[38] NGOs, both local to the affected communities and transnational, were able to apply pressure to politicians in donor countries to get the Bank to start integrating environmental assessments into its funding process and to establish an inspections panel to allow affected citizens a voice.[39] The Bank also established an environment unit within its overall system while also emphasizing the need to mainstream environmental priorities across all its activities. It has, as seen above, been active in funding global environmental initiatives via the GEF and other global funds, and it has pioneered methods of carbon accounting and valuation of ecosystem services. Similar reforms have been put in place across other multilateral development banks, such as the Asian and African Development Banks. The World Bank also pulled out of or refused to fund a number of high-profile projects, including India's controversial Narmada dam project. In that and other cases, independent studies demonstrated that the social and environmental impacts were likely to be far greater than government assessments stated. In the face of losing funding from its highest donor nations, and of widespread publicity, the Bank made a strategic decision to withdraw from many such high-profile projects.

The Bank's reforms have had a mixed reception, and it has remained a target of high-level controversy. While many recognize that the Bank has been far more responsive to public pressure (exerted through its largest donor governments, the United States and the European Union) than other international financial institutions, some have criticized its actions in important areas. For instance, it has retained "brown" lending in its portfolio of investments—including being the leading global investor in coal-fired power plants.[40] Paradoxically, the Bank's withdrawal from controversial projects has led not to the projects necessarily being halted, but to the governments concerned reaching out to other entities—private financial actors or expert credit agencies, for example, that have few or no environmental criteria, meaning that projects go ahead without any supervision.[41] The Bank has, together with the global NGO community, developed voluntary standards for these actors to sign on to, but these, like many voluntary standards programs, have been slow to spread, particularly to the "bad actors" that most need supervision.

Similarly, the global trade regime, governed by the GATT/WTO, has been pressured to take on an environmental governance role (see Chapter 14). From the early 1990s, many observers became concerned that trade liberalization could lead to environmental harm, primarily for two reasons. First, trade liberalization would lead to economic growth, which in turn would lead to environmental degradation along with the negative externalities of increased shipping and transportation. Second, domestic environmental regulations could themselves be seen as barriers to trade: if a country required importers to meet certain environmental standards, that could conceivably be seen as a restriction on trade or as trade discrimination. The GATT/WTO came under fierce criticism in the 1990s for high-profile rulings against U.S. regulatory actions to restrict imports of tuna (from Mexico), shrimp (from Southeast Asia), and gasoline (from Venezuela) on environmental grounds.[42] These cases generated fears that any environment-related trade restrictions, including those under multilateral environmental agreements, might be struck down in the interest of fostering global trade liberalization. In fact, these rulings were either never enforced or overturned on appeal,[43] and over time, the GATT/WTO has demonstrated a shift away from a narrow interpretation of its rules with respect to trade restrictions.[44] Similarly, the results of the unilateral cases referenced above suggest that the WTO is less likely to strike down an environmental rule when there is wide, and possibly universal, support for it among nation-states. The WTO was also a significant presence both at the 2002 World Summit on Sustainable Development and the 2012 Rio+20 summit, and it is actively working with UNEP and treaty secretariats to avoid direct conflict and to explore ways trade and sustainable development agendas can work together for mutual benefit.

Nongovernmental Organizations and the Global Environment

Nongovernmental organizations have come into their own over the past forty years as important players on the international stage, particularly in the context of global environmental politics. NGOs mobilize around different issues to engage in collective action and effect political change.[45] They are recognized as playing important roles in global environmental governance. They are *agitators* and *conscience keepers*, raising concerns about environmental problems and the solutions proffered by, or the slowness of, government and corporate actors. They exert moral force in global environmental governance, providing a voice for marginalized populations or even for nature itself, reminding policy makers of greater responsibilities. They are *witnesses* of actions that lead to environmental degradation, a role played by Greenpeace's small boats in highlighting whaling in the 1980s,[46] and to the activities of the governance system itself, observing and documenting negotiations.[47] They can be *whistle-blowers*, notifying relevant authorities or the world press when governments or private-sector actors violate environmental rules and obligations.[48] Finally, like IGOs, they are *architects* and *entrepreneurs*, suggesting governance solutions, engaging constructively in the negotiation process, and, increasingly, working themselves or with private-sector actors to create their own governance initiatives and their own sphere of nonstate governance.[49] All these examples suggest that NGOs are taking on a critical role in global environmental governance, working with states to achieve their goals and, on occasion, taking on roles that are traditionally associated with governments or international agencies.

NGOs: Definitions and Numbers

There is no universal definition of the term *nongovernmental organization.* Kal Raustiala, in studying the role of NGOs in international law, adopts a broad definition: "non-state organizations that seek to influence international law and policy."[50] NGOs are usually nonprofit, and their memberships consist of individual citizens or organizations, including firms, trade unions, and religious organizations. By some definitions (including under the UN's formal accreditation process), local governments and municipal authorities, although officially "government" entities, count as NGOs, as they are not members of official state delegations and often represent perspectives counter to the positions of their own central or federal governments.[51] Because there are so many types of NGOs, variations are often distinguished for official, and unofficial, purposes by acronyms.[52] Some of these are self-explanatory, and some indicate contradictory purposes—for instance, GONGOs, or government-organized NGOs, are often established by governments to subvert activity by other NGOs. Still other acronyms may be used only because they are clever (e.g., market advocacy NGOs, or MANGOs). Table 2-2 lists

Table 2-2 Subcategories of NGOs

ENGOs	Environmental NGOs, such as Greenpeace International and the African Forest Forum (Kenya)
YOUNGOs	Youth NGOs, such as the UK Youth Climate Coalition and Zero Carbon Africa
BINGOs	Business and industry NGOs, such as the World Business Council on Sustainable Development
RINGOs	Research and independent NGOs, such as the American University delegation (United States) and Pesticide Action Network Asia (Malaysia)
TUNGOs	Trade union NGOs, such as the Norwegian Federation of Trade Unions
LGMAs	Local governments and municipal authorities, such as Asociación Conciencia (Argentina) and the International Council of Local Environmental Initiatives (ICLEI)
IPOs	Indigenous peoples' organizations, such as the Gwichin Council International (Canada)

the NGO subcategories that are officially recognized by the United Nations. They are accredited as such and have their own caucuses at international meetings.[53]

The number of NGOs engaged in global environmental governance has increased dramatically over past decades. For example, 255 NGOs were accredited—that is, recognized by the UN as official observers—at Stockholm in 1972.[54] By contrast, nearly 1,000 nonstate organizations and 20,000 individuals attended the UNFCCC summit in Copenhagen in 2009.[55] Some estimates put the number of international NGOs at more than 50,000 by 2005.[56] The United Nations has officially accredited approximately 3,000 NGOs, and even more are admitted to individual negotiations and meetings.[57] Arriving at an accurate total of the number of NGOs globally is a difficult matter. In addition to different definitions of what constitutes an NGO, it is quite easy for a small group of individuals—or even a single individual—to form an NGO for various reasons (including to obtain funding from Western donor organizations). Also, many NGOs are simply fluid, forming, dissolving, and reforming over time. However, there is little doubt that NGOs are a growing presence in global environmental governance. Although there is some debate over their actual influence on governance processes and outcomes,[58] it is also becoming clear that their influence is significant, despite the fact that they have no formal vote in intergovernmental negotiation processes.

Most NGOs are advocacy organizations, working to further particular causes: the environment, human and political rights, land rights, rights pertaining to sexuality, gender, class, youth, or seniority, to name but a few. They have varying strategies, resources, and support at their disposal, but they all seek to change government action and policy, public opinion and attitudes, and/or corporate action to achieve their goals, ideally framed for the public good. Environmental movement organizations—very generally, "broad networks of people and organisations engaged in collective action in pursuit of environmental benefits"[59]—make up a high percentage of NGOs involved in global environmental governance. They do not, however, have a monopoly, as development, human rights, and other NGOs are demonstrating the ways environmental issues are connected to most of the other important issues of our age.

NGO Characteristics and Differences

NGOs share important similarities and also differ from one another in important ways. These similarities and differences are not absolute. Many NGOs can inhabit different points on organizational and political spectrums at different times and in different political spaces. The characteristics they exhibit, as outlined in this section, apply to both Northern and Southern NGOs, although the large Northern NGOs dominate the entire field in resources and capacity, a situation that creates its own set of tensions when organizations need to work together across borders or in international negotiations.

First, NGOs differ according to their *organizational forms*. Large, professional organizations such as the World Wide Fund for Nature (WWF, formerly the World Wildlife Fund), Conservation International, and Greenpeace are becoming increasingly differentiated from smaller, less well-resourced grassroots organizations in terms of funding, members, and staffing. These large NGOs are able to mount several campaigns at once, establish offices in different cities and countries, and operate at a highly professional level. They are often the most visible face of the environmental movement and drive NGO participation in global environmental governance. Some elite NGOs have gained an almost corporate level of power—including, in the conservation arena, the ability to purchase large swaths of land for preservation purposes.[60]

At the other end of the spectrum, smaller groups, such as those organized around one issue or within a single community, are able to punch above their weight through strategic use of Internet and other media, as well as form alliances with similar groups or larger organizations. Such groups include antidam movements, landless movements, and groups opposing mining, oil production, and other types of resource exploitation.[61] For example, Narmada Bachao Andalan, a coalition of Indian farmers, landless people, and activists, fought both the World Bank and their own government against dam construction, with activists allowing rising waters to come close to drowning them as a public act of defiance. Many such organizations rely on uncertain pools of personnel, including volunteers, and funding resources, as large foundation grants, a key source of NGO funding, become more complex to apply for and maintain.

Second, NGOs differ according to their *strategies* and their *actions*. Some organizations focus on lobbying and other mainstream ways of engaging with political or corporate actors, while others use more confrontational tactics. Many NGOs directly lobby politicians and government officials and may be included in policy-making or advisory bodies,[62] although their access to the policy process and their level of influence vary according to political systems and the party in power. They may also forge partnerships with the corporate sector to ensure sustainable production or use of sustainable goods, as the Rainforest Action Network was able to do with the large hardware chain Home Depot in the 1990s. Sometimes this activity backfires, as when WWF came under fire for certifying "sustainable" palm oil plantations in 2009, despite some scientific and activist consensus that palm oil plantations are unsustainable per se.

NGOs also may engage in public protests against political decisions or lead boycott actions against companies. On-the-street demonstrations remain part of their repertoire, but so are art installations and other visual media, as well as use of social media to arrange flash-mob-style protests, or to spread information about a product or company quickly. Activists dressed as tomatoes and sea turtles at anti-WTO protests in the early 2000s highlighted the dangers of genetically modified organisms and of the bycatch resulting from mass seafood harvesting. In Europe, "climate camps" have helped educate activists, particularly youth activists, about the need for climate justice campaigns and have provided lessons in alternative lifestyles.

Another function that a subset of NGOs has taken on is the generation and dissemination of scientific knowledge about the state of the environment. Think tanks such as the Center for Science and the Environment in India and the U.S.-based World Watch Institute generate information, reports, and indicators across a range of issue areas. Other NGOs, such as Oceana, based in Washington, D.C., undertake research on particular issues expressly to contribute to political debates. The information-provision function extends to the global level, as NGOs document meetings and disseminate the information they collect to broader publics.

In 1989, the World Bank drew a distinction between "operational" and "advocacy" NGOs: operational NGOs "fund, design or implement development-related programs or projects," and advocacy NGOs "defend or promote a specific development cause and . . . seek to influence the development policies and practices of the Bank, governments, and other bodies."[63] This distinction (while clearly not rigid) matters as NGOs become more engaged in projects related to the primary global funding mechanisms, including the GEF, REDD, and the Clean Development Mechanism, where states and IGOs are relying more and more on NGO expertise and ground-level experience. There could, therefore, be some tension between NGOs of different types, as well as tension within NGOs in choosing the directions they should emphasize.

Finally, while NGOs are often assumed to be progressive, individual organizations may lobby for either side of a cause. For example, business and industry NGOs, or BINGOs, representing the U.S. oil industry have played an obstructionist role in climate negotiations.[64] They are now key backers of the climate skeptics movement and its efforts to discredit climate science.[65]

In all cases, NGOs are becoming more transnational, as the scope of environmental issues broadens and environmental governance has shifted to the global level. They have increasing capacity to network easily across borders and to organize systems of representation at different levels.

NGOs across Borders

The international NGO sector has grown significantly, not least because of the emergence and rapid diffusion of cheap global communication technologies. This sector consists of NGOs that attend international negotiations and transnational activist networks (TANs), with significant overlap between these two groups. At negotiations, NGOs attend as individual observers, are represented by peak associations, or both. Peak associations are made up not of individual members but of organizational members sharing a common goal. They can speak for a large number of actors with a common voice and can wield more influence than organizations on their own. For example, the more than seven hundred member organizations of the Climate Action Network (CAN), based in ninety-five countries, have agreed to a common vision

42   Kate O'Neill

with respect to action around climate change.[66] CAN's activities at UNFCCC COPs and other meetings are designed both to raise awareness and to participate constructively in negotiations. Publicly, CAN is probably most well known for its Fossil of the Day award, given out at COPs to the country considered most obstructive in negotiations each day: Canada, Saudi Arabia, and the United States have been frequent recipients. The International Union for the Conservation of Nature (IUCN) represents conservation and biodiversity groups from around the world, including some governmental organizations, at CBD and other relevant meetings.

TANs are made up of groups that network horizontally across borders around specific issues, such as preventing the building of large dams or protecting the rain forests, without necessarily directly targeting international negotiations.[67] Within the TAN arena, organizational structures vary widely. For example, WWF, Greenpeace International, Conservation International, the Third World Network, and others follow a vertical model, with main headquarters in one country and branches in many others. The Pesticide Action Network, Via Campesina, Climate Justice Now!, and other groups that affiliate around particular issues such as dams or biotechnology tend to build horizontal networks, partnering with comparable groups in other countries.

Climate justice TANs have served to represent more radical perspectives on the impacts of climate change, and how it should be addressed.[68] Climate Justice Now! (CJN!) and Climate Justice Action (CJA) are networks that represented "outsider" views at Copenhagen in 2009. They make a direct connection between climate change and its impacts on vulnerable populations, highlighting the need for structural change in the global economy—particularly the global fossil fuel–based economy—to address greenhouse gas emissions. Climate justice networks bring together a diverse set of interests that, while they may overlap with groups within CAN and similar networks, place a different frame on climate action, tend to use less mainstream tactics, and focus more on mobilizing grassroots activists than on working at more elite levels.

NGOs and the International Environmental Policy Process

At every stage of the international policy process NGOs have devised actions and roles for themselves, as well as fulfilling roles that have been formally delineated through international law and practice. While environmental NGOs make up the bulk of participants at global environmental negotiations, development and antipoverty NGOs, agricultural workers, human rights activists, indigenous peoples, and others who would not immediately describe themselves as "environmentalists" are active in negotiation processes.

The global environmental governance arena is one that has been particularly open to participation by nonstate actors (not just environmental NGOs, or ENGOs, but also business groups, scientific experts, and others), in stark comparison to some other global policy arenas, such as international trade and arms control. The provisions of international law—which is not generally known for its openness to nonstate actors—have provided important channels of access for NGOs. The codification of international law—namely, the formalization of international law into treaties and other sorts of documents, which began in the 1920s—gave nonstate actors the information and the opportunities they needed to start weighing in on various negotiation processes.[69] Specific treaties contain language that allows for the incorporation of NGOs. The 1973 Convention on International Trade in Endangered Species was the first MEA to allow the admission of NGOs engaged in related activities,[70] and other major MEAs, such as the CBD and the UNFCCC, have followed suit.[71]

Likewise, the United Nations and its agencies have, as IGOs, been open to participation by nonstate actors, at the very least in an advisory capacity, having granted NGOs accredited consultative status since the UN was created. Accreditation grants group representatives official observer status as well as access to the main building where negotiations are taking place and to many (but not all) meetings and plenary sessions taking place among the parties. Not all NGOs that attend international meetings are accredited. Many meet outside the official convention halls, holding parallel summits and side events of their own—and often protesting the official meeting.

NGOs and agenda setting. Perhaps not surprisingly, NGOs help raise awareness of and concern over particular problems. They do this in many ways, from producing major scientific and technical reports to staging protests such as sit-ins and witnessing events, as with the Sea Shepherd Conservation Society's pursuit and documentation of the actions of Japanese whaling vessels. Greenpeace, for example, collected data on waste dumping in the South by Northern countries in the 1970s and 1980s that was instrumental in kickstarting negotiations that led to the 1989 Basel Convention.[72] WWF and other conservation organizations raise awareness about endangered species—particularly the charismatic megafauna whose plight is likely to trigger widespread public concern. In recent years, environmental health–related organizations have publicized the impacts of mercury on human health as mercury treaty negotiations heated up in 2010 and 2011. Sometimes NGOs' role is to translate scientific concern into public and political awareness, as has been the case with climate change. NGOs also help to set the international political agenda in particular issue areas by providing information and ways to frame problems, sometimes by offering draft texts and focal points for negotiations. IUCN, for example, was instrumental in pushing for, and indeed provided a draft text for, the CBD.

Negotiating at international meetings. NGOs are visible and active participants in all but name at international environmental meetings. They lobby delegates; provide information, data, ideas, and talking points; and report on the meetings' results. Lobbying at the international level has become an important additional channel of influence for NGOs, although it has not yet displaced lobbying at the domestic level.[73]

CAN provides a daily bulletin, ECO, at UNFCCC negotiations, as well as its Fossil of the Day award. The Earth Negotiations Bulletin (ENB) team, an informational NGO rather than an advocacy NGO, provides daily summaries and summary reports across a wide range of international negotiations.[74] The Third World Network, based in Penang, Malaysia, also provides reports on negotiations as they happen. For activists, the rise of social media, giving them the ability to use Twitter, Facebook, and blogging to report on negotiating events as they happen, has generated many opportunities. Youth activists, for example, launched the Adopt a Negotiator project, in which individuals track members of their countries' or regions' negotiating teams and report on their activities.

Sometimes, NGO members have been known to serve as delegates on the negotiating teams of smaller or poorer states, which cannot always afford to send full complements of delegates. On rare occasions (usually in smaller or lower-profile negotiations), NGO representatives have even been able to insert treaty language directly from the floor, or to influence how rules and policy mechanisms are defined. At the UNFCCC negotiations after Kyoto, for example, NGOs were able to suggest mechanisms to help enforce compliance.[75]

Another important role for NGOs at international meetings is in organizing and participating in side events—officially sanctioned panels, roundtables, and other discussions that may bring together actors from across the spectrum of global environmental governance on specific topics. At the major COPs, ENB now provides a separate report on daily side events, as the numbers of these events have grown so much. Likewise, parallel summits, which are not part of the main meeting and are separately organized by civil society groups, are often hailed as the parts of meetings where the most is accomplished, often simply through networking effects of bringing so many groups together who would not otherwise have met.

NGO actions inside the conference halls are matched by equally, and probably louder, activity outside. Sometimes there are protests—at the UNFCCC COP in The Hague in 2000, protesters surrounded the conference hall with flood barriers made of piled sandbags. Organizations have marched, unfurled banners, staged "drown-ins," donned gas masks, dressed up as penguins, and installed highly creative art installations. Unlike the protests surrounding the meetings of the Bretton Woods institutions in the 1990s and 2000s,[76] protests at COPs have not tended to involve violence or property damage—protesters are more interested in pushing the official delegates further than where they might be going than in stopping the process all together. This has not prevented tensions, however. At Copenhagen in 2009, the atmosphere became tense when the COP organizers decided to allow only ninety observers into the final days' high-level talks, at which heads of state would be present.[77] This incident also highlighted the conflicts, as well as the alliances, between so-called insider and outsider NGOs: those that are accredited and allowed access to negotiating spaces and those that are not but are present outside.

NGOs and implementation. NGOs play an important role in the implementation of international environmental agreements. They help to carry out their objectives on the ground, blow the whistle when governments fail to comply with, or violate, their obligations, and engage with the ongoing work of regime strengthening, generating and disseminating new knowledge and information, and pushing their governments to ratify agreements. In these respects they work to supplement the low capacity of global governance organizations to carry out these tasks directly.

NGOs often work in partnership with state, IGO, or private-sector actors.[78] Such partnerships may be on the ground. For instance, NGOs are accorded an important role in implementing GEF projects and projects funded by other donor agencies on the ground. In one example, microcredit NGOs serve as vehicles for the distribution of funds.[79] The GEF-funded International POPs Elimination Network has assisted more than 350 NGOs in sixty-five countries in working with local communities on education about, identification of, and reduction of persistent organic pollutants in local communities.[80] Other sorts of partnerships are designed to do more than implement existing projects or undertake projects under their own steam. Visseren-Hamakers, Leroy, and Glasbergen show how some partnerships actually seek to shape international policy processes, using as cases the Great Apes Survival Project (GRASP) and the Critical Ecosystem Partnership Fund.[81]

In other ways, both direct and indirect, NGOs inform the ongoing work of many international environmental regimes. As with participation at meetings, this engagement varies across regimes and tends not to be formalized. Treaties such as CITES, the 1994 Convention to Combat Desertification, and UNESCO include provisions for NGOs to take on a range of roles at this level.[82] NGOs also operate in consultative roles, as, for instance, in the deliberations of the Open-Ended Technical Working Group of the Basel Convention. The emergence of REDD under the UNFCCC has engaged many NGOs that had sought to have a role in its development from the start. REDD has, however, strongly split the NGO community, with some seeing it as humankind's best opportunity to preserve forests and/or mitigate greenhouse gas emissions and others opposing it on grounds of its social impacts—and likely effectiveness.[83]

Finally, NGOs have been crucial in alerting the international community when, for example, toxic waste from the wealthy North is dumped in a poorer Southern nation, or when illegal trading of endangered species is taking place. They have brought new dimensions of issues to the forefront, including electronic waste trading and increased poaching of ivory in African war zones. The Silicon Valley Toxics Coalition, the Basel Action Network, and Greenpeace published influential reports in the early 2000s on emerging e-waste disposal problems and their impacts in developing countries.[84] TRAFFIC, the main wildlife trade reporting network, has active campaigns on the poaching of elephant and rhino horns for trade in Africa and Asia, information that it submits directly to the CITES secretariat as well as makes available to the general public.

Beyond Regimes: Transnational Networks and Nonstate Market-Driven Governance

A significant part of NGOs' role in global environmental governance goes beyond working within international treaty processes and targeting governments and other state representatives. This chapter has outlined how NGOs have targeted the World Bank and other Bretton Woods institutions, as well as multinational corporations, challenging the "business as usual approach" of economic globalization.[85]

Moving beyond the role of challenger, NGOs have been instrumental in the design and construction of governance regimes beyond the state, usually in partnership with private-sector actors, particularly in issue areas where state-led global environmental governance has failed. Leading examples of this phenomenon are transnational, third-party certification initiatives, through which goods—such as timber, fish, coffee, and cocoa—are certified by independent auditors as being sustainably produced according to environmental, social, or other criteria. Two of the better-known of these initiatives are the Forest Stewardship Council (FSC), which has a twelve-point certification systems for timber production, and the Marine Stewardship Council, which issues certifications of fisheries according to whether or not the stocks are sustainably harvested.[86] As of May 2013 nearly 180 million hectares of forest cover were under FSC certification, out of roughly 4 billion hectares of forest worldwide.

These schemes are seen to fill a governance vacuum and to have the nimbleness that comes from bypassing cumbersome interstate politics. They do, however, face many of the same challenges that traditional regimes face. For example, participation is voluntary and they lack direct enforcement mechanisms, which often means the worst actors simply choose not to participate.[87] Nonetheless, such initiatives are an important new arena for global environmental governance, allowing nonstate actors considerably more agency in shaping and directing the management of critical resources.

IGOs and NGOs in Global Environmental Governance: Current and Future Directions

IGOs and NGOs have been critical in shaping global environmental governance as we know it today and in globalizing environment and sustainable development concerns. As organizations representing nation-states and civil society, respectively, they have proliferated in recent decades and now perform governance functions at and across multiple scales. They have created new spaces of political action and enabled the emergence of transnational as well as global politics. The discussion above has demonstrated how IGOs and NGOs have taken on roles as *agitators, entrepreneurs,* and *architects* in instigating, creating, and implementing global environmental governance. One common theme has been how their respective influences have varied over time and across issue areas.[88] This final section considers some of the dilemmas these organizations face as they move forward, within their own sectors, in their relationships with each other, and in their relationships with nation-states.

The first challenge they face is capacity. As NGOs and IGOs take on more governance functions—as in, for example, the implementation of global funding initiatives—they will find themselves stretched. With personnel, financial, and other resources already tight for all but the most well-financed organizations, this will be a difficult challenge to meet.

A second challenge for these organizations will be to maintain—or acquire—legitimacy in the eyes of wider audiences. This is a challenge for representative organizations, which derive their power and authority from those they represent. In the case of IGOs, such power is delegated by nation-states. If states see IGOs reaching beyond their mandates in ways that affect the states' interests, they are able to pull the plug—on an IGO's funding, its activities, or even its existence. NGOs, on the other hand, choose to represent certain sectors of civil society, yet the sources of their legitimacy are not always clear. NGOs aim to open the democratic spaces in global governance, but whether they themselves can claim they represent more than particular immediate constituencies (members, board members, funders) is an empirical question, not a given.

Third, interorganizational differences and conflicts in each sector create their own sets of issues. As the NGO community broadens, and as NGOs work together across borders, issues of how Northern and Southern NGOs work together equitably start to come to the fore, as does the relationship between "insider" and "outsider" NGOs, as highlighted at the UNFCCC negotiations in Copenhagen in 2009. Likewise, the distinction between advocacy and operational roles, similar to the distinction between mainstream and radical organizations that has long been part of the field, has implications for how environmental NGOs situate themselves, whether inside or outside the implementation process. For IGOs, the proliferation of IGOs and their broadening functions have generated potential for overlap and conflict, as very different IGOs may have responsibility for, and even conflicting rules regarding, the same issue area—such as climate change or genetic resources.[89] This chapter has already highlighted these issues of horizontal linkages and interplay management. They will only become more important as this system moves forward.

Both IGOs and NGOs have changing and evolving relationships with each other and with nation-states. NGOs are moving more and more into traditional intergovernmental spheres of governance and are taking on (sometimes informally, sometimes formally) some of the functions of negotiating, monitoring, and implementing global environmental commitments. They are working quite closely with IGOs, but so far there has been little formal clarification of their roles. How this will change, and whether NGOs can become recognized more formally at all stages of the policy process, remains to be seen. Likewise, the role of IGOs and state-led governance regimes in interacting with or fostering nonstate governance initiatives has potential to expand, as relevant actors recognize complementarities between the two sorts of governance systems.

This leads to a final consideration: whether the center of gravity in global environmental governance is shifting away from states to IGOs and/or NGOs. While some argue that this is so, or is to be desired,[90] it is not clear that states are ceding control in this arena, at least not uniformly (a factor that explains some of the variation in influence across issue areas cited above). States maintain critical functions in the international system, such as the ability to enforce international rules or to fund large-scale scientific research, and have a degree of legitimacy that is not yet accorded to IGOs or NGOs.[91] As Susan Park notes, NGOs are still blocked by states, whose decision-making role remains primary in international negotiations.[92] IGOs have less frequently overstepped their bounds but certainly could, especially in highly politicized issue areas. Still, both groups have taken on roles willingly ceded by governments that lack the will or the capacity to take them on. How all actors within the current system of global environmental governance learn from their experience over the past decades and discover ways to work together and allocate responsibilities will be decisive in determining the form, functions, and effectiveness of global environmental governance as environmental challenges become only more critical in years to come. One thing is certain: the need for IGOs and NGOs to maintain their roles as architects, agitators, and entrepreneurs in global environmental and sustainability politics is going to remain as states' wills and capacities wax and wane and as increasingly complex and dedicated actions are needed to address environmental crises.

Notes

1. This typology follows and expands on that presented in Stanley W. Burgiel and Peter Wood, "Witness, Architect, Detractor: The Evolving Role of NGOs in International Environmental Negotiations," in *The Roads from Rio: Lessons Learned from Twenty Years of Multilateral Environmental Negotiations*, ed. Pamela S. Chasek and Lynn M. Wagner (New York: Routledge, 2012).
2. Kate O'Neill, *The Environment and International Relations* (Cambridge: Cambridge University Press, 2009).
3. Margaret P. Karns and Karen A. Mingst, *International Organizations: The Politics and Processes of Global Governance*, 2nd ed. (Boulder, CO: Lynne Rienner, 2010), 5.
4. The other active principal organs of the United Nations are the International Court of Justice, the Educational, Scientific and Cultural Organization (commonly known as UNESCO), and the Secretariat.
5. Jussi M. Hanhimäki, *The United Nations: A Very Short Introduction* (Oxford: Oxford University Press, 2008).

6. Ibid., 20–23.
7. See Chapter 9 in this volume.
8. Patricia Birnie, Alan Boyle, and Catherine Redgwell, *International Law and the Environment*, 3rd ed. (Oxford: Oxford University Press, 2009).
9. Paul N. Edwards, *A Vast Machine: Computer Models, Climate Data, and the Politics of Global Warming* (Cambridge: MIT Press, 2010).
10. Maria Ivanova, "Designing the United Nations Environment Programme: A Story of Compromise and Confrontation," *International Environmental Agreements* 7 (2007): 337–361.
11. Louis B. Sohn, "The Stockholm Declaration on the Human Environment," *Harvard International Law Journal* 14 (1973): 423–515.
12. Ivanova, "Designing the United Nations Environment Programme"; Maria Ivanova, "UNEP in Global Environmental Governance: Design, Leadership, Location," *Global Environmental Politics* 10, no. 1 (2010): 30–59.
13. Ronald B. Mitchell, International Environmental Agreements (IEA) Database Project, Version 2013.2, accessed April 14, 2013, http://iea.uoregon.edu.
14. Stephen D. Krasner, ed., *International Regimes* (Ithaca, NY: Cornell University Press, 1983); Ken Conca, *Governing Water: Contentious Transnational Politics and Global Institution Building* (Cambridge: MIT Press, 2006).
15. Richard N. Gardner, *Negotiating Survival: Four Priorities after Rio* (New York: Council on Foreign Relations Press, 1992).
16. Ina von Frantzius, "World Summit on Sustainable Development Johannesburg 2002: A Critical Analysis and Assessment of the Outcomes," *Environmental Politics* 13, no. 2 (2004): 467–473.
17. See Maria Ivanova, "The Contested Legacy of Rio+20," *Global Environmental Politics* 13, no. 4 (2013): 1–11; Steven Bernstein, "Rio+20: Sustainable Development in a Time of Multilateral Decline," *Global Environmental Politics* 13, no. 4 (2013): 12–21.
18. John Vidal, "Rio+20: Reasons to Be Cheerful," *Guardian*, Poverty Matters blog, June 27, 2012, http://www.theguardian.com/global-development/poverty-matters/2012/jun/27/rio20-reasons-cheerful.
19. Frank Biermann, "The Emerging Debate on the Need for a World Environment Organization: A Commentary," *Global Environmental Politics* 1, no. 1 (2001): 46–47.
20. Steffen Bauer, "The Ozone Secretariat: The Good Shepherd of Ozone Politics," in *Managers of Global Change: The Influence of International Environmental Bureaucracies*, ed. Frank Biermann and Bernd Siebenhüner (Cambridge: MIT Press, 2009).
21. Ivanova, "UNEP in Global Environmental Governance."
22. Ibid.
23. UNEP/Open-Ended Working Group (OEWG) of the Basel Convention, "Report on International Cooperation and Coordination on the Basel Convention Partnership Programme" (UNEP/CHW/OEWG.8/INF/20), 2012.
24. Bauer, "The Ozone Secretariat"; Ivanova, "UNEP in Global Environmental Governance," 36–37; Adil Najam, "The Case against a New International Environmental Organization," *Global Governance* 9 (2003): 367–384.
25. Ivanova, "UNEP in Global Environmental Governance," 46.
26. Ivanova, "The Contested Legacy of Rio+20."
27. Sikina Jinnah, "Singing the Unsung: Secretariats in Global Environmental Politics," in *The Roads from Rio: Lessons Learned from Twenty Years of Multilateral Environmental Negotiations*, ed. Pamela S. Chasek and Lynn M. Wagner (New York: Routledge, 2012).
28. Ibid.; Sikina Jinnah, "Overlap Management in the World Trade Organization: Secretariat Influence on Trade-Environment Politics," *Global Environmental Politics* 10, no. 2 (2010): 54–79; Biermann and Siebenhüner, *Managers of Global Change*; Miquel Muñoz, Rachel Thrasher, and Adil Najam, "Measuring the Negotiation Burden of Multilateral Environmental Agreements," *Global Environmental Politics* 9, no. 4 (2009): 1–13.

29. Jinnah, "Singing the Unsung."
30. Jinnah, "Overlap Management in the World Trade Organization"; Thomas Gehring, "The Institutional Complex of Trade and Environment: Toward an Interlocking Governance Structure and a Division of Labor," in *Managing Institutional Complexity: Regime Interplay and Global Environmental Change,* ed. Sebastian Oberthür and Olav Schram Stokke (Cambridge: MIT Press, 2011).
31. Steffen Bauer, "The Secretariat of the United Nations Environment Programme: Tangled up in Blue," in Biermann and Siebenhüner, *Managers of Global Change.*
32. Per-Olof Busch, "The Climate Secretariat: Making a Living in a Straitjacket," in Biermann and Siebenhüner, *Managers of Global Change.*
33. Pia M. Kohler, Alexandra Conliffe, Stefan Jungcurt, Maria Gutierrez, and Yulia Yamineva, "Informing Policy: Science and Knowledge in Global Environmental Agreements," in Chasek and Wagner, *The Roads from Rio.*
34. Mike Hulme and Martin Mahony, "Climate Change: What Do We Know about the IPCC?," *Progress in Physical Geography* 34, no. 5 (2010): 705–718.
35. See Global Environment Facility, "What Is the GEF?," http://www.thegef.org/gef/whatisgef.
36. Raymond Clémençon, "What Future for the Global Environment Facility?," *Journal of Environment and Development* 15, no. 1 (2006): 50–74; Charlotte Streck, "The Global Environment Facility: A Role Model for International Governance?," *Global Environmental Politics* 1, no. 2 (2001): 71–94.
37. Peter J. Kanowski, Constance L. McDermott, and Benjamin W. Cashore, "Implementing REDD+: Lessons from Analysis of Forest Governance," *Environmental Science and Policy* 14, no. 2 (2011): 111–117.
38. Jonathan A. Fox and L. David Brown, eds., *The Struggle for Accountability: The World Bank, NGOs, and Grassroots Movements* (Cambridge: MIT Press, 1998).
39. Ibid.; Tamar Gutner, "Evaluating World Bank Environmental Performance," in *Handbook of Global Environmental Politics,* 2nd ed, ed. Peter Dauvergne (London: Edward Elgar, 2012).
40. Ibid.
41. Jennifer Clapp and Peter Dauvergne, *Paths to a Green World: The Political Economy of the Global Environment,* 2nd ed. (Cambridge: MIT Press, 2011), 214–220.
42. For summaries, see Nico Jaspers and Robert Falkner, "International Trade, the Environment, and Climate Change," in *The Handbook of Global Climate and Environment Policy,* ed. Robert Falkner (London: John Wiley, 2013).
43. Kate O'Neill and William C. G. Burns, "Trade Liberalization and Global Environmental Governance: The Potential for Conflict," in *Handbook of Global Environmental Politics,* ed. Peter Dauvergne (Cheltenham, UK: Edward Elgar, 2005).
44. Jaspers and Falkner, "International Trade, the Environment, and Climate Change."
45. For overviews, see O'Neill, *The Environment and International Relations*; Kate O'Neill, "The Comparative Study of Environmental Movements" in *Comparative Environmental Politics,* ed. Paul F. Steinberg and Stacy D. VanDeveer (Cambridge: MIT Press, 2012); Kal Raustiala, "NGOs in International Treatymaking," in *The Oxford Guide to Treaties,* ed. Duncan B. Hollis (Oxford: Oxford University Press, 2012); Michele M. Betsill and Elisabeth Corell, eds., *NGO Diplomacy: The Influence of Nongovernmental Organizations in International Environmental Negotiations* (Cambridge: MIT Press, 2008); Burgiel and Wood, "Witness, Architect, Detractor"; Susan Park, "Transnational Environmental Activism," in Falkner, *The Handbook of Global Climate and Environment Policy.*
46. Paul Wapner, *Environmental Activism and World Civic Politics* (Albany: State University of New York Press, 1996).
47. Burgiel and Wood, "Witness, Architect, Detractor."
48. John McCormick, "The Role of Environmental NGOs in International Regimes," in *The Global Environment: Institutions, Law, and Policy,* ed. Norman J. Vig and Regina S. Axelrod (Washington: CQ Press, 1999).

49. Benjamin Cashore, Graeme Auld, and Deanna Newsom, *Governing through Markets: Forest Certification and the Emergence of Non-state Authority* (New Haven, CT: Yale University Press, 2004); Lars H. Gulbrandsen, *Transnational Environmental Governance: The Emergence and Effects of the Certification of Forests and Fisheries* (Northampton, MA: Edward Elgar, 2010).
50. Raustiala, "NGOs in International Treatymaking," n. 9.
51. Konrad Otto-Zimmermann, "NGO—the Questionable Charm of Being Defined by What You Aren't: A Call for Renaming an Important Group of Actors," International Council of Local Environmental Initiatives, ICLEI Paper 2011-2, 2011, http://local2012.iclei.org/fileadmin/files/ICLEI_Paper_2011-2_NGO_20110830.pdf.
52. David Lewis and Nazneen Kanji, *Non-governmental Organizations and Development* (London: Routledge, 2009), 9.
53. For a list of NGO subtypes recognized by the UNFCCC Secretariat, see United Nations Framework Convention on Climate Change, "Admitted NGO," http://maindb.unfccc.int/public/ngo.pl.
54. Kate O'Neill, "From Stockholm to Johannesburg and Beyond: The Evolving Metaregime for Global Environmental Governance," paper presented at the Amsterdam Conference on the Human Dimensions of Global Environmental Change, May 24–26, 2007.
55. Raustiala, "NGOs in International Treatymaking," 1.
56. Clapp and Dauvergne, *Paths to a Green World*, 80.
57. Raustiala, "NGOs in International Treatymaking," 7.
58. Betsill and Corell, *NGO Diplomacy*.
59. Christopher Rootes, "Environmental Movements: From the Local to the Global," in *Environmental Movements: Local, National and Global*, ed. Christopher Rootes (London: Frank Cass, 1999), 2. See also O'Neill, "The Comparative Study of Environmental Movements."
60. George Holmes, "Conservation's Friends in High Places: Neoliberalism, Networks, and the Transnational Conservation Elite," *Global Environmental Politics* 11, no. 4 (2011): 1–21.
61. Bron Taylor, ed., *Ecological Resistance Movements: The Global Emergence of Radical and Popular Environmentalism* (Albany: State University of New York Press, 1995); Timothy Doyle, *Environmental Movements in Majority and Minority Worlds: A Global Perspective* (New Brunswick, NJ: Rutgers University Press, 2005).
62. Robert J. Duffy, "Organized Interests and Environmental Policy," in *The Oxford Handbook of U.S. Environmental Policy*, ed. Sheldon Kamieniecki and Michael E. Kraft (Oxford: Oxford University Press, 2013).
63. World Bank Operational Directive 14.70 (1989).
64. Simone Pulver, "Organizing Business: Industry NGOs in the Climate Debates," *Greener Management International* 39 (2002): 55–67.
65. Peter J. Jacques, Riley E. Dunlap, and Mark Freeman, "The Organisation of Denial: Conservative Think Tanks and Environmental Scepticism," *Environmental Politics* 17, no. 3 (2008): 349–385.
66. Pulver, "Organizing Business"; Park, "Transnational Environmental Activism."
67. Conca, *Governing Water*; Sanjeev Khagram, *Dams and Development: Transnational Struggles for Water and Power* (Ithaca, NY: Cornell University Press, 2004).
68. Ruth Reitan and Shannon Gibson, "Environmental Praxis, Climate Activism, and the UNFCCC: A Participatory Action Research Approach," *Globalizations* 9, no. 3 (2012): 395–410.
69. Raustiala, "NGOs in International Treatymaking," 4.
70. CITES, Article XI:7.
71. Raustiala, "NGOs in International Treatymaking," 11.
72. Jim Vallette and Heather Spalding, *The International Trade in Hazardous Wastes: A Greenpeace Inventory*, 5th ed. (Washington, DC: Greenpeace International Waste Trade Project, 1990).

73. Park, "Transnational Environmental Activism"; Miranda A. Schreurs and Elizabeth C. Economy, eds., *The Internationalization of Environmental Protection* (Cambridge: Cambridge University Press, 1997).
74. Chasek and Wagner, *The Roads from Rio.*
75. Lars H. Gulbrandsen and Steinar Andresen, "NGO Influence in the Implementation of the Kyoto Protocol: Compliance, Flexibility Mechanisms, and Sinks," *Global Environmental Politics* 4, no. 4 (2004): 54–75, cited in Park, "Transnational Environmental Activism," 280.
76. Kate O'Neill, "Transnational Protest: States, Circuses, and Conflict at the Frontline of Global Politics," *International Studies Review* 6 (2004): 233–251.
77. Dana R. Fisher, "Cop-15 in Copenhagen: How the Merging of Movements Left Civil Society Out in the Cold," *Global Environmental Politics* 10, no. 2 (2010): 11–17.
78. Christopher C. Joyner, "Rethinking International Environmental Regimes: What Role for Partnership Coalitions?," *Journal of International Law and International Relations* 1, nos. 1–2 (2005): 89–119.
79. Richard K. Lattanzio, *Global Environment Facility (GEF): An Overview* (Washington, DC: Congressional Research Service, 2010), 8.
80. Ibrahima Sow, Robert K. Dixon, Jie Pan, Anil Sookdeo, Evelyn Swain, and Laurent Granier, "Financing for Innovative Technologies and Best Practices to Reduce Persistent Organic Pollutants," *Mitigation and Adaptation Strategies for Global Change* (October 2012).
81. Ingrid Jacoba Visseren-Hamakers, Pieter Leroy, and Pieter Glasbergen, "Conservation Partnerships and Biodiversity Governance: Fulfilling Governance Functions through Interaction," *Sustainable Development* 20, no. 4 (2012): 264–275.
82. Raustiala, "NGOs in International Treatymaking"; Sabine von Schorlemer and Peter-Tobias Stoll, eds., *The UNESCO Convention on the Protection and Promotion of the Diversity of Cultural Expressions* (Berlin: Springer, 2012).
83. Burgiel and Wood, "Witness, Architect, Detractor," 142–144.
84. Alastair Iles, "Mapping Environmental Justice in Technology Flows: Computer Waste Impacts in Asia," *Global Environmental Politics* 4, no. 4 (2004): 78–107.
85. Park, "Transnational Environmental Activism," 276.
86. Cashore et al., *Governing through Markets*; Gulbrandsen, *Transnational Environmental Governance.*
87. O'Neill, *The Environment and International Relations,* 2009.
88. Betsill and Corell, *NGO Diplomacy*; Jinnah, "Singing the Unsung."
89. Amandine Orsini, "Multi-forum Non-state Actors: Navigating the Regime Complexes for Forestry and Genetic Resources," *Global Environmental Politics* 13, no. 3 (2013): 34–55.
90. James Gustave Speth, *Red Sky at Morning: America and the Crisis of the Global Environment* (New Haven, CT: Yale University Press, 2004).
91. John Vogler, "In Defense of International Environmental Cooperation," in *The State and the Global Ecological Crisis,* ed. John Barry and Robyn Eckersley (Cambridge: MIT Press, 2005).
92. Park, "Transnational Environmental Activism."

3

International Law and the Protection of the Global Environment

*Jacqueline Peel**

This chapter examines the historical development, central principles, and current implementation of international environmental law. Half a century ago, discussion of this topic would probably have begun with a question as to whether the subject of international environmental law even existed: there were no treaties or journals specifically on the subject, only a very small number of law school seminars were taught, and most public international law texts avoided addressing the environment, with little risk of being criticized for incompleteness.

Today the situation is entirely different. The International Court of Justice (ICJ) has confirmed the "obligations of States to respect and protect the natural environment."[1] Moreover, it has declared that states' "general obligation . . . to ensure that activities within their jurisdiction or control respect the environment of other States or of areas beyond national control is now part of the corpus of international law relating to the environment."[2] This latter obligation is applicable at all times and to all activities, even the use of nuclear weapons.[3] These general obligations have been further developed in the context of the international community's commitment to "integrate environment and development in pursuance of the overall goal of sustainable development."[4]

This chapter is divided into four major sections. The first briefly describes the historical development of international environmental law and the institutional context within which that development has taken place. The second section examines certain general principles of international law that have emerged in relation to environmental matters. The third section summarizes basic rules of international environmental law in fields such as protection of biodiversity, protection of freshwater resources and the marine environment, prevention of air pollution and climate change, and management of waste and hazardous substances. The final section offers a consideration of some of the main challenges facing international environmental law and its future development.

*This chapter is based on an earlier version coauthored with Philippe Sands, which was published in the second edition of this text. The author would like to acknowledge research assistance provided by Ms. Emma Cocks.

International Environmental Law: Context, History, and Sources

International legal efforts to protect the environment go back at least to the 1890s, when a dispute was submitted to international arbitration as a consequence of U.S. efforts to prevent British vessels from exploiting fur seals in the international waters of the Bering Sea. Although the Pacific Fur Seal Arbitral Tribunal did not find in favor of a unilateral U.S. approach to conservation, it did adopt regulations for the "proper protection and preservation" of fur seals.[5] These regulations have served as an important precedent for the subsequent development of international environmental law, reflecting an acknowledgment that environmental problems transcend national boundaries.

In the twenty-first century, as we face problems like climate change, there is even greater recognition of the inherent and fundamental interdependence of the global environment and the challenge of reconciling this with the fact that many land, sea, and air spaces are part of the sovereign areas of independent states.[6] To understand how international rules of environmental protection have developed in this context, it is first necessary to know something of the nature of international society and the structure of the international legal order, as well as the sources of international environmental law.

The International Legal Order

International law and international organizations provide the basis for cooperation among the various members of the international community in their efforts to protect the global environment. At each level the task becomes progressively more complex as new actors and interests are drawn into the process. Whereas just two states, representing the interests of local fishing communities, negotiated the early fisheries conventions in the middle of the nineteenth century, more than 150 states were involved in negotiations sponsored by the United Nations General Assembly that led to the 1992 UN Framework Convention on Climate Change (FCCC) and its 1997 Kyoto Protocol. More than 190 states are participating in the current negotiations for a new climate change treaty to be in effect from 2020 (see Chapter 10).

Whether negotiations are bilateral or multilateral in nature, the principles and rules of public international law are intended to serve similar functions. The overall objective of the international legal order is to provide a framework within which the various members of the international community may cooperate, establish norms of behavior, and resolve their differences. Accordingly, as with domestic law, the functions of international law are legislative, administrative, and adjudicative. The legal principles and rules that impose binding obligations requiring states and other members of the international community to conform to certain norms of behavior are accomplished through the legislative function. These obligations place limits on the activities that may be conducted or permitted because of their actual or potential impact on the environment. Such impact may be entirely within national borders, across territorial boundaries, or in areas beyond national jurisdiction.

The administrative function of international law allocates tasks to the various actors to ensure that standards imposed by the principles and rules of international environmental law are carried out. The adjudicative function of international law aims, in a limited way, to provide mechanisms or forums for the pacific settlement of differences or disputes that arise between members of the international community involving the use of natural resources or the conduct of activities affecting the environment.

These similarities mask some important differences between the international legal order and domestic law. For instance, there is no formal global legislature to carry out the legislative function of international environmental law, nor does any global environmental agency exist to administer and enforce international environmental rules. Whether a country is bound by a particular environmental treaty depends upon whether it has consented to the treaty's terms, signified by the formal process of state ratification of the treaty.[7] Given that not all states ratify all environmental treaties, different states have different sets of international environmental commitments at any one time. When a dispute arises as to whether a state has complied with its commitments, that state's consent is generally also required in order for another state to initiate formal dispute settlement in an international court. The difficulties for compliance and enforcement of international environmental law that this traditional international legal structure creates have spurred the development of new compliance mechanisms and compulsory dispute settlement procedures in some treaty regimes (see Chapter 5).

Actors in International Society

Reflecting the state-centric nature of the international legal order, states remain far and away the most important actors shaping international environmental law. It is still states that create, adopt, and implement international legal principles and rules, establish international organizations, and permit other actors to participate in the process. States encompass both developed ("Northern") and developing ("Southern") countries, which often pursue markedly different agendas in international environmental treaty negotiations. However, this rather simple developed/developing country distinction does not always hold in environmental negotiations as states pursue what they perceive to be vital national interests, including strategic alliances. The current climate change negotiations, for instance, illustrate the extent of the differences that exist both *between* developed and developing countries and *within* the respective developed and developing country blocs on the contentious issue of responsibility for controlling greenhouse gas emissions in order to avoid dangerous anthropogenic global warming.

As with the human rights field, international environmental law provides clear evidence of an evolution from conceptions of the international society as comprising only a community of states to the view that it encompasses individuals, groups, and corporate and other entities within and among those states. This new reality is reflected in the important role played by international organizations and nongovernmental actors in virtually all aspects of the international legal process relating to environment and development.[8]

The international organizations involved in environmental matters make up a complex and unwieldy network at the global, regional, subregional, and bilateral levels. It is unlikely that any international organization today will not have some responsibility for environmental matters. Indeed, emerging as among the most significant international organizations for environmental purposes are those with economic or development mandates, including the World Bank, the International Monetary Fund, and the World Trade Organization (WTO). Nevertheless, the increasing number of international organizations with environmental competence, and the overall lack of coordination among them, presents a major challenge for achieving common policy goals, such as sustainable development.

Nongovernmental organizations (NGOs) have historically played an important role in developing international environmental law and continue to do so in a variety of ways (see Chapter 5). In the past few decades at least six different types of groups have emerged as actors in the development of international environmental law: the scientific community, nonprofit environmental groups and associations, private companies and business concerns, legal organizations, the academic community, and individuals. In addition, transnational corporations are more and more the objects of international environmental regulation, as well as being active participants in negotiations for new international environmental rules. Because they conduct activities across national boundaries in an increasingly interdependent world, the need for minimum international standards of behavior has been recognized. In line with emerging concepts of corporate social responsibility, transnational corporations have themselves begun to consider the need for further development of international environmental law governing their activities, although efforts to date have produced only voluntary guidelines for corporate behavior.[9]

Different types of actors have different roles and functions, both as subjects and as objects of international environmental law. These functions and roles include participating in the lawmaking process; monitoring implementation, including reporting; ensuring enforcement of obligations; and providing independent mechanisms for the resolution of disputes. The nature of each actor's contribution turns upon the extent of the actor's international legal personality and the rights and obligations granted to it by general international law, as well as the rules established by particular treaties and other instruments. For instance, in the case of international organizations, the actual functions of each institution depend to a great extent upon the powers granted to it, as subsequently interpreted and applied by the parties and the practice of the organization.

Sovereignty and Territory

In the traditional international legal order, states are considered sovereign and equal, imbued with equal rights and duties as members of the international community, notwithstanding differences of an economic, social, or political nature. The sovereignty and equality of states means that each has prima facie exclusive jurisdiction over its territory and the natural resources found there. States also have a duty not to intervene in the area of exclusive jurisdiction of other states. In principle, this means that each state has competence to develop policies and laws in regard to the natural resources and environment of its own territory. That territory comprises the following:

- The state's landmass and subsoil
- The state's internal waters, such as lakes, rivers, and canals
- The territorial sea adjacent to the state's coast, including its seabed, subsoil, and the resources thereof
- The airspace above the state's land, internal waters, and territorial sea, up to the point at which the legal regime of outer space begins

States may also have more limited sovereign rights and jurisdiction over other areas, including a contiguous zone adjacent to their territorial seas; the continental shelf, its seabed and subsoil; and "exclusive economic zones" important for fishing rights.

As a result of these arrangements, certain areas fall outside the territory and exclusive jurisdiction of any state. These areas, sometimes referred to as the global commons, include the high seas and their seabed and subsoil, the atmosphere, outer space, and, according to a majority of states, the Antarctic.

This apparently straightforward international legal order was a satisfactory organizing structure until technological developments, and their environmental effects, permeated national boundaries. The traditional structure does not coexist comfortably with an environmental order that consists of a biosphere of interdependent ecosystems that do not respect artificial territorial boundaries between states.[10] As an ecological matter, if not a legal one, many natural resources and their environmental components are shared, and the use by any one state of the natural resources within its territory will invariably have consequences for the use of natural resources and their environmental components in other states. Ecological interdependence therefore poses a fundamental challenge for international law, as no one state, acting within its territorial boundaries, can adequately address global environmental problems. International cooperation and the development of shared norms of behavior are indispensable.

Historical Development

The deficiencies of the traditional international legal order in responding to environmental challenges led to the rapid development of new, "greener" rules of international law. The process of "greening" international law occurred over four periods, responding to particular factors that influenced legal developments.[11] In the early stages of the development of international environmental law, the field lacked a coordinated legal and institutional framework. Attempts to create such a framework came with two global environmental conferences:

the 1972 Stockholm Conference and the Rio Earth Summit in 1992. The latter is best known for establishing the concept of sustainable development as the central objective of international environmental law. Twenty years on from the Earth Summit, the Rio+20 conference in 2012 provided an opportunity for the international community to take stock of the development (or lack thereof) in notions of, and mechanisms for implementing, sustainability.

To 1945. The first distinct period in the greening process began with nineteenth-century bilateral fisheries treaties and the Pacific Fur Seal arbitration. It concluded with the creation of the United Nations and its associated family of international institutions in 1945. This period might be characterized as one in which states first acted internationally upon their understanding that the process of industrialization and the rapid expansion of economic activities relying on natural resources required limits on the exploitation of flora and fauna and the adoption of appropriate legal instruments.

Until the establishment of the United Nations in 1945, no international forum existed in which to raise environmental concerns, and most of the agreements adopted in this initial period did not create arrangements to ensure that legal obligations were complied with or enforced. Many initiatives grew from activities by private citizens, an early harbinger of the more intensive activism of NGOs that marks international negotiations today.

1945–1972. The establishment of the United Nations introduced a second period in the development of international environmental law, culminating in the 1972 Stockholm Conference on the Human Environment. During this period many international organizations with competence in environmental matters were created, and legal instruments were adopted to address particular sources of pollution and the conservation of general and particular environmental resources. These included rules governing oil pollution, nuclear testing, wetlands, the marine environment and its living resources, freshwaters, and the dumping of waste at sea.[12]

The UN provided a forum for discussing the consequences of technological progress and introduced a period characterized by the proliferation of international organizations, engagement with environmental issues, and action to address the causes of pollution and environmental degradation. The relationship between economic development and environmental protection began to be understood. However, the UN Charter did not, and still does not, explicitly address environmental protection or the conservation of natural resources.

Stockholm to Rio. The third period began with the 1972 Stockholm Conference and concluded with the Earth Summit in 1992 (see also Chapter 2). In this twenty-year span the United Nations attempted to put in place a system to address a growing range of environmental issues in a more coordinated and coherent way. A raft of regional and global conventions addressed new issues, and new techniques of regulation were employed.

The 1972 Stockholm Conference, convened by the UN General Assembly, adopted several nonbinding instruments, including a "Declaration of Twenty-six Guiding Principles."[13] The conference represented the international community's first effort at constructing a coherent strategy for the development of international policy and institutions to protect the environment, and the Stockholm Declaration is generally regarded as the foundation of international environmental law.[14]

One of the most significant contributions of the Stockholm Conference has proved to be the creation of the United Nations Environment Programme (UNEP), which has subsequently been instrumental in the establishment and implementation of important global and regional treaties addressing ozone depletion, trade in hazardous waste, biodiversity, and marine protection.

In addition, the Stockholm Conference catalyzed other global treaties adopted under UN auspices, such as the 1982 United Nations Convention on the Law of the Sea (UNCLOS).[15] This treaty established a unique, comprehensive framework of global rules for protection of the marine environment and marine living resources, including detailed institutional arrangements and provisions on environmental impact assessment, technology transfer, and liability. These provisions have had significant influence on the language and approach of many other environmental agreements.

By 1990, when preparations for the Earth Summit formally began, there existed a solid body of rules of international environmental law. States were increasingly subject to limits on the right to allow or carry out activities that harmed the environment. New standards were in place, and a range of techniques sought to implement those standards. Environmental issues, moreover, had begun to intersect with economic matters, especially trade and development lending. But in spite of these relatively impressive achievements, environmental matters remained on the periphery of the international community's agenda and the activities of most institutions.

Earth Summit and Beyond. The 1992 Earth Summit launched a fourth period in the development of international environmental law, requiring that environmental concerns be integrated into all international activities. International environmental law merged with international law in the new field of sustainable development.

The origins of the Earth Summit lay in the UN General Assembly's endorsement of the Brundtland Report in December 1987 and its call the following year for a global conference on environment and development.[16] The Earth Summit, held in Rio de Janeiro, saw participation in environmental negotiations by an unprecedented number of states (176 in total), together with several dozen international organizations and several thousand NGOs. Three nonbinding instruments were adopted at the summit: the Rio Declaration on Environment and Development (the Rio Declaration); the Non-legally Binding Authoritative Statement of Principles for a Global Consensus on the Management, Conservation, and Sustainable Development of All Types of Forests (the Forest Principles); and Agenda 21.[17] Two treaties were also opened for signature: the Convention on Biological Diversity and the FCCC.[18] These two treaties have since formed the basis for further elaboration of international environmental law in their respective fields through the adoption of protocols and implementing arrangements.

Since the Earth Summit, progress in developing and implementing the international concept of sustainable development has not been as promising.[19] The 2002 World Summit on Sustainable Development (WSSD) held in Johannesburg, South Africa, produced a plan of implementation, but in fact it contained few new commitments.[20] This may have been a result of the breadth of the negotiating agenda, which included poverty eradication, agricultural practices, and public health issues. The much-anticipated Rio+20 Summit in 2012 suffered a similar fate. The summit's grandly titled outcome document, "The Future We Want," reaffirms the Rio Declaration principles but does not go much further, with trade concerns associated with the goal of instituting a "global green economy" proving particularly divisive.[21] NGOs meeting at Rio for the parallel People's Summit strongly criticized the official outcome and released their own counterstatement explaining how the text lays the groundwork for "The Future We Don't Want."[22] More broadly, the failure since the original Earth Summit to agree on concrete actions for implementing sustainable development suggests that the concept may function best as an overall policy goal rather than as the basis for prescriptive rules constraining state conduct with respect to the environment.

Post-1992 developments in other key areas of international environmental law, such as within the international climate change regime, also reflect some ambivalence about the future direction of international environmental law. Many point to the 2009 Copenhagen climate change conference as an important turning point. Parties' failure at the conference to deliver on the promise of a new climate change agreement raised important questions over the future of environmental multilateralism. The principal outcome of the Copenhagen meeting—the nonbinding political document known as the Copenhagen Accord[23]—suggests a new way forward for international climate change law based upon "bottom-up" development of emissions targets and actions by states rather than the establishment of prescriptive standards of conduct at the international level.[24]

Sources of International Environmental Law

International law consists of rules, rights, and obligations that are legally binding on states and other members of the international community in their relations with each other. As a branch of general international law, international environmental law relies on the same legal sources, including the following:

- Bilateral or multilateral treaties
- Binding acts of international organizations
- Rules of customary international law
- General principles of law
- Judgments of an international court or tribunal

It is to these sources that international courts look in determining whether a particular legally binding obligation of international environmental law exists,[25] and hence they are generally regarded as "hard law."

Sources of binding obligation with respect to environmental matters (hard law) are supplemented by nonbinding sources of so-called soft law, reflected in guidelines, recommendations, and other nonbinding acts adopted by states and international institutions. Both the 1972 Stockholm Declaration and the 1992 Rio Declaration fall into the category of international environmental soft law. So too do newer instruments like the WSSD Plan of Implementation, the Rio+20 statement "The Future We Want" (elaborating guidelines for the pursuit of sustainable development in various sectors), and the 2009 Copenhagen Accord (setting out common objectives and state actions to address climate change). While not formally binding on states, rules of soft law can play an important role in the field of international environmental law. For instance, soft law may be politically influential, may point to the likely future direction of development of hard law such as treaty rules, may informally establish acceptable norms of behavior, or may serve to "codify" or reflect rules of customary international law.[26]

Treaties. The most important binding sources of international environmental law are treaties—formal international agreements also referred to by such names as conventions or protocols. These can be adopted bilaterally, regionally, or globally. With more than 193 UN member states now in existence, the number of bilateral environmental agreements runs into the thousands, supplemented by dozens of regional agreements and a smaller but increasing number of global treaties. The principal global environmental treaties are listed in Table 3-1.

Countries of the European Union and other industrial nations have adopted a large body of regional environmental rules that frequently provide a basis for measures adopted in other parts of the world. Important regional treaties include the 1979 Convention on Long-Range Transboundary Air Pollution and its implementing protocols, the 1992 Convention for the Protection of the Marine Environment of the North-East Atlantic (OSPAR), and the 1998 Aarhus Convention on Access to Information, Public Participation and Decision-Making and Access to Justice in Environmental Matters. Regional treaties are less well developed in Africa, the Caribbean, and Oceania and are even more limited in Asia and parts of the Americas. Industrial activity in Antarctica is prohibited by treaty.

Environmental treaties share the same general characteristics as other international treaties, although certain special features exist. One such feature is the widespread use of a "framework convention–protocol model" in regulating regional or global environmental problems. Under this model, as the first response to a problem, a general framework treaty is adopted that sets out general obligations, creates basic institutional arrangements, and provides procedures for the adoption of more detailed obligations in a subsequent protocol. Only states that ratified the parent convention are able to ratify any subsequent protocol. Table 3-1 provides

Table 3-1 Major Global Environmental Treaties

Year of conclusion	Treaty and associated instruments
1946	International Whaling Convention
1971	Ramsar Wetlands Convention
1972	London Dumping Convention
	• 1996 Protocol
1972	World Heritage Convention
1973/1978	MARPOL (marine pollution)
1973	Convention on International Trade in Endangered Species (CITES)
1982	United Nations Convention on the Law of the Sea (UNCLOS)
	• 1995 Fish Stocks Agreement
1985	Vienna Ozone Convention
	• 1987 Montreal Protocol
1989	Basel Hazardous Wastes Convention
	• 1999 Liability Protocol
1992	Convention on Biological Diversity
	• 2000 Biosafety Protocol
	• 2010 Nagoya Protocol on Access to Genetic Resources and Fair and Equitable Sharing of Benefits
1992	Framework Convention on Climate Change (FCCC)
	• 1997 Kyoto Protocol
1998	Chemicals Convention
2001	Persistent Organic Pollutants Convention

a number of examples of the framework convention–protocol model, including the 1992 Framework Convention on Climate Change and its Kyoto Protocol adopted in 1997.

The adoption of an environmental treaty is preceded by a series of negotiations that frequently take place over a lengthy period of time. Once an environmental issue has been identified as requiring international legislation (for example, through scientific evidence or concern), states must identify an appropriate legislative forum or institution, such as UNEP, to address the issue. After the forum agrees to participate, that body establishes a negotiating process, which could involve anything from an informal ad hoc group of governmental experts to a formal institutional structure. Negotiations may be open-ended in time or established for a limited period, which may later be extended (as in the case of the ongoing international climate change negotiations). Once a draft treaty text has been negotiated, it is formally adopted and opened for signature by states. For most environmental treaties, signature by a state is insufficient to create binding obligations on that state; instead the treaty must be ratified by the state through the submission of a formal instrument of ratification.[27] Many multilateral environmental treaties contain further provisions regarding the number, or pattern of participation, of states necessary for the treaty to enter into force. Such provisions may result in considerable delays in the entry into force of some treaties; for example, the 1997 Kyoto Protocol did not enter into force until February 2005 because of the opposition of prominent developed countries such as the United States.

Acts of International Organizations. The second principal source of international law in the environmental field is acts of international organizations, including environmentally relevant acts of UN institutions such as the General Assembly and the Security Council.[28] Almost all international environmental agreements establish institutional organs with the power to adopt certain rules, make decisions, and take other measures. Such acts, sometimes referred to as secondary legislation, can be important sources of international law. Some of the more far-reaching international measures affecting the use of natural resources have been adopted in the form of acts of international organizations rather than by treaty.

Many environmental treaties allow the institutions they create to have a choice of adopting acts with or without binding legal effects. Binding acts of international organizations derive their legal authority from the treaty on which their adoption was based and can therefore be considered part of treaty law. Those acts that do not have binding legal consequences could, however, subsequently be relied on as reflecting rules of customary international law.

Customary International Law. The primary place of treaties and acts of international organizations as sources of international environmental law should not obscure the important, albeit secondary, role played by customary international law. Customary law fulfills a number of functions by creating binding obligations and contributing to the codification of obligations in the form of treaty rules and other binding acts. The significance of customary law lies in the fact that, as a general matter, it establishes obligations for all states (or all states within a particular region) except those that have persistently objected to a practice and its legal consequences. Article 38(1)(b) of the statute establishing the ICJ identifies the two elements of customary international law: state practice and *opinio juris*—the belief that the practice is required as a matter of law. Establishing the existence of a rule of customary international law requires evidence of consistent state practice. Such practice rarely provides clear guidance as to the precise content of any particular rule.

General Principles of Law. Alongside customary international law, another source of international law referenced in Article 38 of the ICJ statute is "general principles of law recognized by civilized nations." This allows the consideration and application of widely accepted principles of domestic law by international courts, usually only on occasions when gaps exist. Examples of general principles that may be applied in an environmental context include the principle of good faith in the exercise of rights by a state and the principle of equity, which allows the international community to take into account considerations of justice and fairness in the establishment, operation, or application of an international law rule.[29]

International Case Law. The case law of international courts and tribunals and arguments presented to such bodies identify some general principles and rules of international environmental law. The significance of arbitral awards in the development of international environmental law should not be understated. Important principles were elaborated by arbitral tribunals in the previously mentioned Pacific Fur Seal case, in the Lac Lanoux arbitration between France and Spain (concerning the use of a shared river), and more recently in the Iron Rhine Railway arbitration between Belgium and the Netherlands (clarifying the nature of the concept of sustainable development). Another important arbitral decision is the much-cited Trail Smelter case between the United States and Canada concerning transboundary air pollution from a zinc smelter in British Columbia. This case famously articulated the principle that "no state has the right to use or permit the use of its territory in such a manner as to cause injury by fumes in or to the territory of another or the properties or persons therein, when the case is of serious consequence and the injury is established by clear and convincing evidence."[30]

Judgments of the ICJ have also contributed to the development of international environmental law, although in recent times arguably judgments of other international tribunals, including the International Tribunal for the Law of the Sea (ITLOS) and the WTO Appellate Body, have had greater impact. Important decisions of the ICJ include the Icelandic fisheries cases (on fisheries conservation), the nuclear test cases of 1974 and 1995 (on the legality of atmospheric and underground nuclear tests), the 1997 Gabčikovo-Nagymaros (Danube dam) case (concerning a large hydroelectric project with potential impacts on biodiversity), the opinions on the legality of the use of nuclear weapons, and the 2010 Pulp Mills case (considering the procedural and substantive obligations of states to prevent potential environmental harm to freshwater resources). Another environmental case currently before the Court concerns the legality of Japan's practice of taking protected species of whales for "scientific research" purposes.[31] This case offers the Court an opportunity to contribute to the development of international environmental law in the field of biodiversity conservation.

Principles of International Environmental Law

Several general principles of international law have emerged specifically in relation to environmental matters. They are general in the sense that they potentially apply to all members of the international community, span every range of activities, and address the protection of all aspects of the environment.

They are principles in the sense that they usually operate as broad, overarching objectives rather than as prescriptive rules for state conduct, although if sufficiently well subscribed they may amount to customary international law.[32] While principles do not require particular outcomes, they are designed to direct behavior—often by specifying considerations for decision making—and have a normative quality that distinguishes them from mere policies.[33] In international environmental law, general principles also serve an important structural function, providing the common scaffolding upon which more specific rules affecting different environmental resources are built and implemented.

Sovereignty and Responsibility for the Environment

The rules of international environmental law have developed in pursuit of two principles that pull in opposing directions: that states have sovereign rights over their natural resources and that states must not cause damage to the environment. These objectives are reflected in Principle 21 of the Stockholm Declaration and Principle 2 of the Rio Declaration and provide the foundation of international environmental law.

The first element (sovereignty) reflects the preeminent position of states as primary members of the international legal community. It is tempered by the second element (environmental protection), which places limits on the exercise of sovereign rights. In an environmentally interdependent world, activities in one state almost inevitably produce effects in other states or in areas beyond national jurisdiction (such as the high seas).

In the form presented by Principle 21 and Principle 2, the responsibility to prevent damage to the environments of other states or of areas beyond national jurisdiction has been accepted as an obligation by all states.[34] As noted previously, the ICJ has now confirmed that the second element reflects customary international law.[35]

The emergence of this responsibility has historical roots that predate the Stockholm Conference. These relate to the obligation of all states "to protect within the territory the rights of other states, in particular their right to integrity and inviolability in peace and war"[36] and the principle endorsed by the arbitral tribunal in the Trail Smelter case.

Prevention of Harm

Closely related to the Principle 21/Principle 2 obligation is the principle requiring the prevention of damage to the environment and otherwise to reduce, limit, or control activities that might cause or risk such damage. The preventive principle is distinguishable from the responsibility principle in two ways. First, the latter arises from the application of respect for state sovereignty, whereas the preventive principle seeks to minimize environmental damage as an objective in itself. In the Iron Rhine arbitration, the tribunal recognized that "today, in international environmental law, a growing emphasis is being put on the duty of prevention." It declared that the "duty of prevention" is now "a principle of general international law" that "applies not only in autonomous activities but also in activities undertaken in implementation of specific treaties between the Parties."[37] Second, under the preventive principle, a state may be under an obligation to prevent not only transboundary harm but also damage to the environment within its own jurisdiction. The preventive principle requires action to be taken at an early stage and, if possible, before damage has actually occurred.

This approach was confirmed in the Pulp Mills case, where the ICJ pointed out that "the principle of prevention, as a customary rule, has its origins in the due diligence that is required of a State in its territory." Fulfillment of the obligation to prevent harm is thus tied to the exercise of due diligence, which the ICJ described as "an obligation which entails not only the adoption of appropriate rules and measures, but also a certain level of vigilance in their enforcement and the exercise of administrative control applicable to public and private operators, such as the monitoring of activities undertaken by such operators."[38] Emerging as an essential measure for demonstrating due diligence to prevent harm is the carrying out of an environmental impact assessment.[39]

Even so, it is clear that what amounts to due diligence under international environmental law may vary with the circumstances. For instance, the Seabed Disputes Chamber of ITLOS, in its 2011 Advisory Opinion on Responsibilities and Obligations in the Deep Seabed Area, recognized that a higher standard may be warranted "for the riskier activities" or may be required as a result of developments in scientific and technological knowledge.[40] Conversely, a lower standard might be accepted in the context of a developing country with limited technical and financial capacity to implement preventive measures.

Good Neighborliness and International Cooperation

The principle of "good neighborliness," as enunciated in Article 74 of the UN Charter concerning social, economic, and commercial matters, has been extended to environmental matters by rules promoting international cooperation. It applies particularly to activities carried out in one state that might have adverse effects on the environment of another state or in areas beyond national jurisdiction. The commitment to environmental cooperation is reflected in many international agreements and is supported by state practice. In general, the obligation includes commitments to implement treaty objectives or to improve relations outside a treaty or in relation to certain tasks. Specifically, the obligation can require information sharing, notification, consultation, or participation rights in certain decisions, the conduct of environmental impact assessments, and cooperative emergency procedures, particularly where activities might be ultrahazardous. The construction of nuclear power plants on borders is an example of an area where cooperative obligations are reasonably well developed, although, as examples like the Austria–Czech Republic dispute over the Temelin nuclear power plant illustrate (see Chapter 13), their implementation in practice is often more problematic.

The required extent of cooperation has been a central issue in a number of international environmental disputes, including the case between Hungary and Slovakia over construction of the Gabčikovo Dam, referred to the ICJ in 1993.[41] Construction of the dam, as well as a second dam at Nagymaros, required the diversion of the Danube River, which Hungary claimed would produce dire environmental consequences. Hungary alleged that Slovakia violated its obligation to cooperate in good faith in the implementation of principles affecting transboundary resources. However, in its 1997 judgment, the Court did not address in any detail what the obligation to cooperate entailed beyond calling on the parties to apply an existing 1977 treaty arrangement between them "in a reasonable way and in such a manner that its purpose can be realized."[42]

ITLOS was more forthcoming in a 2002 case considering Ireland's allegation that the United Kingdom failed to cooperate in protecting the Irish Sea by refusing to share information and failing to carry out a proper environmental impact assessment of the proposed operation of a nuclear fuel recycling plant at Sellafield in England. ITLOS affirmed that "the duty to cooperate is a fundamental principle in the prevention of pollution of the marine environment" under UNCLOS and general international law. In the interests of "prudence and caution," the tribunal ordered the parties to cooperate in exchanging information about the environmental risks and effects of the operation of the plant and in devising appropriate measures to prevent pollution of the marine environment.[43]

Sustainable Development

The International Court of Justice in the Gabčikovo-Nagymaros case described the principle of sustainable development as expressing the "need to reconcile economic development with protection of the environment."[44] The ideas underlying the concept of sustainable development have a long history in international law, dating back at least to the Pacific Fur Seal arbitration in 1893. The concept came of age with the Earth Summit and the international agreements that it spawned. It now seems that the principle has acquired a harder legal edge. For instance, in 2005, in the Iron Rhine Railway case, an arbitral tribunal of the Permanent Court of Arbitration declared:

> Environmental law and the law on development stand not as alternatives but as mutually reinforcing, integral concepts, which require that where development may cause significant harm to the environment there is a duty to prevent, or at least mitigate, such harm. . . . This duty, in the opinion of the Tribunal, has now become a principle of general international law.[45]

What the term *sustainable development* means in international law today is a more complicated matter. Where it has been used, it appears to refer to at least four separate but related objectives that, taken together, might constitute the legal elements of the concept of sustainable development as used in the Brundtland Report.[46] First, as invoked in some agreements such as the FCCC, it refers to the commitment to preserve natural resources for the benefit of future generations (the principle of intergenerational equity). Second, in other agreements, it refers to appropriate standards for the exploitation of natural resources such as fisheries based upon sustainable harvest or wise use (the principle of sustainable use). Third, yet other agreements require an equitable use of natural resources such as international watercourses, suggesting that a state must consider the needs of other states and people (the principle of equitable use or intragenerational equity). A fourth category of agreements requires that environmental considerations be integrated with economic and other development plans, programs, and projects and that development needs be taken into account in the application of environmental objectives (the integration principle).

Common but Differentiated Responsibilities

The principle of common but differentiated responsibilities has emerged from application of the broader principle of equity in general international law and recognition that the special needs of developing countries must be considered if these countries are to be encouraged to participate in global environmental agreements. The principle includes two important elements. First, states have a common responsibility to protect certain environmental resources. Second, it is necessary to take account of differing circumstances, particularly in relation to each state's contribution to causing a particular environmental problem and its ability to respond to the threat.

Application of the principle of common but differentiated responsibilities has important, practical consequences. It leads to the adoption and implementation of environmental standards that impose different commitments for individual states, and it establishes a basis for providing financial and technical assistance to developing countries and least developed countries to assist them in implementing their commitments. To date the principle is reflected in a mere handful of agreements, although these include the treaties dealing with climate change that require parties to protect the climate system "on the basis of equity and in accordance with their common but differentiated responsibilities and respective capabilities" and place the burden of reducing greenhouse gas emissions primarily on developed countries.[47] In the ongoing negotiations for a new climate change agreement, continuing adherence to the principle of common but differentiated responsibilities is coming under challenge from some developed countries that stress the need for large emitters in the developing world, such as Brazil, China, and India, to accept greenhouse gas emissions reduction targets (see Chapters 8, 9, and 10). The 2009 Copenhagen Accord reflects this approach, as does the Durban Platform for Enhanced Action, which emerged from the seventeenth Conference of the Parties held in December 2011. The platform launched "a process to develop a protocol, another legal instrument or an agreed outcome with legal force under the [Climate Change] Convention *applicable to all Parties*," whether developed or developing.[48]

Precautionary Principle

The precautionary principle emerged in international legal instruments only in the mid-1980s, although it had previously been relied upon in some domestic legal systems. The core of this legal principle, which some believe reflects customary international law,[49] is reflected in Principle 15 of the Rio Declaration, one part of which provides that "where there are threats of serious or irreversible damage, lack of full scientific certainty shall not be used as a reason for postponing cost-effective measures to prevent environmental degradation." The precautionary principle aims to provide guidance to states and the international community in the development of international environmental law and policy in the face of scientific uncertainty. It continues to generate disagreement as to its meaning and effect. Some invoke it to justify early international legal action to address highly threatening environmental issues such as climate change. Opponents, however, have decried the principle, arguing that it promotes overregulation of a range of human activities.

Notwithstanding the controversy, the principle has been endorsed in a large number of international agreements. Among these is the Biosafety Protocol to the Convention on Biological Diversity (see Chapter 12), which permits parties to ban imports of genetically modified organisms where there is a "lack of scientific certainty due to insufficient relevant scientific information and knowledge" concerning health or environmental impacts.[50] Similar language is found in the provisions of the 2001 Stockholm Convention on Persistent Organic Pollutants (see Chapter 11) regarding the placement of controls on additional chemicals in the future,[51] although the term *precautionary principle* is not used on account of objections raised by the United States, Australia, and other countries.[52]

International judicial acceptance of the precautionary principle has been more cautious. The principle was not mentioned in the majority decision in the Gabčikovo-Nagymaros case, despite considerable scientific uncertainty over the environmental impact of the project.[53] Likewise, the Appellate Body of the WTO, in the Beef Hormones and Apples cases, declined to take a position on whether the principle amounts to customary international law, commenting that the international status of the principle is "less than clear."[54] ITLOS was more forthcoming in the Southern Bluefin Tuna case, citing "prudence and caution" as a basis for its decision requiring Japan to cease an experimental fishing program despite scientific uncertainty as to the impacts of fishing on stocks of the migratory tuna species.[55] On the other hand, the ICJ in the Pulp Mills case took a more stringent approach, recognizing the potential relevance of "a precautionary approach" in the interpretation and application of treaties but stating "it does not follow that it operates as a reversal of proof."[56] Most recently, the Seabed Disputes Chamber of ITLOS, in its Advisory Opinion on Responsibilities and Obligations in the Area, noted that "the precautionary approach is . . . an integral part of the general obligation of due diligence of sponsoring States [under UNCLOS and related instruments]" such that ignoring "plausible indications of potential risk . . . would amount to a failure to comply with the precautionary approach." Invoking the Pulp Mills judgment and the widespread incorporation of the precautionary principle in environmental treaties, the Chamber declared that this has "initiated a trend towards making this approach part of customary international law."[57]

Overall, while the legal status of the precautionary principle continues to evolve, there is now sufficient evidence of state practice to conclude that the principle has received broad enough support to allow a strong argument to be made that it reflects a principle of customary international law, albeit that the precise consequences of its application remain a matter for case-by-case assessment.[58]

Polluter-Pays Principle

The polluter-pays principle states that the costs of pollution should be borne by those responsible for causing the pollution. The precise meaning, international legal status, and effect of the principle remain open to question because international practice based upon the principle is limited. It is doubtful whether it has achieved the status of a generally applicable rule of international law,[59] except perhaps in relation to states in the European Union, the UN Economic Commission for Europe (UNECE), and the Organisation for Economic Cooperation and Development (OECD). It has nevertheless attracted broad support and underlies rules on civil and state liability for environmental damage (for example, the Liability Protocol to the Basel Hazardous Wastes Convention) and on the permissibility of state subsidies. Developed countries have acknowledged the "responsibility that they bear in the international pursuit of sustainable development in view of the pressures their societies place on the global environment" as well as the financial and other consequences that flow from this acknowledgment.[60] Supporting instruments include Principle 16 of the Rio Declaration, OECD Council Recommendations, the Treaty of the European Union (as amended) and related instruments, and UNECE regional treaties such as the 1992 OSPAR Convention.

Basic Rules of International Environmental Law

As international environmental law has developed, standards have been adopted to address a widening range of environmental resources. Integrated concepts of the environment have become prevalent in recent years, but these standards still tend to address particular resources or sectors of the environment, such as biodiversity conservation, water quality, air pollution, hazardous substances, and waste. Hence wide-ranging problems like climate change, which encompasses aspects of biodiversity conservation and water management along with atmospheric pollution, pose significant (and largely unresolved) challenges for the coordination of different bodies of international environmental rules.

For each environmental sector, international environmental law has developed a set of treaties that elaborate the basic rules applicable to that sector. These rules are summarized in Table 3-2. Although such rules cover many issues and resources, they are not comprehensive. Some areas have eluded international agreement, such as forests (where global regulation is strongly opposed by many developing countries), land-based sources of marine pollution, and groundwater conservation.

In certain sectors, acts adopted by international organizations have also contributed significantly to the development of international environmental rules. Notable examples in the marine environment context include the 1982 decision by the International Whaling Commission to adopt a moratorium on commercial whaling and the 1985 decision of the parties to the 1972 London Dumping Convention to adopt a moratorium on the dumping of radioactive wastes at sea.

Where "hard" rules of international environmental law are yet to develop or are incomplete, soft law instruments may play an important role in setting guidelines for state behavior. Two prominent examples in this regard are the nonbinding standards elaborated by the International Atomic Energy Agency governing issues of nuclear safety[61] and the UN Food and Agriculture Organization's Code of Conduct on the Distribution and Use of Pesticides, which was an important precursor to the 1998 Chemicals Convention described in Table 3-2.[62]

The emergence of a novel environmental problem may see efforts to conclude a new treaty regime, as in the case of the 2001 Persistent Organic Pollutants Convention. Other areas potentially on the horizon for international lawmaking include regulation of the health and environmental effects of nanotechnologies,[63] geoengineering options for climate change mitigation,[64] and putting in place a coherent regulatory framework for natural disaster management.[65] However, a feature of the past decade of international environmental law has been the consolidation and augmentation of existing treaty regimes, such as through the adoption of protocols, rather than extensive new lawmaking activity.

Conclusion: Challenges for International Environmental Law

In a relatively short period, a significant body of principles and rules of international law has been put in place for the protection of the environment and conservation of natural resources. These rules have been primarily developed by and are addressed to states, although increasingly international environmental law encompasses a much broader range of actors, including NGOs, treaty bodies, and corporate entities. As international environmental law has developed, its rules have become increasingly complex and technical, particularly as environmental considerations are addressed in economic and other social fields.

Table 3-2 Summary of the Main International Environmental Treaty Rules

Environmental sector	Treaties	Main functions and features
Biodiversity conservation, including flora and fauna protection (see Chapter 12)	Ramsar International Wetlands Convention, adopted Ramsar, February 2, 1971, entered into force December 16, 1975 (UNTS, 996: 245); number of parties, 163	• Parties must designate wetlands in their territories as internationally important wetlands and implement planning to promote conservation of such wetlands.
	Convention Concerning the Protection of World Cultural and Natural Heritage, adopted Paris, November 16, 1972, entered into force December 17, 1975 (UNTS, 1037: 151); number of parties, 187	• Parties must identify and delineate their own cultural and natural heritage sites for nomination for inclusion on the World Heritage List. • Parties are subject to a duty to protect, conserve, present, and transmit heritage on their territories to future generations.
	Convention on International Trade in Endangered Species of Wild Fauna and Flora, adopted Washington, D.C., March 3, 1973, entered into force July 1, 1975 (UNTS, 993: 243); number of parties, 176	• Lists in its appendices species of wild flora and fauna whose conservation status is threatened by international trade. • Once listed, imports and exports of the species are subject to a permit system implemented by national management and scientific authorities.
	Convention on Biological Diversity, adopted Rio de Janeiro, June 5, 1992, entered into force December 29, 1993 (*ILM* 31 [1992]: 822); number of parties, 193	• Three objectives: the conservation of biodiversity, the sustainable use of its components, and the fair and equitable sharing of the benefits arising from the use of genetic resources. • 2000 Biosafety Protocol regulates transboundary movements of genetically modified organisms. • 2010 Nagoya Protocol deals with access to genetic resources and fair and equitable sharing of the benefits from their utilization.

Marine environment, including prevention of pollution and conservation of marine resources such as fisheries	United Nations Convention on the Law of the Sea, adopted Montego Bay, December 10, 1982, entered into force November 16, 1994 (*ILM* 21 [1982]: 1261); number of parties, 162	• Establishes a comprehensive framework to address marine pollution from various sources, including dumping at sea, land-based sources, vessels, and offshore installations, such as oil rigs.
		• Establishes general obligations of states to protect and preserve the marine environment and provisions concerning the conservation and management of marine living resources.
		• Supplemented by the 1995 Fish Stocks Agreement, which concerns conservation measures for straddling and highly migratory fish stocks.
		• Directs states to cooperate in conservation of shared fish stocks either directly or through regional fisheries organizations.
	London Dumping Convention, adopted London, December 29, 1972, entered into force August 30, 1975 (UNTS, 1046: 120); number of parties, 87	• Aims to prevent marine pollution through the dumping of wastes and other hazardous matter.
		• In London on November 7, 1996, the parties to the Dumping Convention agreed to a protocol that is intended eventually to replace the 1972 Convention (see *ILM* 36 [1997]: 1).
		• 1996 protocol takes a more restrictive approach to dumping by generally prohibiting all forms of dumping except for listed substances.
	International Convention for the Prevention of Pollution from Ships, adopted London, September 2, 1973, as modified by the Protocol of 1978 relating thereto, entered into force October 2, 1983 (1340 UNTS, 81, 184); number of parties, 152	• Main international convention regulating pollution from vessels.
		• Six annexes set out detailed rules on topics such as pollution by oil, noxious substances, harmful substances carried by sea in packaged form, sewage from ships, garbage from ships, and maritime air pollution.
		• Program extends to thirteen regional areas, with ten regions the subject of binding international agreements.

(Continued)

Table 3-2 Continued

Environmental sector	Treaties	Main functions and features
	UNEP Regional Seas Conventions and Implementing Protocols	• In total the UNEP Regional Seas program comprises more than 40 framework conventions and protocols, with others under negotiation. • The conventions and protocols deal with issues of marine pollution and dumping at sea.
	International Whaling Convention, adopted Washington, D.C., December 2, 1946, entered into force November 10, 1948 (UNTS, 161: 72); number of parties, 42	• Originally established as a "whaling club," the convention has shifted focus over time to issues of conservation of whale stocks.
Protection of freshwater resources, including rivers, lakes, and groundwaters	Convention on the Law of Non-navigational Uses of International Watercourses, adopted May 21, 1997, not in force (reprinted in *ILM* 36 [1997]: 700)	• Articulates rules of global application for the sustainable use of international watercourses.
	Agreement between the United States and Canada Concerning the Water Quality of the Great Lakes, adopted Ottawa, April 15, 1972 (reprinted in *ILM* 11 [1972]: 694)	• Protective regime for North American lakes threatened by acid rain and other chemical deposits.
Air pollution, including ozone depletion and climate change (see Chapters 4, 5, and 10)	UNECE Convention on Long–Range Transboundary Air Pollution, adopted Geneva, November 13, 1973, entered into force March 16, 1983 (reprinted in *ILM* 18 [1979]: 1442); number of parties, 51	• Seeks to regulate long-range transport of air pollutants causing transboundary environmental damage. • Supplemented by protocols on sulfur dioxide, nitrogen oxides, volatile organic compounds, heavy metals, persistent organic pollutants, and ground-level ozone.

Framework Convention for the Protection of the Ozone Layer, adopted Vienna, March 2, 1985, entered into force September 22, 1988 (reprinted in *ILM* 26 [1985]: 1529); number of parties, 197	• Establishes a framework for the adoption of measures to protect health and the environment against the adverse effects of ozone depletion. • No set targets or timetables for action.
Montreal Protocol to the Vienna Ozone Convention, adopted Montreal, September 16, 1987, entered into force January 1, 1989 (reprinted in *ILM* 26 [1987]: 154); number of parties, 197	• Establishes limitations and required reductions in levels of consumption and production of controlled ozone-depleting substances. • Amendments in 1990, 1992, 1997, and 1999 have expanded the range of substances covered by the protocol and altered the timetables for phaseout of controlled substances.
Framework Convention on Climate Change, adopted New York, May 9, 1992, entered into force March 24, 1994 (1771 UNTS, 107); number of parties, 195	• Aims to limit industrial countries' emissions of carbon dioxide and other greenhouse gases. • Creates a framework for cooperation and commitments to ensure that greenhouse gas concentrations in the atmosphere do not lead to dangerous anthropogenic interference with the climate system.
Kyoto Protocol, adopted Kyoto, December 11, 1997, entered into force February 16, 2005 (*ILM* 31 [1992]: 881); number of parties, 192	• Establishes emission reduction targets for certain developed countries for the commitment period 2008 to 2012. • Parties are permitted to use a range of innovative "flexibility mechanisms" (including emissions trading) to reach their targets, although significant domestic abatement action is still necessary. • The protocol was extended in 2011 for a further commitment period commencing in 2013.

(Continued)

Table 3-2 Continued

Environmental sector	Treaties	Main functions and features
Chemical pollution, hazardous substances, and waste (see Chapter 11)	Basel Convention on the Control of Transboundary Movements of Hazardous Wastes and Their Disposal, adopted Basel, March 22, 1989, entered into force May 5, 1992 (reprinted in *ILM* 28 [1989]: 649); number of parties, 179	• Requires that importing countries be notified of and grant consent for hazardous waste shipments before they occur (prior informed consent). • A proposed amendment known as the Basel Ban would prohibit hazardous waste exports from OECD countries to non–OECD countries (see Chapter 6 for a full discussion) but is not in force as it has not achieved the required level of ratification.
	Convention on Persistent Organic Pollutants (POPs), adopted Stockholm, May 22, 2001, entered into force May 17, 2004 (reprinted in *ILM* 40 [2001]: 532); number of parties, 178	• 1999 protocol establishes a civil liability regime. • Adopted to regulate the production, use, and transboundary movement of POPs (chemicals that remain intact in the environment for long periods and bioaccumulate in living organisms). • Establishes controls on the production, import, export, and disposal of POPs.
	Rotterdam Convention on the Prior Informed Consent (PIC) Procedure for Certain Hazardous Chemicals and Pesticides in International Trade, adopted Rotterdam, September 10, 1998, entered into force February 24, 2004 (reprinted in *ILM* 38 [1999]: 1); number of parties, 149	• Establishes a PIC procedure for international trade in toxic pesticides and other hazardous chemicals. • Allows parties to refuse imports of hazardous chemicals that they cannot manage safely and imposes labeling requirements on exports of these substances to promote their safe use.

Compared with the frenetic treaty-making activity of the early 1970s, the pace of legal development in the twenty-first century has slowed, with the focus moving to the elaboration of existing treaties, such as those dealing with biodiversity and climate change, as well as to issues of implementation and enforcement. Consequently, we are seeing a shift from the legislative domain to the judicial and quasi-judicial domain, with international courts and arbitral bodies filling the gaps left by legislators. Further signs of this trend are the increasingly detailed noncompliance mechanisms adopted under environmental treaties, including those dealing with atmospheric pollution, such as the Kyoto Protocol.[66]

Yet these significant developments cannot hide the fact that environmental protection largely remains on the margins of international policy and that the rules and principles of international environmental law have not yet radically or significantly changed human behavior or led to the institution of sustainable practices. The environmental problems facing international law are still very real, as finite resources are subject to ever-increasing demands.

At the institutional and legal levels, international environmental law also faces a number of difficult challenges in respect to its structures of governance, mechanisms for implementation and enforcement of state obligations, and processes of future regulatory development. Governance challenges center on the capacity for international environmental law to accommodate the needs and aspirations of peoples from both developed and developing countries, and to allow for participation by a vast range of actors and stakeholders extending beyond the states, which have been the traditional subjects of international environmental law. Models for broader participation might be imported from the human rights field, along the lines of the "environmental rights" provisions adopted in the 1998 UNECE Aarhus Convention.[67]

Ensuring adequate and effective implementation and enforcement of international obligations is a long-standing and continuing challenge for international environmental law. The plethora of international environmental rules outlined in this chapter are of little utility in the absence of robust domestic implementation efforts, particularly as international environmental law moves to put in place ever more detailed regulatory requirements. To achieve real advances in domestic implementation and compliance, however, it will be necessary for these procedures to work closely with treaty bodies and other international organizations concerned with facilitating technology transfer and ensuring the provision of financial resources to assist developing countries with compliance.

Where domestic implementation efforts are inadequate, states have shown greater willingness in the past decade to refer environmental disputes to courts and tribunals, which in turn have engaged with environmental issues more closely. Nevertheless, judging by decisions of international tribunals, there is still some way to go before the more established judicial bodies will feel comfortable dealing with environmental questions and providing leadership on enforcement matters. Indeed, it may well be that the greatest contribution to applying the principle of sustainable development will come from bodies traditionally outside the field of international environmental law, such as the dispute settlement bodies of the WTO and the World Bank's Inspection Panel.[68]

That we now look to the WTO and other economic institutions as much as to international environmental organizations for rules governing environmental matters attests to the extent of integration of environmental issues into aspects of economic and development institutions and law. This is a welcome development in that it signals the potential for international environmental law to have a transformative effect on broader international society. At the same time, integration between environmental and other issues, as well as the related question of coordinating different environmental regimes, poses a considerable challenge for the future effectiveness and cohesiveness of international environmental law.

Finally, with recent legal developments such as the 2009 Copenhagen Accord embracing "bottom-up" evolution rather than "top-down" prescription of environmental rules, international environmental law faces an almost existential question: Is a multilateral lawmaking model based on universal participation, consensus decision making, and the desire to articulate comprehensive rules governing a particular subject matter still feasible in the context of a vast increase in the number of states and greater divergence of their interests? It is noteworthy that in the past decade many of the more progressive developments in international environmental law have taken place in regional forums, such as the UNECE and regional seas conventions. If international environmental law in the future does move to embrace a more diversified mode of environmental regulatory development, this is likely to offer more avenues for participation by nonstate actors, including NGOs, corporations, and intergovernmental organizations. At the same time, it will present further challenges to ensuring that different areas of international law are complementary rather than conflictual and achieve overall goals of environmental protection.

Notes

1. "Request for an Examination of the Situation in Accordance with Paragraph 63 of the Court's Judgment of 20 December 1974 in the Nuclear Tests (*New Zealand v. France*) Case," Order of September 22, 1995, *International Court of Justice Reports* (hereafter *ICJ Reports*) (1995): 306, para. 64 (hereafter "Nuclear Tests II").
2. "Legality of the Threat or Use of Nuclear Weapons, Advisory Opinion, July 8, 1996," *ICJ Reports* (1996): 226, para. 29.
3. Ibid., para. 33.
4. See Principle 27 of the Rio "Declaration on Environment and Development," *Report of the UN Conference on Environment and Development*, A/CONF.151/26/Rev.1, 2:3 (1993), reprinted in *International Legal Materials* (hereafter *ILM*) 31 (1992): 874.
5. "Pacific Fur Seal Arbitration (*Great Britain v. United States*)," *Moore's Report of International Arbitration Awards* 1 (1893): 755.
6. Philip Allott, *Eunomia: New Order for a New World* (New York: Oxford University Press, 1990), para. 17.52.
7. Signature of a treaty by a state indicates only a preliminary endorsement of the treaty; it creates no binding obligations. By contrast, ratification is an act by which a state signals its agreement to be legally bound by the terms of the treaty. Processes of ratification differ from country to country. For instance, in the United States, a treaty requires Senate

approval to be ratified, which in practice has had a chilling effect on U.S. participation in international environmental law treaties. Once the president or a designated representative of the U.S. government has signed an international treaty, the treaty must be sent to the Senate Committee on Foreign Relations along with a package of documents explaining any policy benefits and potential risks to the United States and significant regulatory or environmental impacts, as well as an analysis of the issues surrounding the treaty's implementation. The Senate Foreign Relations Committee then considers the treaty and can send the treaty to the full Senate with recommendations. For a treaty to pass the Senate, sixty-seven out of one hundred senators must vote in favor of passage.

8. This is a role called for by United Nations Conference on Environment and Development, "Agenda 21," chap. 38, paras. 38.42–38.44.

9. For example, the OECD Guidelines for Multinational Enterprises (2000), as updated by governments adhering to the guidelines in 2011, available at http://www.oecd.org/daf/internationalinvestment/guidelinesformultinationalenterprises. In contrast to other voluntary international instruments of this kind, such as the UN Global Compact, the OECD Guidelines were negotiated and approved by national delegates. It has been argued that they therefore may reflect the *opinio juris* of adhering states. Elisa Morgera, "An Environmental Outlook on the OECD Guidelines for Multinational Enterprises: Comparative Advantage, Legitimacy, and Outstanding Questions in the Lead up to the 2006 Review," *Georgetown International Environmental Law Review* 18 (2006): 755. See also Foundation for International Environmental Law and Development, "Transnational Corporations: The Environmental Governance Gap," briefing paper, June 2010, http://www.field.org.uk/files/FIELD_Briefing_Paper_TNCs_June2010_1.pdf.

10. See, generally, Philippe Sands, "The Environment, Community, and International Law," *Harvard International Law Journal* 30 (1989): 393–419.

11. For a general history of international environmental law, see Philippe Sands and Jacqueline Peel, *Principles of International Environmental Law*, 3rd ed. (Cambridge: Cambridge University Press, 2012), chap. 2.

12. Important treaties adopted during this period included the Geneva Conventions on the High Seas: "Convention on the High Seas," Geneva, April 29, 1958, United Nations Treaty Series (hereafter UNTS), 450: 82; "Convention on Fishing and Conservation of the Living Resources of the High Seas," Geneva, April 29, 1958, UNTS, 559: 285; "Convention on the Continental Shelf," Geneva, April 29, 1958, UNTS, 499: 311. In 1963 the Nuclear Test Ban Treaty was adopted, paving the way politically for Australia and New Zealand to bring a case before the ICJ calling on France to stop all nuclear testing; see *Australia v. France, ICJ Reports* (1974): 253; *New Zealand v. France, ICJ Reports* (1974): 457.

13. *Report of the UN Conference on the Human Environment*, UN Doc. A/CONF/48/14 at 2–65, and Corr. 1 (1972), reprinted in *ILM* 11 (1972): 1416.

14. Louis B. Sohn, "The Stockholm Declaration on the Human Environment," *Harvard International Law Journal* 14 (1973): 423–515.

15. "United Nations Convention on the Law of the Sea," Montego Bay, December 10, 1982, reprinted in *ILM* 21 (1982): 1261.

16. UN General Assembly Resolution 42/187, December 11, 1987, endorsement of World Commission on Environment and Development, *Our Common Future*; UN General Assembly Resolution 43/196, December 20, 1988.

17. *ILM* 31 (1992): 881; *Report of the United Nations Conference on Environment and Development*, vol. 1.

18. *ILM* 31 (1992): 822, 849.

19. The majority of policy development in the area takes place under the auspices of the UN Commission on Sustainable Development (CSD) pursuant to its Multi-year Programme of Work for CSD: 2004/2005 to 2016/2017; see http://www.un.org/esa/sustdev/csd/policy.htm. This is directed to very broad thematic areas such as agriculture, drought, and Africa.

20. Kevin Gray, "World Summit on Sustainable Development: Accomplishments and New Directions," *International and Comparative Law Quarterly* 52 (2003): 256–268.

21. Andrew Aziz, George Riddell, and Malena Sell, "Critical Voices Drown Out Official Outcome in Rio," *Bridges Trade BioRes Review* 6, no. 3 (2012).

22. Statement—NGOs, United Nations Conference on Sustainable Development, Rio+20, 1st plenary meeting (formal opening), June 20, 2012, http://www.uncsd2012.0rg/content/documents/859RIO20%20Conference%20NGO%20MG%20Statement%20PrepCom%20Statements.pdf.

23. Conference of the Parties to the UN Framework Convention on Climate Change, Decision 2/CP15, March 30, 2010, in the Report of the Conference of the Parties on Its Fifteenth Session, Copenhagen, December 7–19, 2009, FCCC/CP/2009/11/Add.1. The Conference of the Parties merely "took note" of the accord rather than formally adopting it because of the objections of some parties.

24. Jacqueline Peel, Lee Godden, and Rod Keenan, "Climate Change Law in an Era of Multilevel Governance," *Transnational Environmental Law* 1, no. 2 (2010): 245–280.

25. United Nations, *Statute of the International Court of Justice,* April 18, 1946; and International Law Commission, Draft Articles on State Responsibility, Part 2, Art. 5(1), "Report of the ILC to the United Nations General Assembly," UN Doc. A/44/10, 218 (1989).

26. Christine M. Chinkin, "The Challenge of Soft Law: Development and Change in International Law," *International and Comparative Law Quarterly* 38 (1989): 850–866; André Nollkaemper, "The Distinction between Non-legal and Legal Norms in International Affairs: An Analysis with Reference to International Policy for the Protection of the North Sea from Hazardous Substances," *International Journal of Marine and Coastal Law* 13 (1998): 355–371; Alan Boyle, "Some Reflections on the Relationship of Soft Law and Treaties," *International and Comparative Law Quarterly* 48 (1999): 901–913.

27. An instrument of ratification is a formal sealed letter referring to the state's decision, taken according to its own domestic constitutional procedures, to become a party to the treaty concerned. The letter is signed by the state's responsible authority and deposited with the appropriate depository specified in the treaty.

28. UN General Assembly resolutions under Article 25 of UN Charter are "only recommendatory," whereas resolutions of the Security Council are binding "on all states."

29. "North Sea Continental Shelf (Federal Republic of Germany/Denmark)," *ICJ Reports* (1969): 3.

30. "*United States v. Canada,*" *Reports of International Arbitral Awards* 3 (1941): 1907, citing Clyde Eagleton, *Responsibility of States* (New York: New York University Press, 1928), 80.

31. "Whaling in the Antarctic (Australia v. Japan)," General List No. 148. A further environmental case between Ecuador and Colombia concerning pollution caused by aerial herbicide spraying (General List No. 138) was removed from the ICJ list on September 17, 2013, at the request of Ecuador.

32. On the general distinction between rules and principles, see Ronald Dworkin, *Taking Rights Seriously* (Cambridge, MA: Harvard University Press, 1977), 24, 26.

33. Daniel Bodansky, "The United Nations Framework Convention on Climate Change: A Commentary," *Yale Journal of International Law* 18 (1993): 501; Boyle, "Some Reflections on the Relationship of Treaties and Soft Law," 908.

34. "Nuclear Tests II," 306.

35. "Legality of the Threat or Use of Nuclear Weapons," para. 29. See also "Case Concerning the Gabcikovo-Nagymaros Project" (Hungary/Slovakia), *ICJ Reports* (1997): paras. 53 and 112.

36. Permanent Court of Arbitration, Palmas Case (1928), *HCR* 2: 93.

37. "The Iron Rhine (Ijzeren Rijn) Arbitration (Belgium-Netherlands)," *Permanent Court of Arbitration Award Series* (Cambridge: Cambridge University Press, 2005), paras. 59, 222.

38. "Pulp Mills on the River Uruguay (Argentina v. Uruguay) (Judgment)," General List No. 135, April 20, 2010, para. 197.
39. Ibid., para. 204.
40. "Responsibilities and Obligations of States Sponsoring Persons and Entities with Respect to Activities in the Area" (Advisory Opinion), Seabed Disputes Chamber of the International Tribunal for the Law of the Sea, ITLOS Case No. 17, February 1, 2011, para. 117.
41. See original Hungarian application, October 22, 1992, paras. 27, 29, and 30, in *Documents in International Environmental Law*, vol. 2A, ed. Philippe Sands, Richard Tarasofsky, and Mary Weiss (Manchester: Manchester University Press, 1995), 691, doc. 28.
42. "Case Concerning the Gabcikovo-Nagymaros Project," paras. 78–79, 141–142.
43. "MOX Plant Case (*Ireland v. United Kingdom*) (Provisional Measures)," *ILM* 41 (2002): 405, paras. 82, 84, and 89.
44. "Case Concerning the Gabcikovo-Nagymaros Project," para. 140.
45. "The Iron Rhine (Ijzeren Rijn) Arbitration (Belgium-Netherlands)," para. 59.
46. World Commission on Environment and Development, *Our Common Future* (Oxford: Oxford University Press, 1987).
47. "Climate Change Convention," Art. 3(1), *ILM* 31 (1992): 881; "Kyoto Protocol," *ILM* 37 (1997): 22.
48. Conference of the Parties to the UN Framework Convention on Climate Change, Decision 1/CP.17, "Establishment of an Ad Hoc Working Group on the Durban Platform for Enhanced Action," in the Report of the Conference of the Parties on Its Seventeenth Session, Durban, November 28–December 11, 2011, UN Doc FCCC/CP/2011/9/Add.1, March 15, 2012, emphasis added.
49. For discussion see Arie Trouwborst, *Evolution and Status of the Precautionary Principle in International Law* (The Hague: Kluwer International, 2002).
50. "Cartagena Protocol on Biosafety," Art. 10(6), *ILM* 39 (2001): 1027.
51. "Stockholm Convention on Persistent Organic Pollutants," Arts. 8.7(a) and 8.9, *ILM* 40 (2001): 532.
52. A rift has emerged in this respect between the European Union, which supports the idea of the precautionary principle as a principle of international law, and the United States, which sees precaution merely as an approach to decision making. See Jacqueline Peel, *Science and Risk Regulation in International Law* (Cambridge: Cambridge University Press, 2010).
53. See Afshin A-Khavari and Donald R. Rothwell, "The ICJ and the Danube Dam Case: A Missed Opportunity for International Environmental Law?," *Melbourne University Law Review* 22 (1998): 530.
54. "EC Measures Concerning Meat and Meat Products (Hormones)," *Report of the Appellate Body*, WT/DS26/AB/R and WT/DS48/AB/R, January 16, 1998, para. 123; "Japan Measures Affecting the Importation of Apples (Apples)," *Report of the Appellate Body*, WT/DS245/AB/R, November 26, 2003, para. 233. See also "EC Measures Affecting the Approval and Marketing of Biotech Products," *Reports of the Panel*, WT/DS291/R, WT/DS292/R, and WT/DS293/R, September 29, 2006, para. 7.89.
55. "Southern Bluefin Tuna Cases (*New Zealand v. Japan; Australia v. Japan*) (Provisional Measures)," *ILM* 38 (1999): 1624, para. 77. Also see the suggestions of Judge Weeramantry in his dissenting opinion in "Nuclear Tests II," 342.
56. "Pulp Mills on the River Uruguay (Argentina v. Uruguay) (Judgment)," para. 131.
57. "Responsibilities and Obligations of States Sponsoring Persons and Entities with Respect to Activities in the Area," para. 135.
58. Sands and Peel, *Principles of International Environmental Law*, 228.
59. See, for example, the Rhine Chlorides arbitration, where the arbitral tribunal did not view the principle as being a part of general international law. "The Rhine Chlorides Arbitration Concerning the Auditing of Accounts (Netherlands-France)," Award of 2004, *Permanent Court of Arbitration Award Series*, vol. 4, para. 103.

60. Rio Declaration, Principle 7.

61. See, for example, International Atomic Energy Agency, *Siting of Near Surface Disposal Facilities,* Series No. 111-G-3.1 (Vienna: IAEA, 2010). For a complete list of published standards, see International Atomic Energy Agency, "IAEA Safety Standards," http://www-ns.iaea.org/standards.

62. 1985 UN Food and Agriculture Organization Code of Conduct on the Distribution and Use of Pesticides (as revised in 2002); see also 1987 UNEP London Guidelines for the Exchange of Information on Chemicals in International Trade, as amended in 1989.

63. David Leary and Balakrishna Pisupati, "Emerging Technologies: Nanotechnology," in *The Future of International Environmental Law,* ed. David Leary and Balakrishna Pisupati (Tokyo: United Nations University, 2010), 227–245. The diversity of nanoparticles, together with uncertainty over any risks they may pose for human health or the environment, makes it difficult to generalize about the nature of their environmental impact. However, their growing use in many products and fields of manufacture has raised questions concerning the need for precautionary regulation to prevent any unintended adverse environmental consequences.

64. House of Commons, Science and Technology Committee, *The Regulation of Geoengineering,* Fifth Report of Session 2009–2010, March 18, 2010, http://www.publications.parliament.uk/pa/cm200910/cmselect/cmsctech/221/221.pdf.

65. International Federation of Red Cross and Red Crescent Societies, *Law and Legal Issues in International Disaster Response: A Desk Study* (Geneva: International Federation of Red Cross and Red Crescent Societies, 2007).

66. See Decision 24/CP.7, Procedures and Mechanisms Relating to Compliance under the Kyoto Protocol, in *Marrakesh Accords,* in the Report of the Conference of the Parties on Its Seventh Session, Marrakesh, October 29–November 10, 2001, FCCC/CP/2001/13/Add.2.

67. "Convention on Access to Information, Public Participation and Decision-Making and Access to Justice in Environmental Matters," Articles 4–9, *ILM* 38 (1999): 517.

68. Of particular significance are two decisions of the WTO Appellate Body in the Shrimp-Turtle dispute. See "United States—Import Prohibition of Certain Shrimp and Shrimp Products," *Report of the Appellate Body,* WT/DS58/AB/R, reprinted in *ILM* 38 (1999): 118; and "United States—Import Prohibition on Certain Shrimp and Shrimp Products," Recourse to Article 21.5 of the DSU by Malaysia, *Report of the Appellate Body,* October 22, 2001, WT/DS58/AB/RW.

4

International Environmental Regimes and the Success of Global Ozone Policy

David Leonard Downie

International regimes are sector-specific international regulatory and administrative systems. A useful formal definition of such a regime is a system of principles, norms, rules, operating procedures, and institutions that actors create or accept to regulate and coordinate action in a particular issue area of international relations. Principles are beliefs of fact, causation, and rectitude. Norms are general standards of behavior. Rules are specific prescriptions or proscriptions for action. Operating procedures are prevailing practices for work within the regime, including those for making and implementing collective choice. Institutions are mechanisms and organizations for implementing, operating, evaluating, and expanding the regime and regime policy.[1]

Regimes with varying degrees of development, effectiveness, and impact are found in most areas of international relations, including security, trade, finance, environment, human rights, management of the global commons (including the oceans, Antarctica, and outer space), travel, and the Internet.[2] When effective, a regime helps to sharpen international goals in an issue area, shape international behavior toward particular outcomes, manage state interactions, augment policy coordination and collaboration, and facilitate the making of further agreements.[3]

Regime elements are created, structured, and implemented through formal agreements, international organizations, accepted norms of international behavior, private international law, or a combination of these structures. A regime is more than patterned interaction, a single international agreement, or a single organization, although each of these is usually part of one. For example, the key elements of the nuclear nonproliferation regime include the principles, norms, rules, and procedures created by the Partial Test Ban Treaty and the Nuclear Non-Proliferation Treaty as well as the relevant activities of the International Atomic Energy Agency.

States, as the dominant actors in the international system, are the primary and most important creators and implementers of international regimes, but other actors, including international organizations, nongovernmental organizations (NGOs), and multinational corporations, often play critical roles.[4] Similarly, while formal treaties often delineate their key features, regimes can also incorporate or even be based on nonbinding "soft law," private international law, or other arrangements, provided that these are accepted by the actors in the issue areas as creating principles, rules, and procedures that guide their behavior. Examples include product certification programs, such as those that identify wood and wood products harvested from sustainable forests (rather than taken from old-growth forests or rain forests using clear-cutting methods),[5] and international management and manufacturing standards, such as the frameworks developed under the rubric of the International Organization for Standardization (ISO).[6]

While several international wildlife treaties date from early in the twentieth century, modern transnational environmental politics traces its origins to the UN Conference on the Human Environment in 1972 in Stockholm. Today, international environmental policy—of varying specificity, effectiveness, and importance—exists in regard to migratory species, trade in endangered species, global biodiversity, protection of individual species such as whales, wetlands protection, ocean dumping, transnational rivers, regional seas, desertification, hazardous waste, toxic chemicals, climate change, stratospheric ozone, and other issues. Negotiations on these issues continue, as do talks on numerous regional and bilateral issues. Funding for several of these regimes is provided by the Global Environment Facility (GEF), an international organization that distributes funds to developing countries for projects that address biodiversity, climate change, international waters, land degradation, and persistent organic pollutants (POPs). Table 4-1 lists several notable international environmental regimes and some of their most important constituent agreements and institutions. This is by no means an exhaustive list. Many more regimes and treaties exist, and several of the regimes included in the table encompass many more agreements and institutions.[7]

The Ozone Regime

The ozone regime is widely regarded as one of the most effective global environmental regimes.[8] Ozone is a gas composed of three oxygen atoms (O_3). While anthropogenic ozone is a harmful air pollutant at ground level, ozone far above the Earth, in the stratosphere (where 90 percent of naturally occurring ozone resides) helps to shield the Earth from ultraviolet radiation produced by the sun. Depletion of this *ozone layer* would result in increases in human skin cancers and cataracts and serious harm to many plants, animals, and ecosystems.[9] Destruction of the ozone layer would be a planetary disaster.

In the early 1970s, scientists discovered that certain human-made chemicals pose a serious threat to stratospheric ozone.[10] Chemicals that threaten the ozone layer include chlorofluorocarbons (CFCs), once very widely used as refrigerants, industrial solvents, and aerosol propellants, as well as in the manufacture of rigid and flexible foam; hydrochlorofluorocarbons (HCFCs), less ozone-depleting CFC substitutes; halons, widely used for fire control; methyl bromide, an inexpensive, widely used, and very toxic soil and structural fumigant used to kill pests across a wide range of agricultural and shipping sectors; and other substances such as carbon tetrachloride and methyl chloroform.

Table 4–1 International Environmental Regimes

Regime	Goal and key constituent agreements and institutions (indicative list)
Climate change (see Chapter 10)	Prevent dangerous anthropogenic interference with the climate system by limiting anthropogenic emissions of greenhouse gases and protecting sinks. • 1992 UN Framework Convention on Climate Change (UNFCCC) • 1997 Kyoto Protocol • The Conference of Parties (COP) and its subsidiary negotiation bodies (which negotiate on particular sets of issues on behalf of the COP) • Global Environment Facility (GEF) climate program • Technology Executive Committee and Technology Center and Network • Adaptation Committee • Adaptation Fund • Intergovernmental Panel on Climate Change (IPCC)
Hazardous waste (see Chapter 11)	Protect human health and the environment from wastes that are toxic, poisonous, explosive, corrosive, ecotoxic, or infectious. • 1989 Basel Convention on the Control of Transboundary Movements of Hazardous Wastes and Their Disposal • 1995 Ban Amendment (not yet in force) • 1999 Protocol on Liability and Compensation (not yet in force) • Basel Regional Centers • Conference of Parties and subsidiary bodies
Toxic chemicals[a] (see Chapter 11)	Protect human health and the environment from toxic chemicals. • 1989 Basel Convention (elements focused on chemical wastes) • 1998 Rotterdam Convention on the Prior Informed Consent (PIC) Procedure for Certain Hazardous Chemicals and Pesticides in International Trade • 2001 Stockholm Convention on Persistent Organic Pollutants (POPs) • Agreements in 2009, 2011, and 2013 to add a total of eleven more chemicals to the convention • Rotterdam Convention Chemical Review Committee • Stockholm Convention Persistent Organic Pollutant Review Committee • Basel, Rotterdam, and Stockholm COPs and their subsidiary bodies • Strategic Approach to International Chemicals Management (SAICM) initiative

(Continued)

Table 4–1 Continued

Regime	Goal and key constituent agreements and institutions (indicative list)
	• Intergovernmental Forum on Chemical Safety (IFCS) • United Nations Environment Programme (UNEP) Chemicals Branch • GEF POPs program
Ocean pollution	Reduce and prevent ocean pollution dumped from ships and certain land-based sources. • London Dumping Convention • 1973, 1978, and 1990 International Conventions for the Prevention of Marine Pollution from Ships • Relevant activities of the International Maritime Organization
Mediterranean Sea[b]	Reduce and prevent pollution in the Mediterranean Sea. • 1976 Barcelona Convention for the Protection of the Mediterranean Sea against Pollution • 1976 Protocol for the Prevention of Pollution of the Mediterranean Sea by Dumping from Ships and Aircraft • 1976 Protocol Concerning Cooperation in Combating Pollution of the Mediterranean Sea by Oil and Other Harmful Substances in Cases of Emergency • 1980 Protocol for the Protection of the Mediterranean Sea from Land-Based Sources
Long-range transboundary air pollution	Reduce transboundary air pollution in the Northern Hemisphere. • 1979 Convention on Long-Range Transboundary Air Pollution (CLRTAP) • 1984 Protocol for Long-Term Financing of Monitoring • 1985 Protocol to Reduce Sulfur Emissions • 1988 Protocol to Control Nitrogen Oxides • 1991 Protocol to Control Volatile Organic Compounds • 1994 Protocol to Further Reduce Sulfur Emissions • 1998 Protocol on Heavy Metals • 1998 Protocol on Persistent Organic Pollutants • 1999 Protocol to Abate Acidification, Eutrophication, and Ground-Level Ozone • Executive Body of CLRTAP • Implementation Committee • Working Group on Effects and its seven task forces • Working Group on Strategies and Review and its subsidiary bodies • European Monitoring and Evaluation Programme (EMEP) Steering Body and its subsidiary bodies, centers, and task forces

Regime	Goal and key constituent agreements and institutions (indicative list)
Antarctica	Protect Antarctica. • 1972 Convention for the Conservation of Antarctic Seals • 1980 Convention on the Conservation of Antarctic Marine Living Resources • 1988 Convention on the Regulation of Antarctic Mineral Resource Activities • 1991 Protocol on Environmental Protection
Global biodiversity (see Chapter 12)	Protect the global diversity of species, ecosystems, and genes; ensure that biological resources are used in a sustainable fashion; and ensure that the benefits of biological diversity are shared fairly and equitably. • 1992 Convention on Biological Diversity • 2000 Cartagena Protocol on Biosafety • Conference of Parties and its subsidiary bodies • Associated funding activities by the GEF
Trade in endangered species	Protect specific species by limiting or prohibiting their international trade. • 1973 Convention on International Trade in Endangered Species of Wild Fauna and Flora (CITES) • CITES Standing Committee • Animal and Plant Committees • CITES Secretariat
Migratory species	Protect marine, bird, and land-based species that migrate across international borders. • 1979 Bonn Convention on the Conservation of Migratory Species of Wild Animals
Wetlands	Provide a framework for national action and international cooperation to conserve wetlands, diverse natural resources that provide unique habitats and ecosystem services. • 1991 Ramsar Wetlands Convention
Whaling	Originally sought to protect whale stocks for the benefit of the whaling industry but now focuses on prohibiting whaling except for particular species. • 1946 International Convention for the Regulation of Whaling • International Whaling Commission

[a] The Basel, Rotterdam, and Stockholm Conventions can be considered as the centerpieces of individuals regimes, but significant efforts are under way to enhance the coordination and integration of various aspects of their operations. For current details, see Synergies among the Basel, Rotterdam and Stockholm Conventions, http://synergies.pops.int.

[b] Regimes exist for other regional seas as well. For information, see UNEP's Regional Seas Program, http://www.unep.org/regionalseas.

What all these chemicals share is the ability to remain intact and rise high into the atmosphere, where they break down and release chlorine or bromine atoms into the stratosphere; these atoms then destroy ozone molecules.[11]

In the late 1970s, the United States and several other countries (but not the European Union) banned the use of CFCs in aerosol sprays and for other non-essential uses.[12] The first global discussions on possible efforts to protect the ozone layer occurred in the 1970s, but formal global negotiations on options to control CFCs and other ozone-depleting substances (ODSs) did not begin until the mid-1980s. The ozone regime is the set of integrated principles, norms, rules, and procedures that nation-states have created to regulate and coordinate action in an attempt to protect stratospheric ozone from human-made chemicals. The international agreements that delineate the main elements of the regime include the 1985 Vienna Convention for the Protection of the Ozone Layer (a framework convention that did not establish regulations), the 1987 Montreal Protocol on Substances That Deplete the Ozone Layer (a regulatory treaty), and the many amendments and adjustments to the Montreal Protocol agreed to during more than twenty meetings of the parties to the protocol.[13] Of these, the most important are the 1990 London Amendment and Adjustment, the 1992 Copenhagen Amendment and Adjustment, the 1995 Vienna Adjustment, the 1999 Beijing Amendment and Adjustment, and the 2007 Montreal Adjustment.

The 1987 Montreal Protocol established the mechanism to control ODSs and placed binding controls on the production and use of certain CFCs and halons. Subsequent amendments and adjustments to the protocol added restrictions on additional chemicals, such as HCFCs and methyl bromide, and increased the level of controls so that the regime now mandates that countries eliminate the production and use of most of these chemicals. The required phaseout dates for ODSs are listed in Table 4-2. Exemptions exist for some countries to continue the production and consumption of small amounts of some ODSs for "essential uses" after the phaseout dates listed in the table, and larger and more controversial exemptions exist for "critical" agricultural and "quarantine and pre-shipment" uses of methyl bromide.[14]

Also central to the ozone regime are operations of its constituent institutions. The Meeting of the Parties (MOP) is the supreme decision-making authority and can negotiate amendments and adjustments to the protocol as well as make binding decisions on issues related to implementation. The MOP meets annually and includes representatives of all governments that have ratified the protocol as well as observers (who can participate in discussions but cannot take part in the decision-making procedures) from international organizations, environmental NGOs, and industry groups. The Open-Ended Working Group (OEWG) holds discussions in preparation for the MOP. Three independent assessment panels—the Scientific, Environmental Effects, and Technology and Economic Assessment Panels—provide the parties and the general public with periodic comprehensive and authoritative reviews of key issues, under instructions from the parties.[15] The Implementation Committee provides a forum for discussing issues of noncompliance by parties

Table 4-2 Schedule for the Phaseout of Ozone-Depleting Substances

Chemicals	Phaseout schedule Developed countries	Developing countries
CFCs	Phase out by 1996	Phase out by 2010
Halons	Phase out by 1994	Phase out by 2010
Carbon tetrachloride	Phase out by 1996	Phase out by 2010
Methyl chloroform	Phase out by 1996	Freeze by 2003 at average 1998–2000 levels; reduce by 30% by 2005 and 70% by 2010, and phase out by 2015
Hydrobromofluorocarbons (HBFCs)	Phase out by 1996	Phase out by 1996
HCFCs	Reduce by 35% by 2004, 75% by 2010, 90% by 2015, and phase out by 2020, allowing 0.5% for servicing purposes during the period 2020–2030	Freeze by 2013 at average 2009 and 2010 levels; reduce by 10% by 2015, 35% by 2020, 67.5% by 2025, and phase out by 2030, allowing for an annual average of 2.5% for servicing purposes during the period 2030–2040
Methyl bromide (CH$_3$Br)	Phase out by 2005	Freeze by 2002 at average 1995–1998 levels; reduce by 20% by 2005 and phase out by 2015
Bromochloromethane (BCM)	Phase out by 2002	Phase out by 2002

Note: This table is adapted from very similar tables developed by the author, including one in Pamela S. Chasek, David L. Downie, and Janet Welsh Brown, *Global Environmental Politics,* 6th ed. (Boulder, CO: Westview Press, 2014), which contains a more detailed discussion of the development and content of the ozone regime.

(such as not meeting the phaseout requirements) and offers recommendations to the MOP. The Ozone Secretariat provides day-to-day administration of the regime and supports the MOP, OEWG, assessment panels, and Implementation Committee.

The Multilateral Fund is perhaps the regime's most important institution. Created in a landmark agreement as part of the 1990 London Amendment, the Multilateral Fund provides financial assistance to developing countries to aid their transition from using ozone-depleting chemicals.[16] The Executive Committee, composed of representatives from fourteen governments—seven industrialized country donor parties and seven developing country recipient parties—is the decision body for the Fund. The World Bank, United Nations Development Programme (UNDP), United Nations Environment Programme (UNEP), and United Nations Industrial Development Organization

(UNIDO) act as implementing agencies, executing work plans approved by the Executive Committee. The Multilateral Fund Secretariat performs day-to-day administration functions and assists the Executive Committee. Industrialized countries provide new money for the Fund every three years at levels negotiated by the MOP. The total budget for 2012–2014 is $440 million. The Fund has disbursed nearly $3 billion to support projects in more than 140 countries and is widely considered a key ingredient in the success of the ozone regime.[17]

The major principles (beliefs of fact, causation, and rectitude) of the ozone regime are enunciated in the Vienna Convention and the Montreal Protocol, particularly in their preambles. These include statements that the ozone layer is a critical natural system and must be protected; that certain human-made chemicals deplete the ozone layer; that political action should be based on the best scientific and technical information available; that regulations should be guided, in general, by precaution; and that all states have a common responsibility to help protect the ozone layer but have different responsibilities in doing so.

The norms of the ozone regime include the standards of behavior enunciated in the Vienna Convention, the Montreal Protocol, amendments to the protocol, and decisions by the parties or Executive Committee that do not carry the binding nature of rules. The telling difference is the verb used to proscribe the action. For example, "Parties shall" indicates a rule. "Parties should" and "Parties are requested to" indicate attempts to create norms.

The most important regime rules (specific prescriptions or proscriptions for action) are the binding requirements for countries to reduce or eliminate the production and use of ODSs (outlined in Table 4-2). Regime rules also include requirements regarding the provision of technical and financial assistance to developing countries to help them implement the treaty, reporting by countries regarding the production and use of ODSs, when and how the efficacy of the regime is to be reviewed, and other issues. In addition to the rules set out in the Montreal Protocol and its amendments, rules on a variety of policy and procedural issues are created by binding decisions of the MOP and the Executive Committee of the Multilateral Fund—decisions that are within the jurisdiction of these bodies as established by the amended protocol.

The procedures of the ozone regime include provisions for amending the treaty; procedures for deliberating on, agreeing to, and implementing other types of binding and nonbinding decisions made by the MOP and Executive Committee of the Multilateral Fund; and the standard operating procedures of the regime's institutions (the MOP, OEWG, Ozone Secretariat, Executive Committee, Fund Secretariat, assessment panels, Implementation Committee, and implementing agencies). Moreover, because the ozone regime is nearly thirty years old, many operating procedures are fully entrenched and provide clear and well-regarded precedents for considering, developing, deciding upon, mandating, and implementing global ozone policy.

As a result of the ozone regime, the production of many ODSs, including CFCs, halon, carbon tetrachloride, and methyl chloroform, has been almost completely eliminated.[18] The production and use of HCFCs and methyl bromide are declining. As a result, the atmospheric abundance of ODSs is declining, as is the amount of chlorine and bromine in the stratosphere, and ozone depletion has largely stabilized, although severe depletions still occur.[19] If countries continue to implement their commitments, the ozone layer over most parts of the world should fully recover by 2050, with the depletion above the Antarctic disappearing later in the century.[20]

At the same time, however, it is not certain that all countries will fulfill their commitments (see also Chapter 5). Indeed, several problems exist that threaten the ultimate success of the ozone regime. For example, millions of tons of CFCs reside in, and are slowly leaking from, obsolete equipment and other wastes.[21] Unless these CFCs are identified, recovered, and destroyed, they represent an enormous source of ODS emissions even though the production of new CFCs is largely curtailed. HCFCs are being smuggled from several developing countries, where their production and use are less restricted, to the United States and other industrialized countries.[22] Although this also occurred with CFCs and was eventually stopped, this flouting of regime rules could delay and even threaten the complete phaseout of HCFCs.

In addition, exemptions continue to allow the production and use of significant quantities of methyl bromide in quarantine and preshipment applications and in certain agricultural sectors, especially in the United States.[23] Although one can argue that these exemptions were necessary to reach agreement on an earlier overall phase-down for methyl bromide,[24] no firm end point has been set for these exemptions. Thus, even though the overall production and use of methyl bromide continue to decline, it is possible that the same influential agricultural interests that successfully lobbied the U.S. government and other governments to create the exemptions could succeed in preventing the elimination of methyl bromide, threatening stratospheric ozone.[25] More broadly, climate change could produce atmospheric changes that enhance the ability of chlorine and bromine atoms to destroy ozone, increasing the importance of eliminating the remaining ODSs. Donor countries will also have to continue supporting the Multilateral Fund to ensure full implementation of ODS phaseouts in some developing countries, something that is far from certain given the lingering impact of global financial crises and the competition for such funding among different environmental regimes.

Obstacles to Effective Global Environmental Policy

The success to date of the ozone regime and the existence of other environmental regimes issue areas should not obscure the fact that creating and implementing effective global environmental policy are not easy tasks. It took many years to create each of the environmental regimes listed in Table 4-1, and most remain weaker and less effective than their supporters would like. Even the ozone regime, widely considered a success, faces challenges that could forestall full recovery of the ozone layer. It is important, therefore, to understand the obstacles to effective global environmental policy.

This section briefly outlines four broad categories of factors that make it difficult for governments to create and implement effective international environmental policy: (1) systemic obstacles, (2) procedural obstacles, (3) lack of necessary and sufficient conditions, and (4) obstacles that stem from certain characteristics of international environmental issues.[26] These categories are indicative, heuristic, and interrelated, and the individual and relative impacts of the characteristics vary across countries and issues. Nevertheless, the categories are useful starting points for discussing why governments have not created more effective global policy despite increasingly compelling evidence of serious and dangerous environmental problems.

Systemic Obstacles

Several significant impediments to creating and implementing effective global environmental policy can be traced to core elements of the global political, ecological, and legal systems.[27]

The International Political System. Anarchy is one defining characteristic of the structure of the international system. *Anarchy* in this sense does not mean chaos but rather the absence of hierarchy. In international politics, the absence of a world government with recognized authority to create common rules, maintain order, and punish violators demands that states ultimately rely on self-help to ensure their safety. Many theorists and national leaders have argued that the exigencies of this situation and the resulting security dilemma have significant impacts on international politics.[28] Among the most familiar consequences are that states prefer and strive for independence over interdependence, states tend to seek a balance of power, and effective cooperation among states is often difficult to achieve.[29]

The last of these consequences is particularly important for understanding regimes. Strong theoretical arguments and a history of unfortunate examples support the proposition that the structure of the international political system can make it difficult for states to follow cooperative paths. For example, states sometime do not cooperate successfully, or fail to develop effective rules to govern their behavior in particular issue areas, because they fear that other states might not follow the rules and thus will gain an advantage over them (and might even be planning a double-cross).[30] States sometimes fail to cooperate if they fear that another country might benefit more from the arrangement, even if they themselves would benefit, because this would erode their relative economic, military, or political position in relation to that country.[31] Countries are tempted to free ride or gain benefits without paying a fair share of the costs (for example, a country might continue to emit a certain pollutant when others agree to stop) and fear that others might free ride. Such temptations and worries reduce the ability of international actors to create and implement effective rules.[32] Anarchic situations also produce incentives that cause actors to pursue actions that might be rational individually but result in the destruction of a common-pool resource.[33] (Think about the destruction of certain stocks of ocean fish as certain countries and fishing fleets try to get as much as they can even as the resource runs out for all.) In international relations, it is also easy for countries to misperceive the motives, intentions, or actions of other governments, which can contribute to states missing opportunities to make mutually beneficial agreements.[34]

Environmental politics takes place within the international arena. It is not divorced from the pressures that system structure places on state actors. Cooperative solutions do not arise without concerns for comparative costs. The national negotiating positions of many countries on climate change provide numerous examples. States do engage in distributive bargaining—they often try to pay less than the other side and to get more benefits, as many countries did during the ozone negotiations in the 1980s. They do compromise possible solutions by linking them to extraneous political, security, and economic issues. They do fail to locate mutually advantageous policies (market failure). In short, international environmental politics is still international politics, and, therefore, creating and implementing effective global policy and regimes remain difficult.

Global Political and Ecological Systems. Ecological systems have their own logic and laws and exist independent of the international political and legal systems. Simply put, the causes, consequences, and geographic scope of environmental problems do not respect national boundaries. Maps of the two systems do not match up. This somewhat simplistic observation nevertheless captures an important truth: the structure of the global political system, composed of independent sovereign states, is structurally not well suited to address complex, interdependent, international environmental problems whose causes, impacts, and solutions transcend unrelated political boundaries.

Global Legal Systems and the Requirements for Effective International Environmental Policy. Principle 21 from the 1972 UN Conference on the Human Environment in Stockholm is often cited as one of the most important foundations of modern international environmental law. It reads: "States have, in accordance with the Charter of the United Nations and the principles of international law, the sovereign right to exploit their own resources pursuant to their own environmental policies, and the responsibility to ensure that activities within their jurisdiction or control do not cause damage to the environment of other states or of areas beyond the limits of national jurisdiction."[35] Note the profound contradiction between the two halves of this sentence. The fundamental principle of international law is sovereignty. States have, to a significant extent, unfettered legal control over activities within their borders. This has been, and continues to be, particularly true when it comes to economic development and the use of natural resources (as both raw materials and as sinks for pollution).

At the same time, actions taken within a country—from using HCFCs and methyl bromide to emitting greenhouse gases to clearing rain forests to discharging pollutants into the air or water—often have international environmental implications. Legitimate actions within one country can create environmental problems for another. Effective international policy, therefore, often requires limiting what a state can do within its own borders. Climate change presents the classic example. Both China and the United States possess enough coal within their borders to meet their energy needs for two hundred years or more. Blessed with this natural resource, each country has the sovereign right to exploit it for the benefit of its citizens. Burning so much coal, however, would produce massive amounts of carbon dioxide, contributing to climate change that would have dangerous global impacts. Thus the structure of international law, in the form of sovereign legal control of resources within one country's borders, often conflicts with the requirements for effective international environmental policy.

Procedural Obstacles

The structural obstacles outlined above give rise to additional procedural problems when nation-states actually attempt to address international environmental issues. Two problems stand out: the lowest-common-denominator problem and the time-lag problem.

Lowest-Common-Denominator Problem. Because states are sovereign entities, they can choose to join or not join international environmental agreements. At the same time, the active participation of many countries is usually necessary to address a regional or global problem. This often means that the countries most interested in addressing a problem must gain the cooperation of countries with less, little, or even no interest. Thus international and global environmental policy often represents, at least at the start, the lowest-common-denominator measures that the relevant countries are willing to accept.

For example, during the early stages of negotiations on protecting the ozone layer, from 1983 to 1985, there were two major coalitions. The United States, the Nordic states, Canada, and Switzerland supported creating international controls on CFCs and other ODSs, while the European Community and its member states, supported quietly on some issues by Japan and the Soviet Union, opposed them. (Most other countries were either undecided or, as in the cases of China and India, uninterested in regulation and largely uninvolved in the negotiations.) In March 1985, negotiators met in Vienna to review and adopt a framework treaty that affirmed the importance of protecting the ozone layer but did not include control measures. Until the last moment, the United States, Canada, and the Nordic countries considered forcing delegates to vote on adding a protocol mandating binding controls on CFCs. They abandoned this strategy, however, understanding that such controls without participation by the European Community, and probably without Japan and the Soviet bloc, would not have significant impact on the global problem and would probably threaten the ability of the planned framework treaty, the Vienna Convention, to produce a binding protocol in the future. The most reluctant, necessary actor, Europe, set the lowest common denominator for global policy.

We see this today in climate change politics as well. The world cannot prevent dangerous climate change without concerted efforts by all the major emitters of greenhouse gases, including China, Europe, India, and the United States. The greenhouse gases from any one of these countries could eventually lead to significant global climate change, so all must eventually participate for the world to address this issue successfully. However, the United States, China, and India have not yet agreed to binding international agreements to curb their domestic emissions. The European Union has taken strong action domestically, but effective global policy will require the eventual participation of the least willing but necessary actors (see Chapters 7 and 10).

This obstacle also affects the chemical regime. Many countries wanted to eliminate the production and use of most chemicals addressed in the 2001 Stockholm Convention and the agreements in 2009, 2011, and 2013 to control additional chemicals. Other states, however, insisted that they needed to continue using some of the chemicals for specific applications. The need to create a treaty with global participation necessitated accepting the lowest common denominator in the form of exemptions that allowed the continued use of certain chemicals by particular countries (see Chapter 11).[36]

Slow Development and Implementation. The sovereignty of states and the fact that each can choose to join or not join an international environmental agreement contributes to a significant time lag between the identification of an international environmental problem and the impact of international policy. Negotiations must be convened, policies agreed to, treaties formally ratified by governments, treaty implementation initiated, and national policies undertaken effectively and over a long enough period of time to have an impact on the environmental problem.

While this process unfolds, the environmental issue continues to worsen: greenhouse gases continue to pour into the atmosphere, biodiversity continues to decline, toxic pollutants continue to accumulate. Preventing serious and perhaps irreversible environmental damage requires addressing such issues before they pass particular tipping points. Those timelines follow the laws of nature, not those of politics. Thus the years, even decades, required by the global policy-making process, even when it reaches a successful conclusion in a new agreement, present a significant procedural obstacle to effective global environmental policy and regimes, because by the time a policy is put into place, the situation has often grown far worse.

The Absence of Necessary Conditions: Concern, Contractual Environment, and Capacity

As Robert Keohane, Peter Haas, and Marc Levy argue, effective international environmental policy requires three necessary (but not sufficient) conditions.[37] First, government "concern must be sufficiently high." States do not have infinite resources of time, money, and diplomatic attention. For international environmental policy to be successful, many governments must decide to devote resources to addressing a particular problem, resources they could use on other competing political or economic issues. Second, a sufficiently "hospitable contractual environment" must exist. Because of the obstacles associated with the international system (outlined above), international environmental cooperation requires that states "be able to make credible commitments, to enact joint rules with reasonable ease, and to monitor each other's behavior at moderate costs . . . without debilitating fear of free riding or cheating by others." This can be difficult. Third, states must possess the scientific, political, and administrative "capacity" to understand the issue, to negotiate international policies that can address it successfully, and then to implement the policies within their own countries effectively and within the necessary time frame. Capacity in this context is often discussed in terms of the economic, political, and governmental capacity within developing countries to address particular issues, including by officials from many developing countries who argue at international negotiations that their countries require financial and technical assistance to build the capacity necessary to implement particular international environmental regimes. Capacity can be considered more broadly, however, to include, from different perspectives, the political capacity or political will of industrialized states to enact environmental policies even when they run counter to the economic interests of key political and economic constituencies; the ability to make difficult decisions in the presence of considerable uncertainty about future events; and the ability of human society to address very complex, long-term environmental issues through collective decision making and action.

Although the concepts are easy to oversimplify, it is a fact that concern, contractual environment, and capacity encapsulate important, even critical, requirements for successful environmental policy. Thus the absence of any one of them presents significant obstacles to the creation and implementation of effective environmental regimes. Insufficient concern regarding the potential of ODSs to destroy ozone delayed action to address CFCs in Europe and Russia in the 1970s. North-South and East-West conflicts in international relations affected the contractual environmental and hampered negotiations on creating and expanding the Montreal Protocol. Insufficient concern and capacity in China, India, Russia, and other countries contributed to illegal production and use of CFCs a decade ago and of HCFCs today.

Characteristics of International Environmental Issues That Create Obstacles

International environmental issues possess inherent characteristics that can make effective cooperation difficult.[38] Individually or in combination, these characteristics can exacerbate systemic or procedural constraints on international cooperation as well as inhibit the creation of sufficient concern, a hospitable contractual environment, and sufficient capacity. The individual and relative impacts of these characteristics in obstructing effective environmental policies vary across countries and issue areas. This section delineates several interrelated categories of such obstacles.[39]

Scientific Complexity, Uncertainty, and Nonlinearity. Environmental issues often involve complex scientific questions and significant uncertainty about their ultimate impact, particularly early in an issue area's development. For example, the initial discovery in the early 1970s that CFCs threatened the ozone layer introduced new ideas and generated significant scientific debates that continued for many years, some of which were not resolved until the late 1980s.[40] In addition, many environmental issues do not develop in a linear, predictable pattern, making it difficult to predict the timing and impact of specific environmental problems. Scientific complexity and uncertainty concerning the content, scope, severity, and time frame of individual problems can contribute to difficulty in reaching agreement on international policy. Lack of firm knowledge or consensus can undermine concern. Uncertainty about the extent of an environmental problem allows clearer economic interests to remain higher priorities. Complexity can challenge the capacity of governments to understand an issue or design effective policies. Complexity and uncertainty can harm the contractual environment by causing states to reach different conclusions about a problem and thus to place different values on the importance of cooperating. Ozone depletion, climate change, biodiversity loss, depletion of ocean fish stocks, and the use and disposal of toxic chemicals are examples of issues in which complexity and uncertainty have hampered international negotiations despite general agreement that complete inaction would lead to significant if not disastrous outcomes.

Linked Economic and Political Interests. Environmental problems are inextricably linked to economic and political interests. Environmental issues, and therefore environmental negotiations and policy, do not exist independent of other economic and political activities and interests. Rather, environmental issues exist because of these activities and interests. Environmental problems are produced as externalities of individuals, corporations, and nations pursuing other important interests such as energy production, mining, manufacturing, farming, fishing, transportation, livestock husbandry, urbanization, and national security. The fact that individuals, corporations, and countries could pursue many of these activities successfully while producing less environmental degradation does not erase the links between the issues.

Because of these links, effective international policy on environmental issues must also entail effective policy on the economic or social activities that create the environmental problems. Protecting the ozone layer requires developing and utilizing the means to deliver refrigeration and air-conditioning on a global scale without using CFCs and HCFCs. Addressing climate change requires controlling fossil fuel consumption. Preventing more serious declines in stocks of ocean fish requires limiting fishing economies. Safeguarding biodiversity requires addressing the economic pressures that lead to habitat destruction. Protecting or restoring regional seas and waterways, such as the Mediterranean, Baltic, and Red Seas, the Nile, and the Danube, requires cooperative agreements and coordinated regulatory policy among large numbers of states with very different economic interests concerning the use of these waters.

Such issue linkages can exacerbate the lowest-common-denominator problem, augment the inherent difficulties associated with cooperation under anarchy, and have negative impacts on concern, the contractual environment, and capacity. Governments and their constituencies often express greater concern for the underlying economic and political interests than for the environmental consequences. As high economic costs become associated with collaborative action, actors face fears that others might try to free ride, thus harming the contractual environment. Many governments lack the capacity to negotiate, enact, and enforce environmental regulations in the face of significant economic or political costs.

Unequal Adjustment Costs. Addressing the activities that cause environmental problems can produce broad benefits to the environment, human health, and even the economy. For example, replacing fossil fuel power plants with wind, solar, and geothermal energy reduces carbon dioxide emissions that cause climate change; cleans the air of other pollutants that negatively affect human health; reduces energy imports, which improves a country's balance of trade; and creates new, sustainable jobs in the alternative energy industry. At the same time, however, those with economic interests attached to the old, polluting industries will incur economic costs, sometimes very significant costs. Thus solving a common problem does not mean that all actors will bear equal costs. The costs of change—of adjusting to new policies and practices—can vary significantly within a country and across different countries, and this can produce obstacles to effective policy.

Solutions to international environmental problems frequently involve unequal adjustment costs. This accentuates the difficulties inherent in international cooperation, exacerbates the lowest-common-denominator problem, and has significant impacts on the contractual environment. Because states can be concerned with relative or positional advantages, they may reject solutions that ask them to bear burdens that are relatively larger than those borne by other states.[41] Alternatively, they may demand special compensation for joining the regime, such as exemptions, extended time horizons, technical assistance, or financial compensation. Comparative costs vary depending on the environmental issue area, level of industrialization, method of energy production, resource base, transportation policy, and many other factors. Overcoming the impact of unequal adjustment costs is a critical and difficult part of global environmental negotiations.

Extended Time Horizons and Time Horizon Conflicts. For many environmental problems, the most serious impacts will not occur for many years after they are discovered. It can be difficult for societies and policy makers to agree on incurring short-term costs to fix a long-term problem, despite the fact that it is usually most effective and least costly to take action before the most serious consequences occur. In addition, the elected officials and government bureaucrats responsible for making decisions on when and how to address environmental problems operate in much shorter time frames—usually two-, four-, or six-year election cycles and one- or two-year budget cycles—than do global environmental problems. This is not to cast aspersions on these individuals or their priorities but rather to acknowledge that even the most enlightened officials face time pressures and perspectives far different from those required to address a problem with a twenty- or fifty-year time horizon. These conflicts present political difficulties, especially if the threat is not well defined or the costs of abatement measures are very high. Climate change presents an obvious example of this problem, despite evidence that the impacts of climate change are already occurring.

Large-Number Problems. Solutions to international environmental problems often require the participation of a large number of state and private actors. The problems associated with creating cooperation in such situations are wellknown. Large numbers present significant incentives for free riding—not participating in the policy, and thereby avoiding the costs, while hoping to enjoy the benefits. This can be particularly dangerous when the environmental policy aims to manage and protect a common-pool resource—such as the oceans or the atmosphere, which all can use but no one controls—if fears that others will cheat can lead actors to believe they face a use-it-or-lose-it situation.[42] Large numbers can also harm the contractual environment and decrease the possibility of effec- tive environmental cooperation because of increased transaction costs, difficulties in identifying and reaching consensus, increased likelihood of free riding, and problems in detecting and sanctioning violators. Further, large numbers increase the likelihood of significant differences in culture, environmental values, and economic and institutional development among the states. Global issues must also overcome North-South and other divisions. Although neither group is uni- formly cohesive, industrialized and developing nations exhibit strong differences in many global negotiations on issues such as the targets and timetables required for different types of parties, financial assistance, technology transfer, and the relative importance of environmental protection versus other issues.

Different Core Beliefs. States and groups within states (including cultural, reli- gious, regional, economic, and political groups) sometimes possess different beliefs and values relevant to protecting particular species, preventing pollu- tions, pursuing economic development, preserving the environment for future generations, and the relative importance of precaution in setting public policy. Some individuals, for example, believe products from certain endangered ani- mal or plant species have significant medicinal, psychological, or sexual prop- erties. This creates a market for these species and undercuts international controls designed to protect them. Members of particular religious groups oppose certain policies designed to control human population growth. Some countries or groups within them have no ethical concerns in regard to hunting whales; others have very strong concerns. Some groups have strong cultural links to fishing, timbering, or hunting certain animals. Some political ideolo- gies treat economic development and freedom from government regulations as higher priorities than environmental protection. Others take the reverse view. These differences can create obstacles to effective global environmental policy.

They can not only inhibit the identification and implementation of cooperative solutions but also obstruct attempts to begin discussions by limiting concern for particular environmental issues.

Explaining the Ozone Regime

Many explanations have been advanced regarding why actors were largely able to overcome the obstacles outlined above and create and expand the ozone regime.[43] Several broad categories stand out. Each encapsulates a number of important factors that affected the development and the relative success of the ozone regime.[44]

First, advancing scientific knowledge played an important but not a determinative role in the creation and expansion of global ozone policy by helping to increase government concern, inform public opinion, alter perceptions of national self-interest, enhance the contractual environment, and increase the perceived value of the regime.[45] A startling scientific discovery created the issue.[46] Scientific debates in the United States played a role in the U.S. decision to ban CFCs in aerosol sprays (which had an impact on later international negotiations), as well as in U.S. and UNEP efforts to convene the first international discussions.[47] In the 1980s, advancing scientific understanding of the issue undercut European opposition to starting negotiations on a framework convention.[48] The startling discovery of the ozone hole acted as an exogenous shock,[49] swaying public opinion and providing countries that supported a global ban on CFCs the argument they needed to restart negotiations on a binding protocol.[50] Scientific confirmation in 1989 that chlorine released from CFCs was causing the Antarctic ozone hole played a key role in the agreement to strengthen the regime considerably in 1990 (London Amendment and Adjustment). Discovery of the first serious ozone depletion above the Northern Hemisphere and an expanding Antarctic hole contributed to a strengthening of the agreement again in 1992 (Copenhagen Amendment and Adjustment). During the period in which binding controls were established and rapidly expanded (1987–1995), advancing scientific knowledge essentially "framed" the negotiations, constraining policy arguments that appeared to go against the consensus scientific opinion as set forth in the regime's assessment reports.[51] A decade later, the 2007 report of the Intergovernmental Panel on Climate Change on the seriousness of the climate change issue and separate conclusions by the ozone regime's Scientific Assessment Panel that protecting the ozone layer required further action provided a foundation for the surprising decision to accelerate the phaseout of HCFCs, which are both ODSs and powerful greenhouse gases.[52]

Following discussions on conditions that enhance international cooperation ("cooperation under anarchy"), advancing scientific knowledge helped to "alter the payoff structure."[53] Cooperation became more likely as countries learned more about the consequences of ozone depletion and increased the value they attached to protecting stratospheric ozone (altered payoffs). Using a different theoretical vocabulary, advancing scientific knowledge convinced more states that without international action, ozone depletion would have negative impacts on their countries, altering their interests.[54] Increasing knowledge of the long-term nature of the problem also served to "enhance the shadow of the future," augmenting the chances of cooperation as states came to believe that they would be holding discussions for many years.[55] Increased scientific understanding of the issue also confirmed the value and importance of the global ozone policy, increasing the value that actors attached to the ozone regime and enhancing prospects for even more cooperation.[56]

The importance of the complex science to policy discussions also empowered a transnational network of experts, an epistemic community, that favored development of effective international policy.[57] The complexity of the science also allowed those who understood it to shape important discourse on the issues, to introduce or enhance influential frameworks, including precautionary and intergenerational perspectives, and to take other actions that influenced more senior policy makers.[58]

At the same time, while increasing scientific understanding of the issue was important and perhaps necessary for the creation and expansion of the ozone regime, it was not sufficient on its own to produce the current set of norms, rules, and institutions. Comparing the development of the ozone and climate regimes at analogous stages of scientific knowledge and consensus provides evidence for this conclusion.[59]

Thus a second broad set of important causal factors involves the changing economic interests of key actors. In short, changing perceptions regarding the economic costs and benefits of controlling ODSs, particularly adjustment costs, affected calculations of state interests, which in turn had an impact on policy preferences.[60]

Not surprisingly, and as seen in analogous situations in other environmental regimes, the economic interests of important actors often impeded efforts to create stronger ODS controls. Examples include the lack of meaningful CFC regulations in most of Europe prior to the Montreal Protocol[61] and the continued use of methyl bromide by large agricultural enterprises in the United States.[62] Once international negotiations began, many countries advocated international policies similar to their existing domestic policies. During creation of the Vienna Convention and the early stages of the Montreal Protocol negotiations, the United States supported the establishment of a global ban on the use of CFCs in aerosol sprays, a step it had already enacted domestically but most other countries had not. EU countries countered with proposals for caps on CFC production capacity, policies they had already enacted and that would favor European CFC producers because they possessed significant excess capacity while U.S. producers did not. Similar situations emerged during various negotiations to strengthen HCFC and methyl bromide controls and to reduce the amount of methyl bromide used via exemptions. Economic interests also contributed to several lowest-common-denominator compromises. These included Europe preventing the inclusion of control measures in the Vienna Convention; limiting to 50 percent the mandated reductions established by the Montreal Protocol, which allowed the EU countries to meet much of their obligation through inexpensive controls on the use of CFCs in aerosol sprays; expanding developing country grace periods beyond their original ten years; creating exemptions for certain uses of CFCs and halons; and allowing much broader exemption for methyl bromide.

At other times, however, economic interests greatly assisted efforts to create and strengthen the ozone regime. First, the regulation of CFCs in the United States in the late 1970s and then again in the Montreal Protocol in the late 1980s created economic incentives for companies to develop substitutes.[63] The development of effective substitutes then began to alter the economic interests of several important actors. Once the major producers of CFCs in Japan, the European Union, and the United States were certain that they could produce HCFCs and hydrofluorocarbons (HFCs), they changed their position and began to support a gradual global CFC phaseout, as this would create a market for HCFCs and HFCs. Along with new scientific information linking CFCs to the ozone hole, this change in long-term economic interests contributed to an abrupt shift in EU policy in 1989.[64] It also represents a major reason that the large industrialized nations agreed to expand and strengthen the ozone regime so significantly in 1990, 1992, and 1995.

The creation and operation of the Multilateral Fund also affected economic interests in ways that assisted efforts to strengthen the regime. Most obviously, China and India had demanded creation of the Fund as a condition for their joining the regime. Later, developing countries accepted stronger controls on methyl bromide and HCFCs in part because their experience with the Fund had given them confidence that their economic interests would not be seriously compromised.[65] In addition, many companies within developing countries that received support from the Multilateral Fund and transitioned away from CFCs changed their economic interests and became advocates of "stronger domestic action in their own countries as they did not want to get undercut by competitors using less expensive ozone-depleting chemicals."[66]

Third, specific characteristics of the ozone issue contributed to its success. This is not to say that the ozone regime was easy to create or expand (as some revisionists argue). The negotiations were in fact extremely difficult. However, all issues are somewhat different, and individual characteristics can affect outcomes. For example, the potential impacts of ozone depletion, especially increased skin cancers and cataracts, were easily understood by the public. The science of ozone depletion, while complex, could be summarized in general, understandable terms for nonexperts, even before proof had been established. By the late 1980s, CFCs and several other ODSs accounted for relatively small percentages of the profits of their major manufacturers in OECD countries. Moreover, the fact that the manufacturers of CFCs would become the manufacturers of CFC substitutes, which carried higher profit margins, turned some regime opponents into regime proponents. Equally important, while the use of CFCs was truly crucial in many sectors, the development of drop-in substitutes (HCFCs and HFCs) significantly reduced corporate and consumer adjustment costs.

A fourth set of causal factors involves the impact that UNEP, the World Meteorological Organization (WMO), and the Vienna Convention and Montreal Protocol themselves had on efforts to create and then strengthen the ozone regime.[67] This supports the neoliberal institutionalist argument that international institutions can have positive impacts on the development of collective action.[68] In the late 1970s, UNEP worked to increase concern about ozone depletion and helped to initiate international action by organizing the first scientific and political meetings focusing on the problem.[69] European governments that were skeptical of the need even to discuss the possibility of ozone depletion had difficulty opposing UNEP's nascent efforts on the issue. UNEP then sustained international attention on the issue when official interest in ozone depletion waned significantly during the early 1980s.[70] Once substantive negotiations began, UNEP facilitated regime creation by establishing a procedural foundation and reducing transaction costs. UNEP's executive director, Mostafa Tolba, actively pushed the parties toward agreements in Montreal in 1987 and London in 1990 and aggressively and successfully lobbied developing countries in the 1980s and 1990s to join the regime.[71] In the early 1980s, involvement by WMO and UNEP facilitated creation of the coordinating committee on the ozone, which discussed the developing science of the issue, as well as the regime's scientific assessment panel.

The existence and content of regime institutions themselves also played important roles. The process of considering the issue, holding formal negotiations, and reaching the initial agreements helped to raise governmental concern, clarify issues, and correct misperceptions regarding the costs of controlling ODSs.[72] The existence of the Vienna Convention and the Ozone Secretariat provided a forum and a manager to begin global negotiations on regulating CFCs following discovery of the ozone hole, saving considerable time. Similarly, governments could not have agreed in 1990 to eliminate CFCs and halons in response to the 1989 confirmation that CFCs were causing the ozone hole if the Montreal Protocol had not already existed and provided a ready-made regulatory framework. ODS controls could not have been strengthened so significantly in 1990, 1992, 1995, and 2007 if regime rules had not allowed the parties to "adjust" control measures on ODSs already in the protocol and bypass the formal amendment and ratification procedures required by most treaties, a process that would have taken years longer.

The final set of factors to be discussed here are the specific elements of the Montreal Protocol itself. In short, "regime design matters."[73] Several aspects of the ozone regime have been identified as important to its success (see also Chapter 5). These include the following:

- The stated principle that control measures should be guided by scientific understanding of threats to the ozone layer in a precautionary manner and the general, although not absolute, observance of this principle. The original Montreal Protocol embraced precaution, establishing global 50 percent cuts on the most widely used CFCs and halons without evidence of ozone depletion in the Northern

Hemisphere and without scientific confirmation that ODSs were causing the Antarctic ozone hole. This made it easier to reach agreement on eliminating these ODSs once scientists confirmed the connection.

- The design of the control measures, which are concise, clear, and binding and target the production, use, and trade of ODSs.

- The design of the exemptions. Their existence reduced the ability of isolated economic interests to prevent a country from joining the regime, but their rules limited their long-term environmental impact by requiring that countries apply for most exemptions annually and that these applications be reviewed by an assessment panel and the MOP (the methyl bromide exemptions are not bound by these rules).

- The ability of the regime to expand quickly through "adjustments"— decisions taken by the MOP to strengthen controls on ODSs already controlled under the treaty and that became binding immediately, without requiring additional ratification per the normal amendment process.

- The assessment panels. These provide the parties with regular, consensus updates on the ozone depletion issue and the availability of ODS alternatives, information that greatly assisted regime expansion.

- The practice of holding annual MOPs, so the parties can make decisions on a timely basis.

- The Multilateral Fund. Creation of the Fund ensured the participation of large developing countries in the regime. Its existence provided economic and political support and augmented government capacity to implement the regime, its funding of specific projects helped many developing countries to meet and sometime exceed the ODS phaseout schedules, and its impact on the marketplace in some countries created corporate supporters of ODS controls among those that transitioned to alternatives and did not want their competitors to continue using the old chemicals.

- Trade restrictions. The prohibition on parties from exporting ODSs and products containing ODSs to nonparties after a certain date acted as a powerful incentive for importing countries, especially smaller countries, to join the regime.

- Reporting requirements. Parties must report annual data on production, imports, and exports of ODSs. This allows for effective monitoring of regime implementation and helps expose instances of noncompliance.

- A formal but facilitative noncompliance procedure that focuses on identifying instances of noncompliance and working with the noncompliant parties to seek solutions before punitive measures are considered.

Conclusion

International environmental regimes are dynamic, sector-specific international regulatory and administrative systems that states create to manage policy on particular issues. They comprise sets of integrated principles, norms, rules, procedures, and institutions. Some environmental regimes, such as those for protecting stratospheric ozone, reducing trade in endangered species, and addressing pollution in regional seas, are of long standing, are well developed, and have produced some notable successes. However, as many other chapters in this volume illustrate, most environmental regimes have not achieved their objects and face significant challenges. Consequently, it is important to understand the obstacles to effective global environmental policy so that we can better understand past successes and failures and take more effective action in addressing critical long-standing issues, such as climate change and biodiversity loss, as well as new issues such as endocrine-disrupting toxic chemicals.

Notes

1. This is a modified version of the well-known definition in Stephen Krasner, *International Regimes* (Ithaca, NY: Cornell University Press, 1983). As noted in Pamela S. Chasek, David L. Downie, and Janet Welsh Brown, *Global Environmental Politics*, 6th ed. (Boulder, CO: Westview Press, 2014), it can be useful to compare definitions and the use of the term *regime* in John Ruggie, "International Responses to Technology: Concepts and Trends," *International Organization* 29 (1975): 557–583; Ernst Haas, "On Systems and International Regimes," *World Politics* 27 (1975): 147–174; Robert Keohane and Joseph Nye Jr., *Power and Interdependence: World Politics in Transition* (Boston: Little, Brown, 1977); Oran Young, "International Regimes: Problems of Concept Formation," *International Organization* 32 (1980): 331–356; Krasner, *International Regimes*; Robert Keohane, *After Hegemony: Cooperation and Discord in the World Political Economy* (Princeton, NJ: Princeton University Press, 1984); Stephan Haggard and Beth Simmons, "Theories of International Regimes," *International Organization* 41 (1987): 491–517; Thomas Gehring, "International Environmental Regimes," in *Yearbook of International Environmental Law*, vol. 1, ed. G. Handl (London: Graham & Trotman, 1990); and David Downie, "Road Map or False Trail: Evaluating the Precedence of the Ozone Regime as Model and Strategy for Global Climate Change," *International Environmental Affairs* 7 (Fall 1995): 321–345.
2. As a result, regimes have received a good deal of theoretical and empirical attention within the international organization subfield of international relations. Influential early discussions of regimes in international relations include Ernst Haas, "Why Collaborate? Issue-Linkage and International Relations," *World Politics* 32 (1980): 357–405; Robert Keohane, "The Theory of Hegemonic Stability and Changes in International Economic Regimes," in *Changes in the International System*, ed. Ole Holsti (Boulder, CO: Westview Press, 1980); Krasner, *International Regimes*; Keohane, *After Hegemony*; Friedrich Kratochwil and John Gerard Ruggie, "International Organization: A State of the Art on an Art of the State," *International Organization* 40 (1986): 753–776; and Haggard and Simmons, "Theories of International Regimes." A brief examination of progenitor discussions in the international organization literature is provided in Chasek et al., *Global Environmental Politics*.
3. For an influential early discussion, see Keohane, *After Hegemony*.
4. For a recent discussion, see Chasek et al., *Global Environmental Politics*, chap. 6.

5. See, for example, the Forest Stewardship Council's Web site, http://www.fsc.org.
6. See the International Organization for Standardization's Web site, http://www.iso
   .org.
7. Information on these regimes and treaties can be found on the Web sites maintained
   by their secretariats. Also, the International Institute for Sustainable Development's
   site, Linkages (http://www.iisd.ca), and its online publication the Earth Negotiations Bulletin publish reports from ongoing negotiations. For analyses of the development and content of several of these regimes, see Chasek et al., *Global
   Environmental Politics*.
8. This section draws explicitly from three recent analyses by the author: in Chasek et al.,
   Global Environmental Politics, chap. 3; David Downie, "Stratospheric Ozone Depletion," in *Routledge Handbook of Global Environmental Politics*, ed. Paul Harris
   (New York: Routledge, 2013); David Downie, "The Vienna Convention, Montreal
   Protocol, and Global Policy to Protect Stratospheric Ozone," in *Chemicals, Environment, Health: A Global Management Perspective*, ed. Philip Wexler, Jan van der Kolk,
   Asish Mohapatra, and Ravi Agarwal (Boca Raton, FL: CRC Press, 2012). Other
   detailed discussions of the ozone depletion issue and the development of international
   policy include Lydia Dotto and Harold Schiff, *The Ozone War* (New York: Doubleday,
   1978); Peter Haas, "Banning Chlorofluorocarbons: Epistemic Community Efforts to
   Protect Stratospheric Ozone," *International Organization* 46, no. 1 (1992): 187–224;
   David Downie, "Comparative Public Policy of Ozone Layer Protection," *Political Sci-
   ence (NZ)* 45, no. 2 (1993): 186–197; Karen Litfin, *Ozone Discourses* (New York:
   Columbia University Press, 1994); Downie, "Road Map or False Trail"; David Downie,
   "UNEP and the Montreal Protocol," in *International Organizations and Environmental
   Policy*, ed. Robert V. Bartlett, Priva A. Kurian, and Madhu Malik (Westport, CT:
   Greenwood Press, 1995); David Downie, "Understanding International Environmen-
   tal Regimes: The Origin, Creation and Expansion of the Ozone Regime" (Ph.D. diss.,
   University of North Carolina, Chapel Hill, 1996); Richard Benedick, *Ozone Diplo-
   macy*, 2nd ed. (Cambridge, MA: Harvard University Press, 1998); David Downie,
   "The Power to Destroy: Understanding Stratospheric Ozone Politics as a Common
   Pool Resource Problem," in *Anarchy and the Environment: The International Relations
   of Common Pool Resources*, ed. J. Samuel Barkin and George Shambaugh (Albany: State
   University of New York Press, 1999); Stephen Anderson and K. Madhavea Sarma,
   Protecting the Ozone Layer: The United Nations History (London: Earthscan, 2002);
   Edward Parson, *Protecting the Ozone Layer: Science and Strategy* (Oxford: Oxford Uni-
   versity Press, 2003); Ozone Secretariat, *Montreal Protocol on Substances That Deplete
   the Ozone Layer, 2012: A Success in the Making* (Nairobi: UNEP, 2012).
9. For discussion of the impacts of ozone depletion, see United Nations Environment
   Programme, *Environmental Effects of Ozone Depletion and Its Interactions with Climate
   Change: 2010 Assessment* (Nairobi: UNEP, 2011).
10. Mario Molina and F. Sherwood Rowland started this process with their article
    "Stratospheric Sink for Chlorofluoromethanes: Chlorine Atomic Catalyzed Destruc-
    tion of Ozone," *Nature* 249 (June 28, 1974): 810–812, in which they outlined the
    threat posed by chlorofluorocarbons. Subsequent discoveries regarding other chemi-
    cals followed in the 1970s and 1980s.
11. For comprehensive discussions of the ozone layer and the impact of ozone-depleting
    substances, see World Meteorological Organization et al., *Scientific Assessment of
    Stratospheric Ozone: 2010* (Geneva: World Meteorological Organization, 2011).
12. For discussion, see Downie, "Comparative Public Policy of Ozone Layer Protection."
13. Texts of the ozone treaties, amendments, and adjustments, as well as reports from
    each Meeting of the Parties and its subsidiary bodies, are available online from the
    UNEP Ozone Secretariat, http://www.ozone.unep.org.
14. Brian J. Gareau, *From Precaution to Profit: Contemporary Challenges to Environmental
    Protection in the Montreal Protocol* (New Haven, CT: Yale University Press, 2013),
    details the development of, and strongly criticizes, the methyl bromide exemptions.

15. For information on the panels and recent reports, see United Nations Environment Programme, Ozone Secretariat, "Assessment Panels," http://ozone.unep.org/new_site/en/assessment_panels_main.php.
16. See the Multilateral Fund Web site, http://www.multilateralfund.org.
17. See ibid. for these figures and details of the history and operation of the Multilateral Fund.
18. Ozone Secretariat, "Information Provided by Parties in Accordance with Article 7 of the Montreal Protocol on Substances That Deplete the Ozone Layer," UNEP Document UNEP/OzL.Pr0.23/7, September 16, 2011.
19. World Meteorological Organization et al., *Scientific Assessment of Stratospheric Ozone*; Gloria L. Manney et al., "Unprecedented Arctic Ozone Loss in 2011," *Nature* 478 (October 27, 2011): 469–475; Andrew Freedman, "The Rare Arctic Ozone Hole and Global Warming," *Washington Post*, October 4, 2011; Brad Plumer, "Why Do We Still Have Holes in the Ozone Layer?," *Washington Post*, October 3, 2011.
20. World Meteorological Organization et al., *Scientific Assessment of Stratospheric Ozone*.
21. Ibid., executive summary.
22. Elisabeth Rosenthal and Andrew Lehren, "As Coolant Is Phased Out, Smugglers Reap Large Profits," *New York Times*, September 7, 2012.
23. For information on quarantine and preshipment applications, see Secretariats of the Montreal Protocol and International Plant Protection Convention, *Methyl Bromide: Quarantine and Preshipment Uses* (Nairobi: UNEP, 2008), http://ozone.unep.org/Publications/UNEP-Ozone-Secretariat-MP-Brochure.pdf.
24. This is the position of the author, based on discussions and observations made while attending the negotiations that produced these exemptions. Compare the discussion in Gareau, *From Precaution to Profit*, which is very critical of the development and use of the exemptions, to the discussions in Chasek et al., *Global Environmental Politics*, regarding how exemptions are used to overcome the lowest-common-denominator problem.
25. For a detailed discussion of this issue, see Gareau, *From Precaution to Profit*.
26. This section summarizes elements of a longer discussion in Chasek et al., *Global Environmental Politics*.
27. Some argue that the current structure of the international economic system—particularly global capitalist markets that emphasize consumerism, lowest-cost production, globalization, and resource extraction while largely failing to take into account the costs of environmental degradation—presents a structural impediment to effective global environmental policy. These characteristics currently, and obviously, do present serious obstacles to effective policy, but elements of the economic system could be adjusted in ways that would support global environmental policy. For example, externalities could be taxed, or corporations could be helped to speed the introduction of environmentally friendly technology.
28. Classic examples include Thucydides, Machiavelli, and Hobbes. Influential modern examples include Hans J. Morgenthau, *Politics among Nations*, 5th ed. (New York: Knopf, 1973); Robert Jervis, "Cooperation under the Security Dilemma," *World Politics* 30 (1978): 167–186; Kenneth Waltz, *Theory of International Politics* (Reading, MA: Addison-Wesley, 1979); Glenn Snyder, "The Security Dilemma in Alliance Politics," *World Politics* 36 (1984): 461–495.
29. Waltz, *Theory of International Politics*.
30. Glenn Snyder and Paul Diesing, *Conflict among Nations: Bargaining, Decision Making, and System Structure in International Crises* (Princeton, NJ: Princeton University Press, 1977); Jervis, "Cooperation under the Security Dilemma"; Kenneth A. Oye, "Explaining Cooperation under Anarchy: Hypotheses and Strategies," in *Cooperation under Anarchy*, ed. Kenneth A. Oye (Princeton, NJ: Princeton University Press, 1986), 1–22.
31. Joseph M. Grieco, "Anarchy and the Limits of Cooperation," *International Organization* 42 (Summer 1988): 485–507.
32. Mancur Olson, *The Logic of Collective Action* (Cambridge, MA: Harvard University Press, 1965).

33. Garrett Hardin, "The Tragedy of the Commons," *Science* 166 (December 13, 1968): 1103–1107; J. Samuel Barkin and George Shambaugh, eds., *Anarchy and the Environment: The International Relations of Common Pool Resources* (Albany: State University of New York Press, 1999).

34. Robert Jervis, *Perception and Misperception in International Politics* (Princeton, NJ: Princeton University Press, 1976).

35. *Report of the United Nations Conference on the Human Environment*, UN Document A/CONF.48/14, June 1972, 118. This principle later became Principle 2 of the Rio Declaration, but with the words "and developmental" inserted before "policies," thus making it even more self-contradictory.

36. David Downie and Jessica Templeton, "Pesticides and Persistent Organic Pollutants," in Harris, *Routledge Handbook of Global Environmental Politics*; David Downie and Terry Fenge, eds., *Northern Lights against POPs: Combating Toxic Threats in the Arctic* (Montreal: McGill-Queens University Press, 2003).

37. Robert O. Keohane, Peter M. Haas, and Marc A. Levy, "The Effectiveness of International Environmental Institutions," in *Institutions for the Earth: Sources of Effective International Environmental Protection*, ed. Peter M. Haas, Robert O. Keohane, and Marc A. Levy (Cambridge: MIT Press, 1993), 3–24; all quotations in this paragraph are from pp. 19–20.

38. These characteristics are not unique to environmental issues, but they are prominent in, and common to, environmental issues.

39. As with the broader categories of obstacles, the sets of characteristics represent somewhat artificial but useful heuristic divisions whose components and impacts should be seen as interrelated rather than mutually exclusive.

40. Molina and Rowland, "Stratospheric Sink for Chlorofluoromethanes." For discussion of the discovery and early debate, see Dotto and Schiff, *The Ozone War*.

41. Grieco, "Anarchy and the Limits of Cooperation."

42. Downie, "The Power to Destroy."

43. See the discussions cited in note 8 above as well as those cited below.

44. This section explicitly follows, and includes much of the same language as, a similar discussion in Downie, "Stratospheric Ozone Depletion."

45. For discussion and analysis of different aspects of this impact, see Sharon Roan, *Ozone Crisis: The 15-Year Evolution of a Sudden Global Emergency* (New York: John Wiley, 1989); Haas, "Banning Chlorofluorocarbons"; Litfin, *Ozone Discourses*; Downie, "Understanding International Environmental Regimes"; Benedick, *Ozone Diplomacy*; Penelope Canan and Nancy Reichman, *Ozone Connections: Expert Networks in Global Environmental Governance* (Sheffield, UK: Greenleaf, 2002); Anderson and Sarma, *Protecting the Ozone Layer*; Parson, *Protecting the Ozone Layer*; Downie, "Stratospheric Ozone Depletion."

46. Molina and Rowland, "Stratospheric Sink for Chlorofluoromethanes."

47. Dotto and Schiff, *The Ozone War*; Downie, "Comparative Public Policy of Ozone Layer Protection;" Downie, "UNEP and the Montreal Protocol"; Downie, "Understanding International Environmental Regimes."

48. Downie, "Understanding International Environmental Regimes"; Benedick, *Ozone Diplomacy*.

49. For an influential discussion of how exogenous shocks can affect regime development, see Oran R. Young, ed., *The Effectiveness of International Environmental Regimes: Causal Connections and Behavior Mechanisms* (Cambridge: MIT Press, 1999).

50. See, for example, Roan, *Ozone Crisis*; Downie, "Understanding International Environmental Regimes"; Benedick, *Ozone Diplomacy*.

51. Downie, "Understanding International Environmental Regimes."

52. Downie, "The Vienna Convention," 248.

53. Oye, "Explaining Cooperation under Anarchy." Oye discusses the importance of altering the payoffs but does not reference the ozone case.

54. Detlef Sprinz and Tapani Vaahtoranta, "The Interest-Based Explanation of International Environmental Policy," *International Organization* 48, no. 1 (1994): 77–105.
55. Oye, "Explaining Cooperation under Anarchy."
56. For discussion of how states come to value regimes after their creation, see Keohane, *After Hegemony.*
57. Haas, "Banning Chlorofluorocarbons."
58. See the discussions (which use somewhat different vocabularies) in Haas, "Banning Chlorofluorocarbons"; Litfin, *Ozone Discourses*; Downie, "Understanding International Environmental Regimes"; Canan and Reichman, *Ozone Connections.*
59. Downie, "Road Map or False Trail."
60. For examples of different versions of this argument, see Downie, "Comparative Public Policy of Ozone Layer Protection"; Kenneth Oye and James Maxwell, "Self-Interest and Environmental Management," *Journal of Theoretical Politics* 64 (1994): 599–630; Sprinz and Vaahtoranta, "Interest-Based Explanation of International Environmental Policy"; Downie, "Understanding International Environmental Regimes"; Robert Falkner, "The Business of Ozone Layer Protection: Corporate Power in Regime Evolution," in *The Business of Global Environmental Governance,* ed. David Levy and Peter Newell (Cambridge: MIT Press, 2005); Downie, "The Vienna Convention"; Gareau, *From Precaution to Profit.*
61. See, for example, Dotto and Schiff, *The Ozone War*; Roan, *Ozone Crisis*; Downie, "Comparative Public Policy of Ozone Layer Protection"; Downie, "Understanding International Environmental Regimes."
62. Gareau, *From Precaution to Profit.*
63. See, for example, Roan, *Ozone Crisis*; Downie, "Understanding International Environmental Regimes"; Benedick, *Ozone Diplomacy*; Elizabeth Cook, *Marking a Milestone in Ozone Protection: Learning from the CFC Phase-out* (Washington, DC: World Resources Institute, January 1996); Falkner, "The Business of Ozone Layer Protection."
64. See, for example, Downie, "Comparative Public Policy of Ozone Layer Protection"; Oye and Maxwell, "Self-Interest and Environmental Management"; Downie, "Understanding International Environmental Regimes"; Falkner, "The Business of Ozone Layer Protection."
65. Author's personal observations and conversations during the relevant global ozone negotiations.
66. Downie, "The Vienna Convention," 248.
67. Downie, "Understanding International Environmental Regimes."
68. See, for example, Keohane, *After Hegemony.*
69. Downie, "UNEP and the Montreal Protocol."
70. Ibid.
71. Ibid.; Benedick, *Ozone Diplomacy.*
72. United Nations Environment Programme, *Global Environment Outlook 5* (Nairobi: UNEP, 2012).
73. Ronald Mitchell, "Regime Design Matters: International Oil Pollution and Treaty Compliance," *International Organization* 48, no. 3 (1994): 425–458.

5

Compliance with Global Environmental Policy

Climate Change and Ozone Layer Cases

Michael G. Faure and Jürgen Lefevere

The United Nations Conference on the Human Environment, held in Stockholm in 1972, set off an unprecedented development of new international environmental treaties. Before 1972 only a dozen international treaties with relevance to the environment were in force; four decades later more than a thousand such instruments can be counted.

As the use of international treaties as a means to combat environmental degradation has increased, so have concerns regarding the compliance of states with the commitments to which they have agreed. Implementation and effectiveness of international environmental treaties, and compliance with their requirements, remain central issues and will continue to increase in importance as the complexity and strength of commitments grow in the face of the tremendous environmental challenges that remain.

In recent decades international actors have tried new approaches to drafting, implementation, and enforcement in an attempt to improve compliance with international environmental treaties. This activity has been mirrored by advances in the scholarly study of factors that affect state compliance and increased discussion of such factors in both academic and policy-making circles.

This chapter examines the theory and practice of national compliance with international environmental treaties. In doing so, it uses as primary examples the United Nations Framework Convention on Climate Change (FCCC) and its Kyoto Protocol, the European Union environmental regime, and the Montreal Protocol on Substances That Deplete the Ozone Layer (see also Chapters 4, 7, and 10). We begin by discussing the theory of compliance as it has been developed both in the academic literature and in practice.[1] We then provide an overview of sources for compliance and noncompliance. Finally, we examine methods developed to date that seek to improve compliance with international environmental treaties.

Theory of Compliance

The term *compliance* is often used inconsistently and confused with related terminology such as *implementation, effectiveness,* and even *enforcement.* To avoid unnecessary confusion, one should be careful in using these terms. They refer to different aspects of the process of achieving international political and legal cooperation.

Implementation refers to the specific actions (including legislative, organizational, and practical actions) that international actors and states take to make international treaties operative in their national legal systems. Implementation by relevant international actors includes, for instance, the provision of financial resources by the Global Environment Facility (GEF) in accordance with the rules adopted under the FCCC. Implementation by states establishes the link between the national legal system and the international obligations. The aim of establishing this link should be compliance.

Compliance is generally defined as the extent to which the behavior of a state—party to an international treaty—actually conforms to the conditions set out in the treaty. Some authors make a distinction between compliance with the treaty's explicit rules and compliance with the treaty's objective.[2] It is, however, often difficult to assess compliance with the "spirit" of an agreement, since this evaluation can be subjective. The third term, *enforcement,* indicates the methods that are available to force states not only to implement but also to comply with treaty obligations. Whereas compliance and implementation concern the actions of the states themselves, *effectiveness,* as the term indicates, is more concerned with the effects of the treaty as a whole. *Effectiveness* addresses the question of whether a treaty that is correctly complied with actually achieves its stated objectives, or whether the treaty actually helped to reach the environmental goal for which it was designed.

The terms *compliance* and *effectiveness* are often used interchangeably but, in fact, have very distinct meanings. Compliance is in most cases a condition for effectiveness, if by effectiveness we mean the reaching of the treaty's goals. If a treaty is complied with, however, this does not automatically signify that it is effective in reaching the environmental goal for which it was originally designed. Effectiveness also depends on the actual treaty design, the instruments and goals contained in the treaty, as well as other external factors, such as changing political situations or even changing environmental conditions. The Kyoto Protocol is an example: even if it now looks likely that most countries will comply with its targets, it is still insufficient to stop dangerous climate change from occurring. Hence, compliance is only a proxy for effectiveness; greater compliance will usually lead to environmental improvement, but whether this is actually the case will to a large extent depend on the contents of the treaty. One could imagine a treaty that is so badly drafted that noncompliance would even contribute to its effectiveness. For instance, this ironic result could be reached in a treaty that on paper protects the environment (or potential victims) but that, in fact, protects industrial operators, for example, by introducing financial caps on their liability and thus enabling them to continue their activities. One could argue that potential victims would be better off with noncompliance, but this is obviously true only in cases where special interests (not primarily environmental concerns) dictated the contents of the treaty.

We will concentrate here on the issue of compliance as a requirement for an effective treaty. This issue has received increasing attention in scholarly writing and in practice since the mid-1990s. This growing attention has led to the development of a new approach to the compliance issue. The traditional view of compliance was very much connected to the principle of sovereignty of states. According to this principle, states are sovereign actors in the international arena, meaning that they are free to act as they find necessary, unrestricted by any external authority or rules. Based on this principle, one tended to believe that governments therefore accepted only those international treaties that were in their own interest. A breach of these treaties was thus seen as unlikely. If a state was in breach of its treaty obligations, this was usually considered to be intentional. Enforcement measures were thus often limited and were regarded as severe actions. Examples of these enforcement measures are procedures through which states can file an official complaint against the violating state or impose trade sanctions on the state. Because of the gravity of these sanctions, however, they are rarely applied in practice. Even in the European context, direct complaints of one state against another are still highly exceptional.[3]

Toward the end of the 1990s, the traditional view of compliance problems was increasingly criticized in scholarly writings,[4] criticism that goes hand in hand with the new approach to sovereignty. Some argue that states should no longer be seen as completely sovereign entities but as willing to accept limits on their original sovereign rights for the benefit of the environment, future generations, or the international community as a whole.[5] The international community is increasingly organized in *regimes*.[6] These regimes consist of frameworks with relatively well-developed sets of rules and norms concerning specific subjects. The development of regimes can be placed between the traditional concept of sovereignty, leaving the states unbound, and a comprehensive world order, placing the states within a new world governance. Examples of important regimes are the climate change regime, constructed around the FCCC and its Kyoto Protocol, and the international trade regime, based on the agreements concluded under the World Trade Organization (WTO). With the development of these regimes, "sovereignty no longer consists in the freedom of states to act independently, in their perceived self-interest, but in membership in reasonably good standing in the regimes that make up the substance of international life."[7] States' interests are increasingly determined by their membership in, as well as good reputation under, these regimes.[8]

The new approach tries to place compliance problems in this increasingly complicated international context, with a multitude of regimes, interdependent actors, and different interests and obligations. Within this new context many factors can lead countries to conclude treaties. These factors also affect the states' willingness and, more important, ability to comply with the obligations. In this more complex perception of compliance, the actors at the international level can no longer be seen as utilitarian decision makers weighing the benefits and costs of compliance.[9] The compliance record of states is influenced by a large number of factors, in which the willful desire to violate rules plays only a minor role. Often it is practical obstacles, outside the direct will or control of states, that make compliance difficult.

This new concept of compliance also necessitates new solutions to problems. The traditional sanction mechanisms, based on the notion that states intentionally do not comply, have proven largely ineffective. Moreover, some of these are now often unlawful under other international arrangements. The use of military action is strictly regulated under international law, although states obviously observe such regulations unevenly, and force is now allowed in a legal sense in a limited number of situations. Certainly, military action is not seen as a legally appropriate or practical method of seeking compliance with environmental treaties.[10] Economic sanctions have become more difficult to apply since the development of an increasingly comprehensive international trade regime and a rapidly growing number of bilateral trade agreements. It is now necessary to take into account the actual abilities of states to comply, and sanctions for noncompliance need to be developed that fit within the new international regimes. Solutions for compliance problems need to be based more on what is referred to as a "managerial approach" rather than on a more traditional "enforcement approach."[11]

Sources of Compliance and Noncompliance

This section addresses the various factors that may affect compliance with environmental agreements and possible sources of noncompliance. Guzman mentions three factors that can increase the costs of violations and thus promote compliance: reputation, reciprocal noncompliance, and retaliation. Cooperative outcomes can thus be enhanced by increases in the costs of these factors.[12]

Regime Rules

The regime rules are the actual contents of the treaty that the parties have signed. These rules define the behavior that is required of the participating states under the terms of the treaty. The regime rules are directly related to the activity that the environmental accord is supposed to regulate. Even during the negotiations, when the primary rules are defined, the degree of treaty compliance can to a large extent be determined.

A first important aspect of the design of the regime rule system relates to whether it requires any behavioral change and, if so, what the costs of this change will be and by whom this behavioral change is required. It is easier to achieve compliance if the degree of behavioral change and the costs of this change are low. It has therefore been argued, for instance, that it might be harder to achieve compliance with the Kyoto Protocol than with the Montreal Protocol, since more people and industries must make bigger behavioral changes to comply with the former. The Montreal Protocol mainly requires behavioral changes by the producers and corporate users of a limited number of very important but replaceable chemicals. The greenhouse gas emission reduction targets in the Kyoto Protocol, in contrast, require larger-scale behavioral changes, not only by industry but also by individuals, particularly with respect to the production and consumption of energy.[13]

In a number of cases treaty rules require no change in behavior of the industry in a specific country. This is often the case when industries are already meeting specific pollution standards (for example, emissions). Those industries may even lobby in favor of treaties that will impose on their foreign competitors the standards that domestic industries already have to comply with at the national level.[14] In those cases the industries already meeting the specific standard will obviously readily comply, since the treaty merely erects a barrier to entry for the foreign competitors.

In some cases the treaties are clearly in the interest of industry for other reasons. One example is the treaties relating to liability for nuclear accidents and oil pollution. On paper these treaties serve the interests of victims, but, in fact, the contents are often such that the liability of operators is limited (for example, through financial caps). The nuclear liability conventions that originated in the late 1950s came into being as a reaction to the growing nuclear industry's fear of unlimited liability. Hence, compliance with the conventions, which included limited liability of nuclear operators, was relatively high.[15]

The amount of detail or specificity in a treaty may affect future compliance. States can facilitate their own compliance by negotiating vague and ambiguous rules. Examples include agreeing to provisions that on paper seem to be in the environmental interest but are sufficiently vague to allow business as usual. However, primary rules can often increase compliance through greater specificity. Specific obligations make compliance easier by reducing the uncertainty about what states need to do to comply. Specific treaty language will also remove the possibility of the excuse of inadvertence and misinterpretation in case of noncompliance. Moreover, the advantage of conventions with relatively precise obligations (such as the Montreal Protocol) is that it is easier to judge whether states do, in fact, comply. If the obligations are vague, assessing implementation and compliance becomes more difficult.

One obvious remedy for inadvertence as a source of noncompliance is, therefore, to draft specific, detailed obligations. These, together with an information campaign, can at least prevent states from justifying noncompliance on the basis of a lack of information or clarity with respect to their obligations. A general formulation of the obligations may, however, be unavoidable in some cases simply because political consensus may not support more precision. Article 4(2)(a) of the FCCC is an example of diplomatically formulated "obligations." The article leaves unclear whether there is any specific obligation at all.[16]

One source of noncompliance may be the incapacity of states to fulfill the treaty obligations owing to a lack of resources or technological abilities. When these problems are recognized during the drafting stage, noncompliance may be prevented if the primary rules are designed in such a manner that the differing capacities of states are taken into account. Treaty obligations can be differentiated based on the varying capacities of states, or resources or technologies can be transferred. This is, again, an example of a managerial approach; instead of blunt sanctions, instruments are developed in the treaty design stage that take into account the varying capacities of states and thus help to prevent noncompliance.

The idea of differentiated standards according to states' capacities is predominant in the FCCC and its Kyoto Protocol. This treaty regime places its signatory states in different categories and imposes different obligations for each group. All signatory states commit themselves to the general obligations, such as developing national greenhouse gas inventories (albeit with different frequency) and national programs containing measures to mitigate climate change (for example, Article 4[1][a] and [b] of the FCCC). Under the FCCC, only the developed states and states in transition that are listed in Annex I of the FCCC are required to stabilize their carbon dioxide emissions. Under the Kyoto Protocol, only the developed states and states in transition that are listed in Annex B of the protocol are required to limit their greenhouse gas emissions in accordance with the targets contained in that annex. Annex II of the FCCC lists the developed countries that additionally need to provide financial resources to facilitate compliance by developing countries.[17] Although the issue of differentiation, and in particular its scope, is increasingly coming under pressure in the multilateral climate negotiations, discussions on the availability of sufficient "means of implementation" (consisting of financial, technological, and capacity-building assistance) continue to play a central role in those negotiations under the FCCC.[18] The transfer of funds from developed to developing states can also be observed in other treaties. The Montreal Protocol, for instance, provides a framework within which financial support as well as technical assistance are provided. The European Union uses the instrument of structural funds to promote economic and social development of disadvantaged regions within the EU.

A new concept in the area of climate change that also takes into account differing abilities of states is the use of "flexible" or "market-based" mechanisms. These mechanisms allow developed countries to meet their emission limitation targets through buying "emission rights" from countries in which the marginal costs of emission reduction are lower, thus reducing the costs of compliance. The Kyoto Protocol's mechanisms are Joint Implementation (JI), the Clean Development Mechanism (CDM), and International Emissions Trading (IET). The CDM is the most interesting of these mechanisms: it allows developed countries to invest in emission reduction projects in a developing country and in return receive emission rights that they can use to comply with their emission limitation obligations. A well-implemented CDM project can thus help to provide financial aid and technologies to developing countries and hence also help remedy capacity problems, in addition to reducing the compliance costs of the developed country purchasing those emission rights.[19]

The only problem with these various inducements is that they are vulnerable to "moral hazard." That is, incentives for the prevention of emissions may be diluted if states are subsidized through financial or technological transfers.

States may indeed misrepresent their abilities in order to have others pay for their compliance costs. A clear example is the crediting of the destruction of hydrofluorocarbon-23 (HFC-23), a greenhouse gas that is 11,700 times more powerful than carbon dioxide emissions, in the production of hydrochloro-fluorocarbon-22 (HCFC-22), an ozone-depleting substance regulated under the Montreal Protocol, under the Kyoto Protocol's CDM. During the first few years of the operation of the CDM the revenue of the sale of CDM credits for the destruction of HFC-23 by far surpassed the revenue of the sale of the actual product (HCFC-22), leading to a situation in which producers continued the production of HCFC-22 with the main purpose of obtaining CDM credits, not only undermining the effectiveness of the Kyoto Protocol but also delaying the phasing out of HCFC-22 under the Montreal Proto-col.[20] This, in turn, led to a ban on the use of those credits under domestic greenhouse gas emissions trading systems in the EU and a number of other countries. The lessons from this example are clear: any incentive system should explicitly build in safeguards against moral hazard.

The approach of using differentiated standards and financial and techno-logical transfers is the basis of the more comprehensive noncompliance response systems that we discuss below (see Box 5-1 for a discussion of the Montreal Protocol as an example of the managerial approach).

Box 5-1   The Montreal Protocol as a "Managerial" Primary Rule System

The approach to international environmental treaty design has changed in the past decades, mainly because of the new, more realistic "managerial" approach. Prime examples of this new approach are the Vienna Convention for the Protection of the Ozone Layer and, more important, its subsequent Montreal Protocol on Substances That Deplete the Ozone Layer, adopted under this convention.

The Vienna Convention was adopted in 1985. It did not contain substantive commitments for the states but provided for a general framework, including the possibility of adopting protocols in the Conference of the Parties, the main institution set up under the convention. Only two years after the adoption of the convention, the 1987 Montreal Protocol on Substances That Deplete the Ozone Layer was adopted. The Vienna Convention and, more particularly, its Montreal Protocol surprised the international community with their swift adoption, their specific goals, their effectiveness, and the large number of states that have become parties to them (196 countries and the EU had ratified both the Vienna Convention and the Montreal Protocol as of January 2012, making them the first UN treaties to achieve universal ratification). One of the main reasons given for this effectiveness is the design of the treaty system, which has several "modern" characteristics that make it very suitable for dealing with environmental problems in the current international context. In many of the more recent international environmental treaties the Vienna-Montreal system is used as a model, largely because of the flexibility of its primary rule system.

The Vienna Convention establishes the Conference of the Parties (Article 6), which is to meet "at regular intervals," in practice every three years. The Montreal Protocol adds a Meeting of the Parties. Montreal Protocol meetings are now held annually to discuss implementation of the commitments and possible improvements to or adoption of new commitments. They are organized by the Ozone Secretariat, set up under Article 7 of the Vienna Convention and Article 12 of the Montreal Protocol. The regular convening of the Meeting of the Parties has proven very useful in keeping the treaty objectives on the political agenda and has ensured a continuous updating of its goals and standards. This updating was made possible by the framework structure chosen by the Vienna Convention. Although not a new structure (it was also used in the 1979 UNECE Convention on Long-Range Transboundary Air Pollution), it has been particularly effective. Whereas the Vienna Convention does no more than establish the framework for further negotiations, the real commitments are laid down in the Montreal Protocol—the first and, to date, only protocol adopted under this convention. The provisions of the Montreal Protocol are regularly updated by means of amendments. During the two decades of its existence, the Montreal Protocol has seen a total of six "adjustments" regarding the production and consumption of the controlled substances listed in the annexes of the protocol as well as four amendments. This shows how compliance is likely to be influenced in the treaty design stage by the creation of a primary rule system that can develop over time, responding to evolving science and the capacity to deal with environmental problems.

The Montreal Protocol also provides an example of how the individual capacities of states may determine their willingness to accept treaty obligations in the first place. India and China would not become parties to the Montreal Protocol until the agreement about compensatory financing had been adopted at the London meeting in 1990. This agreement provided for financial support to developing states in order to allow them to become parties to the protocol and be financially capable of complying with its obligations.

Under the Montreal Protocol, various instruments have been developed to remedy financial incapacity. The Multilateral Fund was set up (Article 10) to provide financial assistance. The Fund's four implementing agencies—the World Bank, the United Nations Environment Programme (UNEP), the United Nations Development Programme (UNDP), and the United Nations Industrial Development Organization (UNIDO)—have drawn up country programs and country studies that offer financial support, assistance, and training. Furthermore, the Montreal Protocol provides for the transfer of technology under its Article 10A. On the basis of this article, all states party to the protocol "shall take every practicable step" to ensure that "the best available, environmentally safe substitutes and related technologies are expeditiously transferred" to developing countries (as defined in Article 5[1] of the protocol) and that those transfers "occur under fair and most favourable conditions."

With universal participation of nations and robust support from industry, the ozone regime has reduced worldwide use of ozone-depleting chemicals by more than 97 percent, and use is still falling. The ozone regime is therefore considered the first realization of a managerial approach, using policies and institutions that promote learning about the systems being managed and that adapt in response to what is learned for any global environmental issue.

Reporting and Information

The likelihood of compliance also depends on informational issues (see also Chapter 4). Information plays an important role at several stages. First, accurate information on the environmental risks increases the chances of the adoption of a treaty on the specific subject and also the likelihood of compliance. Second, information, through monitoring or reporting systems, serves to increase the transparency of the implementation and compliance records of states.

With regard to the first factor, it is broadly assumed that the more information there is about an environmental issue, the more effective implementation and compliance will be.[21] This understanding is rather straightforward: the clearer the presentation of the activities and risks that are the subject of the treaty, the easier it will be to build political pressure (through, among others, nongovernmental organizations, or NGOs) via public opinion to induce compliance. One of the reasons that the swift adoption of the Montreal Protocol came as a surprise to the international community was that it occurred in a time of still-important scientific uncertainties about the causes and effects of the changes in the ozone layer.[22] The scientific reports of the Intergovernmental Panel on Climate Change (IPCC) play an important role in forming international consensus about the science of climate change as the basis for the international climate negotiations.[23]

With regard to the second factor, information increases the transparency of the implementation and compliance records of states. If it is known that a state does not comply, international and domestic groups can take actions aimed at improving the state's compliance. Transparency with respect to the compliance record will to a large extent depend on the complexity of the issue covered by the treaty as well as the democratic character of the complying state. Transparency can lead to public pressure to increase compliance. In this respect, one can cite the actions of NGOs to identify noncompliance, thereby giving incentives for compliance without a need for formal sanctions. Transparency is considered an almost universal element of compliance management strategy. Indeed, transparency in the form of "naming and shaming" is increasingly being used as a sanction for noncompliance, building on the desire of states and companies to satisfy an environmentally aware electorate, consumers, and shareholders.[24]

Transparency can be achieved through an effective compliance information system that is laid down in the treaty. To a large extent, treaties rely on self-reporting by states. As noted above, in a regime system with sometimes delicate political links and pressures, the status of a state is often very important. States are generally careful about losing face with other states and their own population. Many treaties, including those outside the environmental field, have used this fear of losing face to their advantage by imposing a requirement that each state report on its compliance with the treaty. This reporting allows other states and citizens to hold a state accountable for its compliance record. Although reporting procedures can be found in most environmental treaties, they are often vaguely formulated, and many of the reports are poorly drafted. Hence, the reporting procedure is often criticized for its "weak" character and the absence of sanctions in case of noncompliance with the reporting requirements.

Self-reporting is also criticized because it may lead to self-incrimination. If states take this duty seriously, they should report their own noncompliance. The hesitancy of states to incriminate themselves may be one of the reasons the reporting requirements of environmental treaties are violated. Moreover, governments, particularly of smaller states, are sometimes overburdened with administrative tasks, and filing reports is seen as yet another burden. Reporting can also be difficult for developing countries, which often lack both financial resources and the capacity to comply with detailed reporting obligations. Reporting by states is, therefore, a first step, but obviously no guarantee of compliance.[25]

The likelihood of compliance will to a large extent be influenced by the treaty's provisions for effective monitoring. This in turn depends on the contents of the primary rules. The Montreal Protocol, for instance, regulated the production rather than the consumption of chlorofluorocarbons (CFCs) because it is easier to monitor a few producers than thousands of consumers. Some treaties, such as those on nuclear weapons, allow on-site monitoring. This obviously is one of the most effective instruments to control whether states not only formally adopt legislation implementing a treaty but also comply with the contents. On-site monitoring is, however, still heavily debated because it constitutes an important infringement on state sovereignty.[26] Even in the EU there is no on-site monitoring by a European authority of member state violations of environmental directives.[27]

The compliance record will inevitably depend on the ability to monitor violations. This brought Gro Harlem Brundtland, the former Norwegian prime minister and chair of the World Commission on Environment and Development, to recommend the establishment of "an international authority with the power to verify actual emissions and to react with legal measures if there are violations of the rules" in order to ensure compliance with carbon dioxide emission targets.[28]

The problems with reporting procedures have led to the development of *compliance information systems*.[29] These systems include elaborate procedures for the provision of information by member states, the possible review of this information by independent experts, and the availability of this information to the general public. The development of a more elaborate and transparent system for the provision of information on the compliance of member states automatically increases those states' accountability.

For example, both the FCCC and its Kyoto Protocol contain extensive reporting requirements, including emission inventory reports and national communications setting out broader efforts of countries to implement their commitments. Developed country inventory reports (submitted annually) and national communications (submitted every four to five years) are subject to review by "expert review teams." These teams consist of experts from third countries, and their work is coordinated and supported by the FCCC Secretariat, which also arranges their training and selection from a roster of experts. Most reviews are done during central team meetings at the FCCC Secretariat in Bonn, but every five years a party is subject to an in-country review. The task of these expert review teams is to review the report and prepare a technical assessment of the implementation of the FCCC by the developed country, which is reflected in a review report prepared under the collective responsibility of the team. A draft of the team's report is provided to each party for review and comments before it is finalized and placed on the FCCC Web site. Under the Kyoto Protocol, an expert review team can also raise "questions of implementation." These questions are then automatically put to the Kyoto Protocol's Compliance Committee. Interestingly, one of the main achievements of the review process is not only the improvement of the quality of reports but also the building of the capacity of experts, including from developing countries, participating in the review process. As these experts are usually involved in preparing the reports for their own countries, their exposure to the reporting systems and understanding of the reporting guidelines are extremely valuable.

At the Cancun climate conference in 2010, it was agreed to strengthen the reporting system under the FCCC by means of biennial reports to be submitted by all parties. This agreement provided an important reinforcement of the transparency procedures under the FCCC by also requiring developing countries to provide such reports on a fixed schedule (timing of earlier reports was indicative only) and by subjecting those reports to a process of international consultation and analysis. This process, which will first be applied to developing country reports submitted at the end of 2014, consists of a technical analysis by a team of experts in consultation with the party concerned and a facilitative sharing of views among all parties in one of the FCCC's subsidiary bodies.[30]

The increased attention to information systems and reporting procedures is part of the transformation from an enforcement approach to a managerial approach to compliance. Traditionally, the incentives for states to report their own noncompliance were low because such admissions could lead only to "bad news," such as the imposition of sanctions. The situation totally changes, however, when noncompliance is not necessarily considered the intentional act of a sovereign state but rather the result, for example, of incapacity. In that case, a state's reporting a noncompliance problem may lead other partners in the regime to look for remedies to overcome the difficulty, such as through a transfer of finances or technology. In this managerial approach, reporting noncompliance should not be threatening; in fact, it may well be in the state's interest. The desired result of this new approach is that in the end a higher compliance record is achieved than with traditional enforcement methods. Thus the reporting of noncompliance under the Montreal Protocol leads the Implementation Committee to investigate the possibilities of financial and technical assistance instead of threatening the noncompliant state with sanctions.

Country Characteristics

The characteristics of the parties involved in negotiating and adopting international environmental treaties—that is, the states concerned—will have an impact on the likelihood of treaty adoption; in addition, they will have considerable influence on the probability of compliance.

There may be many reasons states ratify treaties but nevertheless do not comply. A state may ratify an agreement because of international pressure or to serve domestic interests. Domestic interests, however, may also oppose compliance. Hence, it may well be in the state's interest to ratify the agreement but not comply. Moreover, compliance with international environmental agreements is seldom a black-or-white situation: states may view most provisions of a treaty as being in their interest, and they may comply with those provisions but violate a few others.

Other factors that may play a role include the cultural traditions, political system, administrative capacities, and economic factors of the country concerned. Compliance may also be influenced by the strength of NGOs, an issue that will be discussed below.

An important factor is whether a country has a democratic form of government. Many features of democratic governments contribute to improved implementation and compliance. There may be more transparency and hence easier monitoring by citizens who can exert pressure to improve the implementation record. Also, NGOs generally have more freedom to operate in democratic countries. There have also been cases, however, in which a country's democratic institutions have prevented the implementation of necessary measures to enable the country to comply with its internationally agreed obligations—the issue of climate change being a case in point. A considerable role can also be played by individuals, such as the heads of state. In many cases the personal enthusiasm of a particular head of state has facilitated compliance, including through promoting the adoption of domestic legislation that enabled a country to comply with its obligations.[31]

As indicated above, compliance may also fail because of incapacity. This could be due to the country's lack of administrative capacity to implement the treaty, which in turn may have to do with, for example, the level of education and training of the country's bureaucrats. The level of administrative capacity also depends on economic resources. In addition, compliance with treaties sometimes requires investment in technologies that countries with fewer resources simply lack.

Number of States and the International Environment

The greater the number of countries that have ratified an accord, and the greater the extent of their implementation and compliance, the greater the probability of compliance by any individual country, because noncompliance would run counter to the international public opinion.[32] There is also a relationship between the area to be regulated in the environmental treaty and the number of countries that can be expected to comply. For example, the International Whaling Commission faces a trade-off between, on one hand, maintaining a moratorium on commercial whaling in a treaty that fewer countries have been willing to sign and, on the other hand, allowing some commercial whaling in order to keep a larger number of countries within the scope of the treaty and thus achieve a higher compliance record.[33] Conversely, the agreement to a second commitment period under the Kyoto Protocol at the UN climate conference at the end of 2012 was possible only because of its limited coverage, setting binding emission reduction targets for the European Union, Norway, Switzerland, Monaco, and Liechtenstein, and Australia as the only non-European country. Treaty making thus often requires a trade-off between the coverage of a treaty and the strength of the standards set in the treaty—where the effectiveness of the treaty will be determined by the interplay between the two.

The general "international environment" will have an influence on the willingness of a country to engage in the treaty obligations and on the subsequent compliance record as well. This can be analyzed in terms of the problems of free riding and the "prisoner's dilemma."[34] Individual states may hope that others will take the necessary measures to reduce the sources of, for example, a transboundary pollution problem, and thus free ride on those other states' efforts. The game-theoretical concept of the prisoner's dilemma in this context refers to the fact that although mutual compliance may be in the interest of all states (in order, for example, to reduce transboundary industrial pollution), the absence of enforcement may lead all parties to believe that they can violate their obligations. Because of these problems, enforcement was traditionally advocated as a way to guarantee compliance.

Compliance also depends on the distribution of power among nations, which can influence individual states' compliance strategies. A dominant state, perceiving sufficient benefits from complying, may force compliance by other, weaker states.[35] In those cases compliance does not even require explicit enforcement. Obviously, the division of power between states may change, which will also produce changes in the incentives to comply.[36]

States sign numerous international treaties. Negotiations on treaties and compliance often involve situations in which states encounter each other repeatedly in the context of various treaties (often referred to as "repeat-player games"). Such multiple encounters may have a beneficial influence on compliance. Thus the fear of free riding can be overcome if the record of compliance is related to potential benefits for states in existing and future international agreements.[37] In other words, states may comply because future agreements with the same partner states will be possible if they have an acceptable compliance record. An important issue, often stressed in the work of Andrew Guzman, is that when the reputation of states is at stake, this may also induce them toward compliance.[38]

This international environment perspective underscores the point made in the section above on the theory of compliance: states increasingly belong to various regimes that engage them in a repeat-player game. Hence, the incentives to comply may emerge from these regimes, reducing the need for formal enforcement of one particular treaty.[39]

Role of NGOs

NGO activity can beneficially influence the compliance record of a country in various ways (see Chapter 2).[40] International environmental NGOs may influence the international public opinion, shaping the agenda that determines the issues to be dealt with in a treaty. For instance, the number of NGO participants at UN climate meetings usually far exceeds the number of official party delegates.[41] Activities of those environmental NGOs, including through targeted lobbying, media reports, and demonstrations, but also through direct support provided to negotiators, often play an important role in those negotiations and help to determine their outcomes. Once a treaty has come into being, NGOs can play a crucial role in ensuring compliance. As watchdogs, they can pressure their governments to uphold the key provisions of specific regimes. This so-called bottom-up approach to compliance is increasingly stressed in the literature.[42] The role of NGOs here also illustrates that their actions can lead to what is referred to as "compliance as self-interest," or at least not treaty-induced compliance. Through pressure by environmental groups, public opinion may be influenced in such a manner that a country views the costs of a potential violation of treaty provisions as prohibitively high.[43]

Finally, NGOs can also provide information about activities that are addressed in international environmental treaties. Greenpeace, for instance, is an important source of information about ocean dumping, and the Washington-based World Resources Institute (WRI) has regularly provided independent overviews of the extent to which developed countries have fulfilled their financial pledges under the FCCC.[44] Hence, NGO activity may foster transparency both at the negotiation stage and at the implementation and compliance stages.

These factors generally merit the conclusion that stronger and more active NGOs help increase the probability of compliance. This is in line with recent empirical evidence showing that the presence of NGOs generally increases environmental quality.[45]

Responses to Noncompliance

As we have discussed, in the past treaty mechanisms for noncompliance were traditionally restricted to adversarial dispute settlement procedures. These procedures, used generally under international environmental law, mostly involve sequences of diplomatic and legal means of dispute settlement. Diplomatic procedures for settling disputes usually involve negotiation and consultation in a first instance. If negotiation and consultation do not lead to a solution, some form of mediation or conciliation is often prescribed. This involves third parties or international institutions. In cases of deeper conflicts, parties often have recourse to legal means of dispute settlement, either arbitration or the International Court of Justice.

This standard sequence of dispute resolution—negotiation, mediation, and finally arbitration or submission to the International Court of Justice—can still be found in more recent treaties, such as the Vienna Convention for the Protection of the Ozone Layer and the FCCC. Article 11 of the Vienna Convention prescribes negotiation as the first means of dispute resolution (paragraph 1). If this fails, parties must seek mediation by a third party (paragraph 2). As an ultimate remedy, arbitration or submission to the International Court of Justice—or, in absence of agreement over this remedy, a conciliation committee—is prescribed (paragraphs 3–5). Article 14 of the FCCC and Article 19 of the Kyoto Protocol contain similar wording.

The number of cases brought under dispute settlement proceedings is still very limited, especially considering the compliance problems with most environmental treaties. The International Court of Justice has so far never dealt with a purely environmental conflict.[46] Conflicts under dispute settlement proceedings mostly involve either trade relationships or territorial disputes. One of the reasons for the limited use of dispute settlement instruments is that these procedures are characterized by an adversarial relationship between the parties, so they are used only as a last resort. States are rarely willing to risk their relationships with other sovereign international actors by openly challenging them. As noted above, even in a close community of states such as the EU, the state complaints procedure under Article 259 of the Treaty on the Functioning of the European Union has rarely been used. Not only are traditional dispute settlement procedures rarely used, but they are also considered less effective and less appropriate in environmental treaties. The result of noncompliance with environmental treaties is often damage to the global commons in general, affecting all states rather than one or several well-identified parties.

The ineffectiveness of dispute settlement proceedings in international environmental agreements has led to the development of a new system for responding to noncompliance known as noncompliance procedures (NCPs). Such procedures, rather than punishing noncompliance, are aimed at finding ways to facilitate compliance by the state that is in breach of its obligations. They provide a political framework for "amicable" responses to noncompliance that cannot be considered "wrongful." This tendency to use NCPs reflects the new managerial approach, which does not assume that noncompliance is the result of a willful desire to violate.

One of the consequences of shifting from an adversarial approach to a more managerial approach is that sanctions play only a minor role in the noncompliance response system. Three categories of sanctions can be distinguished: treaty-based sanctions, membership sanctions, and unilateral sanctions.[47] The last of these, the category of unilateral sanctions, is now severely restricted under international law. As discussed above, resort to the use of military force is exceptional. Trade sanctions are increasingly difficult to invoke under the rapidly developing international trade regimes. Treaty-based

sanctions have not proven very popular, which can be explained by the political difficulties involved in the use of such a system. The European Union is,
however, an exception to this. Since November 1993, the European Commission (which supervises the application of EU law) has had the competence to
ask for the imposition of a financial penalty on any member state that is in
breach of its obligations (Article 260 of the Treaty on the Functioning of the
European Union). After a slow start, the European Court of Justice has now
imposed financial penalties for noncompliance with EU law in an increasing
number of situations, making it the "sharp end" of the EU's enforcement
procedures.[48] This also has an important preventive effect, as member states
now remedy their violations before the final court decisions are handed
down.

Sanctions against states party to an international treaty, including expulsion
or suspension of rights and privileges, are also not considered to be effective
responses in the case of noncompliance with an environmental treaty, since
one of the aims of these treaties is to achieve global membership. (See Box 5-2
for discussion of noncompliance procedures.)

Box 5-2   Noncompliance Procedures: The Montreal Protocol and the Kyoto Protocol

The more recent environmental treaties have new NCPs, often side by side with
traditional dispute settlement procedures. A prime example of a well-functioning
noncompliance procedure is the one set up under Article 8 of the Montreal Protocol.
This article states that the parties to the protocol "shall consider and approve
procedures and institutional mechanisms for determining noncompliance with the
provisions of this Protocol and for treatment of Parties found to be in noncompliance."

At the Copenhagen meeting in November 1992, the Meeting of the Parties
adopted the procedure under this article. The Implementation Committee was set up,
consisting of ten representatives elected by the Meeting of the Parties, based on
equitable geographic distribution. Although under the NCP a party can also submit
reservations regarding another party's implementation of its obligations under the
protocol, this adversarial action has in practice not become the main function of the
procedure. The focus has instead been on the nonadversarial functions. The procedure
allows states, when they believe they are unable to comply with their obligations, to
report this inability to the Secretariat and the Implementation Committee. The
Implementation Committee also discusses the general quality and reliability of the
data contained in the member states' reports. The Implementation Committee has,
in fact, assumed a very active role in improving the quality and reliability of the data
reported by the member states and, in a cooperative sphere, has sought solutions for
parties with administrative, structural, and financial difficulties, in close cooperation
with the Multilateral Fund set up under the Montreal Protocol and its implementing
agencies to provide assistance to facilitate compliance.

(Continued)

(Continued)

The NCP under the Montreal Protocol has served as an important source of inspiration for the development of the compliance regime under the Kyoto Protocol. This regime, which was finalized at the FCCC meeting in Marrakesh in 2001 (COP-7) and started its operation following its formal adoption after the entry into force of the Kyoto Protocol at the FCCC meeting in Montreal in December 2005, has both a facilitative and an enforcement branch. The enforcement branch will apply the consequences for noncompliance that were agreed between countries in 2001 if a country fails to meet its Kyoto target. Importantly, it deals with "questions of implementation" raised by expert review teams following their review of country reports and determines whether a country is eligible to participate in the Kyoto Protocol's mechanisms. The mandate of the facilitative branch is based on the nonadversarial role that the Compliance Committee of the Montreal Protocol has assumed in practice. The facilitative branch has the task of assisting all countries in their implementation of the protocol.

Of interest is that the facilitative branch has so far played only a very minor role, whereas the enforcement branch has dealt with a growing number of cases (eight cases as of the end of 2012). All of these cases resulted from "questions of implementation" raised by expert review teams in relation to the reports provided by the countries concerned. In most cases the enforcement branch suspended the ability of the country in question to participate in the Kyoto Protocol's mechanisms pending the resolution of the question of implementation. The suspension of eligibility provided a strong incentive for a country to remedy the shortcomings in its reporting.

Although the Kyoto Protocol's compliance regime has thus far been focused more on enforcement and has done little in terms of facilitation, there is evidence that other regimes are learning from the Montreal experiences and are including a more managerial approach in their treaty design. Perhaps most interesting is the compliance system set up in 2002 under the Aarhus Convention on Access to Information, Public Participation in Decision-Making, and Access to Justice in Environmental Matters. This contains a number of unique features, not least of which are the practice of independence of the members of the Compliance Committee, which includes them not as part of the executive branch of government or NGOs, and the ability of the public to trigger the compliance mechanism.[a]

The noncompliance procedures developed under the Montreal Protocol have thus strongly influenced the design of other conventions as well.

Note: For further information on the Kyoto Protocol's compliance system, see René Lefeber and Sebastian Oberthür, "Key Features of the Kyoto Protocol's Compliance System" and Meinhard Doelle, "Experience with the Facilitative and Enforcement Branches of the Kyoto Compliance System," in *Promoting Compliance in an Evolving Climate Regime,* ed. Jutta Brunnée, Meinhard Doelle, and Lavanya Rajamani (Cambridge: Cambridge University Press, 2012), chaps. 4 and 5. For further information on the Montreal Protocol's compliance regime, see also Gilbert Bankobeza, "Compliance Regime of the Montreal Protocol," in *The Montreal Protocol: Celebrating 20 Years of Environmental Progress,* ed. Donald Kaniaru (London: UNEP/Earthprint, 2007), chap. 7.

[a]See Veit Koester, "The Compliance Committee of the Aarhus Convention: An Overview of Procedures and Jurisprudence," *Environmental Policy and Law* 37, nos. 2–3 (2007): 83–96.

Nonadversarial approaches to solving international environmental disputes seem to be gaining in popularity. For example, as far as the management of the Meuse[49] and Rhine Rivers is concerned,[50] international commissions have been installed to promote stakeholder involvement and exchange of information. The consensual approach followed in the Rhine basin has led to a substantially better water quality in the Rhine River than in the Great Lakes of the United States, despite looser regulation.[51] The politics of water protection in the Great Lakes basin has been more adversarial than in the Rhine watershed, a situation that has reduced the willingness of Great Lake firms to invest in water protection.[52]

Toward Comprehensive Noncompliance Response Systems

In this chapter we have provided an overview of the new approaches to compliance with international environmental treaties that have been developed since the beginning of the 1990s. We have observed a clear shift from the old approach, including dispute settlement proceedings and sanctions in treaties, to the managerial approach, which tries to use a more comprehensive system of different methods for solving compliance problems. Increasingly, more recent treaties have included comprehensive combinations of different instruments for responding to noncompliance. These systems, also referred to as comprehensive noncompliance response systems, contain not only methods to sanction violations but also, and perhaps more important, methods to facilitate compliance, improve transparency and reporting procedures, and prevent violations.[53]

The various capacities of states can be taken into account in the design of the primary rule system through provisions that allow financial or technology transfer mechanisms. These differing capacities can also be taken into account in the noncompliance response system. The fact that self-reporting of noncompliance does not automatically result in negative sanctions but can lead to actual support to remedy incapacity can, in turn, also increase the reporting record. Although the managerial approach is proving successful in treaties such as the Vienna Convention and the Montreal Protocol, it is important to remember that we are only at the beginning of new efforts to find solutions to compliance problems. In many other areas it remains difficult to reach any international consensus at all on the protection of our global environment.

Conclusion

International environmental law is increasingly moving from a phase in which the emphasis was on the adoption of standards to one in which the focus is on the implementation of and actual compliance with these standards. It is important to note, however, that it is especially in the phase of adoption that a well-designed noncompliance response system can prove decisive in getting states to agree to new commitments.

Recent developments in the design of the primary rule system, but also in the response to noncompliance, show an increasing awareness among policy makers in the international arena that compliance issues indeed deserve attention from the early drafting stage. We have presented the Montreal

Protocol as an example of how both the primary rule and the compliance system can be designed *ex ante* to increase the probability of compliance (see also Chapter 4). The increasing attention being given to compliance issues (as, for example, in the discussion of the Kyoto Protocol's compliance regime) shows that implementation and compliance issues remain high on the international and national agendas as the number, complexity, and strength of commitments have grown over time. This conclusion holds not only for the Montreal and Kyoto Protocols, presented as examples of those developments in this chapter. Implementation and compliance are crucial conditions for the effectiveness of all international regimes, and therefore the features that may increase compliance deserve greater attention in future research by scholars and students interested in international (environmental) policy.

Notes

1. Harold K. Jacobson and Edith Brown Weiss, "Strengthening Compliance with International Environmental Accords: Preliminary Observations, from a Collaborative Project," *Global Governance* 1 (1995): 119–148. Jacobson and Brown Weiss rightly point to the fact that there are very few studies of compliance with international environmental treaties and even fewer studies that focus on factors at the national level that affect compliance. Their cross-treaty and cross-country evaluation of compliance is an important exception. See also Ronald B. Mitchell, "Compliance Theory: An Overview," in *Improving Compliance with International Environmental Law*, ed. James Cameron, Jacob Werksman, and Peter Roderick (London: Earthscan, 1996), 3–28; David G. Victor, Kal Raustiala, and Eugene B. Skolnikoff, eds., *The Implementation and Effectiveness of International Environmental Commitments: Theory and Practice* (Cambridge: MIT Press, 1998).
2. Jacobson and Brown Weiss, "Strengthening Compliance," 124.
3. Article 259 of the Treaty on the Functioning of the European Union, one of the treaties forming the basis of the EU, contains the possibility of one or more member states bringing another member state before the Court of Justice of the European Union. Since the founding of the European Community, the EU's predecessor, in 1958, this procedure has been used rarely, and usually only in politically controversial cases. Most recently, in October 2012, the Court dismissed a Hungarian action against the Slovak Republic. This action followed the Slovak Republic's refusal to allow the Hungarian president to enter the country to unveil a statue of Saint Stephen I, the first king (and patron saint) of Hungary, on its territory on the same day as the forty-first anniversary of the occupation of Czechoslovakia by the Warsaw Pact (Case C-364/10).
4. This new approach is not followed by all scholars, however. See, for example, Jack L. Goldsmith and Eric A. Posner, *The Limits of International Law* (Oxford: Oxford University Press, 2005). Goldsmith and Posner stress that states will mainly conclude agreements and comply when this is in their self-interest. See also Andrew T. Guzman, "A Compliance-Based Theory of International Law," *California Law Review* 90 (2002): 1823–1888.
5. This new idea is probably best formulated by Abraham Chayes and Antonia Handler-Chayes, *The New Sovereignty: Compliance with International Regulatory Agreements* (Cambridge, MA: Harvard University Press, 1995), especially chap. 1.
6. For a review of the early literature on regimes, see Marc A. Levy, Oran R. Young, and Michael Zürn, "The Study of International Regimes," *European Journal of International Relations* 1, no. 3 (1995): 267–330. See also Oran R. Young, ed., *The Effectiveness of International Environmental Regimes: Causal Connections and Behavioral Mechanisms* (Cambridge: MIT Press, 1999).

7. Chayes and Handler-Chayes, *New Sovereignty*, 27.
8. The role of reputation in complying with international agreements is strongly stressed in the work of Andrew T. Guzman. See Andrew T. Guzman, "The Design of International Agreements," *European Journal of International Law* 16, no. 4 (2005): 579–612; Andrew T. Guzman, *How International Law Works: A Rational Choice Theory* (Oxford: Oxford University Press, 2008), especially chap. 3.
9. See, however, Goldsmith and Posner, *Limits of International Law*. According to these authors, states will conclude agreements only when doing so is in their self-interest.
10. Articles 2(3) and 2(4), in combination with Articles 42 and 51 of the UN Treaty.
11. Chayes and Handler-Chayes, *New Sovereignty*, 22–28.
12. Guzman, *How International Law Works*, 175.
13. For a comparison of these two cases, see David Downie, "Road Map or False Trail: Evaluating the Precedence of the Ozone Regime as Model and Strategy for Global Climate Change," *International Environmental Affairs* 7, no. 4 (Fall 1995): 321–345.
14. Examples of this can be found in European environmental law. See Michael Faure and Jürgen Lefevere, "The Draft Directive on Integrated Pollution Prevention and Control: An Economic Perspective," *European Environmental Law Review* 5 (April 1996): 112–122; Michael G. Faure, "Optimal Specificity in Environmental Standard-Setting," in *Critical Issues in Environmental Taxation: International and Comparative Perspectives*, vol. 8, ed. Claudia Dias Soares, Janet E. Milne, Hope Ashiabor, Larry Kreiser, and Kurt Deketelaere (Oxford: Oxford University Press, 2010), 730–745.
15. See, with respect to nuclear accidents, Tom Vanden Borre, "Shifts in Governance in Compensation for Nuclear Damage, 20 Years after Chernobyl," in *Shifts in Compensation for Environmental Damage*, ed. Michael Faure and Albert Verheij (Vienna: Springer, 2007), 261–311; Michael Faure and Tom Vanden Borre, "Compensating Nuclear Damage: A Comparative Economic Analysis of the U.S. and International Liability Schemes," *William & Mary Environmental Law and Policy Review* 33 (2008): 219–287; Michael Faure and Karine Fiore, "The Civil Liability of Nuclear Operators: Which Coverage for the New 2004 Protocols? Evidence from France," *International Environmental Agreements* 8 (2008): 227–248. With respect to civil liability for marine oil pollution, see Alan Khee-Jin Tan, *Vessel-Source Marine Pollution: The Law and Politics of International Regulation* (Cambridge: Cambridge University Press, 2006); Wang Hui, "Shifts in Governance in the International Regime of Marine Oil Pollution Compensation: A Legal History Perspective," in Faure and Verheij, *Shifts in Compensation for Environmental Damage*, 197–241; Wang Hui, *Civil Liability for Marine Oil Pollution Damage: A Comparative and Economic Study of the International, US and Chinese Compensation Regime* (Alphen aan den Rijn: Kluwer Law International, 2011). For an economic analysis of the marine oil pollution regime, see Michael Faure and Wang Hui, "Economic Analysis of Compensation for Oil Pollution Damage," *Journal of Maritime Law and Commerce* 7 (2006): 197–217. For discussion of recent developments, see Wang Hui, "Prevention and Compensation for Marine Oil Pollution," in *Marine Pollution Liability and Policy: China, Europe and the US*, ed. Michael Faure, Han Lixin, and Shan Hongjun (Alphen aan den Rijn: Kluwer Law International, 2010), 13–40.
16. The article reads as follows: "The developed country Parties and other Parties included in Annex I commit themselves specifically as provided for in the following: (a) Each of these Parties shall adopt national policies and take corresponding measures on the mitigation of climate change, by limiting its anthropogenic emissions of greenhouse gases and protecting and enhancing its greenhouse gas sinks and reservoirs. These policies and measures will demonstrate that developed countries are taking the lead in modifying longer-term trends in anthropogenic emissions consistent with the objective of the Convention, recognizing that the return by the end of the present decade to earlier levels of anthropogenic emissions of carbon dioxide and other greenhouse gases not controlled by the Montreal Protocol would contribute to such modification, and taking into account the differences in these Parties' starting

points and approaches, economic structures and resource bases, the need to maintain strong and sustainable economic growth, available technologies and other individual circumstances, as well as the need for equitable and appropriate contributions by each of these Parties to the global effort regarding that objective. These Parties may implement such policies and measures Jointly with other Parties and may assist other Parties in contributing to the achievement of the objective of the Convention."

17. For details, see Jacob Werksman, "Designing a Compliance System for the UN Framework Convention on Climate Change," in Cameron et al., *Improving Compliance with International Environmental Law*, 85–112. See also Philippe Sands and Jacqueline Peel, *Principles of International Environmental Law* (New York: Cambridge University Press, 2012), 274–298.

18. For an overview of the application of differential treatment in international law and in particular the climate regime, see Lavanya Rajamani, "The Changing Fortunes of Differential Treatment in the Evolution of International Environmental Law," *International Affairs* 88, no. 3 (2012): 605–623.

19. For more in-depth background on the Kyoto Protocol mechanisms, see Sebastian Oberthür and Hermann E. Ott, *The Kyoto Protocol: International Climate Policy for the 21st Century* (Berlin: Springer, 1999).

20. See Lambert Schneider, "Perverse Incentives under the CDM: An Evaluation of HFC-23 Destruction Projects," *Climate Policy* 11, no. 2 (2011): 851–864.

21. Jacobson and Brown Weiss, "Strengthening Compliance," 126.

22. Richard Elliot Benedick, *Ozone Diplomacy: New Directions in Safeguarding the Planet*, enlarged ed. (Cambridge, MA: Harvard University Press, 1998). Benedick describes this process of decision making under scientific uncertainty.

23. The IPCC published its Fourth Assessment Report in 2007. This report, for which the IPCC was awarded a Nobel Peace Prize (together with former U.S. vice president Al Gore for his work on climate change), is available on the IPCC Web site, http://www.ipcc.ch. The Fifth Assessment Report is foreseen for 2014.

24. The European Union's greenhouse gas emissions trading directive (Directive 2003/87/EC), which is the basis of the EU's greenhouse gas emissions trading system, explicitly requires, for example, the publication of the names of companies that do not comply with their obligation to surrender sufficient emission allowances to compensate for their greenhouse gas emissions (Article 16[2]).

25. Several varieties of reporting and data collection are discussed in Chayes and Handler-Chayes, *New Sovereignty*, 154–173.

26. The "international consultation and analysis" on the biennial reports to be provided by developing countries under the FCCC is, for instance, explicitly required to be "non-intrusive, non-punitive, respectful of national sovereignty, facilitative in nature." See FCCC Decision 1/CP.16, para. 63.

27. See European Commission, "Improving the Delivery of Benefits from EU Environment Measures: Building Confidence through Better Knowledge and Responsiveness," Brussels, COM(2012) 95 final, March 7, 2012.

28. Gro Harlem Brundtland, "The Road from Rio," *Technology Review* 96 (1993): 63.

29. Mitchell, "Compliance Theory," 14; Lynne M. Jurgielewicz, *Global Environmental Change and International Law* (Lanham, MD: University Press of America, 1996), 113.

30. See Remi Moncel and Kelly Levin, "Transparency and Accountability (MRV) in the Durban Climate Deal," World Resources Institute, Insights paper, February 13, 2012, http://insights.wri.org/news/2012/02/transparency-and-accountability-mrv-durban-climate-deal.

31. Jacobson and Brown Weiss cite the important role of Brazilian president Fernando Collor at the UN Conference on Environment and Development in 1992. Jacobson and Brown Weiss, "Strengthening Compliance," 142. More recently, the president of the European Commission, José Barroso, played a key role in getting the EU to adopt its "climate change and energy package," the basis for the EU's greenhouse gas

emission reduction target of 20 percent by 2020, in combination with targets to increase the EU's energy efficiency and share of renewable energy by 20 percent. See BBC News, "EU Plans 'Industrial Revolution,'" January 10, 2007, http://news.bbc .co.uk/2/hi/science/nature/6247199.stm.

32. Jacobson and Brown Weiss, "Strengthening Compliance," 129.
33. Mitchell, "Compliance Theory," 24.
34. Jacobson and Brown Weiss, "Strengthening Compliance," 143; Oran R. Young, *International Governance: Protecting the Environment in a Stateless Society* (Ithaca, NY: Cornell University Press, 1994), 110–115.
35. Young, *International Governance*, 37–39.
36. Mitchell, "Compliance Theory," 15.
37. Ibid., 11.
38. See Guzman, "Compliance-Based Theory of International Law."
39. Belonging to a particular regime can thus also increase the reputational losses felt by violating parties, a point often stressed by Guzman. See Guzman, *How International Law Works*, chap. 3.
40. For a general discussion of the role of NGOs in international environmental law, see Foundation for International Environmental Law and Development (FIELD) and Ecologic Institute for International and European Environmental Policy, *Participation of Non-governmental Organisations in International Environmental Governance: Legal Basis and Practical Experience* (Berlin: German Umweltbundesamt, June 2002), http://www.ecologic.eu/download/projekte/1850-1899/1890/report_ngos_en.pdf. See also John McCormick, "The Role of Environmental NGOs in International Regimes," in *The Global Environment: Institutions, Law, and Policy*, 3rd ed., ed. Regina S. Axelrod, Stacy D. VanDeveer, and David Leonard Downie (Washington, DC: CQ Press, 2011).
41. For information on NGO participation in FCCC meetings, including statistics, see United Nations Framework Convention on Climate Change, "Civil Society and the Climate Change Process," http://unfccc.int/parties_and_observers/ngo/items/3667 .php.
42. See, for example, James Cameron, "Compliance, Citizens and NGO's," in Cameron et al., *Improving Compliance with International Environmental Law*, 29–42. More particularly, see the book review by Oran R. Young in *International Environmental Affairs* 9 (Winter 1997): 84.
43. Mitchell, "Compliance Theory," 9.
44. See Jacobson and Brown Weiss, "Strengthening Compliance," 129, 140–142; Clifford Polycarp, Taryn Fransen, Catherine Easton, and Jennifer Hatch, "Summary of Developed Country 'Fast-Start' Climate Finance Pledges," World Resources Institute, November 2012, http://www.wri.org/publication/summary-of-developed-country-fast-start-climate-finance-pledges.
45. See Seth Binder and Eric Neumayer, "Environmental Pressure Group Strength and Air Pollution: An Empirical Analysis," *Ecological Economics* 55 (2005): 527–537. Binder and Neumayer find that environmental NGOs exert a statistically significant impact on sulfur dioxide, smoke, and particulates concentration levels, based on a cross-country time series regression analysis.
46. In 1993, the International Court of Justice created the Chamber for Environmental Matters, which was periodically reconstituted until 2006. As no state ever requested that a case be dealt with by the chamber, the Court decided in 2006 not to hold elections for a bench for the chamber.
47. Chayes and Handler-Chayes, *New Sovereignty*, 30.
48. For a full overview of the EU's penalties under Article 260, see Paul Craig and Gráinne De Búrca, *EU Law: Text, Cases and Materials* (Oxford: Oxford University Press, 2011), 433–439.
49. See Cesare P. R. Romano, *The Peaceful Settlement of International Environmental Disputes: A Pragmatic Approach* (London: Kluwer Law International, 2000), 233–245;

Nicolette Bouman, "A New Regime for the Meuse," *Review of European Community & International Environmental Law* 5, no. 2 (1996): 161–168.
50. See André Nollkaemper, *The Legal Regime for Transboundary Water Pollution: Between Discretion and Constraints* (Utrecht: Martinus-Nijhoff, 1993).
51. Marco Verweij, "Why Is the River Rhine Cleaner Than the Great Lakes (Despite Looser Regulation)?," *Law and Society Review* 34, no. 4 (2000): 1007–1054.
52. Ibid., 1040.
53. Mitchell, "Compliance Theory," 14; Chayes and Handler-Chayes, *New Sovereignty,* 25; Werksman, "Designing a Compliance System," 115–116.

6

Domestic Sources of U.S. Unilateralism

Elizabeth R. DeSombre

The United States has, over the past half century, gone from unambiguously leading efforts at global environmental cooperation to avoiding (at best) and undermining (at worst) international environmental efforts. Despite then president-elect Barack Obama's initial promise to "make the U.S. a leader on climate change,"[1] the domestic pressures he faced once in office prevented any major U.S. environmental effort internationally and relegated domestic action to behind-the-scenes procedural action taken to implement existing policies more fully.

Early U.S. international leadership on environmental issues was notable. Some of the very earliest efforts at international environmental cooperation—such as protecting seals, whales, and other endangered species in the first half of the twentieth century—were led by the United States. Beginning in the early 1970s, the United States was a leader in international efforts to protect endangered species and ecosystems, to prevent ocean pollution, and, later, to protect the ozone layer.

More recently, however, the United States has backed away from international environmental leadership. This change in approach was most apparent at the United Nations Conference on Environment and Development in Rio de Janeiro in 1992. Of the two binding agreements signed there, the United States signed but refused to ratify the Convention on Biological Diversity (and has not signed its Biosafety Protocol) and signed and ratified the United Nations Framework Convention on Climate Change (after working to weaken it); it refused to ratify the Kyoto Protocol to that agreement, negotiated later, which contained actual abatement obligations (see Table 6-1). Even on issues on which it has previously led, the United States has become increasingly reluctant. U.S. agricultural interests, for instance, have persuaded the United States to oppose the strengthening of regulations on methyl bromide, a major ozone-depleting substance, and to ask for continuing exemptions from existing rules concerning the chemical.[2]

It is important to note, however, that U.S. environmental recalcitrance has not all been recent. The lack of U.S. ratification of the Basel Convention on the Control of Transboundary Movements of Hazardous Wastes and Their Disposal (1989) and related treaties on transborder movement of other toxic materials suggests that the United States managed to avoid important global environmental obligations before Rio. Its public and sudden refusal to ratify

Table 6-1 U.S. Signature and Ratification Status of Major Environmental Agreements

Treaty	Year	U.S. signature?	U.S. ratification?
Ramsar Convention on Wetlands	1971	Yes	Yes
London Convention (Dumping at Sea)	1972	Yes	Yes
World Heritage Convention	1972	Yes	Yes
Convention on International Trade in Endangered Species (CITES)	1973	Yes	Yes
MARPOL (Pollution from Ships)	1978	Yes	Yes
Convention on Migratory Species	1979	No	No
Convention on Long-Range Transboundary Air Pollution (CLRTAP)	1979	Yes	Yes
UN Convention on the Law of the Sea	1982	Yes	No
Vienna Convention on the Protection of the Ozone Layer	1985	Yes	Yes
Montreal Protocol on Substances That Deplete the Ozone Layer	1987	Yes	Yes
Basel Convention (Hazardous Waste Trade)	1989	Yes	No
Framework Convention on Climate Change (FCCC)	1992	Yes	Yes
Convention on Biological Diversity (CBD)	1992	Yes	No
Convention to Combat Desertification	1994	Yes	No
Kyoto Protocol (Climate Change)	1997	Yes	No
Rotterdam Convention (PIC)	1998	Yes	No
Stockholm Convention on Persistent Organic Pollutants (POPs)	2001	Yes	No

the United Nations Convention on the Law of the Sea (1982), at least partially for reasons relating to how the convention addressed access to resources of the deep seabed, extends this pattern further back in time.

There are numerous possible explanations for the change in U.S. approaches to international environmental cooperation. Those who blamed—or credited—Republican presidents (most notably George W. Bush) for the decline in U.S. international environmental leadership would have expected a more dramatic change with Obama's election than transpired. Others suggest that the trend is not unique to environmental issues; the United States has increasingly refrained from cooperation on a large number of international issues. Even apart from broader difficulties with the United Nations over Iraq, the United States refused to join the International Criminal Court; to sign the Convention on the Prohibition of the Use, Stockpiling, Production and Transfer of Anti-Personnel Mines and on Their Destruction (1997); and to ratify the Comprehensive Test Ban Treaty (1996). In late 2012, it was one of only a small number of states to refuse to ratify the United Nations Convention on the Rights of Persons with Disabilities,[3] a treaty modeled on existing U.S. legislation. Other explanations focus on broader characteristics of the country or its ideological goals, the degree of uncertainty about environmental problems, the ecological vulnerability of the United States, the costs of taking action on the issues in question, and the domestic political power of industrial actors likely to bear those costs.

Understanding U.S. international environmental behavior is important for those who are concerned about addressing global environmental issues. The United States matters environmentally; among all the world's nations, its population has, by most measures, the largest ecological footprint.[4] The United States combines a large per capita output of substances such as carbon dioxide, consumption of resources, and generation of waste with a large population and a long history of high energy use. It is alone among industrialized countries in having significant population growth,[5] so its per capita impacts continue to increase. It also has the largest economy (measured per capita and overall) and is the largest single-country market internationally, consistently leading in imports and exports. In addition, it is among the largest providers of overseas development assistance.[6] What the United States decides to do environmentally thus reverberates globally.

More important, the size and influence of the United States mean that the actions it takes can provide the critical mass for cooperative efforts internationally. Because environmental issues involve common-pool resources, those who refuse to go along with addressing them may not only fail to contribute to a beneficial outcome but also can actually undermine the ability of those who do to address a given problem successfully. The influence and economic and environmental weight of the United States mean that an initiative it signs on to is well on the way to bringing the majority of relevant environmental behavior under its regulatory umbrella. Conversely, an initiative that the United States refrains from participating in is unlikely to succeed at serious environmental protection.

The recent unwillingness of the United States to lead—or even join—efforts at multilateral environmental cooperation in the post–Cold War world seems overdetermined: it is neither an entirely new phenomenon nor one restricted to environmental issues, and it is certainly not one that can be attributed to the administration of George W. Bush. It is an essential trend to understand, given a U.S. history of strong domestic environmental action, previous U.S. leadership on global environmental issues, the importance of the United States for the world's ability to address global environmental issues, and the Obama administration's promise of increased engagement with the world community.

When does the United States lead in addressing global environmental problems, and when does it refuse even to go along? Ultimately the most promising explanation for the pattern of U.S. unilateralism on international environmental issues involves characteristics of the domestic political system and the way in which national policy making relates to international negotiations. The issues on which the United States leads internationally are those on which it has previously regulated domestically. The intersection between domestic politics and international relations can go a long way toward explaining what we see, and what we should expect, from U.S. environmental leadership. It also suggests that it is less the actions or the party of the president that matter and much more the regulatory processes undertaken by Congress that provide an explanation for U.S. environmental leadership or lack thereof. The increasing polarization of U.S. politics, and the role that environmental issues have played in that polarization, contributes to current and future inaction. If we want to understand what the United States has chosen to pursue or avoid internationally in terms of environmental policy, and predict what future U.S. leadership is likely to do, we need to look at what it has regulated or shunned domestically.

U.S. Environmental Leadership

The United States has traditionally had among the strictest environmental regulations on the domestic level[7] and has often been a leader internationally on environmental issues. It has a reputation for "taking environmental treaties seriously,"[8] suggesting that when it does participate in multilateral environmental efforts it tends to implement the relevant provisions domestically and comply with the obligations of the treaties. Moreover, it has been the driving force behind the negotiations to address a number of international environmental problems. This leadership can be seen in the context of U.S. actions to protect endangered species internationally and to protect the atmosphere from substances that deplete the ozone layer.

Endangered Species

The United States was one of the principal proponents of international action to protect endangered species, beginning in 1900 with the Lacey Act, which prohibited trafficking in animals taken illegally in their countries of origin as well as those killed in violation of any U.S. or international law.[9] Domestically the U.S. Endangered Species Act (and its predecessors) restricted the taking, importing or exporting, and sales of species listed as endangered, and it adopted a variety of increasingly strict regulations to protect species wherever they were found. Early versions of this legislation also called on the United States to negotiate binding international agreements to protect endangered species worldwide.[10] The United States followed this concern by working for international protection of endangered species through the creation of the 1973 Convention on International Trade in Endangered Species of Wild Fauna and Flora (CITES) (see Chapter 12). U.S. participation was important in other early international negotiations to address endangered species, such as the Ramsar Convention on Wetlands of International Importance Especially as Waterfowl Habitat (1972), and in the creation of a moratorium on commercial whaling—agreed to in 1982, begun in the 1985–1986 whaling season—under the International Convention for the Regulation of Whaling (1946).[11]

Ozone Depletion

U.S. leadership on global atmospheric issues was evident in the country's response to ozone depletion (see Chapters 4 and 5). U.S. involvement with the issue of ozone depletion stemmed from scientific research undertaken in the early 1960s to ascertain whether a planned fleet of supersonic aircraft would harm the ozone layer. Much of the other early scientific work on sources of possible harm to the ozone layer took place in the United States.[12] The United States also took the lead in domestic regulation, including in the 1977 Clean Air Act Amendments that required that U.S. industry phase out the use of chlorofluorocarbons (CFCs), the main substances implicated in ozone depletion, in nonessential aerosols beginning in 1978.[13] The United States hosted the 1977 International Conference on the Ozone Layer, the first intergovernmental discussion of the problem of ozone depletion, which produced the World Plan of Action on the Ozone Layer. Although the United States resisted meaningful international regulation during the period shortly following that conference, by the early 1980s it had joined with the Nordic countries, Austria, Canada, and Switzerland in support of deep cuts in international production and use of ozone-depleting substances. This coalition supported such measures in the negotiation of the 1985 Vienna Convention for the Protection of the Ozone Layer.

But staunch opposition from European countries, which had not yet taken any action to regulate their domestic production of ozone-depleting substances, resulted in a framework treaty that simply supported the principle of ozone layer protection without requiring substantive abatement obligations. The United States came out as a clear leader, however, in the negotiation for binding reductions of emissions of ozone-depleting substances that resulted in the 1987 Montreal Protocol on Substances That Deplete the Ozone Layer. U.S. proposals began with a freeze on the use of harmful substances and then suggested a range of further reductions. Along with its negotiating partners (and against the European Community), the United States also insisted that all known ozone-depleting substances be regulated under the protocol. In addition, several bills introduced into the U.S. Congress in 1987 would have prohibited imports of ozone-depleting substances or products that contained them or were made from them if the exporting countries did not adopt domestic measures to protect the ozone layer. (This legislation was abandoned when the protocol was successfully negotiated.)[14]

U.S. International Environmental Reluctance

More recent U.S. refusals to ratify the major international initiatives to address global issues such as climate change and biodiversity protection suggest that the United States is often unwilling to exercise leadership or even participate in some multilateral environmental efforts. In addition to these two issues, it is useful to examine U.S. refusals (some earlier than the Rio conference) to accept a variety of efforts to regulate the international movement of hazardous chemicals and waste or to ratify the Law of the Sea Convention.

Climate Change

The position of the United States on global efforts to mitigate climate change (global warming) has been the most obvious evidence of recent U.S. recalcitrance (see also Chapter 10). The United States participated in the negotiation of the United Nations Framework Convention on Climate Change (FCCC) signed at the Earth Summit in Rio in 1992. Its main goals for the negotiation, however, were to avoid the creation of binding targets and timetables for reduction of greenhouse gas emissions (which European states were willing to negotiate) and to ensure that all major greenhouse gases (rather than just carbon dioxide) be included in any agreement. The United States prevailed in these goals because the other major negotiators did not want to create an agreement without U.S. participation.[15] The convention nevertheless sets out a potentially important set of principles that member states accept by ratification. The agreement's objective is to stabilize atmospheric greenhouse gas concentrations "at a level that would prevent dangerous anthropogenic interference with the climate system," although that level is not specified. The agreement acknowledges the use of the precautionary principle, indicating that lack of full certainty is not to be used to postpone taking action to address the issue, and specifies that "the developed country Parties should take the lead in combating climate change and the adverse effects thereof."[16] The Senate ratified this agreement quickly,[17] and the United States has lived up to its implementation obligations by reporting on its emissions and policies pertaining to climate change.

U.S. interaction with the Kyoto Protocol, the agreement that requires cuts in emissions of greenhouse gases from developed country parties, has been even less productive from the perspective of international environmental cooperation. The United States did take part in the negotiation of the agreement. During negotiations in 1996, Tim Wirth, the U.S. undersecretary of state for global affairs, suggested that negotiations should set "a realistic, verifiable, and medium-term emissions target," making the United States the first major FCCC party to call for binding reductions.[18] In general the United States advocated in the negotiation process that the greatest degree of flexibility (from trade in emissions, joint implementation, and the counting of sinks for greenhouse gases) be included, and most of these issues were written into the agreement in much the way the United States wanted. The one exception concerned the actual abatement obligations; President Bill Clinton originally set the U.S. negotiating position at a freeze at 1990 emissions levels by 2008. In the agreement as negotiated in Kyoto, the United States was persuaded to accept a reduction of its greenhouse gas emissions of 7 percent below 1990 levels.[19]

Several months before the final negotiation at which the agreement was to be signed, the U.S. Senate passed what came to be known as the Byrd-Hagel resolution, indicating the Senate's intention not to ratify any agreement that would require abatement obligations from industrialized countries unless it simultaneously "mandates new specific scheduled commitments to limit or reduce greenhouse gas emissions for developing country parties within the same compliance period." This resolution passed on a vote of ninety-five to zero.[20] The Senate's resolution did not succeed in influencing the agreement's treatment of developing countries, as the entire Kyoto negotiation process had been premised on a lack of specific abatement obligations for developing countries in the first commitment period. It did, however, ensure that the Clinton administration, despite having signed the agreement, could not realistically submit it to the Senate for ratification.

U.S. unwillingness to participate delayed the protocol's entry into force and weakened the agreement. Without the United States, it needed the participation of almost all industrialized countries, many of which also refused to go along until their obligations were made more flexible and less onerous. Lack of U.S. involvement also arguably decreased the likelihood that those states that did take on obligations would meet them. Without serious action by the United States to decrease emissions, other states knew their actions could not make a serious impact on the climate system. In stating its decision to not meet its Kyoto obligations, for instance, Canada made reference to the U.S. absence from the UN climate negotiation process.[21]

Congress also influenced the extent and content of domestic U.S. action in the absence of participation in the Kyoto Protocol. Many members of Congress opposed legislative action that would encourage the cutting of greenhouse gas emissions in general. Former presidential candidate Jack Kemp, for example, argued in opposition to proposed emissions reduction measures, asserting that the United States must "guard against a milder version of the Kyoto treaty that would serve the same purpose, offering concessions to companies that would acquiesce in creating the biggest global regulatory regime yet conceived."[22] Other members of Congress introduced bills to forbid any action on climate change. For example, Representative David McIntosh

(R-Ind.) proposed H.R. 2221, which not only would have prohibited the use of federal funds for advocating, developing, or implementing early credit systems for voluntary emissions reductions but also would have mandated that federal funds not be used "to propose or issue rules, regulations, decrees, or orders or for programs designed to implement, or in preparation to implement, the Kyoto Protocol" before the Senate ratified the agreement. While this legislation did not pass, it inhibited the creation of new policies to give credit for voluntary measures.[23] The more successful effort, however, came from attaching a legislative rider to appropriations bills in 2000 and 2001. Representative Joseph Knollenberg (R-Mich.) inserted language into these bills prohibiting the government from undertaking any action that would contribute to meeting the goals of the Kyoto Protocol before it had been ratified by the Senate.[24]

There were more recent congressional proposals, however, that would have led the United States to take domestic action, outside of the Kyoto framework, to address its emissions of greenhouse gases. Senator Joseph Lieberman (earlier a Democrat, then later an Independent from Connecticut) repeatedly introduced versions of legislation to cap and then reduce U.S. greenhouse gas emissions. The 2003 version (cosponsored with Senator John McCain, R-Ariz.) would have created a cap-and-trade system for greenhouse gases in the United States, with the objective of returning U.S. emissions by 2010 to what they had been in 2000.[25] Subsequent versions of the proposed legislation changed dates and targets; most have not even received a floor vote. The 2008 version, the Lieberman-Warner Climate Security Act, came closer to passing than any previous measures. Although it was subject to procedural jockeying that meant it never received a full vote in the Senate, fifty-four senators indicated their support for cap-and-trade measures for greenhouse gases in the bill's process.[26] A similar approach (the American Clean Energy and Security Act of 2009, H.R. 2454, also called the Waxman-Markey Bill) passed the House of Representatives, but the Senate as a whole did not take up compatible legislation despite efforts by the Energy and Natural Resources Committee and other proposals from individual senators.[27] The 112th Congress also concluded its work in 2012 with no major climate legislation; indeed, there were as many proposals to block action on climate change during the session as there were efforts to address the issue productively, and none of the latter would have involved a cap-and-trade approach.[28]

In the interim, U.S. states have begun their own greenhouse gas emissions reductions mandates, many of them legally binding. Although the states' efforts vary considerably in strength (some taking the form of nonbinding suggestions), thirty-two states have some form of a climate change action plan; others have gone much further to mandate emissions reductions. California took the lead, requiring that by 2010 greenhouse gas emissions be reduced to the level of 2000, and many states since then have created state-level climate policies.[29]

In addition, regional groupings of states have undertaken climate policies. The governors of six New England states created the New England Governors

Climate Change Action Plan, which set forth a goal of collective reduction of greenhouse gas emissions by 2010 to 1990 levels, a further reduction by 10 percent below 1990 levels by 2020, and an ultimate reduction to a level that would not pose a threat to the climate.[30] Another effort in the Northeast, the Regional Greenhouse Gas Initiative (RGGI), began in 2005 with seven states (Connecticut, Delaware, Maine, New Hampshire, New Jersey, New York, and Vermont) and grew to ten states in 2007 (when Rhode Island, Massachusetts, and Maryland joined the initiative). RGGI caps carbon dioxide emissions from power plants (initially at 2009 levels, with a 10 percent reduction by 2019) and allows trading of emissions allowances. Six midwestern states (Illinois, Iowa, Kansas, Michigan, Minnesota, and Wisconsin), along with the Canadian province of Manitoba, created a similar cap-and-trade system in 2007, as did states and provinces in the North American West in the same year.[31] These groups came together in March 2012 under an effort called North America 2050 to coordinate their efforts and work collectively for ways to address climate change.[32] So despite federal inaction, individual U.S. states and regions have taken steps to create climate policy even when a national policy proved unreachable.

In addition, the Obama administration, thwarted by congressional inaction, worked within existing regulatory powers to modify or create regulations with important climate implications. Most important of these was the issuing of a finding by Environmental Protection Agency (EPA) administrator Lisa Jackson in December 2009 that the agency was statutorily required, by the Clean Air Act, to regulate greenhouse gas emissions because they endanger human health and welfare.[33] The U.S. Supreme Court had set the stage for this process in 2007 (in a case brought by Massachusetts and other states and environmental organizations against the then Republican-controlled EPA) when it ruled that greenhouse gas emissions were air pollutants and therefore subject to EPA regulation if they were determined to endanger human health.[34] Using this regulatory power, the Department of Transportation and the EPA also adopted new fuel efficiency standards for automobiles, requiring an average by 2025 of 54.5 miles per gallon, dramatically increased from previous standards. New greenhouse gas emissions requirements were also created for heavy-duty vehicles.[35]

It is certainly true that climate change provides an unusually difficult case for U.S. leadership; U.S. emissions of greenhouse gases on a per capita basis (and, until recently, when China's emissions surpassed them, also in the aggregate)[36] are far higher than those of any other country. Certain demographic characteristics contribute to these high levels of emissions, such as the large size of the country and the long distances U.S. residents travel (particularly without access to public transportation). The large land area of the country also makes possible a number of individual choices, not only about commuting but also about the size and number of residential housing units, that increase greenhouse gas emissions. A tradition of low gasoline prices and easy access to fossil fuels has increased reliance on individual transportation and discouraged fuel efficiency and alternative energy generation. But the level of U.S. unwillingness to entertain national or international efforts to mitigate climate change, in conjunction with evidence of voluntary behavior on the part of industry, especially in the context of other reluctant environmental leadership, needs to be explained.

Biodiversity

The other main issue initiated at the 1992 Earth Summit in Rio on which the United States has resisted international action is that of biodiversity (see Chapter 12). In keeping with its history of concern about the protection of species, the United States helped launch the initial negotiations in the late 1980s, but it became apprehensive at the direction of the negotiations. In particular, the United States feared that the resulting treaty would require strengthening the U.S. Endangered Species Act and the conservation of wetlands, both of which the George H. W. Bush administration was trying to weaken. The United States was also concerned about the principle, favored by developing countries, of the importance of equitable sharing of the benefits of biodiversity. This principle was of concern to the biotechnology and pharmaceutical industries within the United States, which also feared that the treaty would provide inadequate protection for intellectual property rights. It was in response to these concerns that any references to "biosafety" (and efforts to limit the trade in genetically modified organisms) were omitted from the negotiated draft.[37] The United States announced, however, before the Rio conference, that it would not sign the Convention on Biological Diversity (CBD) even in this weakened form. President Bush indicated in particular that he was concerned about the treaty's possible impact on jobs in the United States.[38]

After Bill Clinton was elected president at the end of 1992, a group of nongovernmental organizations and biotechnology and pharmaceutical firms met on their own initiative for several months to determine whether there could be advantages to U.S. participation in the treaty.[39] This group eventually proposed that the United States sign the agreement but issue an interpretive statement to spell out its understanding of its obligations under the treaty. In particular, this group, which included major firms such as Merck, Genentech, and WRI, concluded that the treaty would not create major economic difficulties in the near term and that participating in the process might be better for the United States than remaining outside it. At the same time, the United States conducted an interagency review that determined that the treaty could be implemented within the existing legal framework.[40] President Clinton signed the CBD in 1993 and sent it to the Senate for ratification, along with a letter of submittal that incorporated the interpretive language indicating that the treaty would not endanger essential patent protection or harm research or innovation by industry.

Ratification did not follow, however. Despite a vote of sixteen to three by the Senate Committee on Foreign Relations to support the treaty, a vote was not taken in the Senate in either 1993 or 1994, presumably because the

Senate majority leader (George Mitchell, D-Maine) ascertained that the two-thirds majority needed for approval would not materialize. By the time the issue would have been considered in 1993, thirty-five Republican senators (one more than required to block ratification) had come out against the treaty. The reasons given for opposition to the treaty were varied and included claims that the text was too vague, the treaty was unnecessary, it would hamper U.S. business interests, or it would commit the United States to transfers of funding and technology to developing countries.[41] Subsequent Republican majorities in the Senate meant the issue of ratification was not even considered under Clinton, and it was not a priority in the Senate at the end of George W. Bush's term. The treaty was not taken up for ratification during Obama's first term either. The lack of ratification has reduced the role of the United States to that of an observer at meetings of the parties (although an observer whose interests are nevertheless influential) and in the negotiation protocols to the convention.

Trade in Hazardous Wastes and Other Toxic Materials

The United States generates the overwhelming majority of hazardous waste in the world, although much of it is disposed of within U.S. borders. Nevertheless, the approximately 1 percent of U.S. hazardous waste that is traded still marks the nation as a higher exporter of waste than many major countries.[42] The United States has signed but has refrained from ratifying the main treaty to address trade in hazardous waste, the Basel Convention on the Control of Transboundary Movements of Hazardous Wastes and Their Disposal (1989).

The United States was involved in the negotiation of the Basel Convention and used its role in the negotiation to weaken the proposed agreement. The treaty negotiation was an effort to make formal a set of nonbinding guidelines created by the United Nations Environment Programme governing council in 1987. Many states that were the recipients of hazardous wastes wanted the new binding agreement to go further and actually ban the trade in hazardous wastes; concurrent discussions outside the specific negotiations showed many European states to be sympathetic to a stronger regulatory framework. The United States, however, served as the center of a blocking coalition of developed states that refused to participate if such stringent regulations were enacted. As a result, the eventual treaty created a system by which states need to be notified (and given the opportunity to refuse) before hazardous waste is sent to them. It also included agreement that hazardous waste is to be disposed of in a manner that is "environmentally sound," although that term was not defined.

The United States signed the agreement but did not immediately send it to the Senate for ratification. President Clinton announced his intention to submit the treaty for ratification in 1998, but the treaty has still not been ratified. One of the difficulties for the United States in terms of contemplating the implementation of this agreement is that the definition of hazardous waste under the Basel Convention is broader than that under current U.S. domestic regulation, and industry groups oppose expanding current regulations.[43] Although the United States has reasonably strong existing controls on how it deals with hazardous waste, these measures are in a different format (and thus regulate a somewhat different list of substances) than would be required under the Basel agreement.

In addition, the United States actively opposes the amendment to the convention, referred to as the Basel Ban, that would end all trade in hazardous wastes between rich and poor countries. During the negotiations on the ban the United States made a clear effort to defeat it, even though, as a nonparty to the treaty, its direct forms of influence were limited. It nevertheless worked hard to convince individual states to take leadership positions opposing the ban and allocated funding for international meetings to help persuade others of its possible negative ramifications.[44] The ban ultimately was negotiated in the form of an amendment to the convention, but it has experienced delays in entering into force. Some environmental nongovernmental organizations now actually discourage U.S. ratification of Basel if, as seems inevitable, it would happen without simultaneous ratification of the ban amendment.[45] They fear that U.S. ratification of the agreement without the ban would then allow the United States to work to undermine the ban and enable it to trade with other Basel members that have not accepted the ban.

The United States has also been slow to take action on two other treaties on toxic substances: the Stockholm Convention on Persistent Organic Pollutants (2001) and the Rotterdam Convention on the Prior Informed Consent Procedure for Certain Hazardous Chemicals and Pesticides in International Trade (1998). Although President George W. Bush signed the Stockholm Convention and repeatedly indicated an interest in ratifying it, the United States has been reluctant to create a domestic process that could be used for deciding which chemicals would be restricted under the treaty. This unwillingness has held up the ratification process, even once Obama was elected.[46]

In the negotiations on what became the Rotterdam Convention, moving from a voluntary prior informed consent (PIC) procedure to one that was mandatory for trade in hazardous chemicals and pesticides, the United States supported a proposal that increased the difficulty of including a chemical on the list. In place of a system where any chemical banned in one country would immediately trigger a PIC procedure, the chemical would need to be banned in two different countries representing two different regions; this would prevent a chemical banned only in European countries from making the list.[47] Despite the inclusion of this U.S.-supported measure in the final version of the treaty, the United States has also not ratified this agreement. Legislation has periodically been introduced in the House of Representatives to implement the provisions that the United States would need to have in place in order to comply with both agreements, if ratified. Although the bills have been referred to committee,[48] none have been voted on, and as of late 2013 the treaties had not been brought for ratification to the U.S. Senate.

The Law of the Sea

The United Nations Convention on the Law of the Sea is an additional international agreement on which the United States has resisted action. Negotiation on the treaty, which attempts to address in one agreement all issues relating to oceans, was completed in 1982, but President Ronald Reagan refused to sign the agreement. His administration expressed concern about the redistributive aspects of provisions in the treaty for regulating deep-seabed mining and fears that the United States would not be guaranteed influence in decisions on these issues.[49] When George H. W. Bush was president, the United States worked to negotiate an annex (The Agreement Relating to the Implementation of Part XI of the Convention) that addressed these concerns, after which the United States signed the treaty in 1994 and President Clinton submitted it to Congress for ratification. The treaty received unanimous support from the Senate Committee on Foreign Relations. It was not brought to a vote in the Senate that year, however, owing to strong opposition from a group of conservative senators and the unwillingness of the White House to invest political capital in the issue.[50]

Recent developments have brought new pressure on the United States to ratify the agreement. Jockeying for newly accessible ocean resources (especially in the Arctic as climate change makes previously frozen areas accessible) has intensified. Russia made bold claims to continental shelf resources in the Arctic in 2007 by planting a flag on the seabed in an area it claims as an extension of Russia's landmass,[51] and the melting sea ice is increasing shipping opportunities in the Arctic. The treaty allows for states to claim mineral rights to areas of the continental shelf contiguous with their territory far beyond what had previously been accepted under international law, with the treaty's governing process responsible for adjudicating such claims. Only those states that have ratified the treaty can participate in the process.

There have been more recent efforts to gain ratification of the treaty. In May 2007 President George W. Bush publicly urged the Senate to ratify the agreement. In October 2007 the Senate Foreign Relations Committee voted seventeen to four in favor of ratification.[52] Opposition from some senators remained strong, however, and the full Senate did not take up the question of ratification before Bush left office. The push was renewed during Obama's first term, and in 2012 the Senate Foreign Relations Committee again held hearings on ratification. High-ranking military officials from all branches testified in favor of ratification, as did major business organizations and many Obama administration officials. But thirty-four senators (enough to deny ratification) signed a letter pledging to vote against ratification, so further consideration by the Senate did not transpire.[53]

Understanding U.S. Unilateralism

What explains the variety of U.S. actions? In an examination of only the specific cases discussed here, several possible conclusions emerge about the determinants of U.S. international environmental leadership. These include a consistent ideological approach to international regulation or other elements of U.S. exceptionalism (including a general suspicion of multilateralism), the issue of uncertainty, the severity of the environmental problem for the United States, and the degree to which U.S. industry is affected by proposed regulations. One explanation is that the United States has become more inclined toward unilateral action in recent years, although earlier strong rejection of multilateral cooperation on environmental issues (such as the deep-seabed issues in the law of the sea) and relatively recent U.S. willingness to cooperate on increasingly strict protection of the ozone layer suggest that this is not a sufficient explanation. And to the extent that recent behavior denotes a trend, ascertaining the reasons behind this trend would nonetheless be important.

Before examining a more specifically environmental hypothesis, it is worth exploring the possibility that there is a normative unity to the environmental goals the United States pursues or avoids internationally. There appear to be some ideological consistencies in the international environmental issues on which the United States has avoided serious international participation. Harold Jacobson argues that what the CBD, the Kyoto Protocol, and the Law of the Sea (three of the major international agreements the United States has refused to ratify) have in common is that all contain specific provisions that provide for the redistribution of the benefits of cooperation to developing countries.[54] The Kyoto Protocol eschews abatement obligations for developing countries but includes the promise of funding and technology transfer. The CBD requires that the profits and results from biotechnology development be shared with those states from which the biodiversity resources were obtained. The Law of the Sea created a deep-seabed mining regime in which the benefits of such mining would explicitly be redistributed to developing countries.

Objections to these provisions were stated as the major impediments to U.S. participation in these agreements. These types of policies represent the approaches pursued by developing countries under the rubric of the "new international economic order" in the 1970s and 1980s. It is particularly telling that the United States participated actively in the negotiation of all these agreements and in the case of the Law of the Sea and the CBD explicitly attempted to exclude these redistributive measures but failed. The analysis breaks down somewhat in the context of the Kyoto Protocol, however, since the United States did not actively push for developing country obligations under the agreement. And, as Jacobson points out, the flexibility mechanisms the United States supported so strongly for the Kyoto Protocol would likely result in some level of income redistribution to developing countries:[55] developing countries would be able to receive funding for undertaking actions that reduce global emissions of greenhouse gases. Moreover, other international agreements the United States has avoided, such as the Basel Convention, do not contain these redistributive elements, and some that the United States has joined, such as the Montreal Protocol (under which the United States is the

largest contributor of funding), do. If ideology does not explain U.S. recalcitrance, what does?

A related explanation points to the general U.S. reluctance to accept international norms on a wide range of issues, from human rights to international
security, with environment just one additional manifestation of this approach.
Some identify this issue as "exceptionalism," focusing particularly on the idea
of cultural relativism.[56] If the United States is indeed exceptional, its reluctance to take on unnecessary foreign entanglements may be one side effect of
this phenomenon. A related issue is the possibility that the United States, as
the most powerful state internationally in the post–Cold War era, knows that
it does not need international cooperation to guard its interests. This seems
an unlikely explanation for issues of the global environmental commons,
however, where states cannot protect themselves unilaterally. In any case, as
Andrew Moravcsik points out, identifying exceptionalism, even where relevant, does not explain it.[57]

When the United States chooses not to take action on a given environmental issue, such as global climate change, uncertainty is often given as a
reason for inaction. Attempts to explain U.S. reticence on climate change
frequently mention incomplete knowledge. On the face of it, this explanation for U.S. behavior seems implausible. Although genuine uncertainty may
exist on many of these issues, the United States was willing to act in the face
of uncertainty on ozone depletion but not climate change, and few would
argue that U.S. inaction on biodiversity can be attributed primarily to lack
of information. Moreover, other states have access to the same degree of
information on these issues that the United States does, and they make
different decisions about how to act internationally. That may not damn this
explanation; some have suggested that the ways the United States handles
uncertainty in the political process may be different from the ways other
states do.

In particular, the United States differs from other countries in its approach
to risk. Sheila Jasanoff has compared the different ways states approach risk
on the domestic level, and she notes that the European policy process is more
cautious about accepting risk than is that of the United States.[58] This finding
would not seem to explain U.S. reluctance on the international level on issues
pertaining to risk (such as climate change and biodiversity or biosafety), especially when the main proponents of international cooperation on these issues
are European states. Jasanoff addresses this issue with respect to U.S.
responses to climate change, suggesting that because the scientific community
in the country does not have a clear hierarchy, when there are political actors
who gain from avoiding action, they can make use of existing uncertainty,
implicitly painting the taking of action as riskier than doing nothing. Lawrence Susskind argues that the United States uses scientific evidence to support international action it prefers, but "when we prefer to take a different
political course we attack the available data as insufficient regardless of the
strength of the worldwide scientific consensus."[59] In this context, then, uncertainty is an excuse but not an explanation.

A common explanation for the leadership behavior of states on environmental problems is the extent to which states are likely to be harmed by the problems. Detlef Sprinz and Tapani Vaahtoranta argue that "the worse the state of the environment, the greater the incentives to reduce the ecological vulnerability of a state."[60] They suggest that states will be "leaders" on international environmental issues when they are particularly affected by the issues but will either resist action or simply go along when their ecological vulnerability is low. It is true that the United States is less likely to be harmed by issues such as climate change and biodiversity loss than are those states that are more generally dependent on land-based resources and less able to adapt to environmental change. However, a simple comparison of U.S. vulnerability across even the issues addressed here does not explain why the United States was more willing to act on ozone depletion than on climate change (the latter certainly has a bigger environmental and economic impact on the country than the former) or less willing to act on biodiversity protection than on trade in endangered species. Moreover, the United States is more likely to be harmed economically by its continued refusal to ratify the Law of the Sea Convention.

Another plausible interpretation of U.S. decisions on environmental leadership is that decisions depend on the extent to which domestic industry bears a cost from taking action to address the issue. Sprinz and Vaahtoranta also posit that the costs of abatement play an important role in determining the extent of state leadership on the international level. Although they examine cases where restricting emissions is the abatement cost, it could be argued that the predicted costs of international action on an issue more broadly can play an important role in determining what a state—in this instance, the United States—will choose to undertake internationally.

This logic fits well with anecdotal evidence and domestic theorizing about the particularly important role U.S. businesses play in politics within the United States. It also appears consistent with U.S. avoidance of action on climate change. Sebastian Oberthür and Hermann Ott argue that the U.S. position on climate change is influenced by the country's status as the world's largest producer of coal, oil, and gas.[61] While estimates of the cost to the United States of implementing the Kyoto Protocol vary widely (and with some correlation to the political positions of those making the estimates), it is clear that the cost and disruption, at least initially, to the U.S. way of life from addressing climate change could be large. A U.S. Department of Energy report comparing studies predicting the costs of implementing Kyoto obligations (although not accounting for emissions trading or other flexibility mechanisms) found estimates ranging from $91 billion to $311 billion.[62] (It is also worth noting that the energy intensity of the U.S. economy provides additional opportunities for behavior change not available to other states.)

A straight comparison of costliness of regulatory action does not, however, predict the U.S. pattern of international leadership on environmental issues. While some in the U.S. biotechnology and pharmaceutical industries feared the economic cost of the CBD and urged George H. W. Bush not to sign it on that basis, other similar industries had determined within the space of the year that the economic costs would not be large. Similarly, U.S. action on ozone depletion was likely at least as costly (and the costs were more clearly known in advance) as potential costs from protecting biodiversity. And if one considers the cost to the United States of implementing the provisions of CITES, which includes a set of border controls that would otherwise not be required, they are larger than might have been the case for biodiversity.

A related view is that what matters is the political power of industry within the United States on a given issue. Even if the cost to the country as a whole of an abatement measure for a given environmental problem is not enormous (or is not the main basis on which decisions about international action are made), the cost to the industry that has to adapt is meaningful to that industry. The extent to which that industry has influence within the U.S. political process should then have an impact on the willingness of the United States to take a stand internationally. Detlef Sprinz and Martin Weiß argue that industry interests in opposition to reduction of greenhouse gas emissions had a disproportionate impact on the U.S. negotiating process on the FCCC.[63] We would need to come up with a more sophisticated explanation, however, for what accounts for this disproportionate impact on policy making and how to generalize when and how it will affect U.S. international environmental actions.

A more nuanced view about the extent to which U.S. industry will be able to marshal domestic political efforts to avoid international commitments would focus on specifying aspects of the domestic political process in the United States that allow those opposing international environmental leadership to have influence. One argument made on a different issue is that the United States has a set of decentralized political institutions that "empower small veto groups."[64] Peter Cowhey has suggested that "national politicians have been unlikely to accept any global regime that fails to reinforce the preferred domestic regime."[65] Kal Raustiala points out that states rarely create completely new domestic regulatory structures to address international issues, but rather rely on existing institutional structures domestically. That observation suggests that how domestic institutions are structured "influences what can be implemented, and often what is negotiated."[66] This explanation may help us identify either domestic structural determinants of U.S. global environmental leadership or simply content-based approaches to evaluating the likelihood of eventual U.S. international action on an issue.

The United States also has an admirable tradition of accepting only those international environmental obligations with which it intends to comply, unlike some states, including the European Union, that are more likely to see commitments as goals. Other states frequently accept obligations they have no intention of complying with or know that they will not be capable of fulfilling in the near future (this was often the case with the former Soviet Union).[67] This propensity may influence the degree to which the United States is willing to take on obligations, limiting them to those with which it intends to comply. Structural constraints only serve to magnify this tendency.

Structurally, the separation of powers between the executive and legislative branches of government and the fact that the Senate must ratify treaties by a two-thirds majority can be seen to have the effect of hindering U.S. international environmental action under certain circumstances. Although a domestic ratification process for treaties exists in most countries, the U.S. barrier is doubly high, requiring not only a supermajority vote but also one in a completely different branch of government. As Oona Hathaway notes, the United States is nearly unique in its high barrier to ratification—it is one of only six states worldwide that requires support by a supermajority of a legislative body, and it is one of only a few in which ratification involves automatic incorporation into domestic law.[68] Many other advanced industrialized democracies operate under parliamentary systems in which the head of government is a member of the majority (or largest) party; thus, treaties submitted to parliament for ratification by the prime minister are likely to be accepted. Some have noted that the willingness of Congress to reassert its control over foreign policy increased in the post–Cold War era, when the need for strong central executive leadership lessened.[69] Under this explanation, the two branches of government may be at odds about what a policy should be, resulting in a situation in which the president pushes an international approach that Congress refuses to go along with.

That it is the Senate that ratifies treaties by such a supermajority may be especially important. The U.S. Senate is particularly prone to economic pressure from special interest groups. Elections to the Senate ensure that each state is represented by two senators who are more concerned about the issues that matter to their states than they are about those that affect the country as a whole. This focus is an avenue for industry impact. And, as Hathaway points out, the ideological composition of the Senate also means that the two-thirds ratification threshold requires cooperation among senators on vastly different parts of the political spectrum. If senators serving in the 109th Congress had been lined up on an ideological spectrum, the sixty-seventh senator would have been rated more than twice as conservative as the fifty-first; the same would have been true in the liberal direction.[70] The polarization (and rightward tilt) has only increased since then, most dramatically with the emergency of the so-called tea party as a right-wing political force. Requiring a two-thirds majority makes agreement orders of magnitude more difficult than requiring a simple majority would.

Even for processes that do not require ratification, the current version of the filibuster rule requires consent of three-fifths of the Senate to move a measure forward to a vote. Although this procedure has long existed, its use has increased exponentially in recent years. The separation of executive and legislative branches in the United States and the increased polarization of Congress may serve to explain increased U.S. reluctance on international environmental issues compared with other major industrialized states, but it alone cannot explain the variations in degrees of U.S. unilateralism on different environmental issues.

What is possible, however, is that the role of the Senate intersects with some characteristics of environmental issues to influence the likelihood of

U.S. international leadership on a given issue. The Senate's consideration and adoption of the Byrd-Hagel resolution is itself an indication of the important congressional role in addressing international environmental policy. The Senate took up this issue on its own, not only without direction from the executive branch but also without making President Clinton even aware, until the last minute, that such a debate would happen. At that point the White House could not hope to stop the adoption of the resolution and simply tried to moderate its language.[71] In the case of this particular resolution, Democratic senator Robert C. Byrd represented West Virginia, a major coal producer, and Republican senator Chuck Hagel represented Nebraska, where agriculture, the most important economic sector, is highly mechanized and thus sensitive to the price of oil.[72]

What brings these explanations together is the process of domestic congressional regulation. One notable consistency in U.S. international environmental leadership is the extent to which the United States had already undertaken domestic regulatory action—on the topic and in the form being considered internationally—at the point at which such action was being pushed internationally. Harold Jacobson's description of the U.S. experience with environmental multilateralism is telling: he points to the U.S. wave of multilateral environmental diplomacy in the 1970s with the following description: "As soon as U.S. legislation designed to protect and enhance the environment was in place, the United States typically proposed that multilateral treaties be negotiated to achieve the same objective."[73] Note, for example, that a major concern in the U.S. decision about whether to sign or ratify the CBD was the question of whether it could be implemented within the existing legal framework protecting endangered species and land resources. This understanding is especially useful for explaining the U.S. reluctance on climate change: the United States not only has no preexisting domestic climate change mitigation policy but also has traditionally rejected any sort of tax on energy. This reluctance has been particularly demonstrated in Congress. Similarly, one analyst points out that an important sticking point in the effort to ratify the Stockholm Convention on Persistent Organic Pollutants is that the convention calls for the elimination of chemicals that the United States has not already banned domestically.[74]

This analysis does not imply that U.S. industry is always cheerful about adopting international environmental regulations, but it does suggest that the existence of previous domestic regulations on an industry changes its interests internationally. The example of ozone depletion, a potentially costly regulatory issue with a reasonably high degree of uncertainty at the time of international regulation, is illustrative. Although the history of U.S. regulatory efforts on the subject shows that producers and large consumers of CFCs fought initial regulatory efforts (and invoked scientific uncertainty as well as industrial cost as arguments against regulation), industry eventually acquiesced to international regulation. The process began domestically, when consumer purchasing habits and pressure from domestic environmental organizations persuaded Congress to include a ban on CFCs in nonessential aerosols in the

1977 Clean Air Act Amendments. That regulation, which the main producers of CFCs fought from the beginning (and attempted to get repealed after
it had passed),[75] nevertheless put CFC producers and consumers on notice
that they would have to come up with alternatives for at least some of their
activities. It also fundamentally changed their incentive structure (especially
when they realized that increasingly severe domestic regulations were likely).
They then were more likely to support international controls on CFCs so that
foreign industries with which they competed internationally would have to be
bound by the same costly restrictions.

Conclusion

To the detriment of global environmental cooperation, U.S. leadership (and
even level of participation) in international environmental agreements has
been mixed and can be seen as declining in the past two decades. To attribute
this trend simply to increasing U.S. unilateralism misses the opportunity,
however, to understand when and why the United States is more or less likely
to lead internationally on environmental issues. Within a domestic framework that can make international participation difficult, it is nevertheless
possible for the United States to exercise international leadership. It tends to
do so on issues it has already addressed domestically and where the form of
the domestic regulation fits the format of the international regulation being
considered. Under those circumstances, domestic opposition to international
action is muted or even avoided because domestic industries, which have
disproportionate influence on the senators who have to vote for ratification of
any international agreements, either are not additionally disadvantaged by
new international regulations or even welcome those that restrict the actions
of their international competitors. To the extent that the United States
returns to global environmental leadership under President Obama, this shift
is likely to be attributable at least as much to the change in the composition
of the Senate as it is to executive branch leadership.

The United States took an early lead in the domestic regulation of many
environmental harms in the 1960s and 1970s, and those regulations set the
groundwork for many international efforts to deal with the global versions
of these problems. It is thus no surprise that the United States would be both
willing and able to lead globally in addressing them. To the extent that the
United States has more recently ceased in many issue areas to be a domestic
innovator on environmental policy, it is also no surprise that the country
resists international action on newer international environmental issues.
Although issues such as uncertainty and the effect on the United States of
environmental problems or the costliness of regulatory solutions certainly
contribute to the difficulty of international regulation, where they are particularly important may be at the level of domestic regulation. Those who
would prefer that the United States lead internationally should perhaps
focus their efforts on creating the domestic regulations that give it the incentive to do so.

The issues are rarely so clear-cut, however, and the links between domestic and international action are becoming more porous. The case of climate change particularly bears watching, as U.S. domestic industries are in some instances becoming the major proponents of U.S. action on climate change or are undertaking meaningful voluntary steps themselves to address the problem. The Law of the Sea may have a similar dynamic. The pattern we have traditionally seen, of U.S. action following only from domestic regulation, may be changing with the more diffuse and complex environmental issues that are appearing on the international agenda. It may come to pass that U.S. domestic action on such issues as climate change, regulation of toxics, and ocean governance happens in the reverse, pushed by industry affected by international (or subnational) regulation. Given the central importance of U.S. action for protection of the global environment, pressure is needed, whether the push comes from subnational or supranational actors.

Notes

1. Office of the President-Elect, "Agenda—Energy and the Environment," http://change.gov/agenda/energy_and_environment_agenda/2008.
2. Brian Gareau, *From Precaution to Profit: Contemporary Challenges to Environmental Protection in the Montreal Protocol* (New Haven, CT: Yale University Press, 2013).
3. John B. Bellinger, "Obama's Weakness on Treaties," *New York Times,* December 18, 2012, http://www.nytimes.com/2012/12/19/opinion/obamas-weakness-on-treaties.html?_r=0.
4. Jutta Brunnée, "The United States and International Environmental Law: Living with an Elephant," *European Journal of International Law* 15, no. 4 (2004): 617–649.
5. Central Intelligence Agency, "Country Comparison—Population Growth Rate," *World Factbook,* 2012, https://www.cia.gov/library/publications/the-world-factbook/rankorder/2002rank.html.
6. Anup Shah, "Foreign Aid for Development Assistance," *Global Issues,* April 8, 2012, http://www.globalissues.org/article/35/foreign-aid-development-assistance.
7. Richard B. Stewart, "Environmental Regulation and International Competitiveness," *Yale Law Journal* 102 (1993): 2046.
8. Michael J. Glennon and Alison L. Stewart, "The United States: Taking Environmental Treaties Seriously," in *Engaging Countries: Strengthening Compliance with International Environmental Accords,* ed. Edith Brown Weiss and Harold K. Jacobson (Cambridge: MIT Press, 1998), 197–213.
9. 16 U.S.C. 3372(a)(1) (1988).
10. The Endangered Species Conservation Act of 1969 called on the United States to seek "the signing of a binding international convention on the conservation of endangered species." P.L. 91-135 (Section 5).
11. It should be noted, however, that the United States is not a participant in the Bonn Convention on the Conservation of Migratory Species of Wild Animals (1979).
12. William C. Clark, Jill Jäger, Jeannine Cavender-Bares, and Nancy M. Dickson, "Acid Rain, Ozone Depletion, and Climate Change: An Historical Overview," in Social Learning Group, *Learning to Manage Global Environmental Risks,* vol. 1 (Cambridge: MIT Press, 2001), 35.
13. 43 *Federal Register* 11301; 43 *Federal Register* 11318.
14. Elizabeth R. DeSombre, *Domestic Sources of International Environmental Policy: Industry, Environmentalists, and U.S. Power* (Cambridge: MIT Press, 2000), 94.
15. William A. Nitze, "A Failure of Presidential Leadership," in *Negotiating Climate Change: The Inside Story of the Rio Convention,* ed. Irving M. Mintzer and J. A. Leonard (Cambridge: Cambridge University Press, 1994), 188.

16. United Nations Framework Convention on Climate Change (1992), Articles 2 and 3.
17. U.S. Congress, Senate, 102d Cong., 2d sess., *Senate Congressional Record,* daily ed., October 1992, S.17, 156.
18. Michael Grubb with Christiaan Vrolijk and Duncan Brack, *The Kyoto Protocol* (London: Royal Institute of International Affairs, 1999), 54.
19. Kyoto Protocol (1997), Annex B.
20. U.S. Congress, Senate, 105th Cong., 1st sess., *Congressional Record,* daily ed., July 27, 1997, S8113–S8138.
21. Bill Curry, "Ottawa Now Wants Kyoto Deal Scrapped," *Globe and Mail,* May 20, 2006, http://www.climateark.org/shared/reader/welcome.aspx?linkid=56534.
22. Jack Kemp and Fred L. Smith Jr., "Beware of the Kyoto Compromise," *New York Times,* January 13, 1999, sec. A.
23. Kai S. Anderson, "The Climate Policy Debate in the U.S. Congress," in *Climate Change Policy: A Survey,* ed. Stephen H. Schneider, Armin Rosencranz, and John O. Niles (Washington, DC: Island Press, 2002), 243.
24. Ibid., 244.
25. Joseph I. Lieberman and John McCain, "Tap U.S. Innovation to Ease Global Warming," *Los Angeles Times,* January 8, 2003, Op-Ed, http://articles.latimes.com/2003/jan/08/opinion/oe-lieber8.
26. Pew Center on Global Climate Change, "Analysis of the Lieberman-Warner Climate Security Act of 2008," June 6, 2008, http://www.pewclimate.org/analysis/1-w.
27. Center for Climate and Energy Solutions, "111th Congress Climate Change Legislation," C2ES, n.d., http://www.c2es.org/federal/congress/111.
28. Center for Climate and Energy Solutions, "Climate Debate in Congress," C2ES, 2013, http://www.c2es.org/federal/congress.
29. Pew Center on Global Climate Change, "State Legislation from around the Country," n.d., http://www.pewclimate.org/what_s_being_done/in_the_states/state_legislation.cfm.
30. Henrik Selin and Stacy D. VanDeveer, "Political Science and Prediction: What's Next for U.S. Climate Change Policy," *Review of Policy Research* 24, no. 1 (2007): 1–27.
31. Pew Center for Global Climate Change, "Regional Initiatives," n.d., http://www.pewclimate.org/what_s_being_done/in_the_states/regional_initiatives.cfm.
32. North America 2050, "A Partnership for Progress," http://na2050.org.
33. U.S. Environmental Protection Agency, "Endangerment and Cause or Contribute Findings for Greenhouse Gases under Section 202(a) of the Clean Air Act," 2012, http://www.epa.gov/climatechange/endangerment/index.html.
34. U.S. Supreme Court, *Massachusetts v. EPA,* 549 U.S. 497, 2007.
35. U.S. Environmental Protection Agency, "Transportation and Climate—Regulations and Standards," 2012, http://www.epa.gov/otaq/climate/regulations.htm.
36. "China Surpasses U.S. Emissions," *International Herald Tribune,* June 21, 2007, 12.
37. Kal Raustiala, "The Domestic Politics of Global Biodiversity Protection in the United Kingdom and United States," in *The Internationalization of Environmental Protection,* ed. Miranda A. Schreurs and Elizabeth C. Economy (Cambridge: Cambridge University Press, 1997), 42–73. Issues of biosafety were later included in a separate protocol.
38. Ann Devroy, "President Affirms Biodiversity Stance; Citing Jobs, Bush Firmly Rejects Treaty," *Washington Post,* June 8, 1992, sec. A.
39. Kal Raustiala, "Domestic Institutions and International Regulatory Cooperation: Comparative Responses to the Convention on Biological Diversity," *World Politics* 49, no. 4 (1997): 482–509.
40. Raustiala, "The Domestic Politics of Global Biodiversity Protection Sources"; Raustiala, "Domestic Institutions and International Regulatory Cooperation."
41. Robert L. Paarlberg, "Earth in Abeyance: Explaining Weak Leadership in U.S. International Environmental Policy," in *Eagle Adrift: American Foreign Policy at the End of the Century,* ed. Robert J. Lieber (New York: Longman, 1997), 135–160.

42. Marian A. L. Miller, *The Third World in Global Environmental Politics* (Boulder, CO: Lynne Rienner, 1995), 87–88.
43. Kate O'Neill, "Hazardous Waste Disposal," *Foreign Policy in Focus* 4, no. 1 (January 1999), http://fpif.org.
44. Jim Puckett, "The Basel Ban: A Triumph over Business-as-Usual," Basel Action Network, October 1, 1997, www.ban.org/about_basel_ban/jims_article.html.
45. See, for instance, the Basel Action Network, http://www.ban.org.
46. Kristin S. Schafer, "Global Toxics Treaties: U.S. Leadership Opportunity Slips Away," *Foreign Policy in Focus* 7, no. 11 (September 2002), http://fpif.org.
47. Ibid.
48. See, for example, U.S. Congress, House of Representatives, 109th Cong., 1st sess., "Stockholm and Rotterdam Toxics Treaty Act of 2005," HR 4591; and House of Representatives, 109th Cong., 2d sess., "POPS, LRTAP POPS and PIC Implementation Act of 2006," HR 4800.
49. Don Kraus and John Feffer, "Time to Ratify the Law of the Sea," *Foreign Policy in Focus*, June 6, 2007, http://fpif.org/time_to_ratify_the_law_of_the_sea.
50. William L. Schachte Jr., "The Unvarnished Truth: The Debate on the Law of the Sea Convention," *Naval War College Review* 61, no. 2 (Spring 2008): 119–127.
51. Paul Reynolds, "Russia Ahead in Arctic 'Gold Rush,'" BBC News, August 1, 2007, http://news.bbc.co.uk/2/hi/in_depth/6925853.stm.
52. Schachte, "The Unvarnished Truth," 119.
53. Keith Johnson, "GOP Scuttles Law-of-Sea Treaty," *Wall Street Journal*, Washington Wire blog, July 16, 2012, http://blogs.wsj.com/washwire/2012/07/16/gop-opposition-scuttles-law-of-sea-treaty.
54. Harold K. Jacobson, "Climate Change, Unilateralism, Realism, and Two-Level Games," in *Multilateralism and U.S. Foreign Policy: Ambivalent Engagement*, ed. Shepard Forman and Stewart Patrick (Boulder, CO: Lynne Rienner, 2002), 428.
55. Ibid.
56. David Forsythe, *The Internationalization of Human Rights* (Lexington, MA: Lexington Books, 1991).
57. Andrew Moravcsik, "Why Is U.S. Human Rights Policy So Unilateralist?," in Forman and Patrick, *Multilateralism and U.S. Foreign Policy*, 435–476.
58. Sheila Jasanoff, "American Exceptionalism and the Political Acknowledgment of Risk," *Daedalus* 19, no. 4 (Fall 1990): 395–406.
59. Lawrence E. Susskind, *Environmental Diplomacy: Negotiating More Effective Global Agreements* (Oxford: Oxford University Press, 1994), 65.
60. Detlef Sprinz and Tapani Vaahtoranta, "The Interest-Based Explanation of International Environmental Policy," *International Organization* 48, no. 1 (Winter 1998): 77–105.
61. Sebastian Oberthür and Hermann E. Ott, *The Kyoto Protocol: International Climate Policy for the 21st Century* (Berlin: Springer, 1999), 18.
62. U.S. Department of Energy, "Comparing Cost Estimates for the Kyoto Protocol," Report no. SR/OIAF/98-03 (1998), http://www.eia.gov/oiaf/kyoto/cost.html.
63. Detlef F. Sprinz and Martin Weiß, "Domestic Politics and Global Climate Policy," in *International Relations and Global Climate Change*, ed. Urs Luterbacher and Detlef F. Sprinz (Cambridge: MIT Press, 2001), 67–94.
64. Andrew Moravcsik lists this as one of the four characteristics he sees as explaining U.S. unilateralism on international human rights issues. See Moravcsik, "Why Is U.S. Human Rights Policy So Unilateralist?," 348.
65. Peter F. Cowhey, "International Telecommunications Regime: The Political Roots of Regimes for High Technology," *International Organization* 44 (Spring 1990): 171.
66. Raustiala, "Domestic Institutions and International Regulatory Cooperation," 487.
67. See, generally, Edith Brown Weiss and Harold K. Jacobson, eds., *Engaging Countries: Strengthening Compliance with International Environmental Accords* (Cambridge: MIT Press, 1998).

68. Oona A. Hathaway, "Treaties' End: The Past, Present, and Future of International Lawmaking in the United States," *Yale Law Journal* 117, no. 8 (2008): 1236–1372.
69. Stewart Patrick, "Multilateralism and Its Discontents: The Causes and Consequences of U.S. Ambivalence," in Forman and Patrick, *Multilateralism and U.S. Foreign Policy*, 1–44.
70. Hathaway, "Treaties' End," 1310–1311.
71. Jacobson, "Climate Change, Unilateralism, Realism, and Two-Level Games," 442.
72. Ibid.
73. Ibid., 415.
74. Schafer, "Global Toxics Treaties."
75. The main industry lobbying group, the Alliance for Responsible CFC Policy, did such things as draft legislation to be introduced into Congress to limit the EPA's ability to regulate ozone-depleting substances. "Congress Debates Depletion of Ozone in the Stratosphere," *Christian Science Monitor*, October 14, 1981, 19.

7

Environmental Policy Making and Global Leadership in the European Union

Regina S. Axelrod and Miranda A. Schreurs

The European Union, with a population of close to half a billion, a membership of twenty-eight countries (and still growing), and the largest gross domestic product (GDP) of any economy in the world, has transformed Europe. The establishment of a common internal economic market contributed to the opening of national borders and the harmonization of many policies once in the exclusive domain of individual member states. The EU also has established some of the strongest and most innovative environmental protection measures in the world. In principle, environmental protection now enjoys equal weight with economic development in EU policy making. It is quite remarkable that despite its mix of countries and cultures—some rich, some relatively poor—the EU has managed to become an international agenda setter in relation to climate change, renewable energy, chemicals regulation, product standards, biosafety, and numerous other environmental matters.[1] It is an impressive development that provides valuable lessons for other regions of the world to consider.

Political will and public support have been key factors behind the EU's success in approaching the environment from an integrated perspective. Over time, legal foundations were firmly established, giving the EU the right to take measures to protect the environment. Member states have come to recognize that without common environmental policies, barriers to free trade develop. There is also a growing conviction that future economic well-being is inherently tied to the quality of the environment. And there is concern about the long-term health of the planet and the exhaustion of its resources. Contrary to what one might expect, the political, economic, and geographic diversity that characterize the EU have not brought environmental policy making to a standstill, but instead have challenged policy makers to develop innovative strategies and skills for overcoming differences and sharing burdens equitably, both of which are important at the global level as well.

The EU is therefore an important model to study, both as the most advanced regional organization of states and as a comprehensive environmental policy regime. The EU also is an important actor in global environmental diplomacy, negotiating treaties on behalf of member states. At least since the 1992 United Nations Conference on Environment and Development, the EU has played a leading role in promoting international environmental agreements.

As a result of its enlargement, the EU shapes environmental policy from the Baltic to the Aegean. All states hoping to join the EU are required to transpose the entire body of EU laws, regulations, and directives, collectively known as the *acquis communautaire*, into domestic legislation. Enlargement has both complicated internal negotiations on environmental matters and provided opportunities to strengthen the EU's international reach on environmental issues. This chapter explores the history, institutions, current environmental policies, and future challenges of this unique supranational body.

EU Political Origins: Treaties of the European Union and Environmental Policy

The quest for political and economic union in Europe has its origins in the 1920s and 1930s, when it was recognized that some kind of supranational organization was needed to avoid brutal competition, protectionism, and war. But it was the experience of World War II that convinced statesmen to seek a new type of unity. U.S. economic assistance under the postwar Marshall Plan also called for regional cooperation.

The first step toward building a more integrated Europe was the formation of the European Coal and Steel Community (ECSC). The idea of French economic planner Jean Monnet and foreign minister Robert Schumann, the ECSC was created by the Treaty of Paris on April 18, 1951. The original members were Belgium, France, Germany, Italy, Luxembourg, and the Netherlands. The ECSC's economic goal was to pool the production of coal and steel for the benefit of all six countries. Its other purpose was to lock Germany, politically and economically, into a stable partnership with Western Europe.

As a next step, the six ECSC members decided to move toward closer economic integration as a means to increase industrial and agricultural exports, redistribute resources to economically depressed areas, and encourage travel among countries. The result was the 1957 Treaty of Rome, which established the European Economic Community (EEC), a free trade area or "common market," and the European Atomic Energy Authority (Euratom), for the promotion of nuclear energy in Europe. In the 1970s Denmark, Ireland, and the United Kingdom joined the EEC; Greece entered in 1981, and Portugal and Spain in 1986. Austria, Finland, and Sweden became full members in 1995, bringing the membership to fifteen.[2] In 2004 the membership of the EU expanded to twenty-five with the accession of Cyprus, the Czech Republic, Estonia, Hungary, Latvia, Lithuania, Malta, Poland, the Slovak Republic, and Slovenia. Bulgaria and Romania joined in 2007 and Croatia in 2013.[3] Iceland, the former Yugoslav Republic of Macedonia, Montenegro, Serbia, and Turkey are candidate countries for future membership, although the publics of these countries and those of some EU member states are mixed in their attitudes regarding their joining the EU. Albania, Bosnia and Herzegovina, and Kosovo are potential candidate countries, meaning they also have prospects of EU accession but only in the medium to long term.

Map 7-1 European Union Member States, 2014

The European Union is built on a series of treaties. The Treaty of Rome contained no explicit provisions for protection of the environment. EEC policy on the environment dates from the 1972 Paris summit of the Community's heads of state and government, which was inspired in part by the United Nations Conference on the Human Environment held earlier that year in Stockholm. Under Article 235 of the Treaty of Rome, the summit proposed the creation of an environmental action program setting out environmental protection priorities for the Community. In the following decades, a series of six environmental action programs were adopted covering the period from 1973 to 2012. In addition, numerous environmental directives and regulations were adopted, governing air and water, waste management, noise reduction, protection of endangered flora and fauna, environmental impact assessment, and other topics.

The next milestone in the development of the treaties was the Single European Act of 1986, which accelerated the European integration process by calling for establishment of a single internal economic market by the end of 1992. Equally important, the act added a new section to the Treaty of

Rome that formally defined the goals and procedures of EEC environmental policies and called for "balanced growth" through the integration of environmental policy into all other areas of decision making.

The Maastricht Treaty (also called the Treaty on European Union), which was signed in 1992, advocated closer political and monetary union. It also strengthened the legal basis and procedures for environmental policy making. This trend continued with revisions initiated by the Treaty of Amsterdam in 1997, which stated that "environmental protection requirements must be integrated into the definition and implementation of Community policies and activities . . . in particular with a view to promoting sustainable development."[4]

The 2001 Treaty of Nice dealt primarily with the effects of enlargement on EU institutions but also reaffirmed the Union's commitment to environmental policy. At the December 2000 Nice conference that led to the treaty's formation, a declaration was adopted affirming member states' determination "to see the European Union play a leading role in promoting environmental protection in the Union and in international efforts promoting the same objective at global level."[5]

The growing complexity and size of the EU led to an effort to create a European Constitution that would replace the many treaties governing the union's institutions and member state relations. When this effort failed as a result of referenda in France and the Netherlands, the fallback option was the Treaty of Lisbon, which was signed in 2007 and entered into force on December 1, 2009. The Lisbon Treaty amended earlier treaties without replacing them. It changed voting procedures in the European Council, strengthened the role of the European Parliament in decision making, and created new leadership positions. The treaty specifically states that combating climate change is a goal.

Main EU Institutions

In the Treaty of Lisbon the EU was given legal status and seven formal institutions were named: the European Council, the Council of the European Union, the European Commission, the European Parliament, the Court of Justice of the European Union (or European Court of Justice, ECJ), the European Central Bank, and the Court of Auditors. The treaty also established numerous secondary agencies, including the European Environment Agency (EEA).

The *European Council* is very important as it sets the broad policy agenda for the EU and serves as a forum for building intergovernmental consensus on issues and dealing with points of disagreement among the leaderships of individual member states. The European Council consists of the heads of government and states of the member states, the president of the Council (a position newly created by the Treaty of Lisbon), and the president of the Commission. The high representative of the Union for foreign affairs and security policy also takes part in its work. In addition to the president of the

Council, who is sometimes known as the president of the EU (Herman van Rompuy being the first to hold this post), there is a presidency of the Council. The presidency rotates among the member states every six months, and the country in charge has considerable power to shape the agenda of meetings. The list of countries scheduled to hold the presidency from 2014 through 2020 is as follows: Greece, Italy, Latvia, Luxembourg, the Netherlands, Slovakia, Malta, the United Kingdom, Estonia, Bulgaria, Austria, Romania, and Finland.

More specific policies and proposals are debated and decided upon in the *Council of the European Union* (often referred to simply as the Council of Ministers or just as the Council). Depending on the issue being discussed, different ministers come together. Thus, when environmental issues are being discussed, the EU's twenty-eight environmental ministers may be called together to meet as the Environment Council. This tends to happen about four times a year. During the March 2013 Environment Council meeting, the ministers debated a draft directive on indirect land-use change, proposed amendments to the fuel quality and renewable energy directives, debated a draft regulation on access to genetic resources and the fair and equitable sharing of benefits arising from their use in the EU, and proposed changes to the environmental impact assessment directive that would streamline environmental assessments but also strengthen standards.[6] In some cases, such as with determining EU climate targets for 2030, different groups of ministers (such as energy and environment) might meet together.

A significant change to EU policy making occurred with the introduction of qualified majority voting in the Council by the 1986 Single European Act. For environmental matters this meant that environmental regulations no longer required consensus among all member states to pass, but rather a special type of majority. Qualified majority voting gives greater weight to states with large populations but protects smaller states by requiring a majority of votes. Under this system, the votes of large countries were given more weight than the votes of those with smaller populations. Thus, the votes of Germany, France, the United Kingdom, and Italy weighted at twenty-nine, Spain and Poland at twenty-seven, Romania at fourteen, and so on, with the smallest country, Malta, weighted at three. After the 2007 enlargement, a qualified majority required 74 percent of the (weighted) votes in the Council, plus a coverage of at least 62 percent of the EU's total population. The Treaty of Lisbon introduced a new double majority procedure, in effect as of November 2014. Under this system, for a law to pass, 55 percent of the members of the Council, comprising at least fifteen states and at least 65 percent of the EU's population, will be needed. Qualified majority voting and the new double majority system under the Lisbon Treaty are important institutions that limit the ability of a single or very small number of member states to block action at the Community level that the majority desires. At the same time, they provide minority interests with the ability to prevent large states from pushing through policies with which small states do not agree.[7]

The *European Commission*, which functions partly as an executive branch, partly as an administrative bureaucracy, and partly as a drafter of legislation, is led by appointed commissioners and includes more than forty directorates-general and services that are somewhat analogous to ministries and agencies of national governments.[8] The commissioners and their staffs are international civil servants who are not supposed to serve any national interest. The Commission's tasks include initiating EU legislation and overseeing its implementation by member states. The Commission is also empowered to negotiate international agreements on behalf of the Community on the mandate of the Council. The Treaties of Amsterdam and Nice strengthened substantially the powers of the Commission president. Romano Prodi held this position from 1999 to 2004. Since then the position has been held by José Manuel Barroso. A multinational bureaucracy of more than 32,000 civil servants serves the Commission and its directorates in Brussels.[9]

The Directorate-General for the Environment, with approximately 515 staff members, addresses issues concerning air and water quality, nature conservation, biodiversity, land use, marine affairs, sustainable resources management, eco innovation, and international environmental affairs, among others. The Directorate-General for Climate, newly established in 2010 and with a staff of 150, is responsible for the international climate negotiations, the EU's Emissions Trading System, and the implementation of the EU's climate policy goals. The Commission has been an important agenda setter in many environmental areas.

The *European Parliament* is elected directly by voters in each country and tends to reflect the diverse interests of political parties and groupings across Europe. Because of the accessions of new member states in 2004 and 2007, the number of parliamentarians has been in flux. Since the 2009 election, there have been 736 members of the European Parliament and 18 observers. The next election is scheduled for May 2014, when the Parliament's size will once again increase. There are seven recognized party groupings in the Parliament that bring parties of similar ideological leanings together: the center-right European People's Party and the more left-leaning Party of European Socialists and Democrats are the largest. They are followed in size by the Alliance of Liberals and Democrats for Europe and the Greens-European Free Alliance. The Parliament holds plenary sessions in Strasbourg, France, but much of its staff is in Luxembourg, and most of its committee meetings are held in Brussels.

Initially the Parliament was greatly limited in its ability to influence the shape of legislation. Its main powers were in its abilities to approve or reject the Commission's proposal for a budget and to vote to accept or reject Commission proposals for legislation. Strong criticisms that the restricted role of the Parliament equated to a major democratic deficit in the EU's institutional structures led to a strengthening of the Parliament's powers through treaty amendments. The Treaty of Maastricht initiated a "co-decision" authority, which in subsequent treaties was extended to cover most policy areas, including the environment. The Parliament is now basically on an equal footing with the Council of Ministers in determining most EU laws. The Parliament can vote to approve or reject a Commission proposal or can amend it.

The Committee on the Environment, Public Health and Food Safety (ENVI), the largest legislative committee in the Parliament, studies and debates critical policy issues related to the regulation of toxic chemicals, the preservation of biodiversity, the promotion of a resource-efficient sustainable Europe, climate change, food safety, and many other issues. In 2011, for example, the committee made a proposal to amend a Commission proposal on genetically modified crops that only vaguely stated that a member state could give "other" reasons to ban or restrict a genetically modified organism (GMO) that had been given a green light at the EU (see also Chapter 12). The committee proposed that greater attention be paid to the idea that member states could use health or environmental arguments—such as concerns about pesticide resistance, the invasiveness of crops, or potential loss of biodiversity—as the basis for restricting or banning GMOs.[10]

The *European Court of Justice* (ECJ), located in Luxembourg, considers cases brought before it by the Commission, the Council, or member states concerning the application of EU treaties. It has one judge per member state. Member states' national courts may request that the ECJ provide interpretations of EU law. In 2008, for example, in response to a request by the Federal Administrative Court of Germany for interpretation of a Council directive on air quality assessment and management, the ECJ ruled that individuals have the right to require national authorities to draw up action plans when there is a risk that emission limit values or alert thresholds may be exceeded.[11] The Commission or another EU country also may initiate infringement proceedings in the ECJ against a member state that is failing to fulfill its obligations under EU law. In addition, the ECJ has protected the right of member states to keep national laws that exceed Community-wide standards.

The *European Environment Agency*, approved in 1990, was established in 1994 in Copenhagen after a long battle over its location. The EEA does not have regulatory and enforcement powers; rather, it is tasked with helping the Community and member states make informed decisions about the environment. Its membership includes, in addition to the EU member states, Iceland, Liechtenstein, Norway, Switzerland, and Turkey. The Balkan countries are cooperating partners. The EEA also collects and distributes environmental data through the European Environment Information and Observation Network (EIONET), which consists of about three hundred environmental bodies, agencies, and research centers.[12] It issues a substantial number of reports about the European environment each year, including emissions inventories and many types of environmental assessments and scenarios.

The Policy Process

Policy making within the EU is more "political" than a description of the institutions might suggest. Because the EU is a fluid and developing set of institutions, it is subject to frequent changes in institutional roles, power relationships, and decision-making rules. Although scholars still debate whether the EU is primarily an "intergovernmental" organization dominated by the interests of individual member states or a "functional" regime that represents common transnational interests and actors, it is increasingly regarded as a competent environmental actor functioning as a "multilevel governance structure."[13]

The Commission's proposed legislation tends to favor greater harmonization of European policies. Parliament also tends to favor stronger EU policies, especially in fields that are popular with the electorate, such as environmental and consumer protection. The Council, in contrast, is usually more cautious because of its sensitivity to national political interests and the costs of implementing EU policies (which largely devolve on national governments). The Council is more likely to invoke the principle of *subsidiarity*, under which actions are to be taken at the EU level only if they cannot be carried out more efficiently at the national or local level.[14]

Agenda setting in the EU is complex. Numerous actors at different levels may try to get EU policy makers to pay attention to an issue and frame how issues are viewed and discussed.[15] Being a first mover on an issue can be an important aspect of the agenda-setting process. To stimulate discussion on an issue, the Commission sometimes issues a green paper, such as the one it issued in 2001 that boldly criticized EU fishery policy as being unsustainable and argued for a dramatic shift in policy.[16] This paper was meant to put reform of the common fisheries policy on the agenda while also stimulating stakeholder debate. It led to a series of action plans, communications, and regulations, but as a second green paper in 2009 calling for a major overhaul in the common fisheries policy made clear, there was little improvement in conditions. EU fish stocks are in such a severe state of depletion that major reform is now on the agenda, as discussed further below.

In addition to green papers, the Commission may issue white papers to lay out policy recommendations. Relevant examples include the 2000 white paper "Environmental Liability," the 2009 white paper "Adapting to Climate Change: The European Union Must Prepare for the Impacts to Come,"[17] and the 2011 "Roadmap to a Single European Transport Area—Towards a Competitive and Resource Efficient Transport System," which among other things called for cutting carbon emissions in transport by 60 percent by 2050.[18]

At other times, the Parliament's Environment Committee may push for stronger environmental leadership by the EU.[19] This has been the case with a wide range of issues, including adding the airline industry into the emissions trading scheme, illegal timber imports, packaging waste, and climate. The Parliament, for example, issued a resolution calling upon the Council to speak with one voice on climate change and maintain a leadership role on climate during the Copenhagen climate negotiations in December 2009.[20] Similarly, it passed a resolution calling for the EU to push for an extension of the Kyoto Protocol at the Durban climate negotiations in 2011.[21] An example of a case in which the Parliament did not take a strong pro-environment stance was in its vote to block a reform proposal for the ailing European emissions trading system in April 2013.[22]

Conflicts of interest among the states are most evident in the Council.[23] Industrial and other lobbies within a country or countries might fight to prevent or weaken EU legislation pushed by the Commission or other member states that they see as detrimental to their own interests. This was the case, for example, after the Commission argued for EU carbon dioxide (CO_2) standards for new cars, given that the automobile industry had failed to meet the voluntary targets it had itself earlier established. Germany's and France's powerful automobile industries were opposed to the Commission's proposed timetables and standards, arguing that the costs would be too high in terms of jobs, especially at a time of financial crisis.[24] The French president, Nicolas Sarkozy, and the German chancellor, Angela Merkel, bowed to this pressure and proposed an alternative but weaker proposal. In the end, a coalition of member states led by the Netherlands and backed by Belgium, Denmark, Finland, Sweden, and the United Kingdom opposed the French and German move and backed the Commission's proposal. France and Germany were forced to back down.[25] In April 2009 the countries agreed on a regulation establishing carbon dioxide emission standards for new light-duty vehicles effective as of January 2012, with standards becoming even more stringent for 2020.[26]

Yet it is also the case that industries may have an interest in getting the EU to adopt standards that have been adopted already at the national level—a process tied to "regulatory competition."[27] For example, Germany was influential in pushing for the EU to adopt air pollution controls on large combustion plants (Council Directive 88/609/EEC), packaging waste requirements (Council and Parliament Directive 94/62/EC), and renewable energy standards (Council and Parliament Directive 2009/28/EC). After domestic legislation was put into place, Germany had an interest in ensuring that other member states were subject to similar environmental controls. It has been argued that this is one reason there is not an inevitable downward spiral to lowest-common-denominator legislation.[28] Success is not, however, always guaranteed. Britain, Denmark, Germany, Greece, Portugal, Spain, and Sweden failed in their efforts to push a higher renewable energy target for 2020 at the EU level than the existing 20 percent target because of strong opposition from Poland.[29]

Enlargement and the Acquis Communautaire. One of the principal challenges facing the EU has been finding ways of accommodating different levels of environmental commitment and regulatory capacity without weakening ultimate goals. This has become an even bigger challenge because of the accession of central, eastern, and southern European states that are economically less wealthy than the first 15 EU member states and have different priorities and concerns. Various strategies have been adopted to ease the transition of the new member states into the EU and to bring their environmental programs into line with the demands of the *acquis communautaire*.[30] Particularly important were the assistance programs that were set up to assist accession states in preparing for enlargement. These included instruments such as Poland-Hungary: Assistance for Restructuring Their Economies (PHARE), which was later broadened to include other accession countries, and the Instrument for Structural Policies for Pre-Accession (ISPA), which focused on environmental and transportation infrastructure priorities. For EU member states three main sources of funding exist to help with adjusting to EU regulatory expectations: structural funds (for agriculture, social, and regional development), cohesion funds (for support of environment and infrastructure in the poorest member states), and the financial instrument for the environment, known as LIFE.

Burden Sharing. Another strategy that has been used to deal with member states' differing capacities is the development of burden-sharing agreements. In the case of the Kyoto Protocol, the EU agreed to reduce its combined emissions of greenhouse gases by 8 percent of 1990 levels by 2008–2012. Under an internal burden-sharing arrangement that covered the fifteen member states of the EU at the time the Kyoto Protocol was signed, different national targets were formulated based on a mix of factors that included national capabilities, the existing energy mix, and per capita economic wealth. Some countries were expected to make large cuts relative to their 1990 emissions level, others were given relatively mild targets, and other less economically strong member states were permitted to increase their emissions.

A similar kind of burden-sharing agreement has been formulated to meet the EU's 20 percent renewable energy target as a share of the total energy mix by 2020, which affects all member states. Member states' targets were determined on the basis of a formula that included a flat-rate increase in renewables of 5.5 percent and an additional increase based on per capita GDP.[31] Ten states have renewable energy targets of 10–15 percent, eleven states have targets of 16–25 percent, and six states have targets of 30–49 percent.

Lobbying. Lobbying by private interests is omnipresent in the EU,[32] so much so that the Commission has established a voluntary register of lobby groups.[33] Industry is very concerned about the impact of new environmental legislation on competitiveness and maintains armies of lawyers and lobbyists in Brussels. Both the Commission directorates and parliamentary committees regularly consult such interests, which tend to represent the largest companies and trade associations. Environmental, consumer, and other public interest groups also have representation and actively try to shape policy outcomes.[34] An umbrella organization in Brussels, the European Environmental Bureau, represents more than 140 environmental citizens' organizations from the EU and some neighboring countries.[35] It closely monitors the Directorate-General for the Environment and tries to influence proposed legislation. Other international environmental nongovernmental organizations (NGOs), such as the World Wide Fund for Nature and Greenpeace, also lobby intensely and are regarded as among the most effective pressure groups.[36] A broad range of stakeholders and policy networks influence the EU policy process at all levels.

Environmental policy is closely related to other issues, such as economic competition, taxation, research and development, energy, agriculture, and transportation.[37] Effective policy making therefore requires interaction and cooperation among many EU directorates and parliamentary committees. The development of efficiency standards for electrical appliances, for example, involved a working group of members from the environment and energy directorates. The divergent perspectives of these directorates often lead to different policy preferences. The requirement, introduced first by the Amsterdam Treaty, that environmental protection must be integrated into all fields of EU policy has given new weight to environmental considerations.

Harmonization of Environmental Standards

One general rationale for creating common environmental policies and "harmonizing" standards across member states has been to level the economic playing field. Indeed, an early motivating factor behind the establishment of European environmental legislation was to remove potential trade barriers in the form of different environmental standards. Another reason for harmonization is to set minimum environmental standards and to improve environmental performance across Europe.

To prevent a common environmental policy from being set with the lowest common denominator, the Council has taken various measures to preserve the ability of states to push the EU forward toward continuously higher standards. The Single European Act added to the Treaty of Rome three new articles. The first guarantees that the EU will take action for "preserving, protecting, and improving the quality of the environment, protecting human health, prudent and rational utilization of natural resources, and promoting measures at [the] international level to deal with regional or worldwide environmental problems." The second allows the Council to decide which measures can be decided by qualified majority voting. The third specifies that protective measures taken at the Community level "shall not prevent any member state from maintaining or introducing more stringent protective measures" so long as these measures are compatible with treaty law.[38] This third article enables member states to retain higher environmental standards than exist in EU legislation so long as the Commission or the ECJ does not find them in violation of other treaty rules. Examples of areas in which this occurs include carbon taxes and bans on genetically modified organisms. The EU must then also determine if its standards should be raised to those of the lead state.

Environmental Action Programs

Since 1972 the Commission has developed environmental action programs to guide its activities for multiyear periods. Although these programs are not legally binding, they have had substantial influence on policy development at the EU level and among member states. The first environmental action program (1973–1976) focused on water protection and waste; the second (1977–1982) broadened its scope of coverage but concentrated on nature conservation. At a time when environmental regulations and directives were only beginning to be formulated, these early action programs served especially important functions as they set out European environmental priorities and policy direction.

The three most recent action programs have focused on sustainability concerns, more strongly linking environmental, economic, and social matters than was the case with earlier programs. The fifth environmental action program (1992–2002), "Towards Sustainability," focused on the need to integrate environment into other economic and sectoral policies. In line with this, the commission's "Communication on Environment and Employment," issued in November 1997, spelled out for the first time how environmental protection and job creation can be mutually reinforcing.[39] The sixth program, "Environment 2010, Our Future, Our Choice," continued this theme. It called for the EC to integrate environmental concerns into all its policies and to promote sustainable development within the enlarged Community. The program was based on "the polluter pays principle, the precautionary principle and preventive action, and the principle of rectification of pollution at source." Its four priority areas were climate change, nature and biodiversity, environment and health, and natural resources and waste.[40] In November 2013, the seventh environmental action program, "Living Well, within the Limits of our Planet," was passed into law. It goes through 2020 and has nine priority areas, including the protection of nature and strengthening of ecological resistance; promoting sustainable, resource-efficient, low-carbon growth; and addressing environment-related threats to health.[41]

Legislative Action

With an extensive body of environmental legislation—more than two hundred pieces—the EU has created the most comprehensive regional environmental protection regime in the world.[42] The EU has enacted legislation on many aspects of environmental protection, including noise; environmental impact assessment; control of chemicals and other dangerous substances; hazardous waste transfer and management; development of renewable energy; protection of forests, wildlife, and biodiversity; fisheries; radioactive waste; and action to limit climate change.[43] EU environmental legislation is anything but static; it is characterized by a continual process of amendment and revision.

Regulations, Directives, Action Plans

When the EU passes laws (known as directives and regulations), these take precedence over national law. Under Article 249 of the Consolidated Treaty, directives "shall be binding, as to the result to be achieved, upon each Member State . . . but shall leave to the national authorities the choice of form and methods."[44] In contrast, regulations are directly binding on member states and require no further legislation at the national level; they are used when technical standardization is necessary.

The EU has enacted a growing number of environmental directives. Examples include the Environmental Impact Assessment Directive, the Strategic Environmental Assessment Directive, the Directive on Access to Environmental Information, the Public Participation Directive, the Environmental Liability Directive, and the Waste Electrical and Electronic Equipment Directive.[45] Directives establish comprehensive long-term environmental quality goals and standards that can be used to measure progress across a wide range of specific policy instruments and actions. Framework directives provide mechanisms for consolidating, integrating, and simplifying related pieces of legislation (for example, separate directives on drinking water, bathing water, and protection of shellfish) to encourage more comprehensive and efficient management of resources. While allowing countries greater flexibility in pursuing these goals (because states have discretion to determine strategies for achieving the goals), framework directives can also serve as catalysts to force states to adopt more integrated approaches to environmental protection. It is not uncommon for states to request periods of "derogation" that allow them additional time to comply with EU directives. The Commission does not, however, always consent to such requests.

The EU also issues action plans such as the Commission's Energy Efficiency Plan 2011, setting out steps to be taken to help the EU meet its 2020 energy efficiency goals,[46] and its December 2011 Eco-Innovation Action Plan (Eco-AP), which looks at drivers that could accelerate eco-innovation development and introduction.[47] The evolving nature of EU environmental law and the different rationales behind EU legislative developments provide a fascinating look into how new institutional arrangements and normative understandings can lead to new approaches to environmental protection.[48] Some examples are given below.

The Industrial Emissions Directive. The Industrial Emissions Directive (2010/75/EU) was established as a successor to the Integrated Pollution Prevention and Control Directive of 2008 (Directive 2008/1/EC) and several other more specific directives dealing with various pollutants. The directive imposes common requirements for issuing permits to large industrial and agricultural sources of pollution throughout the EU. It aims to improve environmental and human health conditions by reducing harmful emissions from more than fifty thousand industrial installations. The directive calls for an integrated approach, meaning that the issuing of permits must consider the entire environmental performance of an industrial source, including emissions to air, water, and land; noise levels; material inputs and waste generated; energy intensity; and restoration of a site upon plant closure. Permit conditions related to emission limit values have to be based on best available techniques (BATs).

The larger significance of the directive is that it encourages states to take a comprehensive, integrated approach to pollution reduction at the source, including waste minimization, efficient use of energy, and protection of soil and groundwater as well as surface waters and air. This approach is in line with the shift evident in Europe from end-of-the-pipe controls to pollution prevention; more integrated, long-term environmental management; and greater flexibility in the use of policy instruments.

Air Quality. EU legislation to protect air quality goes back to 1970, when the first directive to regulate emissions from automobiles was passed (70/220/EEC). Since then, dozens of directives on air pollution have been enacted, covering, among other things, diesel engine emissions, the lead and sulfur content of fuels, and emissions from large industrial facilities, power plants, and waste incinerators. Ambient air quality standards also have been set for sulfur dioxide, nitrogen dioxide, particulates, and lead, and regulations to limit chlorofluorocarbons and other ozone-depleting gases have been implemented under the Montreal Protocol.

In 2008, Directive 2008/50/EC on ambient air quality and cleaner air was formulated. It consolidates four earlier directives plus a Council decision with the rationale of incorporating "the latest health and scientific developments and the experience of the Member States" while serving "the interests of clarity, simplification, and administrative efficiency." The earlier directives set limit values for nitrogen dioxide, oxides of nitrogen, sulfur dioxide, lead, particulate matter, carbon monoxide, benzene, and ozone in ambient air. The earlier Council decision addressed reciprocal exchange of information and data from networks and measuring stations. The sixth community environment action program determined that pollution should be reduced to levels that minimize harmful effects on human health, especially for sensitive populations, and the environment. It also called for improved monitoring and assessment of air quality and provision of information to the public. The directive responded to this stating not only that "it is particularly important to combat emissions of pollutants at source and to identify and implement the most effective emission reduction measures at [the] local, national and Community level" but also that "emissions of harmful air pollutants should be avoided, prevented or reduced." A major addition of the directive is its setting of tough standards for fine particulate matter (2.5 micrometers in diameter), which is particularly dangerous for human health.[49]

The Commission has been reviewing existing air quality policies in an effort to assess their effectiveness. The review has involved expert working groups and a multiyear consultation process that uses a questionnaire format to obtain views from stakeholders regarding new potential goals, measures, and implementation options. The review process has led to revisions of the directive dealing with the sulfur content of bunker fuels and of the Convention on Long-Range Transboundary Air Pollution's 1999 Gothenburg Protocol to Abate Acidification, Eutrophication and Ground-Level Ozone. Under the revisions, emission reduction commitments are established for fine particulate matter for 2020.

Other reforms are ongoing or under discussion, such as in relation to automobile emission standards. The European Union has issued emission standards for vehicles that are commonly known as Euro standards. Each new standard is given a new number. The first standard, Euro 1, was issued in 1993. The new Euro 6 emission limits for nitrogen oxides, particulates, and other pollutants for cars and light commercial vehicles go into effect in September 2015. Among the most stringent standards in the world, many other countries orient their own emission standards on the Euro standards.

Water Resources Management. EU water quality has been protected since 1975 by directives covering drinking and bathing water, fish and shellfish, groundwater, urban wastewater, and protection against nitrates from fertilizers and various dangerous chemicals. Other policies cover pollution of European seas and rivers under various international maritime conventions and agreements. A new drinking water directive was adopted in 1998.

In February 1996 the Commission called for a water framework directive that, like the air framework, would establish broad guidelines for the protection and management of all freshwater resources. In October 2000 the EU Water Framework Directive (Directive 2000/60/EC), which replaced seven existing directives, was finally adopted after years of sometimes tense discussion and debate. The directive is based on a river basin management approach, with the idea that water quality can best be protected if an entire ecological system's pollution problems are dealt with in an integrated fashion that combines emission limits and quality standards. The goal is to obtain "good status" for water quality throughout the EU by 2015.[50] Under the directive, water basin management plans were drawn up to meet this goal. In 2012, the Commission issued a communication to the Council and the Parliament, "A Blueprint to Safeguard Europe's Water Resources," noting that by 2015 an estimated 53 percent of European waters will achieve the status. The blueprint considers steps that could be taken to improve water quality in Europe further, addressing pressures from agriculture, dams, chemicals, and the like. The communication emphasizes water efficiency, the greening of waterways, and the need to address point source pollution.[51]

Packaging and Recycling. Beginning in the 1970s, a number of European countries began to enact laws to reduce the volume of solid waste by requiring the use of returnable beverage containers, encouraging recycling of materials, and limiting waste in packaging. Denmark led the way by banning the use of aluminum cans and requiring that beer and soft drinks be sold in reusable bottles. Denmark's action eventually led to the seminal ruling by the ECJ in 1988 that such restrictions on trade may be justified on environmental grounds, provided that they do not unfairly discriminate in favor of domestic producers. Other countries subsequently passed legislation mandating the reduction or recycling of certain materials, including packaging. In 1991 Germany gained international attention for its novel packaging ordinance (*Verpackungsverordnung*), which required retail stores to take back all used packaging materials from consumers and process them. The ordinance allowed business and industry to set up a private collection system (the green dot system) on condition that it could meet ambitious recycling targets for various materials; otherwise a mandatory deposit would be levied on the sale of relevant products. The Netherlands also established an ambitious recycling program that required industry to reduce its volume of packaging by 2000.[52]

The EC had adopted a directive on beverage containers in 1985, but in the wake of the German and Dutch laws and the Danish bottle decision it was moved to draft a packaging directive that would accommodate recycling of other materials while preventing the development of potential trade restrictions. After much haggling over German and Dutch approaches mandating higher recycling targets and a coalition led by the United Kingdom that objected to such rigid quotas, a compromise was reached that lowered the mandatory targets to 50 percent recovery, 25 percent overall recycling, and 15 percent minimum recycling for each material. While states were allowed to exceed these targets, Germany's experience suggested that too-high recovery rates could lead to excessive accumulation and export of waste materials because of inadequate processing capacity. In the end, the EU packing and packaging waste directive (94/62/EC), passed in 1994 over the objections of Denmark, Germany, and the Netherlands, set a "maximum recovery" rate of 65 percent and a recycling rate of 45 percent.[53]

In view of the enlargement of the EU as well as growing pressures to reduce waste further, the European Parliament and the Council agreed on amendments to the directive in February 2004 and March 2005. The 2004 amendments strengthened the recovery and recycling targets for packaging waste to 60 percent recovery and between 55 percent and 80 percent recycling by the end of 2008.[54] The 2005 amendments gave new member states additional time (ranging from 2012 to 2015) to meet the new recovery and recycling targets.[55] In 2008, the newly established Waste Framework Directive set 2020 recycling targets: 50 percent of household waste and 70 percent of construction and demolition waste.

Environmental Liability. The "White Paper on Environmental Liability," issued in February 2000, called for the establishment of a Framework Directive on Environmental Liability that would introduce the possibility of NGOs bringing suits for environmental harms.[56] The subsequently proposed EU Environmental Liability Directive dropped this provision, however, in favor of a system that focuses on environmental restoration and cost recovery.[57] Directive 2004/35/EC of the European Parliament and of the Council became the first EC legislation whose main objectives included the application of the polluter-pays principle in view of preventing and remedying environmental damage. On account of the numerous contaminated sites in the Community that pose health risks and contribute to loss of biodiversity and on the basis of the polluter-pays principle, the directive states that "an operator causing environmental damage or creating an imminent threat of such damage should, in principle, bear the cost of the necessary preventive or remedial measures. . . . It is also appropriate that the operators should ultimately bear the cost of assessing environmental damage and, as the case may be, assessing an imminent threat of such damage occurring."[58]

In 2008, the Council and the Parliament further agreed to Directive 2008/99/EC on the protection of the environment through the body of criminal law. This directive requires member states to treat as criminal offenses activities that breach EU environmental legislation, such as the illegal shipment of waste, trade in endangered species or ozone-depleting substances, and the significant deterioration of wildlife habitats that are part of the Natura 2000 network of protected sites. Other criminal offenses include significant damage to the environment caused by unlawful emissions to the air, water, or soil; the unlawful treatment of waste; and the unlawful manufacture or handling of nuclear materials.[59]

Nuclear Safety. In November 2000, the Commission adopted a green paper on security of the energy supply that raised issues regarding the position of nuclear energy vis-à-vis other energy sources in light of concerns about meeting goals for reduction of greenhouse gas emissions on one hand and concerns about aging nuclear power plants on the other. Starting in December 2001, the Council requested regular reports on nuclear safety, and in December 2002 the ECJ confirmed in a judgment that the Community has the authority to legislate in relation to nuclear safety. In January 2003, the Commission adopted two proposals for directives for a Community approach to issues of nuclear plant safety and radioactive waste disposal.[60] It was not until June 2009, however, that the EU environment ministers agreed on the Nuclear Safety Directive.[61] The directive sets expectations regarding nuclear safety and protection of workers and the general public and establishes the license holder of a nuclear plant as responsible for assuring safety. In response to the accident at the nuclear power plant in Fukushima, Japan, in 2011, the EU decided to reassess the level of safety of European nuclear plants (see also Chapter 13). Common methodologies were developed and assessments of the safety levels of all plants made.[62] The Commission subsequently prepared proposals for a revision of the Nuclear Safety Directive. They include new EU-wide safety objectives, a European system of peer reviews of nuclear facilities, establishment of EU-wide harmonized safety guidelines, a stronger role for independent national regulators, increased transparency, and new provisions for on-site emergency preparedness and response.[63] Efforts supported by Great Britain, the Czech Republic, France, and Lithuania to allow subsidies for the development of nuclear reactors as a form of low-carbon energy were opposed by Austria, Germany and other states shutting down their nuclear industries.[64] The Commission ruled out the use of nuclear subsidies in October 2013. There is little common understanding among EU member states on how to address nuclear energy.

Ecolabeling. Another approach to limiting waste and environmental damage generally is to encourage consumers to purchase the most ecologically benign products available by providing better information. Germany had introduced an ecolabeling system and several other countries were planning to do so when in 1990 the Council asked the Commission to prepare a regulation establishing criteria for an EC labeling scheme. The initial criteria used for granting a "green" label took into account the environmental impact of the product throughout its entire life cycle, including the materials used, manufacturing technologies, health and safety of workers, and ultimate disposal costs. Under the Council regulation (92/880/EEC) of March 23, 1992, member states were authorized to appoint competent bodies to award the EC ecolabel to manufacturers and importers whose products met the criteria. Participation by industry was voluntary, but it was hoped that consumer demand for green products would drive producers to compete for the label (symbolized by a flower) by designing better products.

In July 2000 a revised ecolabeling regulation (1980/2000/EC) was passed. It authorized the new EU Ecolabeling Board, consisting of representatives

from ecolabeling bodies in all member states, consumer groups, environmental NGOs, trade unions, industry, and small and medium-sized enterprises, to
develop ecolabel criteria jointly for different product groups. About thirty
product groups, ranging from furniture and household appliances to cleaning
products, electrical equipment, and bedding, are covered by ecolabeling
requirements. Consumers can learn about products bearing the ecolabel on
the European Commission's Web site.[65] National ecolabeling bodies remain
in charge of implementing the system. Ecolabeling has become very common
across Europe. The European Commission notes that more than seventeen
thousand products now carry the EU Ecolabel, across such categories as hard
floor coverings, indoor paints, cleaners, tissue paper, textiles, electronics, and
even tourist accommodations.[66]

Climate Change

Concern over global climate change owing to the accumulation of carbon
dioxide and other greenhouse gases in the atmosphere has been particularly
strong in Europe and has led to a search for effective means of reducing
dependence on fossil fuels. Climate change (see Chapter 10) has arguably
become the single most important global environmental issue on the EU's
agenda, and the EU has striven to be a global leader not only in the international climate change negotiations, where it has pushed for stronger targets,
but also by the power of example. The EU has become a major force in pushing for global action on greenhouse gas emission reductions, with its goals of
20 percent energy efficiency, 20 percent renewable energy, and 20 percent
greenhouse gas emissions reduction by 2020 (the last of these relative to a
1990 base year). The EU has stated that it will raise its greenhouse gas emissions reduction target to 30 percent if other states take comparable action.

Over time, efforts to address climate change have resulted in increasingly
ambitious new policies and programs. These policies and programs have put
Europe at the forefront of global efforts to tackle climate change. Yet these
efforts have also elicited a degree of resistance from various member states,
and not all member states have been equally enthusiastic about implementing
programs and regulations to reduce greenhouse gas emissions. The EU has
failed, for example, to agree internally on a unilateral 30 percent greenhouse
gas emissions reduction target. The expansion of the EU to an increasingly
large and diverse set of countries could make subsequent EU leadership on
climate change more difficult.[67]

Environmental and Energy Taxes. One way of trying to reduce greenhouse gas
emissions is through environmental and energy taxes. Environmental taxes are
relatively high in the EU in comparison with the United States. They do vary,
however, by member state. Relatively early on, several countries in northern
Europe enacted extensive green taxes to promote waste reduction and energy
saving, both important climate policy measures.[68] In 2010, environmental taxes
accounted for 2.4 percent of GDP and 6.2 percent of all tax revenues and social

contributions in what was then still the EU-27. Environmental tax rates vary among member states in level and content but tend to be in the range of 6–10 percent. Bulgaria and the Netherlands were both greater than 10 percent. The Eastern European countries and Luxembourg gather most of their environmental tax revenues from taxes on energy, whereas in Norway and Malta taxes on transportation constitute the largest share. Only in the Netherlands, Iceland, and Estonia are taxes on pollution and resources more than 10 percent of total environmental tax revenue.[69]

There have also been efforts to introduce new energy taxes in order to level the economic playing field, encourage energy efficiency, and address climate change. In 2003, the Commission proposed the establishment of a directive on energy taxation, which was adopted and came into effect the following year. Directive 2003/96/EC established minimum energy tax rates on various energy products, including mineral oils, coal, natural gas, and electricity, while allowing national governments to offer rebates for environmentally friendly forms of energy production. The minimum rates were intended to curb the use of fossil fuels and encourage sustainable transport. In 2011, the Commission issued a proposal for a revision of the Environmental Tax Directive, calling the rules on the taxation of energy products outdated. The new rules would take the CO_2 emissions and energy content of products into account, with the goal of promoting more energy-efficient and environmentally sustainable products.[70] No further decisions have yet been reached, however.

Energy Efficiency and Renewable Energy. EU policy on electricity and gas markets is premised on the Community's competence for forming a common market. Its competence related to renewable energy is tied to articles on the environment. Improving energy efficiency has become a key component of EU climate policy. This goal has been embodied in a series of action plans, programs, and communications from the Commission. In October 2006, for example, the Commission released a communication titled "Action Plan for Energy Efficiency: Realising the Potential" (COM[2006]545). The plan called for a reduction in primary energy consumption by 20 percent by 2020, corresponding to a 1.5 percent saving per year. A subsequent Commission communication (COM[2008]772) called for reforms in EU legislation related to energy efficiency in the building sector and proposed reforms to the Energy Labelling Directive, the establishment of a directive for the setting of ecodesign requirements for energy-related products, and reinforcement of a directive on cogeneration.

In March 2007, the European Council endorsed a Commission communication that called for a 20 percent target for renewable sources in the overall share of energy and a 10 percent target for energy from renewable sources in the transport sector. Directive 2009/28/EC embodied these goals, setting a common 10 percent target for fuel from renewables in the transport sector for each member state and differentiated national targets for renewables in the overall share of energy owing to the different starting points, renewable energy potential, and energy mix of the different member states. The new directive pointed to the importance of reducing greenhouse gas emissions, promoting the security of the energy supply, promoting technological development and innovation, and providing opportunities for employment and regional development. In 2011, the Commission completed a communication on an energy efficiency plan in which it indicated the EU was not on track to meet its 2020 energy efficiency target. In response, in 2012 a revised directive was issued (2012/27/EU) to try to take the measures necessary to put the EU back on track, including greater emphasis on renovation of buildings in order to improve their energy efficiency, energy-efficient purchasing by government agencies, the establishment of indicative national energy efficiency targets, the introduction of energy efficiency obligations, and metering requirements to enhance transparency for consumers related to their energy consumption.[71]

Emissions Trading. Emissions trading is considered a key approach to meeting greenhouse gas emissions reduction goals in Europe. Ironically, the idea of a carbon emissions trading scheme was originally proposed by the United States during the negotiations leading to the Kyoto Protocol but was initially strongly resisted by the EU. After the George W. Bush administration announced it would withdraw from the Kyoto Protocol in the spring of 2001, however, the EU unanimously resolved to move forward in trying to put the agreement into force even without the United States and began to look more positively at emissions trading schemes.

In October 2001 the Commission proposed a greenhouse gas emissions trading scheme to the Parliament and the Council.[72] Modeled on the successful sulfur dioxide emissions trading system employed in the United States, the EU Emissions Trading System (ETS) is the first international carbon emissions trading scheme in the world. It came into effect in 2005 and covers the member states of the EU as well as members of the EEA. It addresses more than twelve thousand major emissions sources (for example, utilities and manufacturing industries such as the cement industry and the pulp and paper industry) and approximately 40 percent of all EU CO_2 emissions. The first phase of the ETS, which ran from 2005 to 2007, encountered serious problems stemming from an overallocation of permits by individual member states to their industries. The number of permits national governments issued during the second phase, which covered 2008 to 2012, was controlled more closely by the Commission. The third phase started in 2013 and lasts through 2020. It has introduced a single EU-wide emissions cap as opposed to the national caps that existed during the second phase. In the past allowances were provided freely, but now 40 percent of allowances are auctioned, with the percentage set to increase each year.

A major and controversial expansion of the emissions trading scheme to cover emissions from airlines went into effect in 2012. Air transportation is a growing source of greenhouse gas emissions. The system is to apply to both domestic and international carriers, but owing to strong international pressure, international carriers received a temporary exemption pending a decision on a global framework for addressing airline emissions expected in late 2013. With this expansion, the EU ETS covers about 45 percent of EU carbon emissions.[73] A major challenge to the effectiveness of the EU ETS has been the rock-bottom price of a ton of carbon, which has reduced much of the expected incentive for emitters to reduce their emissions. Another major problem is that too many permits were issued, making it relatively easy for industry to continue to pollute. The low carbon prices are the result of an over allocation of certificates by national governments that were trying to protect domestic industries when the EU ETS began. The financial crisis and economic downturn also had an impact. After much contentious debate and despite the resistance of Poland and Cyprus and initially Germany, the European Parliament approved a proposal to delay an auction of 900 million euros worth of additional emissions certificates that were suppose to have been sold during 2013–2015 to 2019–2020. Germany had originally opposed the move but a change in the ruling coalition's membership shifted Germany's stance in favor of the backloading plan. Backloading is intended to bolster the price of carbon by delaying the release of yet more carbon emission allowances. Analysts see this as only a small fix to a complex problem.

Nature Conservation, Marine Environmental Protection, and Biodiversity Protection

Given its dense population and long history of settlement, Europe has relatively little land still in its natural state. Among the most important pieces of legislation aimed at protecting Europe's remaining natural areas are the Birds Directive (79/409/EEC) and the Habitats Directive (92/43/EEC). A new development of significance is Directive 2008/56/EC, which established a framework for Community action in the field of marine environmental policy.

Natura 2000. The Birds Directive, signed in 1979, is the EU's oldest legislation for nature protection. It recognized habitat loss and degradation as the largest threats to bird populations and set up special protection areas. The Habitats Directive, signed in 1992, set up a European ecological network of special conservation areas that was given the title Natura 2000. Each member state is expected to designate and protect areas that are habitats to special plant and animal species as defined by the directive. Since 1994, all of the special conservation areas set up by the Birds Directive have been incorporated into the Natura 2000 ecological network. The aim of Natura 2000 is to ensure the long-term survival of species and habitats that are of special importance to Europe.

Biodiversity Action Plan and the EU Biodiversity Strategy to 2020. As a party to the United Nations Convention on Biological Diversity (see Chapter 12), in 2001 the EU established a biodiversity action plan that called for a halt in the decline of biodiversity within the EU by 2010 and a restoration of habitats and natural systems. A midterm assessment report issued in 2008 concluded, however, that the EU was "highly unlikely to meet its 2010 target of halting biodiversity decline." According to the report, 50 percent of species and as much as 80 percent of habitat types protected under the Habitats Directive had an "unfavourable conservation status." The conclusion was that Europe must do much more to halt the loss of biodiversity and natural habitats caused by conversion of land for agricultural and development purposes and by pollution. In response, in May 2011 the Commission proposed an EU biodiversity strategy to 2020, and the following year the Parliament adopted a resolution on the strategy. The resolution "deplores" the EU for failing to meet its 2010 biodiversity target and points out the serious challenges facing both global and European biodiversity. In Europe, 65 percent of habitat types and 52 percent of the species listed in the annexes to the Habitats Directive are suffering, and 88 percent of fish stocks are being fished beyond their maximum sustainable yield. The resolution calls for greater focus on nature conservation and ocean and marine protection.[74]

Common Fisheries Policy. Fish stocks in European waters are severely depleted. In June 2009, the European Commission issued a green paper calling for reform of the common fisheries policy because of overfishing in European waters and the excess capacity of the fishing fleet. The green paper also highlighted the call made at the World Summit on Sustainable Development in 2002 to restore fish stocks to maximum sustainable yield (MSY) by 2015 and noted that, despite reforms introduced in 2002, "88% of Community stocks are being fished beyond MSY."[75] Two years later, in the summer of 2011, the European Commission issued a proposal for a reform of the common fisheries policy to the European Parliament and Council.[76] In a first reading, the European Parliament debated and voted on an overhaul of the common fisheries policy in February 2013. It passed with a large majority: 502 for and 137 against (with 27 abstentions). The largest share of negative votes came from France (28 for, 39 against) and Portugal (8 for, 14 against), with mixed support from Spain (28 for, 23 against), Italy (30 for, 16 against), the Netherlands (17 for, 7 against), and Romania (23 for, 7 against). The Parliament called for an end to overfishing by 2015, a recovery of fish stocks by 2020, a ban on the discard of dead bycatch, and a quota system based on MSY criteria. In December 2013 in a second reading, the European Parliament approved the texts adopted by the Council in its first reading without further amendment. Thus, the long-debated reform of the Common Fisheries Policy entered into force in 2014. The reforms require that fishing quotas be established based on the concept of maximum sustainable yields in order to protect endangered fish stocks and that steps be taken to limit the discard of unintended catches.

EU Environmental Compliance

The environment is one of the most developed areas of EU law. The EU has done much to protect and improve the quality of the environment in Europe and to slow the rate of environmental deterioration. In some areas, the EU is well on track to meet its goals. On the whole, EU member states have been doing well in meeting their renewable energy and climate change goals, for example. The EU-15 widely exceeded their Kyoto Protocol target to reduce greenhouse gas emissions by 8 percent of 1990 levels by the 2008–2012 period. Combined, emissions were down by more than 14 percent at the end of 2011. Furthermore, most EU member states are making good progress on their goal to reduce emissions by 20 percent of 1990 levels by 2020.[77] More problematic have been efforts to fulfill energy efficiency targets, as noted above.

Still, many compliance problems continue to hinder the overall effectiveness of EU environmental legislation even within the most environmentally conscious of the member states (see also Chapter 5). New challenges for the enforcement of environmental regulations have arisen, moreover, on account of EU enlargement. The Central and Eastern European countries have had far higher levels of pollution than Western European countries because of the failure of their former communist governments to enforce environmental standards. In addition to outdated coal-burning power plants and factories, and in many cases a lack of adequate sewerage and waste disposal systems, several of these countries have relied heavily on Soviet-designed nuclear plants that posed substantial safety risks. The costs of their coming into compliance with EU environmental standards have therefore been very high. This situation, combined with the new member states' strong interest in economic development and their typically more limited environmental capacity, has contributed to compliance problems.[78]

The success of the EU commitment to environmental protection depends on the extent to which member states transpose EU law into national law and apply and enforce the law in practice.[79] EU treaty compliance and enforcement have been matters of concern for decades.[80] The Commission monitors policy implementation and seeks to detect violations of EU law. More than 20 percent of all Commission dossiers are related to the environment. Each year there are hundreds of new cases dealing with noncompliance; many of these are cases opened by citizens and NGOs.[81]

The EU has legal enforcement mechanisms at its disposal. Citizens, local authorities, businesses, and interest groups have the right to make inquiries and lodge complaints on the inadequate application or transposition of EU law directly before the Commission. Once a complaint has been brought, efforts are made to mediate the dispute or to informally persuade the national government to take appropriate action. If a party is found to be in violation of EU law, the Commission can issue a formal notice to the state. If all else fails, an infringement case can be brought before the ECJ to force compliance. ECJ decisions are binding on member states. In 2013, the Commission took several states to the Court of Justice: Belgium over the discharge of untreated urban wastewater in a number of towns, Italy over inadequate treatment of waste destined for landfills in the Lazio region, Greece over illegal landfills, Poland over its failure to transpose European water legislation adequately and over nitrates and water pollution, and Sweden for its failure to comply with e-waste legislation, among many other cases.

Steps have been taken to strengthen the ECJ's reach. The Maastricht Treaty gave the Court the authority to fine member states for noncompliance. In a landmark 2005 ruling, the ECJ fined France 20 million euros for repeated failure to comply with the EU fishery conservation policies described above. France was also subject to a fine of 57.8 million euros for every six additional months that it failed to comply; it chose to pay the initial fine of 20 million euros on time.

Some of the variation in compliance among states is related to differing levels of awareness among the states' citizens and interest groups.[82] Some states may have proportionately more complaints lodged against them because their citizens are alert, informed, and able to bring matters to the attention of the EU. But differential compliance is also the result of variations in the budgets and other resources governments have to carry out EU mandates. Because states choose their own means of compliance, differences are inevitable in the instruments used and in the severity of penalties levied against violators.[83]

The Commission is seeking to manage its high number of noncompliance cases more effectively by targeting serious categories of breaches. These include bad transposition of directives; breaches of core strategic obligations under EC legislation, including concerning the designation of Natura 2000 sites and the adoption of national allocation plans for emissions of greenhouse gases; and breaches concerning big infrastructure projects. In addition, it is focusing on more horizontal approaches, where breaches involve, for example, failure to comply with nature conservation or impact assessment regulations across large numbers of individual cases.[84] The Commission also works with an informal group of national environmental officials known as the European Union Network for the Implementation and Enforcement of Environmental Law (IMPEL).[85]

All in all, the EU does well in international comparison in terms of its environmental performance. The growing ability of the EU to require member states to monitor performance and to penalize noncompliance is certainly an important factor contributing to this outcome.

Conclusion

The European Union has made great strides toward environmental protection during the past four decades. It has done much to strengthen environmental standards in old and new member states alike. The EU's detailed environmental directives and regulations are motivated by the polluter-pays, precautionary, and prevention principles. In many areas, the EU has set standards that have been imitated internationally.[86] EU environmental policies are motivated by concerns about climate change, biodiversity loss, overexploitation of natural resources, human health, and long-term sustainability. They also increasingly link the concepts of environmental protection to economic innovation and the possibilities of green growth.

Member states have pressed for greater freedom in implementing EU legislation while supporting the general principles of sustainable development. The European Commission has responded by turning toward the use of broader framework directives that set long-term environmental goals while allowing flexibility in the choices of means to achieve them, consistent with the principle of subsidiarity; it also has encouraged the introduction of new policy instruments such as emissions trading, burden-sharing agreements, and labeling to improve environmental performance and cost-effectiveness. At the same time, it has backed the Kyoto Protocol over U.S. opposition, developed the world's first international carbon dioxide emissions trading scheme, and challenged the global community with far-reaching proposals going into the Copenhagen and Durban climate negotiations.

Despite these accomplishments, the EU faces major challenges if it is to remain an environmental leader. Economic stagnation, the euro crisis, and high levels of unemployment have dampened public and government enthusiasm for increased environmental protection. Implementation of EU environmental laws at the national level still leaves much to be desired. There are signs of resistance by some member states to the further strengthening of EU renewable energy and greenhouse gas emissions targets. Within the EU generally, sustainable development will require much greater integration of environmental perspectives into other policy areas, such as energy, transportation, agriculture, and tourism.[87] This is a particularly difficult challenge at a time when many member states are being forced to follow austerity plans in response to severe budget problems. Still, despite the many challenges, Europe remains quite strongly convinced of the importance of environmental protection, nature conservation, and sustainable development.

Notes

1. On EU environmental policy in comparative perspective and on the EU as a global environmental leader, see Norman J. Vig and Michael G. Faure, eds., *Green Giants? Environmental Policies of the United States and the European Union* (Cambridge: MIT Press, 2004); Miranda A. Schreurs, Henrik Selin, and Stacy D. VanDeveer, eds., *Transatlantic Environment and Energy Politics: Comparative and International Perspectives* (Farnham, UK: Ashgate, 2009); Rüdiger Wurzel and James Connelly, *The European Union as a Leader in International Climate Change Politics* (New York: Routledge, 2011); David Vogel, *The Politics of Precaution: Regulating Health, Safety, and Environmental Risks in Europe and the United States* (Princeton, NJ: Princeton University Press, 2012).

2. On the general history and development of the EC/EU, see Andreas Staab, *The European Union Explained: Institutions, Actors, Global Impact,* 2nd ed. (Bloomington: Indiana University Press, 2011); John McCormick, *Understanding the European Union: A Concise Introduction,* 5th ed. (New York: Palgrave Macmillan, 2011); Elizabeth Bomberg, John Peterson, and Richard Corbett, *The European Union: How Does It Work?,* 3rd ed. (Oxford: Oxford University Press, 2012); Michelle Cini and Nieves Pérez-Solórzano Borragan, *European Union Politics,* 4th ed. (Oxford: Oxford University Press, 2013); Dick Leonard, *Guide to the European Union: The Definitive Guide to All Aspects of the EU,* 10th ed. (London: Profile Books, 2010); Simon Hix and Bjørn Høyland, *The Political System of the European Union,* 3rd ed. (New York: Palgrave Macmillan, 2011); Helen Wallace, Mark A. Pollack, and Alasdair R. Young, *Policy-Making in the European Union,* 6th ed. (Oxford: Oxford University Press, 2010).

3. On the impact of enlargement on EU institutions, see Edward Best, Thomas Christiansen, and Pierpaolo Settembri, *The Institutions of the Enlarged European Union: Continuity and Change* (Cheltenham, UK: Edward Elgar, 2008).

4. Consolidated Versions of the Treaty on European Union and the Treaty Establishing the European Communities, *Official Journal of the European Communities,* C321, December 29, 2006, E46.

5. See "Treaty of Nice Amending the Treaty on European Union, the Treaties Establishing the European Communities and Certain Related Acts," 2001/C 80/01, *Official Journal of the European Communities,* C80/78, March 10, 2001.

6. Council of the European Union, (7640/13) PR/CO/19, Brussels, March 21, 2013, http://www.consilium.europa.eu/ueDocs/cms_Data/docs/pressData/en/envir/136431.pdf.

7. On the European Council, see Daniel Naurin and Helen Wallace, *Unveiling the Council of the European Union: Games Governments Play in Brussels* (Basingstoke, UK: Palgrave Macmillan, 2008).
8. On the European Commission, see Gerhard Sabathil, Clemens Joos, and Bernd Keβler, *The European Commission: An Essential Guide to the Institution, the Procedures and the Policies* (London: Kogan Page, 2008); Antonis A. Ellinas and Ezra Suleiman, *The European Commission and Bureaucratic Autonomy: Europe's Custodians* (Cambridge: Cambridge University Press, 2012); Hussein Kassim, John Peterson, Michael W. Bauer, Sara Connolly, Renaud Dehousse, Liesbet Hooghe, and Andrew Thompson, *The European Commission of the Twenty-First Century* (Oxford: Oxford University Press, 2013).
9. European Commission, Human Resources Key Figures Card, 2013, http://ec.europa .eu/civil_service/docs/hr_key_figures_en.pdf.
10. Committee on the Environment, Public Health and Food Safety, "GMOs: Environment Committee Strengthens Legal Grounds for Cultivation Bans," European Parliament News Press Service, press release PR/09/174, April 12, 2011, http://www .europarl.europa.eu/news/de/pressroom/content/20110411IPR17409/html/GMOs-Environment-Committee-strengthens-legal-grounds-for-cultivation-bans.
11. Judgment of the Court (Second Chamber) of July 25, 2008 (reference for a preliminary ruling from the Bundesverwaltungsgericht, Germany), *Dieter Janecek v. Freistaat Bayern*, Case C-237/07, *Official Journal of the European Union*, September 13, 2008, 3.
12. Information about the EEA is available on the agency's Web site, http://www.eea .europa.eu.
13. Adrienne Héritier, *Explaining Institutional Change in Europe* (Oxford: Oxford University Press, 2007).
14. See Regina S. Axelrod, "Subsidiarity and Environmental Policy in the European Community," *International Environmental Affairs* 6 (Spring 1994): 115–132.
15. Miranda A. Schreurs and Yves Tiberghien, "Multi-level Reinforcement: Explaining European Union Leadership in Climate Mitigation," *Global Environmental Politics* 7, no. 4 (2007): 19–46; Sebastiaan Princen, *Agenda-Setting in the European Union* (Basingstoke, UK: Palgrave Macmillan, 2009).
16. European Commission, "Green Paper on the Future of the Common Fisheries Policy," vol. 1, COM(2001)135 Final, Brussels, March 20, 2001.
17. European Commission, "Adapting to Climate Change: The European Union Must Prepare for the Impacts to Come," IP/09/519, Brussels, April 1, 2009.
18. European Commission, "White Paper on Transport: Roadmap to a Single European Transport Area," COM(2011)0144 Final, Luxembourg, March 28, 2011, http://ec .europa.eu/transport/themes/strategies/2011_white_paper_en.htm.
19. David Judge, "'Predestined to Save the Earth': The Environment Committee of the European Parliament," in *A Green Dimension for the European Community: Political Issues and Processes*, ed. David Judge (London: Frank Cass, 1993), 186–212.
20. European Parliament Resolution of 11 March 2009 on an EU Strategy for a Comprehensive Climate Change Agreement in Copenhagen and the Adequate Provision of Financing for Climate Change, P6_TA-PROV(2009)0121.
21. "MEPs Push for Strong EU Role in Climate Talks," EurActiv Network, November 17, 2011, http://www.euractiv.com/climate-environment/meps-push-strong-eu-role-climate-news-509004.
22. "MEPs Reject Proposed Reform of Emissions Trading Scheme," EurActiv Network, April 16, 2013, updated April 18, 2013, http:/www.euractiv.com/climate-environment/meps-reject-proposed-reform-emis-news-519155.
23. Mikael Skou Andersen and Duncan Liefferink, eds., *European Environmental Policy: The Pioneers* (Manchester: Manchester University Press, 1997); Duncan Liefferink and Mikael Skou Andersen, "Strategies of the 'Green' Member States in EU Environmental Policy-Making," *Journal of European Public Policy* 5 (June 1998): 254–270.

24. "Commission Snubs German Auto Industry over CO_2 Emissions," EurActiv Network, January 30, 2007, http://www.euractiv.com/transport/commission-snubs-german-auto-ind-news-217834.

25. "French Phase-in Plans for Car CO_2 Opposed," EurActiv Network, October 22, 2008, http://www.euractiv.com/transport/french-phase-plans-car-co2-oppos-news-220691.

26. "Cars & CO_2," EurActiv Network, September 19, 2007; Regulation EC No. 443/2009 of the European Parliament and of the Council, of April 23, 2009, setting emission performance standards for new passenger cars as part of the Community's integrated approach to reducing CO_2 emissions from light-duty vehicles, *Official Journal of the European Union*, L140/16, June 5, 2009, 0001–0014.

27. Adrienne Héritier, Christoph Knill, and Susanne Mingers, *Ringing the Changes in Europe: Regulatory Competition and Transformation of the State—Britain, France, Germany* (New York: Walter de Gruyter, 1996); Katharina Holzinger, Christoph Knill, and Bas Arts, *Environmental Policy Convergence in Europe: The Impact of International Institutions and Trade* (Cambridge: Cambridge University Press, 2008).

28. David Vogel, *Trading Up: Consumer and Environmental Regulation in a Global Economy* (Cambridge, MA: Harvard University Press, 1995).

29. Andrew Willis, "Poland Blocks Climate Efforts in 'Dark Day' for Europe," *EU Observer*, June 22, 2011, http://euobserver.com/news/32529.

30. JoAnn Carmin and Stacy D. VanDeveer, eds., *EU Enlargement and the Environment: Institutional Change and Environmental Policy in Central and Eastern Europe* (New York: Routledge, 2005).

31. Directive 2009/28/EC of the European Parliament and of the Council of April 23, 2009, on the promotion of the use of energy from renewable sources and amending and subsequently repealing Directives 2001/77/EC and 2003/30/EC, *Official Journal of the European Union*, L140/16, June 5, 2009, 16–62.

32. Sonia Mazey and Jeremy Richardson, eds., *Lobbying in the European Community* (Oxford: Oxford University Press, 1993); Sonia Mazey and Jeremy Richardson, "The Logic of Organisation: Interest Groups," in *European Union: Power and Policy-Making*, ed. Jeremy J. Richardson (London: Routledge, 1996).

33. Dave Keating, "EU Lobby Register Fails to Impress," *ENDS Daily Europe*, July 10, 2009.

34. Elizabeth Bomberg, "Policy Learning in an Enlarged European Union: Environmental NGOs and New Policy Instruments," *Journal of European Public Policy* 14 (March 2007): 248–268.

35. See the European Environmental Bureau, http://www.eeb.org.

36. "Pressure Groups Become a Political Force," *European Voice*, June 11–17, 1998.

37. See Andrea Lenschow ed., *Environmental Policy Integration: Greening Sectoral Policies in Europe* (London: Earthscan, 2002).

38. Consolidated Versions of the Treaty on European Union and the Treaty Establishing the European Communities, E1–331.

39. European Commission, "Communication on Environment and Employment," COM(97)592 Final, Brussels, November 18, 1997.

40. "Decision No. 1600/2002/EC of the European Parliament and of the Council of July 22, 2002, Laying Down the Sixth Community Environmental Action Programme," *Official Journal of the European Communities*, L242/1, vol. 45, September 10, 2002.

41. European Union, "Decision of the European Parliament and of the Council on a General Union Environment Action Programme to 2020 'Living Well, Within the Limits of our Planet,'" Strasbourg, 20 November 2013, 2012/0337 (COD) LEX1388, PE-CONS 64/1/13 REV 1, http://ec.europa.eu/environment/newprg/pdf/PE00064_en.pdf.

42. See, for example, John McCormick, *Environmental Policy in the European Union* (Basingstoke, UK: Palgrave, 2001); Vig and Faure, *Green Giants?*; Andrew Jordan and Camilla Adelle, eds., *Environmental Policy in the EU: Actors, Institutions and Processes*, 3rd ed. (New York: Routledge, 2013); Albert Weale, Geoffrey Pridham, Michelle Cini, Dimitrios Konstadakopulos, Martin Porter, and Brendan Flynn, *Environmental Governance in Europe: An Ever Closer Ecological Union?* (Oxford: Oxford University

Press, 2000); Anthony R. Zito, *Creating Environmental Policy in the European Union* (Basingstoke, UK: Palgrave Macmillan, 2000); Elisa Morgera, ed., *The External Environmental Policy of the European Union: EU and International Law* (Cambridge: Cambridge University Press, 2012); Rüdiger K. W. Wurzel, *Environmental Policy-Making in Britain, Germany and the European Union* (Manchester: Manchester University Press, 2006).

43. See Vig and Faure, *Green Giants?*; Schreurs et al., *Transatlantic Environment and Energy Politics.*

44. Consolidated Versions of the Treaty on European Union and the Treaty Establishing the European Communities, E151.

45. For a summary of the programs, see Stanley P. Johnson and Guy Corcelle, *The Environmental Policy of the European Communities*, 2nd ed. (London: Kluwer Law International, 1995). See also David Judge, ed., *A Green Dimension for the European Community: Political Issues and Processes* (London: Frank Cass, 1993); McCormick, *Environmental Policy in the European Union.*

46. European Commission, "Energy Efficiency Plan 2011," COM(2011)109 Final, Brussels, March 8, 2011, http://eur-lex.europa.eu/LexUriServ/LexUriServ.do?uri=C OM:2011:0109:fin:en:pdf.

47. European Commission, "Innovation for a Sustainable Future—The Eco-Innovation Action Plan (Eco-AP)," COM(2011)899 Final, Brussels, December 15, 2011, http://eur-lex.europa.eu/LexUriServ/LexUriServ.do?uri=COM:2011:0899:fin:en:pdf.

48. Maria Lee, *EU Environmental Law: Challenges, Change and Decision Making* (Oxford: Hart, 2005).

49. For a more detailed discussion of auto oil legislation in the 1990s, see Regina S. Axelrod, Norman J. Vig, and Miranda A. Schreurs, "The European Union as an Environmental Governance System," in *The Global Environment: Institutions, Law, and Policy*, 2nd ed., ed. Regina S. Axelrod, David L. Downie, and Norman J. Vig (Washington, DC: CQ Press, 2005).

50. Directive 2000/60/EC of the European Parliament and of the Council of 23 October 2000, *Official Journal of the European Union*, L327, December 22, 2000, 0001–0073.

51. European Commission, "A Blueprint to Safeguard Europe's Water Resources," COM(2012)673 Final, Brussels, November 14, 2012, http://eur-lex.europa.eu/Lex-UriServ/LexUriServ.do?uri=COM:2012:0673:fin:en:pdf.

52. Markus Haverland, "Convergence of National Governance under European Integration? The Case of Packaging Waste" (paper presented at the Fifth Biennial Conference of the European Community Studies Association, Seattle, May 29–June 1, 1997).

53. Thomas Gehring, "Governing in Nested Institutions: Environmental Policy in the European Union and the Case of Packaging Waste," *Journal of European Public Policy* 4 (September 1997): 337–354.

54. Directive 2004/12/EC of the European Parliament and of the Council of 11 February 2004 amending Directive 94/62/EC on Packing and Packaging Waste, *Official Journal of the European Union*, L47, February 18, 2004, 0026–0031.

55. Directive 2005/20/EC of the European Parliament and of the Council of 9 March 2005 amending Directive 94/62/EC on Packing and Packaging Waste, *Official Journal of the European Union*, L70, March 16, 2005, 0017–0018.

56. European Commission, "White Paper on Environmental Liability," COM(2000)66, Brussels, February 9, 2000.

57. Timothy Swanson and Andreas Kontoleon, "What Future for Environmental Liability? The Use of Liability Systems for Environmental Regulation in the Courtrooms of the US and the EU," in Vig and Faure, *Green Giants?*

58. Directive 2004/35/CE of the European Parliament and of the Council of 21 April 2004 on Environmental Liability with Regard to the Prevention and Remedying of Environmental Damage, *Official Journal of the European Union*, L143, April 30, 2004, 0056–0075.

59. Directive 2008/99/EC of the European Parliament and of the Council of 19 November 2008 on the Protection of the Environment through Criminal Law, *Official Journal of the European Union*, 328, December 6, 2008, 0028–0037.
60. Derek M. Taylor, "The Directives of the 'Nuclear Package,'" European Commission, 2004, ftp://ftp.cordis.europa.eu/pub/fp6-euratom/docs/euradwaste04pro_1-taylor_en.pdf.
61. Council Directive 2009/71/Euratom of 25 June 2009 Establishing a Community Framework for the Nuclear Safety of Nuclear Installations, *Official Journal of the European Union*, L172/18, July 2, 2009, 18–22.
62. European Commission, "Two Years after Fukushima—Nuclear Safety in Europe," MEMO/13/182, Brussels, March 7, 2013, http://europa.eu/rapid/press-release_MEMO-13-182_en.htm.
63. See European Commission, "Draft Proposal for a Council Directive Amending Directive 2009/71/EURATOM Establishing a Community Framework for the Nuclear Safety of Nuclear Installations," Brussels, COM(2013)343 Final, June 13, 2013, http://ec.europa.eu/energy/nuclear/safety/doc/com_2013_0343_en.pdf.
64. Dave Keating, "Commission rules out nuclear subsidy guidance," European Voice, October 9, 2013, http://www.europeanvoice.com/article/2013/october/commission-rules-out-nuclear-subsidies-/78358.aspx.
65. See European Commission, "The Ecolabel Catalogue," http://ec.europa.eu/ecat.
66. European Commission, "Ecolabel: Facts and Figures," http://ec.europa.eu/environment/ecolabel/facts-and-figures.html.
67. Carmin and VanDeveer, *EU Enlargement and the Environment*; John W. Maxwell and Rafael Reuveny, eds., *Trade and Environment: Theory and Policy in the Context of EU Enlargement and Economic Transition* (Cheltenham, UK: Edward Elgar, 2005).
68. Mikael Skou Andersen, *Governance by Green Taxes: Making Pollution Prevention Pay* (Manchester: Manchester University Press, 1994); Timothy O'Riordan, ed., *Ecotaxation* (London: Earthscan, 1997).
69. Stela Stamatova and Anton Steurer, "Environmental Taxes Account for 6.2% of All Revenues from Taxes and Social Contributions in the EU-27," European Commission, Eurostat, Statistics in Focus, 53/2012, http://epp.eurostat.ec.europa.eu/cache/ity_offpub/ks-sf-12-053/en/ks-sf-12-053-en.pdf.
70. European Commission, "Legislation: European Commission Proposes to Overhaul Energy Taxation Rules," http://ec.europa.eu/taxation_customs/taxation/excise_duties/energy_products/legislation.
71. Directive 2012/27/EU of the European Parliament and of the Council of October 25, 2012, on energy efficiency, amending Directives 2009/125/EC and 2010/30/EU and repealing Directives 2004/8/EC and 2006/32/EC, *Official Journal of the European Union*, L315/1, vol. 55, November 14, 2012, http://eur-lex.europa.eu/johtml.do?uri=oj:l:2012:315:som:en:html.
72. Commission of the European Communities, "Proposal for a Directive of the European Parliament and of the Council Establishing a Scheme for Greenhouse Gas Emission Allowances Trading within the Community and Amending Council Directive 96/61/EC," COM(2001)581 Final, 2001/0245 (COD), Brussels, October 23, 2001.
73. European Commission, "The EU Emissions Trading System (EU ETS)," Commissioner for Climate Action, http://ec.europa.eu/clima/policies/ets/index_en.htm; European Commission, "Reducing Emissions from the Aviation Sector," Commissioner for Climate Action, http://ec.europa.eu/clima/policies/transport/aviation/index_en.htm.
74. European Parliament Resolution of 20 April 2012 on Our Life Insurance, Our Natural Capital: An EU Biodiversity Strategy to 2020 (2011/2307[INI]), http://ec.europa.eu/environment/nature/biodiversity/comm2006/pdf/EP_resolution_apri12012.pdf.
75. European Commission, "Green Paper: Reform of the Common Fisheries Policy," COM(2009)163 Final, Brussels, April 22, 2009, http://eur-lex.europa.eu/LexUriServ/LexUriServ.do?uri=com:2009:0163:fin:en:pdf.

76. European Commission, "Proposal for a Regulation of the European Parliament and of the Council on the Common Fisheries Policy," COM(2011)425 Final, Brussels, July 13, 2011, http://eur-lex.europa.eu/LexUriServ/LexUriServ.do?uri=com:2011:04 25:fin:en:pdf.
77. European Commission, "Renewable Energy: Progress Report," http://ec.europa.eu/energy/renewables/reports/reports_en.htm.
78. See EcoTec Research and Consulting Limited, "The Benefits of Compliance with the Environmental Acquis," DGENV Contract: Environmental Policy in the Applicant Countries and Their Preparation for Accession, Service Contract B7-8110/2000/159960/MAR/H1, Final Report, Executive Summary, July 2001, C/1849/PtB.
79. See Peter M. Haas, "Compliance with EU Directives: Insights from International Relations and Comparative Politics," *Journal of European Public Policy* 5 (March 1998): 17–37.
80. Alberta Sbragia, "Environmental Policy in the European Community: The Problem of Implementation in Comparative Perspective," in *Towards a Transatlantic Environmental Policy* (Washington, DC: European Institute, 1991); Jeremy Richardson, "Eroding EU Policies: Implementation Gaps, Cheating and Re-steering," in Richardson, *European Union*; Wyn Grant, Duncan Matthews, and Peter Newell, *The Effectiveness of European Union Environmental Policy* (London: Macmillan, 2000).
81. Commission Staff Working Document, *Situation in the Different Sectors*, accompanying European Commission, *25th Annual Report on Monitoring the Application of Community Law (2007)*, COM(2008)777 Final, SEC(2008)2855, Brussels, November 18, 2008.
82. See also Tanja A. Börzel, *Leaders and Laggards in European Environmental Policy* (Cambridge: Cambridge University Press, 2003).
83. See also Jonathan Golub, ed., *New Instruments for Environmental Policy in the EU* (London: Routledge, 1998); Matthieu Glachant, ed., *Implementing European Environmental Policy* (Cheltenham, UK: Edward Elgar, 2001).
84. Commission Staff Working Document, *Situation in the Different Sectors*.
85. For information, see the organization's Web site, European Union Network for the Implementation and Enforcement of Environmental Law, http://ec.europa.eu/environment/impel.
86. See Chapters 10–12 in this volume; see also Schreurs et al., *Transatlantic Environment and Energy Politics*; Henrik Selin and Stacy D. VanDeveer, "Raising Global Standards: Hazardous Substances and E-Waste Management in the European Union," *Environment* 48, no. 10 (2006): 6–17; Paul Steinberg and Stacy D. VanDeveer, eds., *Comparative Environmental Politics: Theory, Practice, and Prospects* (Cambridge: MIT Press, 2012); Carolyn Dudek, "Transmitting Environmentalism? The Unintended Global Consequences of European Union Environmental Policies," *Global Environmental Politics* 13, no. 2 (2013): 109–127; Judith van Leeuwen and Kristine Kern, "The External Dimension of European Union Marine Governance," *Global Environmental Politics* 13, no. 1 (2013): 69–87.
87. See Lenschow, *Environmental Policy Integration*.

8

Energy and Environment in China

National and Global Challenges

Joanna I. Lewis and Kelly Sims Gallagher

China's breakneck economic growth over the past three decades has created extreme environmental challenges, including high levels of air pollution. China is reliant on coal for more than two-thirds of its energy needs, and coal combustion causes most of this pollution, which includes sulfur dioxide and particulates, affecting human health, agriculture, ecology, and infrastructure. In addition, China's energy-related carbon dioxide emissions have led to the nation's becoming the largest source of such emissions in the world and, therefore, a major contributor to global climate change. China's economic development has come at the expense of both the local and the global environment.

China faces serious challenges in addressing the environmental impacts of its energy use. Energy demand is growing so quickly that the government can barely monitor technology decisions, resulting more often than not in the construction of additional conventional coal plants. Despite relatively stringent environmental regulations, enforcement of central government policies is often overlooked at the local level. A lack of capacity and transparency in emissions monitoring and energy consumption data means policy makers do not have in hand all the information they need to make strategic decisions about China's energy future.

Despite these real challenges, China has made significant progress in many key areas, including promoting energy efficiency and renewable energy. Armed with aggressive national-level energy intensity reduction targets, a national renewable energy law mandating and supporting the use of low-emission or emission-free technologies, and a suite of other policies targeting the industrial and transportation sectors, the Chinese government has numerous tools in place to address the environmental impacts of its current energy system. Perhaps most promising is the attention China places on the development of advanced low-emission technologies, including renewable energy technologies and higher-efficiency motor vehicles. Chinese firms have used creative strategies to obtain access to advanced technologies, often from the United States and Europe, and in some instances have been able to leapfrog older technologies, shifting directly to more advanced energy-efficient or cleaner ones.

Examining the successes and failures in China's strategies to address the environmental impacts of its energy consumption can provide insights into where China may be headed in the years to come. Understanding how current domestic challenges shape China's positions in international environmental negotiations is also crucial for productive engagement with China to improve its environmental situation. This chapter demonstrates how China's energy challenges are shaping the way the country's leadership is approaching environmental protection at the domestic level, which in turn is shaping its positioning in international environmental negotiations. The chapter also explores how low carbon development has become positioned at the core of China's overarching national five-year economic plans and examines the twelfth five-year plan's domestic policy framework to implement carbon management programs alongside a low carbon development strategy.

Energy, Environment, and Development

China's economic development during the past thirty years has been remarkable by nearly all metrics. Since 1978, China has consistently been the most rapidly growing country in the world.[1] Already the world's largest exporter, as of 2012 China was the second-largest economy in the world measured in purchasing power parity and the fifth-largest according to market exchange rates.[2] As a result of this steady and rapid economic growth, an estimated 200 million people have been pulled out of absolute poverty since 1979.[3]

Despite these impressive achievements, the Chinese government continues to face difficult economic development challenges. China's overall development statistics reveal that, despite the emergence of modern cities and a growing middle class, China is still largely a developing country. China's gross domestic product (GDP) per capita is still below the world average.[4]

Economic growth is not just a crucial part of China's development strategy, but it is also crucial to the political stability of the country. A fundamental target of the current development plan articulated by China's leadership is an annual economic growth rate of 7.5 percent.[5] Many have argued that continued rapid economic growth in China is critical to the Communist Party's legitimacy. The Communist Party leadership in China "considers rapid economic growth a political imperative because it is the only way to prevent massive unemployment and labor unrest."[6]

Energy is directly tied to economic development. The relationship between energy use and economic growth matters greatly in China. Although China quadrupled its GDP between 1980 and 2000, it did so while merely doubling the amount of energy it consumed during that period. This allowed China's energy intensity (ratio of energy consumption to GDP) and consequently the emissions intensity (ratio of carbon dioxide–equivalent emissions to GDP) of its economy to decline dramatically, marking a dramatic achievement in energy intensity gains not paralleled in any other country at a similar stage of industrialization. This has important implications not just for China's economic growth trajectory but also for the total quantity of China's

Figure 8-1 China's Energy Consumption and Energy Intensity Trends, 1980–2011

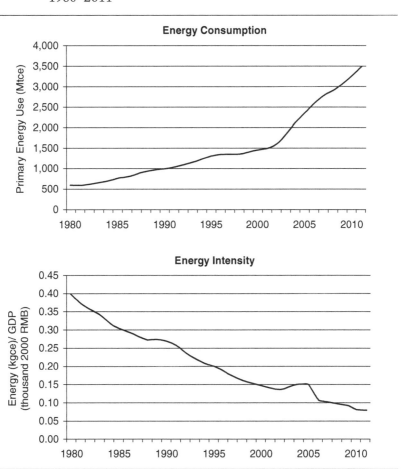

Source: China Energy Group, Lawrence Berkeley National Laboratory, China Energy Databook Version 8.0 (Berkeley, CA: Lawrence Berkeley National Laboratory, 2013).

energy-related emissions. Reducing the total quantity of energy consumed also contributes to the country's energy security. Without this reduction in the energy intensity of the economy, China would have used more than three times the energy it did during this period.

The past decade brought new challenges to the relationship among energy consumption, emissions, and economic growth in China. Starting in 2002, China's declining energy intensity trend reversed, and energy growth surpassed economic growth for the first time in decades. This trend continued until 2005. This reversal has had dramatic implications for energy security and greenhouse gas emissions growth in China during the past few years.

In 2007 China's carbon dioxide (CO_2) emissions were up 8 percent from the previous year, making China the largest national emitter in the world for the first time (surpassing U.S. emissions that year by 14 percent).[7] China's long-term energy security is dependent not only on the country's having sufficient supplies of energy to sustain an incredible rate of economic growth but also on its ability to manage the growth in energy demand without causing intolerable environmental damage.

By 2010, China was emitting almost 50 percent more CO_2 annually than the United States and more than 100 percent more than the European Union. China's increase in energy-related pollution in the past few years has been driven primarily by industrial energy use and a rise in the percentage of coal in the overall energy mix. Industry consumes about 70 percent of China's energy, and China's industrial base supplies much of the world. As a result, China's current environmental challenges are fueled in part by the global demand for its products. China today produces about 70 percent of global iron and steel and about half of the world's cement.[8] The centerpiece goal of the current five-year plan is to promote the service industries—the so-called tertiary sector—over heavy industry because of their higher value to the economy and the energy and environmental benefits associated with less reliance on heavy manufacturing. With this shift, energy use should decline and environmental quality should improve. The recent resurgence in heavy industry in China, responsible for the rapid emissions growth in the past few years, illustrates the challenge of facilitating this transition.

Air Pollution

China's rapidly growing economy, population, and energy consumption are all threatening the country's future environmental sustainability. China faces many environmental challenges, including water scarcity, exacerbated by water pollution, and releases of toxic substances in the environment. Although most sources of pollution in China can be traced back to energy use, we focus in this section on the relationship between energy consumption and air pollution, particularly from coal combustion and oil consumption by motor vehicles.

Coal

Coal is at the heart of China's environmental woes, with major implications for human health. The dominance of coal in China's energy mix is the major cause of high levels of air-polluting emissions. Most of these emissions come from the industrial and electricity generation sectors. By the end of 2010, China had installed 669 gigawatts (GW) of coal power plants.[9] To put this in perspective, the next-largest user of coal power, the United States, has about half the installed capacity of China (336 GW),[10] and India, the next-largest emerging economy that is heavily reliant on coal, has only 100 GW of installed coal capacity.[11] Even as China was attempting to diversify its power sector, coal still contributed to about 80 percent of China's electricity generation in 2011; hydropower contributed 15 percent, nuclear 1.8 percent, and wind 1.5 percent.[12] A net coal importer since 2009, China drives much of global coal demand.

China is building some state-of-the-art coal plants, including many ultra-supercritical, high-efficiency plants. Most of its existing power plants, however, are relatively inefficient (see Table 8-1). The average efficiency of today's coal fleet in China is around 32 percent, but this is expected to increase to 40 percent by 2030. Today, the average efficiency of U.S. coal-fired plants is slightly higher than the average efficiency of Chinese power plants. Some of China's newest plants are more efficient than American plants, however, and China is rapidly closing the gap by using some of the world's most advanced designs.[13]

Particulate matter from coal is a major air pollutant. Concentrations of PM_{10} (particles 10 microns or smaller in size that are capable of penetrating deep into the lungs) in China's cities are extremely high, ranging from the extreme of Panzhihua's average concentration of 255 to 150 in Beijing, 140 in Chongqing, and 100 in Shanghai. These numbers can be compared with concentrations of 45 in Los Angeles and 25 in New York City. PM_{10} can increase the number and severity of asthma attacks, cause or aggravate

Table 8-1 China's Coal Technology Characteristics

Technology	Availability	Cost (dollar per kilowatt)	Efficiency (%)	Use in China
Subcritical	Now	500–600	30–36	Most of current generation fleet
Supercritical	Now	600–900	41	About half of current orders
Ultra-supercritical	Now, but needs further research and development to increase efficiency	600–900	43	Two 1,000-megawatt plants in operation
Integrated gasification combined cycle (IGCC)	Now, but faces high costs and needs more research and development	1,100–1,400	45–55	Twelve units awaiting National Development and Reform Commission approval

Sources: International Energy Agency, CO$_2$ Emissions from Fossil Fuels (Paris: IEA, 2007); International Energy Agency, China Coal Report (Paris: IEA, 2009).

Note: Efficiency is lower heating value, gross output.

bronchitis and other lung diseases, and reduce the body's ability to fight infections. Especially vulnerable to PM$_{10}$'s adverse health effects are children, the elderly, exercising adults, and those suffering from asthma or bronchitis.[14] The health impacts from even smaller particulates, such as PM$_{2.5}$, may be even worse (see Box 8-1). In addition, each year more than four thousand miners die in China's coal mines, mostly in accidents.[15]

Box 8-1   The PM$_{2.5}$ Scandal and "Airpocalypse 2013"

By 2013, "PM$_{2.5}$" had become a household word in Beijing. Particulate matter (PM) includes both solid particles and liquid droplets found in air that stem from all types of combustion activities (e.g., those associated with motor vehicles, power plants, wood burning, and certain industrial processes). Particles less than 2.5 micrometers in diameter (PM$_{2.5}$) are referred to as "fine" particles and are believed to pose the largest health risks because fine particles can lodge deep within the lungs.[a] In 2008, the U.S. embassy in Beijing installed a PM$_{2.5}$ monitor on the building's roof and began posting hourly air quality readings on the embassy's Twitter feed.[b] This feed received little notice until 2011, when a period of particularly poor air quality led to public concern and media attention that pointed out the discrepancy between the readings of the U.S. embassy monitor and the official data being reported by the Beijing Environmental Protection Bureau (EPB). China did not have any standards in place to regulate PM$_{2.5}$ at the time, nor did it monitor or report PM$_{2.5}$ data publicly.[c] On many days the U.S. embassy was reporting pollution levels that were "hazardous" or even exceeded the index altogether (now infamously reported as "crazy bad")[d] while the Chinese official data showed levels that were only "slightly polluted."

These repeated discrepancies led to increasing public concern, not to mention negative publicity for the EPB.[e] Many well-known public figures in China called for the government to measure and regulate PM$_{2.5}$,[f] and the Ministry of Environmental Protection in fact responded by drafting regulations and opening them to public comment in November 2011.[g] The new standard is slated to go into effect in 2016 once sufficient monitoring capacity is in place, although some Chinese provinces and cities (such as Shanghai and Beijing) will begin implementing the standard as early as 2013.[h] Enforcement capacity was further enhanced in 2012, when environmental cadre evaluation was applied to the reduction of fine particulate (PM$_{2.5}$) pollution in Beijing and other cities around China.[i] In January 2013, however, Beijing (and much of eastern China) experienced an extended episode of severe pollution. Spanning several days in mid-January, this so-called Airpocalypse was reportedly the worst pollution recorded since PM$_{2.5}$ monitoring began the previous year, and many believed it to be the worst in history.[j] The worsening air quality situation in Beijing and around eastern China further elevated public concern about inaction and a lack of transparency. Beijing's municipal government responded by releasing a new PM$_{2.5}$ monitoring system in early 2013, likely laying the groundwork for the enforcement of coming regulations.[k]

---

[a]U.S. Environmental Protection Agency, Technology Transfer Network, "PM$_{2.5}$ NAAQS Implementation," accessed February 11, 2013, http://www.epa.gov/ttn/naaqs/pm/pm25_index.html.

[b]BeijingAir on Twitter, accessed February 11, 2013, https://twitter.com/BeijingAir.

[c]Alex L. Wang, "The Search for Sustainable Legitimacy: Environmental Law and Bureaucracy in China," *Harvard Environmental Law Review* 37 (2013): 365–440.

[d]Jonathan Watts, "Twitter Gaffe: US Embassy Announces 'Crazy Bad' Beijing Air Pollution," *Guardian*, November 19, 2010, http://www.guardian.co.uk/environment/blog/2010/nov/19/crazy-bad-beijing-air-pollution.

[e]Ibid.

[f]Ibid.

[g]"Pollution Measures for Public Feedback," Xinhua, November 17, 2011, http://news.xinhuanet.com/english2010/china/2011-11/17/c_131251945.htm.

[h]Deborah Seligsohn, "Chinese Air Pollution Update: Ministry of Environmental Protection Proposes Additional Regulation for Particulates," ChinaFAQs: The Network for Climate and Energy Information, November 22, 2011, http://www.chinafaqs.org/blog-posts/chinese-air-pollution-update-ministry-environmental-protection-proposes-additional-regula.

[i]Wang, "The Search for Sustainable Legitimacy."

[j]Louisa Lim, "Beijing's 'Airpocalypse' Spurs Pollution Controls, Public Pressure," National Public Radio, January 14, 2013, http://www.npr.org/2013/01/14/169305324/beijings-air-quality-reaches-hazardous-levels.

[k]Xinhua, "China Uses PM 2.5 in Weather Alert System," *China Daily*, January 30, 2013, http://www.chinadaily.com.cn/china/2013-01/30/content_16185836.htm; Jaime A. FlorCruz, "Beijing's New Year Surprise: PM 2.5 Readings," CNN, January 27, 2012, http://www.cnn.com/2012/01/27/world/asia/florcruz-china-pollution/index.html.

Sulfur dioxide (SO_2) emissions in China have been estimated to contribute to about one-fourth of global emissions and more than 90 percent of East Asia emissions since the 1990s.[16] Total SO_2 emissions in China increased by 53 percent from 2000 to 2006 (from 21.7 teragrams [Tg] to 33.2 Tg) at an annual growth rate of 7.3 percent, and emissions from power plants (the main source of SO_2 in China) increased from 10.6 Tg to 18.6 Tg over this period.[17] Emissions in northern China increased by 85 percent, while in southern China emissions increased by only 28 percent.[18] Emissions of SO_2 were reported by the Ministry of Environmental Protection to have fallen by about 2 percent in 2011, exceeding the goal of 1.5 percent, while nitrogen oxide emissions rose by 7.2 percent.[19] SO_2 is a precursor to acid rain, which particularly affects southeastern China. Hebei Province is most severely affected, with acid rain accounting for more than 20 percent of crop losses. Hunan and Shandong Provinces also experience heavy losses from acid rain. Some 80 percent of China's total pollution-related losses are estimated to be from damage to vegetable crops.[20]

The economic costs of China's air pollution are very high. According to a recent report from China's government and the World Bank, conservative estimates of morbidity and premature mortality associated with ambient air pollution in China were equivalent to 3.8 percent of GDP in 2003 if premature death was valued at one million yuan per person. Acid rain, caused mainly by sulfur dioxide emissions from coal combustion, is estimated to cost

Table 8-2 Emissions Intensity of Air Pollutants in Eastern China, 2010

Area	Sulfur dioxide emissions intensity (tons per square kilometer)	Nitrogen oxide emissions intensity (tons per square kilometer)
Beijing	6.19	11.79
Tianjin	21.64	30.91
Hebei	7.57	9.02
Jing-Jin-Ji	8.17	10.34
Shanghai	43.97	76.38
Jiangsu	10.86	14.72
Zhejiang	6.84	8.53
Yangtze River Delta	9.84	13.45
Guangdong	4.66	7.35
National average level	**2.36**	**2.37**

Source: Statistics come from the "Notice on the Issuance of the 12th Five-Year Plan of Energy Saving and Emission Reduction Comprehensive Program by State Council" (NDRC [2011]26), as published in Greenpeace, "Ranking Eastern Chinese Cities by Their 'Clean Air' Actions," May 2012, http://www.greenpeace.org/eastasia/publications/reports/climate-energy/2012/ranking-cities-air-action.

Note: Pollution intensity is estimated by dividing pollution emissions in 2010 by the area of administrative divisions.

thirty billion yuan in crop damage (mostly to vegetables) and seven billion yuan in material damage annually. This damage is equivalent to 1.8 percent of the value of the crop output. Although water pollution is less directly tied to coal consumption, it is still fundamental to human well-being, and it too has become a major drag on overall economic growth. Health damage from water pollution is estimated to equal 0.3–1.9 percent of rural GDP, not including the morbidity associated with cancer.[21] A more recent analysis of the health effects of ozone and particulate matter in China determined that these types of pollution led to a 5–14 percent loss of welfare for each year of the study period (1975–2005),[22] and that for 2005 total welfare loss was $111 billion (in 1997 U.S. dollars).[23] A 2012 update of the World Bank study found that the costs of air and water pollution had risen to the equivalent of 10 percent of GDP.[24] The coal mining industry in China is also the deadliest in the world in terms of human safety. It is estimated that thousands of people die every year in China's coal mines, compared with about thirty per year in the United States.[25]

Why does China use so much coal? Coal is China's main energy resource endowment, accounting for 93 percent of the country's remaining fossil fuel resources. In 2012, 78 percent of China's electricity was derived from coal, followed by hydropower (18.3 percent), wind power (2 percent), and nuclear power (1.8 percent). In 2012, wind power generation surpassed nuclear power generation for the first time, making it the third-largest source of electricity in China.[26] Although nuclear and wind power have been growing rapidly in recent years, coal is so dominant that it is unlikely that the current mix of electricity supply can be significantly altered anytime soon. Natural gas is not commonly used for power generation in China owing to its high price and lack of availability because of limited domestic resources, although the government has ambitious plans to increase natural gas use to around fifty million tons of coal equivalent (TCE) annually by 2020.[27] In addition, China has always been reluctant to import natural gas from its most obvious supplier, its neighbor Russia. China is aggressively pursuing renewable energy, and it ranks number one in the world in this pursuit in some respects, such as in its installation of solar water-heating technologies and small hydropower. It ranks fourth in the world in terms of installed wind capacity and fourth in terms of ethanol production.[28] Still, China's non-hydro renewable capacity is a tiny fraction of its primary energy supply, which is completely dominated by coal.

In January 2012 China's Ministry of Environmental Protection (MEP) implemented new national air pollution standards for coal-fired power plants, replacing the prior standards that had been in effect since 2003 and bringing Chinese power plant regulation generally in line with developed world standards.[29] The law gives existing power plants a 2.5-year grace period to meet the new standards, and new plants must meet them upon construction. Compliance with the new MEP standards will require power companies to invest approximately $41 billion to upgrade pollution abatement equipment, and the annual operating cost for nitrogen oxide (NO_x) control equipment alone will be around $9.6 billion, or RMB 61.2 billion.[30] The National Development and Reform Commission (NDRC) raised electricity prices for industrial users by RMB 0.03 (0.47 U.S. cents) per kilowatt hour, including RMB 0.008 for NO_x control, to help pay for the needed upgrades.[31]

Motor Vehicles

In China's biggest cities, including Shanghai and Beijing, most of today's urban air pollution comes from motor vehicles. The car population in China has grown dramatically, from fewer than a total of 100,000 autos in 1990 to approximately 34 million in 2010. In the space of a decade, China also became the world's largest producer of cars and trucks. In 2000 China produced only 605,000, but by 2010 it was producing more than 9 million per year, a change of 1,470 percent.[32] Although the growth in new passenger cars has been astounding, the total number is still quite small compared with the number of vehicles in the United States, which has a car and sport-utility vehicle population of 230 million. With 20 percent of the world's population, the Chinese own only 5 percent of the cars in the world.[33]

The increased demand from all the new cars on the road is causing oil imports to rise. Today, China is the second-largest consumer of oil in the world and the second-largest oil importer.[34] In only the past decade China has emerged as a major global consumer of oil, and there is strong potential for it to become a major natural gas consumer as well, especially if it tries to reduce its greenhouse gas emissions (because natural gas is much less carbon-intensive than coal). About half of China's oil imports come from the Middle East, but Angola became the largest supplier in 2006, and China has invested heavily in energy resources in Africa. Although there have been several new oil discoveries in China recently, Chinese reserves are on the decline.

Many projections about future levels of car ownership in China have been offered—the International Energy Agency, for example, projects there will be 203 million light-duty vehicles and 66 million trucks in China by 2030—but these estimates are speculative.[35] Population, degree of affluence, fuel price levels, and extent of available alternatives are all key factors in the possible levels of future car ownership in China. As China imports greater amounts of energy, the prices of these commodities will rise until supply catches up, and price spikes will be especially likely during supply disruptions. China has imposed aggressive fuel economy standards on cars and other types of motor vehicles, which will significantly reduce demand for oil below what it could

Figure 8-2 Standardized Comparison of Actual and Projected International Fuel Economy and Greenhouse Gas Emissions Standards, 2002–2025 (plans and projections after 2010)

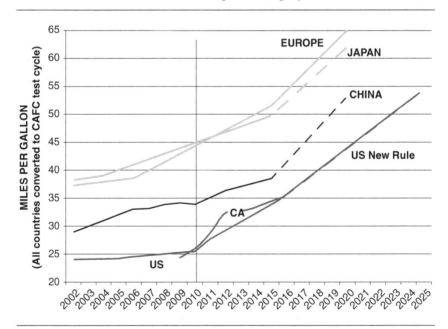

Source: Feng An, Dong Ma, Liping Kang, and Robert Earley, "China Passenger Vehicle Corporate Average Fuel Consumption (CAFC) Trend Report: 2006-2010," Innovation Center for Energy and Transportation, May 2011.

have been absent these policies (see Figure 8-2). China's fuel economy standards are more aggressive than those in the United States, and the government plans to implement new standards that are as much as 18 percent more stringent.[36] These fuel economy standards will greatly benefit the cause of combating global warming, as increased efficiency means reduced fuel consumption and fewer greenhouse gas emissions (unless people drive their cars more because of the lower cost of driving).

Although relatively late in doing so, China has taken many steps to reduce pollution from motor vehicles since 2000. In July 2000, the country banned leaded gasoline, and China's first emission standards were implemented at the Euro I level. In 2005 China moved to the Euro II level, and then to Euro III in 2007. The Chinese standards still lag U.S. and EU standards, however, and a key hurdle has been China's relatively poor fuel quality; emissions cannot be reduced further until fuel quality is improved. Also, public transportation has been scaled up in China's major cities, most notably in Beijing in advance of the 2008 Olympic Games and again through China's economic recovery stimulus package. Despite these actions, emissions of nitrogen oxides, carbon monoxide, and ozone from vehicles continue to increase. As the number of vehicles in China continues to increase, additional regulations will be necessary just to maintain current pollution levels.[37] The rapidly growing vehicle fleet in China is driven by population growth, urbanization, and rising standards of living.

Environmental Regulation in China

In 1972 China signed the United Nations Stockholm Declaration on the Human Environment, which became the impetus for legislative reforms under Deng Xiaoping as the government sought to demonstrate that it could keep its promise to the international community. More immediately, the declaration had the effect of raising environmental concerns among China's leaders, particularly Zhou Enlai.[38] For these reasons, in 1973 the central government held its first national conference on environmental protection. The result of this conference was the publication of the "Rules on the Protection and Improvement of the Environment," which became the blueprint for subsequent environmental lawmaking in China.[39] In 1978 the state's responsibility for the protection of the environment was added to the constitution, but it was not until 1979 that the first comprehensive Chinese environmental law, the Environmental Protection Law, was written.[40]

China now has an extensive range of environmental laws, including six overarching environmental laws, nine natural resources laws, twenty-eight environmental administrative regulations, twenty-seven environmental standards, and more than nine hundred local environmental rules.[41] The key challenge for environmental laws and regulations in China lies in their implementation. Many environmental regulations are top-down in nature, meaning they come from the central government, but their implementation must take place at the local level, where the environmental problems occur.

The relatively weak central government authority that oversees environmental regulation in China has not been very successful at encouraging implementation at the local level. The enforcement of environmental regulations is generally less of a priority for local officials than ensuring that economic growth targets are met.

The idea of incorporating environmental considerations into bureaucratic evaluations has been used in China since the 1980s, but it has not been effective in practice because of the low priority assigned to environmental targets.[42] The 1989 Environmental Protection Law designated the idea of environmental targets as one of eight fundamental "environmental protection systems," and the 1996 ninth five-year plan renewed this idea with an "environmental quality administrative leadership responsibility system."[43] By the eleventh five-year plan these evaluation systems actually began to show results, with strict environmental targets for government leaders leading to greater investment in environmental protection, better coordination of different agencies, and even stronger support for the environmental protection bureau.[44]

Although many of China's laws and regulations are somewhat weaker than their counterparts in the United States and Europe, some of the Chinese government's policies are actually stricter or more far-reaching than most equivalent industrialized countries' policies. Enforcement of China's environmental policies is, however, highly uneven. Some cities—like Beijing in its run-up to the 2008 Olympics—have gone to tremendous lengths and expense to clean up their local factories and reduce air and water pollution. But typical local environmental enforcement is lax and undermines the relatively good policies that have been issued by the central government. For its part, the central government has thus far failed to provide adequate resources to strengthen the MEP so it can improve its own capacity to enforce regulations. There is no adequate system of environmental data collection, distribution, and analysis, and this further complicates the enforcement effort, because without irrefutable data about pollutant emissions and effluent releases, the government lacks the tools that would enable it to judge and act on noncompliance with the law.

All of these deficiencies demonstrate the need for improved environmental governance and, especially, more effective government institutions to promulgate and enforce regulations. Few environmental nongovernmental organizations (NGOs) exist in China because of the government's close control over NGO activities. More and more environmental NGOs are being formed all the time, however, and the Chinese government is increasingly viewing their role as complementary to achieving government goals rather than contradictory. In fact, Chinese environmental NGOs can play an important watchdog role in overseeing the implementation of environmental regulations at the local level and reporting violations to the central government. Even with improving NGO relations, however, in recent years the numbers of protests driven by environmental problems have risen. High-profile incidents driven by environmental catastrophes include the algal bloom in Taihu Lake, caused by factory pollution, that cut off drinking water to thousands of people and a large benzene explosion at a chemical plant that was initially denied by the government, causing public protests.

In March 2009, the State Environmental Protection Agency (SEPA) was upgraded to the Ministry of Environmental Protection. Although it remains to be seen whether this increases the leverage of the environmental mandate or helps with the challenge of implementation of current laws and regulations, the fact that the eleventh five-year plan contained the first "binding" environmental targets is a very positive sign. While environmental targets in the eighth, ninth, and tenth five-year plans were largely not met or even ignored, of the twenty-two key indicators in the eleventh five-year plan, eight received a "binding" designation, and four of these indicators concerned energy or environment.[45]

In Europe and the United States, the environmental movement has been and continues to be critically important to the passage and enforcement of landmark environmental laws. In China, environmental groups are allowed to form, but usually only for the purposes of public education. The government has apparently given the media permission to report on environmental abuses, and it has established hotlines for citizens to call to report environmental infractions. Still, it is clear that criticism of government policies and, especially, the Communist Party itself is not acceptable. Average citizens and NGOs are not yet potent political forces with respect to the formation of environmental policies in China.

There is, however, a growing reliance on academia to inform environmental policy making, and university and research institute experts are encouraged to make suggestions, recommendations, and even relatively modest constructive criticisms to the government. At the beginning of 2009, for example, the government established the new Center for Climate and Environmental Policy under the MEP to conduct policy-related research on climate change, sustainable energy, and environmental protection, and in 2011 the National Center for Climate Strategy and International Cooperation of China (NCSC), a new think tank on climate research under the National Development and Reform Commission, headed by several of China's leading climate change and energy experts, was established. It is difficult to imagine that China will be able to forge a path to sustainability without the help of NGOs and research institutes, given the large size of its economy and population.

Energy and Greenhouse Gas Emissions

Now the world's largest emitter of greenhouse gases, China must play a crucial role in any solution to the global climate change problem. In addition, the impacts of climate change on China are likely to be serious. A synthesis report compiled by China's leading climate change scientists stated, "It is very likely that future climate change would cause significant adverse impacts on the ecosystems, agriculture, water resources, and coastal zones in China."[46] Impacts that are already being observed in China include extended drought in the north, extreme weather events and flooding in the south, glacial melting in the Himalayas endangering vital river flows, declining crop yields, and rising seas along heavily populated coastlines.[47] As a result, China's agricultural system, trade system, economic development engines, and human livelihood all face new risks within a warming world.

Energy and Climate Policy

China has ratified the primary international accords on climate change—the United Nations Framework Convention on Climate Change (FCCC) and the Kyoto Protocol—but as a developing country, China has no binding emissions limits under either accord (see Chapter 10). China is, however, an active participant in the Clean Development Mechanism (CDM) established under the protocol, which grants emissions credits for verified reductions in developing countries that these countries can use toward meeting their Kyoto targets. The Kyoto Protocol requires developing countries to implement measures to mitigate climate change as is feasible for them "in accordance with their common but differentiated responsibilities and respective capabilities."[48]

In the early 1980s, the Chinese government treated climate change primarily as a scientific issue and gave the China Meteorological Administration the responsibility of advising the government on policy options. However, the start of the international climate negotiations meant the engagement of China's Ministry of Foreign Affairs and the gradual politicizing of the climate change issue. As both political awareness and sensitivity surrounding the climate change issue increased, the primary role of representing the Chinese government was shifted to the more powerful NDRC, the main government agency responsible for studying and formulating policies for economic and social development. The move indicated a shift in the relative importance given to the issue as well as a shift in perspective; initially viewed as primarily a scientific issue, climate change had now become recognized as predominantly a development issue.[49]

China's domestic climate strategy remains centered on the nation's energy development strategy as driven by its overall economic development goals. Although attention to climate change has recently increased among China's leadership, climate change has not surpassed economic development as a policy priority. Now the largest emitter of greenhouse gases measured on an annual basis, China can no longer ignore its contribution to this challenge, even with its relatively low per capita emissions rates (see Figure 8-3).

China released its national climate change report on June 4, 2007.[50] Referred to as China's climate change plan, the report has provided a comprehensive synthesis of the policies that China currently has in place that are serving to moderate its growth in greenhouse gas emissions and to help the country adapt to the impacts of climate change. Most of the policies and programs mentioned in the plan are not climate change policies per se, but policies implemented throughout the economy, and particularly in the

Figure 8-3 Global Carbon Dioxide Emissions Shares, 2010 (actual) and 2035 (estimated)

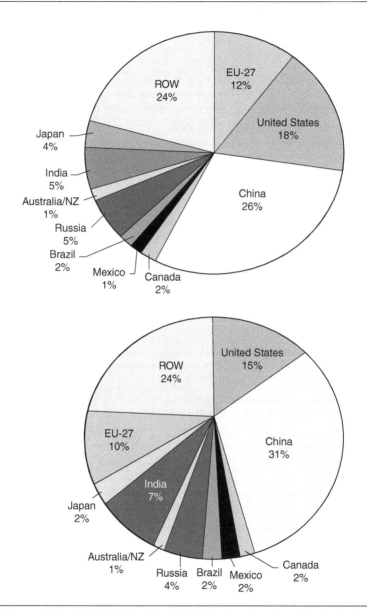

Source: 2010 data, U.S. Energy Information Administration, International Energy Statistics database (as of March 2011), http://www.eia.gov/ies; 2035 projections, U.S. Energy Information Administration, *Annual Energy Outlook 2011*, DOE/EIA-0383, AEO2011 (Washington, DC: U.S. Department of Energy, 2011), http://www.eia .gov/aeo.

energy sector, that have the effect of reducing greenhouse gas emissions. Many of these policies have been enacted to help the country meet its broader economic development strategies and, if implemented effectively, will also serve as policies to mitigate China's greenhouse gas emissions. Three of these key policy areas are energy efficiency, renewable energy, and industrial policy.

The Eleventh Five-Year Plan. With the hope of achieving energy intensity improvements between 2000 and 2020 similar to what it had done the previous two decades, China has a broad national goal of quadrupling economic growth while doubling energy consumption. Beijing's eleventh five-year plan included a near-term goal of reducing national energy intensity 20 percent below 2005 levels by 2010. Implementation of such centrally administered government targets has proven challenging, particularly at the local level. In an attempt to improve local accountability, the NDRC has allocated the target among provinces and industrial sectors, and energy efficiency improvement is now among the criteria used to evaluate the job performance of local officials. The NDRC has reported that the eleventh five-year plan energy intensity target was essentially met, claiming a 19.1 percent rather than a 20 percent reduction, and there is no doubt that much was learned through efforts to improve efficiency nationwide. In addition, many changes were made to enhance enforcement at the local level, including the incorporation of compliance with energy intensity targets into evaluations of local officials.

Under the National Renewable Energy Law, adopted in 2005, China has set a target of producing 15 percent of its primary energy from renewable and other low-emission sources by 2020, up from about 7 percent at present. The Renewable Energy Law offers financial incentives, such as a national fund to foster renewable energy development, discounted lending, and tax preferences for renewable energy projects. Policies to promote renewable energy also include mandates and incentives to support the development of domestic technologies and industries—for instance, by requiring the use of domestically manufactured components. Spurred by a requirement that newly installed wind turbines contain 70 percent local materials, by the end of 2008 Chinese manufacturers were producing about 70 percent of the wind turbines being sold in China. Taxes and other incentives have targeted the solar photovoltaic industry, and by 2008 China produced about 40 percent of the photovoltaic panels used worldwide.

Widespread shutdowns of inefficient coal-fired power plants were conducted during the eleventh five-year plan. In 2006, an estimated 3,140 megawatts (MW) of plants were shut down, followed by 1,409 MW in 2007, 1,655 MW in 2008, 2,615 MW in 2009, and 1,690 MW in 2010. This means that a total of 76.8 GW were shut down during the five-year period—coming close to offsetting the average capacity of new power plants built in China annually over this period (89.8 GW).

The Twelfth Five-Year Plan. Adopted by the Chinese government in March 2011, the twelfth five-year plan set the stage for China's first ever carbon intensity target and pilot cap-and-trade programs, representing a monumental change in the country's approach to global climate change. It also established a new set of targets and policies for the 2011–2015 time frame.[51]

In the twelfth five-year plan the government explicitly identified a new set of high-value strategic industries as essential to the future of the Chinese economy,[52] with many low-carbon energy industries mentioned (including the nuclear, solar, wind, and biomass energy technology industries, as well as hybrid and electric vehicles and energy-saving and environmental protection technology industries).[53] These "strategic and emerging" industries are being promoted to replace the "old" strategic industries such as coal and telecom (often referred to as China's pillar industries), which are heavily state owned and have long benefited from government support. More than 70 percent of the assets and profits of state-owned enterprises are concentrated in the "old" strategic industries. This move to rebrand China's strategic industries likely signals the start of a new wave of industrial policy support for the new strategic industries, which may include access to dedicated state industrial funds, increased access to private capital, and industrial policy support through access to preferential loans or research and development funds. Other targets encourage increased innovative activity, including a target for research and development expenditure to account for 2.2 percent of GDP and for 3.3 patents per 10,000 people. During the eleventh five-year plan period, an estimated 15.3 percent of government stimulus funding was directed toward innovation, energy conservation, ecological improvements, and industrial restructuring.[54]

The twelfth five-year plan builds directly on the energy intensity target and associated programs in the eleventh, setting a new target to reduce energy intensity by an additional 16 percent by 2015. This may seem less ambitious than the 20 percent reduction targeted in the eleventh five-year plan, but it probably represents a much more substantial challenge because the largest and least efficient enterprises have already undertaken efficiency improvements, leaving smaller, more efficient plants to be targeted in this second round. Under preparation is a new Top 10,000 Program, which is modeled on the Top 1,000 Program but adds an order of magnitude of companies to the mix. But as the number of plants grows, so do the challenges of collecting accurate data and enforcing targets.

The twelfth five-year plan also includes a target to increase nonfossil energy sources (including hydro, nuclear, and renewable energy) to 11.4 percent of total energy use (up from 8.3 percent in 2010).[55] Other targets include 100 GW of wind power and 40 GW of solar power by 2015.[56] In early 2013 Chinese officials announced a new solar power target of 40 GW of capacity by 2015. This was substantially larger than the previous target of 21 GW, which had just months before been increased from an earlier target of 5 GW.

To put this new target in perspective, in 2011 Germany (the largest user of solar that year) had installed 24.7 GW in total, and the United States just 4.4 GW. In recent years China has also become a leading manufacturer of wind and solar equipment, and over the past several years it has been the target of several international trade disputes with the United States, the European Union, and others. Several Chinese manufacturers were subjected to antisubsidy tariffs and antidumping duties beginning in late 2012.[57] The United States imposed tariffs ranging from 24 percent to 36 percent on Chinese photovoltaic (PV) manufacturers. Many U.S. solar raw materials manufacturers and installers of solar PV equipment opposed the U.S. government decision to impose the tariffs for fear of Chinese retaliatory tariffs and the worry that solar PV installations would decline in the United States because of increased module prices.[58]

While not formally enshrined in the twelfth five-year plan, another recent notable development is the announcement of a cap on total energy consumption of four billion TCE in 2015.[59] For China to meet this cap on energy consumption, it will have to slow its energy growth to an average of 4.24 percent per year, from 5.9 percent in 2009–2010. The government is also trying to slow GDP growth rates, with a target of 7 percent per year—far below recent growth rates. Lower GDP growth rates make it even more challenging for China to meet energy and carbon intensity targets, since energy and carbon need to grow more slowly than GDP for the country to achieve reductions in energy and carbon intensity.

The twelfth five-year plan includes the goal of gradually establishing a national carbon-trading market, and a handful of provinces have announced the beginnings of pilot carbon-trading schemes. According to an October 2011 NDRC notice, the provinces and municipalities selected to pilot a cap-and-trade program for carbon dioxide are Guangdong, Hubei, Beijing, Tianjin, Shanghai, Chongqing, and Shenzhen.[60] The Tianjin Climate Exchange (TCX), a joint venture of China National Petroleum Corporation Assets Management Co. Ltd., the Chicago Climate Exchange (CCX), and the city of Tianjin, is positioning itself to be the clearinghouse for any future Chinese carbon-trading program, although several other exchanges have been established around the country.

Implementing a carbon-trading scheme in China, even on a small-scale or pilot basis, will not be without significant challenges. Concerns have already been raised by both domestic and foreign-owned enterprises operating in China about how the regulation might affect their bottom lines. But the key challenge is likely technical, resulting from the minimal capacity currently in place to measure and monitor carbon emissions in China. As a result, also promised in the twelfth five-year plan is an improved system for monitoring greenhouse gas emissions, which will be needed to assess compliance with the carbon intensity target and to prepare the national greenhouse gas inventories that, under the Cancun Agreements, are to be reported more frequently and are to undergo international assessment.

Post-2012 International Climate Negotiations

China's positioning in the international climate negotiations has been consistently driven by domestic factors, namely, China's energy and industrial policy objectives. In addition, an increase in China's scientific and technical understanding of its own energy and emissions situation has permitted Chinese leaders to legislate with more confidence domestically. Although China has made significant advances in some areas, the major part of its energy development in the next few decades is likely to be based on fossil fuels and, consequently, will have profound implications for global greenhouse gas emissions. China is showing increasing recognition of a responsibility to engage with the rest of the world on issues related to climate change, but this transition is likely to be a gradual one.

The Chinese government has stated that it is unwilling to accept a firm limit (or cap) on its national greenhouse gas emissions in an international treaty. Despite real evolution in China's negotiating position over the past decade, the negotiating team has not wavered from this position (see Chapters 9 and 10). This has led many to criticize China's position and claim that China is unwilling to take on its fair share of the climate change solution. It is important to understand, however, that while the government may argue against such caps based on an equity principle—after all, a person in China is responsible for far fewer emissions than a person in the United States—China may in fact implement binding domestic policies to limit greenhouse gas emissions in the near term. In such a case, China would be more likely to translate these domestic policies into voluntary commitments under the UNFCCC.

There are also technical reasons China is unlikely to agree to cap its greenhouse gas emissions by committing to an absolute emissions reduction target in a binding international treaty. Committing to a quantifiable emissions limit is challenging for a country that has little prescience into its future emissions pathway, as recent emissions trends well outside the bounds of expert modeling projections have illustrated. In 2004, the U.S. Energy Information Administration projected that China's carbon dioxide emissions would not surpass those of the United States until after 2030. In 2006 this date was revised to approximately 2013, and in reality it happened in about 2007.[61] This inaccuracy is due to the fact that China's emissions grew much more rapidly during this period than anyone had predicted. There is perhaps understandable concern in China about agreeing to bind itself internationally to targets for the future if it is not possible to quantify the country's emissions today.

China still needs international assistance to reduce its greenhouse gas emissions, and not just in the form of the financial assistance and technology transfer it publicly demands at the international climate negotiations. It is therefore critically important for the international community to ratchet up bilateral and multilateral collaboration with China on a wide range of issues, ranging from technology development and cooperation to more basic technical assistance with collecting and processing data, establishing accurate domestic systems to quantify and monitor emissions, and modeling and projecting future emissions growth. Such baseline information is crucial for developing any domestic climate change policies as well as for setting any international climate change commitments. In November 2009, President Hu Jintao and President Barack Obama, in an important first step, announced an initial package of climate and energy agreements to foster cooperation between the two countries, and progress toward implementing these agreements is under way.[62]

It is uncertain how China will respond politically to the climate change threat and to its role in the challenge. While dramatic, path-changing action is unlikely in the near future, it is probable that China will institute gradual changes to begin to address domestic greenhouse gas emissions. The changes most likely to be made, however, will be those that address other pressing issues simultaneously. The Chinese government is already under pressure to reduce severe local air and water pollution, for example, and addressing these pollutants by using less coal could also be a climate change mitigation strategy. Likewise, current policies to promote energy efficiency and renewable energy are in line with domestic priorities and are also crucial for reducing greenhouse gas emissions. Several proposals are being discussed in the context of the post-2012 UN climate negotiations that would require China's commitment to the international community to be in the form of policy actions or sector-specific actions rather than national mandatory emissions limits.[63]

Other studies have attempted to quantify the potential for greenhouse gas mitigation from China through such ongoing policy activities.[64] Because of the country's challenges in quantifying and projecting emissions trajectories, it may be more technically and politically feasible for China to commit to policies that will lead to absolute emissions reductions (or nationally appropriate mitigation actions, or NAMAs) and to carbon intensity targets that are indexed to economic growth. The Chinese leadership announced in November 2009 its intention to implement a domestic carbon intensity target of a 40–45 percent reduction below 2005 levels by 2020. Depending on the stringency of the domestic carbon intensity target, growth in absolute emissions could continue. Whether such a target would reduce emissions below "business as usual" is an open question, and it depends on, among many other factors, future economic growth rates, rates of deployment of low-carbon technologies, the evolving structure of the Chinese economy, and the types of energy supply. For the fifteen-year period from 1991 to 2006, for example, China reduced its carbon intensity by 44 percent, but its carbon dioxide emissions more than doubled.

These win-win actions, or mitigation actions with other cobenefits, may not be sufficient in the eyes of the international community as we approach 2030. Although the EU is the only region in the world to date that has implemented mandatory national measures to reduce greenhouse gas emissions, several countries are expected to follow soon, including Australia, New Zealand, and Japan, as well as certain regions within the United States.[65]

Developing countries have for the most part remained unified over time in their approach to the international climate change negotiations, representing their positions in the context of the Group of 77 (G-77).[66] Additional pressure could mount if other non–Annex I countries (the group of developing countries currently exempt from binding mitigation commitments under the UNFCCC) opt to take on mitigation commitments in the current round of negotiations for the post-2012 period. For example, Brazil and Mexico have already signaled their willingness to pledge national actions in an international framework.[67]

The 2011 climate negotiations in Durban, South Africa, saw two potentially significant changes to long-held elements of China's negotiating position. The first was a potential shift in China's willingness to adopt some form of legally binding commitments, rather than just voluntary commitments, as part of a future climate change agreement. This was reflected in China's support of the Durban Platform, in which UNFCCC parties agreed "to launch a process to develop a protocol, another legal instrument or an agreed outcome with legal force under the Convention applicable to all Parties."[68] The second was a new openness toward discussing absolute greenhouse gas emissions targets, rather than just intensity targets. These changes are very likely results of the programs that have been implemented domestically in the wake of China's carbon intensity target and since the Copenhagen negotiations to both measure and monitor domestic emissions and to implement domestic carbon-trading programs. Since early 2011, China's National Energy Administration has discussed implementing a cap on total domestic energy consumption by the year 2015, which could certainly pave the way for an absolute emissions target as well.[69]

Outlook and Conclusions

Providing modern energy services for 1.3 billion people in an environmentally sustainable manner is a profoundly daunting challenge. Fortunately, the Chinese central government is demonstrating increasing awareness of the problems posed by local pollution and climate change and an interest in altering China's current energy development trajectory. Clearly there is new urgency and opportunity to address climate protection, energy security, and economic development issues, especially among the world's largest energy consumers. It is doubtful, however, that the Chinese government will be able to alter this trajectory significantly without meaningful international engagement during the critical time period of the next one to two decades.

China possesses the ingenuity and the institutional capital to meet certain elements of the climate challenge better than others. It has the technical, engineering, and, increasingly, innovation capacity that many other developing countries lack. China is expected to gain from developing many of the technologies that will be crucial for dealing with climate change. This includes both renewable energy technologies and carbon capture and storage technologies, the latter of which would allow China to continue to rely on fossil fuels while avoiding severe impacts of climate change.

For China to transition to a more environmentally sustainable development pathway, it will need to address several overarching issues. First, because of its reliance on coal, China faces a large incremental cost in moving toward higher-efficiency coal technology and in capturing and storing the emissions from these plants. Large financial resources will be needed because, even though China is already a successful industrializing country, it is confronted with competing demands for available financial resources. Second, key capacity limitations in its ability to collect accurate and transparent energy and emissions data are at the root of China's challenge in enforcing environmental regulations and of its hesitancy to commit to quantifiable reduction targets for greenhouse gas emissions. Third, limitations on the use of foreign investment and foreign technology to achieve China's domestic development goals cause ongoing bilateral trade disputes and tensions in discussions over international technology transfers.

Recognition of the unique challenges that China faces in addressing the transition to a more sustainable development pathway can inform expectations regarding what China will be willing and able to undertake in its own domestic energy and environmental policy and within a multilateral climate agreement.[70] China's local environmental challenges are increasingly global in their impact, and as a result the entire world is watching to see how the nation responds to its challenges. While the interest in China is global, its government still looks primarily inward in shaping its domestic policy decisions; thus, national energy security and local environmental concerns still rank above global greenhouse gas emissions in relative importance. In the end, decisions about how to deal with climate change will hinge on the government's ability to find a way to reduce local and global emissions while continuing to grow the economy and bring a better quality of life to the citizens of the People's Republic of China. Improved human well-being is key to maintaining domestic stability, and that will be the guiding principle for China's leadership in local and global environmental politics.

Notes

1. Barry Naughton, *The Chinese Economy: Transitions and Growth* (Cambridge: MIT Press, 2007).
2. Central Intelligence Agency, "China," *World Factbook,* 2013, https://www.cia.gov/library/publications/the-world-factbook/geos/ch.html.
3. "World Bank Says China Is Poverty Reduction Model," Xinhua, February 25, 2003, http://www.china.org.cn/english/2003/Feb/56694.htm.
4. Central Intelligence Agency, "China."
5. "Facts and Figures: China's Main Targets for 2006–2010," *People's Daily Online,* March 6, 2006, http://english.people.com.cn/200603/06/eng20060306_248218.html.
6. Susan L. Shirk, *China: Fragile Superpower* (New York: Oxford University Press, 2007), 54.
7. Netherlands Environmental Assessment Agency (MNP), "China Contributing Two Thirds to Increase in CO_2 Emissions," press release, June 13, 2008, http://www.pbl.nl/en/news/pressreleases/2008/20080613chinacontributingtwothirdstoincreasein co2emissions.html.
8. "Society Needs Fair Call to Clear Heavy Smog," *Global Times,* January 14, 2013, http://www.globaltimes.cn/content/755570.shtml.

9. Matthias Finkenrath, Julian Smith, and Dennis Volk, *CCS Retrofit: Analysis of the Globally Installed Coal-Fired Power Plant Fleet* (Paris: IEA, 2012).
10. Ibid. Data are for 2010.
11. Ibid. Data are for 2010.
12. China Energy Group, Lawrence Berkeley National Laboratory, *China Energy Databook Version 8.0* (Berkeley, CA: Lawrence Berkeley National Laboratory, 2013).
13. Keith Bradsher, "China Outpaces U.S. in Cleaner Coal-Fired Plants," *New York Times*, May 10, 2009, http://www.nytimes.com/2009/05/11/world/asia/11coal.html.
14. California Air Resources Board, "Air Pollution—Particulate Matter," May 2003.
15. David Biello, "Can Coal and Clean Air Coexist in China?," *Scientific American*, August 4, 2008, http://www.sciam.com/article.cfm?id=can-coal-and-clean-air-coexist-china.
16. Z. Lu, D. G. Streets, Q. Zhang, S. Wang, G. R. Carmichael, Y. F. Cheng, C. Wei, M. Chin, T. Diehl, and Q. Tan, "Sulfur Dioxide Emissions in China and Sulfur Trends in East Asia Since 2000," *Atmospheric Chemistry and Physics* 10 (2010): 6311–6331.
17. Ibid.
18. Ibid.
19. "China Sets Pollution Reduction Targets for 2012," Xinhua, December 21, 2011, http://news.xinhuanet.com/english/china/2011-12/21/c_131320014.htm.
20. World Bank and State Environmental Protection Administration, People's Republic of China, *Cost of Pollution in China: Economic Estimates of Physical Damages* (Washington, DC: World Bank, 2007).
21. Ibid.
22. Welfare loss is a combination of losses in consumption and leisure time.
23. Kira Matus, Kyung-Min Nam, Noelle E. Selin, Lok N. Lamsal, John M. Reilly, and Sergey Paltsev, "Health Damages from Air Pollution in China," *Global Environmental Change* 22, no. 1 (2012): 55–66.
24. World Bank and Development Research Center of the State Council, People's Republic of China, *China 2030: Building a Modern, Harmonious, and Creative High-Income Society* (Washington, DC: World Bank, 2012).
25. Kenneth Rapoza, "Is China Slowly Giving Up on Coal?," *Forbes*, February 10, 2013, http://www.forbes.com/sites/kenrapoza/2013/02/10/is-china-slowly-giving-up-on-coal.
26. Joshua S. Hill, "China Accounted for 35% of Global Onshore Wind Capacity," CleanTechnica, accessed February 11, 2013, http://cleantechnica.com/2013/02/06/china-accounted-for-35-percent-of-global-onshore-wind-capacity.
27. Rapoza, "Is China Slowly Giving Up on Coal?"
28. Eric Martinot, *Renewables 2007 Global Status Report* (Paris: REN21 Renewable Energy Policy Network, 2007).
29. People's Republic of China, Ministry of Environmental Protection, "Emission Standard of Air Pollutants for Thermal Power Plants," GB 13223-2011, 2012, http://english.mep.gov.cn/standards_reports/standards/Air_Environment/Emission_standard1/201201/t20120106_222242.htm.
30. "China Adopts World-Class Pollutant Emissions Standards for Coal Power Plants," ChinaFAQs: The Network for Climate and Energy Information, June 15, 2012, http://www.chinafaqs.org/library/chinafaqs-china-adopts-world-class-pollutant-emissions-standards-coal-power-plants.
31. Hui Lu, "China Hikes Power Tariffs, Adjusts Coal Prices to Ease Power Shortages," Xinhua, November 30, 2011, http://news.xinhuanet. com/english2010/china/2011-11/30/c_131280061.htm.
32. Stacy C. Davis, Susan W. Diegel, and Robert G. Boundy, *Transportation Energy Data Book*, Report No. ORNL-6987 (Oak Ridge, TN: U.S. Department of Energy, Oak Ridge National Laboratory, 2012).
33. Ibid.
34. BP, "Statistical Review of World Energy," June 2012, http://www.bp.com/statistical-review.

35. International Energy Agency, *World Energy Outlook 2007* (Paris: IEA/OECD, 2007), 20.
36. Keith Bradsher, "China Is Said to Plan Strict Gas Mileage Rules," *New York Times*, May 27, 2009, http://www.nytimes.com/2009/05/28/business/energy-environment/28fuel.html.
37. Michael P. Walsh, "Motor Vehicle Pollution and Fuel Consumption in China," in *Urbanization, Energy, and Air Pollution in China: Proceedings of a Symposium* (Washington, DC: National Academies Press, 2004).
38. Stefanie Beyer, "Environmental Law and Policy in the People's Republic of China," *Chinese Journal of International Law* 5, no. 1 (2006): 185–211; Lynn Kirshbaum, "Environmental Law in China: Challenges to Implementation" (paper prepared for Robert Sutter, Georgetown University, December 12, 2008).
39. Kirshbaum, "Environmental Law in China."
40. Beyer, "Environmental Law and Policy in the People's Republic of China"; Kirshbaum, "Environmental Law in China."
41. Xielin Liu, "Building an Environmentally Friendly Society through Innovation: Challenges and Choices" (background paper, China Council for International Cooperation on Environment and Development, Beijing, 2007).
42. Alex L. Wang, "The Search for Sustainable Legitimacy: Environmental Law and Bureaucracy in China," *Harvard Environmental Law Review* 37 (2013): 365–440.
43. Ibid.
44. Ibid.
45. Ibid.
46. Lin Erda, Xu Yinlong, Wu Shaohong, Ju Hui, and Ma Shiming, "Synopsis of China National Climate Change Assessment Report (II): Climate Change Impacts and Adaptation," supplement, *Advances in Climate Change Research* 3 (2007): 6–11. This paper is a synopsis of Section II of China's *National Assessment Report on Climate Change*, published in February 2007.
47. Intergovernmental Panel on Climate Change, *Climate Change 2007: Impacts, Adaptation and Vulnerability* (Working Group II Contribution to the Fourth Assessment Report of the Intergovernmental Panel on Climate Change) (New York: Cambridge University Press, 2007).
48. The Kyoto Protocol to the United Nations Framework Convention on Climate Change, http://unfccc.int/resource/docs/convkp/kpeng.html.
49. Joanna I. Lewis, Jeffrey Logan, and Michael B. Cummings, "Understanding the Climate Challenge in China," in *Climate Change Science and Policy*, ed. Stephen H. Schneider, Armin Rosencranz, Michael D. Mastrandrea, and Kristin Kuntz-Duriseti (Washington, DC: Island Press, 2010).
50. People's Republic of China, National Development and Reform Commission, *China's National Climate Change Programme* (Beijing: NDRC, June 2007), http://en.ndrc.gov.cn/newsrelease/P020070604561191006823.pdf.
51. Government of the People's Republic of China, "12th Five-Year Plan for National Economic and Social Development of the People's Republic of China" (in Chinese), March 16, 2011, http://news.xinhuanet.com/politics/2011-03/16/c_121193916.htm; Joanna Lewis, "Energy and Climate Goals of China's 12th Five-Year Plan," Pew Center on Global Climate Change, March 2011, http://www.pewclimate.org/doc-uploads/energy-climate-goals-china-twelfth-five-year-plan.pdf.
52. Government of the People's Republic of China, "12th Five-Year Plan for National Economic and Social Development."
53. Government of the People's Republic of China, "Decision on Speeding Up the Cultivation and Development of Emerging Strategic Industries" (in Chinese), September 8, 2010, http://www.gov.cn/ldhd/2010-09/08/content_1698604.htm.
54. HSBC Global Research, "China's Next 5-Year Plan: What It Means for Equity Markets," October 2010.

55. Government of the People's Republic of China, "China Announces 16 Pct Cut in Energy Consumption per Unit of GDP by 2015," March 5, 2011, http://www.gov .cn/english/2011-03/05/content_1816947.htm; "Zhang Guobao: 'Twelfth Five' Push to Nonfossil Energy to Account for 11.4 Percent Share of Primary Energy" (in Chinese), People.com.cn, January 6, 2011, http://energy.people.com.cn/GB/13670716 .html.

56. Zachary Shahan, "China's New Solar Target: 40 GW by 2015 (8 Times More Than Its Initial 5 GW Target)," CleanTechnica, December 13, 2012, http://cleantechnica .com/2012/12/13/chinas-new-solar-target-40-gw-by-2015-8-times-more-than-its-initial-5-gw-target; Herman Trabish, "Wind Power in China Sees Enormous Growth, Immense Challenges," Greentech Media, November 29, 2012, http://www .greentechmedia.com/articles/read/will-china-wind-keep-growing-or-outgrow-itself.

57. Brian Wingfield, "U.S. Sets Anti-dumping Duties on China Solar Imports," Bloomberg, October 10, 2012, http://www.bloomberg.com/news/2012-10-10/u-s-sets-anti-dumping-duties-on-china-solar-imports.html.

58. Diane Cardwell and Keith Bradsher, "U.S. Will Place Tariffs on Chinese Solar Panels," *New York Times,* October 10, 2012, http://www.nytimes.com/2012/10/11/business/global/us-sets-tariffs-on-chinese-solar-panels.html?_r=0.

59. Joshua Fellman, "China to Hold Primary Energy Use to 4.2 Billion Tons in 2015, Xinhua Says," Bloomberg, October 20, 2010, http://www.bloomberg.com/news/2010-10-30/china-to-hold-primary-energy-use-to-4-2-billion-tons-in-2015-xinhua-says .html.

60. National Development and Reform Commission, "Guojiafazhangaigewei Bangongting Guanyu Kaizhan Tan Paifangquan Jiaoyi Shi Dian Gongzuo De Tongzhi [NDRC Notice on Pilot Trading Programs for the Development of Carbon Emissions Rights], Notice 2601," October 2011, http://www.ndrc.gov.cn/zcfb/ zcfbtz/2011tz/t20120113_456506.htm.

61. U.S. Energy Information Administration, *International Energy Outlook, 2004–2007* (Washington, DC: U.S. Department of Energy, 2004–2007), http://www.eia.doe .gov/oiaf/ieo/ieoarchive.html. Note that revisions to U.S. emissions projections were also made, but by a much smaller total amount during this time period.

62. U.S. Department of Energy, "U.S.-China Clean Energy Announcements," press release, November 17, 2009, http://www.whitehouse.gov/the-press-office/us-china-clean-energy-announcements.

63. See Joanna Lewis and Elliot Diringer, "Policy-Based Commitments in a Post-2012 Climate Framework," Pew Center on Global Climate Change, May 2007, http:// www.pewclimate.org/working-papers/policy-based-commitments; Jake Schmidt, Ned Helme, Jin Lee, and Mark Houdashelt, "Sector-Based Approach to the Post-2012 Climate Change Policy Architecture," *Climate Policy* 8 (2008): 494–515.

64. Jiang Lin, Nan Zhou, Mark Levine, and David Fridley, "Taking Out 1 Billion Tons of CO_2: The Magic of China's 11th Five-Year Plan?," *Energy Policy* 36 (2008): 954–970; Center for Clean Air Policy, *Greenhouse Gas Mitigation in China, Brazil and Mexico: Recent Efforts and Implications* (Washington, DC: Center for Clean Air Policy, 2007).

65. See the Web site of the Regional Greenhouse Gas Initiative (RGGI), http://rggi.org/ home; California Environmental Protection Agency, Air Resources Board, "Assembly Bill 32: Global Warming Solutions Act," http://www.arb.ca.gov/cc/ab32/ab32.htm.

66. The G-77 was established on June 15, 1964, by seventy-seven developing countries that were signatories to the Joint Declaration of the Seventy-Seven Countries issued at the end of the first session of the United Nations Conference on Trade and Development (UNCTAD) in Geneva. Although the number of members of the G-77 has increased to 130 countries, the original name has been retained because of its historic significance. See Group of 77 at the United Nations, "About the Group of 77," http:// www.g77.org/doc.

67. Government of Brazil, Interministerial Committee on Climate Change, *National Plan on Climate Change: Brazil* (Brasília: Government of Brazil, December 2008), http://www.mma.gov.br/estruturas/imprensa/_arquivos/96_11122008040728.pdf; Government of Mexico, Intersecretarial Commission on Climate Change, *National Strategy on Climate Change: Mexico: Executive Summary* (Mexico City: Government of Mexico, 2007), http://www.un.org/ga/president/61/follow-up/climatechange/Nal_Strategy_MEX_eng.pdf.

68. UN Framework Convention on Climate Change, "Establishment of an Ad Hoc Working Group on the Durban Platform for Enhanced Action Draft Decision (CP.17)," December 2011.

69. Xinhua, "China to Cap Energy Use at 4 Bln Tonnes of Coal Equivalent by 2015," China Radio International, March 4, 2011, http://english.cri.cn/6909/2011/03/04/1461s624079.htm.

70. Joanna I. Lewis, "China's Strategic Priorities in International Climate Negotiations," *Washington Quarterly* 31, no. 1 (Winter 2007–2008): 155–174.

9

The View from the South

Developing Countries in Global Environmental Politics

Adil Najam

This chapter examines the collective behavior of developing countries in global environmental politics. In the now burgeoning literature on global environmental politics no single aspect's importance is acknowledged as consistently, but treated as casually—even shabbily—as the role of developing countries. Although high-quality work is published on the behavior of specific developing countries (particularly large and fast-growing economies within this group) with regard to particular environmental issues, little analysis exists of how this group of countries—often referred to as "the South" or "the Third World"—tends to behave collectively in global environmental politics.

Of course, developing countries are not a monolithic, entirely united bloc. Indeed, this group of countries is and has been from its very beginning a nonhomogeneous group. Individual developing countries often differ, and sometimes bicker, on particular environmental issues. However, despite such specific differences and despite the growing significance of emerging economies within the South (for example, China, India, and Brazil), which has itself brought South-South relations into sharper relief, there is a generally acknowledged, still prevalent, and easily identifiable sense of shared identity and common purpose among the developing countries of the South.[1] Developing countries do not forfeit their national interests in choosing to act collectively, but they do form a distinct and identifiable collective within global environmental politics.

This chapter explores the nature of this shared identity and common purpose and how it manifests in global environmental politics. Its four sections (a) outline a historical and conceptual understanding of "Southness," (b) highlight the motivations and aspirations that developing countries have invested in global environmental politics, (c) review the experience of the developing countries in key aspects of these politics since the UN Conference on Environment and Development (UNCED)—also known as the Earth Summit—held in Rio de Janeiro in 1992, and (d) explain why developing countries continue to harbor a certain sense of frustration with global environmental politics. A core argument of this chapter is that the South's recurrent desire for what could be described as a new international *environmental* order stems from the same hopes and fears that prompted its call in the 1970s for a new international *economic* order. Such reservations notwithstanding, countries of the South have become increasingly engaged and embedded in global environmental politics. They seek major shifts in the priorities of global environmental politics but neither deny nor desist from that politics— indeed, they have become central players in that politics and are now beginning to define some of its essential contours.

Understanding the Collective South

Since the mid-1990s, the term *South* has again become a descriptor of choice for the set of nations variously referred to as developing countries, less developed countries, underdeveloped countries, or the Third World. Especially in the context of global negotiations—and even more so in global environmental negotiations—these countries often choose, and sometimes demand, to be referred to as the South. This is more than a matter of semantics. The term reflects a certain aspect of collective identity and a desire to negotiate as a collective.[2]

The term, and its use in the concept of the North-South divide, was a staple of scholarly and populist political discourse during the 1970s, particularly as a rallying cry in the demand by developing countries for a new international economic order (NIEO).[3] After spending most of the 1980s in hibernation, the phrase again gained currency during the 1990s. In particular, its wide use by governments, nongovernmental organizations, the media, and officials during the Rio conference in 1992 revitalized it in popular environmental contexts. Since then the turning tides of globalization, including the dramatic economic rise of emerging economies in Asia, have brought the distinctions within this group to the fore and given us new groupings and acronyms—most central within them being BRICS (Brazil, Russia, India, China, South Africa) as a motif for emerging economies of fast-growing international influence. While this has sometimes distracted from the salience of "the South" in global environmental politics, it has not yet eroded that salience, as was visible during the negotiation phase of the 2012 Rio+20 conference (formally known as the United Nations Conference on Sustainable Development).

However, the new dynamics within the South have made the articulation of the collective voice of the South more complex. Indeed, a host of new global issues—including the two great challenges of global climatic and global economic change—have added new dimensions of complexity to the once routinized rituals of "Southness" in global political debate.[4] At the same time, globalization, the information revolution, and rapidly rising environmental awareness within developing countries also add new layers of local environmental pressures on developing country negotiators at the global level. The result is a new set of constraints on those negotiating on behalf of the global South in the arenas of global environmental politics. However, at the highest level of global environmental discourse, the collective South—as articulated by the Group of 77 (G-77)—remains an important player, although not as important as it might have been twenty years ago. It deserves our understanding. In short, the politics of the South as operationalized by the G-77 may be less influential today, but not less relevant.

Writing in the 1980s, then secretary-general of the Organisation for Economic Cooperation and Development (OECD) pointed out that the North-South concept, "like all powerful ideas[,] ... has the virtue of grand simplicity" and described it as a divide between the developed countries of the North, which have "advanced or relatively advanced income levels and social conditions and a more or less completed process of national integration," and the developing countries of the South, "where the development process is still very much in train, where dual economies and dual societies are characteristic, and where, in many cases, hunger and poverty remain the dominant way of life for millions of people."[5] This popular view of the North-South divide as a binary distinction between haves and have-nots is a powerful, and not untrue, way of understanding the concept—so long as one remembers that the South seeks not simply economic development but also a say in the political decisions affecting its destiny.[6] The 1990 report of the South Commission defined the term in a decidedly more political context by addressing not merely economic poverty but also the "poverty of influence."[7] For the commission, the defining feature of the South is not just its economic weakness but also its political dependence. The self-definition of the South, therefore, is a definition of exclusion: these countries believe that they have been bypassed and view themselves as existing on the periphery. To redress what they consider to be an imbalance of influence, the developing countries have sought the vehicle of global negotiations, often referred to as the North-South dialogue.[8]

From the moment the term was coined, some considered it largely irrelevant or inaccurate. Such views have been as resilient as the term itself. For example, a 1994 headline in the *New York Times* proclaimed, "The 'Third World' Is Dead."[9] Such unwarranted obituaries have been, and remain, an enduring feature of the collective's decidedly rocky history. For those who define the Third World, or the South, solely in terms of Cold War polarizations, the conclusion is obvious: the emergence of Southern unity, they insist, was a result of Cold War politics; now that the Cold War is dead, the alliance should also be buried.[10] Others who see the term simply as an economic differentiator similarly find it irrelevant as some Southern countries build economic muscle.

Yet at the simplest and most pragmatic level, what Roger Hansen said about the validity of North-South thinking thirty-five years ago seems equally valid today: "If over [130] developing countries time and again, in forum after forum, act as a diplomatic unit, they would seem to merit analysis as a potential actor of major importance in the international system."[11] Current predictions of the South's (and the G-77's) imminent demise should be seen in a similar light. At a deeper level of analysis, it is important to remember that for many of these countries—including for major emerging economies such as China, India, and Brazil—the desire for unity in the face of an international order they believe continues to place them at a systemic disadvantage still outweighs their internal diversity or differences. Most important, even if some Northern observers consider the South's agenda of the 1970s "discredited,"[12] it remains unfinished business for much of the South and a goal believed to be worth pursuing.[13]

A sense of new vulnerabilities, the persistent pangs of an unfinished agenda, and the opportunity to renew a North-South dialogue under environmental auspices serve to rally the countries of the South and translate into a renewed assertiveness, especially around the broad issue of sustainable development.[14] The reinvigoration that the South seems to have enjoyed during and since the 1992 Earth Summit and the prominence it has regained as a relatively cohesive negotiating collective have taken many by surprise. Indeed, at many turns during the 1992 Earth Summit, and in subsequent global negotiations, differences within the developing countries of the G-77 led to apparent fractures and frictions in the collective. This has been evident, for example, in climate change negotiations, where the interests of major oil-producing countries, of growing energy users, and of small island states that belong to the Alliance of Small Island States (AOSIS)—often poorer as well as especially vulnerable to climatic changes—have been at odds.[15] The importance assumed by large and growing countries such as China and India as major energy users and carbon emitters has similarly differentiated their climate change interests from those of many other developing countries.[16] Negotiations on the Biosafety Protocol to the Convention on Biological Diversity Convention (see Chapter 12) saw developing countries take significantly different positions on the basis of their trade priorities.[17] In the negotiations on desertification, a dispute between African and non-African members nearly brought G-77 coordination to a halt.[18] The dramatic economic rise of China, and to a lesser extent India, has also induced speculation about whether the South is disintegrating. Indeed, on the climate change issue there seem to be deliberate efforts from the North to break the Southern coalition by seeking dialogue with components of the South rather than the collective as represented by the G-77.[19]

However, the empirical evidence suggests, at least until now, that even when developing countries have different national priorities on specific issues in global negotiations—something that should not be surprising—they almost always choose to pursue these interests within the framework of the Southern collective, the G-77. At the 2012 Rio+20 conference the G-77 was not as strong a voice of the South as it was twenty years before,[20] yet it was clearly the most important voice of the South in official negotiations. Historically, the collective has remained remarkably resilient in the face of conditions that could have led to its disintegration. This might well change in the future, but it has not changed just yet. Analysts trace this resilience to a common view of the nature of environmental issues and their placement within a North-South framework, which suggests that the collective South will continue to play an important role in future global environmental politics. As Porter, Brown, and Chasek note, "Despite growing disparities among the developing countries between rapidly industrializing countries such as China, India, Malaysia, and Brazil, and debt-ridden countries that have experienced little or no growth since the 1980s, such as most of sub-Saharan Africa, Vietnam, Myanmar, and Nicaragua, developing countries share a common view of the relationship between global environmental issues and North-South economic relations."[21] China and India may well eventually exit the Southern collective, but at this point the benefits of being wooed individually by the North while speaking for and through the larger collective remain in their interest, as well as in the interest of other developing countries.[22]

Institutionally, the South consists of two distinct organizations—the Non-Aligned Movement (NAM) and the Group of 77—that have played different but complementary roles in furthering the Southern agenda. As Sauvant notes, "While the Non-Aligned Countries [have] played a key role in making the development issue a priority item of the international agenda, the Group of 77 has become the principal organ of the Third World through which the concrete actions . . . are negotiated within the framework of the United Nations system."[23] An instrument of political summitry, the hundred-plus members of NAM meet every three years at the summit level to renew (or redefine) their vows. Meetings of foreign ministers are held every eighteen months. Operating through ministerial committees, NAM has no permanent institutional infrastructure to manage its activities between these meetings. On environmental issues, NAM has made some—but relatively few—declaratory statements of aspiration. It is the G-77 that remains the collective voice of the developing countries in global environmental politics.

Julius Nyerere, former president of Tanzania, described the G-77 as the "trade union of the poor."[24] It functions as the negotiating arm of the developing country collective during global negotiations, and it has described its goals as "provid[ing] the means for the developing world to articulate and promote its collective economic interests and enhance its joint negotiating capacity on all major North-South international economic issues in the United Nations system, and promot[ing] economic and technical cooperation among developing countries."[25] Although the G-77 emerged around the same time as NAM, it has distinctive origins. Unlike NAM, it was born within—and was primarily a result of—the changing composition of the United Nations in the 1960s. Starting as a temporary caucus of 77 developing countries, it has grown into an ad hoc but quasi-permanent negotiating caucus of some 130 members, plus China, which has the status of associate member but plays an influential role in the collective (see Map 9-1).

A main historical achievement of the G-77 was its role as chief negotiator for Southern demands for a new international economic order in the 1970s. Although the NIEO never achieved its goals, the G-77 remained a negotiation collective, exerting influence in agenda setting within various UN forums. It enjoyed particular successes in shaping final compromises during the 1992 Earth Summit and in a series of subsequent global environmental negotiations.[26] Indeed, the G-77 remains the main negotiating voice of the Southern collective in major environmental negotiations. As a negotiating

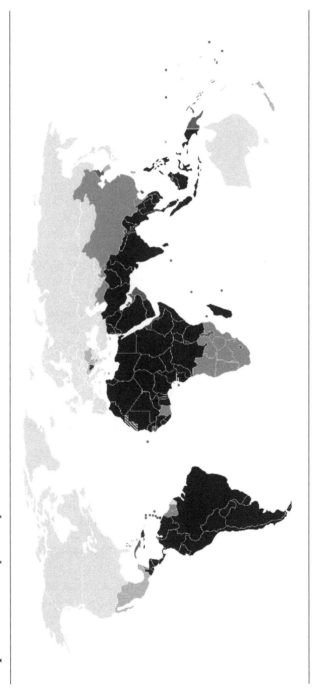

Map 9-1 The Group of 77 plus China

vehicle, the G-77 does not override the individual national interests of its member states; instead it becomes a potent vehicle for national interests on which the member states maintain shared positions.

The G-77 chairmanship rotates on an annual basis among the group's three regional subgroups—Asia, Africa, and Latin America—and the delegation from the chairperson's country serves as the designated spokesperson for the entire caucus in all negotiations during that year. Although the South has emerged as a stable and resilient collective in global environmental politics, it has often been forced to adopt lowest-common-denominator positions because of the impulse for risk reduction, low expectations, assumed habits of collaboration wrought out of a long history, and the need to herd a large and differentiated collective in the face of chronic resource constraints and no management effort. This has limited the G-77's ability to negotiate effectively for the shared goals of the collective or the differentiated interests of its members. The unity of the G-77, while not insignificant, is forever tentative; it is a unity that its members stumbled into—a unity that they have learned to stumble into.

Today, the G-77 is clearly more tentative and stumbling than it was at the 1992 Rio Earth Summit. However, its obituary is as premature today as it has been during so many other historical moments. It may not be the most effective international coalition, but it serves a purpose for its membership—and for global environmental politics itself, as discussed below.

Southern Motivations in Global Environmental Politics

The timing of the 1992 Earth Summit was opportune for the South. The UNCED preparatory process coincided with the withering away of Cold War politics (see Chapters 2 and 3). The end of the Cold War instilled a sense of new vulnerabilities in the developing world and provided the motivation for revitalizing the collective South. Rio offered an opportunity for the South to engage the North in a new dialogue. UNCED gave the South a forum, an issue, and an audience that it had been denied since the 1970s. The South—represented by an energetic G-77—not only succeeded in reopening the North-South dialogue but also effectively made that dialogue the focus of the Rio conference. Ultimately, the achievements at Rio and their legacy did not match the South's exaggerated hopes.[27] However, Rio and subsequent global negotiations provided the South with opportunities to influence the global environmental agenda, particularly within the context of sustainable development.

A close examination of the goals and actions of developing countries during global environmental negotiations suggests that the South seeks what can be described as a new international *environmental* order (NIEnvO) and that this goal stems from the same concerns and ambitions that prompted its call for a new international *economic* order in the 1970s.[28] Roger Hansen defined the original NIEO debate as a conflict over "conceptions about the management of society."[29] Rallying its newfound unity and negotiating as a tight bloc, the G-77 gained a major victory when a 1974 special session of the United Nations General Assembly legitimated the South's demand for the creation of a NIEO by passing a resolution to that effect and drawing up a plan of action. However, the optimism reflected in the UN resolution proved misplaced, and the differences persisted—North accusing South of being confrontational, and South blaming North for perpetuating an unjust order. By the 1980s the momentum was lost and, as Mahbub-ul-Haq put it, "North-South negotiations [had] deteriorated to a ritual and a skillful exercise in *non*-dialogue."[30] In subsequent years, as the North's perception of the economic importance of natural resources in the South (particularly mineral and agricultural products) diminished, so did the perceived leverage enjoyed by the G-77. The NIEO agenda rapidly receded from world attention, as did discussions about North-South dialogue. It wasn't until the Earth Summit in 1992 that the relevance of and need for North-South negotiations again became the subject of broad academic, policy, and public discussion.

However, the environmental issue as an exemplar of the North-South divide predates Rio by at least twenty years. The vast literature on the history of the North-South conflict, as well as the now bulky scholarship on international environmental politics, treats the role of developing countries in the United Nations Conference on the Human Environment (UNCHE), held in Stockholm in 1972, as a mere footnote. In fact, UNCHE was one of the first global forums at which the South consciously negotiated as a unified collective and adopted many of the substantive arguments and negotiation strategies soon to become the hallmark of the NIEO debates.[31]

From the very beginning, many developing countries perceived environmental concerns as a distinctively North-South issue and, in some cases, as an effort to sabotage the South's developmental aspirations. The intellectual leadership of the South very poignantly set out to redefine the environmental issue area in a decidedly North-South context. The most telling example was the so-called 1971 Founex Report, produced by a distinguished group of Southern intellectuals as part of the UNCHE preparatory process.[32] The tone and substance of the report foreshadowed, nearly exactly, what soon became the rhetoric of the South during the 1970s NIEO debates, the 1992 UNCED, and other major environmental forums.

The constancy in the South's position at Stockholm, at Rio, and subsequently is striking, demonstrating that the original NIEO ideals survived and resurfaced in new rounds of global environmental negotiations. Chris Mensah, who served as a G-77 negotiator at UNCED, points out that the Southern leadership explicitly formulated its negotiation strategy around two key goals: first, to "ensure that the South has adequate environmental space for its future development," and second, to "modify global economic relations in such a way that the South obtains the required resources, technology, and access to markets which would enable it to pursue a development process that is both environmentally sound and rapid enough to meet [its] needs and aspirations."[33] Developing countries have consistently contextualized environmental issues as part of the larger complex of North-South concerns, particularly concerns about an iniquitous international order and their desire to bring about structural change in that order. This has become more poignant in recent years as environmental negotiations on issues such as climate change have become increasingly focused on trade and economic aspects. Developing countries have pursued the same types of systemic considerations as during NIEO debates.

The experience in global environmental politics in the past two decades seems to suggest that polarizations across North-South lines are unlikely to disappear if they are simply ignored or wished away.[34] Even as some individual countries become more active on specific environmental issues, they and the G-77 find collective bargaining an effective strategy for those interests that remain broadly shared by the South. The resilience shown by the South in pursuing what it considers its legitimate agenda of economic justice and international systemic change suggests that international environmental negotiations will continue to be influenced by a Southern agenda that looks very much like a call for a new international *environmental* order. As Gareth Porter and Janet Brown note, "Many developing countries, particularly the more radical members of the Group of 77, have viewed global environmental negotiations as the best, if not the only, opportunity to advance a broader agenda of change in the structure of North-South economic relationships."[35] Marc Williams elaborates, "The possibility of linking negotiations on global environmental change with demands for change in other areas of North-South relations is one crucial reason for the continued participation of developing countries in negotiations of environmental problems."[36] He adds, "It is not . . . a question of environment being co-opted into the North-South debate. It already exists in this debate and is conceived in North-South terms."[37]

If the new vulnerabilities brought forth by the end of the Cold War motivated the developing countries to reinvigorate the collective South, the all-encompassing rubric of sustainable development has enabled them to pursue the new North-South dialogue without having (yet) lost the North's attention. For some, the loosely defined global politics of sustainable development provides a broad framework within which to build a global compact to address both the North's concern for environmental sustainability and the South's desire for economic and social development. For others, including many G-77 negotiators, this new politics encompasses "a struggle between the developing and developed countries to define sustainable development in a way that fits their own agendas. The developed countries, most of which are relatively rich, put environment first. By contrast, the developing countries, most of which are poor and still struggling to meet basic human needs, put development first."[38]

Around the time of the Rio Earth Summit, many in the North and South argued that sustainable development might be the trump card the South had been seeking all along. The North's new concern for global environmental problems, it was argued, provided the South with considerable leverage and bargaining power, because without the participation of the developing countries many such problems cannot be addressed effectively.[39] For example, a Caribbean official suggested that "for the first time in more than a decade, the developing countries have an issue [the environment] where they have some real leverage," while India's environment minister went even further to proclaim that "the begging bowl is [now] really in the hands of the Western world."[40]

Such Southern enthusiasm proved decidedly exaggerated, and it mellowed after 1992.[41] Because of the rise of major power centers *within* the South, the G-77 soon found that its leverage lay less in influencing what went into the treaties than it did in deciding what was kept out of them. While the South has some limited leverage in the global politics of sustainable development, this leverage is applied largely to avoid defeat, and its use is conditioned by the existence of a high level of concern in the North for the environmental issue under discussion. Marian Miller's research on global regimes relating to the ozone layer, hazardous waste, and biodiversity found that "when there is a shared perception of environmental vulnerability, the Third World is able to gain a modest bargaining advantage."[42] That "modest bargaining advantage" yielded little for the South at the Rio+20 conference.[43]

From the South's perspective, such assessments are sobering but not melancholy. Although the desire for systemic change endures, it is tempered by more realistic assessments. Moreover, part of the defining essence of the collective South is a desire to minimize risk rather than to maximize gain. From this standpoint, the Southern collective has done what it set out to do: it has minimized the risk of being bulldozed by a Northern environmental agenda, maintained a North-South focus on the global environmental dialogue, and eked out little victories (in terms of global transfers) whenever possible. Importantly, Southern hopes persist for a new North-South bargain constructed around the global politics of sustainable development; the importance that countries like China and India now have in environmental negotiations—for example, on climate change—only underscores this potential further.[44] This potential emanates from two important differences between the first generation of North-South dialogue and its current incarnation, including the growing importance of the South-South dimensions of the emerging global order.[45]

First, unlike its predecessor, this new generation of North-South interaction is characterized by both sides wanting a global dialogue, albeit with differing interests and agendas. For the South, such a dialogue is itself a long-standing goal. For the North, it is necessitated by the realization that global action on the environment, especially in the age of climate change, cannot be successful without the active participation of the developing countries. This is a major sea change from the 1970s, when the South was calling for dialogue and the North actively resisted. Furthermore, a certain sense of urgency exists on both sides as the effects of both environmental devastation and abject poverty compound visibly over time. Second, by their nature, global environmental problems are difficult to conceive of in terms of victory and defeat, especially in the long run. Although the jury is still out on whether and how the global environment might become a win-win issue, all indications suggest that it can easily be transformed into a lose-lose proposition. This also marks a difference from aspects of earlier North-South dialogues, such as the 1970s oil and debt crises, which failed partly because attempts to address the issues were perceived as zero-sum games.

At the heart of North-South politics of sustainable development are debates about the costs to be borne, the ability to bear these costs, the responsibility for causing the problems, and the ability to influence future decisions. These can be reduced to contentions about past responsibility, present ability, and future priorities. Serious differences persist between North and South on all three. Bridging the deep differences is not an easy task and would require, at minimum, innovative strategies from both North and South. One proposed strategy for the South would build upon the lessons of negotiation theory and the experiences of the South. The eight-point strategy can be paraphrased as "Stop feeling angry at the North and sorry for yourself."[46] It recommends that the South focus on interests, not positions; cultivate its own power; be hard on issues, not on people; redefine the international environmental agenda; organize itself; develop its constituency; clean up its own act; and remember that good agreements are more important than "winning." Such a strategy would also lead to a more productive international negotiation process.

Given the South's long pursuit of deeply felt interests, it is unlikely that it will voluntarily forsake its demands or be argued out of them. Given the South's bargaining leverage, it is equally unlikely that the South will browbeat the North into simply accepting its positions. If meaningful headway is to be made, it will have to come through some mechanism that allows the interests of both sides to be met. In this regard, *sustainable development* can be a potentially fortuitous term in that it can (given the right conditions) allow efficient packaging of issues of concern to North and South—issues that they might otherwise be hesitant to deal with individually. Issue linkage, however, can be fraught with both dangers and opportunities. Some observers, such as Christopher Stone, fear that "adding cards to the deck raises the risk that the environment will get lost in the shuffle."[47] However, Lawrence Susskind reminds us that issue linkage can be "crucial to the success of negotiation[s]" that involve complex, multiparty, multi-issue bargaining.[48] While there is certainly the danger of issue linkage turning into blackmail—with the North arm-twisting the South to follow its environmental dictates or the South threatening environmental inaction in the absence of a restructured international system—there is a strong case for both sides to seek issue linkages in their pursuit of meaningful dialogue. After all, the very term *sustainable development* is the embodiment of creative issue linkage.

Southern Views on Global Environmental Politics since Rio

The 1992 UNCED conference is widely viewed as one of the high points of the past thirty years of global environmental politics. Rio's legacy probably owes as much to the many disappointments since that conference as it does to its actual achievements. For example, in a survey of 252 scholars and practitioners from seventy-one countries conducted ten years after Rio, nearly 70 percent of the respondents viewed the Rio Earth Summit as having been "very significant" or "monumental," even though only 6 percent believed that significant progress had been made toward implementing Rio goals. The survey findings suggest that Rio's greatest impact came from its indirect outputs: its success in giving a higher global profile to issues of environment and development; spurring the growth of national and international institutions, policies, projects, and multilateral agreements for environment and development; and giving more prominence to the views of developing countries on global environmental policy.[49]

For developing countries, a key manifestation of these indirect outputs was the so-called Rio bargain. Although difficult to define—and embraced with varying degrees of conviction by various parties—the Rio bargain is generally understood to be an attempt to bridge lingering North-South differences through two key mechanisms: the concept of sustainable development and a set of design principles for global environmental agreements that addressed key concerns of the South.[50]

More than twenty years after Rio, it is easy to forget that the notion of sustainable development—which has since become somewhat of a Southern mantra—was not the South's idea but rather a conceptual device used to appease developing countries apprehensive, since before the 1972 Stockholm Conference, that protection of the environment would be used as a reason to stall their economic development. Indeed, the official name of the Rio Earth Summit—the United Nations Conference on Environment and Development—was crafted, after some debate, to signify that environment and development are complementary rather than contradictory categories.

Still, many in the South came to UNCED and viewed the notion of sustainable development with doubt and in some cases outright trepidation.[51] This was not much different from how others in the South viewed the notion of "green economy" twenty years later at Rio+20. Eventually, however, developing country negotiators came to see sustainable development and the broader Rio process as good opportunities to reopen the North-South dialogue, which had languished through the 1980s, and to move toward a grand North-South bargain for which the South had been striving since the 1970s.[52] Today, it is a concept that is fully "owned" by the developing countries of the South. Indeed, at Rio+20 it was the G-77 that was defending sustainable development vigorously and with gusto.[53]

Thus, for the G-77 (but perhaps not for many in the North), the most important legacy of the Rio process was a global commitment to sustainable development, which the South sees as providing an emphasis on development equal to environmental protection, and to three critical subsidiary principles: additionality, common but differentiated responsibility, and polluter pays.[54] Embodied in the frameworks of various Rio documents, these principles arose out of fears among the countries of the South that even though they had not been historically responsible for creating the major global environmental problems, the costs of global environmental action would somehow be transferred to them, through either forgone developmental opportunities or actual remediation and adaptation costs. This section reviews the state of global environmental politics from the perspective of the South.[55]

Sustainable Development

Sustainable development has never been a clear concept.[56] Indeed, it was never meant to be. It originated as a political compromise, and a rather good one. Its greatest strength was constructive ambiguity; actors that might otherwise not talk to one another could accept the concept for very different reasons and agree to talk. The World Commission on Environment and Development gravitated toward the concept of sustainable development in a conscious attempt to resolve developing countries' apprehension about the environmental agenda. The Earth Summit found the concept useful in getting the North and the South to sit at the same table. As a result, use of the concept began to evolve. By the time Rio ended, many saw sustainable development not as a nebulous ideal or vague goal but as a policy prescription, a desired if not mandatory pathway for future national and international policy.[57]

In practical terms, the good news is that many in the South have totally internalized the concept of sustainable development and have become staunch advocates. This denotes a significant evolution. Many government and citizen organizations in developing countries have adopted sustainable development as a guiding principle for implementation and action. As a result, at the local level the concept of sustainable development is far more real today than it was a decade ago.[58] The bad news is that at the level of intergovernmental debates, the concept has become more, rather than less, murky since Rio. The term stands in danger of being reduced from an innovative framework for negotiation to an empty declaratory aspiration. The rise of the idea of the "green economy" and the overall tone of the Rio+20 deliberations in general were seen by some as an erosion of the concept. This is ironic given that the official name of the Rio+20 conference was the United Nations Conference on Sustainable Development. Thus, while sustainable development was once seen in some quarters as a potentially powerful and even threatening concept—because it suggested the possibility of change in the status quo—it is today on the verge of becoming ineffectual and divorced from its initial action orientation.[59] For those in the South who had come to accept and even embrace the concept because of its embedded promise of systemic change, this dilution has been particularly disturbing.[60] The current climate change debate is a good indicator of this unease. Much of the public discourse, as well as the policy debate, highlights the environmental parameters much more than the developmental impacts. However, the impacts of climate change, and the need for many developing countries to adapt to these impacts, will be a practical test of the concept of sustainable development and of Northern commitment to the concept. Because adaptation policy is mainly about development, it will either force environmentalists to take development concerns more seriously or bring new North-South fissures on sustainable development to the fore.

Additionality

The principle of additionality arose out of the Southern concern that environmental issues would divert international aid from traditional developmental matters. Developing countries feared that instead of raising new funds for dealing with global environmental issues, the North and international institutions would simply transfer to the environment resources previously targeted for development. The principle of additionality seeks to ensure that new moneys are made available to deal with global environmental issues. Despite assurances given to the South, however, this principle was abandoned soon after UNCED, during negotiation of the UN Convention to Combat Desertification (UNCCD). It became clear that few if any new funds would be made available for implementation of the treaty. This dismayed developing countries, particularly those in Africa, and became a major source of contention in the negotiations. Ultimately, a global mechanism was established under the UNCCD in order to, essentially, use existing resources more efficiently to meet the action needs of the UNCCD.[61] While the Global Environment Facility eventually decided to include desertification activities in its funding, the UNCCD negotiations severely damaged the principle of additionality. Since then, negotiations on several other multilateral environmental agreements—including those addressing climate change and toxic chemicals—have included arguments from Northern nations that utilizing market forces and managing existing resources better are adequate substitutes for additionality. Today, additionality is a particular concern in the context of climate adaptation. Many poorer countries fear that climate adaptation will drain their developmental resources away from other immediate needs, even as international assistance for other development issues is diverted to climate-related investments. The climate change issue already diverts attention from issues of more immediate importance for developing countries, and many in the South fear that it will also divert resources.[62]

Common but Differentiated Responsibility

The principle of common but differentiated responsibility acknowledges that some nations have a greater and more direct responsibility for creating and therefore for addressing global environmental problems (see Chapter 3). Although such problems concern all nations, and all should work toward their solution, responsibility for action should be differentiated in proportion to the responsibility for creating the problem and the available financial and technical resources to take effective action. Although this principle places the primary responsibility for action on industrialized countries, it was actually a concession of sorts made by the developing countries. Placing responsibility for action on the North had been a major argument of the South since before the 1972 Stockholm Conference.[63] In accepting this principle, the South agreed that it would also address global environmental issues—provided the primary burden of action, investment, and implementation was not shifted to the very countries least responsible for creating the problems and least able to resolve them.

The principle of common but differentiated responsibility enjoys generally broad support and is explicitly acknowledged in nearly all international environmental agreements since Rio. Yet it faces an important assault in the context of the UN Framework Convention on Climate Change. The United States has taken the position that it cannot accept mandatory targets for reductions of greenhouse gas emissions unless restrictions of some kind are also placed on major developing countries such as China and India. Industrialized countries account for the vast majority of historical greenhouse gas emissions. In addition, although aggregate national greenhouse gas emissions are growing significantly in many developing countries, the per capita emissions in these countries will remain significantly smaller than those in the North for decades to come. Although understanding the need for the growing economies within the South to take on some additional responsibilities, many in the South worry that they have already seen a shift from past responsibility as a yardstick for future action—a change that would, from their perspective, make global environmental regimes even less equitable.[64]

Polluter Pays

The polluter-pays principle, rooted in domestic environmental policy in the North, seeks to ensure that the costs of environmental action are borne by those who created the need for the action. Like common but differentiated responsibility, the polluter-pays principle is rooted in concerns about fairness and constitutes a key component of the Rio bargain. As with other aspects of the Rio bargain, many in the South believe the polluter-pays principle has been steadily diluted through attempts to create a new post-Kyoto climate regime. They point to an increasing pattern of pushing implementation of multilateral environmental agreements steadily Southward, including in the climate, desertification, and biodiversity regimes, by seeking relatively fewer changes in behavior patterns in the North and relatively more in the South— even though Northern behavior gave rise to many problems in the first place.[65] Consider the Clean Development Mechanism (CDM), a provision of the Kyoto climate agreement that allows industrialized countries to meet some of their responsibilities for greenhouse gas reduction by investing in projects in the South. In the name of efficiency, the CDM moves a great deal of climate action to developing countries where emission reductions are likely to be cheaper, rather than imposing greater costs in the countries responsible for past greenhouse gas emissions. Although the logic of economic efficiency is potentially compelling, the CDM arguably threatens the core moral element of the polluter-pays principle in that it allows industrialized countries to avoid taking more significant and expensive action domestically—essentially allowing the polluters to buy their way out of their responsibility. While capturing efficiencies in the South may be enticing in the short term, it leaves subsequent generations in the developing countries with potentially more arduous tasks in the future, having already sold their rights to cheaper solutions. On the other hand, as the developing countries' contributions to carbon emissions increase, the polluter-pays principle should equally apply to them. However, if the principle's integrity is compromised by the North in trying to find cheap and quick fixes for its pollution, we may find the South less willing to accept the principle when its turn comes.

Southern Frustrations in Global Environmental Politics

Global environmental politics yields mixed results for the Southern collective. On the positive side, one could argue that the South, which largely rejected the global environmental agenda at Stockholm in 1972, has now internalized and accepted much or most of that agenda. Indeed, developing countries are far more integrated into the global environmental system than many expected would be possible at Stockholm in 1972 or at Rio in 1992. The concept of sustainable development has allowed developing countries to incorporate long-standing concerns about economic development and social justice into the emerging environmental agenda, and by doing so they have influenced the nature of global environmental discourse. More broadly, global environmental politics affords the South a new arena in which to advance its persistent demand for radical, structural reform of the international system. Indeed, the rise of Southern emerging economies has also given many developing country concerns a new salience and more influence, even if it has weakened institutions such as the G-77.

Yet the dominant feeling within the South remains one of frustration with global environmental politics. The South has few tangible benefits to show for its continuing and increasing involvement and investment in this issue. It has been no more successful in crafting a new international *environmental* order than it was in building a new international *economic* order. Most of the concessions the South thought it had negotiated from the North have proved largely illusory, and the so-called Rio bargain has not exactly delivered. Much of the attention in terms of North-South environmental relations since UNCED has focused on what the South sees as the North's failure to deliver what was promised or implied at Rio, such as additional resources, technology transfers, and capacity building. The North's inability to fulfill these commitments—and the lack of attention to this failure in the policy discourse—is a major contributor to the South's prevailing sense of frustration. The achievements of individual countries notwithstanding, the Southern collective has little to celebrate except its survival. As the concept of sustainable development loses clarity and purpose at the global level, and as the key principles of additionality, common but differentiated responsibility, and polluter pays are steadily eroded (from the South's standpoint), developing countries have a diminishing interest in these processes.[66] These issues defined the raison d'être for the South's engagement in global environmental negotiations. While Southern disenchantment is unlikely to turn into total disengagement, it is certainly not conducive to meaningful North-South partnerships for what remain pressing global environmental challenges.

Parallel to this unraveling of the Rio bargain is the negotiation overload that characterized the world of global environmental policy immediately following the 1992 Rio Earth Summit.[67] It is not without irony that the less we were able to implement existing multilateral environmental agreements, the more frantically we seemed to try to create new ones. Proliferation of such agreements led to a severe negotiation fatigue among all countries, particularly developing countries.[68] The limited and already stretched human resources available to these countries were further thinned by increasing demands of even more, and more complex and demanding, negotiations for multilateral environmental agreements. While major Northern countries have responded to the negotiation proliferation by deploying more human and knowledge resources, most developing countries were unable to do so, compounding the systemic disadvantage they already face in the negotiations.[69] A result was the visible priority placed on implementation concerns, rather than on negotiating new treaties, at Rio+20.

More than four decades after the 1972 Stockholm Conference, developing country negotiators are much more involved in global environmental politics than they expected to be, even if they consider themselves disenchanted, disadvantaged, and disempowered.[70] For the Southern collective, the sense of frustration stems not only from global environmental negotiations having yielded many agreements but very little implementation; it also stems from having seen the North-South bargain, a cherished legacy of the Rio Earth Summit, unravel slowly. Yet the key assumption that led to the forging of the original bargain—that meaningful progress could be made on the great environmental challenges of our times, including climate change but not limited to it—is more valid today than ever before. Such progress is unlikely, if not impossible, however, without the full and active participation of the developing countries. Meaningful participation by the developing countries is less likely to come from efforts to break up the Southern collective (which has been resilient to such attempts) than from efforts to address the acknowledged and often-articulated needs of the developing countries. The view from the South is not without hope, but it contains major challenges that cannot be wished away.

Notes

1. For more on this theme, see Adil Najam and Rachel Thrasher, eds., *The Future of South-South Economic Relations* (London: Zed Books, 2012).
2. For a more elaborate treatment of the argument made in this section, see Adil Najam, "The Collective South in Multinational Environmental Politics," in *Policymaking and Prosperity: A Multinational Anthology*, ed. Stuart Nagel (Lanham, MD: Lexington Books, 2003), 197–240.

3. For discussion, see Craig Murphy, *The Emergence of the NIEO Ideology* (Boulder, CO: Westview Press, 1984).

4. See Najam and Thrasher, *The Future of South-South Economic Relations.*

5. Emile Van Lennep, "North-South Relations in the 80s: A Constructive Approach to New Realities," in *Global Development: Issues and Choices*, ed. Khadija Haq (Washington, DC: North-South Roundtable, 1983), 15.

6. See Stephen D. Krasner, *Structural Conflict: The Third World against Global Liberalism* (Berkeley: University of California Press, 1985); Caroline Thomas, *In Search of Security: The Third World in International Relations* (Boulder, CO: Lynne Rienner, 1987).

7. South Commission, *The Challenge to the South: The Report of the South Commission* (Oxford: Oxford University Press, 1990), 1.

8. See B. P. Menon, *Global Dialogue: The New International Order* (London: Pergamon Press, 1977); Murphy, *The Emergence of the NIEO Ideology.*

9. Barbara Crossette, "The 'Third World' Is Dead, but Spirits Linger," *New York Times*, November 13, 1994, sec. A.

10. Examples include Alan Oxley, "North/South Dimensions of a New World Order," in *Whose New World Order? What Role for the United Nations?*, ed. Mara R. Bustelo and Philip Alston (Annandale, VA: Federation Press, 1991).

11. Roger Hansen, *Beyond the North-South Stalemate* (New York: McGraw-Hill, 1979), 2. See also Marc Williams, "Re-articulating the Third World Coalition: The Role of the Environmental Agenda," *Third World Quarterly* 14, no. 1 (1993): 7–29; Cedric Grant, "Equity in International Relations: A Third World Perspective," *International Affairs* 71, no. 3 (1995): 567–587.

12. James K. Sebenius, "Negotiating a Regime to Control Global Warming," in *Greenhouse Warming: Negotiating a Global Regime*, ed. Jessica Tuchman Mathews (Washington, DC: World Resources Institute, 1991), 87.

13. South Commission, *The Challenge to the South*; Mohammed Ayoob, "The New-Old Disorder in the Third World," *Global Governance* 1, no. 1 (1995): 59–77; Adil Najam, "An Environmental Negotiation Strategy for the South," *International Environmental Affairs* 7, no. 3 (1995): 249–287.

14. Dennis Pirages, *Global Ecopolitics: The New Context for International Relations* (North Scituate, MA: Duxbury Press, 1978); Hayward R. Alker Jr. and Peter M. Haas, "The Rise of Global Ecopolitics," in *Global Accord: Environmental Challenges and International Responses*, ed. Nazli Choucri (Cambridge: MIT Press, 1993), 133–171; Najam, "An Environmental Negotiation Strategy for the South."

15. William R. Moomaw, "International Environmental Policy and the Softening of Sovereignty," *Fletcher Forum of World Affairs* 21 (Summer/Fall 1997): 7–15.

16. Sjur Kasa, Anne T. Gulberg, and Gørild Heggelund, "The Group of 77 in the International Climate Negotiations: Recent Developments and Future Directions," *International Environmental Agreements: Politics, Law and Economics* 8, no. 2 (2008): 113–127.

17. Aaron Cosbey and Stas Burgiel, *The Cartagena Protocol on Biosafety: An Analysis of Results* (Winnipeg: International Institute for Sustainable Development, 2000).

18. Anil Agarwal, Sunita Narain, and Anju Sharma, *Green Politics* (New Delhi: Centre for Science and Environment, 1999); Elisabeth Corell, *The Negotiable Desert: Expert Knowledge in the Negotiations of the Convention to Combat Desertification* (Linköping, Sweden: Linköping University, 1999).

19. John Humphrey and Dirk Messner, "China and India as Emerging Global Governance Actors: Challenges for Developing and Developed Countries," *IDS Bulletin* 37, no. 1 (2006): 107–114. Also see Kasa et al., "The Group of 77 in the International Climate Negotiations."

20. Mark Halle, Adil Najam, and Christopher Beaton, *The Future of Sustainable Development: Rethinking Sustainable Development after Rio+20 and Implications for UNEP* (Winnipeg: International Institute for Sustainable Development, 2013).

21. Gareth Porter, Janet Welsh Brown, and Pamela S. Chasek, *Global Environmental Politics*, 3rd ed. (Boulder, CO: Westview Press, 2000), 179.
22. For related discussion, see Shangrila Joshi, "Understanding India's Representation of North-South Climate Politics," *Global Climate Politics* 13, no. 2 (2013): 128–147; Phillip Stalley, "Principled Strategy: The Role of Equity Norms in China's Climate Change Diplomacy," *Global Climate Politics* 13, no. 1 (2013): 1–8; Humphrey and Messner, "China and India as Emerging Global Governance Actors."
23. Karl P. Sauvant, *The Group of 77: Evolution, Structure, Organization* (New York: Oceana, 1981), 5.
24. Julius K. Nyerere, "Unity for a New Order," in *Dialogue for a New Order*, ed. Khadija Haq (New York: Pergamon Press, 1980), 3–10.
25. Group of 77, *Principles and Objectives of the Group of 77 for the Year 2000 and Beyond* (New York: Office of the Chairman of the Group of 77, 1994), 1.
26. See Najam, "An Environmental Negotiation Strategy for the South"; Adil Najam, "A Developing Countries' Perspective on Population, Environment and Development," *Population Research and Policy Review* 15, no. 1 (1996): 1–19; Tariq Banuri, "Noah's Ark or Jesus's Cross?," Working Paper WP/UNCED/1992/1, Sustainable Development Policy Institute, Islamabad, Pakistan, 1992; Makhund G. Rajan, "Bargaining with the Environment: A New Weapon for the South?," *South Asia Research* 12, no. 2 (1992): 135–147; Agarwal et al., *Green Politics*.
27. See Banuri, "Noah's Ark or Jesus's Cross?"; Najam, "An Environmental Negotiation Strategy for the South"; Halle et al., *The Future of Sustainable Development*; Adil Najam, "The Case for a South Secretariat in International Environmental Negotiation," Working Paper 94-8, Program on Negotiation at Harvard Law School, Cambridge, Massachusetts, 1994; Richard Sandbrook, "UNGASS Has Run Out of Steam," *International Affairs* 73, no. 4 (1997): 641–654.
28. Najam, "An Environmental Negotiation Strategy for the South."
29. Hansen, *Beyond the North-South Stalemate*, vii.
30. Mahbub-ul-Haq, "North-South Dialogue: Is There a Future?," in Haq, *Dialogue for a New Order*, 270.
31. See Wade Rowland, *The Plot to Save the World* (Toronto: Clarke, Irwin, 1973).
32. *Development and Environment*, Report and Working Papers of Experts Convened by the Secretary General of the United Nations Conference on the Human Environment, Founex, Switzerland, June 4–12, 1971 (Paris: Mouton, 1971).
33. Chris Mensah, "The Role of Developing Countries," in *The Environment after Rio: International Law and Economics*, ed. Luigi Campiglio, Laura Pineschi, Domenico Siniscalco, and Tullio Treves (London: Graham and Trotman, 1994), 38.
34. Banuri, "Noah's Ark or Jesus's Cross?"; Caroline Thomas, *The Environment in International Relations* (London: Royal Institute of International Affairs, 1992); Williams, "Re-articulating the Third World Coalition"; Tariq Osman Hyder, "Looking Back to See Forward," in *Negotiating Climate Change: The Inside Story of the Rio Convention*, ed. Irving M. Mintzer and J. Amber Leonard (Cambridge: Cambridge University Press, 1994), 201–226; Agarwal et al., *Green Politics*; Adil Najam, "Trade and Environment after Seattle: A Negotiation Agenda for the South," *Journal of Environment and Development* 9, no. 4 (2000): 405–425.
35. Gareth Porter and Janet Welsh Brown, *Global Environmental Politics* (Boulder, CO: Westview Press, 1991), 129.
36. Williams, "Re-articulating the Third World Coalition," 19.
37. Ibid., 25.
38. Hyder, "Looking Back to See Forward," 205.
39. For example, Gordon J. MacDonald predicted that "the views of the developing nations will determine the direction, and probably the ultimate significance, of UNCED." Gordon J. MacDonald, "Brazil 1992: Who Needs This Meeting?," *Issues in Science and Technology* 7, no. 4 (1992): 41. The *New York Times* (March 17, 1992)

noted that "for the first time . . . the developing countries have an issue where they have some real leverage." Oran Young argued that the South has "substantial bargaining leverage" and that "Northerners will ignore the demands of the South regarding climate change at their peril." Oran R. Young, "Negotiating an International Climate Regime: The Institutional Bargaining for Environmental Governance," in Choucri, *Global Accord*, 447.

40. Both statements quoted in Rajan, "Bargaining with the Environment," 135–136.
41. Ibid., 147.
42. Marian A. L. Miller, *The Third World in Global Environmental Politics* (Boulder, CO: Lynne Rienner, 1995), 141. Others have reached similar conclusions, including Susan Sell, who examined North-South environmental bargaining on ozone depletion, climate change, and biodiversity, and Valérie de Campos Mello, who analyzed the forestry negotiations at UNCED. See Susan Sell, "North-South Environmental Bargaining: Ozone, Climate Change, and Biodiversity," *Global Governance* 2, no. 1 (1996): 97–118; Valérie de Campos Mello, "North-South Conflicts and Power Distribution in UNCED Negotiations: The Case of Forestry," Working Paper WP-93-26, International Institute for Applied Systems Analysis, Laxenburg, Austria, 1993.
43. Halle et al., *The Future of Sustainable Development*.
44. Kasa et al., "The Group of 77 in the International Climate Negotiations"; Joshi, "Understanding India's Representation of North-South Climate Politics"; Stalley, "Principled Strategy"; Humphrey and Messner, "China and India as Emerging Global Governance Actors."
45. See Najam and Thrasher, *The Future of South-South Economic Relations*.
46. Najam, "An Environmental Negotiation Strategy for the South."
47. Christopher D. Stone, *The Gnat Is Older Than Man: Global Environment and Human Agenda* (Princeton, NJ: Princeton University Press, 1993), 115.
48. Lawrence E. Susskind, *Environmental Diplomacy: Negotiating More Effective Global Agreements* (New York: Oxford University Press, 1994).
49. Adil Najam, Janice M. Poling, Naoyuki Yamagishi, Daniel G. Straub, Jillian Sarno, Sara M. DeRitter, and Eonjeong M. Kim, "From Rio to Johannesburg: Progress and Prospects," *Environment* 4, no. 7 (September 2002): 26–38.
50. See, for example, Martin Khor K. Peng, *The Future of North-South Relations: Conflict or Cooperation?* (Penang, Malaysia: Third World Network, 1992).
51. Edward Kufour, "G-77: We Won't Negotiate Away Our Sovereignty," *Third World Resurgence* 14–15 (1991): 17; South Centre, *Environment and Development: Towards a Common Strategy of the South in UNCED Negotiations and Beyond* (Geneva: South Centre, 1991); Banuri, "Noah's Ark or Jesus's Cross?"; Najam, "An Environmental Negotiation Strategy for the South."
52. A. O. Adede, "International Environmental Law from Stockholm to Rio," *Environmental Policy and Law* 22, no. 2 (1992): 88–105; Williams, "Re-articulating the Third World Coalition"; Najam, "An Environmental Negotiation Strategy for the South."
53. Halle et al., *The Future of Sustainable Development*.
54. For more on each, see David Hunter, James Salzman, and Durwood Zaelke, *International Environmental Law and Policy* (New York: Foundation Press, 1998).
55. This section builds on the discussion in Adil Najam, "The Unraveling of the Rio Bargain," *Politics and the Life Sciences* 21, no. 2 (2002): 46–50.
56. Sharachchandra M. Lélé, "Sustainable Development: A Critical Review," *World Development* 19, no. 6 (1991): 607–621.
57. See Adil Najam and Cutler Cleveland, "Energy and Sustainable Development at Global Environmental Summits: An Evolving Agenda," *Environment, Development and Sustainability* 5, no. 2 (2003): 117–138.
58. Tariq Banuri and Adil Najam, *Civic Entrepreneurship: A Civil Society Perspective on Sustainable Development*, vol. 1, *Global Synthesis* (Islamabad: Gandhara Academy Press, 2002).
59. Halle et al., *The Future of Sustainable Development*.

60. Banuri and Najam, *Civic Entrepreneurship*; Wolfgang Sachs, H. Acselrad, F. Akhter, A. Amon, T. B. G. Egziabher, Hilary French, P. Haavisto, Paul Hawken, H. Henderson, Ashok Khosla, S. Larrain, R. Loske, Anita Roddick, V. Taylor, Christine von Weizsäcker, and S. Zabelin, *The Jo'burg Memo: Fairness in a Fragile World* (Berlin: Heinrich Böll Foundation, 2002).

61. Pamela S. Chasek, "The Convention to Combat Desertification: Lessons Learned for Sustainable Development," *Journal of Environment and Development* 6, no. 2 (1997): 147–169; Corell, *The Negotiable Desert*.

62. Adil Najam, David Runnalls, and Mark Halle, *Environment and Globalization: Five Propositions* (Winnipeg: International Institute for Sustainable Development, 2007).

63. *Development and Environment*.

64. See Adil Najam and Ambuj Sagar, "Avoiding a COP-out: Moving towards Systematic Decision-Making under the Climate Convention," *Climatic Change* 39, no. 4 (1998): iii–ix; Adil Najam and Thomas Page, "The Climate Convention: Deciphering the Kyoto Convention," *Environmental Conservation* 25, no. 3 (1998): 187–194; Adil Najam, Saleemul Huq, and Youba Sokona, "Moving beyond Kyoto: Developing Countries, Climate Change, and Sustainable Development," *Climate Policy* 3 (2003): 221–231.

65. See, for example, Anil Agarwal and Sunita Narain, *Global Warming in an Unequal World: A Case of Environmental Colonialism* (New Delhi: Centre for Science and Environment, 1991); Agarwal et al., *Green Politics*.

66. Halle et al., *The Future of Sustainable Development*.

67. Adil Najam, Mihaela Papa, and Nadaa Taiyab, *Global Environmental Governance: A Reform Agenda* (Winnipeg: International Institute for Sustainable Development, 2007).

68. Miquel Muñoz, Rachel Thrasher, and Adil Najam, "Measuring the Negotiation Burden of Multilateral Environmental Agreements," *Global Environmental Politics* 9, no. 4 (November 2009): 1–13.

69. Adil Najam, "Knowledge Needs for Better Multilateral Environmental Agreements," WSSD Opinion Paper, International Institute for Environment and Development, London, 2002.

70. Najam et al., "From Rio to Johannesburg."

10

International Climate Change Policy

Complex Multilevel Governance

Michele M. Betsill

G lobal climate change presents a significant challenge to the international community. Anthropogenic emissions of greenhouse gases (GHGs) are causing a warming of the Earth's surface at an unprecedented rate.[1] Scientists predict that, if left unchecked, climate changes produced by this warming could include disruptions in rainfall and temperature patterns, a global rise in sea level, and an increased frequency of severe weather events such as droughts, hurricanes, and floods.[2] Today, people in many parts of the world are already experiencing the impacts of climate change, with serious implications for food security, freshwater supplies, human health, and species survival. Global greenhouse gas emissions continue to rise, with emissions from developing countries increasing at a faster rate than emissions from developed countries.

Climate change can be understood as a *global* environmental problem. Its causes, effects, and potential solutions transcend state boundaries, creating a need for international cooperation. Achieving such cooperation has proven difficult, however. Indeed, several factors create incentives for states and other actors to avoid taking meaningful steps to control their GHG emissions. For example, political and ethical questions remain regarding who bears responsibility for mitigating the threat. Although industrialized countries emitted the vast majority of GHGs in the past, some developing countries are among the largest emitters today. In 2007 China surpassed the United States as the world's leading emitter of GHGs (see Chapter 8). Second, because most GHGs remain in the atmosphere for a long time, the benefits of reducing emissions today will go to future generations rather than to those who must bear the cost of achieving such reductions. Third, the issue of climate change remains intimately linked with the global energy system. Any requirement to reduce emissions will likely affect the cost and availability of energy, a central component of the global economy.

This chapter examines the development of the international climate change regime, from the agenda-setting phase through the negotiation and operationalization phases.[3] The chapter begins with a brief discussion of how the problem of climate change emerged on the international agenda through a gradual buildup of scientific concern and then the transfer of that concern to the political arena, with a focus on the role of the Intergovernmental Panel on Climate Change (IPCC). The subsequent section examines the negotiation of the two multilateral environmental agreements that make up the international climate change regime—the 1992 United Nations Framework Convention on Climate Change (FCCC) and the 1997 Kyoto Protocol—as well as a set of decisions adopted in 2010 referred to as the Cancun Agreements. The discussion emphasizes those aspects of the negotiations and agreements that are relevant to understanding contemporary climate change politics. The third section examines efforts by national governments to operationalize the commitments contained in these agreements and evaluates the effectiveness of the international climate change regime to date. The regime's significance goes beyond its direct effects on state behavior and GHG emissions; it has given rise to a wide range of activities carried out by both state and nonstate actors at a variety of levels, all aimed at mitigating or adapting to the risk of global climate change. These multilevel governance initiatives are increasingly central components of global climate change governance.

The final section examines current debates and future challenges in international climate change policy. While national governments continue to negotiate the future of the multilateral climate change regime, focusing on developing a new legal instrument for the post-2020 period, some observers are calling for a new approach involving fewer countries or for states to abandon the pursuit of international treaties altogether. Perhaps the greatest challenge revolves around building stronger connections between the multilateral treaty-making process and the emerging complex multilevel system of global climate change governance.

Agenda Setting: From the Scientific to the Political Arena

The agenda-setting phase of the international climate change regime saw the expansion of concern about the problem from the scientific to the political arena (see Table 10-1). The threat of global warming is rooted in what is commonly referred to as the "greenhouse effect." Molecules of particular gases that exist naturally in the atmosphere (GHGs) trap heat like the panes of a greenhouse. This "natural" greenhouse effect keeps the Earth's surface temperature 30 degrees Celsius warmer than would otherwise be the case and is thus essential to preserving life on Earth. Global climate policy—the climate change regime—is concerned with the "enhanced" greenhouse effect, first identified in 1896 by Swedish chemist Svante Arrhenius. Arrhenius claimed that humans were altering the makeup of the atmosphere through the burning of coal, which would increase carbon dioxide concentrations.[4] He speculated that a doubling of CO_2 could lead to a warming of the Earth's surface temperature of 4 to 6 degrees Celsius.

International Scientific Cooperation

The scientific community generally ignored Arrhenius's claim of an enhanced greenhouse effect until the 1950s. In 1957, Roger Revelle and H. E. Seuss raised concern that the oceans would not be capable of absorbing the high levels of CO_2 being emitted through industrialization processes and that these emissions would thus alter the composition of the global atmosphere. They concluded, "Human beings are now carrying out

Table 10-1 Key Events in the International Climate Change Regime

Phase	Dates	Events
Agenda setting	1896	• Arrhenius identifies enhanced greenhouse effect
	1957–1958	• Revelle and Seuss study
		• International Geophysical Year
		• Regular monitoring of atmospheric CO_2 levels begins at Mauna Loa
	1979	• First World Climate Conference
	1980–1985	• Villach scientific conferences
	1987	• Villach and Bellagio policy conferences
	1988	• Toronto Conference
		• IPCC created
	1988–1992	• All industrialized states (except United States) adopt domestic targets and timetables for controlling GHG emissions
	1990	• IPCC First Assessment Report
Negotiation	1991–1992	• UN FCCC negotiations
	1994	• UN FCCC enters into force
	1995–1997	• Kyoto Protocol negotiations on commitments
	1996	• IPCC Second Assessment Report
	1998–2001	• Kyoto Protocol negotiations on rules for flexible mechanisms (Marrakesh Accords)
	2001	• IPCC Third Assessment Report
		• United States withdraws from Kyoto Protocol
	2007–2010	• Cancun Agreements negotiations
Operationalization	2005	• Kyoto Protocol enters into force
		• European Union Emissions Trading Scheme begins
	2007	• IPCC Fourth Assessment Report
	2008–2012	• First commitment period under the Kyoto Protocol
	2009–2010	• Countries make pledges under the Copenhagen Accord/Cancun Agreements

a large scale geophysical experiment of a kind that could not have happened in the past nor be reproduced in the future."[5] Later that same year, the International Council of Scientific Unions launched the 1957–1958 International Geophysical Year (IGY). One of the research activities initiated as part of the IGY was the establishment of an observatory at Mauna

Loa, Hawaii, to monitor atmospheric CO_2 concentrations. These observations, along with other types of data, soon revealed that CO_2 levels had risen significantly since the Industrial Revolution.[6] Observations of higher atmospheric CO_2 concentrations were accompanied by findings of increased mean global surface temperature, as Arrhenius had predicted.

Based on these emergent findings, delegates and scientists attending the 1979 First World Climate Conference, which had been organized by the World Meteorological Organization, established the World Climate Program and called on the world's governments "to foresee and prevent potential man-made changes in climate that might be adverse to the well-being of humanity."[7] In collaboration with the United Nations Environment Programme and the International Council of Scientific Unions, the World Climate Program organized a series of scientific conferences in Villach, Austria, in the early 1980s. By 1985 these meetings had produced an emerging scientific consensus that climate change posed a legitimate threat to the international community.[8] Two follow-up conferences were held in 1987—one in Villach (September 28–October 2) and one in Bellagio, Italy (November 9–13)—to consider what policy steps might be appropriate given the state of scientific knowledge on climate change. As a result, scientists participating in the Bellagio conference recommended that governments "immediately begin to reexamine their long-term energy strategies with the goals of achieving high end-use efficiency, reducing multiple forms of air pollution and reducing CO_2 emissions."[9]

The process of placing climate change on the international political agenda culminated in the World Conference on the Changing Atmosphere, held in Toronto, Canada, in June 1988. Although the Toronto Conference, as it came to be known, was sponsored by the Canadian government, it was organized by individuals who had participated in the Villach and Bellagio conferences and thus built directly on the outcomes of those meetings. Participants, including scientists, policy makers, industry representatives, and environmentalists, suggested the first concrete target and timetable for controlling GHG emissions. The "Toronto target," which continued to figure prominently in international debates for many years, called upon states to reduce their CO_2 emissions 20 percent below 1988 levels by 2005.[10]

In the aftermath of the Toronto Conference, the United Nations convened formal international negotiations. The first session, held in 1991, marked the beginning of the "negotiation phase" of the climate regime (see below). During this period, a number of industrialized countries adopted domestic targets and policies for limiting GHG emissions. By 1992 all but the United States had adopted such targets, with members of the European Union committing to stabilizing their emissions at 1990 levels by 2000.[11] The United States had initiated a domestic debate and a significant research program but had not yet developed an action plan for controlling emissions.[12]

Scientific research continues to play an important role in the climate change regime. In November 1988 the World Meteorological Organization and the United Nations Environment Programme created the Intergovernmental

Panel on Climate Change (IPCC) to synthesize and assess the state of scientific knowledge on climate change and evaluate response strategies. (The IPCC does not conduct original scientific research.) The IPCC has completed four major assessments (1990, 1996, 2001, and 2007)[13] as well as numerous technical reports and is generally viewed as the authoritative scientific body on the issue of climate change, giving it a privileged position in the policy process (see Chapter 2). Although climate change science is contested in some countries, including the United States, political debates at the international level tend to focus on what to do about climate change rather than on whether it is a problem.

Negotiating an International Climate Policy

The process of developing a coordinated international response to climate change has focused on negotiation of the three multilateral agreements that constitute the international climate change regime: the FCCC, the Kyoto Protocol, and the Cancun Agreements. With the first two treaties, countries employed the "framework-protocol" approach, which is common in many areas of international environmental law. As a "framework" convention, the FCCC establishes the basic architecture within which international efforts to address global climate change take place, while the Kyoto Protocol outlines specific obligations consistent with the guiding principles set forth in the FCCC. Together, these two documents set forth the principles, norms, rules, and decision-making procedures that have governed interactions among members of the international community on this issue for the past thirty years. With the Cancun Agreements, countries have tried to develop new rules and institutions within the existing regime in order to deal with the changing nature of the climate change problem. More than 190 countries have participated in international climate negotiations, along with hundreds of nongovernmental organizations (NGOs). In the UN context, countries have primary decision-making authority, but NGO representatives can participate as observers and provide input into the diplomatic process. In the climate change negotiations, NGOs frequently comment on proposals under consideration, provide technical expertise, and make formal statements in plenary sessions.

To make the negotiating process more efficient, many states have organized themselves into negotiating blocs (see Table 10-2), a common strategy in the UN system. These blocs allow groups of states with relatively common interests to share information and coordinate their positions on issues under consideration. The Group of 77 (G-77) and China and the Africa Group (see Chapters 8 and 9) are standing coalitions throughout the UN, while others, such as the Umbrella Group and the Environmental Integrity Group, have been organized on an ad hoc basis specifically for the climate change negotiations.[14] Similarly, NGOs have created "observer constituencies" (see Table 10-3) to facilitate their participation in the negotiation process.[15] In many instances, state negotiating blocs and NGO observer constituencies work together to pursue common interests. These blocs and coalitions between blocs change over time, depending on the particular issues on the negotiating agenda.

Table 10-2 State Negotiating Blocs

Group name	Members	Interests
EU	27 member states of the European Union	Support strict targets and timetables for emissions reductions
Umbrella Group	Russia, Iceland, Ukraine, Japan, United States, Canada, Australia, Norway, and New Zealand	Seek to minimize the negative economic impacts of emissions reduction measures through widespread use of market mechanisms
OPEC	Members of the Organization of Petroleum Exporting Countries	Concerned about the negative impact of emissions reduction regulations on export markets for oil and natural gas, on which the members' economies are heavily dependent
AOSIS	Alliance of Small Island States—43 low-lying or island developing states that are particularly vulnerable to the impacts of climate change, especially sea level rise	Support strict targets and timetables for emissions reductions as a matter of survival
G-77 and China	Developing countries	Priority on social and economic development and securing new financial resources for developing countries
Least developed countries	49 countries identified as least developed by the United Nations	Seek to secure resources to reduce vulnerability to impacts of climate change
Environmental Integrity Group	Mexico, the Republic of Korea, and Switzerland	Promote the environmental integrity of the climate change regime
Africa Group	53 members of the African regional group in the United Nations	Seek to secure resources to reduce vulnerability to impacts of climate change and enhance capacity building
CACAM	Central Asia, Caucasus, Albania, and Moldova	Concerned about clarifying the status of its members in the climate regime because several of them did not exist when the negotiations began

Sources: United Nations Framework Convention on Climate Change, "Party Groupings," 2009, http:// unfccc.int/parties_and_observers/parties/negotiating_groups/items/2714.php; Farhana Yamin and Joanna Depledge, *The International Climate Change Regime: A Guide to Rules, Institutions and Procedures* (Cambridge: Cambridge University Press, 2004).

Table 10-3 NGO Observer Constituencies

Constituency name	Description and interests
Environmental NGOs	Loosely organized under the umbrella of the Climate Action Network; united in desire to set strict emissions reduction targets and timetables and to hold states accountable for their commitments
Business and industry NGOs	Include a range of organizations with interests based in the private sector; considerable variation in support of strict emissions reduction targets but united in support for the use of market mechanisms
Local government and municipal authorities	Represented by ICLEI–Local Governments for Sustainability; seek to gain recognition for the role of local authorities in controlling GHG emissions
Indigenous peoples organizations	Seek to ensure that rules for the use of forests in achieving emissions reductions do not infringe on the rights of indigenous peoples
Research-oriented and independent organizations	Engaged in research and analysis focused on developing solutions to the causes and consequences of climate change
Other	Trade unions, farmer organizations, women and gender organizations, and youth

Source: United Nations Framework Convention on Climate Change, "Non-governmental Organization Observer Constituencies," 2004, http://unfccc.int/resource/ngo/const.pdf.

Negotiating the United Nations Framework Convention on Climate Change

Under a United Nations General Assembly mandate, the Intergovernmental Negotiating Committee for a Framework Convention on Climate Change met six times between February 1991 and May 1992. The negotiations took place as part of the preparations for the 1992 United Nations Conference on Environment and Development (the Earth Summit), held in Rio de Janeiro. The FCCC entered into force in March 1994 and had been ratified by 195 countries as of December 2013. Key elements of the FCCC, and thus of international climate policy, include its objective, principles, and commitments and the creation of an organizational structure for the regime.

Objective. Article 2 of the FCCC establishes the objective of the climate change regime as the

stabilization of greenhouse gas concentrations in the atmosphere at a level that would prevent dangerous anthropogenic interference with the climate system. Such a level should be achieved within a time-frame sufficient to allow ecosystems to adapt naturally to climate change, to ensure that food production is not threatened and to enable economic development to proceed in a sustainable manner.[16]

Note that the FCCC does not state what constitutes "dangerous" interference with the climate system or at what level atmospheric GHG concentrations must be stabilized to avoid such interference. During the FCCC negotiations, countries could not agree on more specific language owing to significant differences on the need for action. It was not until the 2010 Cancun Agreements that the international community agreed that global average temperature should not increase more than 2 degrees Celsius compared to the preindustrial period.

Principles. Article 3 of the FCCC sets forth principles to guide the international community in its efforts to address climate change. Many of the current political debates discussed below revolve around the interpretation of these principles (see Chapters 3, 4, and 9). The principle of common but differentiated responsibilities acknowledges that, although all members of the international community have an obligation to protect the climate for present and future generations, industrialized countries and formerly communist countries with economies in transition have a responsibility to take the lead in addressing climate change. This stems from their historical responsibility for emitting GHGs as well as the assumption that they possess the financial and technological capabilities to control those emissions. This principle has been a source of U.S. objections to the climate change regime because it is seen to give large developing country emitters, such as China, a free ride. In current negotiations, decision makers struggle with the challenge of controlling GHG emissions in the developing world, where emissions are increasing most rapidly, while honoring the principle of common but differentiated responsibilities.

The FCCC also states that *equity* should be a guiding principle in the development of a global response to climate change. Equity has been interpreted in a variety of ways, however, and remains an unsettled matter. Many developing countries argue, for example, that equity would be best achieved through a per capita allocation of GHG emissions rights, noting their low historical contribution to the climate problem, current low levels of per capita GHG emissions compared with industrialized countries, and lack of resources. Per capita emissions allocations would enable developing countries to raise their living standards, thereby reducing their vulnerability to the impacts of climate change.[17] However, achieving a convergence of per capita emissions would require even more significant reductions on the part of industrialized countries than have been adopted thus far.

The FCCC also recognizes the specific needs and special circumstances of developing countries that may be particularly vulnerable to climate change, either because of adverse impacts, such as drought, or because their economies are dependent on the production and export of fossil fuels (states belonging to the Organization of Petroleum Exporting Countries). In addition, the FCCC embraces the *precautionary principle*, stating that the absence of full scientific certainty should not be used as an excuse to avoid taking action to mitigate the threat or impact of climate change.

The principles of the FCCC also reflect the relationship between climate change and economic conditions. Measures taken to deal with climate change should be *cost-effective*, ensuring the greatest benefit at the lowest cost. This has been a particularly important point for members of the Umbrella Group as well as for some of the EU member states. In addition, all countries are seen to have a right to *sustainable development*, and measures to address climate change should promote that objective. This was a particularly important issue for the G-77 and China during the FCCC negotiations and continues to be a central part of their negotiating position today.[18] Finally, the FCCC emphasizes the importance of *maintaining an open international economic system*.

Commitments. The FCCC imposes three types of obligations on parties. First, all Annex I parties (industrialized countries and formerly communist countries with economies in transition) were required to adopt policies and measures aimed at returning their GHG emissions to 1990 levels by 2000 (Article 4.2). Second, Annex I parties must provide "new and additional financial resources" as well as technology to help developing countries meet their commitments under the convention (Article 4[3]). Note that consistent with the principles outlined above, the FCCC differentiates between industrialized and developing countries, placing the primary burden for addressing global climate change on the industrialized countries. Despite repeated efforts to establish new financial mechanisms, funding for developing countries remains inadequate. Third, under Articles 4 and 12, all parties must regularly report on their national emissions inventories and their programs to mitigate climate change. Thus, under these and other articles, developing countries do have a general obligation to address global climate change.

Organizational Structure. The FCCC created the central institutional architecture for international climate policy. Article 7 established the Conference of the Parties (COP) as the supreme body, with responsibility for reviewing the implementation of the FCCC (and any related legal instruments) and making decisions to promote its effective implementation. The COP usually meets annually. The Secretariat (Article 8), located in Bonn, Germany, administers the convention, making meeting arrangements and compiling and transmitting information. The FCCC also established two other important subsidiary bodies, the Subsidiary Body for Scientific and Technological Advice (SBSTA, Article 9) and the Subsidiary Body for Implementation (SBI, Article 10), which meet at least twice a year and assist the COP with assessing the state of scientific and technological knowledge related to climate change as well as the effects of measures taken under the convention and subsequent legal decisions. The FCCC designated the Global Environment Facility (GEF) as the financial mechanism for the treaty on an interim basis (Articles 11 and 21).

Developing countries had argued for the creation of an independent financial mechanism because they feared that industrialized states, as the principal donors to the GEF, would use their leverage to control the allocation of resources.[19]

Negotiating the Kyoto Protocol

At the first Conference of the Parties to the FCCC (COP-1), held in Berlin in 1995, delegates adopted the Berlin Mandate, which stated that commitments contained in the convention were insufficient to meet its long-term objective, and they initiated a process of negotiating a protocol to the FCCC that would contain binding targets and timetables for reducing GHG emissions beyond 2000. Following two years of extremely complex and intense negotiations, parties adopted the Kyoto Protocol to the FCCC at COP-3, held in Kyoto, Japan, in December 1997.[20] Building on the principle of common but differentiated responsibilities, the Kyoto Protocol set specific targets for industrialized countries to reduce their GHG emissions (see below) but left the specific rules and operational details for how countries could achieve those reductions unresolved. These issues were debated in several formal and informal negotiating sessions between 1998 and 2001. The future of the Kyoto Protocol was called into question in spring 2001 when the United States withdrew from the negotiations. Newly elected president George W. Bush viewed the treaty as "fatally flawed" on the grounds that it failed to include emissions reduction commitments for developing countries and would damage the U.S. economy. Owing in large part to leadership from the European Union, the rest of the international community agreed to go forward without the United States and reached final agreement at COP-7 in Marrakesh, Morocco (the Marrakesh Accords). The Kyoto Protocol entered into force in 2005, and 192 countries had ratified the protocol as of June 2013.[21] Whereas the FCCC laid out the general architecture of the climate change regime, the Kyoto Protocol identified mechanisms to be used to achieve its overall objective. The central elements include commitments, rules on flexible mechanisms and compliance, and the creation of new organizations.[22]

Commitments. Article 3 of the Kyoto Protocol required industrialized countries to reduce their aggregate GHG emissions 5.2 percent below 1990 levels within the period 2008–2012. These commitments were differentiated in that each country had an individual target (see Table 10-4). In addition, some countries with economies in transition were permitted to select a year other than 1990 as a baseline. These differentiated targets were widely recognized as "purely political," the result of tough bargaining in closed-door sessions involving the EU leadership, the United States, and Japan during the final days (and ultimately hours) of the Kyoto negotiations. They were not based on scientific or economic analyses and were far below what the IPCC recommended as

Table 10-4 Emissions Reduction Targets and Progress, 2008–2010

Country	Emissions reduction target in Kyoto Protocol (% below 1990 levels)[a]	2010 emissions (relative to 1990 levels)
Australia	+8	+47.5
Austria	−8 (−13)	+22.9
Belgium	−8 (−7.5)	−1.4
Bulgaria	−8	−41.4
Canada	−6	+24
Croatia	−5	−11.9
Czech Republic	−8	−26.2
Denmark	−8 (−21)	−6.8
Estonia	−8	−48.9
Finland	−8 (0)	+15.7
Germany	−8 (−21)	−19.8
Greece	−8 (+25)	+20.2
Hungary	−6	−26.3
Iceland	+10	+2.3
Ireland	−8 (+13)	+29.7
Italy	−8 (−6.5)	+0.3
Japan	−6	+7.4
Latvia	−8	−56.8
Lithuania	−8	−59.6
Luxembourg	−8 (−28)	+1.6
Netherlands	−8 (−6)	+20
New Zealand	0	+31.8
Norway	+1	+38.5
Poland	−6	−10.8
Portugal	−8 (+27)	+22.6
Romania	−8	−54.8
Russia	0	−27.4
Slovakia	−8	−38.3
Slovenia	−8	+22.5
Spain	−8 (+15)	+30.7
Sweden	−8 (+4)	−9.8
Switzerland	−8	+5.9
Ukraine	0	−61.2
United Kingdom	−8 (−12.5)	−12.0
United States	−7	+10.3

Source: International Energy Agency, *CO$_2$ Emissions from Fuel Combustion: Highlights* (Paris: International Energy Agency, 2012), http://www.iea.org/co2highlights/co2highlights.pdf.

[a]EU member countries further differentiated their Kyoto Protocol targets under a burden-sharing agreement, as indicated in parentheses.

necessary to stabilize atmospheric concentrations of GHGs. At COP-18, held in Doha, Qatar, in December 2012, parties adopted an amendment to the protocol for a second commitment period of 2013–2020. However, Russia, New Zealand, and Japan have not planned to take on new targets, and Canada withdrew from the Kyoto Protocol in 2012, so the second commitment period, which had not entered into force as of October 2013, will cover only 15 percent of global greenhouse gas emissions.

Flexible Mechanisms. Consistent with the principle of cost-effectiveness, the Kyoto Protocol gives parties considerable flexibility in choosing how to achieve their emissions reduction commitments. The "Kyoto mechanisms" or "flexible mechanisms" include emissions trading (Article 17), joint implementation (Article 6), and the Clean Development Mechanism (CDM, Article 12). Emissions trading permits countries that exceed their allowed emissions to purchase emissions credits from countries whose emissions are below their allotted amount. Industrialized countries may also invest in emissions reduction activities in other industrialized countries under the rules of joint implementation. The investing country receives emissions reduction units (ERUs) that can be applied toward its target (the ERUs are subtracted from the host country's assigned amount). The CDM allows industrialized countries to invest in emissions-reducing activities in developing countries in return for certified emissions reductions that they may then use toward meeting Kyoto targets.[23]

During the initial negotiation of the Kyoto Protocol, the United States, supported by other members of the Umbrella Group and industry representatives, pushed strongly for a broad set of flexibility measures. The EU, most developing countries, and environmental groups objected, arguing that extensive reliance on such mechanisms would allow rich countries to buy their way out of making any meaningful commitments domestically, thereby violating the polluter-pays principle. In the final hours of the COP-3 in Kyoto, the flexible mechanisms were included in the protocol in exchange for U.S. support of reduction, rather than stabilization, targets. As noted, negotiations to finalize the rules about how these mechanisms could be used were extremely contentious. Of particular concern was the issue of "additionality." While the Marrakesh Accords do not place a specific limit on the use of flexible mechanisms, they clearly state that countries should achieve a significant portion of their emissions reductions through domestic measures. The use of the mechanisms should be in addition to, not instead of, such measures.

Compliance. While the issue of compliance (see Chapter 5) was largely ignored in the Kyoto Protocol, the subsequent Marrakesh Accords set forth a compliance system consisting of a Compliance Committee with two branches—the facilitative and enforcement branches—each having ten members. The facilitative branch helps parties fulfill their commitments under the protocol. The enforcement branch determines whether parties are in compliance with their commitments. Parties that are found to be in noncompliance with their reporting obligations become ineligible to use the flexible mechanisms. Parties that fail to meet their emissions reduction targets in the first commitment period are required to make up the difference during the second commitment period, with a 30 percent penalty.[24]

Organizational Structure. The Kyoto Protocol and Marrakesh Accords added several new institutions to the organizational structure of the international climate change regime. The CDM Executive Board supervises the operation of the CDM.[25] It consists of ten representatives from the various state blocs that participate in the climate change negotiations (see Table 10-2). As of December 2012, the CDM Executive Board had certified 5,511 projects (of the more than 7,500 projects in the pipeline), which are expected to produce 5.7 billion tons of emissions reductions by 2020.[26]

For developing countries, one of the major objectives has been to secure financial resources to assist in meeting current and future commitments under the climate change regime. To that end, the Marrakesh Accords call for an increase in funds to the GEF as well as the creation of three new funds.[27] The Special Climate Change Fund is designed to finance activities related to adaptation, technology transfer, development of policies and measures in a number of different sectors, and diversification of economies. The Least-Developed-Country Fund assists these countries in the preparation and implementation of national action plans as required under the FCCC, while the Adaptation Fund provides resources for activities related to adaptation. Initial progress in mobilizing new resources for developing countries was slow. As of March 2008, the Special Climate Change Fund had received pledges from thirteen countries for a total of $90.3 million and had approved $36.14 million for projects. Nineteen countries had pledged $172.84 million for the Least-Developed-Country Fund, with $13.52 million allocated for approved projects. As discussed below, financing was a major issue in the Cancun Agreements negotiations.

Negotiating the Cancun Agreements

Shortly after the Kyoto Protocol entered into force in 2005, parties began negotiations for the "post-2012" period. By then, it had become clear that controlling global GHG emissions requires action by large developing country emitters such as China, India, and Brazil, and the international community made several efforts in 2005 to engage these countries outside the formal climate regime institutions—for example, through the Asia-Pacific Partnership on Clean Development and Climate and the Group of Eight "Gleneagles Dialogue" process.[28] These discussions appeared to lay the foundation for moving forward on the issue of developing country commitments within the international regime. At COP-13 in 2007, held in Bali, Indonesia, delegates adopted the Bali Roadmap, which established two negotiating tracks: one to consider long-term cooperation under the FCCC (including developing country commitments) and one to establish developed country obligations for the second commitment period under the Kyoto Protocol. However, once negotiations began, significant cleavages between industrialized and developing parties as well as among developing countries were revealed. Not all countries agreed on the need for two separate tracks, noting that the willingness of some industrialized parties to agree on new commitments under the Kyoto Protocol would depend on whether large-emitting developing countries took on commitments under the FCCC. While countries like China and India acknowledged their role as major GHG emitters, they rejected the idea that they should accept binding emissions reduction commitments based on the principle of common but differentiated responsibilities.

The negotiations were to have concluded in 2009 at COP-15 in Copenhagen, Demark, where 115 heads of state convened amid unprecedented levels of public and media attention.[29] In the months leading up to the Copenhagen meeting, diplomats debated over several hundred pages of draft text but reached a stalemate on a number of substantive and procedural issues, and in the final hours of COP-15, a small group of heads of state, led by U.S. president Barack Obama, jettisoned the draft text and negotiated a twelve-paragraph political compromise referred to as the "Copenhagen Accord." At the closing plenary, delegates merely "took note of" the Copenhagen Accord, with many countries voicing strong objection to the lack of transparency in the process. The mandates of the two ad hoc working groups were extended, and at the 2010 COP-16 meeting in Cancun, Mexico, parties adopted a package of decisions known as the "Cancun Agreements," which covered a range of issues, including mitigation, adaptation, financing, technology transfer, emissions from deforestation, and monitoring, reporting, and verification, many of which were also covered in the Copenhagen Accord. The central elements included a shared vision for long-term cooperative action, enhanced action on mitigation, and financing.

Shared Vision for Long-Term Cooperative Action. As discussed above, parties spent two decades debating the meaning of FCCC Article 2 and its call to avoid "dangerous" interference with the climate system. To aid in this discussion, the IPCC developed a series of scenarios to project a range of possible futures, but it soon became clear that this was not solely a scientific or technical issue. Rather, the question of what constitutes dangerous interference is a social and political issue involving debates about the acceptability of different kinds of risk. The Cancun Agreements (Article I, paragraph 4) call for the increase in global average temperature to be held below 2 degrees Celsius above preindustrial levels and establish a process for reviewing the adequacy of the 2-degree target and considering a 1.5-degree goal in the future.[30] This target is meant to guide future policy and action at all levels.

Enhanced Action on Mitigation. In the midst of stalemate over the issues of developing country targets and the second commitment period of the Kyoto Protocol, the 2009 Copenhagen Accord adopted a "bottom-up" strategy whereby all parties would make explicit mitigation pledges based on their individual circumstances, which would then be subject to periodic review. Developed parties were encouraged to establish quantified economy-wide targets, while developing parties were asked to identify "nationally appropriate mitigation actions" (see Table 10-5). Developing country pledges are voluntary and subject to financial, technical, and capacity-building support from industrialized countries. The Cancun Agreements take note of the pledges made by parties in response to the Copenhagen Accord and urge developed countries to increase the ambition of their targets (Article 3). This decision brings the issue of emissions reduction commitments under the FCCC process for the first time and marks a break from the "top-down" approach of establishing a common set of commitments to be adopted by all parties.[31]

Financing. The Copenhagen Accord included a pledge from developed countries to provide $30 billion in "fast-start" financing in the period 2010–2012 for adaptation and mitigation activities in developing countries as well as a long-term commitment to mobilize $100 billion per year by 2020 (Article 4[A]).

Table 10-5 Examples of Pledges under the Copenhagen Accord

Country	Pledge
Australia	5–25% below 2000 (depending on what other countries do)
Canada and United States	17% below 2005 levels
EU-27	20–30% below 1990 levels (depending on what other developed countries do)
Japan	25% below 1990 levels (depending on the establishment of an international framework involving all major economies)
Russia	15–25% below 1990 levels (depending on what other major emitters do and how forests are counted)
Brazil	Reduced deforestation, changes to agricultural practices, energy efficiency measures, and changes in energy supply; expected to reduce emissions 36.1–38.9% below business as usual
China	Reduce emissions intensity 40–45% below 2005 levels, increase share of alternative energy sources to 15%, increase forest cover and stock
India	Reduce emissions intensity 20–25% below 2005 levels (agriculture excluded)
South Africa	Unspecified actions to reduce emissions 34% below business as usual

Sources: United Nations Framework Convention on Climate Change, "Appendix I—Quantified Economy-wide Emissions Targets for 2020," http://unfccc.int/meetings/copenhagen_dec_2009/items/5264.php; United Nations Framework Convention on Climate Change, "Appendix II—Nationally Appropriate Mitigation Actions of Developing Country Parties," http://unfccc.int/meetings/cop_15/copenhagen_accord/items/5265.php.

These resources, which are to be "new and additional" and allocated in a balanced manner toward mitigation and adaptation, may come from public or private sources and may flow through bilateral or multilateral arrangements, such as the Special Climate Change Fund established under the Kyoto Protocol. The Cancun Agreements established institutional mechanisms to enhance the transparency of the process and to facilitate the flow of funds. Developed countries are required to report annually the amount of resources provided as well as how developing countries access these resources. As of November 2012, twenty-three developed countries along with the European Commission had announced pledges totaling $33.92 billion.[32] In addition, parties established the Green Climate Fund to manage multilateral funding for adaptation; it is based in South Korea and overseen by a twenty-four-member board with equal representation from developed and developing countries.

From Commitments to Action: Operationalizing the International Climate Change Regime

The first step in operationalizing the Kyoto Protocol involved ratification and entry into force. Under Article 25, the protocol would enter into force upon ratification by at least fifty-five countries, including parties accounting for 55 percent of 1990 emissions. Meeting this standard was difficult without the United States, which accounted for 36 percent of industrialized country 1990 emissions. Russia, which accounted for 17 percent of 1990 emissions, used its leverage to secure concessions from the EU regarding entry into the World Trade Organization before ratifying the Kyoto Protocol in 2004. The treaty entered into force six months later.

With the completion of the ratification process, industrialized countries began the task of developing policies and programs to meet their emissions reduction commitments. In most cases, this task has proven more difficult than originally anticipated. For example, the European Union embraced the idea of emissions trading in 2003 (despite strong earlier objections) when it became clear that EU member states could not meet their Kyoto targets through traditional policies and measures. Since 2005 the EU Emissions Trading Scheme (also known as the EU Emissions Trading System, or EU ETS) has become the central element in EU climate policy and is currently the world's largest cap-and-trade system for GHGs (see Chapter 7).[33] In addition to the practical challenges of reducing GHG emissions, several countries have had to contend with powerful political opposition. Canadian climate policy has fallen victim to a shift from a Liberal to a Conservative government, with the latter reluctant to impose regulations on large emitters such as the oil industry.[34] Similarly, Japan has had to rely on voluntary action because of opposition from the industrial sector.[35]

Evaluating the effectiveness of international environmental regimes is difficult, as it raises a host of methodological challenges.[36] Of particular import is whether one chooses to focus solely on the direct impacts of a specific cooperative arrangement, such as the Kyoto Protocol and Cancun Agreements, or on targeted actors and ultimately the environment, or if one also includes consideration of more indirect effects that may be generated as a result of the negotiation process and reflected in society more broadly. This section contends that, although the direct effects of the multilateral climate change regime may be limited, the indirect effects have prompted the emergence of a complex multilevel governance system involving actors beyond nation-states and initiatives operating across multiple levels from the global to the local. This system may hold greater promise for meaningful action on climate change in the future.

Effects on Targeted Actors and GHG Emissions

A legalistic definition of *effectiveness* focuses on whether states are complying with the rules of the regime.[37] The vast majority of countries in the world have ratified the FCCC and submitted national communications containing emissions inventories and overviews of policies and measures taken to address climate change. Thus, compliance with this basic requirement is quite high. Critics argue, however, that much of the information in these communications is not useful, is incomplete, and often cannot be compared across states.[38]

In terms of commitments to control GHGs, the performance to date is less encouraging. Only the United Kingdom, Germany, and Russia achieved the goal of stabilizing their GHG emissions at 1990 levels by 2000. In each case, however, this progress had little to do with adopting innovative climate policies and more to do with economic circumstances.[39] In 2010 aggregate emissions from industrialized parties to the Kyoto Protocol (i.e., not including the United States) were 17.3 percent below 1990 levels; however, much of that can be attributed to the fact that emissions from countries with economies in transition were 37.4 percent below the Kyoto baseline and the effects of the global financial crisis (Table 10-4).[40] Emissions from some industrialized country parties were above the 1990 baseline, but overall emissions from all industrialized parties decreased 1.3 percent in the period 2000–2010.

In some cases compliance may be a misleading measure of regime effectiveness. Where standards set in an international treaty are low, high levels of compliance may be meaningless.[41] Alternatively, analysts can consider whether agreements prompt changes in behavior among targeted actors by comparing the actors' behavior with business-as-usual scenarios.[42] For example, although U.S. GHG emissions in 1999 were 11 percent above 1990 levels, the Clinton administration argued that they would have been even higher were it not for the 1993 U.S. Climate Change Action Plan, developed in compliance with the FCCC, which consisted of more than fifty voluntary measures designed to stabilize emissions.[43]

Assessments of regime effectiveness might also consider "the degree to which the degrading or polluting processes and consequences are arrested or reversed."[44] In other words, does the regime actually help ameliorate the problem that gave rise to its creation? On this basis, the short-term effectiveness of the international climate change regime must be called into question. Global GHG emissions continue to increase at alarming rates, and China and India now account for one-third of global emissions, the same share as all industrialized countries combined.[45] In its Fourth Assessment Report, the IPCC estimates that industrialized countries need to reduce emissions 25–40 percent below 1990 levels by 2020 to hold the temperature increase below 2 degrees Celsius.[46] However, the emissions reduction pledges submitted by countries under the Copenhagen Accord are insufficient to meet that goal and are projected to result in an increase in global average temperatures of 3.3 degrees Celsius.[47]

Broader Effects

Despite shortcomings in the near term, it is possible to argue that the processes and institutions created under the multilateral climate change regime will facilitate international action to address climate change in the long term. This optimistic assessment stems from a perspective in which international regimes are viewed as catalysts for learning and generating shared understandings rather than simply as a set of specific rules and obligations.[48] As Underdal argues:

International negotiation processes are often large-scale exercises in *learning*, through which at least some parties modify their perceptions of the problem and of alternative policy options and perhaps see their incentives change as well. As a consequence, the process itself may lead governments as well as nongovernmental actors to make unilateral adjustments in behavior—even in the absence of any legal obligation to do so. The aggregate impact of such side effects may well be more important than the impact of any formal convention or declaration signed in the end.[49]

Through the negotiation of the FCCC, the Kyoto Protocol, and the Cancun Agreements, the international community has come to view the problem of climate change as a legitimate threat. Together, these agreements send a clear message to states as well as to industry that business as usual (for example, unregulated emission of GHGs) is no longer acceptable.[50] Moreover, the climate change regime has given rise to new actors, institutions, and interests that are likely to play significant roles in addressing the threat of climate change over the long term.[51]

Nation-states increasingly behave in ways that suggest they have accepted a responsibility to address climate change by limiting their GHG emissions. During the past decade, all industrialized countries have institutionalized responsibility for addressing climate change within their respective governments and have adopted policies for controlling emissions. This is true even in some oil-producing countries that are attempting to secure resources to protect their economies, as well as in laggard countries such as the United States. Despite the Bush administration's objections to the Kyoto Protocol, the United States remained engaged on the issue of climate change by continuing to participate in ongoing negotiations related to the FCCC and adopting a goal of reducing the GHG intensity of the American economy.[52] Many large developing countries have also institutionalized the need to address climate change and are taking significant steps to limit their emissions even though they are not formally required to do so under the multilateral climate change regime. Countries such as Brazil are increasingly taking on a leadership role in the governance of global climate change.[53]

The international climate change regime has given rise to a new discourse linking economic growth with the achievement of emissions reductions, as illustrated by the striking shift in the positions of many business and industry groups since the early 1990s.[54] During the FCCC negotiations, the business groups that participated in the process consisted primarily of members of the fossil fuel industry that organized themselves under the umbrella of the Global Climate Coalition (GCC) and were united in their opposition to international regulations on GHG emissions. During the Kyoto Protocol negotiations, the business and industry community diversified, with groups representing members of the renewable energy industry as well as the insurance industry coming out in support of international GHG regulations. In addition, a number of companies whose profits derive from the production and consumption of fossil fuels left the GCC (which disbanded in December 2001) and began working to find economically viable ways to control GHG emissions. For example, the Business Environmental Leadership Council, an initiative of the Center for Climate and Energy Solutions in Washington, D.C., works with forty-four major corporations including British Petroleum, DuPont, Boeing, Toyota, and Weyerhaeuser. In the late 1990s, British Petroleum and DuPont voluntarily pledged to reduce GHG emissions within their operations by 10 percent and 65 percent, respectively. In 2002 each company announced that it had met its target eight years ahead of schedule.[55] Today, a growing number of companies, large and small, are following their example, and the international community increasingly talks about the need to "green the economy" by promoting economic growth that reduces carbon emissions.[56]

Perhaps most striking, the international climate change regime has mobilized actors beyond national governments, giving rise to a complex system of multilevel governance.[57] More than one thousand municipal governments around the world (accounting for approximately 15 percent of global GHG emissions) participate in the Cities for Climate Protection campaign sponsored by ICLEI–Local Governments for Sustainability.[58] These communities have committed to developing policies and programs to reduce GHG emissions and in the process have recognized linkages between environmental protection and economic growth. In federal systems, many state and provincial governments have become leaders in developing climate change policies. This has been particularly striking in the United States, where state and local governments have stepped in to fill the void left by weak federal action.[59]

As noted above, the private sector has become an important site of climate change governance as large multinational companies such as Walmart seek to control their own emissions as well as the emissions of their suppliers. Transnational networks linking public and private actors across national borders often promote innovation in ideas and technology development.[60] For example, the Climate Group is a network whose purpose is to catalyze action among leaders in business, government, and the nonprofit sector from around the world.[61]

This trend toward multilevel governance challenges the centrality of the international regime in the governance of global climate change and presents new opportunities for the development of effective responses. This is not to suggest that the multilateral treaty negotiation process is irrelevant. Instead, it highlights the fact that actors at other levels of social organization are not sitting around waiting for negotiators to reach agreement on the next multilateral treaty. This is readily apparent to anyone who attends the international climate change negotiations. While country delegates tediously pour over complicated technical language, many of these actors meet in side events where they showcase the innovative policies and measures they are working on. The palpable energy of these events and the enthusiasm of the participants often stand in stark contrast to the mood in the formal halls of international diplomacy.

Current Debates and Future Challenges

The work of the two ad hoc working groups officially concluded at COP-18 in Doha, Qatar, in 2012. As noted above, parties adopted an amendment to the Kyoto Protocol establishing a second commitment period from 2013 to 2020. At COP-17 in Durban, South Africa, countries initiated a process to develop a new legal instrument under the FCCC to establish new commitments for the post-2020 period. These negotiations are scheduled to conclude by 2015. Meanwhile, some observers question the wisdom of continuing the multilateral process, at least in its current form. For example, a "minilateral" approach focused on the top 20 GHG-emitting countries, which account for nearly 75 percent of global emissions, would alleviate the problem of having to reach consensus among 193 countries on a particular course of action.[62] Alternatively, some suggest it is time to abandon the pursuit of a comprehensive multilateral climate treaty altogether and focus time and resources on building a global response from the ground up.[63]

Ultimately, confronting the challenge of climate change will require a global transition to a low-carbon economy. Achieving this transition will require the mobilization of resources and creativity at all levels of social organization, from the global to the local. The international climate change regime likely will continue to define the core principles and objectives of the global effort to address climate change, but it is increasingly clear that these agreements alone will not solve the problem. Many subnational governments, companies, and transnational networks are working hard to find solutions to the threat of global climate change, but the aggregate impact of these actions is as yet unclear. It is essential that the multilateral treaty-making process be integrated into the complex multilevel process of global climate change governance. As additional actors engage in efforts to address climate change, new opportunities emerge to enhance the effectiveness of the global response through public-private partnerships, bottom-up pressure, and transnational networks.[64] The key challenge is to ensure that all of these pieces work together.

Notes

1. The major greenhouse gases are carbon dioxide (CO_2), methane (CH_4), nitrous oxide (N_2O), chlorofluorocarbons (CFCs), and water vapor. Regulations within the climate change regime focus on a "basket" of six gases: CO_2, CH_4, N_2O, hydrofluorocarbons (HFCs), perfluorocarbons (PFCs), and sulfur hexafluoride (SF_6).
2. Intergovernmental Panel on Climate Change, *Summary for Policy Makers: Climate Change 2007: Synthesis Report* (Cambridge: Cambridge University Press, 2007), http://www.ipcc.ch.
3. Oran R. Young, "Rights, Rules, and Resources in World Affairs," in *Global Governance: Drawing Insights from the Environmental Experience*, ed. Oran R. Young (Cambridge: MIT Press, 1997). Note that these phases are distinguished for analytical purposes only; in practice, there are considerable overlaps and feedbacks between and among them.
4. Svante Arrhenius, "On the Influence of Carbonic Acid in the Air on the Temperature on the Ground," *Philosophical Magazine* 251 (1896): 236–276.
5. Quoted in Michael Oppenheimer and Robert H. Boyle, *Dead Heat: The Race against the Greenhouse Effect* (New York: Basic Books, 1990), 36.
6. Robert T. Watson and Core Writing Team, eds., *Climate Change 2001: Synthesis Report* (Cambridge: Cambridge University Press, 2001), 4–8.
7. World Meteorological Organization, *Proceedings of the First World Climate Conference: A Conference of Experts on Climate and Mankind, 12–23 February 1979* (Geneva: World Meteorological Organization, 1979), 709.
8. World Climate Program, *Report of the International Conference on the Assessment of the Role of Carbon Dioxide and of Other Greenhouse Gases on Climate Variations and Associated Impacts* (Geneva: World Meteorological Organization, 1986).
9. Jill Jaeger, *Developing Policies for Responding to Climatic Change: A Summary of the Discussions and Recommendations of the Workshops Held in Villach (28 September–2 October 1987) and Bellagio (9–13 November 1987), under the Auspices of the Beijer Institute, Stockholm* (Geneva: World Meteorological Organization, 1988), 37.
10. World Meteorological Organization, *Proceedings of the World Conference on the Changing Atmosphere: Implications for Global Security* (Geneva: World Meteorological Organization, 1988), 296.
11. International Energy Agency, *Climate Change Policy Initiatives*, vol. 1, *OECD Countries* (Paris: International Energy Agency, 1994).
12. Loren Cass, *The Failures of American and European Climate Policy* (Albany: State University of New York Press, 2006), chap. 2.
13. The Fifth Assessment Report is scheduled to be completed in 2014.
14. For more detailed treatment of the state negotiating blocs, see Joyeeta Gupta, *Our Simmering Planet: What to Do about Global Warming?* (London: Zed Books, 2001); Sebastian Oberthür and Hermann E. Ott, *The Kyoto Protocol: International Climate Policy for the 21st Century* (New York: Springer, 1999); Farhana Yamin and Joanna Depledge, *The International Climate Change Regime: A Guide to Rules, Institutions and Procedures* (Cambridge: Cambridge University Press, 2004).

15. On the different NGO constituencies, see Michele M. Betsill, "Environmental NGOs and the Kyoto Protocol Negotiations," in *NGO Diplomacy: The Influence of Nongovernmental Organizations in International Environmental Negotiations*, ed. Michele M. Betsill and Elisabeth Corell (Cambridge: MIT Press, 2008), 44–66; Peter Newell, *Climate for Change: Non-state Actors and the Global Politics of the Greenhouse* (Cambridge: Cambridge University Press, 2001); Kal Raustiala, "Nonstate Actors in the Global Climate Regime," in *International Relations and Global Climate Change*, ed. Urs Luterbacher and Detlef F. Sprinz (Cambridge: MIT Press, 2001), 95–118; Yamin and Depledge, *The International Climate Change Regime*.

16. United Nations, *United Nations Framework Convention on Climate Change* (Bonn: FCCC Secretariat, 1992), art. 2, http://www.unfccc.int.

17. Ambuj Sagar, "Wealth, Responsibility, and Equity: Exploring an Allocation Framework for Global GHG Emissions," *Climatic Change* 45 (2000): 511–527; P. R. Shukla, "Justice, Equity and Efficiency in Climate Change: A Developing Country Perspective," in *Fair Weather? Equity Concerns in Climate Change*, ed. Ferenc L. Tóth (London: Earthscan, 1999), 150–155; Gary W. Yohe, David Montgomery, and Ed Balistreri, "Equity and the Kyoto Protocol: Measuring the Distributional Effects of Alternative Emissions Trading Regimes," *Global Environmental Change* 10 (2000): 121–132.

18. Tariq Osman Hyder, "Looking Back to See Forward," in *Negotiating Climate Change: The Inside Story of the Rio Convention*, ed. Irving M. Mintzer and J. Amber Leonard (Cambridge: Cambridge University Press, 1994).

19. Gupta, *Our Simmering Planet*, 75–76.

20. For a detailed discussion of the negotiating process, see Oberthür and Ott, *The Kyoto Protocol*.

21. For more on the U.S. and EU roles, see Chapters 6 and 7.

22. For more detailed analysis of these elements, see Michael Grubb, Christian Vrolijk, and Duncan Brack, *The Kyoto Protocol: A Guide and Assessment* (London: Royal Institute of International Affairs, 1999); Oberthür and Ott, *The Kyoto Protocol*. For a more critical review, see David G. Victor, *The Collapse of the Kyoto Protocol and the Struggle to Slow Global Warming* (Princeton, NJ: Princeton University Press, 2001).

23. Oberthür and Ott, *The Kyoto Protocol*, 165–186.

24. United Nations Framework Convention on Climate Change Secretariat, *A Guide to the Climate Change Convention and Its Kyoto Protocol: Preliminary Version* (Bonn: FCCC Secretariat, 2002), http://unfccc.int/resource/process/guideprocess-p.pdf.

25. United Nations Framework Convention on Climate Change, "Kyoto Protocol Mechanisms," 2003, http://unfccc.int/issues/mechanisms.html.

26. United Nations Framework Convention on Climate Change, "CDM Insights—Intelligence about the CDM at the End of Each Month," 2012, https://cdm.unfccc.int/Statistics/Public/CDMinsights/index.html.

27. Davis A. Wirth, "The Sixth Session (Part Two) and the Seventh Session of the Conference of the Parties to the Framework Convention on Climate Change," *American Journal of International Law* 96, no. 3 (2002): 648–660.

28. Asia-Pacific Partnership on Clean Development and Climate, "About the Asia-Pacific Partnership on Clean Development and Climate," http://www.asiapacificpartnership.org/about.aspx. The Asia-Pacific Partnership concluded its work in 2011. Dries Lesage, Thijs Van de Graaf, and Kirsten Westphal, "The G8's Role in Global Energy Governance since the 2005 Gleneagles Summit," *Global Governance* 15, no. 2 (2009): 259–277.

29. More than forty thousand individuals representing governments, media, and NGOs were accredited to attend the meeting, and thousands more descended on Copenhagen to participate in public protests. In the closing days of the meeting, 115 heads of state assembled for the high-level segment of the negotiations. "Summary of the Copenhagen Climate Change Conference: 7–19 December 2009," Earth Negotiations Bulletin, December 22, 2009, http://www.iisd.ca/download/pdf/enb12459e.pdf.

30. United Nations Framework Convention on Climate Change, *Report of the Conference of the Parties on Its Sixteenth Session, Held in Cancun from 29 November to 10 December 2010. Addendum. Part Two: Action Taken by the Conference of the Parties at Its Sixteenth Session,* FCCC/CP/2010/7/Add.1 (Bonn: FCCC Secretariat, March 15, 2011). The European Union was an early adopter of the 2 degree target. See Commission of the European Communities, "Limiting Global Climate Change to 2 Degrees Celsius: The Way Ahead for 2020 and Beyond," Communication from the Commission to the Council, the European Parliament, the European Economic and Social Committee and the Committee of the Regions, COM(2007)2, Brussels, January 10, 2007, http://ec.europa.eu/development/icenter/repository/env_cc_com_2007_2_en.pdf. In its Fourth Assessment Report, the IPCC estimated this would require stabilizing atmospheric GHG concentrations around 450 parts per million.

31. Jennifer Morgan, Athena Ballesteros, Heather McGray, Kelly Levin, Florence Daviet, Fred Stolle, and Hilary McMahon, "Reflections on the Cancun Agreements," World Resources Institute, December 14, 2010, http://www.wri.org/stories/2010/12/reflections-cancun-agreements.

32. Clifford Polycarp, Catherine Easton, Jennifer Hatch, and Taryn Fransen, "Summary of Developed Country 'Fast-Start' Climate Finance Pledges," World Resources Institute, November 2012, http://www.wri.org/publication/summary-of-developed-country-fast-start-climate-finance-pledges#qanda.

33. Jon Birger Skjærseth and Jørgen Wettestad, *EU Emissions Trading* (Aldershot, UK: Ashgate, 2008). There were several smaller-scale experiments with emissions trading prior to establishment of the EU ETS, and today several other markets are being developed in other jurisdictions, including at the subnational level. See Michele M. Betsill and Matthew Hoffman, "The Contours of 'cap and trade': the evolution of emissions trading systems for greenhouse gases." *Review of Policy Research 28,* no.1 (2011): 83-106..

34. Peter Stoett, "Canada, Kyoto, and the Conservatives: Thinking/Moving Ahead," in *Changing Climates in North American Politics: Institutions, Policymaking, and Multilevel Governance,* ed. Henrik Selin and Stacy D. VanDeveer (Cambridge: MIT Press, 2009).

35. Yves Tiberghien and Miranda A. Schreurs, "High Noon in Japan: Embedded Symbolism and Post-2001 Kyoto Protocol Politics," *Global Environmental Politics 7,* no. 4 (2007): 70–91.

36. See Edward L. Miles, Arild Underdal, Steinar Andresen, Jørgen Wettestad, Jon Birger Skjærseth, and Elaine M. Carlin, *Environmental Regime Effectiveness: Confronting Theory with Evidence* (Cambridge: MIT Press, 2002); David G. Victor, Kal Raustiala, and Eugene B. Skolnikoff, eds., *The Implementation and Effectiveness of International Environmental Commitments: Theory and Practice* (Cambridge: MIT Press, 1998); Oran R. Young, ed., *The Effectiveness of International Environmental Regimes: Causal Connections and Behavioral Mechanisms* (Cambridge: MIT Press, 1999).

37. Harold K. Jacobson and Edith Brown Weiss, "A Framework for Analysis," in *Engaging Countries: Strengthening Compliance with International Environmental Accords,* ed. Edith Brown Weiss and Harold K. Jacobson (Cambridge: MIT Press, 1998), 4–5.

38. Victor, *Collapse of the Kyoto Protocol,* 112–113.

39. Grubb et al., *Kyoto Protocol,* 81; Matthew Paterson, *Global Warming and Global Politics* (London: Routledge, 1996), 69.

40. United Nations Framework Convention on Climate Change Secretariat, Subsidiary Body for Scientific and Technological Advice, "Report on the Implementation of Domestic Action by Parties Included in Annex I to the Convention That Are Also Parties to the Kyoto Protocol Based on the Information Reported in Their National Communications," FCCC/SBSTA/2012/INF.9, November 9, 2012, http://unfccc.int/resource/docs/2012/sbsta/eng/inf09.pdf.

41. Marvin S. Soroos, "Global Climate Change and the Futility of the Kyoto Process," *Global Environmental Politics 1,* no. 2 (2001): 1–9.

42. David G. Victor, Kal Raustiala, and Eugene B. Skolnikoff, "Introduction and Overview," in Victor et al., *Implementation and Effectiveness of International Environmental Commitments*, 7.

43. U.S. Environmental Protection Agency, *Inventory of U.S. Greenhouse Gas Emissions and Sinks: 1990–1999* (Washington, DC: Environmental Protection Agency, 2001).

44. Gabriela Kütting, *Environment, Society and International Relations: Towards More Effective International Environmental Agreements* (London: Routledge, 2000), 36.

45. Jos G. J. Olivier, Greet Janssens-Maenhout, and Jeroen A. H. W. Peters, *Trends in Global CO₂ Emissions: 2012 Report* (The Hague: PBL Netherlands Environmental Assessment Agency Joint Research Centre, 2012), http://edgar.jrc.ec.europa.eu/CO2REPORT2012.pdf.

46. Intergovernmental Panel on Climate Change, "Policies, Instruments and Cooperative Arrangements," in *Climate Change 2007: Mitigation of Climate Change* (Contribution of Working Group III to the Fourth Assessment Report of the Intergovernmental Panel on Climate Change) (Cambridge: Cambridge University Press, 2007), 776. The current concentration of CO_2 in the atmosphere is 383 parts per million.

47. Climate Action Tracker, http://www.climateactiontracker.org, accessed January 19, 2013.

48. Oran R. Young, *The Institutional Dimensions of Environmental Change: Fit, Interplay and Scale* (Cambridge: MIT Press, 2002), 31.

49. Arild Underdal, "One Question, Two Answers," in Miles et al., *Environmental Regime Effectiveness*, 5.

50. Michele M. Betsill, "The United States and the Evolution of International Climate Change Norms," in *Climate Change and American Foreign Policy*, ed. Paul G. Harris (New York: St. Martin's Press, 2000), 205–224; Oberthür and Ott, *The Kyoto Protocol*, 287–300; Hermann E. Ott, *The Kyoto Protocol to the UN Framework Convention on Climate Change: Finished and Unfinished Business* (Wuppertal, Germany: Wuppertal Institute for Climate, Environment and Energy, 1999).

51. Matthew J. Hoffmann, *Climate Governance at the Crossroads: Experimenting with a Global Response after Kyoto* (Oxford: Oxford University Press, 2011); Harriet Bulkeley and Peter Newell, *Governing Climate Change* (London: Routledge, 2010); Liliana Andonova, Michele Betsill, and Harriet Bulkeley, "Transnational Climate Change Governance," *Global Environmental Politics* 9, no. 2 (2009): 52–73.

52. George W. Bush, quoted in "Clear Skies Initiative: Executive Summary," White House press release, February 14, 2002, http://georgewbush-whitehouse.archives .gov/news/releases/2002/02/clearskies.html.

53. Kathryn Hochstetler and Eduardo Viola, "Brazil and the Politics of Climate Change: Beyond the Global Commons," *Environmental Politics* 21, no. 5 (2012): 753–771; William Chandler, Roberto Schaeffer, Zhou Dadi, P. R. Shukla, Fernando Tudela, Ogunlade Davidson, and Alpan-Atamer Sema, *Climate Change Mitigation in Developing Countries: Brazil, China, India, Mexico, South Africa, and Turkey* (Arlington, VA: Pew Center on Climate Change, 2002).

54. Ans Kolk, "Developments in Corporate Responses to Climate Change in the Past Decade," in *Climate Change, Sustainable Development and Risk: An Economic and Business View*, ed. Bernd Hansjurgens and Ralf Antes (New York: Physica, 2008); David L. Levy and Ans Kolk, "Strategic Responses to Global Climate Change: Conflicting Pressures on Multinationals in the Oil Industry," *Business and Politics* 4, no. 3 (2002): 275–399.

55. Eileen Claussen, "Solving the Climate Equation: Mandatory and Practical Steps for Real Reductions" (remarks to Alliant Energy conference, Madison, Wisconsin, April 15, 2003), http://www.pewclimate.org/press_room/speech_transcripts/speech_apri115.cfm.

56. United Nations Environment Programme, "Green Economy," http://www.unep.org/greeneconomy, accessed January 19, 2013.

57. Michele M. Betsill and Harriet Bulkeley, "Cities and the Multilevel Governance of Global Climate Change," *Global Governance* 12, no. 2 (2006): 141–159; Barry G. Rabe, "Beyond Kyoto: Climate Change Policy in Multilevel Governance Systems," *Governance: An International Journal of Policy and Administration* 20, no. 3 (2007): 423–444; Henrik Selin and Stacy D. VanDeveer, "North American Climate Governance: Policymaking and Institutions in the Multilevel Greenhouse," in Selin and VanDeveer, *Changing Climates in North American Politics.*

58. ICLEI–Local Governments for Sustainability, Cities for Climate Protection (CCP), http://www.iclei.org/index.php?id=800; see also Harriet Bulkeley, "Cities and the Governance of Climate Change," *Annual Review of Environment and Resources* 35 (2010): 229–253.

59. Barry G. Rabe, "States on Steroids: The Intergovernmental Odyssey of American Climate Policy," *Review of Policy Research* 25, no. 2 (2008): 105–128.

60. Harriet Bulkeley, Liliana Andonova, Karin Bäckstrand, Michele Betsill, Daniel Compagnon, Rosaleen Duffy, Ans Kolk, Matthew Hoffmann, David Levy, Peter Newell, Tori Milledge, Matthew Paterson, Philipp Pattberg, and Stacy VanDeveer, "Governing Climate Change Transnationally: Assessing the Evidence from a Database of Sixty Initiatives," *Environment and Planning C: Government and Policy* 30, no. 4 (2012): 591–612.

61. Climate Group, "About Us," http://www.theclimategroup.org/who-we-are/about-us, accessed January 19, 2013.

62. Moisés Naìm, "Minilateralism: The Magic Number to Get Real International Action," *Foreign Policy*, July/August 2009, 135–136.

63. Steve Rayner, "How to Eat an Elephant: A Bottom-Up Approach to Climate Policy," *Climate Policy* 10, no. 6 (2010): 615–621.

64. Michele M. Betsill and Harriet Bulkeley, "Transnational Networks and Global Environmental Governance: The Cities for Climate Protection Program," *International Studies Quarterly* 48, no. 2 (2004): 471–493; Philipp Pattberg and Johannes Stripple, "Beyond the Public and Private Divide: Remapping Transnational Climate Governance in the 21st Century," *International Environmental Agreements: Politics, Law and Economics* 8, no. 4 (2008): 367–388; Henrik Selin and Stacy D. VanDeveer, "Canadian-U.S. Environmental Cooperation: Climate Change Networks and Regional Action," *American Review of Canadian Studies* 35 (Summer 2005): 353–378; Elinor Ostrom, "Polycentric Systems for Coping with Collective Action and Global Environmental Change," *Global Environmental Change* 20, no. 4 (2010): 550–557.

11

Global Politics and Policy on Hazardous Chemicals

Henrik Selin

The chemicals regime, designed to mitigate environmental and human health problems caused by hazardous substances, is one of the oldest environmental regimes.[1] The first multilateral instrument addressing hazardous chemicals may have been the St. Petersburg Declaration from 1868. This agreement, which is part of humanitarian law, banned the use of "fulminating or inflammable substances" in military projectiles weighing less than 400 grams.[2] Actions to limit workers' exposure to toxic compounds, including lead and white phosphorus, were taken by the International Labour Organization (ILO) starting in 1919. After the end of World War II, states, intergovernmental organizations (IGOs), and nongovernmental organizations (NGOs) began expanding the chemicals regime based on broader concerns about environmental and human health risks. Contemporary debates involve how to improve governance across global, regional, national, and local scales; ways to better manage risks under conditions of scientific uncertainty and competing interests; and means to provide support to countries lacking necessary resources to take effective action.

Chemicals management concerns fundamental and complex issues of how societies should safely apply pesticides for food production and public health protection against vector-borne diseases; properly use industrial chemicals to produce countless goods, from satellites to cell phones; and target emissions from combustion and manufacturing processes. Multiple aspects of chemicals management make it an international issue. Many chemicals are traded extensively across countries. Total chemicals production (excluding pharmaceuticals) is worth more than $2 trillion, and almost half of this value is traded internationally (including intrafirm trade).[3] A multitude of traded goods also contain hazardous substances. Further, emissions of many hazardous substances can travel long distances from their points of origin, predominantly through the atmosphere. International cooperation can also be a way to generate awareness about the risks of particular chemicals and diffuse information about substitutes and alternative techniques. In addition, international activities can help mobilize resources and trigger domestic actions that may otherwise not be taken.[4]

Some major environmental regimes are structured around framework conventions that outline general policy goals, followed by subsequent protocols that spell out more detailed controls and requirements. The ozone and climate change regimes, among others, follow this governance structure. In contrast, the chemicals regime is structured around several legally independent treaties addressing overlapping policy issues and substances, which creates specific governance challenges of policy coordination and implementation. The different multilateral agreements set controls on the full life cycle of production, use, trade, and disposal of a limited number of industrial chemicals and pesticides, as well as emission controls on by-products of production and combustion processes. The regime also includes structures and mechanisms to assess and regulate additional chemicals, to increase and harmonize information about commercial and discarded chemicals traded across national borders, and to enhance regional and domestic management capacities. The four main treaties of the chemicals regime are as follows:

- The 1989 Basel Convention on the Control of Transboundary Movements of Hazardous Wastes and Their Disposal (regulating international shipments and generation of hazardous wastes)
- The 1998 Rotterdam Convention on the Prior Informed Consent Procedure for Certain Hazardous Chemicals and Pesticides in International Trade (managing exports and imports of hazardous chemicals)
- The 1998 Protocol on Persistent Organic Pollutants (POPs) to the Convention on Long-Range Transboundary Air Pollution (CLRTAP) (controlling production, use, disposal, and release of POPs)
- The 2001 Stockholm Convention on Persistent Organic Pollutants (regulating production, use, trade, disposal, and release of POPs)

Related to the institutionally fragmented nature of the chemicals regime, states and stakeholders in 2006 adopted the Strategic Approach to International Chemicals Management (SAICM). While SAICM is not a framework convention but a voluntary program operating as an umbrella mechanism promoting sound chemicals management and harmonization of controls and activities across major agreements and programs, it is an important part of continuing work on policy coordination and treaty implementation. SAICM works toward the goal that chemicals worldwide should be "used and produced in ways that lead to the minimization of significant adverse effects on human health and the environment" no later than the year 2020, adopted at the World Summit on Sustainable Development (WSSD) in Johannesburg in 2002.[5] This policy goal was reaffirmed at the United Nations Conference on Sustainable Development (also known as Rio+20) in Rio de Janeiro in 2012.[6] Societies are, however, still a long way from realizing this policy goal, which remains a critical sustainable development issue for both industrialized and developing countries.[7]

This chapter examines the creation and continuing implementation of the chemicals regime. The next section gives a brief introduction to the challenges of managing hazardous chemicals. This is followed by an examination of the creation and implementation of the main chemical treaties, including their roles in life-cycle management. The subsequent section provides a discussion of four critical governance challenges for improving environmental and human health protection, focusing on treaty ratification and implementation, risk assessments and controls, management capacity and awareness, and the generation of hazardous substances and waste. Next, the importance of developing more proactive and precautionary approaches to assessing and regulating hazardous chemicals is discussed, with a focus on the role of the European Union as a policy leader on these issues. The chapter ends with a few concluding remarks on the future of multilevel chemical governance.

Managing Hazardous Chemicals

The DuPont slogan "Better Things for Better Living . . . through Chemistry" from the 1930s captured early optimism in the chemicals revolution.[8] It is unknown how many chemicals are used worldwide, but EU data provide a rough approximation: more than 140,000 chemicals are registered on the European market.[9] Between 1970 and 2010, the global chemicals industry's output increased in value from $171 billion to $4.1 trillion (not adjusted for inflation).[10] Historically, European and North American firms have dominated, but Asia (mainly China) recently became the world's largest chemicals producing region. Over the past decade, growth in chemicals production and use has slowed down in many industrialized countries while it has increased greatly in many developing countries. This trend, led by China and India, is expected to continue over the next decade.

Modern chemicals provide numerous benefits, and most commonly used substances are not classified as dangerous. However, there is a huge lack of public risk assessment data, and many substances have caused significant environmental and human health problems after having been used in large quantities over long periods of time. Dangerous chemicals are released through normal use of pesticides, common industrial and manufacturing practices, combustion processes, leakages from a large number of wastes, and industrial and household accidents. Policy makers are tasked with developing and implementing socially acceptable standards in the face of limited scientific data and understanding where firms selling and buying chemicals, workers, regulators, advocacy groups, and local communities may have different perspectives and competing interests. This situation makes effective chemicals management very difficult at both domestic and international levels.

Many problems are related to the persistence, toxicity, bioaccumulation, and biomagnification characteristics of chemicals. Persistence refers to the length of time a substance remains in the environment before it is biodegraded. Persistence per se is not dangerous, but there is cause for concern if a substance exhibits other undesirable qualities with respect to toxicity, bioaccumulation, and biomagnification. Common concerns about toxic substances include their ability to cause cancer, to act as endocrine disrupters, and to hinder human development in early developmental stages. Hazardous substances may also bioaccumulate; that is, they can build up in fatty tissues of organisms over time. Hazardous substances that have bioaccumulated in organisms at a lower trophic level can, moreover, be passed up through food webs in a process known as biomagnification. As a result, species (including humans) at the top of food webs have higher concentrations of many hazardous substances in their bodies than do species lower down the same food webs.

With her book *Silent Spring*, published in 1962, Rachel Carson drew attention to the dangers of the indiscriminate use of DDT (dichlorodiphenyl trichloroethane) and other similar pesticides. There are no exact global data, but one study estimated that as many as three million people may still be hospitalized every year as a result of pesticide poisoning, resulting in more than 200,000 deaths, with 99 percent of these cases occurring in developing countries.[11] Many industrial chemicals, including PCBs (polychlorinated biphenyls) and by-products such as dioxins and furans, are also major environmental pollutants and dangerous to human health. This has been evident in major disasters in, for example, Yusho, Japan, in 1962 (PCBs); Seveso, Italy, in 1976 (dioxins); and Bhopal, India, in 1984 (methyl isocyanate gas). More recently, since the opening of a chemical park with twenty-five industries in Wuli Village in eastern China in the 1990s, Wuli has become one of possibly several hundred Chinese "cancer villages," with a rapid surge in cancer-related illnesses and deaths.[12]

Discarded chemicals and waste products containing hazardous substances can also cause critical waste problems. For example, toxic chemicals dumped in Love Canal in Upstate New York between the 1930s and the 1950s leaked through to buildings built on the old dump site. This caused high rates of birth defects, miscarriages, and liver cancer and an elevated incidence of seizure-inducing nerve disease in children.[13] Leakages of hazardous substances also result from the unsafe handling of rapidly growing levels of electronic waste (e-waste), such as old refrigerators, televisions, computers, and media players. Some e-waste is shipped, legally or illegally, from industrialized countries to developing countries where workers in unregulated recycling and disposal businesses frequently handle toxic substances in unsafe ways while trying to make a basic living. As one policy advocate working to stop the e-waste trade from the United States stated: "You know, it's a hell of a choice between poverty and poison. We should never make people make that choice."[14]

The Chemicals Regime

As they have gradually expanded the chemicals regime, states, IGOs, and NGOs have collaborated to create and implement the four major treaties: the 1989 Basel Convention; the 1998 Rotterdam Convention; the 1998 CLR-TAP POPs Protocol; and the 2001 Stockholm Convention. Table 11-1 contains brief descriptions of the major components of each of these agreements. Although the treaties are legally independent, their creation and implementation are politically and practically connected in multiple ways

Table 11-1 Summary of the Four Main Treaties on Chemicals Management

Basel Convention *Adopted in 1989;* *Entry into force in* *1992; 179 parties as* *of 2013*	• Regulates the transboundary movement and disposal of hazardous wastes; covers chemicals if they fall under the treaty's definition of hazardous wastes • Hazardous waste transfers subject to a prior informed consent (PIC) procedure in which a party must give explicit consent before a shipment can take place • Exports of hazardous wastes prohibited to Antarctica and to parties that have taken domestic measures banning imports • Exports of hazardous wastes to nonparties must be subject to an agreement at least as stringent as the Basel Convention • 1995 Ban Amendment (not yet in force) bans export of hazardous wastes from parties that are members of the OECD or the EU, as well as Liechtenstein, to other parties • 1999 Protocol on Liability and Compensation (not yet in force) identifies financial responsibilities in cases of waste transfer accidents • Basel Convention regional centers address management and capacity-building issues
Rotterdam Convention *Adopted in 1998; Entry* *into force in 2004; 150* *parties as of 2013*	• Regulates the international trade in commercial chemicals using a PIC scheme • Forty-three chemicals covered by 2012 • Exporting party must receive prior consent from importing party before the export of a regulated chemical can take place • Parties are obligated to notify the Secretariat when they ban or severely restrict a chemical • Contains a mechanism for evaluating and regulating additional chemicals under the treaty
CLRTAP POPs Protocol *Adopted in 1998;* *Entry into force in* *2003; 31 parties as of* *2013*	• Regulates production and use of persistent organic pollutants (POPs), pesticides, and industrial chemicals listed in the treaty • Outlines provisions regarding environmentally sound transport and disposal of POPs, pesticides, and industrial chemicals, consistent with Basel Convention • Sets technical standards for controlling emissions of unintentionally produced by-product POPs • Twenty-five chemicals regulated by 2012 • Contains a mechanism for evaluating and regulating additional chemicals under the treaty

(Continued)

Table 11-1 Continued

Stockholm Convention *Adopted in 2001; Entry into force in 2004; 178 parties as of 2013*	• Regulates production, use, trade, and disposal of POPs, pesticides, and industrial chemicals listed under the treaty
	• Sets technical standards for controlling release of by-product POPs listed under the treaty
	• Parties required to ban import or export of controlled POPs except for purposes of environmentally sound disposal
	• Contains a mechanism for evaluating and regulating additional chemicals under the treaty
	• Twenty-two chemicals regulated by 2012
	• Stockholm Convention regional centers support capacity building and implementation

because of their overlapping scope, controls, and membership. The adoption of these global treaties was possible only after contentious political negotiations regarding which specific chemicals were to be controlled, how they were to be regulated, and what kinds of management structures were to be created. Further, the continuing implementation of each agreement is influenced by its connections to the others and by efforts to capture regulatory and management synergies.

Basel Convention on the Transboundary Movement and Disposal of Hazardous Wastes

The Basel Convention targets the generation and international shipment of hazardous wastes, which have increased sharply since the 1960s. Industrialized, high-consumption societies generate the vast majority of hazardous wastes, and most waste trade has historically taken place between industrialized countries.[15] However, it was the North-South waste trade between industrialized and developing countries that was the main impetus for the creation of the Basel Convention. Several high-profile cases of firms located in industrialized countries illegally dumping hazardous wastes, including discarded chemicals, in developing countries in the 1970s and 1980s drew much attention.[16] This is not just a historical problem, however. For example, during the night of August 19, 2006, the Greek-owned and Panama-registered vessel *Probo Koala*, chartered by the Dutch-based company Trafigura, illegally dumped near the city of Abidjan in the Ivory Coast an estimated 500 tons of "a fuming mix of petrochemicals and caustic soda" that originated in the Mediterranean region.[17] This resulted in several deaths and severe health problems for tens of thousands of people. In response, local civil servants were fired, and the Dutch firm agreed to pay $200 million in compensation to the Ivorian government.[18]

In an early international policy effort, the Organisation for Economic Cooperation and Development (OECD) in the 1980s developed guidelines for managing the trade in hazardous wastes among its industrialized country members that included a prior informed consent (PIC) mechanism. Under this scheme, an exporting country needed permission from the importing country prior to shipment. The Governing Council of the United Nations Environment Programme (UNEP) in 1987 adopted the first global standards, the Cairo Guidelines and Principles for the Environmentally Sound Management of Hazardous Wastes. These guidelines introduced a voluntary PIC scheme for all transnational transport of hazardous wastes. Many developing countries and environmental NGOs, however, did not think that these guidelines were stringent enough and pushed for legally binding controls. The resultant Basel Convention, which seeks to minimize the generation of hazardous wastes and to control and reduce their transboundary movement, was adopted in 1989.[19]

The Basel Convention prohibits exports of hazardous wastes to Antarctica and to parties that have taken domestic measures to ban imports. Waste transfers to other parties are subject to a mandatory PIC procedure; that is, a party cannot export hazardous wastes to another party without the prior consent of the importing state. Waste exports to nonparties are prohibited unless subject to an agreement between the exporter and importer that is at least as stringent as the requirements under the Basel Convention. Discarded chemicals are covered by the treaty if they meet definitions of "hazardous." Wastes are designated as hazardous if they come from certain waste streams (for example, wood-preserving chemicals), belong to certain categories (for example, mercury compounds), or exhibit certain characteristics (for example, are poisonous or toxic). The Basel Convention relies on domestic legislation to define "waste," which typically includes substances or objects that are intended for or are required to be disposed of by law.

Even if the Basel Convention introduced a legally binding PIC scheme following its entry into force in 1992, many developing countries, supported by NGOs such as Greenpeace and the Basel Action Network, as well as the Nordic countries were disappointed that it did not include a ban on North-South trade. Following some minor policy developments in the early 1990s, the ban supporters convinced the parties in 1995 to adopt the Ban Amendment despite opposition from some industrialized countries and industry organizations.[20] The Ban Amendment prohibits the export of hazardous wastes for final disposal and recycling from countries listed in Annex VII (members of the OECD and the EU as well as Liechtenstein) to all other parties (primarily developing countries). However, because of a continuing desire by at least some countries to maintain the economically valuable trade in hazardous wastes, ratification of the Ban Amendment has been slow. There has also been lingering uncertainty around the number of ratifications needed for entry into force.

In 1999, the parties adopted the Basel Protocol on Liability and Compensation. This was based on concerns among developing countries that they lack sufficient funds and technologies for coping with illegal dumping or accidental spills. The protocol identifies who is financially responsible in the event of an incident during the transboundary movement of hazardous wastes. However, the protocol has not yet entered into force owing to a short-age of ratifications. In addition, the parties have created fourteen regional centers located in different parts of the world to focus on capacity building and technology transfer in support of treaty implementation, mainly in devel-oping countries.[21] The regional centers, for example, help train customs offi-cials and other stakeholders in identifying and handling hazardous wastes, promote environmentally sound waste management, support the application of cleaner production technologies, aid in data collection and reporting to the Basel Secretariat, and engage in public education and awareness raising. While off to a slow start, many developing countries hope that the regional centers can become increasingly active in treaty implementation.[22]

At their meeting in 2011, the parties adopted a ten-year strategic framework on implementation outlining goals and performance indicators to measure progress on waste management (something that was previously lacking).[23] The meeting also clarified how many ratifications the Ban Amendment on North-South trade needs to enter into force. While this is legally and politically sig-nificant, it may have limited on-the-ground impact going forward. Global data are incomplete and difficult to compare but indicate that more than 95 percent of hazardous wastes subject to PIC requirements are transported within geo-graphic regions.[24] The majority of this trade takes place in Europe and North America, falling outside the scope of the Ban Amendment. The EU has already banned exports to developing countries, many of which also prohibit imports. There is no current evidence of systematic waste transfers from industrialized to developing countries (although instances of illegal dumping remain a con-cern). Such exports also seem to be declining while the reverse trade may be growing; some developing countries are increasingly exporting wastes to indus-trialized countries for environmentally safe disposal.

Rotterdam Convention on Trade in Commercial Chemicals

The Rotterdam Convention regulates the international trade in commercial chemicals. Despite the fact that most industrial chemicals and pesticides were traded among firms in industrialized countries, it was largely unregulated North-South trade that acted as the main stimulus for international controls (similar to the hazardous wastes case; both trade issues emerged on the politi-cal agenda in the 1970s). As under the Basel Convention, North-South politics has shaped much of the implementation of the Rotterdam Convention. Con-cerns about the mishandling and unsafe use of pesticides were validated by emerging scientific data on high levels of pesticide poisonings among farmers and other handlers, particularly in many developing countries. Even if some risks have been reduced, many problems remain. A study of one hospital in the Indian state of Andhra Pradesh found that approximately 8,000 patients were admitted with severe pesticide poisoning between 1997 and 2002—more than 20 percent (over 1,800 people) died as a result of this exposure.[25]

Developing countries, working with IGOs, led attempts to regulate the trade in hazardous chemicals.[26] In 1977, the UNEP Governing Council adopted a resolution stating that hazardous chemicals should not be exported without the knowledge and consent of the importing country. In 1982, a UN General Assembly resolution called for the establishment of a PIC procedure governing the export of domestically banned chemicals. The OECD Council in 1984 adopted a recommendation that member states implement a PIC system for trade in chemicals. In 1985, the United Nations Food and Agriculture Organization (FAO) adopted its Code of Conduct on the Distribution and Use of Pesticides. Similarly, the UNEP Governing Council in 1987 adopted the London Guidelines for the Exchange of Information on Chemicals in International Trade. None of these initiatives, however, included formal PIC requirements, which were rejected by major chemical-producing countries and industry organizations.

Nevertheless, as pressure from developing countries increased, the UNEP Governing Council in 1989 adopted the Amended London Guidelines to create a first voluntary global PIC procedure. The same year, the FAO Council made similar changes to the FAO Code of Conduct. The PIC scheme was managed jointly by the FAO in Rome for pesticides and by UNEP Chemicals in Geneva for industrial chemicals. The PIC procedure operated in three sequential steps. First, the government of an exporting country, on behalf of a domestic firm, had to notify an importing country of any control action that it had taken to ban or severely restrict a chemical for human health or environmental reasons. Second, the government of the importing country was obligated to respond to this notification, stating whether or not it would accept the import. Third, the exporting country government was responsible for communicating this response to the firm seeking export permission and for ensuring that the company complied with the decision of the importing country's government.

In the 1990s, many developing countries and environmental NGOs, as well as a growing number of industrialized countries, argued that it was necessary to convert the voluntary PIC scheme into a treaty to strengthen environmental and human health protection. These efforts were further influenced by parallel efforts to expand regulations under the Basel Convention. Chapter 19 of Agenda 21—adopted at the United Nations Conference on Environment and Development in 1992—called on states to create a legally binding PIC instrument. The FAO Council (in 1994) and the UNEP Governing Council (in 1995) approved the start of treaty negotiations, which began in 1996. The Rotterdam Convention was adopted in 1998. During the negotiations, some developing countries proposed a ban on the export of nationally prohibited chemicals from OECD countries (in other words, from industrialized countries) to other countries (to developing countries), but such a ban received little support. As a result, the negotiations largely transformed the voluntary procedure into a similar legally binding mechanism.[27]

Consequently, the Rotterdam Convention stipulates that a party, through the national government, can respond in three different ways after having received a formal request to accept the importation of a particular chemical on the PIC list. First, the government can declare that it consents to receive the import of the chemical and any other shipments within the same calendar year; second, the government may reject the request; or third, the government may consent to the import, but only if specific conditions are met by the exporting party. The government of the potential exporter must abide by any decision made by the potentially receiving country. The Secretariat, which is divided between UNEP Chemicals and FAO, acts as facilitator and communicator throughout this process and distributes all the responses between the parties. National governments are responsible for communicating all information and decisions from the other party to all relevant domestic firms.

A party that has domestically banned or severely restricted the use of a chemical is required to notify the Secretariat about this action.[28] When the Secretariat has received notification from parties from at least two different geographic regions—or a single party that is a developing country or a country with an economy in transition experiencing domestic problems—it forwards all this information to the Chemical Review Committee, made up of thirty-one government-appointed experts. Based on its assessment according to procedures outlined in the Rotterdam Convention, the committee submits a recommendation to the Conferences of the Parties, which make all final decisions regarding the inclusion of a new chemical on the PIC list by consensus.[29] However, the PIC procedure applies only to Rotterdam Convention parties and is not mandatory in trade with nonparties. Thus a party may avoid PIC requirements by using a nonparty country as an intermediary—a practice that does not formally violate any treaty rules.[30]

The PIC procedure operated on a voluntary basis between 1998 and 2006, before the Rotterdam Convention made it mandatory. Originally, twenty-seven substances were listed under the Rotterdam Convention, carried over from the earlier procedure. Following multiple additions, the Rotterdam Convention as of 2012 covered forty-three chemicals. Several of these are also controlled by the two POPs agreements. Many additional substances are lined up for review. Often the Conferences of the Parties have followed the recommendations of the Chemical Review Committee, but there are signs that the process is becoming more politicized. The inclusion of endosulfan on the PIC list was blocked for several years by a minority of parties despite the Chemical Review Committee's support for adding it. Similarly, chrysotile asbestos has yet to be added despite the committee's recommendation that it be listed. Both these cases suggest that future debates on at least some economically important chemicals may be increasingly contentious, as it is also possible that any given chemical may be assessed and considered for regulation under more than one treaty.

CLRTAP Protocol on Persistent Organic Pollutants

The CLRTAP POPs Protocol was the first international treaty that specifically targeted POPs as a separate category of particularly hazardous chemicals. It is a regional agreement that operates under the auspices of the United

Nations Economic Commission for Europe (UNECE), which comprises North America and Europe as far east as Russia and Kazakhstan. The CLR-TAP POPs Protocol was born out of concerns regarding the long-range atmospheric transport of emissions to northern latitudes, in particular the Arctic. Reports by the Arctic Monitoring and Assessment Programme (AMAP) state that the majority of chemicals found in the Arctic environment and wildlife come from distant sources outside the region. AMAP assessments have also concluded that subtle health effects are occurring in the human population in the Arctic as a result of chemical contamination of food sources. Scientific reports express the greatest concern for fetal and neonatal development risks.[31]

CLRTAP actions on POPs are closely linked with scientific and political concerns about Arctic pollution, as identified by the AMAP assessments. The Arctic was long viewed as too remote from industrial societies to be at serious environmental risk. Studies in the 1980s, however, established three interrelated issues: systematic long-range atmospheric transport of emissions to the Arctic, high environmental contamination levels throughout the Arctic region, and actual and potential environmental and human health implications.[32] It is now recognized that the sensitive Arctic environment functions as a window to the future, as the first to react to environmental hazards. Indigenous peoples' exposure to POPs is mainly a result of dietary intake of contaminated wildlife. Taking into consideration the physiological and nutritional benefits of traditional food systems, as well as their social and cultural importance, public health authorities have developed dietary recommendations to minimize local communities' exposure to POPs.

In Canada more than any other country, the POPs issue has become integrated with more general scientific and political concerns about Arctic environmental contamination and health risks of indigenous peoples.[33] Indigenous peoples' rights became a hot political issue in Canada in the 1980s, and the inclusion of indigenous groups in scientific and political work on chemicals increased the sensitivity and status of the chemicals issue in Canada. Indigenous groups were active participants in Canadian and circumpolar research programs, producing results that prompted Canada and other Arctic countries to push for international policy responses. Indigenous groups also lobbied successfully for the Arctic region to be recognized as particularly sensitive to POPs. As a result of their lobbying, the preamble of the CLRTAP POPs Protocol gives special recognition to the exposed situation of the Arctic environment and human populations.

CLRTAP POPs assessments in the 1990s identified a set of priority POPs found extensively and at relatively high concentrations in the environment throughout the Northern Hemisphere. Following the start of political negotiations in 1997, the CLRTAP POPs Protocol was adopted in 1998. It entered into force in 2003. The CLRTAP POPs Protocol is designed to reduce the release and long-range transport of POPs emissions within the UNECE region. Regulated chemicals are divided into three annexes. The production and use of pesticides and industrial chemicals listed in Annex I are banned. Annex

II lists pesticides and industrial chemicals for which some uses are permitted. Parties are required to apply best available techniques and best environmental practices for controlling emissions of POPs by-products listed in Annex III. The CLRTAP POPs Protocol also mandates the environmentally sound transport and disposal of POPs, consistent with the Basel Convention.

Following a long assessment process and tough political negotiations in which countries disagreed on which chemicals should be included and how they should be regulated, sixteen POPs were originally covered by the CLR-TAP POPs Protocol.[34] Similar to the two mechanisms under the Rotterdam and Stockholm Conventions, the CLRTAP POPs Protocol contains a system for assessing additional chemicals for possible controls (as well as reviewing and potentially limiting granted exemptions of chemicals already regulated). In 2009, the parties added seven more substances to the CLRTAP POPs Protocol, but this amendment has yet to enter into force. As other chemicals are already under review, it is likely that more chemicals will be regulated in the future. Furthermore, there are many legal, political, regulatory, and management overlaps between the CLRTAP POPs Protocol and the Stockholm Convention, as parties expand the list of regulated chemicals simultaneously under the two agreements.

Stockholm Convention on Persistent Organic Pollutants

The Stockholm Convention, which was adopted in 2001 and entered into force in 2004, seeks to protect human health and the environment from POPs. In comparison with the CLRTAP POPs Protocol, which includes only countries located in the Northern Hemisphere, the Stockholm Convention also includes developing countries often facing difficult domestic management problems. For example, the government of Tanzania reported in a 2005 national assessment that the country basically had no fully operational POPs waste management facilities, whether for storage, transportation, or disposal. Many workers who handled equipment possibly containing high levels of PCBs did not use any kind of protective gear. Tanzanian government officials also noted that spillage of transformer oil likely to contain PCBs was frequent and that waste transformer oil was usually kept in open areas or was burned or discharged "haphazardly into the environment."[35]

In 1995, the UNEP Governing Council called for global assessments of twelve POPs (known as "the dirty dozen").[36] Based on these assessments, treaty negotiations began in 1998, the same year the CLRTAP POPs Protocol was adopted and the Rotterdam Convention was finalized. Many issues during the negotiations concerned the situations of developing countries with respect to domestic chemicals use and local management problems. The International POPs Elimination Network, a group of more than four hundred NGOs founded in 1998, lobbied in support of the global elimination of POPs. The same Arctic indigenous peoples' groups that influenced the CLRTAP negotiations again advocated for controls on the long-range transport of POPs to mitigate human health risks.[37] Their concerns are also reflected in the preamble of Stockholm Convention, which recognizes that Arctic ecosystems and indigenous communities are particularly at risk because of the biomagnification of POPs and the contamination of traditional foods.

The Stockholm Convention originally covered the dirty dozen, all of which were also regulated by the CLRTAP POPs Protocol. Similar to the CLRTAP agreement, the Stockholm Convention divides POPs into three annexes. The production and use of pesticides and industrial chemicals listed in Annex A are generally prohibited, but parties may apply for country-specific and time-limited exemptions. Annex B lists pesticides and industrial chemicals subject to restrictions under which only specified uses are allowed for all parties. Annex C lists by-products regulated through the setting of best available techniques and best environmental practices for their minimization. The import and export of pesticides and industrial chemicals are permitted only for substances subject to use exemptions or for the environmentally sound management and disposal of discarded chemicals. On these issues, the Stockholm Convention is designed to be legally compatible with the Rotterdam Convention and the Basel Convention.

The Stockholm Convention process for evaluating additional chemicals is carried out under the auspices of the POPs Review Committee, which consists of thirty-one government-designated experts. Any party can submit a proposal to regulate a new chemical. The POPs Review Committee then examines the proposal according to a set of scientific criteria specified in the treaty text.[38] The committee also conducts a management evaluation, which is submitted to the next Conference of the Parties making all final regulatory decisions. In 2009 and 2011, the parties added ten more POPs, making a total of twenty-two POPs that are covered by the Stockholm Convention (many of which are also covered by the Rotterdam Convention and/or the CLRTAP POPs Protocol). More are likely to be added in the future, but, as under other treaties, these discussions may be controversial when they concern chemicals that are still in extensive production and use and are therefore economically important to some firms and countries.

One highly divisive issue concerns DDT. In 1955 the World Health Organization (WHO) launched the Global Malaria Eradication Programme, which relied heavily on the use of DDT. Because eradication turned out to be difficult in large parts of the tropics, the WHO in 1992 shifted focus from eradication to management through the Global Malaria Control Strategy. Building on this effort, the WHO, UNICEF (United Nations Children's Fund), the UN Development Programme, and the World Bank in 1998 launched the Roll Back Malaria Partnership to fight malaria. Consistent with the Roll Back Malaria Partnership, the Stockholm Convention allows for the use of DDT for disease vector control against malaria mosquitoes. The WHO estimates that more than one million people die from malaria every year, with 90 percent of these deaths occurring in Africa.[39] If indirect effects of the disease (such as malaria-induced anemia, maternal pathology, and hypoglycemia) are taken into consideration, as many as three million people may die annually from malaria in Africa alone.[40]

By 2013 eighteen countries had issued notifications for continuing DDT production, use, or both.[41] However, other countries may also use DDT. Three countries were known to be producing DDT as of the early 2000s. India was the largest producer, followed by China and South Korea. Although the use of DDT has been politically and scientifically controversial since the 1960s and it is becoming clear that malaria-carrying mosquitoes in many areas are developing resistance to DDT, parties in 2009 concluded that countries that still use DDT for disease vector control may need to continue doing so until better, cost-effective local alternatives become available. Thus issues relating to the ongoing use of DDT and the advancement of alternatives will be discussed under the Stockholm Convention in the future. These discussions are further linked to DDT debates under the CLRTAP POPs Protocol and by the WHO, as the global community works to support both chemical and nonchemical alternatives to DDT use.

Parties are working to establish a monitoring program to evaluate implementation progress. Countries are also developing technical guidelines for the environmentally sound management of stockpiles and wastes. This work is carried out in collaboration with the Basel Convention Secretariat, as Basel Convention parties are simultaneously formulating technical guidance documents on handling POPs wastes. Parties are also establishing guidelines for best available techniques and best environmental practices for controlling by-products. Furthermore, the parties have established fifteen Stockholm Convention regional centers to support treaty implementation (six of which are also operating as Basel Convention regional centers).[42] The different centers engage in a wide range of efforts to raise awareness, strengthen administrative ability, and diffuse scientific and technical assistance and information.[43] In addition, parties are engaged in discussion with the Rotterdam Convention Secretariat on issues relating to the legal and illegal trade in POPs.

Additional Treaties

In addition to the four main treaties, many other agreements address region-specific problems with hazardous chemicals. Under UNEP's Regional Seas Programme, thirteen action plans targeting pollution problems were created by 2009; they involved more than 140 countries.[44] There are also several other regional seas agreements. For example, the 1972 Convention for the Prevention of Marine Pollution by Dumping from Ships and Aircraft and the 1974 Convention for the Prevention of Marine Pollution from Land-Based Sources cover the northeast Atlantic. In 1974, the Convention on the Protection of the Marine Environment of the Baltic Sea Area was adopted. Canada and the United States signed the Great Lakes Water Quality Agreement in 1972. Updating the agreement in 1978, the two countries pledged the virtual elimination of discharges of all persistent and toxic substances. Many shared rivers are also covered by pollution-related legal provisions.

In addition, several regional waste trade treaties operate alongside the global agreements. Reacting to the lack of a North-South trade ban under the

Basel Convention, African countries negotiated the 1991 Convention on the Ban of the Import into Africa and the Control of Transboundary Movement and Management of Hazardous Wastes within Africa, the so-called Bamako Convention. This convention seeks to prevent the dumping of hazardous wastes in Africa by banning the import of hazardous wastes from any outside country. Additional regional measures initiated by developing countries linked to the Basel Convention include the adoption of the Lomé IV Convention in 1991. This treaty bans the trade in hazardous wastes between members of the EU and former colonies in Asia, the Caribbean, and the Pacific. The 1995 Waigani Convention bans the import of hazardous and radioactive wastes to the island countries in the South Pacific region.

Multilevel Challenges for Improved Management

Multilevel governance, involving many levels of social organization and policy forums, is needed to manage the many environmental and human health problems associated with hazardous chemicals. Although some important progress in regulating highly dangerous substances can be noted, several multilevel governance issues are critical for improved management. Four governance challenges in particular stand out: to enhance treaty ratification and implementation, to expand risk assessments and controls, to improve management capacity and raise awareness, and to minimize the generation of hazardous chemicals and waste.

First, enhanced ratification of the main treaties would increase the number of states that take on formal responsibilities to address problems with hazardous chemicals as well as strengthen the treaties' position under international law. Although nearly 180 countries have ratified the Basel Convention, the United States—one of the world's largest generators of hazardous wastes and exporters of discarded goods and e-waste for recycling and disposal—is not a party. The Basel Convention Ban Amendment also has not received sufficient ratification to enter into force, and even fewer countries have ratified the Protocol on Liability and Compensation. While almost 180 countries have ratified the Stockholm Convention, the Rotterdam Convention after fifteen years has only 150 parties. The United States again is not party to either of these agreements or to the CLRTAP POPs Protocol, and many developing countries have yet to join the Rotterdam Convention, weakening efforts to manage the trade in toxic chemicals.

As recognized by SAICM, better policy coordination across treaties would make it easier for countries to meet their commitments. The parties to the three global conventions have also taken steps to coordinate the meetings of the Conferences of the Parties—the conventions' supreme policy-making bodies. Further, all three global conventions started out with their own independent secretariats providing legal and managerial support. However, in 2011 the Conferences of the Parties established the position of executive secretary as a joint overseeing administrative function for the Basel, Rotterdam, and Stockholm Convention Secretariats. In addition, the secretariats have taken steps to create joint legal, financial, and administrative services. These are all positive political steps to capture synergies across different agreements, but there is an important continuing need to address problems associated with policy fragmentation and differences in ratifications.

It is well established that regimes that use monitoring mechanisms and periodically review parties' compliance records and publish compliance reports tend to perform better than those that do not. Although it is rare to find strong monitoring and compliance programs in environmental regimes, states have sometimes been willing to accept such mechanisms to improve transparency and treaty implementation. Statements and actions by many industrialized and developing countries under all major chemical treaties, however, demonstrate that so far they have been unwilling to cede sovereignty and give much independent authority to secretariats and regional centers to undertake data collection and monitoring, and even less so to give them the right to initiate political or legal actions against states that do not fulfill their treaty obligations and commitments.[45] Continuing debates on these issues, which are central to regime effectiveness, are likely to remain as contentious under the chemicals regime as they are under many other environmental regimes.

Second, countries need to expand international risk assessments and regulations. For most commercial chemicals, only scant data are available on emissions, environmental dispersion, and ecosystem and human health effects. This hinders the conduct of risk assessments that are adequate to inform policy making. While substances have been added to the agreements since their adoption, several at least partially unregulated POP-like chemicals have been detected in remote areas. Many pesticides that may not meet the POPs criteria still fall under the WHO Class I (extremely and highly hazardous) and Class II (moderately hazardous) categories of toxic pesticides that are strong candidates for inclusion under the Rotterdam Convention. There is also a need to increase participation by IGOs such as the FAO, the WHO, and the United Nations Institute for Training and Research in the area of integrated pest management, which involves using a combination of environmentally friendly methods to significantly reduce or even eliminate the use of pesticides.

Despite important legal and organizational developments since the 1990s, hazardous waste management, including the handling of e-wastes, also suffers from important shortcomings. To address the hazardous waste problem more successfully, countries need to develop more extensive management guidelines for additional waste streams and continue their efforts to minimize human health and environmental risks from the transport, reuse, recycling, and disposal of discarded products and hazardous wastes. Waste management techniques need to be improved, as does the monitoring of international shipments of hazardous wastes and environmentally sound disposal of such wastes. To these ends, the Basel Convention, building off the strategic framework on implementation adopted in 2011—and in conjunction with regional waste treaties—can be an important mechanism for monitoring international transports and national disposal practices, setting sound management standards, raising public awareness and supporting training of public officials, and disseminating information about the latest disposal technologies.

Further, countries in 2013 concluded the first global treaty on a heavy metal, the Minamata Convention on Mercury, covering a large set of issues related to the mining, use, trade, release, and discharge of mercury.[46] Provisions address concerns ranging from coal-fired power plants and other major stationary sources to the use of mercury in artisanal and small-scale gold mining, industrial processes, and consumer goods. The Minamata Convention requires the environmentally sound management of mercury wastes consistent with the Basel Convention (which also covers mercury wastes). As global policy moves into the realm of heavy metals, it will be important to review treaty-related and other actions on mercury abatement in the coming years. Some countries and advocacy groups may also try to use the Minamata Convention as a means for expanding international controls on other heavy metals. This, however, will undoubtedly meet significant political resistance from industrialized and developing countries as well as from industry organizations seeking to avoid internationally mandated restrictions on the mining and use of metals.

Third, better connections among global, regional, national, and local efforts to build management capacities are required to improve environmental and human health protection in both Northern and Southern Hemispheres. In particular, many developing countries have difficulties ensuring the safe handling of hazardous chemicals and wastes in the face of both legal and illegal trade. The release of by-products also poses a major management challenge. Working with treaty secretariats, the Basel Convention and Stockholm Convention regional centers can enhance multilevel governance as they aid information generation and sharing, human training and public education, technology transfer, and the building of domestic management capabilities for emissions prevention and remediation of contaminated sites. The regional centers could also operate more ambitious monitoring mechanisms, which would increase opportunities to enhance compliance across major treaties (including through the use of treaty-specific mechanisms for reviewing and measuring implementation progress).

Many debates around better management are closely linked with critical disagreements over funding issues between developing and industrialized countries; such disagreements are common in North-South environmental politics. While developing countries are pushing for mandatory financing mechanisms to support domestic capacity building, the chemical treaties contain provisions only for voluntary contributions because of resistance from industrialized countries to compulsory financial contributions. Effective operation of the Basel Convention and Stockholm Convention regional centers also requires human, financial, and technical resources, and acquiring such resources from the Global Environment Facility, Northern donor countries, and developing countries in each region continues to be a problem. Nevertheless, multilevel management of hazardous chemicals and wastes in many regions of the world would benefit from stronger financial support of the regional centers.[47]

Better management of hazardous substances and wastes also requires raising public awareness. This involves expanding education about environmental and human health hazards among local populations exposed to chemical risks and providing better training for handlers and users of hazardous chemicals in selecting safe control strategies based on which specific substances are used and their intended purposes. Key issues for improving local handling include the appropriate application of pesticides for public health purposes (that is, in targeting vector-borne diseases), effective use of pesticides in agriculture, and the wearing of proper and workable protective gear such as overalls, boots, hats, gloves, and face masks. Increased awareness about integrated pest management approaches would also help reduce risks from pesticides. Similar education efforts are also needed for many workers who handle industrial chemicals and heavy metals.

Fourth, efforts to minimize the generation of hazardous substances and wastes should be intensified, and such efforts need to involve expanded collaboration between public- and private-sector actors. The most effective way to protect human health and the environment from risks posed by hazardous substances is, of course, to avoid producing and using these substances in the first place. However, global political efforts to date have focused on the management of known or suspected hazardous substances rather than on finding effective ways to reduce demand. The same is true for hazardous wastes: although the best long-term hazardous waste management policy is waste reduction, parties under the Basel Convention have focused largely on developing controls on the transboundary movement of wastes and technical guidelines for waste management. They have paid much less or little attention to treaty stipulations on waste minimization.

Rapidly increasing global levels of e-waste—and the development of associated policy and management efforts—further connect the management of dangerous substances with the management of hazardous wastes. The introduction of market-based incentives and different kinds of supportive governmental regulations making firms increasingly responsible for their products—including electronic and electrical goods—throughout the products' entire life cycles could play a significant role in stimulating more effective waste management and minimization efforts. E-waste is also attracting more attention under the Basel Convention, as countries struggle to deal with rapidly growing volumes of such waste. The Basel Convention parties have also engaged in partnerships with private-sector actors such as the Mobile Phone Partnership Initiative, through which multinational mobile phone manufacturers have committed to recover used mobile phones. This and other corporate responsibility efforts, however, remain limited in scope and are also entirely voluntary.

More Proactive and Precautionary Approaches Needed

Although many legal and political actions on hazardous chemicals have been taken since the 1960s, more fundamental changes are ultimately needed to effectively minimize environmental and human health risks posed by hazardous chemicals.[48] Typical regulatory frameworks have assumed that a particular chemical is harmless until scientifically proven dangerous. Furthermore, the burden of proof has traditionally been on regulators to show that a chemical is not safe, rather than on producers or sellers to produce data demonstrating that a substance is not likely to cause adverse environmental and human health effects. Regulators also have often been unable to restrict or ban a chemical until its harm has been extensively documented, as very little risk assessment data have been publicly available. Such a reactionary approach has resulted in much damage, as it has taken authorities a long time to regulate many hazardous substances (and they have not introduced any regulations at all for some).[49] It has also created few incentives for phasing out the use of hazardous substances and focusing on waste minimization.

The EU has taken on a leadership role in efforts to design a more precautionary approach to risk assessment and regulation (see Chapter 7). As defined in Principle 15 of the 1992 Rio Declaration on Environment and Development, this approach is based on the idea that "where there are threats of serious or irreversible damage, lack of full scientific certainty shall not be used as a reason for postponing cost-effective measures to prevent environmental degradation." In the early 1970s, Germany and Sweden were among the first countries to introduce the precautionary principle in domestic legislation and regulation of risk, and EU treaties since the 1990s state that precaution should guide all EU environmental policy making, including on hazardous substances.[50] The EU is also a strong supporter of the precautionary principle under the different chemical treaties, arguing that application of the principle is critical to the parties' ability to meet the 2020 goal on the safe production and use of chemicals (and the EU earlier had formulated a similar regional goal, as it also was a strong force behind the adoption of the global goal at the WSSD).

The EU in 2007 adopted the regulation on Registration, Evaluation, Authorisation and Restriction of Chemicals (REACH), which is to be fully implemented by 2018. REACH puts the burden on producers and sellers of chemicals to provide authorities with risk assessment data to show that there is no cause for concern.[51] Commercial handling of chemicals covered by REACH is prohibited unless it is proven that the chemicals are harmless, that they are adequately controlled, or that the societal benefits outweigh the costs. REACH specifically targets chemicals that are CMR (carcinogenetic, mutagenic, and toxic for reproduction), PBT (persistent, bioaccumulative, and toxic), or vPvB (very persistent and very bioaccumulative). The regulation also contains guidelines for substituting less harmful substances or nonchemical alternatives for hazardous chemicals. Early implementation has produced much risk assessment data (published online) and resulted in more restrictive classifications of some chemicals. There are also indications that firms have withdrawn particular CMR chemicals from the market and that substitution is starting to take place throughout commodity chains.[52]

The EU is also leading in banning the use of specific hazardous substances in electronic goods and in improving the management of e-wastes.[53] More than one thousand chemicals are routinely used in the manufacturing of common electronic products such as mobile phones and computers.[54] EU directives adopted in the early 2000s on the restriction of the use of certain hazardous substances in electrical and electronic equipment (RoHS) and on the management of waste electrical and electronic equipment (WEEE) are designed to phase out the use of several of the more hazardous substances, including mercury and brominated flame retardants, in most kinds of electronic goods and to increase the recycling of electronic products. European consumers are required to return many kinds of discarded electronic goods to the producers (rather than discard them in municipal waste streams); the producers are responsible for establishing management systems for the safe recycling, reprocessing, and disposal of the goods. In this respect, the continuing development of the WEEE and RoHS directives—together with the REACH regulation—will increase producer responsibility and take a more preventive approach to managing hazardous substances and e-wastes.

As the EU pushes for the adoption of similar policy ideas and approaches in international forums, REACH, RoHS, and WEEE are attracting the attention of politicians and policy makers around the globe. National governments of major producers and users of chemicals and electronic goods, such as China, Japan, and South Korea, are drawing from EU initiatives to adopt similar policies and regulations, in effect helping to raise global standards.[55] Several U.S. states, including California, are also copying European policy ideas (but U.S. federal laws remain unchanged, despite strong advocacy pressure for change). EU leadership in these policy developments is engendering changes in the private sector that are helping to drive changes worldwide. Firms that are adjusting to comply with new product and waste standards in the EU and elsewhere are changing their production processes and also the goods they sell in other markets. Similarly, advocacy organizations use policy innovations regarding chemicals and wastes in other jurisdictions to advocate for similar regulatory changes within their own jurisdictions.

Still a Long Way to Go

Improving global, regional, national, and local management of hazardous chemicals remains a critical sustainable development issue. This involves both dealing with existing chemicals and better screening the many hundreds of new chemicals that are introduced on commercial markets each year (in some cases replacing older ones).[56] Working together under SAICM and multiple treaties, states, IGOs, and NGOs over several decades have taken important implementation steps toward enhanced environmental and human health protection from hazardous chemicals. This has included the creation of expanded legal and organizational structures for risk assessment and policy making, leading to controls on a small set of hazardous chemicals (the same chemicals are often regulated under several treaties). The establishment of regional centers under the Basel and Stockholm Conventions to better connect global policy making with national management needs could be an important step forward, but it is too early to evaluate fully the effectiveness of the centers' activities.

Although there is a need to regulate additional substances as well as strengthen existing regulations, there have been—and continue to be—notable disagreements among states over the possible regulation of specific chemicals, expressed during meetings of chemical review committees and in heated debates at meetings of the Conferences of the Parties. Furthermore, many countries protective of their national sovereignty oppose the establishment of strong and independent treaty mechanisms for monitoring and enforcement, even though many studies show that such mechanisms are important to treaty implementation and effectiveness. While all countries struggle to reduce environmental and human health risks of hazardous substances, many developing countries face particular problems because of a lack of data and resources. Building management capacities and increasing awareness in developing countries are consequently important environmental justice and human security issues linked to international policy developments.[57]

In addition to better environmental and human health protection, more effective and precautionary regulations reduce the long-term financial costs of cleaning up contaminated areas. The U.S. Comprehensive Environmental Response, Compensation, and Liability Act (commonly known as the Superfund Act) was passed in 1980 to deal with contaminated sites like Love Canal. There are currently more than 1,300 unaddressed sites on the Superfund national priority list (and more will be added). In 2007, the Superfund Act listed 275 priority chemicals and heavy metals commonly found at contaminated sites. The U.S. Environmental Protection Agency estimated cleanup costs of $335 million to $681 million each year for the period 2010–2014; the actual costs were likely to be even higher.[58] Global cleanup costs are unknown but enormous—and they will keep on growing as long as societies continue to allow large-scale production and use of hazardous substances coupled with inadequate waste management capabilities.

Finally, societies need to rethink the ways in which chemicals are made even before they are used. Green chemistry—the utilization of principles that reduce or eliminate the use or generation of hazardous substances in the design, manufacture, and application of chemicals—is an effort to incorporate environment and health concerns into the development of chemicals.[59] To target the problem of hazardous chemicals at its source, green chemistry proponents stress the importance of synthesizing substances with little or no environmental toxicity. Further, as part of a broader effort to create a more sustainable use of materials, chemicals should be designed so that at the end of their functional lives they break down into innocuous degradation products.[60] Public- and private-sector acceptance of green chemistry is a critical step toward ensuring chemical safety. Both voluntary industry-led programs and mandates set by governments can play important roles in bringing about a world where hazardous chemicals pose less risk.

Notes

1. Henrik Selin, *Global Governance of Hazardous Chemicals: Challenges of Multilevel Management* (Cambridge: MIT Press, 2010).
2. Malcolm Shaw, "The United Nations Convention on Prohibitions or Restrictions on the Use of Certain Conventional Weapons, 1981," *Review of International Studies* 9, no. 1 (1983): 109–121.
3. European Chemical Industry Council (CEFIC), *Facts and Figures: The European Chemical Industry in a Worldwide Perspective* (Brussels: CEFIC, December 2006).
4. Jonathan Krueger and Henrik Selin, "Governance for Sound Chemicals Management: The Need for a More Comprehensive Global Strategy," *Global Governance* 8, no. 3 (2002): 323–342.
5. World Summit on Sustainable Development, *Plan of Implementation of the World Summit on Sustainable Development* (Johannesburg: WSSD, 2002), para. 22.
6. United Nations Conference on Sustainable Development, *The Future We Want* (Rio de Janeiro: United Nations Conference on Sustainable Development, 2012), para. 213.
7. United Nations Environment Programme, *Yearbook 2013: Emerging Issues in Our Global Environment* (Nairobi: UNEP, 2013).
8. John Kenly Smith, "DuPont: The Enlightened Organization," n.d., http://www.dupont.com/Heritage/en_US/Enlightened/Enlightened.html.
9. United Nations Environment Programme, *Global Chemicals Outlook: Towards Sound Management of Chemicals* (Nairobi: UNEP, 2013), 10.
10. Ibid., 11.
11. C. H. Srinivas Rao, V. Venkateswarlu, T. Surender, Michael Eddleston, and Nick A. Buckley, "Pesticide Poisoning in South India: Opportunities for Prevention and Improved Medical Treatment," *Tropical Medicine and International Health* 10, no. 6 (2005): 581–588.
12. Jean-François Tremblay, "China's Cancer Villages," *Chemical & Engineering News* 85, no. 44 (2007): 18–21.
13. Judith A. Layzer, *The Environmental Case: Translating Values into Policy*, 2nd ed. (Washington, DC: CQ Press, 2006), 54–80.
14. "The Electronic Wasteland," *60 Minutes*, November 10, 2008.
15. Kate O'Neill, *Waste Trading among Rich Nations: Building a New Theory of Environmental Regulation* (Cambridge: MIT Press, 2000).
16. Jennifer Clapp, *Toxic Exports: The Transfer of Hazardous Wastes from Rich to Poor Countries* (Ithaca, NY: Cornell University Press, 2001).
17. "Cote d'Ivoire: Dumping Ground," *Africa Research Bulletin: Economic, Financial and Technical Series* 43, no. 9 (2006): 17107–17108.
18. Lisa Bryant, "Ivory Coast Still Suffering from Toxic Spill," Voice of America, December 15, 2007.
19. Katharina Kummer, *International Management of Hazardous Wastes: The Basel Convention and Related Legal Rules* (Oxford: Clarendon Press, 1995); Berndt H. Brikell, "Negotiating the International Waste Trade: A Discourse Analysis" (Ph.D. diss., Örebro University, 2000), *Örebro Studies in Political Science* 2.
20. Jonathan Krueger, *International Trade and the Basel Convention* (London: Royal Institute for International Affairs, 1999), 32–35; Brikell, "Negotiating the International Waste Trade," 181–189.
21. The regional centers are located in Argentina, China, Egypt, El Salvador, Indonesia, Iran, Nigeria, Senegal, Slovak Republic, Russian Federation, Samoa, South Africa, Trinidad and Tobago, and Uruguay.
22. Henrik Selin, "Global Environmental Governance and Regional Centers," *Global Environmental Politics* 12, no. 3 (2012): 18–37.
23. "Summary of the Tenth Meeting of the Conference of the Parties to the Basel Convention: 17–21 October 2011," Earth Negotiations Bulletin, October 24, 2011, http://www.iisd.ca/download/pdf/enb2037e.pdf.

24. Basel Convention, *Waste without Frontiers: Global Trends in Generation and Transboundary Movements of Hazardous Wastes and Other Wastes* (Geneva: Secretariat of the Basel Convention, 2010).
25. Rao et al., "Pesticide Poisoning in South India."
26. Robert L. Paarlberg, "Managing Pesticide Use in Developing Countries," in *Institutions for the Earth: Sources of Effective International Environmental Protection*, ed. Peter M. Haas, Robert O. Keohane, and Marc A. Levy (Cambridge: MIT Press, 1993), 309–350; David G. Victor, "Learning by Doing in the Nonbinding International Regime to Manage Trade in Hazardous Chemicals and Pesticides," in *The Implementation and Effectiveness of International Environmental Commitments: Theory and Practice*, ed. David G. Victor, Kal Raustiala, and Eugene B. Skolnikoff (Cambridge: MIT Press, 1998), 221–281; Marc Pallemaerts, *Toxics and Transnational Law: International and European Regulation of Toxic Substances as Legal Symbolism* (Portland, OR: Hart, 2003).
27. Katharina Kummer, "Prior Informed Consent for Chemicals in International Trade: The 1998 Rotterdam Convention," *Review of European Community & International Environmental Law* 8, no. 3 (1999): 323–330.
28. The Rotterdam Convention explicitly excludes, among others, pharmaceuticals, narcotic drugs, food additives, radioactive materials, wastes, chemical weapons, and chemicals used in research (Article 3). Some of these are covered by other treaties, whereas others were left out because it is believed that they are not likely to be subject to any significant environmental releases.
29. Kummer, "Prior Informed Consent for Chemicals in International Trade"; Pia M. Kohler, "Science, PIC and POPs: Negotiating the Membership of Chemical Review Committees under the Stockholm and Rotterdam Conventions," *Review of European Community & International Environmental Law* 15, no. 3 (2006): 293–303.
30. Ted L. McDorman, "The Rotterdam Convention on the Prior Informed Consent Procedure for Certain Hazardous Chemicals and Pesticides in International Trade: Some Legal Notes," *Review of European Community & International Environmental Law* 13, no. 2 (2004): 187–200.
31. Arctic Monitoring and Assessment Programme, *Arctic Pollution 2009* (Oslo: AMAP, 2009).
32. Henrik Selin, "Regional POPs Policy: The UNECE/CLRTAP POPs Agreement," in *Northern Lights against POPs: Combatting Toxic Threats in the Arctic*, ed. David Leonard Downie and Terry Fenge (Montreal: McGill-Queen's University Press, 2003), 111–132.
33. Henrik Selin and Noelle Eckley Selin, "Indigenous Peoples in International Environmental Cooperation: Arctic Management of Hazardous Substances," *Review of European Community & International Environmental Law* 17, no. 1 (2008): 72–83; Charles Thrift, Ken Wilkening, Heather Myers, and Renata Raina, "The Influence of Science on Canada's Foreign Policy on Persistent Organic Pollutants (1985–2001)," *Environmental Science and Policy* 12, no. 7 (2009): 981–993.
34. Selin, "Regional POPs Policy."
35. Government of Tanzania, National Implementation Plan (NIP) for the Stockholm Convention on Persistent Organic Pollutants, 2005.
36. David Leonard Downie, "Global POPs Policy: The 2001 Stockholm Convention on Persistent Organic Pollutants," in Downie and Fenge, *Northern Lights against POPs*.
37. Sheila Watt-Cloutier, "The Inuit Journey towards a POPs-Free World," in Downie and Fenge, *Northern Lights against POPs;* Selin and Selin, "Indigenous Peoples in International Environmental Cooperation."
38. Annex D contains basic scientific criteria for persistence, bioaccumulation, potential for long-range transport, and adverse effects that a substance has to meet in order to qualify as a POP.
39. World Health Organization, "Malaria," January 2009, http://www.who.int/mediacentre/factsheets/fs094/en/index.html.
40. Joel Breman, Martin S. Alilio, and Anne Mills, "Conquering the Intolerable Burden of Malaria: What's New, What's Needed—A Summary," *American Journal of Tropical Medicine and Hygiene*, supplement, 71, no. 2 (2004): 1–15.

41. These countries were Botswana, China, Eritrea, Ethiopia, India, Madagascar, Marshall Islands, Mauritius, Morocco, Mozambique, Namibia, Senegal, South Africa, Swaziland, Uganda, Venezuela, Yemen, and Zambia.

42. The centers are located in Algeria, Brazil, China, Czech Republic, India, Iran, Kenya, Kuwait, Mexico, Panama, Russia, Senegal, Spain, South Africa, and Uruguay. The six centers that operate under both the Basel and the Stockholm Conventions are those in China, Iran, Russia, Senegal, South Africa, and Uruguay.

43. Selin, "Global Environmental Governance and Regional Centers."

44. The thirteen action plans are the Mediterranean Action Plan (adopted in 1975), Red Sea and Gulf of Aden Action Plan (adopted in 1976, revised in 1982), Kuwait Action Plan (adopted in 1978), West and Central African Action Plan (adopted in 1981), Caribbean Action Plan (adopted in 1981), East Asian Seas Action Plan (adopted in 1981), South-East Pacific Action Plan (adopted in 1981), South Pacific Action Plan (adopted in 1982), Eastern Africa Action Plan (adopted in 1985), Black Sea Strategic Action Plan (adopted in 1993), North-West Pacific Action Plan (adopted in 1994), South Asian Seas Action Plan (adopted in 1995), and North-East Pacific Action Plan (adopted in 2001).

45. Selin, *Global Governance of Hazardous Chemicals.*

46. Henrik Selin, "Global Environmental Law and Treaty-Making on Hazardous Substances: The Minamata Convention and Mercury Abatement," *Global Environmental Politics* 14, no. 1 (2014): 1–19.

47. Selin, "Global Environmental Governance and Regional Centers."

48. Selin, *Global Governance of Hazardous Chemicals.*

49. Poul Harremoës, David Gee, Malcolm MacGarvin, Andy Stirling, Jane Keys, Brian Wynne, and Sofia Guedes Vaz, eds., *The Precautionary Principle in the 20th Century: Late Lessons from Early Warnings* (London: Earthscan, 2002).

50. Noelle Eckley and Henrik Selin, "All Talk, Little Action: Precaution and European Chemicals Regulation," *Journal of European Public Policy* 11, no. 1 (2004): 78–105.

51. Henrik Selin, "Coalition Politics and Chemicals Management in a Regulatory Ambitious Europe," *Global Environmental Politics* 7, no. 3 (2007): 63–93.

52. Risk & Policy Analysts Limited, *Assessment of the Health and Environmental Benefits of REACH* (Loddon, Norfolk: Risk & Policy Analysts Limited, April 2012).

53. Henrik Selin and Stacy D. VanDeveer, "Raising Global Standards: Hazardous Substances and E-Waste Management in the European Union," *Environment* 48, no. 10 (2006): 6–18.

54. UNEP, *Global Chemicals Outlook,* 14.

55. Katja Biedenkopf, "Hazardous Substances in Electronics: The Effects of European Union Risk Regulation on China," *European Journal of Risk Regulation* 3, no. 4 (2012): 477–488; Henrik Selin, "Minervian Politics and International Chemicals Policy," in *Leadership in Global Institution Building: Minerva's Rule,* ed. Yves Tiberghien (New York: Palgrave Macmillan, 2013).

56. UNEP, *Global Chemicals Outlook,* 10.

57. David Naguib Pellow, *Resisting Global Toxics: Transnational Movements for Environmental Justice* (Cambridge: MIT Press, 2007).

58. U.S. Government Accountability Office, *Superfund: EPA's Estimated Costs to Remediate Existing Sites Exceed Current Funding Level, and More Sites Are Expected to Be Added to the National Priority List* (Washington, DC: Government Accountability Office, May 2010).

59. Paul T. Anastas and John C. Warner, *Green Chemistry: Theory and Practice* (Oxford: Oxford University Press, 1998).

60. Kenneth Geiser, *Materials Matter: Toward a Sustainable Materials Policy* (Cambridge: MIT Press, 2001).

12

Global Biodiversity Governance

Genetic Resources, Species, and Ecosystems

G. Kristin Rosendal

B iological diversity, or biodiversity, has been defined as the total variety of all ecosystems and species in the world, including the genetic variation within species. Biodiversity links all organisms on Earth in interdependent ecosystems in which all species have their roles. All life, including human life, depends on this diversity for food, medicines, building materials, water and air purification, climate stabilization, and pollination of food plants, as well as for its contribution to recreation and aesthetic experiences. These benefits are known collectively as the ecosystem services. The Earth's biodiversity has declined by more than a quarter in the past generation and continues to decline rapidly, primarily as the result of human activities such as landuse changes. The Millennium Ecosystem Assessment has estimated that the loss of biodiversity translates into annual loss of ecosystem services worth about US$250 billion.[1] This speaks of an economic interest as well as a moral responsibility for humankind to seek ways and means to halt the loss of biodiversity (see Box 12-1).

Box 12-1   Loss and Value of Biodiversity

Frog populations have been dramatically reduced since the 1950s. More than one-third of frog species are threatened with extinction. Habitat loss is a central cause of the decline, along with pollutants. Amphibians are excellent biological indicators of broader ecosystem health because of their position in food webs, their permeable skins, and their typically biphasic life cycles (aquatic as larvae and terrestrial as adults).

The secretions from the skins of many frog species have properties that combat bacteria, fungi, and parasites. Potential applications of these substances for medicine include nontoxic glue for human organ surgery. Some of the most exciting possibilities are drugs to treat cancer, especially one of the deadliest forms of skin cancer. It has recently been discovered that frog peptides can kill bacteria that are resistant to conventional antibiotics. These peptides eliminate bacteria by destroying their cell membranes, making the frog-derived antibiotics more permanently effective.

Hence, in addition to the frogs' interest in avoiding extinction, human well-being would benefit from keeping frogs alive.

This chapter looks further into what biodiversity is, why it matters, and how global political institutions are seeking to address and remedy the loss of biodiversity. It begins with discussion of the early international efforts to address specific losses, such as wetlands and migratory species. The bulk of the chapter describes the contents, negotiations, and ongoing politics and conflicts relating to the Convention on Biological Diversity (CBD). This convention was established in 1992 and has since been made more specific through its Nagoya Protocol on Access and Benefit Sharing (ABS) and the Cartagena Protocol on Biosafety.

Throughout, the chapter sheds light on actor interests and major differences that characterize the international biodiversity negotiations. Interactions between the CBD and related international regimes are also pointed out. A deep-seated moral conflict is posed by ABS issues regarding how to share the benefits from the use of genetic materials as well as how to share the burden of biodiversity conservation. This pertains in particular to the North-South axis, because the North generally has a higher capacity in biotechnology to produce, for example, pharmaceuticals and high-yielding food plants, while the South is predominantly richer in terrestrial species diversity, including the bulk of input factors for biotechnology.

The chapter then addresses some of the problematic aspects of developing international instruments and financial mechanisms to deal with environmental crosscutting issues pertaining to energy, climate change, and forest conservation. Together, deforestation and forest degradation are the source of about 20 percent of greenhouse gas emissions related to climate change.[2] Given that more than 80 percent of the world's terrestrial species diversity is found in forests, the design of forest policies is central to biodiversity conservation in general. These conflicts cut across the North-South axis in the sense that development and energy issues have strong proponents all over the world, while the conservation and environment movement is comparatively weak globally.

Finally, the chapter examines the Cartagena Protocol, which raises issues of risk and precaution in relation to international trade involving genetically modified organisms (GMOs). The advent of GMOs has raised conflicts not only between North and South, following the tracks of the major multinational seed corporations, but also along North-North and South-South axes, as the world's largest producers and exporters of genetically modified plants are the United States, Argentina, Brazil, Canada, and China.

Brief History of Global Biodiversity Governance: Loss, Value, and International Response

Biodiversity denotes the variation among all living organisms from all sources, including the diversity within species, between species, and of ecosystems (CBD, §2). The loss of biological diversity, which constitutes one of today's greatest environmental challenges, entered the international negotiation agenda for two main reasons: acknowledgment of loss and value. First, concerns about biodiversity stem largely from increased awareness and scientific agreement that the current rate of species extinction is one hundred to one thousand times faster than the natural average rate.[3] Similarly, a rapid loss of genetic diversity in domesticated plants is taking place, resulting in the risk of reduced food security.[4] Since 1900, about 50 percent of the world's wetlands have disappeared,[5] and some 30 percent of coral reefs have been seriously damaged.[6] Over the past two decades, 35 percent of mangroves have disappeared.[7] Of the estimated 7 million to 100 million species on Earth, only 1.9 million have been scientifically described.[8] Most of what is lost is scientifically unknown.

Farming, plantation forestry, road building, industrial developments, and deforestation represent the most serious threats to diversity through land-use change and degradation. The introduction of alien (that is, nonnative) species and various forms of pollution of air, soil, and water are other prominent factors. Industrial methods of capture (e.g., bottom trawling and other fishing methods that increase the likelihood of bycatch) and direct overexploitation can also cause biodiversity loss. Climate change is an increasing danger for biodiversity, and in agro-industry, high-yielding, monoculture plant varieties are driving out local varieties adapted to local conditions. The result is an escalation in the loss of diversity.

Biodiversity is the source of basic natural services.[9] Nature or ecosystems can be viewed as providers of services that humans need for their well-being. Ecosystem services can be divided into four categories: supply services, regulatory services, cultural services, and support services. Supply services are the production of food, fibers, medicines, clean water, and the like. Regulatory services comprise flood regulation, pollination, climate regulation, erosion protection, pollution mitigation, and so on. Cultural services are the possibilities afforded by nature for recreation, aesthetic pleasure, spiritual fulfillment, and preservation of culture. Support services operate within such fundamental natural processes as photosynthesis, decomposition of organic material, and recycling of essential nutrients.[10] The innovations of modern biotechnology have greatly enhanced the potential utility of some of the world's genetic resources, increasing the economic interests linked to these resources.[11] It has been estimated that U.S. biotechnology generates an annual revenue of US$13 billion,[12] and the estimated value of products derived from genetic resources worldwide is between US$500 billion and US$800 billion.[13] Other scholars argue that the economic value of biodiversity is rather low, because biodiversity remains plentiful relative to the demand for it.[14]

The concept of biodiversity dates back to the 1980s,[15] but efforts aimed at nature conservation and awareness of species loss have a much longer history. Human-induced species loss was first recognized with the extinction of the dodo (*Raphus cucullatus*), a large, flightless bird, in the mid-seventeenth century.[16] The United States pioneered in conservation work by establishing the world's first national park, Yellowstone, in 1872.

Formal international cooperation responding to biodiversity loss emerged from cooperation on natural resources management. Establishment of the International Whaling Commission in 1946 and the signing of the Treaty for the Preservation and Protection of Fur Seals in 1911 were among the first such efforts. The latter, responding to the hunting and subsequent loss of fur seals, is seen as one of the most successful international environmental treaties, with its transparent system of incentives and enforcement mechanisms.[17] A central characteristic of these early management regimes is that the users were cooperating on improving the management of resources in order to create integrative results—that is, win-win situations, where all participants might obtain a larger share as a result of cooperation.[18]

Several of the international environmental conventions negotiated during the 1970s focused on the protection of specific endangered species or habitats (see Table 12-1). The most important of these with a global scope include the Ramsar Convention on Wetlands of International Importance (1971), the Bonn Convention on the Conservation of Migratory Species of Wild Animals (CMS, 1979), the UNESCO Convention Concerning the Protection of the World Cultural and Natural Heritage (the World Heritage Convention, or WHC, 1972), the Convention on International Trade in Endangered Species of Wild Fauna and Flora (CITES, 1973), and the United Nations Food and Agriculture Organization (FAO) International Undertaking on Plant Genetic Resources for Food and Agriculture (1983). Many of these were motivated in part by the UN Conference on the Human Environment, held in Stockholm in 1972.[19] In addition, many regional agreements have been

Table 12-1 Major Results from International Cooperation on Biodiversity Loss

Convention/protocol/key parties	Objectives and achievements
1971 Ramsar Convention on Wetlands of International Importance *Entry into force in 1975; 163 parties, including Brazil, China, most of the European countries, India, Russia, United States*	**Objectives:** • Specific target: wetlands • To promote the conservation and wise use of all wetlands through local and national actions and international cooperation, as a contribution toward achieving sustainable development throughout the world **Achievements:** • 2,065 sites designated, almost 200 million hectares
1972 World Heritage Convention (WHC) *Entry into force in 1975; 190 parties, including Brazil, China, most of the European countries, India, Russia, United States*	**Objectives:** • To link together in a single document the concepts of nature conservation and the preservation of cultural properties • To recognize the ways in which people interact with nature and the fundamental need to preserve the balance between the two **Achievements:** • 962 properties designated in 157 states

Table 12-1 Continued

Convention/protocol/key parties	Objectives and achievements
1973 Convention on International Trade in Endangered Species of Wild Fauna and Flora (CITES) *Entry into force in 1975; 177 parties, including Brazil, China, most of the European countries, India, Russia, United States*	**Objectives:** • Specific target: trade in endangered species • To ensure, through international cooperation, that international trade in specimens of wild animals and plants does not threaten the survival in the wild of the species concerned • To protect endangered species from overexploitation by means of a system of import-export permits issued by a management authority under the advice of a scientific authority **Achievements:** • 5,000 species of animals and 29,000 species of plants protected against overexploitation (through domestic institutions licensing and monitoring international trade)
1979 Bonn Convention on the Conservation of Migratory Species of Wild Animals (CMS) *Entry into force in 1983; 118 parties, including European Union and most of the European countries, India*	**Objectives:** • Specific target: migratory species • To conserve terrestrial, aquatic, and avian migratory species throughout their range • To conserve those species of wild animals that migrate across or outside national boundaries by developing and implementing cooperative agreements, prohibiting the taking of endangered species, conserving habitat, and controlling other adverse factors **Achievements:** • Framework for 7 agreements, 19 memorandums of understanding, and 11 action plans between range states, protecting migratory species
1992 Convention on Biological Diversity (CBD) *Entry into force in 1993; 193 parties, including Brazil, China, European Union and most of the European countries, India, Russia*	**Objectives:** • Comprehensive scope: all biodiversity • To promote the conservation of biological diversity, the sustainable use of its components, and the fair and equitable sharing of the benefits that arise out of the utilization of genetic resources, including by appropriate access to genetic resources and by appropriate transfer of relevant technologies, taking into account all rights over those resources and to technologies, and by appropriate funding
2000 Cartagena Protocol on Biosafety, under the CBD *Entry into force in 2003; 89 parties, including Brazil, European Union and most of the European countries, India*	**Objectives:** • To contribute to ensuring an adequate level of protection in the field of the safe transfer, handling, and use of living modified organisms resulting from modern biotechnology that

(Continued)

Table 12-1 Continued

Convention/protocol/key parties	Objectives and achievements
	may have adverse effects on the conservation and sustainable use of biodiversity, taking into account the risk to human health and specifically focusing on transboundary movements
2001 International Treaty on Plant Genetic Resources for Food and Agriculture (ITPGRFA) *Entry into force in 2004; 125 parties, including Brazil, India, European Union and most of the European countries*	**Objectives:** • Specific target: limited list of seeds for certain food plants • To ensure the conservation and sustainable use of plant genetic resources for food and agriculture and the fair and equitable sharing of the benefits arising out of their use, in harmony with the CBD, for sustainable agriculture and food security **Achievements:** • Multilateral system puts 64 of the most important crops (accounting for 80 percent of the food derived from plants) into a global pool of genetic resources freely available to users in the treaty's ratifying nations for some uses
2010 Nagoya Protocol on Access to Genetic Resources and the Fair and Equitable Sharing of Benefits Arising from Their Utilization, under the CBD *Will enter into force 90 days after the date of deposit of the 50th instrument of ratification; 25 ratifications, including India, Indonesia, and South Africa (Brazil and European Union are signatories)*	**Objectives:** • To promote sharing of the benefits arising from the utilization of genetic resources in a fair and equitable way, including by appropriate access to genetic resources and by appropriate transfer of relevant technologies, taking into account all rights over those resources and to technologies, and by appropriate funding, thereby contributing to the conservation of biological diversity and the sustainable use of its components

Note: As this chapter devotes extensive discussion to the comprehensive achievements of the CBD and its two protocols, this table does not include those achievements.

established, such as the Bern Convention on the Conservation of European Wildlife and Natural Habitats (1979) and the African Convention on the Conservation of Nature and Natural Resources (1968).

The United Nations Environment Programme (UNEP) is central in the establishment and organization of the bulk of international biodiversity activities, providing secretariat functions for several of the biodiversity-related conventions and managing conservation programs and projects (concerning species and ecosystems from great apes to coral reefs). Through this work a number of memorandums of understanding and joint work programs have been established among these conventions, seeking to enhance synergy and coordination among them. The CBD, CITES, CMS, Ramsar, WHC, and International Treaty on Plant Genetic Resources for Food and Agriculture also meet in the Biodiversity Liaison Group to explore opportunities for cooperation and collaboration. In the end, however, the aim is to achieve actual implementation of the conventions' objectives in terms of suitable policies and legislation in member countries. As no world government is present to enforce compliance with environmental agreements, UNEP is faced with a formidable task.[20] This makes the incentive structures within the treaties all the more important.

A common trait in many of these cooperative responses is that the owners of the scarce resources are to some extent compensated for restricting their use of the resources. Since most of the diversity of terrestrial species is located in developing countries in the South and the strongest concern for biodiversity loss is voiced in the North, the North-South conflict runs through all of these conventions.[21] Another challenge to the more traditional conservation treaties is the increasing emphasis on the social dimension of conservation, along with issues of legitimacy and equity.[22]

As is apparent in Table 12-1, the CBD is far from the first international treaty to address species or habitat conservation. The treaties of the 1970s and 1980s were, however, seen to be incapable of stemming the loss of biodiversity worldwide. The table also shows that the United States has not ratified any global biodiversity-related treaty since the 1970s. Andorra, the Holy See, and the United States remain the only nonparties to the CBD. Almost all European countries, Brazil, and India are party to all the biodiversity-related conventions. The CBD is the first convention to address the conservation of all biological diversity worldwide and the first to include the objective of the sustainable utilization of biological resources. It also provides a link to questions concerning access to genetic resources and property rights over such resources. The CBD objectives are still subject to political strife, more than twenty years after its completion. The sections that follow discuss the background of these prolonged controversies, the convention text, and the ensuing negotiations on more specific protocols and other instruments to tackle the loss of biodiversity.

The Basic North-South Conflict of the CBD: Access, Ownership, and Equity

The growing realization that biodiversity loss has been accelerating was followed by a new awareness of the economic value of biodiversity—as new biotechnologies make it possible for humans to utilize the full potential of the world's genetic resources, the economic incentives to conserve biological diversity increase. Hence, the interest in genetic material arises both from environmental concerns and from the fact that technological developments have enabled financial gains from the exploitation of that material. Genetic resources are defined by the CBD as genetic material with actual or potential use or value for humanity.[23] Genetic resources are the hereditary material (genes) in all animals, plants, and microorganisms. Modern biotechnology, or gene technology, emerged at the same time as the wider privatization of plant breeding and medical research in the 1970s. Modern biotechnology also made it possible for scientists and corporations to fulfill the legal criteria for patenting inventions involving biological material.[24] This initiated a trend of companies taking out patents on naturally occurring organic material, as well as debate regarding whether such patents run counter to moral and equity concerns. The central aim of patent law, within the life sciences as in other fields, is to provide incentive for innovation. Because patents within biotechnology are arguably defined broadly, the costs of accessing this basic material are high.

Access to the genetic variation represented by seeds is a prerequisite of food security. The genetic material (later dubbed *genetic resources* by the CBD) constitutes the building blocks of all development and breeding of plants and animals. Genetic diversity or variability is necessary to sustain vitality in both wild and domesticated plants and animals, and also for the development of new and improved products. For instance, wild relatives of domestic crops provide genetic variability that can be crucial for overcoming disease outbreaks or for adjusting to climatic changes. Access to the great variety of seeds that have been collected in international gene banks is also essential for development and breeding.[25]

Another reason it is important to conserve biodiversity is that species may contain compounds that can generate valuable pharmaceuticals or other products at some future date. The products may be in the form of genes that are useful to biotechnology, chemicals that are useful as, for instance, enzymes, and structures and constructions from nature that can be used in industry. Microbial diversity may rival the diversity of all other species and is largely unknown. Furthermore, the diversity of marine species is largely unknown; the deep sea may rival tropical forests in species diversity.[26]

The essence of the North-South conflict that has permeated the biodiversity negotiations concerns property rights over genetic resources and who shall reap the benefits from the use of these resources. The international debate on biodiversity that began with the CBD negotiation process in 1989–1992 came to concern not only conservation but also, and equally, the distribution of benefits derived from the use of biological resources (see Chapter 9). The bulk of the world's terrestrial species biodiversity is found in the South, but it is the developed countries that possess the (bio)technology to do "bioprospecting" and reap the economic benefits from these resources on a large scale (see Box 12-2). Patenting is a very costly business, and the South holds only 1–2 percent of the world's biotechnology patents. The World Commission on Environment and Development recognized this potential conflict in 1987, when it urged, "Industrial nations seeking to reap some of the economic benefits of genetic resources should support the efforts of Third World nations to conserve species," stating further that "developing countries must be ensured an equitable share of the economic profit from the use of genes for commercial purposes."[27]

The years preceding the conclusion of the CBD saw fundamental changes in the internationally accepted approach to ownership over genetic resources.

During the late 1980s and early 1990s, property rights went from nonexclusiveness (based on the "common heritage of mankind" principle) for all genetic material to exclusive rights (intellectual property rights/patents) to parts of the genetic material. These changes took place within the UN Food and Agricultural Organization and the World Trade Organization (WTO). During what have been coined the seed wars in the FAO, it was seen as a victory for the developing world when the FAO Undertaking of 1983 acknowledged the traditional approach of the common heritage of mankind principle in stating that *all* categories of plant genetic resources should be subject to free exchange for conservation, plant breeding, and scientific research.[28] Responding to the emerging application of intellectual property rights within the life sciences, however, an agreed interpretation of the undertaking was signed in 1989. This signified an acceptance of the principle of payment for legally protected varieties, hence making intellectual property rights (such as patents and breeders' rights) compatible with the Undertaking. Developing countries reacted by abandoning the common heritage of

---

Box 12-2   Bioprospecting: An Example

The rosy periwinkle is a native plant of Madagascar. Two traits from the plant were patented and turned into a medicine for treating leukemia. The drug reportedly brought in an annual $200 million for Eli Lilly, the U.S. pharmaceutical company that patented it. None of these revenues were returned to the plant's country of origin. When the story of the rosy periwinkle appeared in the international magazine *New Scientist* in 1992, it greatly affected negotiations concerning the Convention on Biological Diversity (CBD).

Traditional knowledge has been found to have a significant impact on the success ratio of bioprospecting. The American company Shaman Pharmaceuticals revealed that of the plant samples it had found with promising chemical activity, 75 percent had possible applications that correlated with the plants' original ethnobotanical uses—that is, the plants' traditional medicinal uses as practiced by indigenous peoples with knowledge of the plants. Other stories of bioprospecting include the hunger-suppressing properties of hoodia, used by the San people in southern Africa, and the antibacterial properties of the neem tree in India.[a]

Against this background, the CBD parties tried to find a balance among conservation, access, and equitable sharing of benefits from the use of genetic resources.

It later became apparent that the rosy periwinkle is also native to Jamaica, illustrating one of the difficulties involved in pinpointing the countries of origin/providers of particular genetic resources (and thus who should be the recipients of eventual benefit sharing).

---

[a]Vandana Shiva, *Biopiracy: The Plunder of Nature and Knowledge* (Cambridge, MA: South End Press, 1997).

mankind strategy and started pointing to national sovereignty over natural resources in the CBD negotiations.[29] At the same time, the developed countries negotiated strengthening and harmonization of patent legislation in the WTO through the Agreement on Trade-Related Aspects of Intellectual Property Rights (TRIPS) (see also Chapter 14). This was accompanied by an expansion of the patent system into the area of biotechnology, which led to the problematic relationship between the CBD and TRIPS.[30]

In effect, the property rights regime immediately preceding the biodiversity negotiations gave rise to asymmetries between actor interests along two dimensions. First, the increased technological and economical ability to exploit genetic resources gave the North the major benefits from use, with few or no benefits accruing to the South. Second, the global distribution of terrestrial species diversity gave the South the major burden of conservation costs, with few costs falling directly on the North. A peculiar situation arose in that the (primary) users of the resources asked the (primary) owners to change their behavior. The users (North) demanded that the providers (South) carry the burden of biodiversity conservation as well as provide for stronger domestic patent legislation.[31]

This situation gave rise to the South's strategy of emphasizing benefit sharing from use of genetic resources in the CBD negotiations. From 1989 to 1992 this position gathered widespread acceptance and culminated with the threefold objectives of the CBD, of which equitable sharing of benefits arising from utilization of genetic resources remains the most controversial and difficult to put into actual practice.

The history of the CBD is in some parts the history of a breach between traditional preservation ideals and novel principles underpinning conservation, with a greater emphasis on sustainable use and an accepted place for human activities. The CBD was originally envisaged as a nature preservation convention, as advocated by major international nongovernmental organizations (such as the International Union for Conservation of Nature and the World Wide Fund for Nature), several European countries (France, the United Kingdom, and Germany), and the United States. It was precisely the loss of this goal that made the United States opt out and remain one of the three nonparties to the CBD. It could not contend with bringing domesticated genetic material and traditional knowledge into the CBD, as this made the case for reimbursing provider countries for their contributions to agriculture (plant genetic resources/seeds) and the pharmaceutical industry. The European Union later turned and supported the South in arguing for fair compensation (benefit sharing) for access to genetic resources as well as for shared responsibility for the conservation of biodiversity, acknowledging that the South harbors the bulk of the world's terrestrial species diversity.

The CBD: Negotiation Results

The Convention on Biological Diversity was signed in Rio de Janeiro in 1992, entered into force the following year, and has been ratified by 193 states. Against the backdrop of the rise in biotechnology and the equity issues that followed, the CBD establishes access to genetic resources and the sharing of benefits from their use. The three objectives of the CBD are the conservation of biodiversity, the sustainable use of biodiversity, and the fair and equitable sharing of benefits arising out of the utilization of genetic resources. Equitable sharing is regarded as a prerequisite of achieving the two first objectives. The CBD reconfirms national sovereignty rights to genetic resources and emphasizes equitable sharing of benefits from the use of those resources. Access to the resources is to be based on mutually agreed terms and subject to prior informed consent.

CBD parties also agree to develop national biodiversity strategies, to integrate biodiversity conservation in all policy levels and sectors, to identify and monitor biodiversity, to establish systems of protected areas, and to identify activities that are likely to have adverse effects on biodiversity. Moreover, the parties must adopt economically and socially sound measures to act as incentives for conservation and sustainable use, establish programs for scientific and technical education and training for identification and conservation, and provide support for such training in developing countries. The CBD is equipped with a monitoring mechanism in the form of national reporting and an incentive mechanism in the form of the Global Environment Facility (GEF), which assists developing countries.

The CBD constitutes an agreement that is open for further developments and specifications. For example, the parties committed themselves to consider the elaboration of a protocol to protect biodiversity from potential risks from genetically modified organisms. On this basis, the parties negotiated the Cartagena Protocol on Biosafety (2000). The protocol builds on a precautionary approach and establishes an advance informed agreement procedure to help countries make decisions about importing such organisms into their territory.

The CBD has initiated work on seven thematic work programs. These address marine and coastal biodiversity, agricultural biodiversity, forest biodiversity, island biodiversity, the biodiversity of inland waters, the biodiversity of dry and subhumid lands, and mountain biodiversity. In addition, work has been initiated on biosafety; access to genetic resources; traditional knowledge, innovations, and practices; intellectual property rights; indicators; taxonomy; public education and awareness; incentives; and alien species. The ecosystem approach is the primary framework for action under the convention. It is a strategy for integrated management of land, water, and living resources that aims to promote conservation and sustainable use in an equitable manner. The ecosystem approach recognizes that humans, with their cultural diversity, are an integral component of ecosystems. As the greatest threat to biodiversity lies in the replacement of undeveloped land by alternative systems of land use, the approach recommends management in an economic context in order to reduce market distortions that undervalue natural systems and provide perverse incentives and subsidies.

The CBD's first and second objectives concerning conservation and sustainable use were later translated, by the Conference of the Parties in 2002, into a goal of halting and reversing the loss of biodiversity by 2010. When that failed, the Conference of the Parties came up with a strategic plan in 2010 that included the following: cutting in half or, where feasible, bringing close to zero the rate of loss of natural habitats, including forests; establishing a conservation target of 17 percent of terrestrial and inland water areas and 10 percent of marine and coastal areas; and making special efforts to reduce pressures on coral reefs. The biodiversity-related treaties have also been bolstered by the establishment in 2010 of the Intergovernmental Panel on Biodiversity and Ecosystem Services (IPBES), which aims to provide them with greater scientific support. The IPBES aims to strengthen the scientific call for action and advance the message of biodiversity loss on political agendas.

The third objective of the CBD has been further negotiated in the Nagoya Protocol on ABS, which was adopted in October 2010. The Nagoya Protocol reestablishes the CBD objective of sharing fairly the benefits arising from the utilization of genetic resources between providers and users; it aims to remedy the lack of implementation of the ABS regime. A central remaining controversial item in the CBD and the Nagoya Protocol pertains to how users of genetic material could be made instrumental in supporting ABS. Efforts to link ABS to patent legislation include the call for disclosure of the origins of genetic material used in patent applications, but this has so far been largely unsuccessful.[32] Only eleven developed (user) countries have so far introduced such amendments in their patent legislation.[33] In response to biotechnology patents, the majority of developing countries have enacted ABS legislation in order to secure a share of the benefits from the use of their genetic resources. These efforts are unlikely to succeed without corresponding legislative changes in user countries in the North to ensure a fairer distribution with provider countries in the South. At the same time, developing countries have been criticized for adopting ABS laws because such laws allegedly obstruct access to genetic material, such as seeds and pathogens. The tendency of users to take out ever wider patents and of providers to increase access control has created a situation like a race between opponents with increasingly powerful means.[34]

A number of other international forums are also relevant for international ABS governance, including the World Trade Organization, the World Intellectual Property Organization (WIPO), and the UN Food and Agriculture Organization.[35] Drawing the lines between the CBD/ABS regime and its relationship to other international agreements remains a contested issue. The harmonization of domestic patent legislation through the WTO and WIPO negotiations will benefit the dominating multinational corporations in the life sciences.[36] Multinational corporations have strong economic means and interest in pursuing broader patent protection; at the same time, they can evade governmental control and regulations that would be necessary to enforce ABS behavior.[37]

Compared to the slow rate of progress on climate change, the Nagoya Protocol has been considered a major achievement of global environmental governance, but it has also been described as a "masterpiece in creative ambiguity."[38]

There is also confusion regarding whether the ABS regime should be based on a moral (equitable benefit sharing based on use) or an environmental (generally sharing of the burden of conservation) foundation. The link between equitable benefit sharing and nature conservation is inherent in the ideology underpinning the CBD, and the ABS may play a role in increasing the awareness of the benefits from ecosystem services provided by biodiversity.[39] Improved ABS governance however, depends on the parties' willingness to comply with the international obligations, especially in the user countries.

International Environmental Funding Mechanisms to Halt the Loss of Biodiversity

The CBD objectives of conservation and sustainable use are also far from being successfully achieved. The UN Millennium Ecosystem Assessment concluded that the ecosystems that have predominantly increased worldwide are agriculture and aquaculture.[40] While protected areas have had a small increase, most are "paper tigers," and only one-fourth of the assessed protected areas are subject to sound management.[41]

Why, in spite of the scientific consensus and political agreement about the gravity of the global problem of biodiversity loss, has so little progress been made toward solving the problem? This question is also raised in the central report from a study on the economics of ecosystems and biodiversity launched by the EU Commission and UNEP.[42] The value of biodiversity and the ecosystem services it provides has also been addressed in various proposals for payment for ecosystem services.

Involving the private sector to a greater extent, a system in which users pay for ecosystem services could potentially add substantially to earlier conservation efforts (such as the establishment of debt-for-nature swaps and biodiversity offsets as part of industrial projects with detrimental effects on ecosystems) and might even exceed conservation projects cofunded by the GEF. ABS could represent one such payment system, and a central debate is currently concerned with how payment for ecosystem services and ABS systems compares to other international environmental financial mechanisms, such as those emanating from the climate and energy arenas.[43]

In 2007, the United Nations Framework Convention on Climate Change decided to consider measures known as Reducing Emissions from Deforestation and forest Degradation (REDD) in developing countries.[44] The following year, the UN-REDD Programme was launched to support national REDD+ strategies. According to the UN-REDD Programme, the plus in REDD+ refers to the program's targeting of conservation and sustainable management of forests in addition to its original focus on carbon stocks and capture. This may imply that protecting biodiversity and securing local livelihoods can be an indirect result of REDD+ investments, although the program's predominant focus still seems to be on carbon capture and carbon stocks.[45] At the international level, the monitoring and evaluation of

UN-REDD Programme projects are currently geared toward carbon levels, and some observers have argued that it will be difficult for the program to implement REDD+ strategies without also developing criteria and principles to use in evaluating the conservation and livelihood aspects of the projects.[46] Great expectations are tied to the potential amount of international funding allocated by REDD+, but some uncertainty exists regarding whether the program will contribute to biodiversity conservation in a major way, as discussed below.

As both climate change and biodiversity are complex, controversial, and multiscale problems, payment for ecosystem services and REDD+ schemes face huge challenges. Thus it is important that these two mechanisms are developed so as to be mutually supportive. Biodiversity loss is even more difficult to deal with than climate change for several reasons. First, climate change has loomed large on the international political agenda for many years and has risen almost to the level of high politics, not the least because of linkages to key issues such as security, energy, and trade.[47] Although achievements in addressing climate change have been modest, the issue has received considerable attention, as well as strong interest from business and associated technology sectors concerning climate change–related projects. By comparison, loss of biodiversity has attracted less international political attention. This does not mean that loss of biodiversity is less of a problem than climate change—on the contrary, several experts have argued that the two are equally important.[48] Second, the problem of biodiversity loss may seem less attractive than the problem of climate change because it is less amenable to technological solutions.[49]

A third reason biodiversity loss receives less attention than climate change has to do with economic considerations. There is a direct connection between forest preservation and biodiversity conservation.[50] Nevertheless, in practice, implementation of the link between REDD+ and biodiversity protection is lacking. Ebeling and Yasué conclude that countries with high biodiversity index values (that is, high levels of endemism and threatened species) do not have high income potential from REDD+. Carbon markets value carbon, not biodiversity; since these markets are designed to focus on the lowest cost options for generating emissions reductions, they tend to favor areas with low land-use opportunity costs.[51] These may not coincide with areas of high conservation priorities (so-called global biodiversity hot spots), since such areas typically have high land-use conversion rates.[52]

The estimated annual need for funding to meet the biodiversity targets is US$78 billion, while annual conservation spending is less than one-tenth of that.[53] For its first ten to fifteen years, the GEF divided its allocations equally between the focal areas of climate change and biodiversity, with smaller shares going to international environmental problem solving relating to international waters and chemicals. The current division is 24 percent to biodiversity and 47 percent to climate change. This is mostly because of the much larger financial resources allocated to climate change–related projects through cofunding from the private sector. Compared with biodiversity projects,

projects related to climate change and energy are much more attractive to commercial interests, as energy production is likely to have a higher economic potential than conservation.[54] At the same time, biofuel production and the establishment of plantations for carbon fixing constitute potential threats to biodiversity, unless the areas chosen for this type of land-use change are properly assessed.

Cartagena Protocol on Biosafety: Precaution and Sound Science in Regulating GMOs

In environmental politics, the concept of precaution implies that lack of full scientific certainty shall not be used as a reason for postponing measures to prevent an environmental threat. The use of trade measures based on such precaution remains controversial. While the ABS-patent debate primarily engages North and South as a largely stable conflict line, the issue of genetically modified organisms crosses between North and North, and may increasingly also be found between South and South. However, while the predominant conflict between the United States and the European Union over biosafety constitutes a breach with the North-South axis, the dominant position of multinational seed corporations implies that this axis may persist to a greater extent than a mere look at countries' GMO production would indicate. In 2007, Monsanto's biotech seeds accounted for an estimated 87 percent of the total world area devoted to genetically engineered seeds.[55]

Today there is no broad international consensus as to what is at risk from genetically modified foods and crops. Considerable scientific uncertainty attends the effects of GMOs with regard to both the environment and human health. The uncertainties regarding environmental effects pertain to the risk of GMOs' affecting or displacing native species and to the risk of "genetic contamination" in the event of cross-breeding between GMOs and related native species. Alien invasive species are ranked among the four main threats to biodiversity, explaining why this issue has been addressed within the CBD. There are also uncertainties about the potential effects of genetically modified food products on human health, most seriously including the threat of creating greater resistance to antibiotics.[56] On the other hand, it is recognized that gene technology has the potential to benefit the environment: it could reduce the need for pesticides and reduce the pressure on scarce land resources while at the same time increasing agricultural yields. Gene technology also has great potential for developing new medicines and vaccines. The debate involves legal, technological, trade-related, and political considerations and has engaged actors at all levels, from the local to the global.

The Cartagena Protocol on Biosafety under the CBD was adopted in 2000 and entered into force in 2003. It concerns the right of a country to apply import restrictions and the precautionary principle in the governance of genetically modified organisms. Under the protocol, a country that wants to export living modified organisms (LMOs) for "intentional introduction into the environment" (such as seeds for planting) must seek advance informed agreement from the importing country before the first shipment takes place.[57] International law also includes the World Trade Organization's demand for "sound science" as opposed to precaution as a basis for restricting international trade in GMOs. Then there is international soft law, made up of the developing standardization on the level of protection together with the decisions of individual countries on risk assessments and risk management based on the precautionary principle.

Several of the world's emerging economies, such as Brazil and China, are joining the United States, Canada, Argentina, Australia, Chile, and Uruguay as major producers and exporters of genetically modified plants. The six latter were the most ardent opponents of the Cartagena Protocol, seeking to subordinate it to the WTO trade rules. They argue that genetically modified products are "substantially equivalent" to those produced by traditional agriculture. Meanwhile, most African countries have tried to avoid the pressure from the multinational seed companies to introduce GMOs in their fields and have even refused to accept GMOs as part of food aid.[58] Along with the EU and Norway, they were among the supporters of developing precaution as a central trait of the international Protocol on Biosafety and successfully argued that the protocol and WTO should be mutually supportive, rather than the protocol being subordinate to the WTO.

Within the sphere of the Organization for Economic Cooperation and Development, the EU has enacted some of the most restrictive rules in this field, matched only by Norway's GMO legislation. (While it is not part of the EU, Norway still receives all the same applications for import of genetically modified plants as do the countries of the EU.) The Norwegian Gene Technology Act represents the most ambitious step toward precaution yet taken. The act stipulates that processing and use of GMOs must be "ethical," have a "public utility," and contribute to "sustainable development." European biotechnology industries have pushed for deregulation in the hope of getting a level playing field with their counterparts in the United States; nevertheless, the EU's GMO regulations have become increasingly stringent.[59] The process has led to environmental risk assessment, mandatory postmarket monitoring of genetically modified products, obligatory provision of information to the public, and requirements for labeling and traceability at all stages of the marketing process. One of the remaining controversial issues in the EU's GMO regulations is how to regulate coexistence between genetically modified crops and traditional and, in particular, ecological, or sustainable, agriculture.

In the past decade, restrictive practice in the approval of import of genetically modified plants in the EU, known as the "de facto moratorium," prompted a reaction from the United States and Argentina. They argued that the EU used the "moratorium" for protectionism in violation of the WTO agreement.[60] The political controversy here revolves around the interpretation of the precautionary approach as elaborated within EU regulations and the Cartagena Protocol on Biosafety, as against the stronger emphasis on scientific evidence of risk (sound science) articulated in WTO agreements. Several

EU members argued that no approvals of new genetically engineered products should be issued unless companies could demonstrate that the products would have no adverse effects on the environment or on health.[61] It has been argued that the regulatory polarization between the European Union and the United States has helped to open up political space in key developing countries, as it displays two different policy models—one based on the precautionary principle and one regarding GMOs as "substantially equivalent" to organisms produced by traditional breeding methods.[62]

The dispute between "precaution" and "sound science" can be observed in the following practical examples. One of the health risks associated with GMO technology has to do with the widespread use of antibiotics as a means to multiply and isolate the material needed. Acknowledging the need for a precautionary approach, industries applying GMO technology increasingly strive to find technical solutions that avoid potential antibiotic resistance. However, some of these technical solutions use antibiotics that are no longer administered in Western and Northern societies but are still used in poorer countries in the South. This has constituted a basis for Norway's rejection of GMO applications; the argument is that if the GMOs cause antibiotic resistance for these particular types, this would be harmful to the poor countries where the genetically modified plants are actually grown.[63] The example points to a weak spot in the industry's dispute with the precautionary principle and questions the argumentation for the "sound science" approach: the GMO industry seems inclined to apply the precautionary principle in areas where it is forced to do so by tough regulations; in countries with weak regulations, however, not even scientific evidence of risk (the threat of antibiotic resistance) is sufficient to stop harmful use of antibiotics in GMO technology.

Another illustration concerns the relationship between science and politics and the legitimacy of the knowledge produced in this particular issue area. Globally, GMO risk assessments have been carried out largely by the multinational corporations that dominate the fields of agrobiotechnology and pharmaceuticals. Most studies on genetically modified plants and other products are based on information provided by research laboratories and/or released by the industry engaged in genetic engineering.[64] A broad study of the documentation that follows applications for import of genetically modified plants showed that it is generally poorly supplied with peer-reviewed reference,[65] raising the question of whether the scientific evidence produced by the GMO industry would itself pass for "sound science."

Highlights: Future Challenges for Biodiversity

There is no scientific dispute regarding the gravity of loss of biodiversity and its serious effects on human well-being worldwide, but the issue is still controversial in political terms. The fair sharing of benefits from the use of genetic resources and how GMOs should be regulated are examples of biodiversity issues that raise political controversy among states. These issues also serve to keep attention on the need for concerted action to resolve global environmental problems.

In spite of multiple efforts, loss of biodiversity has been and still is a difficult problem to solve collectively or internationally. The score across nations is low with regard to implementation effectiveness. Protected areas have increased worldwide, but the majority are still paper tigers. Loss of biological diversity continues to undermine many of the ecosystem services on which humans depend, compromising human well-being in many areas. The reasons for poor implementation are as complex as the drivers of biodiversity loss.

First, despite successful negotiation of two protocols, the CBD remains in many ways a framework convention. It lacks the specified, concrete implementation commitments that are necessary to reverse the negative trend in biodiversity loss. Second, there is not enough political or legal force behind the resolutions passed by the conferences of the parties. It remains to be seen whether the IPBES can affect this situation in a positive direction with a view to implementation. Many observers hope that this newly established scientific panel will be able to play a role similar to that of the Intergovernmental Panel on Climate Change, advancing the issue of biodiversity loss on international political agendas.

Third, there is a technological side to why biodiversity loss is very hard to tackle, even harder than issues related to climate change. Biodiversity politics has no technological engine pulling it forward, unlike policy areas where pollution is involved. Simple technological solutions aimed at easing the constant pressure on land use are harder to envisage compared to the development of substitutes for polluting chemicals. High-rise buildings have been proposed as one way to free land for increased food production, and another exception to this "rule" is the potential of gene technology to intensify food production, itself a controversial issue.

Most important, the conflict level remains high. Basically, the problem of biodiversity loss is delinked from the North-South axis in the sense that short-term development interests tend to trump long-term conservation interests. The GMO issue also engages countries across the North-South divide, but generally the biodiversity issue appears mostly as a North-South conflict through the ABS-patent controversy. The increasingly broad protection rights granted by patents leave developing countries with few incentives to conserve the rich diversity of species in their territories. The principles of access, equitable sharing, incentives to promote innovation, and conservation are difficult—but important—to harmonize in practical politics. These principles have all been recognized by the international community in various forums, but implementation efforts are not necessarily pulling in the same direction. Better understanding of the conflict and synergy between international commitments and processes of cooperation is important if the world's nations are to achieve a working balance between these objectives and principles.

The core and contentious issues of the Nagoya Protocol include its scope in terms of defining genetic resources (affecting the extent to which the ABS system may be able to capture the future potential value of genetic material), how the compliance of users of genetic resources should be secured (e.g., should users disclose the origins of genetic materials in patent applications or not?), and the uneasy relationship between the Nagoya Protocol and other relevant international agreements such as that of the WTO. The problem of instigating compliance in user countries is enhanced by the increasing dominance of multinational corporations in the life sciences sectors, including agriculture, aquaculture, and pharmacy. Still, the norms and principles of the ABS regime are spreading to a wide set of institutions and arenas, such as the WTO and FAO.[66]

We have seen how conservation and biodiversity policies have moved from taking a primarily regulatory approach to including stronger elements of market-based instruments, as illustrated by ABS and various payments for ecosystem services schemes, as well as the link to climate change and REDD+. The rationale for this is that as long as the values of biodiversity and ecosystem services are not integrated into the general economy, consideration for biodiversity will rarely be weighty enough against more immediate development interests. On the other hand, some fear that putting price tags on biodiversity and its ecosystem services will not provide better or quicker solutions to the problem of biodiversity loss. Prioritizing among the various ecosystem services may involve not only economic choices but also choices of societal values. Would price tags make it easier to judge the recreational value of a watershed, or the watershed's value as a habitat for threatened species, against the hydropower that the region could produce? How does one compare the monetary value of carbon captured by (monoculture) plantations today against the value of leaving species-rich, pristine forests to future generations? As the idea of ecosystem services spreads into political debates about biodiversity, there will be an increasing need for discussion of the noncommercial values of the services provided and the extent to which monetary valuation can improve efforts to stem the loss of biodiversity.

Notes

1. Millennium Ecosystem Assessment, *Ecosystems and Human Well-Being: Biodiversity Synthesis* (Washington, DC: World Resources Institute, 2005). The Millennium Ecosystem Assessment is a United Nations–headed group of 1,360 scientists that includes representatives from every continent.
2. Nicholas Stern, *The Economics of Climate Change* (London: H.M. Treasury, 2007).
3. E. O. Wilson, ed., *Biodiversity* (Washington, DC: National Academy Press, 1988); V. H. Heywood, ed., *Global Biodiversity Assessment* (Cambridge: Cambridge University Press, 1995), 232.
4. United Nations Food and Agriculture Organization, *The State of the World's Plant Genetic Resources for Food and Agriculture* (Rome: FAO, 1998).
5. Michael Moser, Crawford Prentice, and Scott Frazier, "A Global Overview of Wetland Loss and Degradation," Ramsar Convention on Wetlands, March 1996, http://www.ramsar.org/cda/en/ramsar-news-archives-2002-a-global-overview-of/main/ramsar/1-26-45-87%5E16905_4000_0__.
6. Clive Wilkinson, *Status of Coral Reefs of the World: 2004* (Townsville, Queensland: Australian Institute of Marine Science, 2004).
7. Millennium Ecosystem Assessment, *Ecosystems and Human Well-Being*.
8. Wilson, *Biodiversity*.
9. Pim Martens, Jan Rotmans, and Dolf de Groot, "Biodiversity: Luxury or Necessity?," *Global Environmental Change* 13 (2003): 75–81.

10. Millennium Ecosystem Assessment, *Ecosystems and Human Well-Being*.
11. "Modern biotechnology" denotes biotechnology that involves direct dependence on human intervention, such as recombinant DNA techniques and genomics. Biotechnology is a broader concept, including activities such as baking bread and brewing beer, where the interaction of different organisms (such as that between yeast and wheat) combine to create a new product.
12. Jasemine Chambers, "Patent Eligibility of Biotechnological Inventions in the United States, Europe, and Japan: How Much Patent Policy Is Public Policy?," *George Washington International Law Review* 34, no. 1 (2002): 237–239.
13. Kerry ten Kate and Sarah A. Laird, *The Commercial Use of Biodiversity: Access to Genetic Resources and Benefit-Sharing* (London: Earthscan, 1999).
14. David R. Simpson, Roger A. Sedjo, and John W. Reid, "Valuing Biodiversity: An Application to Genetic Prospecting," *Journal of Political Economy* 104, no. 1 (1996): 163–185.
15. Wilson, *Biodiversity*.
16. David Quammen, *The Song of the Dodo: Island Biogeography in an Age of Extinction* (London: Random House, 1996).
17. Scott Barrett, *Environment and Statecraft: The Strategy of Environmental Treaty Making* (Oxford: Oxford University Press, 2003).
18. Arild Underdal, *The Politics of International Fisheries Management: The Case of the Northeast Atlantic* (Oslo: Universitetsforlaget, 1980).
19. John Lanchbery, "The Convention on International Trade in Endangered Species of Wild Fauna and Flora (CITES): Responding to Calls for Action from Other Nature Conservation Regimes," in *Institutional Interaction in Global Environmental Governance: Synergy and Conflict among International and EU Policies*, ed. Sebastian Oberthür and Thomas Gehring (Cambridge: MIT Press, 2006).
20. Steinar Andresen and Kristin Rosendal, "The Role of the United Nations Environment Programme in the Coordination of Multilateral Environmental Agreements," in *International Organizations in Global Environmental Governance*, ed. Frank Biermann, Bernd Siebenhüner, and Anna Schreyögg (Abingdon, UK: Routledge, 2009).
21. The general North-South dichotomy has been persistent in the CBD negotiations and is useful in shedding light on the asymmetries that affect parties' behavior. Still, the distinction is problematic, as there are certainly (growing) differences within these categories, both in regard to biodiversity endemism and levels and in regard to technology levels.
22. Jon Hutton and Barnabas Dickson, eds., *Endangered Species, Threatened Convention: The Past, Present and Future of CITES* (London: Earthscan, 2000).
23. Convention on Biological Diversity, Rio de Janeiro, June 5, 1992.
24. Stephen Crespi, *Patents: A Basic Guide to Patenting in Biotechnology* (Cambridge: Cambridge University Press, 1988).
25. Jack Kloppenburg Jr. and Daniel Lee Kleinman, "The Plant Germplasm Controversy," *BioScience* 37, no. 3 (1987): 190–198; Jack Ralph Kloppenburg Jr., *First the Seed: The Political Economy of Plant Biotechnology, 1492–2000*, 2nd ed. (Madison: University of Wisconsin Press, 2004).
26. Bruce Aylward, "The Role of Plant Screening and Plant Supply in Biodiversity Conservation, Drug Development and Health Care," in *Intellectual Property Rights and Biodiversity Conservation: An Interdisciplinary Analysis of the Values of Medicinal Plants*, ed. Timothy M. Swanson (Cambridge: Cambridge University Press, 1995), 105.
27. World Commission on Environment and Development, *Our Common Future* (Oxford: Oxford University Press, 1987), 156–157, 160.
28. G. Kristin Rosendal, *The Convention on Biological Diversity and Developing Countries* (Dordrecht, Netherlands: Kluwer Academic Publishers, 2000); Regine Andersen, *Governing Agrobiodiversity: Plant Genetics and Developing Countries* (Aldershot, UK: Ashgate, 2008).
29. Rosendal, *The Convention on Biological Diversity and Developing Countries*.

30. G. Kristin Rosendal, "The Convention on Biological Diversity: Tensions with the WTO TRIPS Agreement over Access to Genetic Resources and the Sharing of Benefits," in Oberthür and Gehring, *Institutional Interaction in Global Environmental Governance*, 79–102.
31. Rosendal, *The Convention on Biological Diversity and Developing Countries*.
32. Morten W. Tvedt, "Elements for Legislation in User Countries to Meet the Fair and Equitable Benefit-Sharing Commitment," *Journal of World Intellectual Property* 9, no. 2 (2006): 189–212.
33. Convention on Biological Diversity, "List of Countries and Regions with Measures," accessed October 22, 2013, http://www.cbd.int/abs/measures/groups.shtml.
34. G. Kristin Rosendal, "Regulating the Use of Genetic Resources: Between International Authorities," *European Environment* 16, no. 5 (2006): 265–277.
35. Kal Raustiala and David G. Victor, "The Regime Complex for Plant Genetic Resources," *International Organization* 58 (2004): 277–309.
36. Robin Pistorius and Jeroen van Wijk, *The Exploitation of Plant Genetic Information: Political Strategies in Crop Development* (New York: CABI, 1999).
37. Niels Louwaars, Hans Dons, Geertrui van Overwalle, Hans Raven, Anthony Arundel, Derek Eaton, and Annemiek Nelis, *Breeding Business: The Future of Plant Breeding in the Light of Developments in Patent Rights and Plant Breeders' Rights*, CGN Report 2009-14 (Wageningen, Netherlands: Centre for Genetic Resources, 2009).
38. "Summary of the Tenth Conference of the Parties to the Convention on Biological Diversity: 18–29 October 2010," Earth Negotiations Bulletin, November 1, 2010, 26, http://www.iisd.ca/download/pdf/enb09544e.pdf.
39. Sebastian Oberthür and G. Kristin Rosendal, eds., *Global Governance of Genetic Resources: Access and Benefit Sharing after the Nagoya Protocol* (Abingdon, UK: Routledge, 2013).
40. Millennium Ecosystem Assessment, *Ecosystems and Human Well-Being*.
41. Fiona Leverington, Katia Lemos Costa, José Courrau, Helena Pavese, Christoph Nolte, Melitta Marr, Lauren Coad, Neil Burgess, Bastian Bomhard, and Marc Hockings, *Management Effectiveness Evaluation in Protected Areas: A Global Study*, 2nd ed. (Brisbane: University of Queensland, 2010).
42. European Communities, *The Economics of Ecosystems and Biodiversity* (Wesseling, Germany: Welzel and Hardt, 2008).
43. Fariborz Zelli, "Regime Conflicts in Global Environmental Governance: A Framework for Analysis," Global Governance Working Paper 36, Global Governance Project, 2008, http://www.glogov.org/images/doc/WP36.pdf; Arild Underdal, "Complexity and Challenges of Long-Term Environmental Governance," *Global Environmental Change* 20 (2010): 386–393.
44. United Nations Framework Convention on Climate Change, Decision 2/CP.13, 2007.
45. Michelle Kovacevic, "Durban Talks Both Good and Bad for REDD+, Says Expert," Forests News, December 14, 2011, http://blog.cifor.org/6507/durban-talks-both-good-and-bad-for-redd-says-expert; Toby A. Gardner, Neil D. Burgess, Naikoa Aguilar-Amuchastegui, Jos Barlow, Erika Berenguer, Tom Clements, Finn Danielsen, Joice Ferreira, Wendy Foden, Valerie Kapos, Saiful M. Khan, Alexander C. Leesm, Luke Parry, Rosa Maria Roman-Cuesta, Christine B. Schmitt, Niels Strange, Ida Theilade, and Ima C. G. Vieira, "A Framework for Integrating Biodiversity Concerns into National REDD+ Programmes," *Biological Conservation* 154 (2012): 61–71; Constance L. McDermott, Lauren Coad, Ariella Helfgott, and Heike Schroeder, "Operationalizing Social Safeguards in REDD+: Actors, Interests and Ideas," *Environmental Science and Policy* 21 (2012): 63–72; David O'Connor, "Governing the Global Commons: Linking Carbon Sequestration and Biodiversity Conservation in Tropical Forests," *Global Environmental Change* 18 (2008): 368–374.
46. G. Kristin Rosendal and Steinar Andresen, "Institutional Design for Improved Forest Governance through REDD: Lessons from the Global Environment Facility," *Ecological Economics* 70, no. 11 (2011): 1908–1915.

47. Sebastian Oberthür and Claire Roche Kelly, "EU Leadership in International Climate Policy: Achievements and Challenges," *International Spectator* 43, no. 3 (2008): 35–50.
48. European Communities, *The Economics of Ecosystems and Biodiversity*; Secretariat of the Convention on Biological Diversity, *Global Biodiversity Outlook 3* (Montreal: Secretariat of the CBD, 2010).
49. Martin Jänicke and Stefan Lindemann, "Governing Environmental Innovations," *Environmental Politics* 19, no. 1 (2010): 127–141.
50. William F. Laurance, "A New Initiative to Use Carbon Trading for Tropical Forest Conservation," *Biotropica* 39, no. 1 (2007): 20–24.
51. Johannes Ebeling and Maï Yasué, "Generating Carbon Finance through Avoided Deforestation and Its Potential to Create Climatic, Conservation and Human Development Benefits," *Philosophical Transactions of the Royal Society B* 363 (2008): 1917–1924.
52. Norman Myers, Russell A. Mittermeier, Cristina G. Mittermeier, Gustavo A. B. da Fonseca, and Jennifer Kent, "Biodiversity Hotspots for Conservation Priorities," *Nature* 403 (February 24, 2000): 853–858.
53. Donal P. McCarthy, Paul F. Donald, Jörn P. W. Scharlemann, Graeme M. Buchanan, Andrew Balmford, Jonathan M. H. Green, et al., "Financial Costs of Meeting Global Biodiversity Conservation Targets: Current Spending and Unmet Needs," *Science* 338, no. 6109 (November 16, 2012): 946–949.
54. Rosendal and Andresen, "Institutional Design for Improved Forest Governance through REDD."
55. ETC Group, "Who Owns Nature? The Seed Industry" (extracts), GMWatch, accessed October 11, 2013, http://www.gmwatch.org/gm-firms/10558-the-worlds-top-ten-seed-companies-who-owns-nature.
56. Anne Ingeborg Myhr and Terje Traavik, "The Precautionary Principle: Scientific Uncertainty and Omitted Research in the Context of GMO Use and Release," *Journal of Agricultural and Environmental Ethics* 15, no. 1 (2002): 73–86.
57. The Cartagena Protocol uses the term *living modified organisms*; the term *genetically modified organisms*, or *GMOs*, is more widely used.
58. G. Kristin Rosendal, "Governing GMOs in the EU: A Deviant Case of Environmental Policy-Making?," *Global Environmental Politics* 5, no. 1 (2005): 82–104.
59. Thomas Bernauer, *Genes, Trade, and Regulation: The Seeds of Conflict in Food Biotechnology* (Princeton, NJ: Princeton University Press, 2003); Rosendal, "Governing GMOs in the EU."
60. Sarah Lieberman and Tim Gray, "The So-Called Moratorium on the Licensing of New Genetically Modified (GM) Products by the European Union 1998–2004: A Study in Ambiguity," *Environmental Politics* 15, no. 4 (2006): 592–609.
61. Bernauer, *Genes, Trade, and Regulation*.
62. Robert Falkner and Aarti Gupta, "The Limits of Regulatory Convergence: Globalization and GMO Politics in the South," *International Environmental Agreements* 9 (2009): 113–133.
63. G. Kristin Rosendal, "Interpreting Sustainable Development and Societal Utility in Norwegian GMO Assessments," *European Environment* 18, no. 4 (2008): 243–256.
64. George Gaskell, Nick Allum, and Sally Stares, *Europeans and Biotechnology in 2002: Eurobarometer 58.0* (report to the EC Directorate General for Research from the project Life Sciences in European Society), 2nd ed. (Brussels: EC Directorate, 2003).
65. Rosendal, "Interpreting Sustainable Development and Societal Utility in Norwegian GMO Assessments."
66. Sebastian Oberthür and Justyna Poarowska, "The Impact of the Nagoya Protocol on the Evolving Institutional Complex of ABS Governance," in Oberthür and Rosendal, *Global Governance of Genetic Resources*.

13

Democracy and the Global Nuclear Renaissance

From the Czech Republic to Fukushima

Regina S. Axelrod

Nuclear energy has been providing electricity for more than fifty years and is often perceived as a technological breakthrough without negative environmental impacts. It was promoted in the capitalist world as cheap energy, and nuclear power plants were built in communist countries as monuments to the socialist industrial state. Today, the cost-effectiveness of nuclear energy has been challenged, and there is opposition to its continued use and development for environmental and security-related reasons.

This chapter explores the completion of the 1,000-megawatt Temelin nuclear power plant in the Czech Republic (two additional units have been proposed). It examines the extent to which sustainable development policy is addressed in a country undergoing political transformation and also offers insights into the problems associated with building democratic institutions. In 1989 the Iron Curtain fell in Central and Eastern Europe (CEE), but the transition to democracy and a market economy in this region has been more complex than most Westerners anticipated. The chapter begins by examining energy policy and nuclear policy in the CEE region, where the European Union plays an increasingly important role. The chapter next addresses sustainable energy and environmental policy in the Czech Republic, utilizing the Temelin controversy as a focus for analysis. The Czech experience is then compared to that of the United States. The 2011 disaster at Japan's Fukushima nuclear facility is also examined here because of its influence on global nuclear policy and demands for greater safety. The chapter concludes with a brief assessment of the prospects for a nuclear renaissance.

The Czech Case

The Czech Republic has been a proponent of nuclear energy expansion in the EU, since it became a member in 2004, as a means to reduce dependence on fossil fuels. This argument has been adopted by numerous states and other actors, and it is in this changed global context of potential nuclear energy renewal that this analysis takes place. States seeking to expand or develop nuclear energy—including India, China, Belarus, Vietnam, Egypt, Jordan, Turkey, Qatar, Saudi Arabia, Venezuela, Chile, and Morocco—can look to the

Czech Republic example. The argument that nuclear energy could help solve the problem of climate change/global warming has been taken up by nuclear industries. Ironically, nuclear energy expansion was promoted in the 1980s and 1990s with no reference to climate change. In fact, former Czech president Vaclav Klaus, prime minister in the early 1990s, was a proponent of the view that global warming has been exaggerated by left-thinking environmentalists who want to destroy the free market.[1] In the Czech case nuclear power has been promoted because of the revenue from electricity exports it provides the government and the opportunities it creates for construction and industrial companies and developers. Various interests also want nuclear energy to be the key to Czech energy independence from Russia, seeing it as an opportunity for the Czech Republic to be a technology leader in Europe. Czech governmental leaders have also promised to retire the polluting coal-burning power plants, but the reality has been quite different.

The Czech Republic was in the first group of CEE candidates to join both the European Union and the North Atlantic Treaty Organization. The Czech Republic harmonized its environmental and energy legislation with the EU's laws as a prerequisite of its 2004 membership. The country's ability to develop the necessary democratic attributes familiar to Western Europe was also a prerequisite. The adoption of the *acquis communautaire*—the body of European Community law—presented financial difficulties for the CEE nations because of the huge monetary investment they needed to make to meet EU standards. Austria, a nonnuclear EU state, has consistently and aggressively opposed construction of the Temelin nuclear power plant. As Temelin is approximately fifty miles from their border, the Austrians made this proximity an issue in the Czech accession proceedings. Other states, such as Germany, which closed its Soviet-made nuclear plants in the eastern part of the country, also have a stake in the future of Temelin. The Czech experience with nuclear power is a test case affecting the viability and future marketability of nuclear power in CEE. The international nuclear community also has a stake in the outcome, as there is intense competition among American and European nuclear engineering companies for contracts to upgrade, build, and complete new nuclear plants in the region. As a condition of EU accession, CEE states pledged to decommission their Soviet-designed nuclear plants or upgrade the more modern ones, using loans from the European Atomic Energy Authority (Euratom) and aid from the PHARE and TACIS programs—programs that assisted states in the transition to market economies and democratic political systems. Without the prospect of joining the EU, many countries would never have taken these actions.

Energy Policy in Central and Eastern Europe

Building large nuclear power plants to produce electricity was consistent with the former Soviet Union's communist vision of progress. Throughout the CEE region, energy-intensive industries were supported by cheap energy: the higher the energy intensity, the greater the inefficiency in the use of energy and the higher the energy demand for a given level of output. The former Soviet Union controlled the natural gas and oil pipelines and could close them without notice. This power was a type of blackmail, and the CEE regimes took the threat seriously. This situation continues today as the Czech Republic fears that its supply of Russian oil and gas may be cut if the country acts against Russia's interests in other areas.

The soft brown coal with high sulfur content used in many CEE countries is a source of severe air pollution. Crude mining practices, large plant size, and absence of desulfurization equipment led to a catastrophic situation in northern Bohemia in the Czech Republic—this "Black Triangle" extends to the German and Polish borders. Nuclear power advocates saw opportunities. The Soviet Union, with compliance or agreement from the CEE states, planned dozens of nuclear power plants for the region. Skoda, a Czech company, was named the prime contractor. The Temelin project would give the Czech electrical utility Ceske energeticke zavody (CEZ) and Skoda a future in the modernization of these partially completed plants throughout the region.

The former Soviet Union's monopoly over nuclear reactors in the CEE region left enormous problems. The reactors built by the Soviets are considered poorly engineered, and they lack many of the safety features mandatory in the West. To restore public confidence in the safety and reliability of nuclear power, CEE states sought foreign assistance to improve safety through the upgrading or closing of these plants, located in Bulgaria, the Czech Republic, Hungary, Lithuania, Slovakia, and Ukraine. One of the major problems the nuclear industry encountered was the difficulty of grafting Western technology onto Soviet-designed reactors. Temelin was to be the first such redesign project on a Soviet VVER 1,000-megawatt plant. Skeptics were concerned that Russian reactor containment designs could not be properly retrofitted. A 1993 study of the VVER 440 and 230 reactor models by the International Atomic Energy Agency (IAEA) concluded that the containment structure was unsafe.[2]

Sustainable Development and the Environment in the CEE

The most widely used definition of sustainable development is "development that meets the needs of the present without compromising the ability of future generations to meet their own needs."[3] It was popularized by the 1987 UN Brundtland Commission report, *Our Common Future* (see Chapter 1).

From Communism to a Free Market

In the CEE region, the transition from a centralized economy run by an economic and technocratic elite to one based on free market principles and pluralism has been swift and often painful. The demise of central planning left a vacuum in policy direction. Decisions about energy production, supply, and consumption were made in the absence of environmental criteria. As Jehlicka and Kara have observed, "The application of Marxist ideology in practice led to environmental devastation in all Communist countries but its low point was probably reached in the Czech Republic."[4] Under communism, environmentalists were labeled right-wing, accused of trying to destroy socialist dreams by imposing costly demands on the government. After 1992 they were branded as left-wing extremists trying to ruin the free market economy by advocating a role for the state in protecting the environment.

Compared to publics in communist systems and states undergoing political transformation, publics in the West have more opportunities to influence policy making. Greater public participation encourages problems to surface and solutions to be considered earlier in the decision-making process. However, active civil society, transparency, and existing environmental remediation programs were not available in the Czech Republic. As Carmin and VanDeveer note, "Environmental transition, like the more general political and economic transitions, engenders needs for different skills, information and knowledge as well as different organisational structures and social institutions than were common in the communist era."[5]

Embracing Sustainable Development in the Czech Republic

The first postcommunist government of Czechoslovakia (which split into the Czech Republic and Slovakia in 1993) enthusiastically developed policies consistent with the principles of sustainable development. Environmental issues had been part of the pre-1989 opposition, and some dissidents held government positions. Bedrich Moldan, the Czech environment minister, instituted a Green Parliament, a forum for environmental interests to discuss and recommend proposals. The period was full of optimism and a sense of mission. Influenced by the Brundtland Commission, the new government issued a report, "Concept of State Ecological Policy" (also known as the Rainbow Program), calling for the integration of environmental considerations into all policy sectors. Air and water pollution, solid waste disposal, and the cleanup of highly contaminated areas were given priority.[6]

During this period an environmental code of ethics for business was endorsed; it called for the rational use of natural resources, the internalization of environmental costs, and the establishment of a Czech environmental protection agency. The overall strategy was to use economic and financial instruments to change the behavior of polluters rather than rely on end-of-the-pipe solutions. The Federal Committee for the Environment wanted to make environmental recovery a central concern in the shift to a market economy. Its chair hosted a pan-European EU-sponsored conference on the environment at Dobris Castle in 1991. The conference produced a notable EU report on the state of Europe's environment, known as the "Dobris Assessment," in 1995.

All of this changed following the elections of 1992, which brought a new Czech government headed by Vaclav Klaus. Institutional capacity never developed. The Czech Environment Ministry became demoralized and lost political clout. The ministry's dedicated environmentalists were replaced, and monitoring systems and inspection programs were cut. Issues such as crime, inflation, and the Czech-Slovak split replaced the environment on the government agenda, although a majority of people still believed environmental problems were urgent.[7]

The Klaus government ignored the work of the earlier government, focusing instead on free market rationalizations for ignoring the environment. Prime Minister Klaus refused to allow the use of the term *sustainable development*.[8] The government's position was that the market would solve environmental problems and environmentalists were the problem.[9] The optimal level of pollution was proclaimed to be whatever was socially acceptable.

The 1995 State Environmental Policy document referred to the Temelin nuclear facility as a remedy for the air pollution caused by coal-burning units, projecting that the Czech Republic would achieve a level of environmental quality comparable to that of Western Europe by the year 2005—an unrealistic expectation given the state of the environment and the level of administrative infrastructure, resources, and expertise necessary to realize that goal. The *2005 Report on the Environment in the Czech Republic* admitted that it would be very difficult for the country to meet limits for suspended particulates, carbon dioxide, and ground-level ozone.[10] The report did not mention sustainability and did not articulate any plans for increasing renewable and alternative energy.

After 1992, nongovernmental organizations (NGOs) no longer had access to the Environment Ministry. Some environmental groups were on a list of extremist NGOs (with skinheads and anarchists) compiled by the Security Information Services, presumably to discredit them. The list was given to the police, who apologized and said that the responsible persons would be punished. Many of these environmental activists were pre-1989 dissidents and had been labeled enemies of the state.

Perhaps the diminished interest in environmental issues was related to a "lack of social basis for the pursuit of advanced environmental policies typical of the first two years of the 1990s."[11] Czech scholar Petr Jehlicka maintains that the lack of public involvement and information provided by the media and government, as well as the absence of an educated and economically secure middle class, strongly influenced the public perception that environmental concern meant no more than reducing pollution.[12] Capacity building was also lacking, including well-functioning institutions and human resources encompassing skilled personnel to run programs and monitor performance in the public sector at all levels of government.[13] Moreover, embracing the free market system and "neoliberalism" (or liberalization) resulted in both the closure of inefficient plants and increased consumerism, with its negative environmental impacts.[14] The Ministry of Industry and Trade offered subsidies to encourage Czechs to switch to home electric heating, which had the unfortunate consequence of increasing electricity consumption.

Temelin Upgrades and the U.S. Role

The Temelin nuclear facility was approved in 1978, and construction started in 1986. Because of the 1986 accident at the Chernobyl nuclear plant in

Ukraine, construction of Temelin was suspended in 1989 pending a review of the reactor design after concerns about Soviet-designed reactors led to pressure on the Czech government to take action. The plan was scaled back in 1990 because the government used the opportunity to build ties to the West, the Russians could not deliver the designs on schedule, and environmental problems surfaced. During this period Petr Pithart, the first postcommunist Czech prime minister, complained about the lack of information essential to decision making about the plant's future. He reduced the number of reactors from four to two, tried to initiate a public debate, and left the final decision to the next government. In 1992 data indicated that energy consumption would not increase substantially from 1989 to 2005. The Klaus government could have decided that Temelin was unnecessary, but it favored the nuclear facility. Parliament could not initiate a public discussion of the issue.

A 1990 analysis by the IAEA found design flaws in the VVER 1,000-megawatt plant and recommended changes, including replacement of the instrumentation and control systems and fuel assembly. This provided a rationale for upgrading Temelin. In 1992 CEZ and Westinghouse signed letters of intent for supplying nuclear fuel and replacing the instrumentation and control systems subject to U.S. Export-Import Bank (Exim Bank) loan guarantees. In 1993 CEZ awarded the contract to Westinghouse. Controversy erupted over the bidding process in 1996, when it was revealed that information may have been leaked to Westinghouse about the bids of competitors, allowing it to enter a second bid just under the next-lowest bid.[15]

U.S. support for Westinghouse's bid to upgrade Temelin was critical, with intense lobbying by Westinghouse to get the Exim Bank to approve the loan guarantees for a seventeen-bank consortium headed by Citibank. CEZ and the Czech Ministry of Industry and Trade told the United States that the Temelin project could lead to additional upgrading contracts. The United States promised that if Westinghouse won the contract, it would encourage increased cooperation between U.S. and Czech firms in the nuclear industry and other industries as well.[16] The U.S. embassy in Prague assured Czech officials that Westinghouse would have access to competitive financing through the Exim Bank. Both the Czechs and the Americans were interested in making the deal.

The U.S. National Security Council undertook an interagency review of the Temelin reactor design and the technical ability of the Czech regulatory authorities to ascertain compliance with U.S. environmental policy. The unified procedures established for interagency review of projects were not triggered, however, because the exports for Temelin did not include "the entire nuclear reactor or nuclear steam supply system."[17] An environmental impact assessment (EIA) of the redesigned Temelin project was therefore never performed. The Exim Bank reviewed the project to assess safety, environmental risks, and feasibility. To learn about Soviet reactors, the bank relied on U.S. Department of Energy (DOE) reports, IAEA analyses, information from Czech officials in Prague and Temelin, and a DOE study of VVER reactors. Officials at the IAEA and DOE later denied that "any such assessment had actually been made."[18] Although the U.S. Nuclear Regulatory Commission (NRC) did not perform its own evaluation of the reactor design, it lent its support. Temelin opponents alleged that the NRC's cautious report was rewritten to obtain the approval of Vice President Al Gore. Moreover, the Exim Bank found its consultations with Czech officials frustrating because the information the bank requested was not forthcoming. One bank official complained, "It is absolutely unacceptable to have a situation where we don't get a document or are not otherwise informed of something because we didn't ask exactly the 'right' question in the 'right way.'"[19] Nevertheless, in 1994 the Exim Bank's board of directors approved the loan.

Under pressure from NGOs and Austria, the U.S. Congress decided to investigate. By then, more than one million Austrians had signed a petition protesting the loan. The Austrian government had offered to pay the Czech government to switch from nuclear power to natural gas at Temelin. It had also called for an EIA with public comment, or at least a preliminary safety review—procedures that would be followed if the reactors were located in Cuba or Mexico. Thirty-two members of the U.S. Congress sent a letter to Kenneth Brody, the Exim Bank chairman, strongly recommending that Temelin be required to meet Western health and safety standards as a condition for the loan guarantee.[20] Congress expressed concern about potential liability in the event of a nuclear accident, as well as about the potential costs of more projects to upgrade Soviet plants with American tax dollars. Representative John Dingell (D-Mich.), chair of the House Committee on Energy and Commerce, was concerned about an information gap "because the Russians refused to relinquish the documentation with design specifications of the Temelin plant."[21] Dingell requested access to all communications between the Exim Bank, the Czech Republic, the DOE, the NRC, and Westinghouse concerning safety and cost. The Czech government refused to produce any documents.

In 1995, the newly elected Republican-controlled Congress replaced Dingell as committee chair, and Congress was no longer interested in pursuing the issue of safety at Temelin. Exim Bank officials recommended that in the future "unified nuclear procedures"—which require extensive analysis and an environmental assessment—should be applied to the export of major parts of nuclear power plants, with the participation of relevant U.S. agencies. In 1996, the Exim loan guarantee was signed in Prague.

Temelin Problems and Opposition

The many delays in the construction of Temelin contributed to an escalation of costs, and they exceeded the break-even point established by CEZ. Westinghouse asked for increased compensation, claiming it had underestimated its expenses because of safety and design changes, salary increases, and prolonged labor contract negotiations.[22] CEZ blamed Westinghouse for insisting on about two thousand design changes—Temelin went through six major rounds of changes. CEZ admitted that experts had underestimated the amount of work needed to upgrade the Russian design to meet Western standards.[23] Box 13-1 presents a summary list of the administrative, safety, and technical problems at Temelin. The first unit finally came online in October 2000. Even after the plant opened, problems continued to plague it, including leaks in the steam supply pipes. The Czech solution, which used restraints or covers for the pipes, would not have met American or German standards, which require separation by a wall. Other problems surfaced in the nonnuclear part of the system, including improperly fitted safety valves (Soviet designed) and improperly connected welded pipes. Technical problems caused Unit 1 to be shut down numerous times, and Unit 2, launched in May 2002, was also shut down frequently for repairs, including replacement of its turboset rotors. Leakage of low-level radioactive water occurred as well.[24]

Furthermore, little public discussion surrounded the decision to resume construction of Temelin. Two groups, Hnuti Duha (Rainbow Movement) and the South Bohemian Mothers against Temelin, developed a small but substantial

---

Box 13-1   Summary of Administrative, Safety, and Technical Problems at the Temelin Plant

1. Lack of adequate documentation from the Russians necessitated the redrawing of designs.

2. Safety goals were not well defined. Too many suggestions were made and standards were insufficient to enable accurate assessment of the degree of change necessary.

3. CEZ underestimated the magnitude and complexity of integrating Western and Russian technology.

4. Westinghouse had no incentive for timely completion.

5. Communication and coordination of activities were inadequate, both on-site and between the site and Westinghouse's Pittsburgh headquarters.

6. Russian and American cables were incompatible, requiring total replacement.

7. Russian and American safety codes differed.

8. Russian and American assumptions about equipment capabilities differed.

9. The Westinghouse designs lacked the level of detail familiar to Czech workers.

10. Plans for long-term storage of nuclear waste were absent.

11. Westinghouse misplaced two nuclear fuel rods, which were later found at the airport.

12. State Office of Nuclear Safety inspections revealed some noncompliance with safety standards.

13. The release of tritium into the Vltava River, which supplies drinking water to Prague, was a possibility.

presence. Within sight of the plant, the Temelin Nuclear Power Plant Civic Association tried to arouse interest among members of the local community. Numerous protests against the Temelin plant occurred in the 1990s, especially each year on the anniversary of the Chernobyl accident. In 1995, former prime minister Pithart was among the demonstrators. Civilian groups such as Children of the Earth, Citizens against Temelin, and Greenpeace often cooperated in the protests. The Austrian Green Party, accompanied by citizens from Germany, Denmark, and Austria, also held demonstrations. Petitions were presented to the government, which made no official response.

Austria had a strong interest in the plant because of Temelin's close proximity to its border. Low-level radiation and the risk of major accidents make the location of nuclear power plants a transboundary issue. The Greens in Austria were vocal in their opposition to Temelin. They wanted the Austrian government to make the decommissioning of Czech nuclear plants a condition for EU membership. The provincial governor of Upper Austria supported antinuclear groups.

Government studies in the late 1990s opened up public discussion of the future of energy policy in the Czech Republic, including Temelin. Public hearings were held and covered by the media. Temelin's construction continued.

EU Membership as a Force for Change

EU membership was a catalyst for change in the Czech Republic. As part of the accession process, the country had to demonstrate that it had adopted European Community legislation. Environmental and energy legislation presented the greatest challenges. Although EU law was transposed into national law, it was not an easy task because Czech legal practices and culture were incompatible with some EU directives.[25]

By 2000 the conflict over Temelin switched from a domestic debate to the international arena in the context of EU enlargement. Protests by Germany and Austria, with blockades of the Czech-Austrian border at various sites, increased when Temelin was launched in October 2000. Austrian protesters demanded that Austria veto the closing of the energy chapter of the *acquis communautaire*, thereby preventing the Czech Republic from joining the EU unless it closed Temelin.[26] Austrians, as inhabitants of a nuclear-free state, claimed the right to protect their citizens against a potential nuclear threat. Relations between Austria and the Czech Republic became strained. In 2000 the EU enlargement commissioner volunteered to serve as a mediator, and a process began that included hearings in both countries, an EIA completed by the Czech government, and an expert trilateral mission to assess safety issues. The Czech Republic agreed to establish a hotline between the two countries to exchange information. On November 21, 2001, the heads of government of Austria and the Czech Republic signed an agreement, concluding "the Melk process" (after the city in which the document was signed). The Czechs agreed to improve security at Temelin. The commission report stated that the environmental impacts of the plant were minimal. This was the only case in the EU in which a finished project was assessed using an EIA. The EIA process left Austrians still dissatisfied with the level of safety guarantees. The two reactors at Temelin have been operational since 2000, but not without continuing problems, such as defective fuel rods.[27] Austrian and German opposition to Temelin provided the EU with a unique opportunity to broker a solution that resulted in the Melk Protocol.[28]

Entry into the EU gave the Czech Republic a prominent role in promoting nuclear energy. The lack of harmonized EU safety standards for nuclear reactors allowed the country to showcase its nuclear expertise. Most of the electricity the Czech Republic generates is exported to EU countries, and EU membership gave the country improved access to an expanded electricity market and greater opportunities for nuclear collaboration.

Building Democracy and Environmental Protection through Public Participation and Accountability

When democratic attributes such as public participation are compared across CEE countries, similarities in deficiencies may be traced to the influence of Soviet political and bureaucratic structures and patterns of interaction. Nevertheless, one must keep in mind that these states have distinctive histories and cultures that temper the Soviet influence. Much of their citizens' reluctance to participate directly in politics can be traced to the dearth of real opportunities for public involvement prior to 1989.[29] Under Soviet rule, individuals were punished if they challenged or questioned government decisions. There were no institutions to link people to their leaders, other than through the Communist Party.

The public lacked experience in civic life, including membership in intermediary organizations such as NGOs and political parties. Information was the property of technical elites, and criticism was denied to citizens. General apathy and passiveness were pervasive.

Some experts on the CEE region point out the difficulty of changing this political culture.[30] Since the political transformation of 1989, the average Czech citizen has been preoccupied with economic issues. Membership in political parties and NGOs is still low; political parties are still considered a dirty business.[31] Government corruption scandals are common. The problem is how to create political efficacy so that the public has the resources and motivation to play an active role in the policy-making process, given individuals' reluctance to seek information or challenge authorities. The hierarchical government structure that originated in the Austro-Hungarian Empire and was reinforced under communist rule discouraged public participation and influenced bureaucratic behavior. Bureaucrats were not regarded as public servants, but as servants of the state. Bureaucratic accountability meant that no one took responsibility.[32] Administrators could be severely disciplined, even at the local level, for small deviations. Administrators disliked making decisions for which they might be blamed and held accountable. Therefore, most orders were passed orally, with no written record. The reluctance to take responsibility for actions is typical of the communist legacy.

The Czech political culture influenced policy making at Temelin. The low level of information about nuclear power contributed to the belief that it was safe. The media were timid about carrying out investigative reporting concerning the plant, and they often discredited NGOs and others involved in protest activities related to issues of nuclear power, giving them minimum coverage. The lack of public debate left decision making to special stakeholders, and civil society was considered an impediment to government decision making.

Since 1989, the Czech people have been encouraged to take more responsibility for themselves, yet the policy-making process has not provided them with sufficient opportunities to make decisions about their future. Many people hesitate to become involved in problems they do not believe they can solve or assess properly because they lack expertise. Most information is controlled by the government and CEZ.

Comparison with the American Nuclear Experience

The United States and the Czech Republic have nuclear ties through U.S. loan guarantees and technical assistance to the Czechs and U.S. Nuclear Regulatory Commission manuals, held up as models on the desks of Czech nuclear inspectors. The Czech Republic has six nuclear reactors and the United States has about one hundred, with several scheduled for retirement because of their age and the costs of maintaining them; thus the total number continues to decline.[33] Nuclear energy's share of electricity generation in the United States is still around 17 percent, but most of the reactors currently in operation will need to be retired in the coming years unless officials take steps to extend the lives of these plants. Many of these are similar to Japan's Fukushima plant. For nuclear energy to maintain its share of the market, new plants would have to be built fast enough to replace them, but that is not feasible. As of March 2012, seventy-two U.S. plants had received license extensions and fifteen applications for extensions were under review.[34] Some plants wanting license extensions and experiencing leaks are Oyster Creek and Salem in New Jersey, Indian Point in New York, and Braidwood in Illinois. Although the Vermont Yankee Plant received an extension, it is being closed because of costs and competition with natural gas.

The U.S. nuclear industry has been dormant for more than thirty years. The NRC provides safety oversight to U.S. nuclear power plants, most of which are privately owned. The safety records of these plants are varied, and the NRC needs additional resources to be more effective. Box 13-2 lists several examples of ongoing safety issues in U.S. nuclear plants.

More than 120 million Americans live within fifty miles of a nuclear power plant. Accidents are not one-time events, and their consequences continue far into the future. The NRC has faced criticism for not forcing the nuclear industry to address safety problems. Frank von Hippel has asserted

---

Box 13-2   Safety Issues in U.S. Nuclear Power Plants

1. Guards have been found sleeping. Fatigue among guards has been a problem because of excessive overtime.

2. Plants are vulnerable to attacks from the air; the price tag for instituting extra containment measures is in the millions of dollars.

3. Plants are understaffed, with staffing at such low levels that power-downs or brown-outs are possible.

4. Fire protection regulations have been violated at some plants.

5. Drought could force plant shutdowns because of a lack of needed cooling water; a rarely discussed problem is that twenty-four U.S. plants are located in potential drought areas.

6. Clear data on safe limits of radioactive exposure—that is, acceptable levels of frequency and amount of exposure—are lacking. Spent fuel rods stored in overcrowded pools are potentially larger sources of radiation than reactors themselves.

7. Fuel rods have been lost at some plants.

8. Plants routinely fail in exercises involving mock attacks.

9. A culture of safety is lacking at some plants.

10. Many cities use drinking water from areas located near plants where radioactive tritium has been found.

11. In 2009, cracks appeared in the containment building of the plant at Crystal River, Florida. This plant has a history of structural weakness, as steel reinforcements were added to the dome instead of the walls during construction. The problem is too expensive to fix, so the plant will be decontaminated or put in safe storage for sixty years. This is the first plant in the southeastern United States to be shut down.

12. Two reactors at the San Onofre, California, plant have been shut down because their steam tubes were damaged by excessive vibration and friction, leading to the leaking of radioactive water. The problem is too expensive to fix.

13. The Millstone plant in Waterford, Connecticut, closed temporarily because the water in Long Island Sound was too warm and could not be used for cooling.

14. A Braidwood unit in Illinois received special permission to operate when the cooling water rose to more than 102 degrees; the unit was designed to run at no more than 98 degrees.

Source: List compiled by the author from various sources in the period 2008–2013.

---

that the "NRC appears to have informally established an unreasonably high burden of requiring absolute proof of a safety problem, versus lack of a reasonable assurance of maintaining public health and safety."[35]

Currently, the three major problems associated with the expansion of nuclear energy in the United States are safety and security (in particular protection against terrorism), cost, and the long-term disposal of nuclear waste. The second issue, financial cost, is not a major concern in the Czech Republic because the utility, CEZ, is owned primarily by the government and provides substantial revenues through the export of most of the electricity generated to the rest of Europe. That could change with an expansion of Temelin. If new plants require heavy subsidies that cannot be transferred to consumers, cost could become an issue.

In the United States, the DOE supports the nuclear industry by funding research and development projects. Legislation caps the liability of private utilities that operate nuclear plants, and some critics argue that the maximum payouts would not cover the damage from a plant meltdown.[36] Decommissioning a nuclear power plant may cost even more than building a new one. The nuclear industry itself considers investment in new plants risky and expensive, and without government aid—in the form of loan guarantees and tax credits, for example—such investment is a hard sell. Note that the industry refers to government "incentives," not subsidies. Either way, they amount to billions of dollars of support. According to the chief executive officer of Exelon, a Chicago-based corporation that owns seventeen nuclear power plants: "We're not big enough to build nuclear plants into the market without the initial government assistance that's in the loan guarantee program. Exelon has taken a very clear position that unless we get the federal loan guarantees of equivalent financing we will not go forward."[37] Moreover, costs are rising owing to shortages of skilled labor and increases in the prices of materials, including cement, steel, and copper.[38] Insurance companies also consider investment in nuclear power plants to be risky. The bottom line is that American consumers of electricity pay more if the utility regulators in their states allow utilities to institute rate hikes to cover the costs of the construction of nuclear power plants.

Georgia and Florida allow such costs to be borne by the ratepayers—perhaps that is why two new plants are under construction in each of these states. Nuclear energy may now be the most costly form of electric generation. According to Peter Bradford, former NRC commissioner, "The 'renaissance' was always a bubble because new nuclear has always been too expensive."[39]

The safety of nuclear plants and their protection from terrorists have been ongoing issues in both the Czech Republic and the United States. The problem of the disposal of nuclear waste took on a new aspect after the terrorist attacks on New York City and Washington, D.C., on September 11, 2001. Fears arose that trains transporting nuclear waste material—spent fuel, which needs to be safely stored for hundreds of thousands of years—could be attacked by terrorists with shoulder-fired weapons that could pierce protective casks and cause explosions resulting in radioactive emissions. Another problem is that trains laden with nuclear waste travel on tracks through cities on their way to waste disposal sites. Issues of terrorism and nuclear waste disposal are thus intimately related.

No country has yet successfully developed or implemented a long-term program for the storage of nuclear waste. In the United States, most of this waste is stored in cooling ponds or aboveground casks. In the Czech Republic, spent fuel is stored on-site in casks. Some critics assert that until the waste problem is solved, the idea of a nuclear renaissance makes no sense. The accumulation of thousands of tons of additional radioactive material without safe disposal creates a problem as serious as global warming. Some scientists have confidence that geologically safe sites for waste storage will be found. The Czech Republic has identified six potential sites but has faced opposition from citizens living near the sites. The government is supposed to locate a facility by 2065. The Czech Nuclear Waste Repository Authority would like the EU to change its legislation so that states could share sites instead of each state having to locate its own sites within its boundaries. The authority has stated that it would even consider having a Czech site designated as a host EU site.[40]

In the United States, plans to use Yucca Mountain in Nevada as the only designated long-term waste disposal site have been disrupted by opposition from Nevada's government and concerns that the site is unsuitable because of leakage and other environmental uncertainties. This situation has left nuclear waste dangerously accumulating on-site at individual plants, increasing the potential for sabotage and terrorism. If the waste keeps piling up, the building of new plants in the United States and the Czech Republic could be delayed. In 2007, Tomihiro Taniguchi, deputy director-general for nuclear safety and security at the IAEA, noted, "If this doubt is not ameliorated soon, it could well lead to all the ambitious plans to expand the use of nuclear power on a global scale being significantly delayed."[41] In 2009, President Barack Obama announced the withholding of funds from Yucca Mountain and stated that he wanted an alternative plan for the disposal of existing nuclear waste. A proposal to store high-level waste on an Indian reservation in Utah was also killed by public opposition in 2012. However, support for using Yucca Mountain as a waste site lingers as the ultimate solution, especially since the President's Blue Ribbon Commission on the Future of Nuclear Waste recommended in 2012 that a centralized interim site be designated so that the dangerously high levels of spent fuel in pools at various sites could be moved. Industry executives continue to wait for a solution to the waste disposal problem.

The alternative to waste disposal is recycling, but that has problems of its own. A major one, and the reason the United States has banned recycling of nuclear waste, is that it produces plutonium. The risk is that plutonium and other transuranic materials could be used to develop nuclear weapons. American physicists are concerned "that countries with the intent to proliferate can covertly use the associated or reprocessing plants to produce the essential material for a nuclear explosive."[42] The list of countries aspiring to begin nuclear energy programs includes those with oil resources as well as countries in the Middle East and Africa where political instability is increasing. States want to compete with India, Pakistan, and Iran for the political stature that a nuclear arsenal provides. States need skilled technicians, engineers, and specialized personnel to construct and run nuclear plants. Moreover, the more nuclear fuel supplies and spent fuel are transported, the greater the opportunity for the materials to be diverted for weaponization. This is a particularly serious problem if enrichment facilities are available.

The Energy Policy Act of 2005 (P.L. 109-58) directed the DOE to offer financial incentives to the nuclear sector to develop more nuclear plants, offering utilities compensation for license applications and loan guarantees. The NRC approved the construction of four plants—two at Vogtle, Georgia, and two at Summer, South Carolina, near Jenkensville—with loan guarantees. Already $300 million over budget because of increased safety standards, the projects are protected against default by low-interest-rate loans from Treasury financing (i.e., credit subsidy). However, critics say taxpayers are unprotected because of inadequate oversight of the process.[43] No company would undertake new construction without a government subsidy. On the horizon are proposals to design and commercialize small nuclear reactors that would be built underground and so would be less vulnerable to earthquakes and would require fewer operators and less security than larger, aboveground plants. Babcock & Wilcox, with the Tennessee Valley Authority, and Bechtel have received grants from the DOE, which has more than $400 million to spend to develop small modular reactors that could be put together like Legos. They could be transported easily all over the world to replace aging plants or sold to states unable to afford $15 billion nuclear plants. The problem is that such modular reactors would be more difficult to inspect and maintain than traditional reactors, as key components would be located inside the pressure vessels and more vulnerable to flooding.[44] While they could be exported and used on sites that cannot support large reactors, they would lack economies of scale and produce less electricity. Massive numbers of such reactors would have to be built to be economically competitive,[45] and their development would rely on DOE financing and congressional support.[46]

Fukushima

On March 11, 2011, another disaster shook global confidence in nuclear energy. This accident occurred in a technologically advanced democratic state, and the plant involved had state-of-the-art equipment identical to that used worldwide. Had the same type of incident taken place in some other part of the world, in a country lacking a safety culture, oversight, and careful regulatory regimes, the results might have been much worse.[47]

The early response to the damage to the plant in Fukushima, Japan, caused by an 8.9 magnitude earthquake and resulting tsunami, was confusion and chaos. Plant personnel were inadequately prepared for the unprecedented situation confronting them and were reluctant to reveal its reality to their superiors in Tokyo. With no visual of the reactors available, workers could not assess the danger and extent of the problem.[48] Electricity to the plant was knocked out, triggering a series of events in the four Fukushima reactors. Pumps that provided coolant water failed, as did backup generators and pumps, which had been flooded. Nuclear fuel in the reactor cores as well as in the spent-fuel pool overheats if coolant water evaporates and fuel rods are exposed. The reactors and spent fuel could not be cooled because cooling water was unavailable. Steam built up in the containment buildings, and the reduced water left rods exposed. The heat caused explosions, and three reactors experienced meltdowns. A hydrogen explosion also disabled electrical controls in the reactor core container. The plant workers did not communicate the increase in radiation in the buildings to the government in a timely fashion. Vents needed to be opened to release pressure in the containment chambers, but the vents could not be operated either manually or remotely. When the water level in Reactor 3 dropped, it was not reported for over an hour. Fire hoses were too short. The third day of the disaster was devoted solely to how to avoid a hydrogen explosion and how to deal with pleas from Japanese business sectors for exemptions from rolling blackouts. Fuel rods were exposed in Reactor 3, and when the pressure got too high, the reactor blew.[49]

Unit 4 was especially dangerous because hydrogen leaked into its spent-fuel pool through ventilation systems shared with Reactor 3.[50] It was suggested that car batteries could be used to provide power, but none were available (a thousand were ordered, but their delivery was delayed because of the absence of permits to use expressways). Plant workers donated a few used batteries, but these failed.[51] The workers were not told of the danger they incurred by remaining at the plant site. Some were told to ignore dosimeter alerts. The Tokyo Electric Power Company (TEPCO) changed the rule defining the safe level of radiation exposure so it would not run out of workers.[52] Eventually workers were evacuated. People from the surrounding area fled north to avoid the plume, not having been informed that contamination had spread northward. Many workers and citizens were subjected to high degrees of radiation exposure. Japan's prime minister distrusted TEPCO and state bureaucrats, given the nuclear establishment's close ties with the Ministry of Economy, Trade and Industry.[53] He said that he was not given accurate information. TEPCO refused help from the United States, including water pump trucks and technical advice. The prime minister stated: "Given the enormity of the risks associated with nuclear power generation, I have realized nuclear technology is not something that can be managed by conventional safety measures alone. I believe we should aim for a society that is not dependent on nuclear power generation."[54]

The environmental impact of the Fukushima disaster was immense. The Pacific Ocean was contaminated as tons of water used to cool the reactors was dumped into it.[55] Four months after the accident, tainted beef was found in shops and restaurants hundreds of miles from the plants.[56] Two years after the accident, hastily constructed tanks that held contaminated water used for cooling the reactors leaked tens of thousands of gallons into the soil; with no way to stop the flow, much of this water reached the Pacific.[57] Japan has admitted that tons of radioactive water continue to leak into groundwater. The source of the leaking is unknown, so efforts to stop the contamination have failed. "It's difficult to find a solution," said the head of the Nuclear Regulatory Authority, Shunichi Tanaka.[58] Radioactive material and debris from Fukushima have been found as far away as the U.S. West Coast and throughout Pacific countries. Radioactive gas has traveled hundreds of miles from Japan. The full health and environmental impacts of the disaster, including massive soil contamination, will not be known for decades. Since fuel melted down into the ground in three of the reactors, the groundwater was contaminated.[59] Evacuees may not be able to return to the area for many years. A more daunting problem may be how to stabilize the spent fuel in Reactor 4, where any misstep in the removal of the fuel assembly could result in explosion, fire, and catastrophic radionuclide releases.

How could this catastrophe have happened? TEPCO admitted that it could have taken greater precautions, but it did not want to jeopardize the myth that Japanese nuclear technology was infallible. If TEPCO took preventive measures against extreme accidents, the company reasoned, the public might be prompted to question the safety of nuclear power. TEPCO and Japan's Nuclear and Industrial Safety Agency were aware of a potential problem at Fukushima in 2006, when they participated in a conference on the 2004 Sumatra earthquake and tsunami,[60] but they took no preventive action. Proponents of nuclear energy responded to questions about the Fukushima accident by saying it was premature to draw conclusions; they asserted that the plant's designs were excellent and that the employees were effective in handling the emergency.[61] That was not in fact the case.

Could Japan's technologists have been better prepared? Projections about the effects of tsunamis and earthquakes on nuclear power plants were based on what was known. The government never asked TEPCO to go "beyond the probable maximum" that could occur even if it had a low probability. Planning for simultaneous accidents was never done. Critics have asserted that in order to avoid future nuclear disasters, Japan needs to create more backup systems, institute better crisis management, and acknowledge problems in the corporate culture.[62]

Japan's nuclear future rests on national politics. The two major political parties are in opposite camps. The new Nuclear Regulation Agency has proposed stringent regulations that would ban reactors from operating if they are on active earthquake faults, require off-site emergency command centers, and raise the height of seawalls.[63] Agency members cannot have ties to the nuclear industry. Nuclear proponents fear that a cessation of nuclear energy production in Japan would kill the country's spent-fuel recycling program. Japan has yet to open its Rokkasho nuclear waste recycling plant successfully because of mechanical problems. The country has no long-term waste disposal site or plans to build one. Nuclear power plants are needed to produce the spent fuel for the recycling plant, and vice versa. As noted above, the danger of recycling nuclear waste is that the process produces plutonium, along with mixed oxide fuel, and these materials could be used for weapons. Japan is allowed to enrich uranium and extract plutonium. Without nuclear power plants, it would have to stockpile its existing plutonium, and it already has tons of plutonium with no use.[64]

Japan is currently debating its nuclear energy future and has announced its intention to buy natural gas from the United States.[65] The nuclear community and the business sector continue to pressure the government to restart nuclear reactors to produce electricity, and some observers argue that Japan has learned its lessons and should continue its nuclear program. Business interests have raised concerns about economic growth. In 2012 a trade deficit was attributed to an increase in the importing of fossil fuels. Others argue that Japan should, like Germany, serve as a model for the development of renewable energy. TEPCO has announced plans to restart two reactors at Kashiwazaki-Kariwa, located on a seismic fault.[66] The global nuclear community anxiously awaits further study of the environmental and health impacts of the Fukushima disaster for the Japanese and for the world. The Czech reaction to Fukushima was that such an accident could not happen in the Czech Republic. No one had died as the result of any problems with Czech nuclear plants, and nuclear energy was promoted on TV. Foreign Minister Karel Schwarzenberg said, "The last tsunami hit Czech lands some 500 million years ago."[67] The EU asked for stress tests and found shortcomings at the two power plants at Temelin and Dukovany. Its report cited lack of equipment to prevent hydrogen explosions, lack of filtration systems to relieve pressure, and insufficient equipment to deal with an accident.[68] CEZ responded by promising to strengthen seismic resistance in some buildings, increase module diesel generators to supply electricity if the grid was no longer viable, and strengthen resistance to floods. The kind of situation that occurred in Fukushima was considered a "beyond design accident," and the Czechs considered the EU's demands overly stringent. The EU has issued increasingly demanding rules on nuclear safety, from transparency requirements to technical specifications.[69] In the United States, following the Fukushima disaster the NRC ordered that the venting systems be upgraded in thirty-one reactors that are similar in design to the Fukushima units. It also required that plants be able to run without power for a long period of time and that they install instrumentation to track water levels in spent-fuel pools.[70] According to NRC chair Allison Macfarlane, "Strengthened vents will help these plants continue to protect the public and environment even if emergency systems can't immediately stop an accident."[71]

Global Implications

Global warming has emerged as the strongest argument supporting the continued use of nuclear energy. Other arguments made by nuclear proponents include relief from increasing fuel prices and independence from fossil fuel suppliers—Russia in the Czech Republic and Middle Eastern countries in the United States. But oil supplies will eventually be depleted. Middle Eastern states such as Jordan, Morocco, Egypt, Saudi Arabia, Libya, and the United Arab Emirates may recognize that, but instead of investing in solar and renewable energy, they also want to join the nuclear club. States seeking to offset fossil fuels that produce greenhouse gases do not advocate reducing demand or increasing investments in renewable technologies. The IAEA publicly supports increasing the expansion of nuclear energy. An increase in the number of nuclear states will overstretch the IAEA's ability to monitor and regulate the transport and use of nuclear materials and waste disposal procedures. Individual states will need to create independent national authorities to regulate reactor safety, personnel training, licensing, siting, and overall oversight—something that will be problematic in authoritarian states. As one analyst has observed, "In countries where you have an authoritarian, personalized power system . . . , the very idea of a completely independent oversight body is anathema."[72]

As of July 2012, the world had 429 nuclear reactors in thirty-one countries, 15 less than in 2002.[73] In 2011, 19 reactors were closed, 18 because of concerns raised by the Fukushima event.[74] There are approximately 59 reactors currently under construction (28 in China).[75] In 1979, there were 234 under construction.[76] Many plants categorized as "under construction" remain in that status for many years, and because of increasing safety concerns, construction delays are common. Belgium, Lithuania, Kazakhstan, and Germany are phasing out their nuclear power; the Netherlands, Italy, the Philippines, and Switzerland have abandoned construction of nuclear projects; and Spain has shifted its energy focus away from nuclear. Jordan has dropped its nuclear ambitions and is now concentrating on renewable energy.[77] China, which has the world's largest planned nuclear expansion program, scaled back after Fukushima, increasing its support and development of renewables.[78] The evidence shows that, with fewer nuclear plants in operation today than in 2002, a "nuclear renaissance" is not happening.

In the European Union there were 177 reactors operating in 1984 and 134 in February 2012. Fourteen EU states have nuclear power plants.[79] Eight reactors in Eastern Europe were closed as part of a deal for EU accession.[80] New plants are too expensive. The Finnish plant at Olkiluoto, with its new 1,600-megawatt European Pressurized Reactor, has experienced serious delays and cost overruns because of poor-quality concrete, inexperienced contractors, and inadequate communication among thousands of workers speaking eight different languages.[81] This illustrates how difficult and important it is to have adequate expertise and a "safety culture" with qualified technicians—conditions lacking in many aspiring nuclear energy states. Key to any nuclear renaissance is the ability to replace existing plants as they are retired. This means replacing some 287 plants by 2025. If all the plants currently under construction become operational, 18 more plants would still have to be built, or one new plant every three months, to meet the 2025 date.[82] But it now takes at least ten years to complete construction of a new nuclear plant. A nuclear renaissance would require government subsidies to offset huge construction costs, the ability to manufacture large pressure reactors, sufficient numbers of technical experts and engineers (a global problem), and a solution to the spent-fuel disposal issue.

One of the fears of the nuclear industry is the effect of a major accident on the solvency of the company involved. Globally, financial institutions have increased their scrutiny of the nuclear industry, and nuclear companies are finding that capital has become tighter and more expensive. The French company Areva saw its credit rating decline from A to BBB– in 2009, barely above junk status.[83] TEPCO has lost 96 percent of its share value since 2007. After Fukushima, its financial strength rating moved from AA to B+.[84] It is near bankruptcy.

In both the Czech Republic and the United States, the nuclear industry and government regulators have proposed building more nuclear power plants. In the Czech Republic the level of public debate on this issue is low, and the situation is similar in the United States, even though thirty years ago NGOs and the public were able to thwart the building of new plants. In fact, in the Czech Republic public support for nuclear energy has increased.[85] In contrast, two-thirds of Americans surveyed say that they do not want to see a nuclear power plant built anywhere in the United States, and 84 percent oppose one being built near where they live.[86]

Temelin Controversy Continues

In 2008, CEZ announced that it planned to construct two more 1,000-megawatt reactors at Temelin. The Russian-Czech consortium of Atomstroyexport, Skoda JS, and Gidropress is competing with the U.S. firm Westinghouse, a division of Toshiba, for the construction contract. There is concern that the cost of adding reactors at Temelin will be too high because the price of electricity is declining and yielding insufficient revenue. CEZ suggested that the state guarantee a fixed price, but the finance minister rejected the idea.[87] The cost of Temelin's expansion could be covered by "indirect subsidy," which means an increase in the price of electricity paid by the consumer.

CEZ has now become a major exporter of electricity to the rest of Europe and one of the most profitable energy producers in the world.[88] While the current two units at Temelin export 50 percent of electricity produced, 100 percent of electricity generated by the two proposed reactors would be exported. There has been discussion of opening new uranium mines in the Czech Republic to support the growth of nuclear energy. CEZ and the Czech government are discussing a new energy scenario. The Czech Republic did not meet the targets for renewable energy that were set in 2003, and sustainable energy development is not on the agenda. CEZ considers nuclear energy to be a renewable source. An important alternative to nuclear, and consistent with EU policy, would be for the Czech Republic to produce 20 percent renewable energy by 2020.[89] In 2005, legislation was passed guaranteeing a feed-in price for renewable energy by CEZ for fifteen years, with an inflation tariff to provide stability for bank loans. The system encouraged many investors to support renewables. The biggest renewable plants were owned by CEZ, which had the largest share of the market. The government was required to buy back the renewable energy, but it was so lucrative that the Czech Republic became the third-largest producer of solar energy in Europe. The problem for the government was that the scheme was too successful because of the high feed-in tariff and the strength of the crown. The cost of solar production fell, but the tariffs continued at the same level. CEZ had raised the price of electricity to cover payment to the renewable investors. Moreover, the amount of electricity produced began to exceed the national grid's capacity, which was especially dangerous at peak periods, making the entire system unstable. A backlash against renewables emerged. CEZ blamed the Greens and the EU. In March 2010, the Czech parliament cut the price incentives.[90]

The Energy Regulatory Office reduced more than half the feed-in tariff to discourage investments.[91] A 26 percent tax on revenues from solar power was also imposed.[92] The result was a decline in the growth of solar and connections to the grid. Other states, such as Spain, Germany, and Slovakia, had similar situations, but none had to pull out of supporting renewables because their feed-in tariffs had been more realistic. Without sustained growth of domestic renewables, the Czech government could return its focus to nuclear and coal.

Conclusion

The nuclear industry frames the nuclear energy renaissance as environmental stewardship.[93] It portrays nuclear energy as a "green" solution contributing to the reduction of greenhouse gases. Nevertheless, there are problems with nuclear energy. First, nuclear power plants cannot be built fast enough to fulfill all the energy needs of developing economies. Countries with existing plants need to retire older plants that are no longer safe and efficient, and the hundreds of plants needed to replace current plants will not be online in time to meet projected demands. Second, any increase in the number of states with nuclear energy capacity increases the likelihood of nuclear proliferation through weaponization of civilian nuclear energy. Third, no state has found a solution to the problem of long-term disposal of nuclear waste. Fourth, nuclear energy may be the most expensive way to produce electricity. Fifth, there are unknown safety and environmental risks associated with nuclear energy production that may have long-term consequences that cannot be predicted.

There has been little discussion among states about reducing electricity demand, which would benefit the environment by leading to the production of fewer harmful by-products and waste. The myth that nuclear energy has low environmental impacts persists. A false choice has been put forward, that one has to choose between fossil fuels and nuclear energy, when ultimately renewable alternative energy sources will be needed, because the Earth's supplies of fossil fuels are limited. Both the public and private sectors should focus massive investment on the development of such renewables. In the United States, the challenge is whether the nuclear industry can find a market niche for nuclear energy. Nuclear energy is less price competitive when all costs are factored in. The rush to natural gas may also dampen nuclear expansion. In this respect there is potential for change in both the United States and the Czech Republic.

Sustainability as a concept requires group or collective action with a concern for the public interest; it is future oriented. Sustainable development can succeed only if public support emerges and Czechs, Japanese, and Americans participate more fully in the debate about energy policy. Public participation transfers legitimacy to the goal of sustainability. The challenge for all governments is to develop energy policies that are consistent with sustainable environmental goals; in democracies, that includes a greater role for the public through a variety of participatory mechanisms. The Czech Republic, Japan, and the United States currently lack coherent energy policies as well as developed mechanisms for public scrutiny and debate. If Japan shuts down its nuclear plants, a move the business sector and communities receiving government subsidies oppose, it will be forced to develop alternative sources of energy. In the United States, delays and cost overruns in the four new plants under construction will be yet another test. It may be that the future of energy is in renewable, smaller, and decentralized sources—a renaissance of a different kind that is worthy of global attention. As former NRC commissioner Peter Bradford commented in 2010, "The 'nuclear renaissance' has proven to be a promotion that cannot pass economic muster."[94]

Notes

1. Regina S. Axelrod, "Reflections on the Writings of President Vaclav Klaus," *Listy* 38, no. 3 (2008): 105–107.
2. Colin Woodward, "Western Vendors Move East," *Transition* 17 (November 1995): 24.
3. World Commission on Environment and Development, *Our Common Future* (London: Oxford University Press, 1987), 43.
4. Peter Jehlicka and Jan Kara, "Ups and Downs of Czech Environmental Awareness and Policy: Identifying Trends and Influences," in *Protecting the Periphery: Environmental Policy in Peripheral Regions of the European Union*, ed. Susan Baker, Kay Milton, and Steven Yearly (London: Frank Cass, 1994), 154. See also Barbara Jancar-Webster, "Environmental Politics in Eastern Europe in the 1980s," in *To Breathe Free: Eastern Europe's Environmental Crisis,* ed. Joan DeBardeleben (Washington, DC: Woodrow Wilson Center, 1991), 25–56; Andrew Tickle and Ian Welsh, eds., *Environment and Society in Eastern Europe* (New York: Longman, 1998).
5. JoAnn Carmin and Stacy D. VanDeveer, "Enlarging EU Environments: Central and Eastern Europe from Transition to Accession," in *EU Enlargement and the Environment: Institutional Change and Environmental Policy in Central and Eastern Europe*, ed. JoAnn Carmin and Stacy D. VanDeveer (London: Routledge, 2005), 9.
6. Richard Andrews, "Environmental Policy in the Czech and Slovak Republics," in *Environment and Democratic Transition: Policy and Politics in Central and Eastern Europe*, ed. Anna Vari and Pal Tamas (Dordrecht, Netherlands: Kluwer Academic Publishers, 1995), 28.
7. "Status of National Environmental Action Programs in Central and Eastern Europe," in *Country Reports* (Szentendre, Hungary: Regional Environmental Center, May 1995), 28.
8. Brian Slocock, "Paradoxes of Environmental Policy in Eastern Europe," in *Country Reports* (Szentendre, Hungary: Regional Environmental Center, May 1995), 43.6
9. For an excellent discussion of environmental policy in the Czech Republic, see Bedrich Moldan, "Czech Republic," in *The Environmental Challenge for Central European Economies in Transition,* ed. Jurg Klarer and Bedrich Moldan (West Sussex, UK: John Wiley, 1998), 107–130.
10. Ministry of Environment, Czech Republic, *2005 Report on the Environment in the Czech Republic* (Prague: Ministry of Environment, 2006).

11. Peter Jehlicka, "The Development of Czech Environmental Policy in the 1990s: A Sociological Account" (paper presented at the Summer Symposium of the University of Bologna, July 1997), 14.
12. Ibid., 12–14.
13. Carmin and VanDeveer, "Enlarging EU Environments," 12.
14. Ibid., 8.
15. Czech News Agency (CTK), May 11, 1996; *Prague Post,* June 5, 1996.
16. U.S. Government Accounting Office, *Nuclear Safety: U.S. Assistance to Upgrade Soviet-Designed Nuclear Reactors in the Czech Republic,* Report of the Ranking Minority Member, Committee on Commerce, House of Representatives (Washington, DC: Government Accounting Office, June 1995).
17. Ibid., 7.
18. S. Jacob Scherr and David Schwarzbach, "Turning Points," *Amicus Journal* (Winter 1995): 14.
19. Quoted in U.S. Government Accounting Office, *Nuclear Safety,* 11.
20. *East European Reporter,* March 25, 1994.
21. *Energy Daily,* March 17, 1994.
22. *Prague Post,* January 14, 1998.
23. *Nucleonics Week,* August 24, 1995.
24. CTK, April 3, 2008.
25. See Eva Kruzikova, "EU Accession and Legal Change: Accomplishments and Challenges in the Czech Case," in Carmin and VanDeveer, *EU Enlargement and the Environment,* 99–113.
26. For a comprehensive analysis of the Austrian opposition to the Temelin nuclear power plant, see Michael Getzner, *Nuclear Policies in Central Europe* (Frankfurt: Peter Lang, 2003).
27. BBC Monitoring International Reports, December 20, 2007.
28. For a fuller discussion of the role of the EU in relation to Temelin, see Regina Axelrod, "Nuclear Power and EU Enlargement: The Case of Temelín," in Carmin and VanDeveer, *EU Enlargement and the Environment,* 153–171.
29. Adam Fagin and Petr Jehlicka, "Sustainable Development in the Czech Republic: A Doomed Process?," *Environmental Politics* 7 (Spring 1998): 119.
30. Keith Crawford, *East Central European Politics Today* (New York: St. Martin's Press, 1996); Piotr Sztompka, "The Intangibles of the Transition to Democracy," *Studies in Comparative Communism* 24, no. 3 (1991).
31. Z. Vajdova, "Politicka kultura lokalnich politickych elit: Srovani ceskeho a vychodonemeckeho mesta [Political culture of local political elites: A comparison of Czech and East German cities]" (working paper, Institute of Sociology, Academy of Sciences of the Czech Republic, 1997), 38.
32. Jehlicka and Kara, "Ups and Downs of Czech Environmental Awareness and Policy," 156.
33. *New York Times,* June 14, 2013.
34. Mycle Schneider and Antony Froggatt, "2011–2012 World Nuclear Industry Status Report," *Bulletin of the Atomic Scientists,* September 22, 2012, 11.
35. Frank von Hippel, "Second Chances: Containment of a Reactor Meltdown," *Bulletin of the Atomic Scientists,* March 14, 2011.
36. *Wall Street Journal,* May 12, 2008.
37. "An Interview with John Rowe," *Bulletin of the Atomic Scientists,* September/October 2008, 10.
38. *Wall Street Journal,* May 12, 2008.
39. Quoted in Scott DiSavino, "U.S. Clears Another Hurdle toward Nuclear Renaissance," Reuters, December 22, 2011, http://www.reuters.com/article/2011/12/22/us-utilities-nrc-westinghouse-ap-idUSTRE7BL1FN20111222.
40. *Prague Post,* April 9–15, 2008.
41. *International Herald Tribune,* November 8, 2007.
42. John F. Ahearne, "Prospects for Nuclear Energy," *Energy Economics* 33, no. 4 (2011): 574.

43. Mark Clayton, "Georgia Nuclear Power Plant Could be Solyndra Redux, Report Says," *Christian Science Monitor,* January 30, 2013, http://www.csmonitor.com/Environment/2013/0130/Georgia-nuclear-power-plant-could-be-Solyndra-redux-report-says.
44. Matt Smith, "U.S. Backs Project for Small Nuclear Reactors," CNN, November 21, 2012, http://www.cnn.com/2012/11/21/us/small-nukes/index.html.
45. Wendy Koch, "Nuclear Industry Looks toward Smaller Reactors," *USA Today,* November 27, 2012, http://www.usatoday.com/story/news/nation/2012/11/26/nuclear-small-modular-reactors/1727001.
46. *New York Times,* February 21, 2012.
47. *Bulletin of the Atomic Scientists,* March 21, 2011.
48. *New York Times,* November 3, 2011.
49. "TEPCO Fits New Thermometer to Melted-Down Reactor," *Asahi Shimbun,* October 4, 2012, http://ajw.asahi.com/article/0311disaster/fukushima/AJ201210040042.
50. "Fukushima Daiichi 4 Frame Takes Shape," World Nuclear News, January 15, 2012, http://www.world-nuclear-news.org/RS-Fukushima_4_frame_takes_shape-1501138.html.
51. "Inside Fukushima: How Workers Tried but Failed to Avert a Nuclear Disaster," *Asahi Shimbun,* October 14, 2012, http://ajw.asahi.com/article/0311disaster/fukushima/AJ201210140034.
52. *Japan Times,* November 14, 2012.
53. *New York Times,* June 13, 2011.
54. Quoted in Kiyoshi Takenaka and Yoko Kubota, "PM Kan Wants to Wean Japan from Nuclear Power," Reuters, July 13, 2011, http://www.reuters.com/article/2011/07/13/us-japan-nuclear-kan-idUSTRE76C19O20110713.
55. *The Guardian* (London), May 3, 2011.
56. *Wall Street Journal,* July 10, 2011.
57. *New York Times,* April 11, 2013, and August 7, 2013.
58. *New York Times,* July 11, 2013, and August 7, 2013.
59. "Crooked Cleanup (1): Radioactive Waste Dumped into Rivers during Decontamination Work in Fukushima," *Asahi Shimbun,* January 4, 2013, http://ajw.asahi.com/article/0311disaster/fukushima/AJ201301040058.
60. *Japan Times,* May 16, 2012.
61. National Energy Institute (U.S.), "Talking Points: Implications to U.S. Nuclear Energy Program of the Japanese Earthquake," March 13, 2011.
62. *New York Times,* October 13, 2012.
63. *New York Times,* February 1, 2013.
64. Mari Yamaguchi, "Nowhere to Use Japan's Growing Plutonium Stockpile," AP News, December 28, 2012, http://bigstory.ap.org/article/nowhere-use-japans-growing-plutonium-stockpile.
65. *Washington Post,* February 7, 2013.
66. *New York Times,* July 3, 2013.
67. CTK, January 7, 2013.
68. BBC Worldwide Monitoring Europe, October 12, 2012.
69. *European Voice,* June 6, 2013.
70. "What's Next for the NRC? A Conversation with Allison Macfarlane," *Bulletin of the Atomic Scientists,* November 1, 2012, 1–5.
71. "U.S. Orders New Safety Upgrades at Nuclear Plants," CNN, June 6, 2013, http://www.cnn.com/2013/06/06/us/nuclear-reactors-upgrades.
72. Samuel Ciszuk, IHS Energy analyst, quoted in Nick Carey, "After Japan, Where's the Next Nuclear Weak Link?," Reuters, June 10, 2011, http://www.reuters.com/article/2011/06/10/idUS419961224420110610.
73. Schneider and Froggatt, "2011–2012 World Nuclear Industry Status Report," 10.
74. Ibid., 13.
75. *South China Morning Post,* December 9, 2013.

76. Schneider and Froggatt, "2011–2012 World Nuclear Industry Status Report," 10.
77. Paul Gipe, "Jordan Adopts Renewable Energy Feed-in Tariffs, Shelves Nuclear," *Renewable Energy World*, December 12, 2012, http://www.renewableenergyworld .com/rea/news/article/2012/12/jordan-adopts-renewable-energy-feed-in-tariffs-shelves-nuclear.
78. Lutz Mez, "Nuclear Energy—Any Solution for Sustainability and Climate Protection?," *Energy Policy* 48 (2012): 58.
79. Ibid., 57.
80. Ibid., 58.
81. Ahearne, "Prospects for Nuclear Energy," 580.
82. Lutz Mez, "Nuclear Energy—Any Solution for Sustainability and Climate Protection?," Energy Policy 48 (2012): 59.
83. Schneider and Froggatt, "2011–2012 World Nuclear Industry Status Report," 15.
84. Ibid.
85. *Czech and Slovakia Business Weekly,* May 2, 2008.
86. *Washington Post,* April 30, 2011.
87. CTK, March 18, 2012.
88. *Prague Post,* November 4, 2009.
89. CTK, March 28, 2012.
90. *Prague Post,* March 24, 2010.
91. *Prague Post,* November 17, 2010.
92. *Prague Post,* July 6, 2011.
93. PR Newswire, June 3, 2008.
94. Peter Bradford, "Honey, I Shrunk the Renaissance: Nuclear Revival, Climate Change, and Reality," Electricity Policy, October 11, 2010, http://electricitypolicy.com/ articles/2553-honey-i-shrunk-the-renaissance-nuclear-revival-climate-change-and-reality.

14

Free Trade and Environmental Protection

Daniel C. Esty

No mention was made of the word *environment* in the original General Agreement on Tariffs and Trade (GATT)—the central pillar of the international trading system—put into place just after World War II. At that time, no one saw much connection between trade liberalization and environmental protection. For the next forty years, trade and environmental policy makers pursued their respective agendas on parallel tracks that rarely, if ever, intersected. In recent decades, however, trade and environmental policy making have increasingly appeared to be linked, and the two realms have often seemed to collide. Environmental advocates have come to fear that freer trade means increased pollution and resource depletion. Free traders worry that protectionism in the guise of environmental policy will obstruct efforts to open markets and integrate economies around the world.

This chapter explores the trade-environment relationship. It traces the origins of the tension between trade liberalization and environmental protection and identifies the events that triggered the conflict. It examines why environmentalists worry about free trade and why free traders worry about unrestrained environmentalism. Ways to reconcile trade and environmental goals are highlighted, and the North American Free Trade Agreement (NAFTA) is explored as a model in this regard.

Freer trade and economic integration more broadly offer the promise of improved social welfare, as do programs aimed at pollution abatement and improved natural resource management. While not theoretically inconsistent, in practice, these goals are often not in perfect alignment. Only through concerted policy attention and efforts to overcome conflicts and tensions can both aims be addressed simultaneously and progress be made toward sustainable development.

Origins of the Trade and Environment "Conflict"

The trade and environmental policy agendas have been driven together by a number of factors. First, environmental issues have taken on increased salience in recent years. Climate change, drinking-water safety, chemical exposures, and other pollution problems have become a major focus of public concern. Trying to accommodate new issues on the public agenda often creates strain.[1] Because the precise focus of the public's environmental interest varies from nation to nation, and particularly from industrialized to developing countries, aligning trade and environmental policy is even more difficult.

Second, scientific advances have transformed the environmental policy landscape. In particular, recognition of a set of inherently global pollution and resource problems has further propelled environmental issues up the international policy agenda. From the threat of global climate change arising from a buildup of greenhouse gases in the atmosphere to ozone layer destruction, from emissions of chlorofluorocarbons (CFCs) and other related chemicals to the depletion of fisheries in most of the world's oceans, overexploitation of the "global commons" has added to the sense of urgency about international environmental issues.[2]

Third, a policy focus on "sustainable development" has led to an appreciation that environmental progress is easier to achieve under conditions of prosperity—and long-term economic growth depends on careful stewardship of the natural environment. The 1992 Earth Summit in Rio de Janeiro (formally known as the United Nations Conference on Environment and Development) highlighted the link between economic development and environmental protection generally, and trade and the environment more specifically.[3] When a new round of global trade negotiations was launched in 2001 in Doha, Qatar, the trade-environment relationship was made an explicit element of the negotiating agenda.[4] The 2002 World Summit on Sustainable Development in Johannesburg consolidated the focus on the trade-environment linkage. And the 2012 United Nations Conference on Sustainable Development (known as Rio+20) advanced this agenda further, mandating the creation of the new intergovernmental Open Working Group, which will submit a report to the United Nations General Assembly on sustainable development that meets a number of criteria, including universal applicability to countries at all stages of economic development.[5]

Finally, economic integration has also helped to transform environmental protection from a clearly domestic, highly localized issue into one of inherently international scope. Advocates of free trade point to the classic economic benefits associated with productivity gains, the efficient allocation of resources, and the increased ability of individual countries to capitalize on comparative advantage.[6] However, in this world of liberalized trade, where the competition for market share is global, the stringency of environmental regulations in each nation, state, or province becomes an important determinant of the competitiveness of the enterprises located within that territory. These worries take on added significance in the context of efforts to open markets and promote economic integration.

In the past two decades, free trade initiatives and commitments to liberalized investment regimes have sharpened the trade-environment debate. Because the primary barriers to international free trade are domestic policies, such as import tariffs and quotas, multilateral international treaties are necessary to facilitate trade across borders. President George H. W. Bush's 1989 announcement that he intended to negotiate a free trade agreement between the United States and Mexico first brought "trade and environment" issues to the fore. Environmentalists worried that such a trade agreement might mean an expansion of the highly polluted "maquiladora" (duty-free) zone along the U.S.-Mexico border, lowering U.S. environmental standards (through "harmonization" with lax Mexican regulatory requirements). Pressed by Congress, the Bush administration committed to a program of environmental efforts in parallel with the trade negotiations with Mexico and Canada that led to NAFTA.[7]

While NAFTA set the environmental pot on the trade fire, the decision of a GATT dispute resolution panel in the 1991 "tuna/dolphin" case caused a simmering issue to boil over. The GATT panel declared the U.S. law requiring an embargo on Mexican tuna that were caught in nets that killed dolphins to be illegal under the rules of international trade.[8] U.S. environmentalists saw the decision as an affront to American environmental "sovereignty."[9] The environmental community saw this decision as proof that, in a conflict between trade and environmental goals, trade liberalization principles would trump environmental values.

Protests against the effects of globalization, including the environmental impacts of economic integration, have become a fixture at almost every meeting of international economic officials. In fact, the push for further free trade agreements, including a Free Trade Area of the Americas and new commitments to multilateral trade liberalization through the World Trade Organization (WTO), has continued to make "trade and environment" a hot issue on the international agenda.[10]

Some success has been achieved in making trade and environmental policy making more mutually supportive.[11] For example, through the Dominican Republic–Central America–United States Free Trade Agreement (CAFTA-DR), the United States has initiated $20 million toward cooperative environmental projects in the region.[12] In 2012, the Asia-Pacific Economic Cooperation Forum (APEC) agreed on a list of environmental goods on which APEC member states will cut tariffs to 5 percent or less by 2015.[13] Policy makers have learned, furthermore, that they ignore the trade-environment link at some peril. For example, negotiations within the Organisation for Economic Cooperation and Development (OECD) to establish a multilateral agreement on investment faltered in the face of environmentalists' outcries over the lack of attention to pollution control and resource management issues in the draft treaty.

Efforts to make trade and environmental policies more compatible continue to face significant obstacles. The trade and environmental communities have distinct goals, traditions, operating procedures, and even languages. The ultimate good for environmentalists, "protection," sounds a lot like the consummate bad, "protectionism," that free traders seek to avoid. In both terminology and substance, bringing these two worlds together continues to be a challenge.[14]

Core Environmental Concerns about Free Trade

Environmentalists worry that economic integration and more globalized markets will make environmental protection harder to achieve. Their concerns can be boiled down to a few key propositions.[15]

Expanded trade will cause environmental harm by promoting economic growth that, without environmental safeguards, will result in increased pollution and the unsustainable consumption of natural resources. Environmentalists who adhere to a traditional "limits to growth" perspective would reject the possibility that environmental safeguards might make trade liberalization environmentally acceptable. They see free trade as inescapably resulting in environmentally damaging economic growth. Of course, many environmentalists today adhere to the "sustainable development" paradigm, which accepts the possibility that environmental improvements might arise from economic growth so long as pollution control and natural resource consumption issues are expressly addressed.[16] They also recognize that poverty leads to short-term decision making that is often environmentally harmful. Thus, to the extent that trade promotes growth and alleviates poverty, it can yield environmental benefits.

Many environmentalists fear that the "disciplines" to which countries bind themselves as part of trade agreements will result in a loss of regulatory sovereignty. Specifically, they worry that the market access obligations and other trade principles designed to permit the free flow of imports and exports will override environmental policies and goals, resulting in the harmonization of environmental standards at or below baseline levels.[17] This outcome might arise, they believe, through negotiated commitments to common regulatory rules. Alternatively, they fear that a free trade zone might make it hard for high-standard countries to keep their strict environmental requirements in the face of industry claims of competitive disadvantage from producers in low-standard jurisdictions whose environmental compliance costs are lower.

Even where pollution does not spill across national borders, countries with lax environmental standards will have a competitive advantage in a global marketplace, putting pressures on countries with high environmental standards to reduce the rigor of their environmental requirements. Fear that the United States would be competitively disadvantaged in an integrated North American marketplace was the central trade and environment issue in NAFTA. Ross Perot's memorable suggestion that low labor costs and lax environmental standards in Mexico would result in the "giant sucking sound" of U.S. factories and jobs going down the drain to Mexico resonated broadly.[18] Similar concerns have been an issue in virtually all of the recent trade agreement ratification debates.[19]

Although there is little empirical evidence of companies moving to "pollution havens," academics continue to debate the seriousness of fears about a "race toward the bottom" in setting environmental standards.[20] Variations in the stringency of regulations are not necessarily a problem. Differences in environmental standards can be seen as an important component of comparative advantage. Indeed, the fact that countries have different levels of commitment to environmental protection—and thus different pollution control costs—makes gains from economic exchange and trade possible. Competitiveness pressures may also induce "regulatory competition" among jurisdictions as governments work to make their locations attractive to industry. In some circumstances, these pressures will induce governments to provide services and to regulate efficiently. Competition of this sort enhances social welfare.[21] But in other circumstances, competition among horizontally arrayed jurisdictions (national governments versus national governments) may precipitate a welfare-reducing cycle of weakening environmental commitments as political leaders seek to relax their environmental standards to attract investment and jobs.[22] In practice, governments rarely lower their environmental standards to improve their competitive position. They may, however, relax the enforcement of their standards or fail to raise standards to optimal levels for fear of exposing their industries to higher costs than foreign competitors face.[23]

The critical issue, therefore, is why environmental standards diverge. If the stringency of the rules varies because of differences in climate, weather, population density, risk preferences, level of development, or other "natural" factors, the variations in regulatory vigor should be considered legitimate and appropriate. Any competitive pressure created is simply the playing out of socially beneficial market forces. In contrast, divergent standards may also arise from regulatory authorities' failure to monitor fully the harms that spill across their borders into other jurisdictions. These spillovers may result in the "externalization" of part of the costs of pollution control. In addition, regulatory "incapacity" may lead to suboptimal environmental standards or lax enforcement of environmental requirements. And special interest manipulation of the regulatory process or other distortions in environmental policy making may result in regulations that deviate from what would be the optimal environmental policies (what academics call "public choice" failures).

Underregulation that permits pollution to spill over into neighboring jurisdictions or into a global commons represents an unfair (and economically inefficient) basis on which to establish a competitive advantage. Likewise, suboptimal standards that arise from regulatory failures—including results driven by weak government performance and inadequate environmental decision making or outcomes manipulated by special interests through lobbying, campaign contributions, or outright corruption of public officials—break the promise of improved social welfare through interjurisdictional competition. And where competitors have selected, for whatever reason, suboptimal environmental policies, governments often respond strategically and set their standards with an eye on those adopted by their competition. In each of these circumstances, international cooperation in response to environmental challenges promises to improve policy outcomes. Insofar as trade negotiations generate the competitive pressures that trigger a "race to the bottom," they also provide an occasion to advance the collective action required to avoid a welfare-reducing regulatory chill.

The likelihood of a "race" dynamic increases as economic integration deepens. If Jurisdiction A is a comparatively unimportant destination of Jurisdiction B's exports, or if Jurisdiction A is an insignificant international competitor, then differentiated environmental standards matter very little. B will be relatively unaffected by environmental policy choices in A. But if the level of interaction grows, so does B's exposure to "economic externalities" arising from suboptimal environmental policies in A. For example, in 1985, U.S. exports to China totaled $7 billion, and imports from China stood at $3 billion. In 2011, Chinese exports to the United States topped $399 billion, and U.S. exports to China amounted to $103 billion.[24] This extraordinary growth in U.S.-China trade makes U.S. industries much more sensitive to cost disadvantages that they suffer in relation to Chinese competitors. Increasing attention as to whether these disadvantages arise from environmental conditions or other factors that are inappropriate and illegitimate has thus emerged.

If countries fail to carry out their international environmental obligations, trade restrictions may need to be used to limit "free riding." Yet the market-opening commitments made in the course of trade agreements may reduce the availability of trade measures as an environmental enforcement tool. Environmentalists fear that commitments to trade liberalization will limit the international community's leverage over countries that are refusing to sign on to or are not living up to international environmental agreements. This issue, prominent in the early 1990s, has returned to salience in the context of climate change as well as efforts to ensure that countries sign on to (and uphold) obligations to limit greenhouse gas emissions.

While recognizing the need to discipline free riders (those who are benefiting from but not paying for pollution control or shared resource management), trade officials often argue that it is not appropriate to use trade measures as a way of achieving environmental goals. They reason that it is hard enough to keep markets open without trying to carry environmental burdens at the same time. Environmentalists respond that there are very few ways of exerting pressure in the international domain and that trade measures must be available as an enforcement tool.

The Free Trade Response

Free traders worry that the environmentalists' critiques of trade are misplaced and could result in the disruption of efforts to promote trade liberalization and to obtain the benefits promised by more open markets around the world. Trade advocates note, in particular, that trade and environmental policy goals can be made compatible. As the members of the World Trade Organization declared at the launch of the WTO in 1994:

> There should not be, nor need be, any policy contradiction between upholding and safeguarding an open, nondiscriminatory and equitable

multilateral trading system on the one hand, and acting for the protection of the environment and promotion of sustainable development on the other.[25]

Free traders note that both trade liberalization and environmental protection efforts are aimed at promoting efficiency and reducing waste. They posit that, to the extent that environmental policies seem to be in tension with freer trade, the conflict generally arises from poorly constructed environmental policies rather than from any inherently antienvironmental bias embedded in the trading system. Trade experts further observe that environmental policies that seek to internalize externalities through the application of the polluter-pays principle represent virtually no conflict with freer trade.[26]

Trade supporters also maintain that, as an empirical matter, as the wealth of a society increases, its spending on environmental protection almost always goes up. Thus they contend that environmentalists should support freer trade as a way of achieving economic growth and greater wealth, some part of which can be devoted to expanded pollution control and resource conservation programs. More dramatically, trade advocates observe that poverty is the source of a great many environmental harms. And indeed, poor people often make bad environmental choices because of the short-term time frame forced upon them. For example, those who lack modern conveniences must cut down nearby trees to cook their evening meals. They are unable to focus on the longer-term consequences of deforestation, such as soil erosion and pollution of nearby bodies of water.

Professors Gene M. Grossman and Alan B. Krueger have demonstrated that some environmental problems seem to worsen during the early stages of development, peak at a per capita gross domestic product of about $8,000, and improve as countries become wealthier beyond that point.[27] Some problems are so localized and pressing that even the poorest countries will be under pressure to address them as economic growth begins and incomes start to rise. Governments, for example, seek to provide safe drinking water to their people at even the lowest levels of development. Other problems appear to follow the inverted-U "Kuznets curve" that Grossman and Krueger hypothesize, rising in the initial stages of industrialization but falling as wealth increases. Local air pollution problems seem to fall into this category. But other environmental problems continue to worsen even as incomes rise.[28] For instance, greenhouse gas emissions may go up at a less rapid rate when high income levels are achieved, but they do not fall. Other scholars have argued that the relationship between environmental harms and income is somewhat more complicated.[29]

A more nuanced understanding of the relationship between economic growth and environmental protection leads to the conclusion that trade can be a mechanism for advancing economic growth and social welfare, but this result is not guaranteed. Economic gains *can* permit resources to be made available for investments in environmental protection, but welfare losses from trade-exacerbated environmental harms could outweigh the benefits of freer trade. To maximize the chances of net welfare gains, environmental policy must evolve in tandem with commitments to trade liberalization.[30]

NAFTA: First Steps

The need to address environmental issues in the NAFTA context led to a commitment to a set of environmental negotiations alongside the trade negotiations—a "parallel track." These talks generated a joint U.S.-Mexican commitment to address pollution issues along the two countries' shared border. The "integrated border environmental plan" cataloged comprehensively for the first time the spectrum of environmental concerns arising along the 2,000-mile U.S.-Mexico border. The initiative also produced a game plan for addressing the issues identified and a set of priorities to be undertaken jointly by Mexican and U.S. environmental officials.

In addition to the border plan, the parallel-track negotiations led to the Environmental Side Agreement to NAFTA. The Side Agreement, concluded during the Clinton administration, set up a "development bank" to promote environmental infrastructure investments along the U.S.-Mexico border and established the Commission for Environmental Cooperation (CEC) to oversee the environmental issues associated with closer trade links across North America.[31] The CEC provides a mechanism for facilitating cooperation among the NAFTA countries on the full range of environmental issues and resource challenges facing them. It serves as a forum for regular high-level meetings, provides an independent secretariat to report on significant environmental issues confronting the NAFTA parties, ensures that environmental enforcement remains a priority in all three countries, and offers opportunities for public participation in the development and implementation of environmental laws and programs in Mexico, the United States, and Canada.

In addition to the parallel-track environmental negotiations, environmental officials were included, for the first time, in the trade negotiations themselves. Negotiators from the U.S. Environmental Protection Agency (EPA) participated in several of the issue-specific working groups. A senior EPA official served on the high-level negotiating team of the U.S. Trade Representative (USTR). Likewise, nongovernmental organizations (NGOs), including environmental groups, were considered an important constituency in the course of the NAFTA debate—a role they had never played before. In addition, trade representative Carla Hills placed four environmental group leaders on her public advisory committees on various aspects of trade policy making.[32]

Perhaps the most important procedural advance associated with NAFTA was the decision to undertake an environmental review of issues associated with freer trade across North America. This analysis helped to focus the negotiators on both large and small issues, ranging from the benefits of broadening Mexico's economic development beyond the maquiladora zone to finding ways to reduce the traffic jams (and resulting air pollution) caused by backups at customs in Texas, New Mexico, Arizona, and California. The value of this type of analysis is now widely recognized. In fact, the Clinton administration issued an executive order in 1999 requiring the USTR to carry out environmental reviews in advance of all future trade agreements.[33]

Substantive advances in the integration of environmental sensitivity into the trade system were also made in the course of the NAFTA process. The preamble to the agreement makes environmental considerations a central focus of the effort to promote freer trade. It calls on the parties to pursue their program of trade liberalization so as to promote "sustainable development" and to "strengthen the development and enforcement of environmental laws and regulations."[34]

The NAFTA parties further agreed that major environmental agreements with trade provisions should be given precedence if a conflict ever develops between a party's obligations under an environmental agreement and its obligations under NAFTA. Similarly, the NAFTA negotiations made clear in their chapter on "sanitary and phytosanitary" provisions that each party to the agreement retains an unrestricted right to set and maintain environmental health and safety standards at its own chosen level of protection. By clarifying that the parties remain free to make their own risk assessments and apply their own risk policies, NAFTA acknowledges that some legitimate national environmental policies will have impacts on trade but should still be permitted.

NAFTA's investment chapter also broke new ground in addressing environmental issues.[35] Specifically, the investment provisions assured each country the right to adopt and enforce any pollution control or resource management measure it deems necessary to protect its environment. This language prevents trade commitments from trumping environmental policies and programs as long as the policies are based on scientific foundations and are not disguised barriers to trade. The treaty also contains a "pollution haven" proviso that declares that a NAFTA party cannot seek to attract investments by relaxing environmental standards or cutting back on enforcement. A structure of binding arbitration and the possibility of trade penalties being imposed for noncompliance back this provision.

NAFTA also established more environmentally sensitive dispute resolution procedures. Specifically, where environmental issues become part of a trade dispute, the agreement provides procedures for convening a board of scientific or technical experts to advise the dispute settlement panel. It also forbids countries to take disputes out of NAFTA and into the WTO to obtain less environmentally protective ground rules.

The NAFTA efforts to make trade liberalization and environmental protection mutually compatible have generally worked quite well.[36] The feared industrial migration to Mexico based on a promise of lax environmental standards has not materialized. Rather, NAFTA's broadly based program of environmental cooperation has greatly increased the focus on pollution control in Mexico. While many problems remain, and the mechanism set up to finance environmental projects on the U.S.-Mexico border moves too slowly, environmental conditions across large parts of Mexico are beginning to improve.

Some environmentalists remain concerned that environmental issues are still not being taken seriously in the trade context. Over the past twenty years, there have been instances when this complaint was valid. The Clinton administration's proposals in 1997–1998 for a Free Trade Area of the Americas were devoid of any environmental provisions—representing a significant step back from NAFTA. Perhaps not coincidentally, the president failed to win the trade-negotiating authority he sought.

In 2002 the George W. Bush administration won approval for legislation to allow the White House to negotiate trade agreements and submit them to Congress for straight up-or-down votes within ninety days with no amendments. However, as part of the package approved by Congress, the Bush administration agreed to binding negotiating objectives related to the environment.[37] In 2007, this so-called trade promotion authority expired, and the Obama administration did not seek to renew the legislation. The lack of trade progress, never mind further integration of environmental goals into the trade regime, became an issue of some note during the 2012 U.S. presidential election campaign.[38]

In negotiations of recent agreements and amendments to previous agreements, the NAFTA environmental provisions have provided a template. However, none of these later agreements includes a strong institutional structure such as that found in the U.S.-Mexico-Canada context. Of course, the NAFTA Side Agreement's Commission for Environmental Cooperation has not been an unmitigated success. The CEC has undertaken several studies designed to ensure that environmental considerations are factored into trade policy across North America. But the CEC has also faced pressure not to

Table 14-1 U.S. Free Trade Agreements with Environmental Chapters

Dominican Republic–Central America–United States Free Trade Agreement (CAFTA-DR)

North American Free Trade Agreement (NAFTA)

U.S.-Australia Free Trade Agreement

U.S.-Bahrain Free Trade Agreement

U.S.-Chile Free Trade Agreement

U.S.-Colombia Free Trade Agreement

U.S.-Jordan Free Trade Agreement

U.S.-Morocco Free Trade Agreement

U.S.-Oman Free Trade Agreement

U.S.-Panama Free Trade Agreement

U.S.-Peru Free Trade Agreement

U.S.-Republic of Korea Free Trade Agreement (KORUS FTA)

U.S.-Singapore Free Trade Agreement

pursue its environmental goals too aggressively. The lack of clear political support has driven the CEC to back away from several controversial trade and environment issues, including questions about a Mexican cruise ship pier in Cozumel that threatened to damage coral reefs and efforts to address clear-cutting in the U.S. Northwest as well as British Columbia. Whether the CEC will mature into an effective mechanism for environmental coordination among the United States, Mexico, and Canada remains to be seen.[39]

The Broader Policy Response in the WTO

The World Trade Organization, the international body set up in 1994 to implement the General Agreement on Tariffs and Trade and to manage international trade relations, has come under criticism for its slow progress in building environmental sensitivity into the trading system. The WTO has a Committee on Trade and the Environment, and, as WTO director-general Pascal Lamy has observed, the organization has made some advances toward the goal of more mutually supportive trade and environmental policies.[40] Most notably, the WTO's interpretation of GATT Article XX, which provides an exception to GATT antiprotectionist requirements for policy measures that "are necessary to protect human, animal or plant life or health," was more forgiving to environmental regulations than some had anticipated.[41] In 2001, the WTO allowed France to maintain its ban on the importation of asbestos in order to protect its citizens from potentially inhaling the dangerous particulates this substance releases into the air.[42] Moreover, in the now famous "Shrimp-Turtle dispute," the WTO insisted that the parties collaborate to develop a cooperative environmental and trade policy solution for the protection of sea turtles, which led to the Memorandum of Understanding on the Conservation and Management of Marine Turtles and Their Habitats in the Indian Ocean.[43] These few, but prominent, WTO dispute resolutions under GATT Article XX provide real evidence that the trade regime can provide space for effective environmental policies.

At the same time, new disputes have increased the tension between trade and environment. Notably, the European Union challenged U.S. efforts to block the import of wines containing procymidone, an unregistered fungicide used on grapes.[44] The EU also challenged the U.S. Corporate Average Fuel Economy (CAFE) car mileage standards, arguing that this policy tool unfairly penalized European automobile manufacturers (for example, BMW, Mercedes, and Volvo) that sell only at the upper (low-gas-mileage) end of the car market. The United States brought a successful WTO claim against the EU for obstructing exports to Europe of U.S. beef found to contain growth hormones.[45] Canada forced the EU to back off on plans to forbid imports of fur from animals that had been caught through the use of leghold traps. Brazil and Venezuela won a case against the United States based on a claim of discrimination against foreign oil refiners in the EPA's implementation of the reformulated gasoline regulations under the 1990 Clean Air Act. And

Map 14-1 World Trade Organization Membership

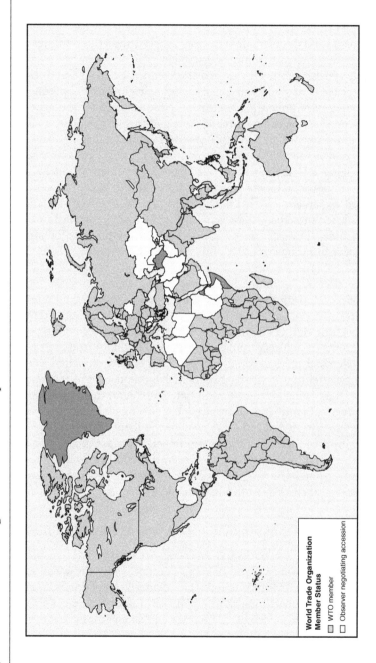

World Trade Organization
Member Status
☐ WTO member
☐ Observer negotiating accession

Thailand and several other countries in Southeast Asia got a WTO panel to agree that U.S. trade limitations imposed on shrimp fishermen who refused to use turtle excluder devices (TEDs) to protect endangered sea turtles were illegal under the GATT, although the WTO Appellate Body decision in this case endorsed the use of trade measures as a last resort to reinforce internationally agreed-upon environmental standards.[46]

China, which historically has had to defend itself in WTO disputes primarily because of its trade imbalance caused by its low cost of production and Chinese monetary policy, has increasingly found itself on the other side of WTO disputes at the intersection of trade and the environment. In 2012, the Chinese government filed a complaint with the WTO alleging that some EU countries had violated "WTO prohibitions on import replacement subsidies" by subsidizing EU producers of solar panels and thereby undercutting the makers of imported Chinese panels.[47] China and the United States have also threatened to initiate a WTO challenge to the EU Emissions Trading System, which requires that all aircraft landing in and departing from EU airports purchase allowances to cover their emissions, ultimately forcing the EU to back away from the extension of its carbon allowance rules to international air travel.[48]

As the pace of economic integration increases, so does the number of trade-environment conflicts. The pressure for a more systematic commitment to building environmental considerations into the international trading system shows little sign of abating. In fact, the WTO has been criticized generally for failing to advance trade-environment harmony and specifically for focusing almost exclusively on the trade effects of environmental policy while paying little attention to the environmental consequences of trade policy.

At the 2001 launch of a new round of multilateral trade talks—the Doha Development Round—the European Union insisted that environmental issues be added to the agenda.[49] Although the identified issues are carefully circumscribed, the fact that the environment is on the global trade agenda represents a break with the past. However, in 2008 the Doha Round broke down, and despite some progress in 2012, it has not yet concluded, rendering the "greening" of the WTO still incomplete.[50]

Strengthening the Global Environmental Regime

Many observers of the trade and environment debate have concluded that part of the explanation for the ongoing conflict lies in the weakness of the international environmental regime. The centerpiece of international environmental protection efforts, the United Nations Environment Programme (UNEP), is in serious disarray.[51] Moreover, global environmental responsibilities are spread across a half dozen other UN agencies (including the United Nations Development Programme, the United Nations Commission on Sustainable Development, and the World Meteorological Organization), the secretariats to various international environmental treaties (including the UN Framework Convention on Climate Change, the Montreal Protocol, the UN

Convention to Combat Desertification, and the Basel Convention), as well as the Bretton Woods institutions (the World Bank, the regional development banks, and the WTO). This fragmented institutional structure results in disjointed responses to global pollution and resource challenges, difficulty in clarifying policy and budget priorities, insufficient coordination across related problems, and lost opportunities for synergistic responses.

The presence of a global environmental organization able to operate in tandem with the WTO and to provide some counterbalance to the WTO's trade emphasis would be advantageous.[52] But fears of lost national sovereignty and concerns about creating a new UN bureaucracy make the prospect of establishing a comprehensive and coherent international umbrella environmental institution any time soon seem remote. In the absence of a functioning global environmental management system capable of addressing trade and environment issues, much of the responsibility for integrating these two policy realms will continue to fall to the WTO.

A serious effort to make the international trading system more environmentally sensitive would require action on many fronts. First, the activities of the WTO would need to become more transparent—that is, more open and easily followed by average people. Although some steps have been taken to open up the WTO,[53] most of the activities of the international trading system still occur behind closed doors. This secrecy generates hostility from those who feel excluded from WTO processes or who are simply put off by the fact that important decisions are being made without public input or understanding. The WTO could broadly enhance its legitimacy and authoritativeness by allowing representatives of NGOs to participate in or at least observe its proceedings.[54] The United States has advanced this logic with a series of proposals to open up the WTO, but to date these efforts to promote transparency have been blocked by WTO representatives from various developing countries.

This opposition reflects many concerns. Most notably, many free traders fear that the presence of environmentalists and others within the walls of the WTO would result in special interest manipulation of trade policy making. It seems unlikely, however, that the presence of outside observers would really distort the decision-making processes of the international trading system. The system is not free of special interest manipulation now, and inviting environmental groups might produce some influence to counteract that of the existing producer and business lobbying and other activities. Allowing NGOs to make submissions when they have positions on issues being addressed by dispute settlement panels, or more broadly by the WTO governing council, would improve the knowledge base of the WTO and might assist the organization's decision making, especially in relation to environmental policy outcomes, which are often fraught with uncertainty.[55]

Over the longer term, the WTO must find a more refined way of balancing trade and environmental goals. The current mechanism (found in Article XX of the GATT) requires a country whose environmental policies have been challenged as an obstacle to free trade to demonstrate that it has selected the "least GATT-inconsistent" policy tool available. This standard sets an almost impossibly high hurdle for environmental policies, because in almost every case there is some environmental strategy or approach that would intrude less on trade. A variety of proposals have been advanced that would amend Article XX and make it easier for countries to maintain legitimate environmental policies in the face of trade challenges.[56]

In addition, while the trade system permits restrictions on imports when the product itself fails to meet national environmental standards, current GATT rules forbid discrimination against imports based on the environmental conditions associated with their production process or method (PPM). This means that imports of cars without the requisite pollution control devices can be banned. Similarly, imports of strawberries containing chemical residues can be barred. But GATT rules do not permit a country to block imports of cars because the steel that goes into them was made in polluting mills. Nor do the rules allow countries to turn back imported strawberries because the farmers who grew the crops polluted nearby rivers with pesticides and fertilizers. The prohibition against PPM-based environmental requirements is, however, untenable in a world of ecological interdependence.

Today the issue of *how* things are made is just as important as *what* is traded. If a semiconductor is produced using CFCs in violation of the ozone layer protection provisions of the Montreal Protocol, GATT rules would not permit an importing nation to bar the offending chip.[57] Even if the current blanket prohibition on PPM-based regulation was swept aside, the WTO would face lingering questions at the trade-environment interface.[58] Whose regulatory standards should be adopted? Who should determine compliance with agreed-upon standards? And who should assess penalties or take other enforcement actions when a violation is uncovered?

These questions persist even if the standards in question arise from an international agreement. The WTO remains vulnerable to challenges arising from the imposition of trade measures under multilateral environmental agreements. This is especially true in those cases where a WTO member is not a party to the environmental accord. A strong possibility exists that, under current interpretations of the GATT, a country facing trade penalties for failing to sign or adhere to a multilateral environmental agreement would be able to argue that those imposing the trade sanctions for environmental reasons are in violation of their GATT obligations. Thus a nation that failed to join the Montreal Protocol banning the use of ozone-depleting chemicals might be able to free ride on the environmental protection efforts of others and dodge trade sanctions imposed by parties to the protocol. In response to this issue, the WTO could adopt a provision such as the one found in NAFTA that declares that trade measures taken in accordance with multilateral environmental agreements are not NAFTA violations. Beyond finding ways to balance conflicting trade and environmental goals more effectively, those seeking to make trade and environmental policies more mutually reinforcing could identify many places where the aims of these policies dovetail.

Notably, the elimination of subsidies for timber, water, agriculture, and energy and the more careful regulation of fisheries would yield both substantial trade benefits and environmental improvements. Agricultural price supports, for instance, encourage farmers to plant on marginal lands, which often require heavy doses of chemicals to be productive. Cutbacks in agricultural subsidies would diminish incentives to farm marginal lands and reduce trade distortions, thus providing new agricultural export opportunities for many developing countries.

Managing Interdependence

Despite the breadth of activities linking trade and environment policies in recent years and the reasonably favorable results arising on this score from NAFTA, some policy makers continue to dismiss the significance of the trade-environment relationship. The call for economic and environmental interests to be kept separate is not just normatively wrong—it is practically impossible to achieve such a separation. The relationship between environmental issues and trade issues in the context of deepening economic integration is inescapable and multilayered. Ignoring these linkages threatens to reduce social welfare, limit the gains from trade, and cause unnecessary environmental degradation. Ignoring the environmental implications of trade policy making poses an acute threat to current and future economic integration efforts, not to mention environmental programs.

The fundamental challenge is to manage interdependence on multiple levels, representing both shared natural resources and a common economic destiny. Governance in this context requires working across divergent priorities—North versus South, economic growth versus environmental protection, and present interests versus future ones. *Sustainable development* has emerged as the shorthand term for a way of refining a systems-oriented policy approach that considers these conflicting needs simultaneously. Making trade and environmental policies work together, therefore, stands as a classic example of the on-the-ground challenge of sustainable development.

Notes

1.   Kym Anderson and Richard Blackhurst, "Trade, the Environment, and Public Policy," in *The Greening of World Trade Issues,* ed. Kym Anderson and Richard Blackhurst (Ann Arbor: University of Michigan Press, 1992), 3.
2.   Daniel C. Esty, *Greening the GATT: Trade, Environment, and the Future* (Washington, DC: Institute for International Economics, 1994), 17–20; Andrew Hurrell and Benedict Kingsbury, *The International Politics of the Environment* (Oxford: Clarendon Press, 1992).
3.   Richard N. Gardner, *Negotiating Survival: Four Priorities after Rio* (New York: Council on Foreign Relations, 1992); "Rio Declaration on Environment and Development," UNCED, UN Doc. A/Conf. 151/5/Rev. 1, reprinted in *International Legal Materials* 31 (1992): 874, 878; "Agenda 21," UNCED, UN Doc. A/Conf. 151/26/ Rev. 1 (1992).

4. Doha WTO Ministerial Declaration, WT/MIN(01)/DEC/1, November 14, 2001, paras. 31–33.
5. "The Future We Want—Rio+20 Outcome Document," A/RES/66/288, September 11, 2012, paras. 247–248.
6. Douglas A. Irwin, *Free Trade under Fire*, 3rd ed. (Princeton, NJ: Princeton University Press, 2009), 5.
7. John J. Audley, *Green Politics and Global Trade: NAFTA and the Future of Environmental Politics* (Washington, DC: Georgetown University Press, 1997); "Binational Statement on Environmental Safeguards That Should Be Included in the North American Free Trade Agreement," issued by Canadian Nature Federation, Canadian Environmental Law Association, Sierra Club–Canada, Rawson Survival–Canada, Pollution Probe–Canada, National Audubon Society, National Wildlife Federation, Community Nutrition Institute, and Environmental Defense Fund, May 28, 1992.
8. Robert Housman and Durwood Zaelke, "The Collision of the Environment and Trade: The GATT Tuna/Dolphin Decision," *Environmental Law Reporter* 22 (April 1992): 10268.
9. Steve Charnovitz, "Environmentalism Confronts GATT Rules," *Journal of World Trade* 28 (January 1993): 37–54.
10. André Dua and Daniel C. Esty, *Sustaining the Asia Pacific Miracle* (Washington, DC: Institute for International Economics, 1997); Yoichi Funabashi, *Asia-Pacific Fusion: Japan's Role in APEC* (Washington, DC: Institute for International Economics, 1995); William H. Cooper, *Free Trade Agreements: Impact on U.S. Trade and Implications for U.S. Trade Policy* (Washington, DC: Congressional Research Service, 2010).
11. For discussion of NAFTA's environmental dimensions and effects, see Carolyn L. Deere and Daniel C. Esty, eds., *Greening the Americas: NAFTA's Lessons for Hemispheric Trade* (Cambridge: MIT Press, 2002).
12. J. F. Hornbeck, *The Dominican Republic–Central America–United States Free Trade Agreement (CAFTA-DR)*, CRS Report for Congress RL31870 (Washington, DC: Congressional Research Service, January 16, 2008), http://nationalaglawcenter.org/wp-content/uploads/assets/crs/RL31870.pdf.
13. Vladivostok Declaration, APEC, September 8–9, 2012, Annex C.
14. Daniel C. Esty, "Bridging the Trade-Environment Divide," *Journal of Economic Perspectives* 15 (Summer 2001): 113–130.
15. Esty, *Greening the GATT*, 42–55.
16. It is interesting to see how "trade and environment" issues have split the environmental community, separating those who accept the promise of sustainable development from those who believe that economic growth is inherently environmentally harmful. See Audley, *Green Politics and Global Trade*.
17. For instance, in the debate over NAFTA, some environmentalists expressed concerns regarding the likelihood of a deterioration in meat inspection standards along the U.S.-Mexico border. See Lori Wallach, *The Consumer and Environmental Case against Fast Track* (Washington, DC: Public Citizen, 1991), 16. Other scholars contend that trade can uplift product standards. See Alan O. Sykes, *Product Standards for Internationally Integrated Goods Markets* (Washington, DC: Brookings Institution, 1995); David Vogel, *Trading Up: Consumer and Environmental Regulation in a Global Economy* (Cambridge, MA: Harvard University Press, 1995). Further excellent considerations of harmonization issues are provided in Jagdish Bhagwati and Robert E. Hudec, eds., *Fair Trade and Harmonization: Prerequisites for Free Trade?* (Cambridge: MIT Press, 1996).
18. Ross Perot, *Save Your Job, Save Our Country: Why NAFTA Must Be Stopped—Now!* (New York: Hyperion, 1993); Esty, *Greening the GATT*.
19. This includes the U.S. free trade agreements with Chile, Singapore, Jordan, Morocco, Bahrain, and Oman.
20. Various aspects of this debate are reviewed in Daniel C. Esty and Damien Geradin, eds., *Regulatory Competition and Economic Integration: Comparative Perspectives*

(Oxford: Oxford University Press, 2001). See also Daniel C. Esty, "Governing at the Trade-Environment Interface," in *The WTO and Global Governance: Future Directions*, ed. Gary P. Sampson (Tokyo: United Nations University Press, 2008).

21. Charles M. Tiebout, "A Pure Theory of Local Expenditures," *Journal of Political Economy* 64 (October 1956): 416–424; Wallace E. Oates and Robert M. Schwab, "Economic Competition among Jurisdictions: Efficiency Enhancing or Distortion Inducing?," *Journal of Public Economics* 35 (April 1988): 333–354; Richard L. Revesz, "Rehabilitating Interstate Competition: Rethinking the 'Race-to-the-Bottom' Rationale for Federal Environmental Regulation," *New York University Law Review* 67 (December 1992): 1210–1254.

22. Daniel C. Esty, "Revitalizing Environmental Federalism," *Michigan Law Review* 95 (December 1996): 629–634.

23. Lyuba Zarsky and Jason Hunter, "Environmental Cooperation at APEC: The First Five Years," *Journal of Environment and Development* 6 (September 1997): 222–251.

24. U.S. Census Bureau, "Foreign Trade: Trade in Goods with China," http://www.census.gov/foreign-trade/balance/c5700.html.

25. Marrakesh Decisions Concurrent to Establishing the WTO, "Decision on Trade and Environment," April 14, 1994, reprinted in *International Legal Materials* 33 (1994): 1255.

26. Steve Charnovitz, "Free Trade, Fair Trade, Green Trade: Defogging the Debate," *Cornell International Law Journal* 27 (1994): 459–525; Sanford Gaines, "The Polluter-Pays Principle: From Economic Equity to Environmental Ethos," *Texas International Law Journal* 26 (Summer 1991): 463–496.

27. Gene M. Grossman and Alan B. Krueger, "Economic Growth and the Environment," *Quarterly Journal of Economics* 110 (May 1995): 353, 369.

28. Dua and Esty, *Sustaining the Asia Pacific Miracle*, 73–77.

29. Theodore Panayotou, "Demystifying the Environmental Kuznets Curve: Turning a Black Box into a Policy Tool," *Environment and Development Economics* 2 (1997): 465–484; M. A. Cole, A. J. Rayner, and J. M. Bates, "The Environmental Kuznets Curve: An Empirical Analysis," *Environment and Development Economics* 2 (1997): 401–416; S. M. DeBruyn, J. C. J. M. van den Bergh, and J. B. Opschoor, "Economic Growth and Emissions: Reconsidering the Empirical Basis of Environmental Kuznets Curves," *Ecological Economics* 25 (1998): 161–175.

30. Esty, "Bridging the Trade-Environment Divide," 119.

31. NAFTA Supplemental Agreements, "North American Agreement on Environmental Cooperation," September 13, 1993, reprinted in *International Legal Materials* 32 (1993): 1480.

32. *Inside U.S. Trade*, August 23, 1991, 7; Trade and Environment Committee of the National Advisory Council for Environmental Policy and Technology, *The Greening of World Trade*, Report to the EPA (Washington, DC: Environmental Protection Agency, 1993).

33. Executive Order 13141, Environmental Reviews of Trade Agreements, November 16, 1999.

34. NAFTA Preamble, December 17, 1992, reprinted in *International Legal Materials* 32 (1993): 296, 605.

35. NAFTA Chapter 11 became a source of controversy, however, because its loose drafting seemed to create a risk that legitimate environmental regulation might trigger compensation requirements. For further discussion on this point, see Howard Mann and Mónica Araya, "An Investment Regime for the Americas: Challenges and Opportunities for Environmental Sustainability," in Deere and Esty, *Greening the Americas*.

36. Gary C. Hufbauer, Daniel C. Esty, Diana Orejas, Luis Rubio, and Jeffrey J. Schott, *NAFTA and the Environment: Seven Years Later* (Washington, DC: Institute for International Economics, 2000); Carolyn L. Deere and Daniel C. Esty, "Trade and Environment: Reflections on the NAFTA and Recommendations for the Americas," in Deere and Esty, *Greening the Americas*,

37. John Audley, "Environment's New Role in U.S. Trade Policy," Trade, Equity, and Development Policy Brief 3, Carnegie Endowment for International Peace, September 2002.

38. "Obama vs. Romney: China, Other Trade Issues," Reuters, November 5, 2012, http://www.dnaindia.com/world/report_obama-vs-romney-china-other-trade-issues_1760603.

39. Hufbauer et al., *NAFTA and the Environment*; Laura Carlsen and Hilda Salazar, "Limits to Cooperation: A Mexican Perspective on the NAFTA's Environmental Side Agreement and Institutions," in Deere and Esty, *Greening the Americas*.

40. Pascal Lamy, "The WTO and Its Agenda for Sustainable Development" (address at Yale University, October 24, 2007).

41. General Agreement on Tariffs and Trade, October 30, 1947, 55 U.N.T.S.194.

42. Lamy, "The WTO and Its Agenda for Sustainable Development."

43. Ibid.

44. An "unregistered" fungicide is one that has not gone through EPA safety testing to establish a safe residue level under the Federal Insecticide, Fungicide, and Rodenticide Act, 7 U.S.C. §136 et seq. (1996).

45. Michael B. Froman, "International Trade: The United States–European Community Hormone Treated Beef Conflict," *Harvard International Law Journal* 30 (Spring 1989): 549–556.

46. For descriptions of many important and interesting trade disputes, see Esty, *Greening the GATT*, app. C, 257–274. See also Carrie Wofford, "A Greener Future at the WTO: The Refinement of WTO Jurisprudence on Environmental Exceptions to the GATT," *Harvard Environmental Law Review* 24, no. 2 (2000): 563–592.

47. "China Files EU Solar Subsidy Complaint with WTO," BBC News, November 5, 2012.

48. Jennifer M. Freedman, "EU's Emissions Trading System Would Beat WTO Challenge," Bloomberg, April 13, 2012; Proposed Decision 2012/328 of the European Parliament and of the Council of November 2012, on derogating temporarily from Directive 2003/87/EC of the European Parliament and of the Council establishing a scheme for greenhouse gas emission allowance trading within the Community.

49. Doha WTO Ministerial Declaration, paras. 31–33.

50. Pascal Lamy, "Report by the Chairman of the Trade Negotiations Committee to General Council," WTO, May 1–2, 2012.

51. Even UNEP acknowledges that "global governance structures and global environmental solidarity remain too weak to make progress a world-wide reality. . . . The gap between what has been done thus far and what is realistically needed is widening." See United Nations Environment Programme, *Global Environment Outlook* (New York: Oxford University Press, 1997).

52. For a review of global environmental governance issues, see Daniel C. Esty and Maria Ivanova, eds., *Global Environmental Governance: Options and Opportunities* (New Haven, CT: Yale School of Forestry and Environmental Studies, 2002).

53. Lamy, "The WTO and Its Agenda for Sustainable Development."

54. Steve Charnovitz, "Two Centuries of Participation: NGOs and International Governance," *Michigan Journal of International Trade* 18 (Winter 1997): 183–286; Daniel C. Esty, "Non-governmental Organizations at the World Trade Organization: Cooperation, Competition, or Exclusion," *Journal of International Economic Law* 1 (1998): 123–147; James Cameron and Ross Ramsey, "Participation by NGOs in the WTO," Working Paper, Global Environment and Trade Study (GETS), New Haven, Connecticut, 1995.

55. Christophe Bellmann and Richard Gerster, "Accountability in the WTO," *Journal of World Trade* 30 (December 1996): 31–74. On the advantages of NGO "co-opetition," see Daniel C. Esty and Damien Geradin, "Regulatory Co-opetition," in Esty and Geradin, *Regulatory Competition and Economic Integration*.

56. Daniel C. Esty, "Making Trade and Environmental Policies Work Together: Lessons from NAFTA," in *Trade and Environment: The Search for Balance*, ed. James Cameron, Paul Demaret, and Damien Geradin (London: Cameron, 1994), 382.
57. Duncan Brack, *International Trade and the Montreal Protocol* (London: Royal Institute of International Affairs, 1996).
58. Some softening of the WTO rules has begun to emerge, especially in the Appellate Body decision in the Shrimp-Turtle case. See Wofford, "A Greener Future at the WTO."

15

Consumption, Commodity Chains, and Global and Local Environments

Stacy D. VanDeveer

Our Material World*

Consumption uses things up. By now it is well known that we humans are consuming vast quantities of natural resources and changing our local, national, and global environments in the process. Furthermore, everything comes from somewhere. Whether the things we consume are grown, captured, mined, or manufactured—or some combination of all of these—they come from somewhere. People and communities are involved in the complex processes that create, harvest, distribute, and sell the things we use in our daily lives. Every transaction along these chains or webs of economic and social relations consumes resources. And frankly, the social and environmental conditions in which things are grown, harvested, and mined are often quite grim—in ecological and humanitarian terms—and often unregulated.

Concern about global ecological limits and the ramifications of scarcity date back to at least the 1970s, continuing through the end of the twentieth century with a spike in interest around the 1992 Rio Earth Summit and since 2005 with higher and more volatile commodities prices and increased concern among policy makers and firms about international resource competition.[1] For much of this same period, resource politics was central to understanding global geopolitics and interdependence as energy, environmental, food, and other natural resource issues grew in importance among many political and economic elites in the "North" and "South."[2] By the early twenty-first century, the global environmental movement and the international social justice movement were beginning to see more shared interests and concerns under broader conceptions of sustainable development.[3]

Contemporary concern about consumptive and social justice aspects of globalization has resulted in a host of state and nonstate attempts to address the negative environmental and social conditions in producer communities around the globe. In recent years, scholars' attention to consumption issues has grown as the aggregate demand of our species continues to increase and as the environmental and human health implications of global resource consumption mount.[4] Environmental and social justice advocates have also

---

*I am grateful for valuable research assistance on this topic from Eric Nitschke and from the insights and information produced during several years of teaching global resources and energy politics to students at the University of New Hampshire and the Harvard University Summer School.

turned their attention to combating overconsumption and the ecological and humanitarian costs of unregulated, or badly regulated, agricultural production, mining, and manufacturing around the world.[5] Organizations such as the Worldwatch Institute, Friends of the Earth, Oxfam, the World Wide Fund for Nature (WWF), Global Witness, Fair Trade International, and thousands of other nongovernmental organizations (NGOs) are working tirelessly to reduce the environmental damage and human exploitation accompanying the growth of global wealth and trade (see also Chapters 2 and 14). Furthermore, some states are working together and with international organizations, NGOs, and private-sector organizations to attempt to reduce corruption and improve governance in areas such as diamond mining and the oil and gas sector.

Social critics from Socrates to Madonna remind us that we live in a material world, and environmental analysts have become increasingly concerned about the scale of human material consumption. According to one recent estimate, humans now consume about 50 percent more natural resources than they did thirty years ago, with people in wealthier countries consuming five to ten times as many resources as those in poorer ones.[6] The same study also notes that we have become more economically efficient over time, using 30 percent fewer resources to produce each dollar or euro of gross domestic product. North American consumerism begets a lifestyle associated with ravenous consumption of resources—energy, minerals, foods, and products of all types.[7] We also know that such consumptive patterns and institutions are being replicated around the world by (mostly) wealthy urbanites in many countries as, for example, consumption of fossil fuels, beef, and bottled water continues to grow and the number of automobiles in the world passes one billion on its way to two billion.[8]

Such lifestyle choices globalize some of the most ecologically damaging and inefficient aspects of Northern consumer culture. Can this process continue? By 2005 Americans had used fifty billion bottles of water—this in a country where tap water is safe to drink in almost every location.[9] How many bottles will be used around the world if the taste for bottled water globalizes? How many bottles will end up floating in the oceans and littering ecosystems, or incinerated, or piled in landfills? In addition to the increase in material throughput, biodiversity is declining, deforestation and habitat loss continue, and greenhouse gas emissions continue their global climb. In North America and Europe some debate is again emerging about the ways that consumerism may harm the consumers as well as the Earth's ecosystems.[10]

On top of growing global consumption of resources, the world is a very unequal place. About 40 percent of the world's seven billion people live in poverty (defined by the World Bank as living on less than $2 per day). Almost a billion people live in even more desperate poverty—on less than $1 per day. In fact, about 80 percent of the global population lives on less than $10 per day—about what it costs to see a movie or buy two beers in the United States. About fifty countries (more than one-quarter of the total number of countries in the world) are actually poorer, per capita, than they were in the 1970s.

Hundreds of millions have no access to clean water or medical care, regularly experience hunger and malnutrition, and live with little or no hope of improvement in these conditions.[11] These people's lives are nearly unimaginable for most North Americans and Europeans: try to imagine living every day on less than the cost of a Starbucks coffee. Chronic hunger would be normal for you, and large portions of your time would be taken up by efforts to get water to drink and fuel for cooking and heating. The "bottom billion" tend to live in countries without good government, economic opportunity, or much help from the international community.[12] These countries are "falling behind and falling apart."[13] And it is not, generally speaking, consumption by the world's poorest people that drives ever-growing consumption of the Earth's resources.

If global sustainable development is also about improving the lives of the world's poorest and most marginalized, then addressing issues of overconsumption in some societies cannot simply mean consigning others to perpetual, grinding poverty. The challenge of global sustainability is to ensure or engender a high quality of life for all seven-plus billion people of today and the nine to ten billion expected in midcentury, without exceeding the capacity of our planet's ecosystems.

The next two sections outline some basic concepts used to understand how globalizing patterns of consumption and production operate. Next, three brief sections present basic information about environmental and humanitarian concerns related to agricultural commodities; extractive industries such as mining, oil, and natural gas exploration; and finished goods. The final section reviews a number of possible policy responses to the challenges of consumption presented here.

Consumption, Commoditization, and Social Embeddedness

Consumption proves to be one of the most difficult issues to confront in environmental politics—for individuals and for authorities from local to global levels. Who benefits from curbing consumption? Consumers like cheap and plentiful products, and leaders of wealthy consumer societies are unlikely to curb consumption, as are the globe's most prominent business leaders and corporations. After the terrorist attacks on New York City and Washington, D.C., on September 11, 2001, President George W. Bush told Americans to get out there and spend money to help fight international terrorism. Americans' consumer debt is credited with slowing the economic recovery from the 2007–2009 recession. Meanwhile, Chinese are criticized at home and abroad for saving too much and spending (read consuming) too little. We are living in a material world.

Because the total human population has grown so dramatically over the past century, it is tempting to blame the number of humans for our species' growing global impacts on the environment. Yet the evidence suggests otherwise. While the human population has grown more than fourfold in the past one hundred years, per capita use of resources has grown much more.[14]

Globally, our consumption of most foods, water, fossil fuels, forest products, fish, and most other resources grows faster than our numbers. Furthermore, in the unequal world of the early twenty-first century, it is in the poorest parts of the world where human population is growing most rapidly, while consumption is driven by the wealthy societies and the urbanites around the world (in the North and the South) whose consumption increasingly mirrors that of North America and Europe. It is not the world's poor and lower-income citizens who drive growing consumption around the world.

Carbon emissions serve as an example. While the average U.S. citizen emits a bit less than twenty metric tons of carbon each year, the average European or Japanese citizen, with a similarly high standard of living, emits less than half of that. Chinese per capita emissions are about five metric tons, and average per capita emissions for India and most of Africa are less than two metric tons per year.[15] So, while the African population grows faster than the populations in North America, Europe, and China, it is not Africans whose consumption is rapidly changing the global climate. Yet Africans will suffer the consequences of the global climate change they did not cause.

North Americans, Europeans, and Japanese have used up billions of barrels of oil—not to mention coal and natural gas—from all around the globe and flushed the pollution into the global atmosphere. They have also depleted their own oil and gas supplies. Now joined by China, India, and a small number of other rapidly growing economies, they are engaged in a mad rush to secure access to the remaining oil from offshore and on-land oil reserves around the world.[16] Again, the significance of North American consumptive lifestyles should not be lost in this example. Although Chinese consumption has grown rapidly (like the Chinese government's involvement in global petro-politics), China's 1.3 billion people consume about 10 million barrels of oil per day, while 300 million Americans use more than 20 million barrels per day.

Many factors cause our collective material consumption to grow over time. This chapter highlights two aspects of contemporary consumer societies and economies: *commoditization* (or *commodification*) and the *social embeddedness of consumption*.[17] One of the many impressive characteristics of capitalism is its endless capacity to induce commoditization. Capitalism gives us concrete incentives to develop goods and services most suited to buying and selling—such goods and services can be entirely new, or they can replace things that used to be free or were less amenable to buying and selling. Capitalism engenders creativity and innovation for new goods and services, but it also means that we tend to convert things that are not commodities into things that are.[18]

The example of children's play illustrates the implications. Children (like other mammal youth) have been playing as part of their development, as far as we know, for thousands of years. Our grandparents tell stories of playing things like stickball, of having one doll, of making a toy gun, or of pretending to be cops and robbers or cowboys and Indians with sticks. They did not grow up in 2,000-plus-square-foot houses with several rooms strewn with hundreds of toys—most made with petrochemicals and transported thousands of miles via fossil fuel–based transportation. This image of contemporary North American childhood reveals a number of things about the typical North American lifestyle: the material throughput of everyday life tends to grow over time, as does the size of the average house, although the size of the average North American family has gone down over time. We have larger houses for fewer people, and a lot more stuff.

Commoditization dynamics may also facilitate inequality and injustice in the world, even as they drive impressive levels of innovation and wealth creation. Thus water privatization may shift water resources from local community control to the control of firms or the state, further marginalizing poorer citizens or communities.[19] Perhaps the best example of commodification's frequently unequal outcomes is found in medical research and product development. Much more money is invested in the development of treatments for the maladies of the world's wealthy than is spent curing and treating things that kill people in the world's poorest societies. Growing markets for treatments for balding and erectile dysfunction, and diet programs and pills, offer enormous potential for the development of profitable products. The profit potential for treatments of diarrheal and other treatable diseases that sicken or kill many of the world's poorest is much lower. So too is the profit potential for preventive treatment regimes for people in the North and the South.[20]

Similar dynamics play out in agricultural production, research, and investment. It is common for people to be malnourished in communities where coffee, roses, or other international commodities are grown for export. Attention to commoditization dynamics is not about spinning conspiracy theories, but about understanding that institutionalized incentives have consequences and outcomes in the world.

Patterns of North American material consumption and related commoditization processes also reveal the importance of our second concept, the social embeddedness of consumption. What individuals consume is heavily determined by a host of social influences and institutions. Unlike the assumptions often made in economic theories and models, social embeddedness suggests that "a consumer's choices are not isolated acts of rational decision making."[21] Rather, what we consume helps us find meaning, social status, or aspects of our identity. Furthermore, our consumer choices are shaped by advertising and myriad media images, and they are very much influenced by a complex, larger web of social and political institutions around us. For example, think of a decision to purchase a car, a phone, or an item of clothing. Which of the choices seems cooler? Sexier? More eco-friendly? More professional? More fun? Which choice seems more like you (or me) or more like the person you want to be? The answers to these questions and the perceptions on which they rest connect our buying decisions to the social worlds around us. We live in a material world.

Beyond individual purchasing choices among the options before us, consumption is embedded in broad social and political institutions. The cars, phones, and clothing available to us are shaped by government policies, corporate structures and cultures, long histories of product development, and a host of other interrelated social, political, and economic factors. Thus consumer choices are not determined simply by the aggregate preferences of consumers but also by myriad other factors. Can I choose not to have a car if there are no transportation alternatives? I can reduce the energy I use in my dorm room or apartment, but I usually have no control over whether my electricity is generated with wind power or the dirtiest coal. Through my individual choices I can reduce my ecological footprint somewhat, by changing my purchasing and other behaviors. Doing so may positively affect the environment, my life, and the lives of others. Yet, because consumption is socially embedded, I can make a substantial impact on the consumption levels of my lifestyle and my community only by working to change social and political institutions. As Michael Maniates observes, we cannot simply recycle cans, plant trees, and buy a few green products and save the Earth.[22] Political and social change is required.

Chains, Chains, Chains

Commodity chains have long been of interest to business practitioners and scholars alike.[23] Traditionally, a commodity chain was viewed as a set of connections or processes through which a product went, from the provision of raw materials at one end of a chain to the final purchase and use of a product at the other end. Processes along the chain might include harvesting or mining, processing, manufacturing, distribution, marketing, and so on. Then, at some point, a product is likely to be discarded. If we are trying to understand the ever-expanding use of material resources, several problems arise with this traditional understanding of commodity chains. First, the traditional notion suggests that consumption happens only at the end of the chain—when we buy something or use it. But, if we are to understand ever-expanding material throughput in our world, we must remember that *consumption happens at every stage or within every transaction along these chains*.[24] At every stage, with every interaction, things are used up.

The traditional formulation also downplays the social embeddedness discussed above. In other words, every point or transaction along a chain of relations involves, and is shaped by, social interaction and institutions. So, for example, how resources are grown or extracted from the earth—whether in ways that are wasteful, environmentally sensitive, or dangerous to the workers and community members—is contingent in large part on social institutions. The same is true of how things are manufactured and transported. These aspects of social embeddedness mean that commodity chains are better thought of as complex webs of social relations connecting people, institutions, and ecosystems across geographies, societies, and markets.

Thought of as complex webs of social relations that consume resources at every point or transaction, commodity chains help us understand the growing complexity of our globalizing world. Through these chains, the environmental and social implications of the things people consume are hidden or distanced from their everyday lives. *Distancing* of the implications of consumption severs feedback of information and ideas between social groups involved in commodity chains. It obscures the costs (often called the ecological and human externalities) of our activities.

Tom Princen argues that distancing has multiple facets or dimensions—including geographic, cultural, bargaining power, and agency dimensions—in the contemporary global political economy.[25] In other words, information feedback or knowledge about the costs of our consumption is inhibited by the sheer physical distances (and the geographic complexity) that separate us from the origins of the things we use. Culturally, most modern consumers know almost nothing about the communities or the practices used in agriculture, mining, or even manufacturing. For example, if we do not associate agriculture with massive amounts of industrial chemicals and the need for stringent regulation of their use, we may not think about whether particular foods come from communities where such regulation (and knowledge about chemical risks) exists. The bargaining power and multiple agency dimensions refer to social and economic institutions associated with complex transnational commodity chains. For example, if local farmers growing fruits or coffee in developing countries have no choice about to whom they sell their crops, they have no leverage over the prices they can ask. There is no competition to buy their goods. Too often, each is forced to take whatever low price is offered. If local workers do not have enforceable rights to organize themselves in attempts to raise their wages, the prices they are paid for the goods, or the standards in which they work, they cannot bargain for their interests. Transnational commodity chains are now so complex and so dynamic, they experience constant change. Usually neither the buyers of a finished good (at one end of the chain) nor the growers or miners or manufacturers at earlier stages in the chain could ever hope to trace the relations or the costs throughout the entire chain.

The commodity chains of the early twenty-first century are complex webs of relations that result in the distancing or obscuring of cost information from consumers. And the impediments to improving these feedback breakdowns are significant. If, for example, we assume that each of us reading this chapter wants to be an informed, environmentally and socially conscious consumer, what would we need to know and do? First, we might want to find out where everything we consume comes from (geographic dimension). For a start, we would need to determine the origins of every ingredient in the food and drink we consume; every component of the clothing, books, and electronics we purchase; and every electron of electricity and transportation fuel we use (to say nothing of where the energy used to make and transport the things we buy comes from). Probably none of us could accomplish this task. Even if we managed to find out where most of these components originated, to make decisions regarding which products are environmentally and socially superior, we would also need to know about the environmental and social conditions in which every component was made and assembled.

An example of the challenges presented to the environmentally and socially concerned consumer can be found in a pair of blue jeans. In 2001, the British newspaper the *Guardian* published a story about the writers' attempts to trace a pair of jeans from their point of sale in a shop in the United Kingdom to the origins of the jeans and their components.[26] They found that cotton for the jeans was grown in Pakistan and Benin; the copper and zinc used for the rivets and buttons came from Namibia and Australia, respectively; and the pumice for the stonewashing came from a volcano in Turkey. Furthermore, where the jeans were made included synthetic indigo made in Germany, thread made in Northern Ireland and dyed in Spain, polyester tapes and wires made in France and Japan, and denim made in Italy. The jeans were sewn in Tunisia by Ejallah Dousab, who made less than $1.00 an hour, and they were stonewashed there as well (not an environmentally benign process, for the record).

What should a tag in these jeans say about where they were made? Would it list all twelve countries noted above? How many geographic locations are involved in even a handful of the many hundreds of things each of us owns right now? Or the hundreds more we will purchase in the coming weeks or months? How many consumers know enough about dyes, pumice, copper mining, stonewashing, Tunisian garment factories, minimum wages, and labor rights to determine the environmental and social costs of the jeans? And the jeans story did not look into the resources consumed by energy generation and transportation, marketing and retailing, and a host of other consumptive aspects associated with consumer goods. Finally, how much more complex than a "simple" pair of jeans is the chain of relations behind a laptop, a cell phone, or an automobile likely to be?

The *Guardian*'s "Story of the Blues" told of cotton cultivation, zinc and copper mining, and the production of the finished product. Building on the chain described in the story, the next three sections briefly discuss three overlapping types of commodity chains: agricultural commodities, extractive industries in mining and oil and gas sectors, and finished consumer goods of all kinds.

Bitter Harvests

The foods we eat and the beverages we drink come from somewhere. So too do a host of other agricultural commodities, from feedstock for the beef and poultry we consume to cut flowers for our dates and weddings and many forest products for the construction industry and finished goods. Some are grown and shipped as is, like many fruits and vegetables. Other agricultural commodities, such as wheat, sugar, coffee, tea, cocoa, and palm oil, require extensive processing before humans use or consume them. This processing, like their growth and transportation, involves the consumption of material resources. Frequently, agricultural commodity chains also involve substantial ecological harm and human exploitation.

That agricultural commodities are associated with massive environmental degradation and exceedingly high humanitarian costs is not a new story and is not confined to the twentieth and twenty-first centuries. Coffee, tea, sugar, spices, and bananas, to name only five of the most famous examples, have been associated for centuries with empire building, colonial oppression, economic dependence, and large-scale environmental change.[27] Today, such commodities

are associated less with explicitly imperialist rule and more with the environmental and humanitarian costs that their growth and production may involve.

Chief among the environmental concerns related to agricultural commodities are ecological harms caused by the widespread use of herbicides and
pesticides and excess nutrients engendered by fertilizer use; deforestation,
land-use changes, and biodiversity losses associated with converting lands
into industrial-scale agriculture; overuse of surface water and groundwater
resources; soil degradation and desertification; and the growing demand for
fossil fuels engendered by the industrialization of agriculture around the
world.[28] This diverse list of environmental harms illustrates that no one policy
or behavioral change is likely to supply the magic bullet for a transformation
to more sustainable agriculture. So, for example, less chemical use or bet-
ter-regulated use of chemicals is unlikely to slow the deforestation or soil
degradation or water exploitation engendered by expanding agricultural
demands. Multiple strategies are needed, and many must be specific to sector,
commodity, or place.

The humanitarian and public health concerns associated with agriculture
that are most frequently listed by activists and analysts alike include the following: human health risks from widespread and often unsafe use of chemical
pesticides and herbicides, exploitation of child labor, the general lack of labor
rights and worker safety institutions, and the widespread low pay and poverty
in grower-producer communities. For example, the International Labour
Organization (ILO) estimates that 69 percent of child laborers work in agriculture.[29] The fair trade movement and fair trade certification were launched
to try to address the widespread poverty in developing country agricultural
communities, as well as the lack of labor rights, bargaining power, and information common in such communities. Table 15-1 lists a number of illustrative examples of agricultural commodities and the environmental and
humanitarian implications associated with them.

NGOs such as Oxfam and Fairtrade Labelling Organizations International and its affiliates and international organizations like the ILO have
cataloged myriad examples: Liberian children working with their parents in
rubber tapping, more than a million Egyptian children handpicking pests
from cotton, more than three hundred thousand children weeding and pick-
ing commercial crops in the United States, and the well-documented and
extensive use of child labor and child trafficking in the West African cocoa
industry.[30] The last of these examples led some NGO activists to ask consumers if they knew whether their chocolates were made by child slaves. In
2004 the ILO estimated that child laborers numbered about 218 million,
with more than 125 million of these engaged in work quite hazardous to
their health.[31]

One review of the environmental issues raised by global agricultural commodities covers the ecological and human health risks of twenty-one major
commodities: bananas, beef, cashews, cassava, cocoa, coffee, corn, cotton,
oranges, palm oil, rice, rubber, salmon, shrimp, sorghum, soybeans, sugarcane,
tea, tobacco, wheat, and wood pulp.[32] Yet even this daunting list is incomplete.

Table 15-1

Commodity	Associated environmental issues	Associated social issues	Major producer areas
Bananas	• Deforestation and habitat loss • Unregulated pesticide, fungicide, and fertilizer use • Soil degradation • Solid waste • Water use	• Low wages and impoverished communities • Child labor • Environmental health and worker safety • Corporate-state collusion and government corruption • Militia funding and violence • Gender discrimination	• Coastal areas across Central America, the Caribbean, South America, India, South Pacific, Central Africa
Cocoa and chocolate	• Deforestation and habitat loss • Unregulated pesticide, fungicide, and fertilizer use • Soil degradation	• Low wages and impoverished communities • Child labor, child slavery, and child trafficking • Lack of labor rights • Environmental health and worker safety	• West Africa (Ivory Coast, Ghana, Nigeria, Cameroon) • Latin America
Coffee	• Deforestation and habitat loss • Unregulated pesticide, fungicide, and fertilizer use • Soil degradation	• Low wages and impoverished communities • Lack of labor rights • Environmental health and worker safety	• Tropical zones of Latin America, Asia, and Central Africa
Tea	• Deforestation and habitat loss • Unregulated pesticide, fungicide, and fertilizer use • Soil degradation	• Low wages and impoverished communities • Lack of labor right • Environmental health and worker safety	• China, India, Sri Lanka, Kenya, Indonesia, Turkey

Sources: Jason Clay, *World Agriculture and the Environment: A Commodity-by-Commodity Guide to Impacts and Practices* (Washington, DC: Island Press, 2004); and information compiled by the author.

One might add grapes, apples, and many other fruits as well as cut flowers, various horticultural products, sugar beets, and cultured pearls. With each of these, ecological risks and harms are incurred, and the people involved in growing, harvesting, and processing may suffer health and/or human rights degradation. Take, for example, the often little-known risks to agricultural workers in parts of Latin America and Africa who cultivate fresh flowers for homes and businesses in North America and Europe and for bouquets used to express love. Few labor rights, poor working conditions, and repeated exposure to dangerous chemical pesticides are all too common for the (mostly) women cultivating and processing the flowers. Conditions in parts of the cut-flower industry illustrate the overlapping nature of ecological risks and humanitarian concerns.

In addition to those listed in Table 15-1, other commodities are experiencing global overconsumption. Perhaps most famous among these are the world's fisheries and tropical forests, around which the record of international cooperation for environmental protection or sustainable use remains exceedingly poor.[33] For example, the seemingly intractable combination of complex transnational commodity chains associated with forest products, growing global demand for most such products, and poor governance in many exporting countries continues to drive massive environmental degradation, human health risks, and oppression in many countries within tropical forest export sectors.[34]

Few agricultural challenges illustrate the growing material throughput and the social embeddedness of consumer culture better than the global growth in beef consumption. For decades, consumer tastes have increasingly turned to beef as consumers have become wealthier. The beef industry engages in debates about World Trade Organization rules and the use of genetically modified organisms and antibiotics in industrial production and often drives land degradation, deforestation, and increased use of myriad agricultural chemicals.[35] Large areas of agricultural land must be devoted to growing the feed for cattle, for example, and the chemical inputs, deforestation, and transportation involved in the global beef market drive enormous quantities of greenhouse gas emissions.

The news about seafood is no better. Since 1950 seafood consumption has grown almost eightfold as nearly all major fish stocks around the globe have experienced dramatic decline.[36] Note that although a vegetarian diet is more carbon efficient than beef and reduces pressure on fish stocks, it does not address the many environmental externalities and humanitarian issues associated with globalized and industrialized agriculture.

Finally, imagine the aggregate environmental and humanitarian harm associated with a simple date on Valentine's Day: cut flowers, chocolates, dinner (seafood or beef), dessert, and coffee. As in the jeans example above, imagine trying to trace the origins, environmental externalities, and working conditions associated with this one night out. Individual consumers, whether carnivores, vegetarians, or green buyers, cannot change the world simply by choosing to buy different things. We can reduce our individual contributions to problems with our purchasing decisions, but political action and social change are required if we are to consume less of our environment and do less harm to each other as we eat and drink.

Still Digging

Extracting resources from the earth is essential to contemporary economies and societies around the globe, and the accompanying ecological and human costs are high. Things like stone, iron, and bronze are so important to human history that whole eras are named after them.[37] The environmental externalities associated with mining have long been of concern. One group of minerals comprises the metals iron, bauxite, copper, lead, nickel, zinc, silver, gold, mercury, cadmium, cobalt, titanium, tin, manganese, chromium, tungsten, coltan, lithium, and a host of others—some quite rare and highly valuable. But metals are not the only commodities mined from the earth: others include stone, sand, and gravel; clays; salt; phosphates; potash; lime; gypsum; and soda ash. Large-scale mining operations take place on every inhabited continent, often involving some of the largest multinational corporations in the world. While mining and oil and gas externalities have long been known, the growing scale of mining operations and increasing demand for oil and natural gas mean that the cumulative effects of extractive industries are unprecedented.

In the mining industry, environmental and humanitarian concerns are tightly coupled. Extractive industries require the movement of massive quantities of earth, and they produce stunning amounts of a diverse set of pollutants. One estimate puts the movement of earth worldwide at 57 billion tons, an amount that rivals estimates of all erosion around the globe.[38] In other words, humans now move more earth each year, just for mining and quarrying, than the global hydrological cycle does. Added to global agriculture and urbanization and construction, this helps illustrate the massive land-use and habitat changes human activities unleash around the globe. These changes do not even consider the impacts of climate change.

Extractive industries are waste-intensive and frequently highly polluting of local and regional environments. Mining wastes degrade surface waters and groundwater across the global North and the global South. North America is littered with areas of local and regional ecological damage from mining, and the contemporary scale of mining operations around the world often dwarfs mining operations in North America. Today, a single mine can be extremely large, or small shallow mines may dot a landscape by the hundreds or thousands. Furthermore, most extracted commodities have to be refined substantially in order to be of value. Here too, resources are used up and wastes produced. The ecological damage does not stop there. As extraction has moved deeper into mountain and tropical forest regions, thousands of workers and the development of previously undeveloped areas have gone with it. Mining is therefore also a driver of broader regional and global ecosystem and social changes.[39]

In terms of social and humanitarian implications, the record of extractive industries is poor. Mining and oil and gas extraction are frequently associated with serious human health risks posed by pollutants released into local and regional environments as well as with damage to indigenous peoples and other groups whose environments, communities, and social and political organization may be substantially altered by the arrival of extractive industries.[40] In fact, the human security and humanitarian-related issues associated with the mining sector and the oil and gas industries are legion.[41] High-profile examples include the following:

- **Diamonds:** Phrases like *blood diamonds* and *conflict diamonds* became famous as African diamond mining became increasingly enmeshed with civil war, state oppression, widespread environmental degradation, and severe human rights abuses. Estimates suggest that more than a million unregulated miners were toiling in conditions similar to enslavement while funds from the diamond trade were fueling weapons transfers, war, and terrorism.[42]

- **Coltan:** The technology boom of the 1990s and 2000s drove boom-and-bust cycles in columbite-tantalite, or coltan, a mineral commonly used in cell phones and other electronics. When the price of coltan spiked, a rush to mine it spread rapidly in parts of the Democratic Republic of the Congo. To extract the mineral individuals and groups dug thousands of giant pits in national parks and reserves, on agricultural lands, and in streams and river basins. Money from the coltan trade fueled militias, arms transfers, and activities of local warlords, mixing violence and oppression with ecological damage and dangerous working conditions. After the price collapsed, mining declined, but the ecological damage, many weapons, and the legacy of civil violence remained.[43]

- **Gold:** The gold industry, like most industries involving mining, is plagued by reports of substantial ecological damage on a local and regional scale, pollution releases, adverse human and ecological health effects, and violations of basic human and labor rights in a host of countries. Gold is no longer mined by pickax-carrying pioneers; rather, miners are employees of (or contractors to) multinational corporations who work in massive open pits that generate staggering quantities of waste. Working conditions are often unsafe, indigenous peoples and other local communities are often overrun, and funds from mining operations can make their way to militias and oppressive public officials.

- **Oil:** It is difficult to overstate the importance of oil in the economic and political history of the past century. Nations, corporations, and individuals have accrued tremendous wealth from oil. Oil's ecological costs include damage via pollution (of land, freshwater, oceans, seas, and air) of local environments and the global atmosphere, ecological changes driven by extraction itself, and damage from pipelines and other transportation modes. In terms of oil's connection to human rights violations, recent reviews include all of the following problems: damage to human health from pollution and climate change, the common connection between oil interests and revenues with public- and private-sector corruption, lack of transparency and accountability, violation and abuse of indigenous peoples' rights, militarization and violent conflict, organized crime, and damage to community development.[44]

Global competition in the mining sector and the growth in global demand for many minerals have resulted in the dramatic expansion of mining operations and the consolidation and growth of a number of large multinational mining conglomerates, often owned primarily by North American, European, Chinese, Australian, and South African investors. These companies often construct what amount to armed camps around mining and oil and gas extraction operations to protect their investments and workers from militias and violence engendered by community resentment. Such camps can be seen in many African, Asian, and Latin American countries.

Perhaps the clearest evidence of political and economic damage related to the extraction of oil and gas resources is found in the extensive research done on the "resource curse."[45] The concept of the resource curse refers to the observed relationship between a country's high level of export dependence on a valuable resource and the likelihood that the country will have poorer-than-average economic performance over time and undemocratic, often corrupt, or ineffective governance. Such oil-exporting states are often called petro-states. For example, of the twenty largest oil exporters in 2000, eighteen were undemocratic. Economically, many highly indebted countries are oil exporters; oil-rich Nigeria ranks among the poorest countries on Earth, and mineral-exporting countries tend to have high levels of poverty and child mortality.[46]

Analysts differ on the exact mix of causes of the resource curse and on the utility of the concept, but important factors include the economic damage done by boom-and-bust dynamics that tend to plague commodity prices and commodity-dependent economies, a lack of economic diversification, and the presence of corruption. Also, political institutions in petro-states tend to be weak and heavily entangled in patronage networks and corruption. State institutions tend to have little independent authority over the oil sector and comparatively low levels of capacity to deliver services to citizens or to build or command their loyalty. Nigeria, Bolivia, Angola, Chad, and several states in the Caspian and Central Asian region are most often mentioned when petro-states are discussed, and many of the dynamics are also seen in the oil-rich states of the Persian Gulf. Perhaps the most valuable insight comes from those most critical of the resource curse concept, who argue that the key problems lie in ownership structure and state control of resources.[47] In other words, it is not that having resources is a curse, but rather that states with resources must avoid particular social and political institutional arrangements. Political action can influence such arrangements.

Environmental and humanitarian challenges are not simply particular to a small number of extracted commodities in a few places; they are endemic in many parts of the sector and across many countries. So, for example, although the coltan price collapse deprived some Congolese militias of a major source of funding in early 2002, by 2008 the mining of tin ore was funding militia activities. Workers' human and labor rights are exploited, and virtually no environmental regulation exists. In this example, militias make money both by selling the tin (often to the multinational corporation that ostensibly owns the concession for the tin) and by taxing the sales of mineral traders and bars, brothels, and peddlers of everyday goods used by the miners and other people around the mine.[48] Congolese "conflict minerals" remain a serious international, domestic, and regional issue.

Furthermore, mining is not simply about "old" products and technologies like steel, tin, and aluminum. Concern about the scarcity and concentrated control of some rare minerals used in electronics, wind power, electric and hybrid cars, and missile technologies has led to a rapid global search for additional deposits and increasing investment on several continents.[49] Lithium, which is used in many types of batteries, is another resource that may also bring new, greener technologies together with the resource curse and geopolitical concerns outlined above, as Bolivia contains perhaps half of the world's lithium deposits even as it already manifests many of the political and economic dynamics common in petro-states.

Most of us have heard the phrase, "When you find yourself in a hole, stop digging." But we cannot simply stop using oil, gas, coal, and dozens of minerals from the earth. Many new and old technologies rely on minerals. Yet halting the escalating ecological and human costs of these activities and reducing environmental and humanitarian externalities is possible. We know it can be done because some mines already meet much higher environmental and labor standards. High-standard mining operations still have ecological and human health effects, of course, but they can substantially minimize such effects. Also possible are substantial increases in energy and materials efficiency—and recycling and reuse. We can use less of things, rather than always using more.

Products, Chains, and Ecological Shadows

Peter Dauvergne calls global patterns of harm, both ecological and human, the "shadows of consumption."[50] He traces these shadows through five products: automobiles, leaded gasoline, refrigerators, beef, and harp seals. Although these products have brought substantial benefits to humans, their use also engenders substantial costs. As Dauvergne notes, people are "dying of consumption." The automobile, for example, extracts a heavy environmental and human price as it transforms societies around the world and increases urban air pollution and risks to drivers, passengers, and pedestrians—to say nothing of its growing contributions to global climate change. As environmental social movements and government policies demand fewer pollutants and safer vehicles in Northern consumer societies, these risks move— sometimes they are clearly pushed—into populations and ecosystems in the developing world. This dynamic also is clear in Dauvergne's treatment of leaded gasoline, about which safety concerns were raised when it was introduced in the 1920s. It was the end of the twentieth century before lead was taken out of gasoline in much of the developed world, and only in the first two decades of the twenty-first century is this happening in much of Africa and parts of Asia.

Dauvergne shows that automobile efficiency and safety have improved globally over time and that leaded gas and ozone-depleting substances are being phased out. These developments are very good news for humans and ecosystems. Yet the globalization of other risks and harms continues apace: climate change, beef consumption, e-waste, and the seemingly endless growth in material throughput of consumer societies in the global North and South. Dauvergne's work on a small number of products, like the blue jeans story above, illustrates that all goods and the chains of consumption that produce and distribute them cast ecological shadows. Although contemporary goods may have very clear benefits for humans in terms of our health, prosperity, entertainment, and knowledge, all also have ecological and humanitarian costs. These costs are usually hidden by the various distancing dynamics discussed above.

Another way to conceptualize the idea that consumption takes place at every point along a product's commodity chain is offered by political scientist Ronnie Lipschutz, who outlines the "waste chain" that parallels literally every aspect of a commodity chain, from product design or conceptualization through the mining, growing, processing, and manufacturing associated with the good.[51] This waste chain includes wastes generated by all of the energy consumed throughout the chain of consumption as well as the eventual disposal of the product itself. A mobile phone (or any other consumer electronics item) illustrates the point. Wastes are generated—in other words, things are consumed or used up—from the mining of minerals and extraction of petroleum used to make both plastics and energy all the way through the toxic e-waste that the phone becomes at the end of its life.

The European Union has taken a leadership role in the reduction of e-waste and the regulation of its reuse, recycling, and disposal. Yet, without political action in other jurisdictions such as the United States, which lacks similar standards, and without aggressive European and global standards and enforcement, e-wastes will continue to grow in quantity and continue to be disposed of legally and illegally in ways that damage ecological and human health.[52]

What Can Be Done?

People who grow the bananas, coffee, flowers, and other crops sold in international markets live in impoverished and ecologically damaged communities. The same is true of people who work to extract minerals and fossil fuels from the earth. A reasonable estimate is that nearly 150 million nonretail production workers and nearly 500 million households depend on production of these commodities, and millions more are indirectly related to them.[53]

These numbers do not include the additional millions who are dependent on the production of the thousands of categories of finished goods. Even if it were possible for higher-income societies and consumers to stop consuming these commodities, throwing hundreds of millions of families out of work and leaving them without any means of support would not beget sustainable development either.

The commodity chains discussed here are complex webs of social relations connecting people and markets across great distances (geographic and otherwise). Thus citizens and governments in the South and the North share responsibility for the ecological and humanitarian effects of global markets. We are all consumers—although some of us consume a lot more than others—sharing a measure of responsibility for sustainable development in our own countries and around the world.

The list below presents only a few sets of policy options that could reduce aggregate material throughput in consumer societies or address specific aspects of the ecological and humanitarian damage engendered by today's globalizing political economy. Most of these options can be deployed at multiple levels of government in the public sector, within the private or civil society sector, or through some combination of public, private, and NGO actors and institutions. They can be used by national and local governments, colleges and universities, and firms.

- **Command-and-control regulations:** With policies that reduce the generation of waste, increase recycling, engender cleaner product design, and encourage energy efficiency and renewable energy development, government mandates remain common and often prove effective. EU law, for example, mandates reducing the use of hazardous substances in a host of products, pushing product redesign to facilitate recycling and reuse, and reducing packaging and other household and consumer wastes. The U.S. federal government mandates automobile fleet fuel efficiency and many vehicle emissions reductions, many U.S. states and several European countries mandate increases in the amount of renewable energy in electricity grids, and governments around the world mandate product energy efficiency. Other examples include banning individual items (such as disposable bags, leaded gasoline, or inefficient products) and regulating and enforcing standards for international corporations.

- **Adjust subsidies:** States or companies can reduce subsidies and incentives that encourage waste and inefficient use, or they can subsidize more efficient technologies. For example, states in both the North and the South use tax codes and other incentives to subsidize oil, mining, and forestry extraction sectors by hundreds of billions of dollars. For example, the International Energy Agency estimated that in 2010 global subsidies for fossil fuel extraction and consumption exceeded $400 billion (and were increasing)—a figure considerably larger than total global investment in the renewable energy sector for 2012. Similarly, U.S., EU, and Japanese domestic agricultural subsidies damage development prospects in the global South and distort trade in ways that disadvantage the world's poorest economies. Subsidies can also be used to encourage research and development in cleaner technologies as well as investment in or purchase of efficient technologies or renewable energy.

- **Taxation:** Although citizens dislike taxes, many economists view them as one of the most efficient ways to reduce pollution and other externalities. If, for example, the cost of emitting carbon or other pollutants or of extracting resources and degrading ecosystems is substantially increased through taxation, we can expect less pollution, waste, resource use, or biodiversity loss as a result. Taxes can be applied to packaging, disposable goods of all kinds, toxic hazards in the workplace, food wastes, and a host of hazardous or unhealthy activities, such as smoking. Globally, the evidence is generally clear; for example, the less energy and carbon are taxed, the less efficiently we use them. And, as noted above, the more the prices of these and other goods are subsidized, the more of them we tend to consume.

- **Certification and labeling schemes:** Certification schemes have proliferated rapidly over the past decade or more; they have been developed by nonstate actors to address the environmental and humanitarian consequences of international markets. Probably the most widely known of these are the Fair Trade certification scheme and the Forest Stewardship Council (FSC) certification system.[54] Many thousands of people live in communities where fair trade–certified products may help to raise living and working standards, and vast tracts of forests have been certified by the FSC process in dozens of countries. Consumers and decision makers in almost any organization can seek to advance the influence of certified products by choosing to buy them or by encouraging organizations such as governments, universities, and companies to set fair trade purchasing policies. In addition to the largely non-state-driven certification programs, such schemes can also be state driven or state backed. Examples of state-coordinated certification systems include the UN- and state-backed Kimberley Process, designed to certify diamonds that do not fund armed conflict and violent oppression, and the Energy Star program operated by the U.S. Environmental Protection Agency (and used or copied in many other countries), which rates the energy efficiency of home appliances, office equipment, and heating and air-conditioning equipment. Like all policy options, certification schemes have critics and limitations. From the consumer's perspective, the ever-growing list of certification schemes—each including a large and complex set of criteria—makes them difficult to keep straight. Each scheme must build credibility and legitimacy with consumers over time.[55] Yet most analysts have concluded that certification schemes and other aspects of the corporate social responsibility movement, although they have the capacity to build niche markets and alter some environmental and humanitarian conditions, rarely alter the dominant incentives and practices in the global market.[56] In other words, fair trade coffee may well benefit the participating pickers and their families and communities, but it constitutes a small fraction of the global coffee market, and it has little impact on most of the market.

368 Stacy D. VanDeveer

- **Capacity building and improved governance:** In many parts of the world where ecological degradation is accelerating and humanitarian exploitation is extensive, government lacks the capacity or the will, or both, to curb these problems. Sustainable development, from alleviating poverty and meeting the UN Millennium Development Goals to reversing environmental damage of all types, requires public institutions that work. Multilateral environmental agreements must be implemented if they are to shape outcomes; so too must the other policy options discussed in this chapter and throughout the volume. Lessons can be drawn from successful cases of public and civil society capacity building around the world, and they can be applied more widely to the dual challenge of environmental and social sustainability.[57] North and South share a need for expanded and enhanced capacity development assistance to build states and civil societies that can effectively and sustainably govern people and resources.[58] Improvements in governance capacity—knowledge, information, effectiveness, efficiency, and so on—would benefit both the global North and the global South.

This partial list leaves out many other possibilities, including government- and NGO-led consumer awareness campaigns, international standards for financial and governance transparency to reduce corruption and improve effective governance, and a host of options that engage global treaties and other forms of international agreements, possibly involving existing environmental institutions as well as those associated with the World Trade Organization, the ILO, development banks, or myriad other organizations and institutions.

Let us also be clear that not all ideas or initiatives related to environmental governance and sustainable development do (or will) come from the North. The notion that environmental and sustainability policies, movements, ideas, and norms are the purview of the North has been put to rest by activists and policy makers in (and analysts of) countries of Central and Eastern Europe, Brazil, Costa Rica, India, and China, to name only a few.[59] It is also clear that environmental and resource politics are high politics in the transatlantic relationship, between North and South, and for dozens of commodity-dependent countries.[60] Resource scarcity or conflict can turn violent, or it can engender deepening cooperation and peace building.[61] The stakes can be high.

Consumption issues and trends, like global inequality and the set of global environmental concerns and institutions discussed in this volume, can be shaped by collective action and individual choices and behaviors. As the introduction to this volume notes, whether we are up to dual challenges of globalizing greater and more sustainable prosperity without overwhelming the planet's ecosystems and other species remains to be determined.

Notes

1. See, for example, Donella H. Meadows, Dennis Meadows, and Jorgen Renders, *Beyond the Limits* (White River Junction, VT: Chelsea Green, 1992); William Ophuls and A. Stephen Boyan Jr., *Ecology and the Politics of Scarcity Revisited* (New York: W. H. Freeman, 1992); Philip Andrews-Speed, Raimund Bleischwitz, Tim Boersma,

Corey Johnson, Geoffrey Kemp, and Stacy D. VanDeveer, *The Global Resource Nexus: The Struggles for Land, Energy, Food, Water, and Minerals* (Washington, DC: Transatlantic Academy, 2012).

2. Joseph Nye Jr. and Robert Keohane, *Power and Interdependence: World Politics in Transition* (Boston: Little, Brown, 1977); Dennis Pirages, *Global Ecopolitics: The New Context for International Relations* (Pacific Grove, CA: Duxbury Press, 1978); James Harf and B. Thomas Trout, *The Politics of Global Resources* (Durham, NC: Duke University Press, 1986).

3. Kate O'Neill and Stacy D. VanDeveer, "Transnational Environmental Activism after Seattle: Between Emancipation and Arrogance," in *Charting Transnational Democracy: Beyond Global Arrogance*, ed. Janie Leatherman and Julie Webber (New York: Palgrave, 2005).

4. Thomas Princen, Michael Maniates, and Ken Conca, eds., *Confronting Consumption* (Cambridge: MIT Press, 2002); Thomas Princen, *The Logic of Sufficiency* (Cambridge: MIT Press, 2005); Peter Dauvergne, *The Shadows of Consumption: Consequences for the Global Environment* (Cambridge: MIT Press, 2008); Worldwatch Institute, *State of the World 2004: The Consumer Society* (Washington, DC: Worldwatch Institute, 2004); Dennis Pirages and Ken Cousins, eds., *From Ecological Scarcity to Ecological Security: Exploring New Limits to Growth* (Cambridge: MIT Press, 2005).

5. Sustainable Europe Research Institute (SERI), *Overconsumption: Our Use of the World's Natural Resources* (Vienna: SERI, 2009); World Wide Fund for Nature, *Living Planet Report 2008* (Washington, DC: WWF, 2008); Stacy D. VanDeveer, *Still Digging: Extractive Industries, Resource Curses, and Transnational Governance in the Anthropocene* (Washington, DC: Transatlantic Academy, January 2013), http://www.transatlanticacademy.org/publications/still-digging-extractive-industries-resource-curses-and-transnational-governance-anthro; Stacy D. VanDeveer, "Resource Curses: Redux, Ex-Post, or Ad Infinitum?," in *Backdraft: The Conflict Potential of Climate Change Adaptation and Mitigation* (Environmental Change & Security Program Report vol. 14, no. 2), ed. Geoffrey D. Dabelko, Lauren Herzer, Schuyler Null, Meaghan Parker, and Russell Sticklor (Washington, DC: Woodrow Wilson International Center for Scholars, 2013).

6. SERI, *Overconsumption*.

7. Andrews-Speed et al., *Global Resource Nexus*.

8. Worldwatch Institute, *Vital Signs 2007–2008* (Washington, DC: Worldwatch Institute, 2007); Daniel Sperling and Deborah Gordon, *Two Billion Cars: Driving toward Sustainability* (New York: Oxford University Press, 2009).

9. David Abel, "Battle to Expand Bottle Law Heats Up," *Boston Globe*, October 8, 2009.

10. Princen, *Logic of Sufficiency;* John de Graaf, David Wann, and Thomas H. Naylor, *Affluenza: The All-Consuming Epidemic*, 2nd ed. (San Francisco: Berrett-Koehler, 2005); Andrews-Speed et al., *Global Resource Nexus*.

11. Joseph Stiglitz, *Making Globalization Work* (New York: Penguin, 2006).

12. Paul Collier, *The Bottom Billion: Why the Poorest Countries Are Failing and What Can Be Done about It* (New York: Oxford University Press, 2007).

13. Ibid., 3.

14. Princen et al., *Confronting Consumption*; SERI, *Overconsumption*.

15. Netherlands Environmental Assessment Agency, "Global CO_2 Emissions: Increase Continued in 2007," June 13, 2008, http://www.pbl.nl/en/publications/2008/GlobalCO2emissionsthrough 2007.html.

16. Michael T. Klare, *Rising Powers, Shrinking Planet: The New Geopolitics of Energy* (New York: Metropolitan Books, 2008); Christopher Flavin and Gary Gardner, "China, India and the New Global Order," in Worldwatch Institute, *State of the World 2006* (Washington, DC: Worldwatch Institute, 2006).

17. Princen et al., *Confronting Consumption*.

18. Jack Manno, "Commoditization: Consumption Efficiency and the Economy of Care and Connection," in Princen et al., *Confronting Consumption,* 67–100.

19. Vandana Shiva, *Water Wars: Privatization, Pollution and Profit* (Cambridge, MA: South End Press, 2002).
20. Ibid.
21. Thomas Princen, Michael Maniates, and Ken Conca, "Confronting Consumption," in Princen et al., *Confronting Consumption*, 14.
22. Michael Maniates, "Individualization: Plant a Tree, Buy a Bike, Save the World?," in Princen et al., *Confronting Consumption*, 43–66.
23. Alex Hughes and Suzanne Reimer, eds., *Geographies of Commodity Chains* (London: Routledge, 2004).
24. Princen et al., *Confronting Consumption*.
25. Thomas Princen, "Distancing: Consumption and the Severing of Feedback," in Princen et al., *Confronting Consumption*, 103–131.
26. Fran Abrams and James Astill, "Story of the Blues," *Guardian*, May 29, 2001; see also Louise Crewe, "Unraveling Fashion's Commodity Chains," in Hughes and Reimer, *Geographies of Commodity Chains*, 195–214.
27. For recent examples from this large literature on coffee, see Antony Wild, *Coffee: A Dark History* (New York: W. W. Norton, 2005); Mark Pendergrast, *Uncommon Grounds: The History of Coffee and How It Transformed the World* (New York: Basic Books, 1999); Stewart Lee Allen, *The Devil's Cup: A History of the World According to Coffee* (New York: Ballantine Books, 2003). On sugar, see Sidney Mintz, *Sweetness and Power: The Place of Sugar in Modern History* (New York: Penguin, 1986). On bananas, see James Wiley, *The Banana: Empires, Trade Wars, and Globalization* (Lincoln: University of Nebraska Press, 2008). On tea, see Roy Moxham, *Tea: Addiction, Exploitation, and Empire* (New York: Carroll & Graf, 2003).
28. Jason Clay, *World Agriculture and the Environment: A Commodity-by-Commodity Guide to Impacts and Practices* (Washington, DC: Island Press, 2004).
29. International Labour Organization, *The End of Child Labor: Within Reach* (Geneva: ILO, 2006), 8.
30. Worldwatch Institute, *Vital Signs 2007–2008*, 112–113.
31. Ibid.
32. Clay, *World Agriculture and the Environment*.
33. Elizabeth R. DeSombre and J. Samuel Barkin, *Fish* (London: Polity Press, 2012); Peter Dauvergne and Jane Lister, *Timber* (London: Polity Press, 2011).
34. Peter Dauvergne, *Loggers and Degradation in the Asia Pacific: Corporations and Environmental Management* (New York: Cambridge University Press, 2001); Peter Dauvergne, *Shadows in the Forest: Japan and the Politics of Timber in Southeast Asia* (Cambridge: MIT Press, 1997). See also extensive information available on the Web site of the NGO Global Witness, http://www.globalwitness.org.
35. See, for example, Geoff Tansey and Joyce D'Silva, eds., *The Meat Business: Devouring a Hungry Planet* (Boston: St. Martin's Press, 1999); Brian Halweil and Danielle Nierenburg, "Meat and Seafood: The Global Diet's Most Costly Ingredients," in Worldwatch Institute, *State of the World 2008* (Washington, DC: Worldwatch Institute, 2008); Dauvergne, *Shadows of Consumption*.
36. Worldwatch Institute, *Vital Signs 2007–2008*, 26; Boris Worm et al., "Impacts of Biodiversity Loss on Ocean Ecosystem Services," *Science*, November 3, 2006, 787–790.
37. John E. Young, *Mining the Earth*, Worldwatch Paper 109 (Washington, DC: Worldwatch Institute, 1992).
38. Gavin Bridge, "Contested Terrain: Mining and the Environment," *Annual Review of Environment and Resources* 29 (2004): 205–259.
39. Ibid.
40. Ibid.; Michael J. Watts, "Righteous Oil? Human Rights, the Oil Complex, and Corporate Social Responsibility," *Annual Review of Environment and Resources* 30 (2005): 373–407; Dara O'Rourke and Sarah Connelly, "Just Oil? Environmental and Social Impacts of Oil Production and Consumption," *Annual Review of Environment and Resources* 28 (2003): 587–617.

41. VanDeveer, "Still Digging"; VanDeveer, "Resource Curses."
42. For detailed histories and information, see the many Web-based reports by Global Witness (http://www.globalwitness.org) and the UN-sponsored Kimberley Process (http://www.kimberleyprocess.com).
43. "Under-mining Peace," Global Witness, June 2005; Carol Albertyn, "Environment and Conservation, Wildlife and Animals," Carte Blanche Interactive, 2004.
44. Watts, "Righteous Oil?"; VanDeveer, "Still Digging."
45. Paul Stevens and Evelyn Dietsche, "Resource Curse: An Analysis of Causes, Experiences and Possible Ways Forward," *Energy Policy* 36 (2008): 56–65; Erika Weinthal and Pauline Jones Luong, "An Alternative Solution to Managing Mineral Wealth," *Perspectives on Politics* 4, no. 1 (2006): 35–53; Stiglitz, *Making Globalization Work*, 133–159; Collier, *Bottom Billion*, 38–52; Terry Lynn Karl, *The Paradox of Plenty: Oil Booms and Petro-States* (Berkeley: University of California Press, 1997); Michael L. Ross, *The Oil Curse: How Petroleum Wealth Shapes the Development of Nations* (Princeton, NJ: Princeton University Press, 2012); VanDeveer, "Resource Curses."
46. Weinthal and Luong, "Alternative Solution to Managing Mineral Wealth."
47. Pauline Jones Luong and Erika Weinthal, *Oil Is Not a Curse: Ownership Structure and Institutions in Soviet Successor States* (Cambridge: Cambridge University Press, 2010).
48. Lydia Polgeen, "Congo's Riches, Looted by Renegade Troops," *New York Times*, September 16, 2008.
49. Keith Bradsher, "Chinese Threat Reinvigorates Efforts to Mine Rare Minerals," *New York Times*, September 26, 2009.
50. Dauvergne, *Shadows of Consumption*.
51. Ronnie D. Lipschutz, *Global Environmental Politics: Power, Perspectives, and Practice* (Washington, DC: CQ Press, 2004), 122–126.
52. See Chapter 11, this volume; Henrik Selin and Stacy D. VanDeveer, "Raising Global Standards: Hazardous Substances and E-Waste Management in the European Union," *Environment* 48, no. 10 (2006): 6–17; Elisabeth Rosenthal, "Smuggling Europe's Waste to Poorer Countries," *New York Times*, September 27, 2009.
53. Figures compiled by author.
54. Benjamin Cashore, Graeme Auld, and Deanna Newsom, *Governing through Markets: Forest Certification and the Emergence of Non-state Authority* (New Haven, CT: Yale University Press, 2004); David Vogel, *The Market for Virtue: The Potential and Limits of Corporate Social Responsibility* (Washington, DC: Brookings Institution Press, 2005).
55. Cashore et al., *Governing through Markets*.
56. Vogel, *Market for Virtue*.
57. Stacy D. VanDeveer and Geoffrey D. Dabelko, "It's Capacity, Stupid: International Assistance and National Implementation," *Global Environmental Politics* 1, no. 2 (2001): 18–29.
58. Ambuj D. Sagar and Stacy D. VanDeveer, "Capacity Development for the Environment: Broadening the Focus," *Global Environmental Politics* 5, no. 3 (2005): 14–22.
59. See, for example, Chapter 8, this volume; JoAnn Carmin and Stacy D. VanDeveer, eds., *EU Enlargement and the Environment: Institutional Change and Environmental Policy in Central and Eastern Europe* (London: Routledge, 2005); Paul F. Steinberg and Stacy D. VanDeveer, eds., *Comparative Environmental Politics: Theory, Practice, and Prospects* (Cambridge: MIT Press, 2012); Paul F. Steinberg, *Environmental Leadership in Developing Countries: Transnational Relations and Biodiversity Policy in Costa Rica and Bolivia* (Cambridge: MIT Press, 2001); Sanjeev Khagram, *Dams and Development: Transnational Struggles for Water and Power* (Ithaca, NY: Cornell University Press, 2004); Kelly Sims Gallagher, *China Shifts Gears: Automakers, Oil, Pollution, and Development* (Cambridge: MIT Press, 2006); Kathryn Hochstetler and Margaret E. Keck, *Greening Brazil: Environmental Activism in State and Society* (Durham, NC: Duke University Press, 2007); Jeannie L. Sowers, *Environmental Politics in Egypt: Activists, Experts, and the State* (London: Routledge, 2013).

60. On transatlantic relations, see Miranda A. Schreurs, Henrik Selin, and Stacy D. VanDeveer, eds., *Transatlantic Environment and Energy Politics: Comparative and International Perspectives* (Farnham, UK: Ashgate, 2009).
61. Geoffrey D. Dabelko, "An Uncommon Peace: Environment, Development, and the Global Security Agenda," *Environment* 50, no. 3 (2008): 32–45; Ken Conca and Geoffrey D. Dabelko, eds., *Environmental Peacemaking* (Baltimore: Johns Hopkins University Press, 2002).

Index

Aarhus Convention on Access to Information, Public Participation and Decision-Making and Access to Justice in Environmental Matters (1998), 61, 77
Abel, David, 369
Abidjan, Ivory Coast, 264
Abrams, Fran, 370
Acid rain, 193–194
Acquis communautaire, 158, 165–166, 306, 313
Across-regime environmental IGOs, 34–35
Acselrad, H., 233
Adaptation Fund, 246
Additionality principle, 226
Adede, A. O., 232
Adelle, Camilla, 183
Adopt a Negotiator project, 44
Advisory Opinion on Responsibilities and Obligations in the Deep Seabed Area, 66, 69–70
Africa
  agricultural commodity chains, 359 (table), 360
  carbon emissions, 353
  mining industry, 362
Africa Group, 238, 239 (table)
African Convention on the Conservation of Nature and Natural Resources (1968), 288
African Development Bank, 36
African Forest Forum (Kenya), 38 (table)
Africa Research Bulletin, 280
Agarwal, Anil, 230, 231, 233
Agarwal, Ravi, 106
Agenda 21, 2, 9, 31 (table), 32, 59, 79, 267
Agreement between the United States and Canada Concerning the Water Quality of the Great Lakes, 74 (table)
Agreement on Trade-Related Aspects of Intellectual Property Rights (TRIPS), 292

Agricultural commodity chains, 356–358, 359 (table), 360–361
Agricultural price supports and subsidies, 345, 366–367
Agro-industry, 285
Aguilar-Amuchastegui, Naikoa, 303
Ahearne, John F., 327, 329
Air pollution
  biodiversity impacts, 285
  China, 190–197, 194 (table)
  coal-fired power plants, 307
  international environmental treaty rules, 74–75 (table)
  radioactive gas, 320–321
  see also Convention on Long-Range Transboundary Air Pollution (CLRTAP)
Air Quality Directive, 170
A-Khavari, Afshin, 81
Akhter, F., 233
Albania, 158, 239 (table)
Albertyn, Carol, 371
Alien species, 285, 297
Alilio, Martin S., 281
Alker, Hayward R., Jr., 230
Allen, Stewart Lee, 370
Alliance of Liberals and Democrats for Europe, 162
Alliance of Small Island States (AOSIS), 216, 239 (table)
Allott, Philip, 78
Allum, Nick, 304
Alston, Philip, 230
Amended London Guidelines, 267
American Clean Energy and Security Act (2009), 140
American University delegation, 38 (table)
Amon, A., 233
Anarchy, 92
Anastas, Paul T., 282
Andersen, Mikael Skou, 182, 185
Andersen, Regine, 302
Anderson, Kai S., 154

Anderson, Kym, 345
Anderson, Stephen, 106, 108
Andhra Pradesh, India, 266
Andonova, Liliana B., 23, 25, 257, 258
Andorra, 289
Andresen, Steinar, 52, 256, 302, 303, 304
Andrews, Richard, 326
Andrews-Speed, Philip, 23, 368, 369
An, Feng, 196 (figure)
Angola, 196, 363
Antarctica, 87 (table), 100, 265
Antes, Ralf, 257
Apples, 69, 360
Araya, Mónica, 347
Arctic Monitoring and Assessment
    Programme (AMAP), 269, 281
Arctic resources, 145, 269, 270–271
Argentina, 284, 298
Argentina v. Uruguay (2010), 81
Arrhenius, Svante, 235, 237, 254
Arundel, Anthony, 303
Asahi Shimbun, 328
Ashiabor, Hope, 129
Asia, 359 (table)
Asian Development Bank, 36
Asia-Pacific Economic Cooperation
    Forum (APEC), 332
Asia-Pacific Partnership on Clean
    Development and Climate,
    246, 255
Asociación Conciencia (Argentina), 38
    (table)
Association of Southeast Asian Nations
    (ASEAN), 27
Astill, James, 370
Atomstroyexport, 324
Audley, John J., 25, 346, 348
Auld, Graeme, 51, 371
    see also Cashore, Benjamin W.
Australia
    carbon dioxide (CO$_2$) emissions,
        201 (figure)
    commodity chains, 357
    Copenhagen Accord, 248 (table)
    emissions reduction targets and
        progress, 244 (table)
    free trade agreements, 339 (table)
    genetically modified organisms
        (GMOs), 298
    greenhouse gas emissions, 206
    international environmental
        agreements, 122
    state negotiating blocs, 239 (table)

Australia v. France (1974), 79
Australia v. Japan (1999), 81
Australia v. Japan (2013), 80
Austria
    emissions reduction targets and
        progress, 244 (table)
    European Council, 161
    European Union membership, 158
    international environmental
        agreements, 137
    nuclear power plants, 66, 173, 306, 311,
        313–314
Automobile emissions standards, 141,
    165, 170
Automobile industry, 364
Automobile mileage standards, 340
Avant, Deborah D., 23
Axelrod, Regina S., 14, 15, 18–19, 24, 50,
    131, 182, 184, 326, 327
Aylward, Bruce, 302
Ayoob, Mohammed, 230
Aziz, Andrew, 80

Babcock & Wilcox, 319
Bäckstrand, Karin, 258
Bahrain, 339 (table)
Baker, Susan, 24, 25, 326
Bali Roadmap, 246
Balistreri, Ed, 255
Ballesteros, Athena, 256
Balmford, Andrew, 304
Balsiger, Joerg, 23
Bamako Convention (1991), 273
Ban Amendment (1995), 85 (table), 265,
    266, 273
Bananas, 357, 358, 359 (table)
Bankobeza, Gilbert, 126
Banuri, Tariq, 231, 232, 233
Barcelona Convention for the Protection
    of the Mediterranean Sea against
    Pollution (1976), 86 (table)
Barkin, J. Samuel, 106, 108, 370
Barlow, Jos, 303
Barrett, Scott, 302
Barroso, José Manuel, 162
Barry, John, 52
Bartlett, Robert V., 106
Basel Action Network, 45, 265
Basel Ban, 144
Basel Convention on the Control of
    Transboundary Movements of
    Hazardous Wastes and their
    Disposal (1989), 281

background information, 260
basic principles, 263 (table), 264–266
basic treaty rules, 76 (table)
constituent agreements and institutions,
    85 (table)
electronic waste, 276
framework convention–protocol model,
    62 (table)
functional role, 17, 18
global environmental responsibility, 343
multilateral international agreements
    (MEAs), 29
nongovernmental organizations
    (NGOs), 43, 45
persistent organic pollutants
    (POPs), 272
United States signature and ratification,
    3, 13, 133, 134 (table), 143–144
Basel Protocol on Liability and
    Compensation (1999), 265–266
Bates, J. M., 347
Bauer, Michael W., 182
Bauer, Steffen, 49, 50
Bauxite, 361
BBC Monitoring International
    Reports, 327
BBC News, 131, 348
BBC Worldwide Monitoring Europe, 328
Beaton, Christopher, 230
    see also Halle, Mark
Bechtel, 319
Beef consumption, 340, 351, 358, 360
Beef hormones, 69
Beets, sugar, 360
Beijing Amendment and Adjustment
    (1999), 88
Beijing, China, 192–193 (box), 204
Belarus, 305
Belgium
    carbon dioxide (CO_2) emissions, 165
    emissions reduction targets and
        progress, 244 (table)
    European Commission (EC), 162
    European Environmental Bureau, 166
    European Union compliance, 179
    European Union membership, 158
    nuclear power plants, 323
Bellagio, Italy, 237
Bellinger, John B., 153
Bellmann, Christophe, 348
Bell, Simon, 24
Benedick, Richard Elliot, 22, 106, 108,
    109, 130

Benin, 357
Berenguer, Erika, 303
Berlin Mandate, 243
Bernauer, Thomas, 304
Bern Convention on the Conservation
    of European Wildlife and Natural
    Habitats (1979), 288
Bernstein, Steven, 24, 49
Best, Edward, 181
Betsill, Michele M., 17, 23, 50, 51, 52,
    255, 256, 257, 258
Beverage packaging, 171–172
Beyer, Stefanie, 210
Bhagwati, Jagdish, 346
Bhopal, India, 262
Biedenkopf, Katja, 282
Biello, David, 209
Biermann, Frank, 49, 50, 302
Bilateral environmental agreements
    global environmental governance,
        2, 10
    international legal sources, 61–63
Binder, Seth, 131
Bioaccumulation, 261–262, 277
Biodiversity Action Plan, 177–178
Biodiversity/biodiversity protection
    agricultural commodity chains, 358,
        359 (table), 360–361
    basic concepts, 284–286
    basic treaty rules, 72 (table)
    definition, 283
    economic factors, 285, 289
    environmental politics, 18, 29
    European Union, 177–178
    future challenges, 299–301
    genetic resources, 289–293
    goals and objectives, 286–288 (table)
    historical perspective, 285–286,
        288–289
    influencing factors, 1
    international agreement negotiations,
        284, 288–289, 292–295
    international environmental funding
        mechanisms, 295–297
    international environmental regimes,
        87 (table)
    losses, 283 (box), 283–285, 299–301
    North-South conflict, 289–292
    threats, 285
    United States environmental policy,
        142–143, 289
    see also Convention on Biological
        Diversity (1992)

Biodiversity Liaison Group, 289
Biomagnification, 261–262
Bioprospecting, 290, 291 (box)
Biosafety Protocol (2000), 13, 62 (table),
 69, 87 (table)
Biotechnology patents, 290
Birds Directive (79/409/EEC), 177
Birnie, Patricia, 49
Blackhurst, Richard, 345
Black Triangle, 307
Bleischwitz, Raimund, 23, 368
 see also Andrews-Speed, Philip
Blogs, 44
Blood diamonds, 362
Blue jean commodity chain study,
 356–357
Bodansky, Daniel, 80
Boeing, 252
Boersma, Tim, 23, 368
 see also Andrews-Speed, Philip
Bohemia, 307
 see also Czech Republic
Bolivia, 363, 364
Bomberg, Elizabeth, 181, 183
Bomhard, Bastian, 303
Bonn Convention on the Conservation of
 Migratory Species of Wild Animals
 (1979), 87 (table), 134 (table), 153,
 286, 287 (table)
Borre, Tom Vanden, 129
Börzel, Tanja A., 186
Bosnia and Herzegovina, 158
Bottled water, 351
Bouman, Nicolette, 132
Boundy, Robert G., 209
Boyan, A. Stephen, Jr., 368
Boyle, Alan, 49, 80
Boyle, Robert H., 254
Brack, Duncan, 154, 255, 349
 see also Grubb, Michael
Bradford, Peter, 317, 326, 329
Bradsher, Keith, 209, 210, 211, 371
Braidwood nuclear power plant, 315
Brazil
 biodiversity protection, 289
 carbon dioxide (CO$_2$) emissions,
  201 (figure)
 climate change policies, 252
 Copenhagen Accord, 248 (table)
 genetically modified organisms
  (GMOs), 284, 298
 global environmental politics, 214,
  217, 368

greenhouse gas emissions, 68, 207, 246
 trade-environment conflicts, 340
Breman, Joel, 281
Bretton Woods institutions, 35, 44, 343
BRICS (Brazil, Russia, India, China,
 South Africa) group, 214
Bridge, Gavin, 370
Brikell, Berndt H., 280
British Petroleum (BP), 209, 252
Brody, Kenneth, 311
Bromochloromethane (BCM), 89 (table)
Brown, Donald A., 23
Brown, Janet Welsh, 89 (table), 105,
 216–217, 221, 231
 see also Chasek, Pamela S.
Brown, L. David, 50
"Brown" lending, 36
Brown Weiss, Edith, 8, 24, 128, 130, 131,
 153, 155, 256
Brundtland Commission, 1–2, 8, 59, 68,
 307, 308
Brundtland, Gro Harlem, 2, 119, 130
Brunnée, Jutta, 126, 153
Brussels, Belgium, 166
Bryant, Lisa, 280
Bryner, Gary C., 24
Buchanan, Graeme M., 304
Buckley, Nick A., 280
 see also Rao, C. H. Srinivas
Bulgaria
 emissions reduction targets and
  progress, 244 (table)
 environmental taxes, 175
 European Council, 161
 European Union membership, 158
 nuclear power plants, 307
Bulkeley, Harriet, 23, 257, 258
Bulletin of the Atomic Scientists, 327, 328
Burden-sharing agreements, 166
Bureaucratic accountability, 314–315
Burgess, Neil, 303
Burgiel, Stanley W., 48, 50, 52
Burgiel, Stas, 230
Burns, William C. G., 50
Busch, Per-Olof, 50
Bush, George H. W., 142, 145, 148,
 331–332
Bush, George W., 257
 economic policies, 352
 environmental policies, 3, 13, 135, 136,
  143, 144, 145, 176
 Kyoto Protocol, 3, 176, 243
 trade agreements, 19, 339

Business and industry NGOs (BINGOs), 38 (table), 41, 240 (table)
Business Environmental Leadership Council, 252
Bustelo, Mara R., 230
Bycatch, 178, 285
Byrd-Hagel resolution, 139, 151
Byrd, Robert C., 151

Cadmium, 361
Cairo Guidelines and Principles for the Environmentally Sound Management of Hazardous Wastes, 265
Caldwell, Lynton K., 23
California Air Resources Board, 209
California Environmental Protection Agency, 211
Cameron, James, 128, 131, 348, 349
Cameroon, 359 (table)
Campiglio, Luigi, 231
Canada
  carbon dioxide (CO$_2$) emissions, 201 (figure)
  Copenhagen Accord, 248 (table)
  emissions reduction targets and progress, 244 (table)
  free trade agreements, 337–340
  genetically modified organisms (GMOs), 284, 298
  international environmental agreements, 94, 137
  Kyoto Protocol (1997), 245, 249
  persistent organic pollutants (POPs), 269
  state negotiating blocs, 239 (table)
  trade-environment conflicts, 340
Canadian Environmental Law Association, 346
Canadian Nature Federation, 346
Canan, Penelope, 108, 109
Cancun Agreements, 246–249, 251
Capacity building and improved governance, 368
Capacity, economic, political, and governmental, 96
Cap-and-trade system, 140, 141, 203, 204, 249
Capitalism, 353
Carbon dioxide (CO$_2$) emissions, 141, 165, 176–177, 187, 190, 201 (figure), 205–206, 235–237, 254
Carbon emissions, 353

Carbon tetrachloride, 84, 89 (table), 90–91
Carcinogens, 261, 262, 277
Cardwell, Diane, 211
Caribbean Region, 359 (table)
Carlin, Elaine M., 256
Carlsen, Laura, 348
Carmichael, G. R., 209
Car mileage standards, 340
Carmin, JoAnn, 25, 183, 185, 308, 326, 327, 371
"Cars & CO$_2$," 183
Carson, Rachel, 262
Cartagena Protocol on Biosafety (2000)
  background information, 18, 29
  constituent agreements and institutions, 87 (table)
  framework convention–protocol model, 62 (table)
  genetically modified organisms (GMOs), 297–299
  goals and objectives, 287–288 (table), 293, 297–299
  international agreement negotiations, 284
  precautionary principle, 69, 297–298
  United States signature and ratification, 13
Case Concerning the Gabcikovo-Nagymaros Project, 64, 67, 69, 81
Case law, international, 64
Cashews, 358
Cashore, Benjamin W., 50, 51, 52, 371
Cassava, 358
Cass, Loren, 254
Cattle industry, 360
Cavender-Bares, Jeannine, 153
Center for Climate and Energy Solutions, 154, 252
Center for Climate and Environmental Policy, 199
Center for Science and the Environment, 41
Central America, 359 (table)
Central and Eastern Europe (CEE)
  communist legacy, 314–315
  environmental politics, 18–19
  free market economies, 307–308
  global environmental governance, 368
  nuclear power plants, 307–308
  political culture, 314–315
  sustainable development, 307
Central Asia, Caucasus, Albania, and Moldova (CACAM), 239 (table)
Central Intelligence Agency (CIA), 153, 208

Certification and labeling schemes, 367
Ceske energeticke zavody (CEZ), 307,
    310, 311, 312 (box), 317, 322,
    324–325
Chad, 363
Chambers, Jasemine, 302
Chandler, William, 257
Charnovitz, Steve, 346, 347, 348
Chasek, Pamela S., 48, 49, 50, 52, 89
    (table), 105, 106, 107, 216–217,
    231, 233
Chayes, Abraham, 128, 129, 130, 131, 132
Chemicals Convention (1992),
    62 (table), 71
Chemicals management regimes
    Basel Convention on the Control of
        Transboundary Movements of
        Hazardous Wastes and their
        Disposal (1989), 260, 263 (table),
        264–266
    chemical production growth, 261
    European Union, 277–278
    future research challenges, 278–279
    governance challenges, 259–260
    historical perspective, 259–260
    management challenges, 261–262
    monitoring and compliance programs,
        274–275
    multilevel governance initiatives and
        challenges, 273–276
    primary treaties, 260, 262, 263–264
        (table), 264
    Protocol on Persistent Organic
        Pollutants to the Convention on
        Long-Range Transboundary Air
        Pollution (CLRTAP), 260, 263
        (table), 268–270
    public awareness programs, 276
    ratification issues, 273
    regional agreements, 272–273
    Rotterdam Convention on the Prior
        Informed Consent Procedure for
        Certain Hazardous Chemicals and
        Pesticides in International Trade
        (1998), 260, 263 (table), 266–268
    Stockholm Convention on Persistent
        Organic Pollutants (2001), 260,
        264 (table), 270–272
Cheng, Y. F., 209
Chicago Climate Exchange (CCX), 204
Child labor/child trafficking, 358,
    359 (table)
Children of the Earth, 313

Chile
    free trade agreements, 339 (table)
    genetically modified organisms
        (GMOs), 298
    nuclear energy programs, 305
China
    air pollution challenges, 190–197,
        194 (table)
    carbon dioxide (CO_2) emissions, 187,
        190, 201 (figure), 205–206
    carbon emissions, 353
    chemical production, 261, 272
    climate change policies, 200–204,
        216, 222
    coal-fired power plants, 187, 190–195,
        191 (table), 202
    Copenhagen Accord, 248 (table)
    economic policies, 352
    Eleventh Five-Year Plan, 202
    energy and environmental challenges,
        187–188, 207–208
    energy consumption/energy intensity
        trends, 189, 189 (figure)
    energy-economic development
        relationship, 188–190
    environmental policies, 15, 21, 278
    environmental regulation and
        enforcement, 197–199
    fuel economy standards, 196 (figure),
        196–197
    genetically modified organisms
        (GMOs), 284, 298
    global environmental politics, 214,
        217, 368
    greenhouse gas emissions, 68, 95,
        187, 196 (figure), 199–207, 234,
        246–247, 251
    gross domestic product (GDP), 188,
        193–194, 204
    international climate negotiations, 200,
        205–207
    international environmental
        agreements, 94, 96, 102
    motor vehicle use, 195–197,
        196 (figure)
    nitrogen oxide (NO_x) emissions,
        194 (table), 195
    nuclear energy programs, 305
    nuclear power plants, 323
    oil imports, 195–196
    particulate matter (PM) health impacts,
        192, 192–193 (box), 194
    state negotiating blocs, 238, 239 (table)

sulfur dioxide (SO_2) emissions, 187, 193, 194 (table)
summary discussion, 207–208
trade-environment conflicts, 342
Twelfth Five-Year Plan, 203–204
China Energy Group, 189 (figure), 209
ChinaFAQs, 209
China Meteorological Administration, 200
China National Petroleum Corporation Assets Management Co. Ltd., 204
"China Surpasses U.S. Emissions," 154
Chinkin, Christine M., 80
Chin, M., 209
Chlorofluorocarbons (CFCs)
    chemical phase-out schedule, 89 (table), 90–91
    compliance records, 119
    international environmental negotiations, 88, 94
    ozone depletion, 84
    regulation background, 100–104
    trade-environment relationship, 331
    United States environmental policy, 137, 151–152
Chongqing, China, 204
Choucri, Nazli, 230
Christiansen, Thomas, 181
Chromium, 361
Cini, Michelle, 181, 183
Ciszuk, Samuel, 328
CITES
    see Convention on International Trade in Endangered Species of Wild Fauna and Flora (CITES)
Citibank, 310
Cities for Climate Protection (CCP), 240 (table), 252, 258
Citizens against Temelin, 313
Clapp, Jennifer, 50, 51, 280
Clark, William C., 153
Claussen, Eileen, 257
Clay, Jason, 359 (table), 370
Clays, 361
Clayton, Mark, 328
Clean Air Act (1977), 137, 141, 152
Clean Air Act (1990), 340
Clean Development Mechanism (CDM), 34, 41, 115–116, 200, 227–228, 245–246
Clémençon, Raymond, 50
Clements, Tom, 303
Cleveland, Cutler, 232

Climate Action Network (CAN), 41–42, 44
Climate Action Tracker, 257
Climate change
    basic treaty rules, 74–75 (table)
    biodiversity impacts, 285, 295–297
    Chinese policies, 200–204
    climate justice networks, 42
    compliance standards, 114–115
    developing countries, 216, 222, 226
    emissions trading, 176–177
    energy efficiency and renewable energy, 175–176
    environmental and energy taxes, 174–175
    environmental impacts, 234
    European Union policies, 174–177
    global environmental politics, 16–17
    global summits, 60
    influencing factors, 1
    international environmental policy process, 68–69, 93–94
    international environmental regimes, 85 (table), 234–254
    nuclear energy programs, 322
    ozone depletion, 74–75 (table), 84, 100–101
    scientific cooperation, 235–237
    trade-environment relationship, 330–331
    United States environmental policy, 138–142
Climate Change Action Plan, 250
Climate Group, 253, 258
Climate Justice Action (CJA), 42
Climate Justice Now! (CJN!), 42
Clinton, Bill, 139, 142, 143, 145, 151, 250, 337–339
CMR (carcinogenetic, mutagenic, and toxic for reproduction) chemicals, 277
CNN, 328
Coad, Lauren, 303
Coal-fired power plants, 187, 190–195, 191 (table), 202, 307
Cobalt, 361
Cocks, Emma, 53
Cocoa industry, 357, 358, 359 (table)
Code of Conduct on the Distribution and Use of Pesticides, 267
Coffee, 357, 358, 359 (table), 367
Cold War politics, 28, 215
Cole, M. A., 347
Collier, Paul, 369, 371

Colombia, 339 (table)
Columbite-tantalite (coltan), 361, 362
Command-and-control regulations, 366
Commercial chemicals
    see Rotterdam Convention on the Prior
        Informed Consent Procedure for
        Certain Hazardous Chemicals and
        Pesticides in International Trade
        (1998)
Commission for Environmental
    Cooperation (CEC), 337, 339–340
Commission of the European
    Communities, 185, 256
"Commission Snubs German Auto
    Industry over CO$_2$ Emissions," 183
Commission Staff Working Document,
    186
Committee on the Environment, Public
    Health and Food Safety (ENVI),
    163, 182
Committee on Trade and the
    Environment, 340
Commoditization processes, 352–355
Commodity chains, 355–357, 364–366
Common but differentiated responsibilities
    principle, 68–69, 226–227
Common Fisheries Policy, 178
Communist legacy, 314–315
Community Nutrition Institute, 346
Compagnon, Daniel, 23, 258
Compliance, definition of, 111
Comprehensive Test Ban Treaty (1996), 135
Conca, Ken, 51, 369, 370, 372
    see also Princen, Thomas
Conference of the Parties (COP), 10, 30,
    33, 44, 85 (table), 273, 293–294
Conference of the Parties to the UN
    Framework Convention on Climate
    Change, 68–69, 80, 81, 242–243, 253
Conflict diamonds, 362
"Congress Debates Depletion of Ozone
    in the Stratosphere," 156
Conliffe, Alexandra, 50
Connecticut, 141
Connelly, James, 181
Connelly, Sarah, 370
Connolly, Sara, 182
Conservation International, 40, 42
Constructivism, 5–6
Consumerism
    background information, 20
    capacity building and improved
        governance, 368

certification and labeling schemes, 367
command-and-control regulations, 366
commoditization processes, 352–355
commodity chains, 355–357, 364–366
global ramifications, 350–352
mining impacts, 361–364
social embeddedness, 354–355, 360
subsidy adjustments, 366–367
sustainable development policies, 20,
    351–352, 358, 360, 366–368
taxation programs, 367
Convention Concerning the Protection
    of World Cultural and Natural
    Heritage, 72 (table)
Convention for the Conservation of
    Antarctic Seals (1972), 87 (table)
Convention for the Prevention of Marine
    Pollution by Dumping from Ships
    and Aircraft (1972), 272
Convention for the Prevention of Marine
    Pollution from Land-Based Sources
    (1974), 272
Convention for the Protection of the
    Marine Environment of the North-
    East Atlantic (OSPAR), 61
Convention on Biological Diversity
    (1992), 302, 303
    background information, 60
    basic treaty rules, 72 (table)
    constituent agreements and institutions,
        87 (table)
    establishment, 284
    framework convention–protocol model,
        62 (table)
    functional role, 18
    genetic resources, 289–293
    global summits, 30, 31 (table)
    goals and objectives, 87 (table), 287
        (table), 292–295
    international agreement negotiations,
        292–295
    international environmental funding
        mechanisms, 295–297
    multilateral international agreements
        (MEAs), 29
    nongovernmental organizations
        (NGOs), 43
    North-South conflict, 289–292
    precautionary principle, 69
    treaty secretariats, 33–34
    United States signature and
        ratification, 3, 13, 133, 134
        (table), 142–143, 146

Convention on International Trade in
    Endangered Species of Wild Fauna
    and Flora (CITES), 51
  basic treaty rules, 72 (table)
  constituent agreements and institutions,
    87 (table)
  framework convention–protocol model,
    62 (table)
  goals and objectives, 287 (table)
  international agreement negotiations,
    286
  multilateral international agreements
    (MEAs), 29
  nongovernmental organizations
    (NGOs), 43, 45
  United States environmental policy,
    137
  United States signature and ratification,
    134 (table)
Convention on Long-Range
    Transboundary Air Pollution
    (CLRTAP)
  background information, 61, 260
  basic principles, 263 (table), 268–270
  basic treaty rules, 74 (table)
  constituent agreements and institutions,
    86 (table)
  European Union directives, 170
  framework convention–protocol model,
    62 (table)
  functional role, 17–18
  multilateral international agreements
    (MEAs), 29
  United States signature and ratification,
    134 (table), 144
Convention on the Ban of the Import
    into Africa and the Control of
    Transboundary Movement and
    Management of Hazardous Wastes
    within Africa (1991), 273
Convention on the Conservation of
    Antarctic Marine Living Resources
    (1980), 87 (table)
Convention on the Law of Non-
    navigational Uses of International
    Watercourses, 74 (table)
Convention on the Prohibition of the Use,
    Stockpiling, Production and Transfer
    of Anti-Personnel Mines and on
    Their Destruction (1997), 135
Convention on the Protection of the
    Marine Environment of the Baltic
    Sea Area (1974), 272

Convention on the Regulation of
    Antarctic Mineral Resource
    Activities (1998), 87 (table)
Convention to Combat Desertification,
    45, 134 (table)
Cook, Elizabeth, 109
Cooperation, 93–95, 100
Cooper, William H., 346
Copenhagen Accord, 247–248, 248
    (table), 251
Copenhagen Amendment and
    Adjustment (1992), 88, 100
Copenhagen Climate Change Summit
    (2009), 21, 60, 61, 68, 247
Copenhagen, Denmark, 163
Copper, 361
Coral reefs, 285
Corbett, Richard, 181
Corcelle,Guy, 184
Corell, Elisabeth, 50, 51, 52, 230,
    233, 255
Core Writing Team, 254
Corn, 358
Cosbey, Aaron, 230
Costa, Katia Lemos, 303
Costa Rica, 368
Côte d'Ivoire, 264, 359 (table)
Cotton, 358
Council of the European Union, 161, 181
Country Reports, 326
Courrau, José, 303
Court of Auditors, 160
Court of Justice of the European Union,
    125, 163
Cousins, Ken, 369
Cowhey, Peter, 149, 155
Craig, Paul, 131
Crawford, Keith, 327
Crespi, Stephen, 302
Crewe, Louise, 370
Critical Ecosystem Partnership Fund, 45
Croatia
  emissions reduction targets and
    progress, 244 (table)
  European Union membership, 158
Cross-border NGOs, 41–42
Crossette, Barbara, 230
Cultural services, 285
Cultured pearls, 360
Cummings, Michael B., 210
Curry, Bill, 154
Customary international law, 63
Cut-flower industry, 360

Cyprus, 158, 177
Czech and Slovakia Business Weekly, 329
Czech News Agency (CTK), 327,
   328, 329
Czech Nuclear Waste Repository
   Authority, 318
Czech Republic
   communist legacy, 314–315
   emissions reduction targets and
      progress, 244 (table)
   environmental policies, 306, 308–309
   environmental politics, 18–19
   European Union membership, 158,
      313–314
   free market economy, 308
   nuclear power plants, 66, 173, 305–306,
      307, 315, 317, 322, 324, 326
   nuclear waste disposal, 317–318
   political culture, 314–315
   sustainable development, 308–309
   Temelin nuclear power plant, 18, 66,
      305, 307, 309–314, 312 (box), 322,
      324–325

Dabelko, Geoffrey D., 369, 371, 372
Dadi, Zhou, 257
da Fonseca, Gustavo A. B., 304
Danielsen, Finn, 303
Dauvergne, Peter, 24, 50, 51, 364–365,
   369, 370, 371
Davidson, Ogunlade, 257
Daviet, Florence, 256
Davis, Stacy C., 209
DeBardeleben, Joan, 326
DeBruyn, S. M., 347
De Búrca, Gráinne, 131
"Decision No. 1600/2002/EC of the
   European Parliament and of the
   Council of July 22, 2002, Laying
   Down the Sixth Community
   Environmental Action
   Programme," 183
"Decision of the European Parliament
   and of the Council on a General
   Union Environment Action
   Programme to 2020 `Living Well,
   Within the Limits of our
   Planet," 183
Deere, Carolyn L., 346, 347, 348
Deforestation, 284, 285, 358, 359 (table),
   360
de Graaf, John, 369

de Groot, Dolf, 301
Dehousse, Renaud, 182
Deketelaere, Kurt, 129
Delaware, 141
Demaret, Paul, 349
Democratic Republic of the Congo
   (DRC), 362, 364
Deng Xiaoping, 197
Denmark
   beverage container packaging and
      recycling, 171–172
   carbon dioxide (CO_2) emissions, 165
   emissions reduction targets and
      progress, 244 (table)
   European Environment Agency
      (EEA), 163
   European Union membership, 158
   nuclear power plants, 313
Department of Energy (DOE), 310, 311,
   317, 319
Depledge, Joanna, 239 (table), 254, 255
DeRitter, Sara M., 24, 232
Dernbach, John C., 24
Desertification, 358
DeSombre, Elizabeth R., 14, 153, 370
Developed nations
   environmental policies, 55
   environmental threats, 7–8
Developing countries
   common but differentiated
      responsibilities principle, 226–227
   common goals and interests, 215–216
   environmental policies, 15, 55
   environmental threats, 7–8
   frustrations and challenges, 228–229
   global environmental politics, 213–229
   greenhouse gas emissions, 234
   hazardous waste management, 270
   historical perspective, 214–217, 219
   international environmental
      negotiations, 219–222
   member states, 218 (map)
   motivations and aspirations, 219–223
   Non- Aligned Movement (NAM), 217
   North-South concept, 214–215
   North-South polarization, 219–221
   polluter-pays principle, 227–228
   post-Rio legacy, 223–228
   principle of additionality, 226
   sustainable development policies,
      221–226
   see also Group of 77 (G-77)

Development and Environment, 231, 233
Devroy, Ann, 154
Diamonds, 362
Dias Soares, Claudia, 129
Dichlorodiphenyl trichloroethane (DDT), 262, 271–272
Dickson, Barnabas, 302
Dickson, Nancy M., 153
Diegel, Susan W., 209
Diehl, Paul F., 23
Diehl, T., 209
Diesing, Paul, 107
Dieter Janecek v. Freistaat Bayern (2008), 182
Dietsche, Evelyn, 371
Dingell, John, 311
Dioxins, 262
Directive 70/220/EEC, 170
Directive 79/409/EEC, 177
Directive 88/609/EEC, 165
Directive 92/43/EEC, 177
Directive 92/880/EEC, 173
Directive 94/62/EC, 165, 172
Directive 96/61/EC, 185
Directive 1980/2000/EC, 173–174
Directive 2000/60/EC, 171, 184
Directive 2001/77/EC, 183
Directive 2003/30/EC, 183
Directive 2003/87/EC, 348
Directive 2003/96/EC, 175
Directive 2004/12/EC, 184
Directive 2004/35/CE, 184
Directive 2004/35/EC, 172
Directive 2004/8/EC, 185
Directive 2005/20/EC, 184
Directive 2006/32/EC, 185
Directive 2008/1/EC, 169
Directive 2008/50/EC, 170
Directive 2008/56/EC, 177
Directive 2008/99/ EC, 172
Directive 2008/99/EC, 185
Directive 2009/125/EC, 185
Directive 2009/28/EC, 165, 175–176, 183
Directive 2009/71/Euratom, 185
Directive 2010/30/EU, 185
Directive 2010/75/EU, 169
Directive 2012/27/EU, 176, 185
Directive on Access to Environmental Information, 169
Directorate-General for Climate, 162
Directorate-General for the Environment, 162, 166

Diringer, Elliot, 211
DiSavino, Scott, 327
Dispute settlement procedures, 12, 338, 340, 343
Distancing concept, 355–356
Dixon, Robert K., 52
Dobris Assessment, 308
Documents in International Environmental Law, 81
Dodo (*Raphus cucullatus*), 285
Doelle, Meinhard, 126
Doha Development Round, 342
Doha, Qatar, 245, 253, 331
Doha WTO Ministerial Declaration, 346, 348
Dolphins, 332
Domesticated plants, 285, 290
Dominican Republic–Central America–United States Free Trade Agreement (CAFTA-DR), 332
Donald, Paul F., 304
Dons, Hans, 303
Dotto, Lydia, 106, 108, 109
Dousab, Ejallah, 357
Downie, David Leonard, 6, 12, 89 (table), 105, 106, 108, 109, 129, 131, 184, 281
    see also Chasek, Pamela S.
Doyle, Timothy, 51
D'Silva, Joyce, 370
Dua, André, 346, 347
Dudek, Carolyn, 186
Duffy, Robert J., 51
Duffy, Rosaleen, 258
Dukovany nuclear power plant, 322
Dunlap, Riley E., 51
DuPont, 252
Durban Platform for Enhanced Action, 68, 207
Dworkin, Ronald, 80

Eagleton, Clyde, 80
Earley, Robert, 196 (figure)
Earth Negotiations Bulletin (ENB), 44, 280
Earthquakes, 320, 321, 322
Earth Summit (1992)
    background information, 2
    biodiversity protection, 142
    climate change policies, 138
    environmental policies, 55
    historical perspective, 58–59

international climate negotiations, 240
legacy, 223–228
sustainable development policies, 9, 16,
    58–59
trade-environment relationship, 331
    see also Global South
Earth Summits, 26, 29–32, 31 (table)
Eastern European countries
    see Central and Eastern Europe (CEE)
East European Reporter, 327
Easton, Catherine, 131, 256
Eaton, Derek, 303
Ebeling, Johannes, 296, 304
Eckersley, Robyn, 52
Eckley, Noelle, 282
    see also Selin, Noelle E.
Eco-Innovation Action Plan (Eco-AP), 169
Ecolabeling Directive, 173–174
Ecological systems, 93
Ecologic Institute for International and
    European Environmental Policy, 131
Economic sanctions, 113, 124–125
Economy, Elizabeth C., 24, 52, 154
Ecosystem services, 283, 285
    see also Biodiversity/biodiversity protection
EcoTec Research and Consulting
    Limited, 186
Eddleston, Michael, 280
    see also Rao, C. H. Srinivas
Edwards, Paul N., 49
Effective international policy, 93–94
Effectiveness
    definition, 111
    international climate change regime,
        250–253
Egypt
    child labor, 358
    nuclear energy programs, 305, 322
Egziabher, T. B. G., 233
Electrical and electronic equipment
    (RoHS) Directive, 278
Electricity production, 324–325
Electronic waste, 262, 276, 277–278
Eli Lilly, 291 (box)
Ellinas, Antonis A., 182
Emissions Trading System (ETS), 162,
    176–177, 245, 249, 342
Endangered Species Act (1973), 136–137,
    142
Endangered species protection
    see Convention on International Trade
        in Endangered Species of Wild
        Fauna and Flora (CITES)

Energy Daily, 327
Energy efficiency and renewable energy,
    175–176, 187–188
Energy Efficiency Plan 2011, 169
Energy Policy Act (2005), 319
Energy Regulatory Office, 325
Energy Star program, 367
Enforcement, definition of, 111
Environmental and energy taxes, 174–175
Environmental change, 1
Environmental Defense Fund, 346
Environmental health risks, 357–358, 359
    (table), 360–363
Environmental Impact Assessment
    Directive, 169
Environmental Integrity Group, 238,
    239 (table)
Environmental issues
    differing core beliefs and values, 99–100
    large-number problems, 99
    linked economic and political interests,
        97–98
    scientific complexity and uncertainty, 97
    time horizon impacts, 98–99
    unequal adjustment costs, 98
Environmental justice, 8
Environmental Liability Directive,
    169, 172
Environmental NGOs (ENGOs),
    38 (table), 42, 240 (table)
Environmental Protection Agency (EPA),
    141, 154, 192 (box), 257, 279, 337,
    340, 367
Environmental Protection Bureau (EPB),
    192 (box)
Environmental Protection Law (China),
    197–198
Environmental Side Agreement, 19,
    337, 339
Environmental treaties
    environmental protection, 19, 337
    hazardous substances, 17–19
    historical perspective, 11–12
Equity principle, 241
Erda, Lin, 210
Estonia
    emissions reduction targets and
        progress, 244 (table)
    European Council, 161
    European Union membership, 158
Esty, Daniel C., 19–20, 25, 345, 346, 347,
    348, 349
    see also Hufbauer, Gary C.

ETC Group, 304
European Atomic Energy Authority
    (Euratom), 158, 306
European Central Bank, 160
European Chemical Industry Council
    (CEFIC), 280
European Coal and Steel Community
    (ECSC), 158
European Commission (EC), 125, 130,
    162, 182, 183, 184, 185, 186, 295
European Communities, 303, 304
European Council, 160–161
European Court of Justice (ECJ), 125, 163
European Economic Community (EEC),
    14, 158
European Environment Agency (EEA), 163
European Environmental Bureau, 166, 183
European Environment Information and
    Observation Network (EIONET), 163
European Parliament, 162–163
European Parliament Resolution, 182, 185
European People's Party, 162
European Pressurized Reactor, 323
European Union, 183
    action plans, 169, 175, 177–178
    biodiversity protection, 177–178, 289
    carbon dioxide (CO_2) emissions,
        201 (figure)
    carbon emissions, 353
    climate change policies, 174–177
    compliance standards, 178–180
    conflicts of interest, 165
    Copenhagen Accord, 248 (table)
    directives and regulations, 168–174,
        277–278
    environmental action programs,
        167–168
    environmental policies, 14–15, 18, 21,
        157–181, 313
    environmental standard harmonization,
        167
    fuel economy standards, 196 (figure)
    genetically modified organisms
        (GMOs), 298–299
    greenhouse gas emissions, 95, 237
    hazardous substances management,
        277–278
    hazardous substances trade, 266
    international environmental
        agreements, 94, 96, 101–102, 122
    Kyoto Protocol (1997), 245, 249
    legislative action, 168–178
    member states, 158, 159 (map)
    nature conservation, 177–178
    noncompliance procedures, 125
    nuclear power plants, 323
    policy-making process, 163–167
    political origins, 158–160
    polluter-pays principle, 70
    primary institutions, 160–163
    state negotiating blocs, 239 (table)
    success factors, 157–158
    summary discussion, 180–181
    trade-environment conflicts, 340, 342
    treaty development, 158, 159–160
European Union Network for the
    Implementation and Enforcement
    of Environmental Law (IMPEL),
    179, 186
European Voice, 328
E-waste disposal, 45–46, 365
Executive Order 13141, 347
Exelon, 317
Exim Bank, 310, 311
Extractive industries, 361–364

Facebook, 44
Fagin, Adam, 327
Fair Trade International, 351
Fairtrade Labelling Organizations
    International, 358
Fair trade movement, 358, 367
Falkner, Robert, 50, 109, 304
Farmer organizations, 240 (table)
Farming impacts, 285
Faure, Michael G., 12, 23, 24, 25, 129,
    181, 183, 184
Federal Register, 153
Feffer, John, 155
Fellman, Joshua, 211
Fenge, Terry, 108, 281
Ferreira, Joice, 303
Finkenrath, Matthias, 209
Finland
    carbon dioxide (CO_2) emissions, 165
    emissions reduction targets and
        progress, 244 (table)
    European Council, 161
    European Union membership, 158
    nuclear power plants, 323
Finnemore, Martha, 23
Fiore, Karine, 129
First World Climate Conference
    (1979), 237
Fisher, Dana R., 52
Fishing methods, 285

Fish stock conservation, 178, 179, 331, 332, 345, 360
Fish Stocks Agreement (1995), 62 (table)
Flavin, Christopher, 369
FlorCruz, Jaime A., 193 (box)
Florida, 317
Flynn, Brendan, 183
Foden, Wendy, 303
Food and Agriculture Organization (FAO), 71, 82, 267, 286, 291, 294, 301
Foreign oil refiners, 340
Forest degradation, 284, 285
Forest Principles, 59
Forest Stewardship Council (FSC), 46, 106, 367
Forman, Shepard, 155
Former Soviet Union, 306–307
Forsythe, David, 155
Fossil fuel consumption, 322, 351, 353–354, 366
Fossil of the Day award, 42, 44
Foundation for International Environmental Law and Development (FIELD), 79, 131
Founex Report (1971), 220
Fox, Jonathan A., 50
Framework Convention for the Protection of the Ozone Layer, 75 (table)
Framework Convention on Climate Change (FCCC), 51, 131, 154, 212, 255, 256, 303
  background information, 54, 60
  basic treaty rules, 75 (table)
  biodiversity protection, 295–297
  Cancun Agreements, 246–249
  China, 200
  commitments and obligations, 242
  compliance standards, 115, 250
  constituent agreements and institutions, 85 (table)
  Copenhagen Accord, 247–248, 248 (table)
  dispute resolution, 124
  framework convention–protocol model, 62, 62 (table)
  global environmental responsibility, 342
  global summits, 30, 31 (table)
  goals, 85 (table)
  international climate negotiations, 240–243
  key objectives and principles, 240–242
  multilateral international agreements (MEAs), 29
  organizational structure, 242–243
  policy impacts, 17
  regime effectiveness, 250–253
  regime organizations, 112
  reporting requirements, 119–120
  state negotiating blocs, 239 (table)
  treaty secretariats, 33
  United States signature and ratification, 133, 134 (table), 138–140
Framework convention–protocol models, 61–63, 62 (table)
France
  carbon dioxide (CO_2) emissions, 165
  commodity chains, 357
  common fisheries policy, 178
  European Commission (EC), 162
  European Council, 161
  European Union membership, 158
  genetic resources, 292
  nuclear power plants, 173, 323–324
Fransen, Taryn, 131, 256
Frantzius, Ina von, 49
Frazier, Scott, 301
Freedman, Andrew, 107
Freedman, Jennifer M., 348
Freeman, Mark, 51
Free rider problem, 92, 122, 241, 335, 344
Free trade agreements
  agreements with environmental chapters, 339 (table)
  competitive pressures, 334–335
  free trader concerns, 335–337, 343
  future challenges, 345
  historical perspective, 331–332
  international environmental regimes, 342–344
  key environmental concerns, 333–335, 343
  North American Free Trade Agreement (NAFTA) negotiations, 337–340
  policy challenges, 19, 330–332
  production process or method (PPM)-based regulations, 344
  regulatory challenges, 334–335, 343–345
  World Trade Organization (WTO), 340, 342–344
Free Trade Area of the Americas, 332, 339
French, Hilary, 22, 233
"French Phase-in Plans for Car CO2 Opposed," 183
Freshwater resources protection, 74 (table)
Fridley, David, 211
Friends of the Earth, 351

Froggatt, Antony, 327, 328, 329
Frog habitat loss, 283 (box)
Froman, Michael B., 348
Fruits, 360
Fukushima nuclear reactor disaster, 19,
    173, 319–322
Funabashi, Yoichi, 346
Fungicide use, 340
Furans, 262
Fur trade, 340
"Future We Want, The," 31 (table), 32,
    60, 61

Gaines, Sanford, 347
Gallagher, Kelly Sims, 15, 371
Game theory, 122
Gardner, Gary, 369
Gardner, Richard N., 49, 345
Gardner, Toby A., 303
Gareau, Brian J., 106, 107, 109, 153
Gaskell, George, 304
Gasoline regulations, 340
Gee, David, 282
Gehring, Thomas, 50, 105, 184, 302
Geiser, Kenneth, 282
Gender discrimination, 359 (table)
Genentech, 142
General Agreement on Tariffs and Trade
    (GATT), 20, 35–36, 37, 330, 332,
    340, 342, 344, 348
General principles of law, 63–64
Gene technology, 297
Genetically modified organisms (GMOs),
    163, 284, 297–299
Genetic resources, 289–293
Geneva Conventions on the High Seas, 79
Georgia, 317
Geradin, Damien, 346, 348, 349
Germany
    beverage container packaging and
        recycling, 171–172
    carbon dioxide (CO_2) emissions, 165
    commodity chains, 357
    emissions reduction targets and
        progress, 244 (table)
    emissions trading, 177
    environmental policies, 277
    European Council, 161
    European Union membership, 158
    genetic resources, 292
    nuclear power plants, 173, 306, 313,
        314, 323
    renewable energy, 325

Gerster, Richard, 348
Getzner, Michael, 327
Ghana, 359 (table)
Gibson, Shannon, 51
Gidropress, 324
Gipe, Paul, 329
Glachant, Matthieu, 186
Glasbergen, Pieter, 45, 52
Glennon, Michael J., 153
Global Atmospheric Research Program, 28
Global biodiversity
    see Biodiversity/biodiversity protection
Global Climate Coalition (GCC), 252
Global consumerism, 20
Global ecological systems, 93
Global environmental policy compliance
    behavioral changes, 113–116
    compliance information systems, 119–120
    comprehensive noncompliance response
        systems, 127
    country characteristics, 121
    differentiated standards, 114–116
    dispute resolution, 123–127
    influencing factors, 113–116, 118–125
    information and reporting systems,
        118–120
    Montreal Protocol, 116–117, 125–126
    noncompliance procedures, 113,
        123–127
    nongovernmental organizations
        (NGOs), 123
    number of countries, 121–123
    regime organizations, 112
    regime rule systems, 113–116
    summary discussion, 127–128
    terminology, 111
    theoretical perspectives, 110–113
    transparency, 118–119
Global Environmental Politics, 23
Global Environment Facility (GEF), 50
    across-regime environmental IGOs,
        34–35
    biodiversity protection, 293, 295–296
    characteristics and functional role, 11
    funding responsibilities, 84, 85 (table),
        226
    global summits, 31 (table)
    and nongovernmental organizations
        (NGOs), 41
    partnerships, 45
    United Nations Framework
        Convention on Climate Change
        (FCCC), 242–243

Global legal systems, 93–94
Global Malaria Control Strategy, 271
Global Malaria Eradication Programme, 271
Global People's Forum, 2
Global political systems, 93
Global South
    common but differentiated
        responsibilities principle, 226–227
    common goals and interests, 215–216
    environmental policies, 15, 55
    environmental threats, 7–8
    frustrations and challenges, 228–229
    global environmental politics, 213–229
    historical perspective, 214–217, 219
    international environmental
        negotiations, 219–222
    member states, 218 (map)
    motivations and aspirations, 219–223
    Non- Aligned Movement (NAM), 217
    North-South concept, 214–215
    North-South polarization, 219–221
    polluter-pays principle, 227–228
    post-Rio legacy, 223–228
    principle of additionality, 226
    sustainable development policies,
        221–226
    see also Group of 77 (G-77)
Global Times, 208
Global warming
    global environmental politics, 16–17,
        138–142
    influencing factors, 1
    nuclear energy programs, 322
    see also Climate change
Global Witness, 351, 371
Godden, Lee, 80
Gold, 361, 362
Goldsmith, Edward, 25
Goldsmith, Jack L., 128, 129
Golub, Jonathan, 186
Good neighborliness/cooperation
    principle, 66–67
Gordon, Deborah, 369
Gore, Al, 130, 311
Gothenburg Protocol to Abate
    Acidification, Eutrophication and
    Ground-Level Ozone (1999), 170
Government of Brazil, 212
Government of Mexico, 212
Government of Tanzania, 281
Government of the People's Republic of
    China, 210, 211

Government-organized NGOs
    (GONGOs), 38
Granier, Laurent, 52
Grant, Cedric, 230
Grant, Wyn, 186
Grapes, 360
Gravel, 361
Gray, Kevin, 80
Gray, Tim, 304
Great Apes Survival Project (GRASP), 45
Great Britain v. United States (1893), 78
Great Lakes Water Quality Agreement
    (1972), 272
Greece
    carbon dioxide (CO$_2$) emissions, 165
    emissions reduction targets and
        progress, 244 (table)
    European Council, 161
    European Union compliance, 179
    European Union membership, 158
Green chemistry, 279
Green Climate Fund, 34, 249
Green Customs Initiative, 35
Green economy, 224, 225
Greenhouse gases
    beef industry, 360
    China, 68, 95, 187, 196 (figure), 199–207,
        234, 251
    emissions trading, 176–177
    environmental impacts, 234, 235
    European Union policies, 174–177
    global environmental politics, 16–17,
        138–142
    influencing factors, 1
    international environmental
        negotiations, 246–247, 249
    regime effectiveness, 250–253
    scientific monitoring, 235–237
    trade-environment relationship, 331
Green, Jonathan M. H., 304
Green Parliament, 308
Green Party (Austria), 313, 325
Greenpeace International, 194 (table)
    Ban Amendment (1995), 265
    functional role, 37, 43, 45, 123, 166
    nuclear power plants, 313
    organizational form, 38 (table),
        40, 42
Greens-European Free Alliance, 162
Grieco, Joseph M., 107, 108
Grossman, Gene M., 336, 347
Groundwater contamination, 320–321,
    358

Group of 77 (G-77), 231
  background information, 8, 16, 28, 207
  climate change policies, 216
  establishment, 211
  functional role, 217, 219
  global environmental politics, 214–215
  international environmental
      negotiations, 219–222
  member states, 218 (map)
  state negotiating blocs, 238, 239 (table)
  sustainable development policies, 224
Group of Eight, 246
Growth hormones, 340
Grubb, Michael, 154, 255, 256
Guangdong Province, China, 204
Guardian, The, 328, 356–357
Guedes Vaz, Sofia, 282
Gulberg, Anne T., 230
  see also Kasa, Sjur
Gulbrandsen, Lars H., 51, 52
Gupta, Aarti, 304
Gupta, Joyeeta, 254, 255
Gutierrez, Maria, 50
Gutner, Tamar, 50
Guzman, Andrew T., 113, 122, 128,
    129, 131
Gwichin Council International (Canada),
    38 (table)
Gypsum, 361

Haas, Ernst, 105
Haas, Peter, 6, 23, 95, 106, 108, 109, 186,
    230, 281
Haavisto, P., 233
Habitat loss, 359 (table)
Habitats Directive (92/43/EEC), 177–178
Hagel, Chuck, 151
Haggard, Stephan, 105
Haigh, Nigel, 24
Hale, Thomas, 23
Halle, Mark, 230, 231, 232, 233
Halons, 84, 88, 89 (table), 90–91
Halweil, Brian, 370
Handler-Chayes, Antonia, 128, 129, 130,
    131, 132
Handl, G., 105
Hanhimäki, Jussi M., 48
Hansen, Roger, 215, 219, 230, 231
Hansjurgens, Bernd, 257
Haq, Khadija, 230, 231
Hardin, Garrett, 108
Hard law, 61, 70–71
Harf, James, 369

Harmonization, 167
Harremoës, Poul, 282
Harris, Paul G., 24, 106, 108, 257
Harvard University Summer School, 350
Hatch, Jennifer, 131, 256
Hathaway, Oona, 150, 156
Haverland, Markus, 184
Hawken, Paul, 233
Hazardous substances management
  Basel Convention on the Control of
      Transboundary Movements of
      Hazardous Wastes and their
      Disposal (1989), 260, 263 (table),
      264–266
  chemical production growth, 261
  environmental treaties, 17–19
  European Union, 277–278
  future research challenges, 278–279
  governance challenges, 259–260
  historical perspective, 259–260
  international environmental law,
      76 (table)
  international environmental regimes,
      85 (table), 259–279
  management challenges, 261–262
  monitoring and compliance programs,
      274–275
  multilevel governance initiatives and
      challenges, 273–276
  nuclear waste disposal, 317–319
  primary treaties, 260, 262, 263–264
      (table), 264
  Protocol on Persistent Organic
      Pollutants to the Convention on
      Long-Range Transboundary Air
      Pollution (CLRTAP), 260,
      263 (table), 268–270
  public awareness programs, 276
  ratification issues, 273
  regional agreements, 272–273
  Rotterdam Convention on the Prior
      Informed Consent Procedure for
      Certain Hazardous Chemicals and
      Pesticides in International Trade
      (1998), 260, 263 (table), 266–268
  Stockholm Convention on Persistent
      Organic Pollutants (2001), 260,
      264 (table), 270–272
  United States environmental policy,
      143–144
Heavy metals wastes, 275
Hebei Province, China, 193
Hecht, Joy E., 24

Heggelund, Gørild, 230
  see also Kasa, Sjur
Helfgott, Ariella, 303
Helme, Ned, 211
Henderson, H., 233
Herbicides, 358, 359 (table)
Héritier, Adrienne, 182, 183
Herzer, Lauren, 369
Heywood, V. H., 301
Hill, Joshua S., 209
Hills, Carla, 337
Hippel, Frank von, 315–316, 327
Hix, Simon, 181
Hnuti Duha (Rainbow Movement), 312
Hochstetler, Kathryn, 257, 371
Hockings, Marc, 303
Hoffmann, Matthew J., 23, 256, 257, 258
Holland, Alan, 23
Hollis, Duncan B., 50
Holmes, George, 51
Holsti, Ole, 105
Holy See, 289
Holzinger, Katharina, 183
Home Depot, 40
Hongjun, Shan, 129
Hooghe, Liesbet, 182
Hornbeck, J. F., 346
Horticultural products, 360
Houdashelt, Mark, 211
House Committee on Energy and
    Commerce, 311
House of Commons, Science and
    Technology Committee, 82
Housman, Robert, 346
Høyland, Bjørn, 181
HSBC Global Research, 210
Hubei Province, China, 204
Hudec, Robert E., 346
Hufbauer, Gary C., 347, 348
Hughes, Alex, 370
Hui, Wang, 129
Hu Jintao, 206
Hulme, Mike, 50
Human-induced species loss, 285
Human-made chemicals, 84, 88,
    89 (table)
Human rights violations, 360, 362–363,
    364
Humphrey, John, 230, 231, 232
Hunan Province, China, 193
Hungary
  emissions reduction targets and
    progress, 244 (table)

European Union membership, 158
  international environmental
    disputes, 67
  nuclear power plants, 307
Hunter, David, 232
Hunter, Jason, 347
Huq, Saleemul, 233
Hurrell, Andrew, 345
Hutton, Jon, 302
Hyder, Tariq Osman, 231, 255
Hydrobromofluorocarbons (HBFCs),
    89 (table)
Hydrochlorofluorocarbon- 22 (HCFC-22),
    116
Hydrochlorofluorocarbons (HCFCs), 84,
    88, 89 (table), 90–91, 101
Hydrofluorocarbon-23 (HFC-23), 116
Hydrofluorocarbons (HFCs), 102, 254
Hydropower, 194

Iceland
  emissions reduction targets and
    progress, 244 (table)
  European Environment Agency (EEA),
    163
  European Union membership, 158
  state negotiating blocs, 239 (table)
ICLEI–Local Governments for
    Sustainability, 240 (table),
    252, 258
Iles, Alastair, 52
Illegal chemical dumping, 264, 265–266
Illinois, 141, 315
Implementation, definition of, 111
India
  agricultural commodity chains, 359
    (table)
  biodiversity protection, 289
  carbon dioxide (CO_2) emissions, 201
    (figure)
  carbon emissions, 353
  chemical production, 261, 272
  climate change policies, 216, 222
  coal-fired power plants, 190
  Copenhagen Accord, 248 (table)
  global environmental politics, 214,
    217, 368
  greenhouse gas emissions, 68, 95,
    246–247, 251
  international environmental
    agreements, 94, 96, 102
  nuclear energy programs, 305, 318
  pesticide poisonings, 266

Indian Point nuclear power plant, 315
Indigenous peoples' organizations (IPOs),
    38 (table), 240 (table), 269, 270–271
Indonesia, 359 (table)
Industrial chemicals, 259–262, 267,
    269–271, 358, 360
    see also Protocol on Persistent Organic
    Pollutants to the Convention on
    Long-Range Transboundary Air
    Pollution (CLRTAP); Rotterdam
    Convention on the Prior Informed
    Consent Procedure for Certain
    Hazardous Chemicals and Pesticides
    in International Trade (1998)
Industrial development impacts, 285
Industrial Emissions Directive, 169–170
Initiative funding, 34–35
Inside U.S. Trade, 347
Instrument for Structural Policies for Pre-
    Accession (ISPA), 166
Instrument of ratification, 80
Insufficient concern and capacity, 95–96
Integrated Pollution Prevention and
    Control Directive, 169
Intellectual property rights (IPRs),
    291–292, 294
Intergovernmental Forum on Chemical
    Safety (IFCS), 86 (table)
Intergovernmental organizations (IGOs)
    across-regime environmental IGOs,
        34–35
    characteristics and functional role,
        10–11, 26, 27
    chemicals management regimes, 259
    current and future challenges, 46–48
    global summits, 29–32, 31 (table)
    international environmental policy
        process, 55–56
    nonenvironmental IGOs, 35–37
    treaty secretariats, 33–34
    United Nations Environment
        Programme (UNEP), 32–33
    United Nations system, 27–29
Intergovernmental Panel on Biodiversity
    and Ecosystem Services (IPBES),
    294
Intergovernmental Panel on Climate
    Change (IPCC), 210, 254, 256, 257
    climate change policies, 100, 118
    constituent agreements and institutions,
        85 (table)
    establishment, 35, 237–238
    functional role, 10, 11, 238

greenhouse gas emissions assessment
    report, 251
policy impacts, 17
treaty secretariats, 33
International Atomic Energy Agency
    (IAEA), 71, 82, 307, 310, 322–323
International climate change regime
    agenda-setting phase, 235–238, 236
        (table)
    Cancun Agreements, 246–249
    commitment and operationalization,
        236 (table), 249–253
    compliance standards, 250
    future challenges, 253–254
    historical perspective, 235–238,
        236 (table)
    international climate negotiations,
        236 (table), 238–249
    Kyoto Protocol (1997), 243, 244 (table),
        245–246
    multilevel governance initiatives,
        252–253
    NGO observer constituencies,
        240 (table)
    regime effectiveness, 250–253
    state negotiating blocs, 239 (table)
    United Nations Framework
        Convention on Climate Change
        (FCCC), 240–243
International Conference on the Ozone
    Layer (1977), 137
International Convention for the
    Prevention of Pollution from Ships
    (MARPOL), 35, 62 (table), 73
    (table), 86 (table), 134 (table)
International Convention for the
    Regulation of Whaling (1946), 29,
    62 (table), 74 (table), 87 (table), 137
International Council of Local
    Environmental Initiatives (ICLEI),
    38 (table), 51
International Council of Scientific
    Unions, 28, 236, 237
International Court of Justice (ICJ), 11,
    48, 53, 63–64, 124
International Court of Justice Reports, 78, 80
International Criminal Court (ICC), 135
International Energy Agency (IEA), 191
    (table), 196, 210, 244 (table), 254,
    366
International environmental governance
    challenges, 2–3, 20–22, 368
    compliance, 12

consumer awareness campaigns, 368
enforcement, 12–13
national policies, 13–16
research scope, 4–5
sustainable development, 7–10
theoretical perspectives, 5–7
International environmental law
  acts of international organizations, 63
  air pollution prevention, 74–75 (table)
  basic treaty rules, 70–71, 72–76 (table)
  biodiversity protection, 72 (table)
  challenges, 71, 77–78
  climate change, 74–75 (table)
  common but differentiated
    responsibilities principle, 68–69,
    226–227
  customary international law, 63
  formal treaties, 61–63, 62 (table)
  freshwater resources, 74 (table)
  general principles of law, 63–70
  good neighborliness/cooperation
    principle, 66–67
  hard law versus soft law, 61, 70–71
  historical perspective, 54, 57–60
  international case law, 64
  international legal order, 54–57
  legal sources, 60–64
  marine environment, 73–74 (table)
  nongovernmental organizations
    (NGOs), 42–43, 56
  polluter-pays principle, 70, 227–228
  precautionary principle, 69–70, 241–242
  prevention of harm principle, 65–66
  signatures versus ratification, 78–79
  sovereignty and territorial jurisdiction,
    56–57, 65
  state organizations and participants,
    55–56
  sustainable development, 67–68, 225–226
  waste and hazardous substances
    management, 76 (table)
International environmental policies
  challenges and controversies, 16–17
  compliance, 110–128, 178–180
  effective international policy, 93–94
  regimes, 12
  trade-environment relationships,
    330–345
International environmental politics, 92–93
International environmental regimes
  absence of necessary and sufficient
    conditions, 95–96
  basic concepts, 83, 112

hazardous substances, 259–279
issue-related obstacles, 96–100
key participants, 83–84
notable examples, 85–87 (table)
procedural obstacles, 94–95
regime success factors, 100–104
summary discussion, 105
systemic obstacles, 92–94
trade-environment relationships, 342–344
see also Ozone regime
International environmental treaties
  biodiversity protection, 284–286,
    286–288 (table), 288–289
  compliance considerations, 121–123
  hazardous substances, 17–19, 259–260,
    272–273
  historical perspective, 11–12
  least-common denominator problem,
    94, 101–102
  ozone-depleting substances (ODSs),
    137–138
  pollution regulation, 86 (table), 272
  sustainable development, 260
  see also Ozone regime; specific treaty
International Federation of Red Cross
  and Red Crescent Societies, 82
International Geophysical Year (IGY),
  28, 236
International Herald Tribune, 327
International Institute for Sustainable
  Development, 106
International Joint Commission, 10
International Labour Organization (ILO),
  259, 358, 368, 370
International Legal Materials (ILM), 78,
  79, 81, 82
International Maritime Organization
  (IMO), 10, 35, 86 (table)
International Monetary Fund (IMF), 11,
  35, 56
International NGOs, 41–42
International Organization for
  Standardization (ISO), 84, 106
International political systems, 92–93
International POPs Elimination Network,
  45, 270
International relations theory, 5–7
International trade agreements, 19
International Treaty on Plant Genetic
  Resources for Food and Agriculture
  (ITPGRFA), 288 (table)
International Tribunal for the Law of the
  Sea (ITLOS), 64, 66, 67, 81

International Tropical Timber
    Organization (ITTO), 10
International Union for Conservation of
    Nature (IUCN), 8, 9, 42, 43, 292
International Whaling Commission (IWC),
    10, 27, 71, 87 (table), 122, 285
International Whaling Convention, 29,
    62 (table), 74 (table), 87 (table), 137
Intertemporal/intergenerational equity, 8
Invasive species, 285, 297
Iowa, 141
Iran, 318
Ireland
    emissions reduction targets and
        progress, 244 (table)
    European Union membership, 158
    international environmental disputes, 67
Ireland v. United Kingdom (2002), 81
Irish Sea case, 67
Iron, 361
Iron Rhine Railway arbitration case, 64,
    65–66, 67
Irwin, Douglas A., 346
Italy
    commodity chains, 357
    common fisheries policy, 178
    emissions reduction targets and
        progress, 244 (table)
    European Council, 161
    European Union compliance, 179
    European Union membership, 158
    nuclear power plants, 323
Ivanova, Maria, 24, 49, 348
Ivory Coast, 264, 359 (table)

Jackson, Lisa, 141
Jacobson, Harold K., 24, 128, 130, 131,
    146, 151, 153, 155, 156, 256
Jacques, Peter J., 51
Jaeger, Jill, 254
Jäger, Jill, 153
Jamaica, 291 (box)
Jancar-Webster, Barbara, 326
Jänicke, Martin, 304
Janssens-Maenhout, Greet, 257
Japan
    carbon dioxide (CO_2) emissions,
        201 (figure)
    carbon emissions, 353
    commodity chains, 357
    Copenhagen Accord, 248 (table)
    emissions reduction targets and
        progress, 244 (table)

environmental policies, 278
fuel economy standards, 196 (figure)
Fukushima nuclear reactor disaster, 19,
    173, 319–322
greenhouse gas emissions, 206
international environmental
    agreements, 94
Kyoto Protocol (1997), 245, 249
nuclear energy issues, 19, 173, 326
state negotiating blocs, 239 (table)
Japan Times, 328
Jasanoff, Sheila, 147, 155
Jaspers, Nico, 50
Jehlicka, Peter, 307–308, 309, 326, 327
Jenkensville, South Carolina, 319
Jervis, Robert, 107, 108
Jinnah, Sikina, 49, 50
Johannesburg, South Africa, 2, 9, 19, 30,
    31 (table), 60
Johnson, Corey, 23, 369
    see also Andrews-Speed, Philip
Johnson, Huey D., 24
Johnson, Keith, 155
Johnson, Stanley P., 184
Joos, Clemens, 182
Jordan
    free trade agreements, 339 (table)
    nuclear energy programs, 305, 322
    nuclear power plants, 323
Jordan, Andrew, 183
Joshi, Shangrila, 231, 232
Joyner, Christopher C., 52
JS, 324
Judge, David, 182, 184
Judgment of the Court, 182
Ju Hui, 210
Jungcurt, Stefan, 50
Jurgielewicz, Lynne M., 130

Kamieniecki, Sheldon, 51
Kang, Liping, 196 (figure)
Kaniaru, Donald, 126
Kanji, Nazneen, 51
Kanowski, Peter J., 50
Kansas, 141
Kapos, Valerie, 303
Kara, Jan, 307–308, 326, 327
Karl, Terry Lynn, 371
Karns, Margaret P., 48
Kasa, Sjur, 230, 232
Kassim, Hussein, 182
Kazakhstan, 323
Keating, Dave, 183, 185

Keck, Margaret E., 23, 371
Keenan, Rod, 80
Kelly, Claire Roche, 304
Kemp, Geoffrey, 23, 369
    see also Andrews-Speed, Philip
Kemp, Jack, 139, 154
Kent, Jennifer, 304
Kenya, 359 (table)
Keohane, Robert O., 23, 95, 105, 108,
    109, 281, 369
Kern, Kristine, 186
Keßler, Bernd, 182
Keys, Jane, 282
Khagram, Sanjeev, 51, 371
Khan, Saiful M., 303
Khosla, Ashok, 233
Kimberley Process, 367, 371
Kim, Eonjeong M., 24, 232
Kingsbury, Benedict, 345
Kirshbaum, Lynn, 210
Klare, Michael T., 369
Klarer, Jurg, 326
Klaus, Vaclav, 306, 308–309, 310
Kleinman, Daniel Lee, 302
Kloppenburg, Jack Ralph, Jr., 302
Knill, Christoph, 183
Knollenberg, Joseph, 140
Koch, Wendy, 328
Koester, Veit, 126
Kohler, Pia M., 50, 281
Kolk, Ans, 257, 258
Konstadakopulos, Dimitrios, 183
Kontoleon, Andreas, 184
Korea
    see South Korea
Kosovo, 158
Kousis, Maria, 24
Kovacevic, Michelle, 303
Kraft, Michael E., 24, 51
Krasner, Stephen D., 49, 105, 230
Kratochwil, Friedrich, 105
Kraus, Don, 155
Kreiser, Larry, 129
Krueger, Alan B., 336, 347
Krueger, Jonathan, 280
Kruzikova, Eva, 327
Kubota, Yoko, 328
Kufour, Edward, 232
Kummer, Katharina, 280, 281
Kuntz-Duriseti, Kristin, 210
Kurian, Priva A., 106
Kütting, Gabriela, 257
Kuznets curve, 336

Kyoto Protocol (1997), 154, 210
    background information, 54
    basic treaty rules, 75 (table)
    burden-sharing agreements, 166
    China, 200
    Clean Development Mechanism
        (CDM), 34, 41, 115–116, 200,
        227–228, 245–246
    commitment and operationalization,
        243, 245, 249
    compliance standards, 115–116,
        245–246
    constituent agreements and institutions,
        85 (table)
    dispute resolution, 124
    emissions reduction targets and
        progress, 244 (table), 250
    European Union compliance, 178
    expiration, 10
    flexible mechanisms, 245, 246
    framework convention–protocol model,
        62 (table), 62–63
    goals, 85 (table)
    international climate negotiations, 243
    International Emissions Trading (IET),
        115
    Joint Implementation (JI), 115
    multilateral international agreements
        (MEAs), 29
    noncompliance procedures, 125–126
    organizational structure, 246
    policy impacts, 17
    regime effectiveness, 250–253
    regime organizations, 112
    reporting requirements, 119–120
    treaty compliance, 111
    treaty secretariats, 33
    United States environmental policy,
        176
    United States signature and ratification,
        3, 13, 133, 134 (table), 138–140,
        146
    see also Cancun Agreements

Labor rights, 358, 359 (table), 360,
    362, 364
Lacey Act (1900), 136
Lac Lanoux arbitration case, 64
Lafferty, William M., 24
Laird, Sarah A., 302
Lamsal, Lok N., 209
Lamy, Pascal, 340, 348
Lanchbery, John, 302

Land-use changes, 358, 359 (table), 360, 361
Large-scale mining operations, 361
Larrain, S., 233
Latin America, 359 (table), 360
Lattanzio, Richard K., 52
Latvia
    emissions reduction targets and progress, 244 (table)
    European Council, 161
    European Union membership, 158
Laurance, William F., 304
Law of the Sea, 13
Lawrence Berkeley National Laboratory, 189 (figure), 209
Layzer, Judith A., 280
Lead, 361
Leaded gasoline, 364–365
Lead phosphorus compounds, 259
Leary, David, 82
Least developed countries, 239 (table)
Least-Developed-Country Fund, 246
Leatherman, Janie, 369
Lee, Jin, 211
Lee, Keekok, 23
Lee, Maria, 184
Leesm, Alexander C., 303
Lefeber, René, 126
Lefevere, Jürgen, 12, 129
Legal systems, 93–94
Lehren, Andrew, 107
Lélé, Sharachchandra M., 232
Lemons, John, 23
Lemos Costa, Katia, 303
Lenschow, Andrea, 183, 186
Leonard, Dick, 181
Leonard, J. A., 153, 231
Leonard, J. Amber, 255
Leroy, Pieter, 45, 52
Lesage, Dries, 255
Leverington, Fiona, 303
Levine, Mark, 211
Levin, Kelly, 130, 256
Levy, David, 109, 257, 258
Levy, Marc A., 95, 108, 128, 281
Lewis, David, 51
Lewis, Joanna I., 15, 210, 211, 212
Liability Protocol (1999), 62 (table)
Liberalism, 5
Liberia, 358
Libya, 322
Lieberman, Joseph, 140, 154
Lieberman, Sarah, 304

Lieberman-Warner Climate Security Act (2008), 140
Lieber, Robert J., 154
Liechtenstein, 122, 163
Liefferink, Duncan, 182
Lime, 361
"Limits to growth" perspective, 333
Lim, Louisa, 193 (box)
Lindemann, Stefan, 304
Lin, Jiang, 211
Lipschutz, Ronnie D., 22, 23, 365, 371
Lister, Jane, 24, 370
Litfin, Karen, 106, 108, 109
Lithium, 361, 364
Lithuania
    emissions reduction targets and progress, 244 (table)
    European Union membership, 158
    nuclear power plants, 173, 307, 323
Liu, Xielin, 210
Living modified organisms (LMOs), 297–298
Lixin, Han, 129
Lobbying, 166
Local governments and municipal authorities (LGMAs), 38 (table), 240 (table)
Logan, Jeffrey, 210
Lomé IV Convention (1991), 273
London Amendment and Adjustment (1990), 88, 89, 100
London Dumping Convention, 62 (table), 71, 73 (table), 86 (table), 134 (table)
London Guidelines for the Exchange of Information on Chemicals in International Trade, 267
Long-range transboundary air pollution, 86 (table)
Loske, R., 233
Louwaars, Niels, 303
Love Canal, New York, 262, 279
Lowest-common-denominator problem, 94–95
Lu, Hui, 209
Luong, Pauline Jones, 371
Luterbacher, Urs, 155, 255
Luxembourg
    emissions reduction targets and progress, 244 (table)
    environmental taxes, 175
    European Commission (EC), 162
    European Council, 161

European Court of Justice (ECJ), 163
European Union membership, 158
Lu, Z., 209

Maastricht Treaty (1992), 14, 160, 162, 179
MacDonald, Gordon J., 231
Macedonia, 158
Macfarlane, Allison, 322
MacGarvin, Malcolm, 282
Madagascar, 291 (box)
Ma, Dong, 196 (figure)
Mahbub-ul-Haq, 220, 231
Mahony, Martin, 50
Maine, 141
Malaria control, 271–272
Malaysia, 217
Malik, Madhu, 106
Malta, 158, 161, 175
Man and the Biosphere program, 28
Mander, Jerry, 25
Manganese, 361
Mangroves, 285
Maniates, Michael, 355, 369, 370
    see also Princen, Thomas
Manitoba, Canada, 141
Manney, Gloria L., 107
Mann, Howard, 347
Manno, Jack, 369
Maquiladora zones, 332, 338
Marine environment protection,
    73–74 (table), 177–178
Marine Stewardship Council, 46
Market advocacy NGOs (MANGOs), 38
MARPOL (marine pollution) convention
    see International Convention for the
    Prevention of Pollution from
    Ships (MARPOL)
Marrakesh Accords, 82, 243, 245, 246
Marrakesh Decisions Concurrent to
    Establishing the WTO, 347
Marr, Melitta, 303
Marshall Plan, 158
Martens, Pim, 301
Martinot, Eric, 209
Maryland, 141
Ma Shiming, 210
Massachusetts, 141
Mass extinctions, 1
Mastrandrea, Michael D., 210
Material consumption
    background information, 20
    capacity building and improved
        governance, 368

certification and labeling schemes, 367
command-and-control regulations, 366
commoditization processes, 352–355
commodity chains, 355–357, 364–366
global ramifications, 350–352
mining impacts, 361–364
per capita use, 352
social embeddedness, 354–355, 360
subsidy adjustments, 366–367
sustainable development policies, 20,
    351–352, 358, 360, 366–368
taxation programs, 367
Mathews, Jessica Tuchman, 230
Matthews, Duncan, 186
Matus, Kira, 209
Mauna Loa, Hawaii, 236–237
Maxwell, James, 109
Mayer, Judith, 23
Mazey, Sonia, 183
Mazmanian, Daniel A., 24
McCain, John, 140, 154
McCarthy, Donal P., 304
McCormick, John, 25, 50, 131, 181,
    183, 184
McDermott, Constance L., 50, 303
McDorman, Ted L., 281
McGray, Heather, 256
McIntosh, David, 139–140
McMahon, Hilary, 256
McNeill, Desmond, 23
Meadowcroft, James, 24
Meadows, Dennis, 368
Meadows, Donella H., 368
Mearsheimer, John J., 23
Medical research and product
    development, 354
Mediterranean Sea, 86 (table)
Meeting of the Parties (MOP), 88–90, 104
Melk Protocol, 313–314
Mello, Valérie de Campos, 232
Membership sanctions, 124
Memorandum of Understanding on the
    Conservation and Management of
    Marine Turtles and Their Habitats
    in the Indian Ocean, 340
Menon, B. P., 230
Mensah, Chris, 220, 231
"MEPs Push for Strong EU Role in
    Climate Talks," 182
"MEPs Reject Proposed Reform of
    Emissions Trading Scheme," 182
Merck, 142
Mercury, 361

Mercury wastes, 2, 29, 275
Merkel, Angela, 165
Messner, Dirk, 230, 231, 232
Metal commodities, 361
Methane (CH₄), 254
Methyl bromide, 84, 88, 89 (table), 90–91, 101, 133
Methyl chloroform, 84, 89 (table), 90–91
methyl isocyanate gas, 262
Meuse River, 127
Mexico
    carbon dioxide (CO_2) emissions, 201 (figure)
    climate change policies, 207
    free trade agreements, 337–340
    state negotiating blocs, 239 (table)
Mez, Lutz, 329
Michigan, 141
Microbial diversity, 290
Middle East, 196, 305, 322
Migratory species protection, 87 (table)
Miles, Edward L., 256
Military action, 113
Milledge, Tori, 258
Millennium Development Goals, 26, 32, 368
Millennium Ecosystem Assessment, 283, 295, 301, 302, 303
Miller, Marian A. L., 155, 222, 232
Mills, Anne, 281
Milne, Janet E., 129
Milton, Kay, 326
Minamata Convention on Mercury (2013), 2, 29, 275
Mineral commodities, 361
Mingers, Susanne, 183
Mingst, Karen A., 48
Mining industry, 361–364
Ministry of Environmental Protection (MEP), 195, 199
Ministry of Environment (Czech Republic), 308–309, 326
Ministry of Industry and Trade (Czech Republic), 309, 310
Minnesota, 141
Mintzer, Irving M., 153, 231, 255
Mintz, Sidney, 370
Mitchell, George, 143
Mitchell, Ronald B., 22, 49, 109, 128, 130, 131, 132
Mittermeier, Cristina G., 304
Mittermeier, Russell A., 304
Mobile Phone Partnership Initiative, 276

Modular nuclear reactors, 319
Mohapatra, Asish, 106
Moldan, Bedrich, 308, 326
Moldova, 239 (table)
Molina, Mario, 106, 108
Monaco, 122
Moncel, Remi, 130
Monnet, Jean, 158
Monsanto, 297
Montenegro, 158
Montgomery, David, 255
Montreal Adjustment (2007), 88
Montreal Protocol on Substances that Deplete the Ozone Layer (1987)
    background information, 1
    compliance standards, 115–116
    framework convention–protocol model, 62 (table)
    functional role, 88
    global environmental responsibility, 342
    as a managerial primary rule system, 116–117
    multilateral international agreements (MEAs), 29
    noncompliance procedures, 125–126
    ozone regime principles, 90, 101–104
    trade-environment conflicts, 344
    United States signature and ratification, 134 (table), 137–138
Montreal Protocol to the Vienna Ozone Convention, 75 (table)
Moomaw, William R., 230
Moore's Report of International Arbitration Awards, 78
Moral hazards, 115–116
Moravcsik, Andrew, 147, 155
Morgan, Jennifer, 256
Morgenthau, Hans J., 23, 107
Morgera, Elisa, 79, 184
Morocco
    free trade agreements, 339 (table)
    nuclear energy programs, 305, 322
Morse, Stephen, 24
Moser, Michael, 301
Mosquito control, 271–272
Motor vehicles, 195–197, 196 (figure)
Moxham, Roy, 370
Multilateral environmental agreements (MEAs)
    characteristics and functional role, 29–30
    global environmental governance, 2, 10, 26, 368
    international legal sources, 61–63

Multilateral Fund, 89–91, 102, 104, 107, 117, 125
Multinational mining conglomerates, 363
Multinational seed companies, 297–298
Muñoz, Miquel, 49, 233
Murphy, Craig, 230
Myanmar, 217
Myers, Heather, 281
Myers, Norman, 304
Myhr, Anne Ingeborg, 304

Nagel, Stuart, 229
Nagoya Protocol on Access to Genetic Resources and the Fair and Equitable Sharing of Benefits Arising from their Utilization, 18, 29, 62 (table), 284, 288 (table), 294–295, 300–301
Naím, Moisés, 258
Nairobi, Kenya, 32
Najam, Adil, 15–16, 24, 49, 229, 230, 231, 232, 233
  see also Halle, Mark
Namibia, 357
Nam, Kyung-Min, 209
Narain, Sunita, 230, 233
  see also Agarwal, Anil
Narmada Bachao Andalan, 40
Narmada dam project, 36, 40
National Academy of Sciences, 9
National Audubon Society, 346
National Center for Climate Strategy and International Cooperation of China (NCSC), 199
National Development and Reform Commission (NDRC), 194 (table), 195, 199, 200, 202, 211
National Energy Administration (China), 207
National Energy Institute, 328
National environmental policies, 13–16
Nationally appropriate mitigation actions (NAMAs), 206
National Renewable Energy Law (China), 202
National Security Council (NSC), 310
National Wildlife Federation, 346
Natura 2000 network, 172, 177, 179
Natural gas, 195, 307, 353
Nature conservation, 177–178
Naughton, Barry, 208
Naurin, Daniel, 182
Naylor, Thomas H., 369
Nelis, Annemiek, 303

Netherlands
  beverage container packaging and recycling, 171–172
  carbon dioxide (CO_2) emissions, 165
  common fisheries policy, 178
  emissions reduction targets and progress, 244 (table)
  environmental policies, 13
  environmental taxes, 175
  European Council, 161
  European Union membership, 158
  nuclear power plants, 323
Netherlands Environmental Assessment Agency, 208, 369
Neumayer, Eric, 131
Nevada, 318
Newell, Peter, 23, 109, 186, 255, 257, 258
New England Governors Climate Change Action Plan, 140–141
New Hampshire, 141
New international economic order (NIEO), 214, 217, 219–221
New international environmental order (NIEnvO), 219
New Jersey, 141, 315
Newsom, Deanna, 51, 371
  see also Cashore, Benjamin W.
New York, 141, 315
New York Times, 215, 327, 328
New Zealand
  carbon dioxide (CO_2) emissions, 201 (figure)
  emissions reduction targets and progress, 244 (table)
  environmental policies, 13
  greenhouse gas emissions, 206
  Kyoto Protocol (1997), 245
  state negotiating blocs, 239 (table)
New Zealand v. France (1974), 79
New Zealand v. France (1995), 78
New Zealand v. Japan (1999), 81
Nicaragua, 217
Nickel, 361
Nierenburg, Danielle, 370
Nigeria, 359 (table), 363
Niles, John O., 154
9/11 terrorist attacks, 317, 352
Nitrogen oxide (NO_x) emissions, 194 (table), 195, 254
Nitschke, Eric, 350
Nitze, William A., 153
Nollkaemper, André, 80, 132
Nolte, Christoph, 303

Non- Aligned Movement (NAM), 217
Nonenvironmental IGOs, 35–37
Nongovernmental organizations (NGOs)
  agreement implementation, 45–46
  categories, 38 (table), 38–39
  characteristics and functional role, 11,
    26, 37–41
  chemicals management regimes, 259
  China, 198
  cross-border NGOs, 41–42
  current and future challenges, 46–48
  Czech Republic, 309
  environmental policies, 21, 337
  environmental policy compliance, 123
  functional role, 123
  global environmental governance, 2, 368
  information dissemination, 41, 43
  international climate negotiations,
    238–239, 240 (table)
  international environmental policy
    process, 42–46, 56
  international negotiations, 43–45
  lobbying, 40, 41, 43–44
  nonstate market-driven governance, 46
  nuclear power plants, 311
  number of organizations, 39
  organizational structures, 40
  partnerships, 45–46
  resource consumption, 351, 358
  strategies and actions, 40–41, 43
  transnational networks, 46
Non-legally Binding Authoritative Statement
  of Principles for a Global Consensus on
  the Management, Conservation, and
  Sustainable Development of All Types
  of Forests, 59
Nonnative species, 285, 297
Nordic countries, 94, 137
North America 2050, 141, 154
North American Free Trade Agreement
  (NAFTA), 19, 330, 332, 337–340,
  339 (table), 347
North American lifestyle, 353–354
Northern Ireland, 357
North-South politics
  Basel Convention on the Control of
    Transboundary Movements of
    Hazardous Wastes and their
    Disposal (1989), 264–266
  basic concepts, 214–217, 219
  biodiversity protection, 284, 289–292,
    300
  biosafety debate, 297–299

  common but differentiated
    responsibilities principle, 226–227
  Convention on Biological Diversity
    (1992), 289–292
  funding disagreements, 275
  global biodiversity, 18
  global environmental negotiations,
    219–225
  hazardous substances trade, 266
  international environmental
    agreements, 99
  international equity, 8
  North-South dialogue, 219–225
  ozone-depleting substances (ODSs), 96
  political frustrations and challenges,
    228–229
  polluter-pays principle, 227–228
  principle of additionality, 226
  Rotterdam Convention on the Prior
    Informed Consent Procedure for
    Certain Hazardous Chemicals and
    Pesticides in International Trade
    (1998), 266
  sustainable development policies, 16,
    225–226
  waste trade treaties, 264–266, 272–273
  see also Global South
Norway
  emissions reduction targets and
    progress, 244 (table)
  environmental taxes, 175
  European Environment Agency
    (EEA), 163
  genetically modified organisms
    (GMOs), 298, 299
  international environmental
    agreements, 122
  state negotiating blocs, 239 (table)
Norwegian Federation of Trade Unions,
  38 (table)
Norwegian Gene Technology Act, 298
Nuclear and Industrial Safety Agency
  (Japan), 321
Nuclear power
  challenges, 325–326
  China, 194–195, 323
  Czech Republic, 305–306, 307, 315,
    317, 322, 324, 326
  economic factors, 317
  environmental politics, 18–19
  former Soviet Union, 306–307
  Fukushima nuclear reactor disaster, 19,
    173, 319–322

global implications, 322–324
long-term waste storage programs,
      317–319
modular reactors, 319
monitoring and regulatory programs,
      322–324
nuclear waste disposal, 317–319
safety issues, 316 (box), 316–318
sustainable development, 325–326
Temelin nuclear power plant, 18, 66,
      305, 307, 309–314, 312 (box), 322,
      324–325
United States, 315–319, 316 (box),
      324, 326
Nuclear Regulation Authority (Japan),
      320, 321
Nuclear Regulatory Commission (NRC),
      311, 315–318, 319, 322
Nuclear Safety Directive, 173
Nuclear Tests II, 64, 80, 81
Nucleonics Week, 327
Null, Schuyler, 369
Nye, Joseph S., Jr., 23, 105, 369
Nyerere, Julius K., 217, 231

Oates, Wallace E., 347
Obama administration
   climate change policies, 206, 247
   environmental policies, 133, 136, 141,
      143, 145
   global environmental governance
      policies, 3
   nuclear waste disposal funding, 318
   trade agreements, 339
"Obama vs. Romney: China, Other Trade
      Issues," 348
Oberthür, Sebastian, 50, 126, 130, 148,
      155, 254, 255, 257, 302, 303, 304
Oceana, 41
Ocean pollution, 86 (table), 272, 285, 320
   see also International Convention for
      the Prevention of Pollution from
      Ships (MARPOL)
O'Connor, David, 303
OECD Guidelines for Multinational
      Enterprises, 79
Office of the President-Elect, 153
Oil and gas industry, 353, 362–363
Oil pipelines, 307
Oil reserves, 353
Olivier, Jos G. J., 257
Olkiluoto nuclear power plant, 323
Olson, Mancur, 107

Oman, 339 (table)
O'Neill, Kate, 11, 23, 48, 50, 51, 52, 155,
      280, 369
Open-Ended Technical Working Group, 45
Open-Ended Working Group
      (OEWG), 88
Ophuls, William, 368
Oppenheimer, Michael, 254
Opschoor, J. B., 347
Oranges, 358
Orejas, Diana, 347
   see also Hufbauer, Gary C.
Organisation for Economic Cooperation
      and Development (OECD), 9, 70,
      215, 265, 267, 298, 332
Organization of Petroleum Exporting
      Countries (OPEC), 239 (table)
O'Riordan, Timothy, 24, 185
O'Rourke, Dara, 370
Orsini, Amandine, 52
Ostrom, Elinor, 258
Ott, Hermann E., 130, 148, 155, 254,
      255, 257
Otto-Zimmermann, Konrad, 51
Overfishing, 178, 285, 360
Oxfam, 351, 358
Oxley, Alan, 230
Oye, Kenneth A., 107, 108, 109
Oyster Creek nuclear power plant, 315
Ozone-depleting substances (ODSs),
      84, 88, 89 (table), 90–91, 94, 96,
      100–104, 116, 137–138
Ozone depletion, 74–75 (table), 84,
      100–101, 137–138, 331
Ozone hole discovery, 100
Ozone regime
   absence of necessary and sufficient
      conditions, 95–96
   background information, 84, 88
   chemical phase-out schedule, 89 (table),
      90–91
   control mechanisms and policies,
      88–89, 89 (table), 101
   economic factors, 101–102
   issue-related obstacles, 96–100
   key principles and rules, 89 (table), 90
   Multilateral Fund, 89–91, 102, 104
   procedural obstacles, 94–95
   regime success factors, 100–104
   scientific complexity and uncertainty,
      97, 100–101
   systemic obstacles, 92–94
Ozone Secretariat, 106, 107

Paarlberg, Robert L., 154, 281
Pacific Fur Seal Arbitral Tribunal, 54, 58, 64, 67, 78
Pacific Ocean contamination, 320
Packaging and Recycling Directive, 171–172
Page, Thomas, 233
Pakistan, 318, 357
Pallemaerts, Marc, 281
Palmas Case (1928), 80
Palm oil plantations, 40, 357, 358
Paltsev, Sergey, 209
Panama, 339 (table)
Panayotou, Theodore, 347
Pan, Jie, 52
Papademetriou, Demetrios G., 25
Papa, Mihaela, 233
Parker, Meaghan, 369
Park, Susan, 48, 50, 52
Parris, Thomas M., 24
Parry, Luke, 303
Parson, Edward A., 22, 106, 108
Particulate matter (PM), 192, 192–193 (box)
Party of European Socialists and Democrats, 162
Patent system, 290–292, 294
Paterson, Matthew, 23, 256, 258
Patrick, Stewart, 155, 156
Pattberg, Philipp, 258
Pavese, Helena, 303
PBT (persistent, bioaccumulative, and toxic) chemicals, 277
Peak associations, 41–42
Pearls, cultured, 360
Peel, Jacqueline, 11, 79, 80, 81, 130
Pellow, David Naguib, 282
Pendergrast, Mark, 370
Peng, Martin Khor K., 232
People's Daily Online, 208
People's Republic of China, Ministry of Environmental Protection, 209
People's Republic of China, National Development and Reform Commission, 210
Pérez-Solórzano Borragan, Nieves, 181
Perfluorocarbons (PFCs), 254
Permanent Court of Arbitration, 67
Permanent Court of Arbitration Award Series, 80, 81
Perot, Ross, 346
Persian Gulf states, 363
Persistence of chemicals, 261, 277

Persistent organic pollutants (POPs)
    see Protocol on Persistent Organic Pollutants to the Convention on Long-Range Transboundary Air Pollution (CLRTAP); Stockholm Convention on Persistent Organic Pollutants (2001)
Peru, 339 (table)
Pesticide Action Network Asia (Malaysia), 38 (table), 42
Pesticides, 259–262, 266, 269–271, 274, 297, 358, 359 (table), 360
    see also Protocol on Persistent Organic Pollutants to the Convention on Long-Range Transboundary Air Pollution (CLRTAP); Rotterdam Convention on the Prior Informed Consent Procedure for Certain Hazardous Chemicals and Pesticides in International Trade (1998)
Peters, Jeroen A. H. W., 257
Peterson, John, 181, 182
Petro-states, 363
Pew Center on Global Climate Change, 154
Pharmaceutical industry, 291 (box)
Philippines, 323
Phosphates, 361
Photovoltaic (PV) equipment, 204
Pineschi, Laura, 231
Pirages, Dennis, 8, 230, 369
Pistorius, Robin, 303
Pisupati, Balakrishna, 82
Pithart, Petr, 310, 313
Plantation forestry, 285
Plumer, Brad, 107
Plutonium, 318, 321
Poarowska, Justyna, 304
Poland
    emissions reduction targets and progress, 244 (table)
    emissions trading, 177
    European Council, 161
    European Union compliance, 179
    European Union membership, 158
Poland-Hungary: Assistance for Restructuring Their Economies (PHARE), 165–166, 306
Polaski, Sandra, 25
Polgeen, Lydia, 371
Poling, Janice M., 24, 232
Political systems, 93

Pollack, Mark A., 181
Polluter-pays principle, 70, 227–228
Pollution Probe–Canada, 346
Pollution regulation
    air pollution protections, 74–75 (table)
    international environmental
        agreements, 86 (table), 272
    mining industry, 361–362
    North American Free Trade Agreement
        (NAFTA) negotiations, 338
    trade-environment relationships,
        330–331
    see also Convention on Long-Range
        Transboundary Air Pollution
        (CLRTAP); International
        Convention for the Prevention of
        Pollution from Ships (MARPOL)
Polycarp, Clifford, 131, 256
Polychlorinated biphenyls (PCBs),
    262, 270
Porter, Gareth, 216–217, 221, 231
Porter, Martin, 183
Portney, Kent E., 24
Portugal
    carbon dioxide (CO_2) emissions, 165
    common fisheries policy, 178
    emissions reduction targets and
        progress, 244 (table)
    European Union membership, 158
Posner, Eric A., 128, 129
Potash, 361
Poverty rates, 351–352, 358, 359 (table)
Prague Post, 327, 329
Precautionary principle, 69–70, 241–242
Prentice, Crawford, 301
President's Blue Ribbon Commission on
    the Future of Nuclear Waste, 318
Prevention of harm principle, 65–66
Pridham, Geoffrey, 183
Princen, Sebastiaan, 182
Princen, Thomas, 356, 369, 370
Principle of additionality, 226
Prior informed consent (PIC), 265,
    267–268
Prisoner's dilemma problem, 122
PR Newswire, 329
Probo Koala, 264
Procymidone, 340
Prodi, Romano, 162
Production process or method
    (PPM)-based regulations, 344
Project funding, 34–35
Property rights, 291–292, 294

Proposed Decision 2012/328, 348
Protocol Concerning Cooperation
    in Combating Pollution of the
    Mediterranean Sea by Oil and Other
    Harmful Substances in Cases of
    Emergency (1976), 86 (table)
Protocol for Long-Term Financing of
    Monitoring (1984), 86 (table)
Protocol for the Prevention of Pollution of
    the Mediterranean Sea by Dumping
    from Ships and Aircraft (1976),
    86 (table)
Protocol for the Protection of the
    Mediterranean Sea from Land-Based
    Sources (1980), 86 (table)
Protocol on Environmental Protection
    (1991), 87 (table)
Protocol on Heavy Metals (1998),
    86 (table)
Protocol on Liability and Compensation
    (1999), 85 (table)
Protocol on Persistent Organic Pollutants
    to the Convention on Long-Range
    Transboundary Air Pollution
    (CLRTAP)
    background information, 61, 260
    basic principles, 263 (table), 268–270
    basic treaty rules, 74 (table)
    constituent agreements and institutions,
        86 (table)
    European Union directives, 170
    framework convention–protocol model,
        62 (table)
    functional role, 17–18
    multilateral international agreements
        (MEAs), 29
    United States signature and ratification,
        134 (table), 144
Protocol to Abate Acidification,
    Eutrophication, and Ground-Level
    Ozone (1999), 86 (table)
Protocol to Control Nitrogen Oxides
    (1988), 86 (table)
Protocol to Control Volatile Organic
    Compounds (1991), 86 (table)
Protocol to Further Reduce Sulfur
    Emissions (1994), 86 (table)
Protocol to Reduce Sulfur Emissions
    (1985), 86 (table)
Public interest groups, 166
Public Participation Directive, 169
Public protests, 40–41, 44
Puckett, Jim, 155

Pulp Mills case, 64, 66, 69–70, 81
Pulver, Simone, 51

Qatar, 305
Quammen, David, 302

Rabe, Barry G., 25, 258
Radioactive gas, 320–321
Raina, Renata, 281
Rainbow Movement, 312
Rainbow Program, 308
Rainforest Action Network, 40
Rajamani, Lavanya, 126, 130
Rajan, Makhund G., 231, 232
Ramsar Wetlands Convention, 33,
    62 (table), 72 (table), 87 (table),
    134 (table), 137, 286, 286 (table)
Ramsey, Ross, 348
Rao, C. H. Srinivas, 280, 281
Raphus cucullatus, 285
Rapoza, Kenneth, 209
Raustiala, Kal, 24, 38, 50, 51, 52, 128,
    149, 154, 155, 255, 256, 257,
    281, 303
Raven, Hans, 303
Rawson Survival–Canada, 346
Rayner, A. J., 347
Rayner, Steve, 258
Reagan, Ronald, 145
Realism, 5
Recycling, nuclear waste, 318
Redgwell, Catherine, 49
Reducing Emissions from Deforestation
    and forest Degradation (REDD),
    34–35, 41, 45, 295–296
Reformulated gasoline regulations, 340
Regime secretariats, 33–34
Regional Greenhouse Gas Initiative
    (RGGI), 141, 211
Regional Seas Programme, 272
Registration, Evaluation, Authorisation
    and Restriction of Chemicals
    (REACH), 277, 278
Regulatory services, 285
Reichman, Nancy, 108, 109
Reid, John W., 302
Reilly, John M., 209
Reimer, Suzanne, 370
Reitan, Ruth, 51
Renders, Jorgen, 368
Renewable energy, 175–176, 187–188,
    322, 324–325
Repeat-player games, 122

Report of the Appellate Body, 81, 82
*Report of the UN Conference on
    Environment and Development*, 78
*Report of the UN Conference on the Human
    Environment*, 79
*Report of the United Nations Conference on
    the Human Environment*, 108
*Report on the Environment in the Czech
    Republic (2005)*, 309
Reports of International Arbitral Awards, 80
Reports of the Panel, 81
Republic of Korea (ROK)
    see South Korea
Research and independent NGOs
    (RINGOs), 38 (table)
Resource consumption
    background information, 20
    capacity building and improved
        governance, 368
    certification and labeling schemes, 367
    command-and-control regulations, 366
    commoditization processes, 352–355
    commodity chains, 355–357, 364–366
    global ramifications, 350–352
    mining impacts, 361–364
    per capita use, 352
    social embeddedness, 354–355, 360
    subsidy adjustments, 366–367
    sustainable development policies, 20,
        351–352, 358, 360, 366–368
    taxation programs, 367
Resource curse, 363, 364
Revelle, Roger, 235
Revesz, Richard L., 347
Reynolds, Paul, 155
Rhine Chlorides arbitration, 81
Rhine River, 127
Rhode Island, 141
Rice, 358
Richardson, Dick, 24
Richardson, Jeremy, 183, 186
Riddell, George, 80
Rio+20 Conference, 280, 346
    environmental policy negotiations,
        21, 214
    global environmental governance, 2
    global summits, 30
    international environmental soft law, 61
    legacy, 224–228
    policy goals, 260
    sustainable development policies, 9–10,
        16, 58, 60, 225–226
    trade-environment relationship, 331

Rio bargain, 224, 227–229
Rio Declaration on Environment and
    Development, 2, 9, 31 (table), 59, 65,
    69, 82, 133, 142
Rio de Janeiro, Brazil, 2, 9, 30, 31 (table)
Rio Summit (1992)
    see Earth Summit (1992)
Risk & Policy Analysts Limited, 282
Road building impacts, 285
Roan, Sharon, 108, 109
Roddick, Anita, 233
Roderick, Peter, 128
Roger, Charles, 23
Roll Back Malaria Partnership, 271
Roman-Cuesta, Rosa Maria, 303
Romania
    common fisheries policy, 178
    emissions reduction targets and
        progress, 244 (table)
    European Council, 161
    European Union membership, 158
Romano, Cesare P. R., 131
Rompuy, Herman van, 161
Rootes, Christopher, 51
Rosencranz, Armin, 154, 210
Rosendal, G. Kristin, 18, 302,
    303, 304
Rosenthal, Elisabeth, 107, 371
Ross, Michael L., 371
Rosy periwinkle, 291 (box)
Rothwell, Donald R., 81
Rotmans, Jan, 301
Rotterdam Convention on the Prior
    Informed Consent Procedure for
    Certain Hazardous Chemicals and
    Pesticides in International Trade
    (1998), 281
    background information, 260
    basic principles, 263 (table), 266–268
    basic treaty rules, 76 (table)
    constituent agreements and institutions,
        85 (table)
    functional role, 17, 18
    United States signature and ratification,
        134 (table), 144
Rowland, F. Sherwood, 106, 108
Rowlands, Ian H., 23
Rowland, Wade, 231
Rubber, 358
Rubio, Luis, 347
    see also Hufbauer, Gary C.
Ruggie, John, 105
Runnalls, David, 233

Russia
    carbon dioxide (CO_2) emissions, 201 (figure)
    Copenhagen Accord, 248 (table)
    emissions reduction targets and
        progress, 244 (table)
    energy production, 306–307
    global environmental politics, 214
    Kyoto Protocol (1997), 245, 249
    state negotiating blocs, 239 (table)

Sabathil, Gerhard, 182
Sachs, Wolfgang, 233
Sagar, Ambuj, 233, 255, 371
Salazar, Hilda, 348
Salem nuclear power plant, 315
Salmon, 358
Salt, 361
Salzman, James, 232
Sampson, Gary P., 347
Sand, 361
Sandbrook, Richard, 231
Sands, Philippe, 53, 79, 81, 130
Sarkozy, Nicolas, 165
Sarma, K. Madhavea, 106, 108
Sarno, Jillian, 24, 232
Saudi Arabia, 305, 322
Sauvant, Karl P., 217, 231
Sbragia, Alberta, 186
Schachte, William L., Jr., 155
Schaeffer, Roberto, 257
Schafer, Kristin S., 155, 156
Scharlemann, Jörn P. W., 304
Scherr, S. Jacob, 327
Schiff, Harold, 106, 108, 109
Schmidt, Jake, 211
Schmitt, Christine B., 303
Schneider, Lambert, 130
Schneider, Mycle, 327, 328, 329
Schneider, Stephen H., 154, 210
Schorlemer, Sabine von, 52
Schott, Jeffrey J., 347
    see also Hufbauer, Gary C.
Schreurs, Miranda A., 14, 15, 23, 24, 52,
    154, 181, 182, 184, 186, 256, 372
Schreyögg, Anna, 302
Schroeder, Heike, 303
Schumann, Robert, 158
Schwab, Robert M., 347
Schwarzbach, David, 327
Schwarzenberg, Karel, 322
Scientific, Environmental Effects,
    and Technology and Economic
    Assessment Panels, 88

Seafood consumption, 360
Sea Shepherd Conservation
    Society, 43
Sea turtle protection, 340, 342
Sebenius, James K., 230
Secretariats, 33–34
Sedjo, Roger A., 302
Self-reports, 118–119
Seligsohn, Deborah, 193 (box)
Selin, Henrik, 17–18, 23, 154, 181, 186,
    256, 258, 280, 281, 282, 371, 372
Selin, Noelle E., 209, 281
Sell, Malena, 80
Sell, Susan K., 23, 232
Sema, Alpan-Atamer, 257
Senate Foreign Relations Committee, 79,
    142, 145
September 11, 2001 terrorist attacks,
    317, 352
Serbia, 158
Settembri, Pierpaolo, 181
Seuss, H. E., 235
Seveso, Italy, 262
Shabecoff, Philip, 22
Shah, Anup, 153
Shahan, Zachary, 211
Shaman Pharmaceuticals, 291 (box)
Shambaugh, George, 106, 108
Shandong Province, China, 193
Shanghai, China, 204
Sharma, Anju, 230
    see also Agarwal, Anil
Shaw, Malcolm, 280
Shenzhen, China, 204
Shirk, Susan L., 208
Shiva, Vandana, 291 (box), 370
Shrimp, 358
Shrimp-Turtle dispute, 340, 342
Shukla, P. R., 255, 257
Siebenhüner, Bernd, 49, 50, 302
Sierra Club–Canada, 346
Sikkink, Kathryn, 23
Silent Spring (Carson), 262
Silicon Valley Toxics Coalition, 45
Silver, 361
Simmons, Beth, 105
Simpson, David R., 302
Singapore, 339 (table)
Single European Act (1986), 159–160,
    161, 167
Siniscalco, Domenico, 231
60 Minutes, 280
Skjærseth, Jon Birger, 256

Skoda, 307, 324
Skolnikoff, Eugene B., 24, 128, 256,
    257, 281
Slocock, Brian, 326
Slovakia
    emissions reduction targets and
        progress, 244 (table)
    European Council, 161
    European Union membership, 158
    international environmental
        disputes, 67
    nuclear power plants, 307
    renewable energy, 325
Slovenia
    emissions reduction targets and
        progress, 244 (table)
    European Union membership, 158
Small Grants Programme, 34
Smith, Fred L., Jr., 154
Smith, John Kenly, 280
Smith, Julian, 209
Smith, Matt, 328
Snyder, Glenn, 107
Snyder, Jack, 23
Soares, Claudia Dias, 129
Social embeddedness, 354–355, 360
Social justice movement, 350–351
Social media, 44
Soda ash, 361
Soft law, 61, 70–71, 83–84
Sohn, Louis B., 49, 79
Soil pollution, 285, 321, 358, 359 (table)
Sokona, Youba, 233
Solar power, 203–204, 324–325
Sookdeo, Anil, 52
Sorghum, 358
Soroos, Marvin S., 256
South
    see Global South
South Africa
    Copenhagen Accord, 248 (table)
    global environmental politics, 214
South America, 359 (table)
South Bohemian Mothers against
    Temelin, 312
South Centre, 232
South Commission, 230
Southern Bluefin Tuna case, 69
South Korea
    chemical production, 272
    environmental policies, 278
    free trade agreements, 339 (table)
    state negotiating blocs, 239 (table)

South Pacific Region, 359 (table)
Sovereignty
    international environmental law,
        56–57, 65
    international environmental policies,
        93–95, 343
    treaty compliance, 111
Soviet Union
    Cold War politics, 28
    international environmental
        agreements, 94, 96
    nuclear power plants, 306–307
Sowers, Jeannie L., 371
Sow, Ibrahima, 52
Soybeans, 358
Spain
    carbon dioxide (CO₂) emissions, 165
    commodity chains, 357
    common fisheries policy, 178
    emissions reduction targets and
        progress, 244 (table)
    European Council, 161
    European Union membership, 158
    nuclear power plants, 323
    renewable energy, 325
Spalding, Heather, 51
Special Climate Change Fund, 246, 249
Species extinctions, 283–285
Spent fuel storage and disposal,
        317–319
Sperling, Daniel, 369
Speth, James Gustave, 22, 25, 52
Spices, 357
Sprinz, Detlef, 109, 148, 149, 155, 255
Sri Lanka, 359 (table)
Staab, Andreas, 181
Stalley, Phillip, 231, 232
Stamatova, Stela, 185
Stares, Sally, 304
State Environmental Protection Agency
        (SEPA), 199
Steinberg, Paul F., 22, 24, 50, 186, 371
Stern, Nicholas, 301
Steurer, Anton, 185
Stevens, Paul, 371
Stewart, Alison L., 153
Stewart, Richard B., 153
Sticklor, Russell, 369
Stiglitz, Joseph E., 369, 371
Stirling, Andy, 282
Stockholm Conference on the Human
    Environment, 1, 7, 58–59, 61, 84, 93,
    110, 228–229

Stockholm Convention on Persistent
    Organic Pollutants (2001), 81
    background information, 260
    basic principles, 264 (table), 270–272
    basic treaty rules, 76 (table)
    constituent agreements and institutions,
        85 (table)
    functional role, 18
    international environmental
        negotiations, 71
    multilateral international agreements
        (MEAs), 29
    precautionary principle, 69
    United States signature and ratification,
        134 (table), 144
Stockholm Declaration, 29, 65, 197
Stockholm, Sweden, 31 (table)
Stoett, Peter, 256
Stokke, Olav Schram, 50
Stolle, Fred, 256
Stoll, Peter- Tobias, 52
Stone, 361
Stone, Christopher D., 232
"Story of the Blues," 356–357
St. Petersburg Declaration (1868), 259
Strange, Niels, 303
Strasbourg, France, 162
Strategic Approach to International
    Chemicals Management (SAICM)
    initiative, 85 (table), 260
Strategic Environmental Assessment
    Directive, 169
Straub, Daniel G., 24, 232
Streck, Charlotte, 50
Streets, D. G., 209
Stripple, Johannes, 258
Sub-Sahara Africa, 217
Subsidiary Body for Implementation
    (SBI), 242
Subsidiary Body on Scientific, Technical
    and Technological Advice
    (SBSTTA), 33–34, 242
Subsidy adjustments, 366–367
Sugar, 357, 358
Sugar beets, 360
Suleiman, Ezra, 182
Sulfur dioxide (SO₂) emissions, 187, 193,
    194 (table)
Sulfur hexafluoride (SF₆), 254
"Summary of the Tenth Conference of
    the Parties to the Convention on
    Biological Diversity: 18–29 October
    2010," 303

Summer, South Carolina, 319
Superfund Act (1980), 279
Supply services, 285
Support services, 285
Surender, T., 280
    see also Rao, C. H. Srinivas
Susskind, Lawrence, 147, 155, 223, 232
Sustainable development
    basic concepts, 8–9, 225–226
    Central and Eastern Europe (CEE), 307
    Czech Republic, 308–309
    environmental threats, 7–8
    future challenges, 20–22
    international environmental law, 67–68,
        225–226
    intertemporal/intergenerational equity, 8
    national policies, 13–16
    North-South dialogue, 221–226
    nuclear energy programs, 325–326
    policy initiatives, 9–10
    resource consumption, 20, 351–352,
        358, 360, 366–368
    trade-environment relationship, 331
Sustainable Europe Research Institute
    (SERI), 369
Swain, Evelyn, 52
Swanson, Timothy, 184, 302
Sweden
    carbon dioxide (CO_2) emissions, 165
    emissions reduction targets and
        progress, 244 (table)
    environmental policies, 277
    European Union compliance, 179
    European Union membership, 158
Switzerland
    emissions reduction targets and
        progress, 244 (table)
    European Environment Agency
        (EEA), 163
    international environmental
        agreements, 94, 122, 137
    nuclear power plants, 323
    state negotiating blocs, 239 (table)
Sykes, Alan O., 346
Sztompka, Piotr, 327

Taiyab, Nadaa, 233
Takenaka, Kiyoshi, 328
Tamas, Pal, 326
Tanaka, Shunichi, 320
Tan, Alan Khee-Jin, 129
Taniguchi, Tomihiro, 318
Tan, Q., 209

Tansey, Geoff, 370
Tanzania, 217, 270
Tarasofsky, Richard, 81
Taxation, 367
Taxes, environmental and energy, 174–175
Taylor, Bron, 51
Taylor, Derek M., 185
Taylor, V., 233
Tea, 357, 358, 359 (table)
Technical Assistance to the
    Commonwealth of Independent
    States (TACIS) program, 306
Temelin nuclear power plant, 18, 66,
    305, 307, 309–314, 312 (box), 322,
    324–325
Temelin Nuclear Power Plant Civic
    Association, 313
Templeton, Jessica, 108
ten Kate, Kerry, 302
Tennessee Valley Authority, 319
Terrorism, 317, 352
Thailand, 342
"The Electronic Wasteland," 280
The Guardian, 328
Theilade, Ida, 303
Thiele, Leslie Paul, 24
Third-party certification initiatives, 46
Third World countries
    see Global South
Third World Network, 42, 44
Thomas, Caroline, 230, 231
Thompson, Andrew, 182
Thrasher, Rachel, 49, 229, 230, 232, 233
Thrift, Charles, 281
Tianjin Climate Exchange (TCX), 204
Tiberghien, Yves, 182, 256, 282
Tickle, Andrew, 326
Tiebout, Charles M., 347
Time-lag problem, 95
Tin, 361, 364
Titanium, 361
Tobacco industry, 358
Tokyo Electric Power Company
    (TEPCO), 320, 321, 322, 324
Tolba, Mostafa, 103
Toronto, Canada, 237
Toronto Conference, 237
Toshiba, 324
Tóth, Ferenc L., 255
Toxic chemicals, 85–86 (table), 133,
    143–144, 277
    see also Chemicals management regimes;
        Hazardous substances management

Toyota, 252
Traavik, Terje, 304
Trabish, Herman, 211
Trade-environment relationship
    competitive pressures, 334–335
    free trade agreements with
        environmental chapters,
        339 (table)
    free trader concerns, 335–337, 343
    future challenges, 345
    historical perspective, 331–332
    international environmental regimes,
        342–344
    key environmental concerns, 333–335,
        343
    North American Free Trade Agreement
        (NAFTA) negotiations, 337–340
    policy challenges, 330–332
    production process or method (PPM)-
        based regulations, 344
    regulatory challenges, 334–335,
        343–345
    World Trade Organization (WTO),
        340, 342–344
Trade sanctions, 124–125
Trade union NGOs (TUNGOs), 38
    (table), 240 (table)
TRAFFIC (wildlife trade monitoring
    network), 46
Trafigura, 264
Trail Smelter case, 64
Transnational activist networks (TANs),
    41–42
Transnational commodity chains, 20, 356
Transuranic materials, 318
Treaty-based sanctions, 124–125
Treaty for the Preservation and Protection
    of Fur Seals (1911), 285–286
Treaty of Amsterdam (1997), 160, 162
Treaty of Lisbon (2007), 160, 161
Treaty of Maastricht (1992), 14, 160,
    162, 179
Treaty of Nice (2001), 160, 162
"Treaty of Nice Amending the Treaty
    on European Union, the Treaties
    Establishing the European
    Communities and Certain Related
    Acts," 181
Treaty of Paris (1763), 158
Treaty of Rome (1957), 14, 158, 159–160,
    167
Treaty on European Union (1992), 14,
    160, 162

Treaty secretariats, 33–34
Tremblay, Jean-François, 280
Treves, Tullio, 231
Tropical forests, 360
Trout, B. Thomas, 369
Trouwborst, Arie, 81
Trzyna, Thaddeus C., 24
Tsunamis, 320, 321, 322
Tudela, Fernando, 257
Tuna fishing, 332
Tungsten, 361
Tunisia, 357
Turkey
    agricultural commodity chains, 359 (table)
    commodity chains, 357
    European Environment Agency
        (EEA), 163
    European Union membership, 158
    nuclear energy programs, 305
Turtle excluder devices (TEDs), 342
Tvedt, Morten W., 303
Twitter, 44

Ukraine
    emissions reduction targets and
        progress, 244 (table)
    nuclear power plants, 307
    state negotiating blocs, 239 (table)
UK Youth Climate Coalition, 38 (table)
Umbrella Group, 238, 239 (table), 245
Underdal, Arild, 251, 256, 257, 302, 303
UN Doc. A/Conf. 151/26/ Rev. 1, 345
UN Doc. A/Conf. 151/5/Rev. 1, 345
UNEP/Open-Ended Working Group
    (OEWG) of the Basel Convention, 49
UNEP Regional Seas Conventions and
    Implementing Protocols, 74 (table)
UNESCO Convention Concerning the
    Protection of the World Cultural and
    Natural Heritage
    see World Heritage Convention (1972)
Unilateral sanctions, 124
United Arab Emirates, 322
United Kingdom
    carbon dioxide (CO_2) emissions, 165
    emissions reduction targets and
        progress, 244 (table), 250
    European Council, 161
    European Economic Community
        (EEC), 158
    genetic resources, 292
    international environmental disputes, 67
    nuclear power plants, 67, 173

United Nations Charter, 11
United Nations Children's Fund
(UNICEF), 271
United Nations Commission on
Sustainable Development (CSD), 9,
79, 342
United Nations Conference on
Environment and Development
(UNCED), 79, 345
background information, 2
global summits, 30, 31 (table)
hazardous waste agreements, 267
international climate negotiations, 240
international environmental
negotiations, 133
North-South dialogue, 16, 219,
223–228
sustainable development policies, 9, 16
United Nations Conference on
Sustainable Development
see Rio+20 Conference
United Nations Conference on
Sustainable Development
(UNCSD), 2, 30, 31 (table), 80
United Nations Conference on the
Human Environment (UNCHE), 1,
29, 31 (table), 220
United Nations Conference on Trade and
Development (UNCTAD), 28, 211
United Nations Convention on the
Law of the Sea (UNCLOS), 59,
62 (table), 73 (table), 79, 134, 134
(table), 145, 146
United Nations Convention on the Rights
of Persons with Disabilities (2012),
135
United Nations Convention to Combat
Desertification (UNCCD), 226, 343
United Nations Development Programme
(UNDP), 22, 34, 89, 117, 271, 342
United Nations Economic Commission
for Europe (UNECE), 70, 77,
268–269
United Nations Educational, Scientific
and Cultural Organization
(UNESCO), 28, 45, 48, 286
United Nations Environment Programme
(UNEP), 106, 107, 109, 257, 280,
282, 348
biodiversity protection, 295
climate change policies, 237
constituent agreements and institutions,
86 (table)

establishment, 1, 29, 31 (table)
functional role, 11, 32–33, 288–289
global environmental responsibility, 342
hazardous waste agreements, 143,
265, 267
Multilateral Fund, 89, 117
multilateral international agreements
(MEAs), 29
ozone regime, 103
Regional Seas Programme, 272
sustainable development policies, 8, 9, 59
United Nations Food and Agriculture
Organization Code of Conduct
on the Distribution and Use of
Pesticides, 71, 82
United Nations Food and Agriculture
Organization (FAO) International
Undertaking on Plant Genetic
Resources for Food and Agriculture
(1983), 286
United Nations Framework Convention
on Climate Change (FCCC), 51,
131, 154, 212, 255, 256, 303
background information, 54, 60
basic treaty rules, 75 (table)
biodiversity protection, 295–297
Cancun Agreements, 246–249
China, 200
commitments and obligations, 242
compliance standards, 115, 250
constituent agreements and institutions,
85 (table)
Copenhagen Accord, 247–248, 248 (table)
dispute resolution, 124
framework convention–protocol model,
62, 62 (table)
global environmental responsibility, 342
global summits, 30, 31 (table)
goals, 85 (table)
international climate negotiations,
240–243
key objectives and principles, 240–242
multilateral international agreements
(MEAs), 29
organizational structure, 242–243
policy impacts, 17
regime effectiveness, 250–253
regime organizations, 112
reporting requirements, 119–120
state negotiating blocs, 239 (table)
treaty secretariats, 33
United States signature and ratification,
133, 134 (table), 138–140

United Nations General Assembly, 11, 27, 79, 80, 220, 331
United Nations Industrial Development Organization (UNIDO), 89–90, 117
United Nations Institute for Training and Research (UNITAR), 35
United Nations Millennium Summit (2000), 26
United Nations-REDD Programme, 295–296
United Nations Regional Seas Programme and the European Union, 2
United Nations Security Council, 27
United Nations (UN), 80, 255
  characteristics and functional role, 27–29
  global summits, 29–32, 31 (table)
  historical perspective, 27–29
  treaty secretariats, 33–34
United States
  carbon dioxide (CO₂) emissions, 201 (figure)
  carbon emissions, 353
  child labor, 358
  Cold War politics, 28
  Copenhagen Accord, 248 (table)
  emissions reduction targets and progress, 244 (table)
  environmental policies, 13–14, 135–136
  free trade agreements, 331–332, 337–340, 339 (table)
  fuel economy standards, 196 (figure)
  genetically modified organisms (GMOs), 284, 298
  genetic resources, 292
  greenhouse gas emissions, 95, 138–142, 206, 237, 250
  international environmental agreements, 94, 101–102, 289
  international environmental leadership, 133–153
  Kyoto Protocol (1997), 249
  nuclear energy issues, 19
  nuclear power plants, 315–319, 316 (box), 324, 326
  state negotiating blocs, 239 (table)
  trade-environment conflicts, 340, 342
United States unilateralism
  agreement signature and ratification status, 134 (table), 289
  biodiversity protection, 142–143, 289
  climate change, 138–142
  determinant factors, 145–152
  endangered species protection, 133, 136–137
  hazardous waste agreements, 143–144
  historical perspective, 133–135
  leadership reluctance, 138–152
  ozone depletion response, 137–138
  participation issues, 135–136
  political issues, 150–151
  summary discussion, 152–153
  treaty objections, 146
United Nations Convention on the Law of the Sea (UNCLOS), 134, 134 (table), 145, 146
United States v. Canada (1941), 80
University of New Hampshire, 350
Uranium enrichment, 321
Uruguay, 298
U.S.-Australia Free Trade Agreement, 339 (table)
U.S.-Bahrain Free Trade Agreement, 339 (table)
U.S. Census Bureau, 347
U.S.-Chile Free Trade Agreement, 339 (table)
U.S. Climate Change Action Plan, 250
U.S. Code, 348
U.S. Code of Federal Regulations, 153
U.S.-Colombia Free Trade Agreement, 339 (table)
U.S. Comprehensive Environmental Response, Compensation, and Liability Act (1980), 279
U.S. Congress, 154, 155, 311
U.S. Corporate Average Fuel Economy (CAFE), 340
U.S. Department of Energy (DOE), 148, 155, 211, 310, 311, 317, 319
U.S. Energy Information Administration, 201 (figure), 205, 211
U.S. Environmental Protection Agency, 141, 154, 192 (box), 257, 279, 337, 340, 367
U.S. Export-Import Bank (Exim Bank), 310, 311
U.S. Government Accountability Office, 282
U.S. Government Accounting Office, 327
U.S.-Jordan Free Trade Agreement, 339 (table)
U.S.-Mexican trade agreement
  see North American Free Trade Agreement (NAFTA)

U.S.-Morocco Free Trade Agreement, 339 (table)
U.S. National Academy of Sciences, 9
U.S. National Security Council, 310
U.S. Nuclear Regulatory Commission (NRC), 311, 315–318, 319, 322
U.S.-Oman Free Trade Agreement, 339 (table)
U.S.-Panama Free Trade Agreement, 339 (table)
U.S.-Peru Free Trade Agreement, 339 (table)
U.S.-Republic of Korea Free Trade Agreement (KORUS FTA), 339 (table)
U.S.-Singapore Free Trade Agreement, 339 (table)
U.S. Supreme Court, 141, 154
U.S. Trade Representative (USTR), 337–338
Utah, 318

Vaahtoranta, Tapani, 109, 148, 155
Vajdova, Z., 327
Valentine's Day impacts, 360
Vallette, Jim, 51
Van de Graaf, Thijs, 255
van den Bergh, J. C. J. M., 347
van der Kolk, Jan, 106
VanDeveer, Stacy D., 20, 22, 23, 24, 25, 50, 131, 154, 181, 183, 185, 186, 256, 258, 282, 308, 326, 327, 369, 371, 372
    see also Andrews-Speed, Philip
van Leeuwen, Judith, 186
Van Lennep, Emile, 230
van Overwalle, Geertrui, 303
van Wijk, Jeroen, 303
Vari, Anna, 326
Vaughan, Scott, 25
Venezuela
    nuclear energy programs, 305
    trade-environment conflicts, 340
Venkateswarlu, V., 280
    see also Rao, C. H. Srinivas
Verheij, Albert, 129
Vermont, 141
Vermont Yankee nuclear power plant, 315
Verpackungsverordnung, 171
Verweij, Marco, 132
Via Campesina, 42
Victor, David G., 24, 128, 255, 256, 257, 281, 303
Vidal, John, 30, 49

Vieira, Ima C. G., 303
Vienna Adjustment (1995), 88
Vienna Convention for the Protection of the Ozone Layer (1985)
    background information, 1
    dispute resolution, 124
    establishment, 35
    framework convention–protocol model, 62 (table)
    as a managerial primary rule system, 116–117
    multilateral international agreements (MEAs), 29
    ozone regime principles, 88, 90, 101–103
    procedural obstacles, 94
    United States signature and ratification, 134 (table), 137
Vietnam
    global environmental politics, 217
    nuclear energy programs, 305
Vig, Norman J., 23, 24, 25, 50, 181, 183, 184
Villach, Austria, 237
Viola, Eduardo, 257
Visseren-Hamakers, Ingrid Jacoba, 45, 52
Vladivostok Declaration, 346
Vogel, David, 181, 183, 346, 371
Vogler, John, 52
Vogtle, Georgia, 319
Voisey, Heather, 24
Volk, Dennis, 209
von Hippel, Frank, 315–316, 327
von Schorlemer, Sabine, 52
von Weizsäcker, Christine, 233
vPvB (very persistent and very bioaccumulative) chemicals, 277
Vrolijk, Christiaan, 154, 255
    see also Grubb, Michael
VVER nuclear reactors, 307, 310

Wagner, Lynn M., 48, 49, 50, 52
Waigani Convention (1995), 273
Wallace, Helen, 181, 182
Wallach, Lori, 346
Wall Street Journal, 327, 328
Walmart, 253
Walsh, Michael P., 210
Waltz, Kenneth N., 23, 107
Wang, Alex L., 193 (box), 210
Wang, S., 209
Wann, David, 369
Wapner, Paul, 50

Warner, John C., 282
Washington Post, 328, 329
Waste chain, 365
Waste Electrical and Electronic Equipment
    (WEEE) Directive, 169, 278
Waste exports
    see Hazardous substances management
Waste Framework Directive, 172
Water exploitation, 358
Water Framework Directive, 171
Water pollution, 86 (table), 194, 272, 285
Water Resources Management Directive,
    171
Water vapor, 254
Watson, Robert T., 254
Watt-Cloutier, Sheila, 281
Watts, Jonathan, 193 (box)
Watts, Michael J., 370, 371
Waxman-Markey Bill, 140
Weale, Albert, 183
Webber, Julie, 369
Wei, C., 209
Weinthal, Erika, 371
Weiss, Edith Brown, 8, 24, 128, 130, 131,
    153, 155, 256
Weiß, Martin, 149, 155
Weiss, Mary, 81
Weizsäcker, Christine von, 233
Welsh, Ian, 326
Werksman, Jacob, 128, 130
Westinghouse, 310, 311, 312 (box), 324
Westphal, Kirsten, 255
Wetland protection, 33, 62 (table),
    72 (table), 87 (table), 134 (table),
    137, 142, 285
Wettestad, Jørgen, 256
Wexler, Philip, 106
Weyerhaeuser, 252
Whaling regulations, 29, 62 (table),
    74 (table), 87 (table)
Wheat, 357, 358
Whistle-blowers, 37
White papers, 164
White phosphorus compounds, 259
Wild, Antony, 370
Wiley, James, 370
Wilkening, Ken, 281
Wilkinson, Clive, 301
Williams, Marc, 221, 230, 231, 232
Willis, Andrew, 183
Wilson, E. O., 301, 302
Wind power, 194–195, 203
Wine imports, 340

Wingfield, Brian, 211
Wirth, Davis A., 255
Wirth, Tim, 139
Wisconsin, 141
Wofford, Carrie, 348, 349
Women and gender organizations,
    240 (table)
Wood, Peter, 48, 50, 52
Wood pulp, 358
Woodward, Colin, 326
Worker safety, 358, 359 (table)
Working conditions, 358, 359 (table), 360,
    362, 364
World Bank
    Chinese air and water pollution, 193–194
    establishment, 35
    functional role, 11
    funding programs, 34, 36–37
    global environmental responsibility, 343
    international environmental policy
        process, 56
    malaria control programs, 271
    Multilateral Fund, 89, 117
    and nongovernmental organizations
        (NGOs), 40–41, 46
    sustainable development policies, 9, 78
    voting procedures, 10
World Bank and Development Research
    Center of the State Council, 209
World Bank and State Environmental
    Protection Administration, 209
World Bank Operational Directive
    14.70, 51
World Business Council on Sustainable
    Development, 38 (table)
World Climate Program, 237, 254
World Commission on Environment and
    Development (WCED), 1–2, 8, 22,
    24, 81, 225, 290, 302, 326
World Conference on the Changing
    Atmosphere (1988), 237
World Conservation Union, 9
World Health Organization (WHO),
    271, 281
World Heritage Convention (1972), 35,
    62 (table), 134 (table), 286,
    286 (table)
World Intellectual Property Organization
    (WIPO), 294
World Meteorological Organization
    (WMO), 106, 107, 254
    climate change research, 33, 35, 237
    functional role, 10

global environmental responsibility, 342
historical perspective, 28
ozone regime impacts, 103
World Nuclear News, 328
World Plan of Action on the Ozone
    Layer, 137
World Resources Institute (WRI), 123,
    131, 142, 256
World Summit on Sustainable
    Development (WSSD), 280
background information, 2
global summits, 30, 31 (table)
goals and objectives, 9–10, 60, 61, 331
international environmental
    agreements, 260
United States environmental policy, 19
World Trade Organization (WTO)
biodiversity protection, 301
environmental protection agreements,
    19–20, 294
environment-related trade restrictions, 37
functional role, 11
genetically modified organisms
    (GMOs), 298
genetic resources, 291–292
global environmental responsibility,
    343, 368
international environmental policy
    process, 56, 78
member states, 341 (map)
production process or method
    (PPM)-based regulations, 344
regime organizations, 112
trade-environment relationships, 332,
    335–336, 340, 342–344
transparency, 343
Worldwatch Institute, 41, 351, 369, 370
World Wide Fund for Nature, 8, 40, 42,
    166, 292, 351, 369

World Wildlife Fund (WWF), 8, 40, 42
Worm, Boris, 370
Wuli Village, China, 262
Wurzel, Rüdiger, 181, 184
Wu Shaohong, 210
Wynne, Brian, 282

Xinhua, 193 (box), 208, 209, 212
Xu Yinlong, 210

Yamagishi, Naoyuki, 24, 232
Yamaguchi, Mari, 328
Yamineva, Yulia, 50
Yamin, Farhana, 239 (table), 254, 255
Yasué, Maï, 296, 304
Yearly, Steven, 326
Yellowstone National Park, 285
Yohe, Gary W., 255
Young, Alasdair R., 181
Young, John E., 370
Young, Oran R., 23, 105, 108, 128, 131,
    232, 254, 257
Young, Stephen, 24
Youth NGOs (YOUNGOs), 38 (table),
    240 (table)
Yucca Mountain, Nevada, 318
Yusho, Japan, 262

Zabelin, S., 233
Zaelke, Durwood, 232, 346
Zarsky, Lyuba, 347
Zelli, Fariborz, 303
Zero Carbon Africa, 38 (table)
Zhang, Q., 209
Zhou Enlai, 197
Zhou, Nan, 211
Zinc, 361
Zito, Anthony R., 184
Zürn, Michael, 128

⊛SAGE research**methods**

The essential online tool for researchers from the
world's leading methods publisher

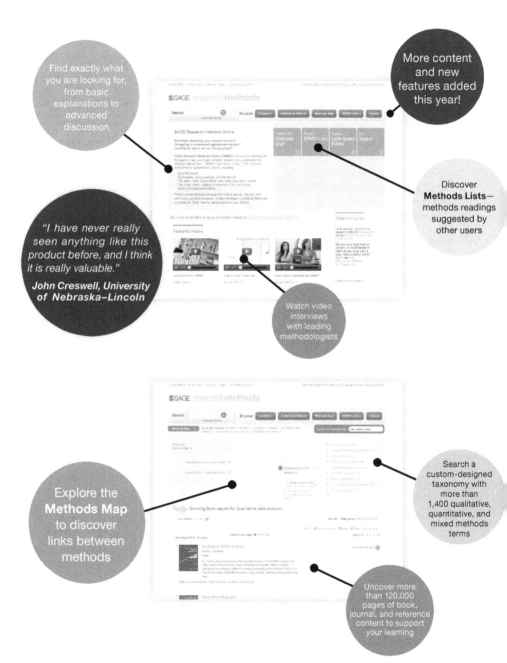

More content
and new
features added
this year!

Find exactly what
you are looking for,
from basic
explanations to
advanced
discussion

Discover
Methods Lists—
methods readings
suggested by
other users

"*I have never really
seen anything like this
product before, and I think
it is really valuable.*"
**John Creswell, University
of Nebraska–Lincoln**

Watch video
interviews
with leading
methodologists

Search a
custom-designed
taxonomy with
more than
1,400 qualitative,
quantitative, and
mixed methods
terms

Explore the
Methods Map
to discover
links between
methods

Uncover more
than 120,000
pages of book,
journal, and reference
content to support
your learning

Find out more at
www.sageresearchmethods.com

CPSIA information can be obtained
at www.ICGtesting.com
Printed in the USA
BVHW042123180119
538225BV00012B/111/P

9 781452 241456